MODERN STRUCTURED ANALYSIS

Edward Yourdon

Prentice-Hall International, Inc.

© 1989 by Prentice-Hall, Inc.
A Division of Simon & Schuster
Englewood Cliffs, NJ 07632

Printed in the United States of America

10 9 8 7 6 5 4 3 2

ISBN 0-13-598632-X

Prentice-Hall International (UK) Limited, *London*
Prentice-Hall of Australia Pty. Limited, *Sydney*
Prentice-Hall Canada Inc., *Toronto*
Prentice-Hall Hispanoamericana, S.A., *Mexico*
Prentice-Hall of India Private Limited, *New Delhi*
Prentice-Hall of Japan, Inc., *Tokyo*
Simon & Schuster Asia Pte. Ltd., *Singapore*
Editora Prentice-Hall do Brasil, Ltda., *Rio de Janeiro*
Prentice-Hall, Inc., *Englewood Cliffs, New Jersey*

CONTENTS

PREFACE

> What is valuable is not new, and what is new is not valuable.
> Henry Peter, Lord Brougham
> *The Edinburgh Review,*1802

Let me begin by addressing a very obvious question: *does the world really need another book on systems analysis?* This may seem like a rhetorical question, but there have been many times—usually late at night—as I have worked on this book when I have asked myself, "Why am I bothering with this? What's wrong with all the books that everyone has been reading for the past ten years? How can I possibly hope to add anything to the body of literature?"

Obviously, people other than me will have to pass judgment on the results. But I do think that there is a need for a book that updates some of the classic material on structured analysis that was first published in the late 1970s. When Tom DeMarco wrote *Structured Analysis and Systems Specification* and Chris Gane and Trish Sarson wrote *Structured Systems Analysis: Tools and Techniques,* there were no fourth generation programming languages, and there were no prototyping tools available for systems developers. Personal computers did not exist in those days, notwithstanding some of the early, primitive machines from Apple and Radio Shack. There were no workstation-based software products that would help the systems analyst create dataflow diagrams.

Developments in these areas have had quite an impact on the overall acceptance of structured analysis: many people argue whether structured analysis is relevant in an environment where users can create their own applications in a matter of hours or days. This alone is one reason for a new book on the subject of systems analysis: the vastly more powerful technology available to systems analysts and users alike has changed our focus and perspective.

In addition, systems developers have had to cope with issues of database systems and real-time systems, in addition to the "function-oriented" systems originally addressed by structured analysis in the late 1970s. This book discusses entity-relationship diagrams and state-transition diagrams, in addition to the classical dataflow diagrams, and shows how all three models can be integrated; this integration of models will become more and more important over the coming years. Several other recent developments in structured analysis—including event partitioning, and the de-emphasis of modeling current physical systems—have been included in this book.

There is one more reason for writing another book on systems analysis: most of the "classical" structured analysis books were written for adult, veteran systems analysts—with little or no provision for the younger person just beginning in the field.

At the same time, most college textbooks on systems analysis written during the past ten years paid scant attention to the new techniques of structured analysis and have continued to devote far too many pages to discussions of punched cards and the Hollerith code; aside from the fact that many of these topics are obsolete, a superficial understanding of computer hardware, software, and programming is generally provided by an "Introduction to Computers" course that would precede the student's exposure to an in-depth coverage of systems analysis. This book tries to strike a balance by recognizing that some introductory material is necessary for the student who has had an introduction to computers, but has never done *any* systems analysis, while also realizing that the concepts of structured analysis are simple enough that they can be presented in substantial detail at the high school and college level. Meanwhile, much of the introductory material is placed in appendixes so that it can be skipped by the practitioner in industry.

The book should be appropriate for a one-semester undergraduate course on systems analysis; it covers the agenda for course CIS-86/5 in the "CIS 86" DPMA Model Curriculum for Undergraduate Computer Information Systems. However, it does *not* attempt to cover both the topics of systems analysis and systems design, even though many colleges attempt to cover both subjects in a single semester. My feeling is that there is more than enough material to discuss in each of the two areas; for a one-semester course on structured design, I suggest that the reader consider either *Practical Guide to Structured Systems Design,* 2nd edition, by Meilir Page-Jones (YOURDON Press, Englewood Cliffs, N.J., 1988), or *Structured Design,* 2nd edition, by Ed Yourdon and Larry Constantine (YOURDON Press, Englewood Cliffs, N.J., 1989).

Battle-scarred veterans of systems analysis may want to read the first chapter to get an orientation, and then skip the rest of Part I; the first seven chapters are essential reading for new students. Veterans will find much of the discussion of dataflow diagrams, data dictionary, and the like, familiar; however, there is material in Chapter 9 on the extensions to DFDs for real-time systems that may be new to those who have worked exclusively on business-oriented systems. The discussion of entity-relationship diagrams may be new, too, for those more familiar with "data structure diagrams," and the discussion of state-transition diagrams in Chapter 13 introduces a major new modeling tool. Most important for the veteran: Chapters 19 and 20 introduce an approach for building the essential model (sometimes known as the *logical* model) that is in stark contrast to the rigid top-down approach followed by systems analysts for so many years; it is an approach known as *event partitioning*, based on the work of McMenamin and Palmer. *And Chapter 17 recommends that the classical approach of modeling the user's "current physical" system be eliminated;* this should be studied carefully by the systems analysts whose techniques are based on textbooks of the 1970s.

Among the appendixes are two case studies that illustrate the various tools and techniques discussed in the book. The first case study is a typical "business-oriented" application based on the YOURDON Press publishing operation; the second is a more typical example of a "real-time system" based on an elevator control system. Both are presented in substantial detail, even though it increases the size of the book: it is important for the student to see a fairly complete example of a specification. Both these models can be used for discussions and exercises in a classroom environment.

Modern Structured Analysis draws from many years of experience with hundreds of consulting clients, thousands of seminar students, and dozens of colleagues at YOURDON inc. and other consulting organizations; I am indebted to all these people, far too numerous for me to mention by name. But there are some people who deserve special mention, for they helped make this a far better book than it might otherwise have been. Nobody can write a book on structured analysis today without acknowledging the pioneering books of Tom DeMarco, Chris Gane, and Trish Sarson. And I feel equally indebted to Steve McMenamin and John Palmer, whose *Essential Systems Analysis* represented a major step forward from the first exposition of structured analysis; similarly, Paul Ward and Steve Mellor introduced a number of important concepts and modeling tools for real-time systems in their three-volume set *Structured Development for Real-Time Systems.* I have also benefited greatly during the past year from discussions with colleagues with whom I taught structured analysis seminars in the United States and England: John Bowen, Julian Morgan, Bob Spurgeon, Nick Mandato, and Alex Gersznowicz deserve special thanks for showing me eloquent ways of explaining structured analysis concepts that I surely would never have found on my own. Meanwhile, Professor Peter Brown and a group of his students at Duquesne University debugged the book by using it as a textbook in a systems analysis course; I thank them for suffering through the typographical errors in early drafts.

I would also like to thank Dennis Stipe of the Washington, D.C., office of YOURDON inc. for the enormous amount of work he contributed to the structured analysis model of the elevator system in Appendix G. Most textbooks today contain only case studies of business-oriented systems; this book contains both a business-oriented case study (Appendix F) and a real-time example based on a classic problem description provided by the ACM. Dennis originally developed the structured analysis model for a "design wars" seminar sponsored in 1986 by the Washington chapter of the ACM to show how different software engineering methodologies would deal with the problem of a scheduler and controller for four elevators; it has been modified since then.

Peter Brown, Pete Coad, Bob Spurgeon, Steve Weiss, Ron Teemley, and Dale Brown improved the draft of this book *enormously* with their thorough review and helpful comments; obviously, I take full responsibility for any remaining errors of omission and commission. Meanwhile, my wife and children supported my efforts by providing endless supplies of Diet Coke and tortilla chips (and a cognac when the occasion called for it); by the time I finished the book, I had gained twenty pounds and had to go on a diet.

Several people at YOURDON Press/Prentice-Hall made the production of this book a delightful experience—in stark contrast to what most of us paranoid authors suffer from publishers! Pat Henry and Ed Moura watched over the project from the beginning and gave me encouragement when I most needed it. Sophie Papanikolaou supervised the production of the book and was a joy to work with. Bill Thomas copyedited the book and ferreted out thousands—no, millions!—of typos and grammatical errors. My wife, Toni, then cheerfully made all of the copyediting corrections on the computer, though I heard her muttering under her breath that someone trained as a mathematician should never pretend he knows how to write.

Finally, I would like to thank my Macintosh computer(s) for struggling valiantly with this huge manuscript. Most of the writing was done with Microsoft Word (versions 1.0, 1.05, 3.0, and 3.01), but I also drew upon MacPaint, Fullpaint, SuperPaint, MacDraw, Microsoft Chart, MacProject, Microsoft Multiplan, ChessMaster, ConcertWare, Living Videotext's MORE, StarSys Inc.'s MacBubbles, and Meta Software's Design, not to mention several pieces of "clip art" from T/Maker and various other publishers. Anybody who tries to write a book with anything other than a Macintosh should have his head examined.

Edward Yourdon
New York, August 1988

PART 1: INTRODUCTION

1 INTRODUCTION

The beginnings and endings of all human undertakings are untidy, the building of a house, the writing of a novel, the demolition of a bridge, and, eminently, the finish of a voyage.

John Galsworthy
Over the River, 1933

In this chapter, you will learn:

1. Why systems analysis is interesting.

2. Why systems analysis is more difficult than programming.

3. Why it is important to be familiar with systems analysis.

Okay. Here we are at the beginning of a long book. The prospect of reading such a long, technical book probably terrifies you; but if it's any consolation, it's even more terrifying when you're at the beginning of *writing* a long book. Fortunately, just as long journeys take place one day at a time, and ultimately one step at a time, so long books get read one chapter at a time, and ultimately one sentence at a time.

1.1   WHY IS SYSTEMS ANALYSIS INTERESTING?

Long books are often dull; hopefully, this one won't be. Fortunately, the subject matter of this book—*systems analysis*—is interesting. In fact, systems analysis is more interesting than anything I know, with the possible exception of sex and certain types of Australian wine. Without a doubt, it is more interesting than computer programming (not that programming is dull) because it involves studying the interactions of people, and disparate *groups* of people, and computers and organizations.

1

As Tom DeMarco said in his delightful book, *Structured Analysis and Systems Specification* [DeMarco, 1978],

> [systems] analysis is frustrating, full of complex interpersonal relationships, indefinite, and difficult. In a word, it is fascinating. Once you're hooked, the old easy pleasures of system building are never again enough to satisfy you.

This may come as a surprise to you if you have any experience writing computer programs.[1] Programming is fun, and it's intellectually challenging; it's hard to imagine anything more rewarding and satisfying than seeing one's program run successfully, especially after spending several hours (or days!) debugging it. It's hard to imagine that things could be even more rewarding and exciting when you begin to move away from the computer and the writing of computer programs to study the overall system in which the programs play a part. But by the end of this book, I hope to have convinced you that the real challenge, and the real joy, of working with computer systems is that of carrying out systems analysis.

No matter what profession you decide to pursue, it will be important for you to understand what systems analysis is all about. If you work in the computer industry as something other than an electrical engineer or hardware designer, there is a good chance that your career will progress from programmer to systems designer to systems analyst before you finally move on to the ranks of management.[2]

1.2   WHO THIS BOOK IS INTENDED FOR

I am writing this book for two audiences: *first,* the person who is new to the field of systems analysis, and, *second,* the experienced systems analyst who needs to

---

1 If you are under 30 years of age, it's hard to imagine that you have *not* written a computer program; after all, virtually every school and college now teaches something about computer programming. But you may not have written a really complicated computer program. If you haven't spent at least a month working on the same program—working 16 hours a day, dreaming about it during the remaining 8 hours of restless sleep, working several nights straight through trying to eliminate that "one last bug" from the program— then you haven't really written a complicated computer program. And you may not have the sense that there is something exhilarating about programming. (By the way, everyone in the industry will tell you that you should not be building large, complex computer programs—and that the object of the game is to build simple, comprehensible programs. This is true: but imagine the mental energy and the sleepless nights that must have gone into the creation and development of something like the Macintosh *MacPaint* program, or the first version of Lotus 1-2-3.)

2 There are a variety of other career paths that you might follow, too. You might specialize in the area of telecommunications and network design; or you might concentrate on database design, or "data administration." While most of this book assumes that you will be concerned with *application* systems (payroll, inventory, accounting, or real-time applications like missile guidance, telephone switching, and process control), you might also concentrate on *systems programming* projects—for example, compilers or operating systems. *All* of this is likely to represent your *second* or *third* job in the computer industry: chances are that you'll start in the business as a junior programmer (where you will be expected to know how to write relatively simple programs, or make maintenance changes to existing programs), and then progress to senior programmer before finally being promoted to the position of systems analyst. As a systems analyst, you will be expected to have broader skills than that of a programmer: in addition to knowledge of computer hardware and software, you will be expected to be able to communicate well with noncomputer people, and you will be expected to be familiar with their business applications.

acquaint himself with systems modeling tools and techniques that have evolved over the past five to ten years. Many readers will be university computer science students who have completed earlier courses on computer programming; some may be students in a business training program.

However, the book should be equally readable by people who have finished their university training and who are now working in industry. Many people in the computer industry spend their first several years working as a computer programmer, and then suddenly find themselves promoted (or reassigned) to a position of systems analyst, without ever being told what systems analysis is all about or what a systems analyst does. If you are in such a position, this book is for you. You should also find the book useful if you began working as a systems analyst in the 1960s or 1970s and never had an opportunity to learn about such structured analysis techniques as dataflow diagrams, entity-relationship diagrams, and data dictionaries.

More and more often today, people outside the computer profession are finding it necessary to become familiar with the field of systems analysis. If you are a business person or a manager (or any one of a number of other professions described by computer people as a user), there is a good chance that you will be involved in a systems analysis activity. You will have systems analysts working for you, spending their time trying to understand what kind of automated system you want them to build. Similarly, if you are an administrator, a clerk, a scientist, a politician, an engineer, or an accountant—or virtually any other professional in today's society—there is a good chance that you will spend a significant amount of time during your career interacting with people (systems analysts) who will be designing and specifying sophisticated computer systems for you. The more you know about what these people do, and what they expect of you, the better off you will be.

Even if you have no expectation of working in a white collar job—that is, even if you expect to be an artist, a writer, a musician, or an athlete—you should know what systems analysis is all about. Citizens in every walk of life are affected by computer systems of all sorts. Even if you never intend to build a computer system or have one built for you, it is inevitable that you will be using computer systems for your banking, for your education, for your interactions with the IRS and Social Security, and for virtually every aspect of your interactions with modern society. As John Gall says in *Systemantics* [Gall, 1977],

> No one, these days, can avoid contact with systems. Systems are everywhere: big systems, little systems, systems mechanical and electronic, and those special systems that consist of organized associations of people. In self-defense, we must learn to live with systems, to control *them* lest *they* control *us*. As Humpty Dumpty said to Alice (though in another context): "The question is: which is to be master—that's all."

To emphasize this point even more, keep in mind that the computer industry represented approximately 8% of the United States GNP in 1985; by 1990, it is expected to represent as much as 15% of the GNP.[3] Almost every product built today

---

3 For more details on this, as well as other discussions of the impact of computers on society, see *Nations at Risk* [Yourdon, 1986].

by American business has one or more computers embedded within it, and almost every service provided to the marketplace by American business is based on or controlled by a computer system.

1.3   WHAT THE BOOK WILL DO FOR YOU

As you have guessed by now, a major purpose of this book is to teach you about systems analysis: what it is and how one goes about doing it. But there is more: my real purpose is to *excite* you, to make you so eager to begin practicing systems analysis that you will want to rush through the last pages of the book and begin working on your first project. Seymour Papert recalls in *Mindstorms* [Papert, 1980],

> I found particular pleasure in such systems as the differential gear, which does not follow a simple linear chain of causality since the motion in the transmission shaft can be distributed in many different ways to the two wheels depending on what resistance they encounter. I remember quite vividly my excitement at discovering that a system could be lawful and completely comprehensible without being rigidly deterministic.

And as Sir Arthur Stanley Eddington said in [Eddington, 1987],

> We have found that where science has progressed the farthest, the mind has but regained from nature that which the mind put into nature.
>
> We have found a strange footprint on the shores of the unknown. We have devised profound theories, one after another, to account for its origin. At last we have succeeded in reconstructing the creature that made the footprint. And lo! it is our own.

Another purpose of the book is to make you understand and appreciate that we live in a world of systems—and systems within systems, which are part of even larger systems. Thus, everything we do in our personal and professional lives has an impact (often unanticipated and unexpected!) on the various systems of which we are a part. This "systems thinking" approach is not only vital for professional systems analysts, but for all members of modern society.

Alas, this book cannot make you an experienced systems analyst, any more than a book on music theory can make you an experienced pianist. By the end of the book, you will be armed with a tremendous amount of technical information that will help you develop accurate *models* of complex systems, and you will know the step-by-step techniques for carrying out a systems analysis effort. But you will still need a great deal of real-world work to learn the people skills: how to interview a variety of disparate users to understand the true essence of a system; how to present the results of your systems analysis work so that everyone can see the true costs and benefits of developing a new system; how to distinguish problems from symptoms. As Barry Boehm pointed out in his classic work, *Software Engineering Economics* [Boehm, 1981]:

> Each of us as individual software engineers has an opportunity to make a significant positive impact on society, simply by becoming more sensitive to the long-range human relations implications of our work, and by incorporating this sensitivity into our software designs and products.

It takes some practice to do this well, and to learn how to balance human relations concerns with programming and quantitative economic concerns. The big thing to remember in doing so is to keep our priorities straight between programming, budgetary, and human considerations.

1.4   THE ORGANIZATION OF THIS BOOK

This book is organized in four major parts, followed by a series of appendixes. Part I serves as an introduction to the entire book; it begins, in Chapter 2, with an introduction to the concept of systems and to the nature of systems analysis; in this chapter, we will see that information systems are usually composed of people, hardware, software (computer programs), procedures, data, and information. Chapter 3 describes the people who are typically involved in the development of a modern information system—the users, managers, operations personnel, members of the quality assurance group, and the like—as well as the special role and responsibilities of the systems analyst. Chapter 4 introduces the modeling tools that the systems analyst uses, including dataflow diagrams, entity-relationship diagrams, and state-transition diagrams. Chapter 5 introduces the procedures (or methodology) that the systems analyst follows when developing a system.

Even if you think you know many of these things already, there are some chapters in Part I that are important for you to read, for they set the tone for the rest of the book. Chapter 2, for example, introduces and discusses the fundamental axioms and principles that we can expect to find in all systems analysis work: the development of system *models,* the notion of iteration, and the notion of top-down partitioning. And Chapter 6 outlines the major issues facing systems analysts today: issues of productivity, system quality, maintainability, and strategic use of information. Finally, Chapter 7 summarizes the major changes that have taken place in the field of systems analysis in the past ten years.

Part II discusses systems modeling tools in detail. Individual chapters cover the topics of dataflow diagrams (Chapter 9), data dictionaries (Chapter 10), process specifications (Chapter 11), entity-relationship diagrams (Chapter 12), and state-transition diagrams (Chapter 13). Chapters 15 and 16 discuss various other modeling tools that systems analysts use when studying a system: PERT charts, Gantt charts, flowcharts, HIPO diagrams, structure charts, and so on. As we will see, these modeling tools allow us to selectively focus on individual aspects of a system whose characteristics are important to understand: the functions that the system must perform, the data that it must keep track of, and its time-dependent behavior.

Even if you never see a computer after you finish reading this book, the modeling tools in Part II will be useful in whatever you do. You will find that modeling tools can be useful to model (or describe or "picture") virtually *any* kind of system: biological systems, business systems, ecosystems, manufacturing systems, political systems, material-flow systems, and so on. We live in a world of systems, and much of our daily life is spent trying to comprehend and work with the many different systems with which we come in contact; modeling tools are enormously helpful in this respect.

Part III is concerned with the *process* of systems analysis—that is, the steps that a systems analyst goes through when constructing a system model. Here, too, the information you learn in this part of the book will be useful regardless of your ultimate profession; but the material is definitely slanted toward the construction of automated information systems. We will see that the process, or methodology, for building a system involves the development of several different types of models, the last of which is the product or output of systems analysis. In many business organizations, this product is known by such names as a "functional specification," or a "business requirements document," or a "business systems design." Regardless of its name, it becomes the input to the person (or people) who are responsible for actually *building* the system—that is, designing the overall architecture of computer hardware and software and ultimately writing and testing the computer programs.

This leads us to Part IV: life after systems analysis. We will explore the transition from systems analysis to systems design and briefly discuss the final details of programming and testing. Since most automated information systems have a lifetime of several years (and often several decades), we will also discuss the subject of maintenance in Chapter 24; but our concern will not be with maintenance *programming,* but rather with the maintenance of the product of systems analysis. The last chapter deals with the future: evolutionary changes in the field of systems analysis that we can expect to see during the 1990s and on into the next century.

Appendixes at the end of the book deal with separate issues that may or may not affect you when you begin working as a systems analyst. Appendix A, for example, deals with the subject of automated PC-based workstations for systems analysis—which few systems analysts have access to in the late 1980s, but which will become increasingly common in the 1990s. Appendix B discusses estimating formulas and metrics used to calculate the size, duration, and cost of a project. Appendix C discusses the economics of cost-benefit calculations. Appendix D covers the subject of walkthroughs and inspections, which are often used to review the technical products of systems analysis. Appendix E discusses interviewing and data-gathering techniques, particularly those interviews that take place between user and systems analyst. All of these have been arranged as appendixes so that experienced systems analysts can skip them easily; beginning students can turn to the appendixes whenever convenient to cover topics that will surely emerge during real-world projects.

Appendixes F and G present two case studies: one is a business-oriented system, and one is a real-time system. If you are a first-time student, at the end of each chapter you should look at these case studies to see how newly learned principles can apply in real-world situations. In fact, you should read the introduction and background of each case study now so that you will be familiar with the nature of each application.

Each chapter has a number of questions and exercises to help you review what you have learned. Some exercises are labeled "Research Project," which means that they address issues that are not covered directly in the chapter but that are relevant in the real world of systems analysis. Some of the questions are intended for classroom discussion; there are no right or wrong answers, but there are answers that are more easily defended than others!

So much for introductions. Let's get started! We will begin by talking about the nature of systems.

REFERENCES

1. Tom DeMarco, *Structured Analysis and Systems Specification*. Englewood Cliffs, N.J.: Prentice-Hall, 1979, page 6.

2. John Gall, *Systemantics*. New York: Quadrangle/The New York Times Book Company, 1977, page xiii.

3. Barry Boehm, *Software Engineering Economics*. Englewood Cliffs, N.J.: Prentice-Hall, 1981.

4. Seymour Papert, *Mindstorms*. New York: Basic Books, 1980.

5. Edward Yourdon, *Nations at Risk.* Englewood Cliffs, N.J.: YOURDON Press, 1986.

6. Sir Arthur Stanley Eddington, *Space, Time and Gravitation: An Outline of the General Theory.* London: Cambridge University Press, 1987.

QUESTIONS AND EXERCISES

1. Explain how systems analysis might be useful in your job or profession even if you are not planning to become a programmer or systems analyst.

2. Research Project: How many people are employed as systems analysts in the United States today? What is their average salary? What is their average level of education?

3. Research Project: Is there a shortage of programmers and systems analysts in the United States? Try to find industry surveys or government surveys (e.g., from the U.S. Commerce Department or the National Science Foundation) that predict the nation's requirements for systems analysts over the next ten years.

4. Give ten examples of systems that you deal with or interact with in your day-to-day life.

5. Would you be studying the subject of systems analysis if you didn't have to? If your answer is "No," explain why you think the material won't be useful or relevant. Find someone else studying this same material and engage in a constructive debate about the general usefulness of systems analysis.

6. Do you think it is important for noncomputer people (people who do not work in the computer field as a profession) to study systems analysis? How expert do you think they should be in the subject?

7. Why is systems analysis likely to be more interesting than programming? Do you agree with this point of view?

8. What things must a systems analyst learn besides the technical skills of building system models?

9. Why can modeling tools of the kind presented in this book be useful for studying noncomputer systems?

2 THE NATURE OF SYSTEMS

Finally, we shall place the Sun himself at the center of the Universe. All this is suggested by the systematic procession of events and the harmony of the whole Universe, if only we face the facts, as they say, "with both eyes open."

Nicholas Copernicus,
De Revolutionibus Orbium Coelestium, 1543

In this chapter, you will learn:

1. What the definition of a system is.

2. The difference between natural systems and man-made systems.

3. The 19 major subsystems found in all living systems.

4. The five major reasons why some systems should not be automated.

5. The five major components of a typical automated information system.

6. The definition and characteristics of several specific types of systems.

7. The definition of and three examples of general system principles.

We can't say very much about systems analysis until we have a clear idea of what a *system* is; that is the purpose of this chapter. As we will see, there is an "official" dictionary definition of the term, which will seem rather abstract. But there are many common usages of the term that will be quite familiar to you, and there are many common *types* of systems that we come into contact with every day.

"So what?" you might be asking yourself. It is important to be familiar with different kinds of systems for at least two reasons. First, even though your work as a systems analyst will probably focus on one kind of system—an automated, computerized information system—it will generally be a part of a larger system. Thus, you may be working on a payroll system, which is part of a larger "human resources" system, which in turn is part of an overall business organization (which is, in itself, a system), which is, in turn, part of a larger economic system, and so forth. Or you may be working on a process control system that is part of a chemical refinery, or an operating system that is part of a vendor-supplied "package" of system software. Thus, to make *your* system successful, you must understand the other systems with which it will interact.

Many of the computer systems that we build are replacements, or new implementations of, *non*computerized systems that are already in existence; also, most computer systems interact with, or interface with, a variety of existing systems (some of which may be computerized and some which may not). If our new computer system is to be successful, we must understand, in reasonable detail, how the current system behaves.

Second, even though many types of systems appear to be quite different, they turn out to have many similarities; there are common principles and philosophies and theories that apply remarkably well to virtually *all* kinds of systems. Thus, we can often apply what we have learned about other systems—based on our own day-to-day experience, as well as the experience of scientists and engineers in a variety of fields—to systems that we build in the computer field. For example, one of the important systems principles first observed in the field of biology is known as the law of specialization: the more highly adapted an organism is to a specific environment, the more difficult it is for the organism to adapt to a different environment. This helps explain the disappearance of dinosaurs when the Earth's climate changed dramatically[1]; it also helps systems analysts understand that if they optimize a computerized system to take maximum advantage of a specific CPU, programming language, and database management system, they are likely to have great trouble adapting that system to run on a different CPU or with a different database management system.[2]

---

1 Paleontologists are still arguing about this issue: some feel that dinosaurs vanished in a relatively brief period of time after a massive meteor hit the earth, creating such a dense dust cloud that most plant life died. Others argue that the change was much more gradual, occurring over a period of nearly a million years. In any case, dinosaurs were highly adapted to one kind of environment and eventually proved unable to adapt to a different one.

2 It can also help the systems analyst understand the phenomenon of a user whose current practices are so specialized that there is no way to change them even if they are computerized. And it reminds the systems analyst that if he or she develops a computer system that is highly specialized for the user's *current* application, it will be difficult to adapt as the user's requirements (and the external environment in which the user operates) change and evolve.

Thus, if we understand something of *general systems theory*, it can help us better understand computerized (automated) information systems. This is more and more important today, because we want to build *stable*, reliable systems that will function well in our complex society—and there are, of course, many examples of non-computer systems that have survived for millions of years: the humble cockroach is likely to outlast every computer system ever built, and all of humanity as well.

So, let us begin with a definition of the basic term system. Every textbook covering some aspect of systems contains such a definition; I have chosen Webster's *New Collegiate Dictionary*.[3] It provides several definitions:

1. a regularly interacting or interdependent group of items forming a unified whole <a number ~>: as

   a.
   (1) a group of interacting bodies under the influence of related forces <a gravitational ~>
   (2) an assemblage of substances that is in or tends to equilibrium <a thermodynamic ~>

   b.
   (1) a group of body organs that together perform one or more vital functions <the digestive ~>
   (2) the body considered as a functional unit

   c. a group of related natural objects or forces <a river ~>

   d. a group of devices or an organization forming a network, especially for distributing something or serving a common purpose <a telephone ~> <a heating ~> <a highway ~> <a data processing ~>

2. an organized set of doctrines, ideas, or principles, usually intended to explain the arrangements or working of a systematic whole <the Newtonian ~ of mechanics>

3. a. an organized or established procedure <the touch ~ of typing>

   b. a manner of classifying, symbolizing, or schematizing <a taxonomic ~> <the decimal ~>

4. harmonious arrangement or pattern: ORDER

5. an organized society or social situation regarded as stultifying: ESTABLISHMENT

---

3 Webster's *New Collegiate Dictionary,* Springfield, Mass.: G. & C. Merriam Company, 1977.

2.1   COMMON TYPES OF SYSTEMS

As we can see from the definition above, there are many different types of systems; indeed, virtually everything that we come into contact with during our day-to-day life is either a system or a component of a system (or both).

Does this mean that we should study all kinds of systems, or hope to become experts in social systems, biological systems, and computer systems? Not at all! However, it is useful to organize the many different kinds of systems into useful categories. Many different categorizations are possible; indeed, the dictionary definition at the beginning of the chapter shows one categorization. Since our ultimate focus is on computer systems, we will begin by dividing all systems into two categories: *natural systems* and *man-made systems*.

2.2   NATURAL SYSTEMS

The vast majority of systems are not made by people: they exist in nature and, by and large, serve their own purpose. It is convenient to divide natural systems into two basic subcategories: *physical systems* and *living systems*. Physical systems include such diverse examples as:

- Stellar systems: galaxies, solar systems, and so on

- Geological systems: rivers, mountain ranges, and so on

- Molecular systems: complex organizations of atoms

Physical systems are interesting to study because, as pesky humans, we sometimes want to modify them. We also develop a variety of man-made systems, including computer systems, that must interact harmoniously with physical systems; so it is often important to be able to model those systems to ensure that we understand them as fully as possible.

Living systems, of course, encompass all of the myriad animals and plants around us, as well as our own human race. And, as James Miller elaborates in his monumental work, *Living Systems* [Miller, 1978], this category also includes *hierarchies* of individual living organisms, for example herbs, flocks, tribes, social groups, companies, and nations.

The study of living systems is a career in itself; a brief perusal of Miller's work will show what a massive subject it is. The purpose of this book is not to study living systems *per se;* but some of the properties and characteristics of familiar living systems can be used to help illustrate and better understand man-made systems. We often use an *analogy* to better understand something unfamiliar; among the more eloquent examples of living systems as an analogy of business systems and organizational systems is Stafford Beer's *Brain of the Firm* [Beer, 1972], and *The Heart of Enterprise* [Beer, 1978].

A more elaborate analogy can be drawn from Miller's categorization of the 19 critical subsystems of all living systems. Miller argues that living systems, whether at the level of the cell, the organ, the organism, the group, the organization, the society, or the supranational system, all contain the following subsystems:

- The *reproducer,* which is capable of giving rise to other systems similar to the one it is in. In a business organization, this might be a facilities planning division that makes new plants and builds new regional offices.

- The *boundary,* which holds together the components that make up the system, protects them from environmental stresses, and excludes or permits entry to various sorts of matter-energy and information. In a business organization, this might consist of the physical plant (office building, factory, and so on) and the guards and other security personnel who prevent unwanted intrusion.

- The *ingestor,* which brings matter-energy across the system boundary from its environment. In a business organization, this might be the receiving or the purchasing department, which brings in raw materials, office supplies, and the like. Or it might consist of the order entry department, which receives verbal and written orders for the organization's products and services.

- The *distributor,* which carries inputs from outside the system or outputs from its subsystems around the system to each component. In a business organization, this could be telephone lines, electronic mail, messengers, conveyor belts, and a variety of other mechanisms.

- The *converter,* which changes certain inputs to the system into forms more useful for the special processes of that particular system. Again, one could imagine a number of examples of this in a typical business organization.

- The *producer,* which forms stable associations that endure for significant periods among matter-energy inputs to the system or outputs from its converter, the materials synthesized being for growth, damage repair, or replacement of components of the system, or for providing energy for moving or constituting the system's outputs of products or information markets to its suprasystem.

- The *matter-energy storage* subsystem, which retains in the system, for different periods of time, deposits of various sorts of matter-energy.

- The *extruder,* which transmits matter-energy out of the system in the form of products or wastes.

- The *motor,* which moves the system or parts of it in relation to part or all of its environment or moves components of its environment in relation to each other.

- The *supporter,* which maintains the proper spatial relationships among components of the system, so that they can interact without weighing each other down or crowding each other.

- The *input transducer,* which brings markers bearing information into the system, changing them to other matter-energy forms suitable for transmission within it.

- The *internal transducer,* which receives, from other subsystems or components within the system, markers bearing information about significant alterations in those subsystems or components, changing them to other matter-energy forms of a sort that can be transmitted within it.

- The *channel and net,* which are composed of a single route in physical space, or multiple interconnected routes, by which markers bearing information are transmitted to all parts of the system.

- The *decoder,* which alters the code of information input to it through the input transducer or internal transducer into a private code that can be used internally by the system.

- The *associator,* which carries out the first stage of the learning process, forming enduring associations among items of information in the system.

- The *memory,* which carries out the second stage of the learning process, storing various sorts of information in the system for different periods of time.

- The *decider,* which receives information inputs from all other subsystems and transmits to them information outputs that control the entire system.

- The *encoder,* which alters the code of information input to it from other information processing subsystems, from a private code used internally by the system into a public code that can be interpreted by other systems in its environment.

- The *output transducer,* which puts out markers bearing information from the system, changing markers within the system into other matter-energy forms that can be transmitted over channels in the system's environment.

Figure 2.1(a) and 2.1(b) show an example of the 19 major subsystems for the communications team in a modern ocean liner; Figure 2.2(a) and 2.2(b) show the major subsystems for the ocean liner itself; and Figure 2.3(a) and 2.3(b) show the major subsystems for the entire country of Holland. These are worth studying, for they illustrate that if you look at any system that has living components, the major subsystems can be found.

Keep in mind that many man-made systems (and automated systems) interact with living systems; for example, computerized pacemakers interact with the human heart. In some cases, automated systems are being designed to replace living systems; and in other cases, researchers are considering living systems (known as organic computers) as components of automated systems. See [Hall, 1983], [DeYoung, 1983], [Shrady, 1985], and [Olmos, 1984] for discussions of this viewpoint. Living systems and man-made systems are often part of a larger metasystem, and the more we understand about both, the better we will be as systems analysts.

2.3   MAN-MADE SYSTEMS

As we saw from the definition at the beginning of the chapter, a number of systems are constructed, organized, and maintained by humans. These include such things as:

- Social systems: organizations of laws, doctrines, customs, and so on.

- An organized, disciplined collection of ideas: the Dewey decimal system for organizing books in libraries, the Weight-Watcher's system for shedding ugly extra pounds, and so on.

- Transportation systems: networks of highways, canals, airlines, ocean tankers, and the like.

- Communication systems: telephone, telex, smoke signals, the hand signals used by stock market traders, and so on.

- Manufacturing systems: factories, assembly lines, and so on.

- Financial systems: accounting, inventory, general ledger, stock brokerage, and the like.

Most of these systems include computers today; indeed, many could not survive without computers. However, it is equally important to point out that such systems existed *before* there were computers; indeed, some of these systems are still completely noncomputerized and may remain that way for many more decades. Others contain a computer as a component, but also include one or more noncomputerized (or manual) components.

Consider, for example, the common phrase, "John has a system for doing this job" or "Mary sure does have a systematic way of going about her work." Such phrases do not necessarily suggest that Mary has computerized her work or that John has used some of the formal modeling tools discussed in Chapters 9 and 10 to document (or model) how he proposes to do his job. But certainly the phrases imply that John and Mary have broken their work into a series of discrete steps, the cumulative sum of which will accomplish some overall purpose.

Whether or not a man-made system should be computerized is a question that we will discuss throughout this book; *it is not something you should take for granted.* As a systems analyst, you will naturally assume that *every* system that you come in contact with should be computerized; and the customer or user, (the owner of the system in question) with whom you interact will generally assume that you have such a bias. As we will see in later chapters, your primary job as a systems analyst will be to analyze, or study, the system to determine its *essence*: its required behavior *independent* of the technology used to implement the system.[4] In most cases, we will be in a position to determine whether it makes sense to use a computer to carry out the functions of the system only after modeling its essential behavior.

Why should some information processing systems *not* be automated? There may be many reasons, but here are some of the more common ones:

- *Cost*—it may be cheaper to continue carrying out the system functions and storing the system's information manually. It's not always true that computers are faster and cheaper than the "old-fashioned" way!

- *Convenience*—an automated system may take up too much room, make too much noise, generate too much heat, or consume too much electricity, or, in general, it may be a pain in the neck to have around. This is becoming less true with the pervasive influence of microprocessors—but it's still a factor.

- *Security*—if the information system is maintaining sensitive, confidential data, the user may not feel that an automated system is sufficiently secure. The user may want the ability to keep the information physically protected and locked up.

- *Maintainability*—the user might argue that a computerized information system would be cost-effective *except* that there is nobody on the staff that can maintain the computer hardware and/or software, so nobody would be able to repair the system if it broke down nor would anyone be able to make changes and enhancements.

- *Politics*—the user community may feel that computers threaten their jobs or make their jobs too boring and "mechanical," or they may have a dozen other reasons that the system analyst may regard as irrational. But since it's the users' system, their feelings are paramount. If they don't want an automated system, they will do their best to make it fail if it gets shoved down their throats.

2.4   AUTOMATED SYSTEMS

Most of this book will concentrate on *automated* systems, that is, man-made systems that interact with or are controlled by one or more computers. No doubt you have seen many different examples of automated systems in your day-to-day life: it seems that almost every aspect of our modern society is computerized. As a result, we can distinguish many different kinds of automated systems.

---

4 We will discuss the *essence* of a system and *essential models* in Chapter 17.

Subsystems that process both matter-energy and information: Boundary (Bo), wall of radio room (artifact).

Subsystems that process matter-energy: Ingestor (IN), stewardess who brings food into radio room from ship's galley; Distributor (DI), steward who hands out food to members of communications team; Converter (CO), steward who cuts bread, meat, and cheese for sandwiches; Producer (PR), steward who makes sandwiches and coffee; Matter-Energy Storage (MS), steward who stores various sorts of artifacts, including food in refrigerator, coats and hats of team members in closet, blankets and pillows in closet, and tools and equipment in chest of drawers; Extruder (EX), steward who removes used dishes, wastepaper, and other wastes from radio room; Supporter (SU), floor, walls, ceiling, furniture of radio room (artifacts).

Subsystems that process information: Input Transducer (it), radio operator who receives radio messages; Internal Transducer (in), day-shift foreperson who reports to chief signal officer on efficiency and morale of team members on his or her shift; Channel and Net (cn), all members of group who intercommunicate by speech that travels through the air of the radio room; Decoder (dc), radio operator who transcribes into English messages received in Morse code; Memory (me), secretary who keeps records of all messages received and transmitted; Decider (de), chief signal officer, who commands communications team; Encoder (en), radio operator who encodes English messages into Morse code; Output Transducer (ot), radio operator who transmits radio messages.

Figure 2.1(a): **Subsystems for an ocean liner communications team**

Even though there are many different kinds of automated systems, they all tend to have common components:

- *Computer hardware*—CPUs, disks, terminals, printers, magnetic tape drives, and so on.

- *Computer software*—systems programs such as operating systems, database systems, and telecommunication control programs, plus application programs that carry out the functions that the user wants.

- *People*—those who operate the system, those who provide its inputs and consume its outputs, and those who provide manual processing activities in a system.

- *Data*—the information that the system remembers over a period of time.

- *Procedures*—formal policies and instructions for operating the system.

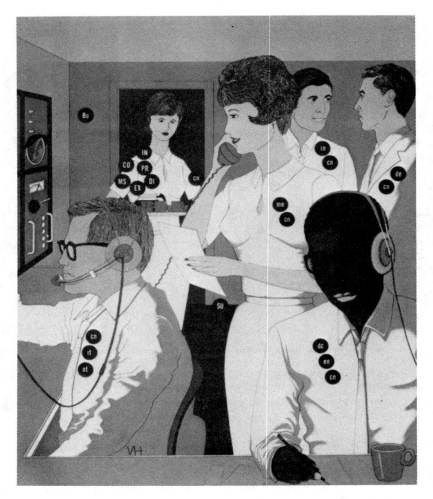

Figure 2.1(b): **Subsystems for an ocean liner communications team**

One way of categorizing automated systems is by *application*: manufacturing systems, accounting systems, military defense systems, and so on. However, this turns out not to be terribly useful, for the techniques that we will discuss in this book for analyzing, modeling, designing, and implementing automated systems are generally the same regardless of the application.[5]

---

[5] However, each application does have its own vocabulary, and culture, and set of procedures. The user generally expects that the systems analyst will know something about the details and business policy and procedures of his or her application so that everything won't have to be explained from the beginning. Thus, if you're going to be a systems analyst in a bank, it will probably be very useful to learn as much as you can about the business of banking. This is not a one-way street: bankers are learning more about the technology of information systems each day.

Subsystems that process both matter-energy and information: Reproducer (Re), representatives of the owning corporation; Boundary (Bo), ship's hull and personnel who guard and maintain it.

Subsystems that process matter-energy: Ingestor (IN), hatchway into ship's hold and personnel who load passengers, baggage, and freight into the ship; Distributor (DI), gangways, decks, staircases, and stewards, waiters, and porters who carry food, beverages, baggage, and various other sorts of matter-energy on them, as well as passengers who move about the ship on them; Converter (CO), galley personnel peeling vegetables and preparing other food for cooking; Producer (PR), chefs cooking food and bakers baking in ship's galley; Matter-Energy Storage (MS), ship's hold and fuel tanks and personnel in charge of them; Extruder (EX), smokestack for gaseous wastes, garbage and sewage outlets for liquid and solid wastes, and operating personnel responsible for seeing that wastes are properly removed; Motor (MO), ship's engines, drive shaft, propellors, and the entire hull of the ship, which moves passengers, crew, and freight in the sea, as well as engineers responsible for managing this movement; Supporter (SU), hull, sides, walls, and decks of ship and personnel who maintain them.

Subsystems that process information: Input Transducer (in), radio operator and other members of communications team who receive messages to ship; Internal Transducer (in), officer who reports to senior officer of the watch on states of various components that make up the ship; Channel and Net (cn), air between watch officers on the bridge of the ship over which they transmit and receive messages; Decoder (dc), radio operator in communications team who decodes Morse code messages into English after they are received; Memory (me), logbooks of past trips, charts of the seas, and those personnel who consult them in the ship's chart room; Decider (de), captain and other ship's officers; Encoder (en), radio operator in communications team who encodes English messages into Morse code in order to transmit them; Output Transducer (or), radio operator and other members of communications team who transmit messages from ship.

Figure 2.2(a): **Major subsystems for an ocean liner**

Figure 2.2(b): **Major subsystems for an ocean liner**

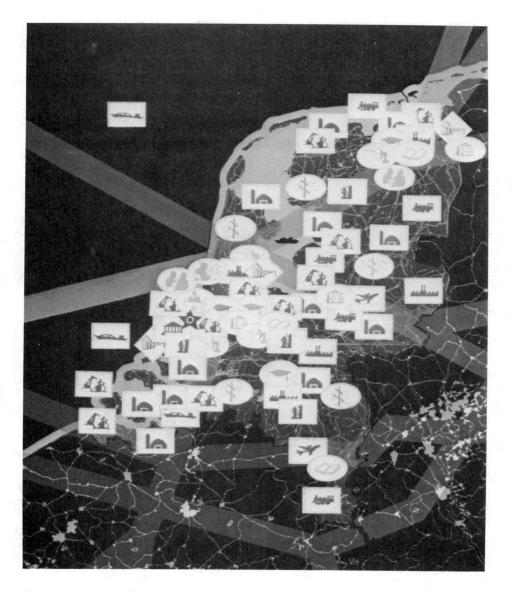

Figure 2.3(a): **Major subsystems of the country of Holland**

Subsystems which process both matter-energy and information: Boundary , organizations defending, guarding, or policing the national border.

Subsystems which process matter-energy: Ingestor , organizations, such as airlines, railroads, trucking companies or steamship lines, which import various forms of matter-energy into the country; Distributor , national organizations which transport various forms of matter-energy by water, road, railroad, or airline; Converter , organizations which convert raw forms of matter-energy into other forms useful to the society; Producer , manufacturing organizations which make products for the society or for export; Matter-Energy Storage , organizations like warehouses, reservoirs, and electric power plants which store various forms of matter-energy; Extruder , organizations which export products of the Netherlands to other nations or eject wastes into the sea and agencies which deport unwanted persons; Motor , units of transportation or construction industry, armed forces, or space agency; Supporter , public buildings and land.

Subsystems which process information: Input Transducer , organizations that receive telegraph, cable, telephone, or radar signals or foreign news from outside borders of the Netherlands; Internal Transducer representative legislature, political party officials, or public opinion polling organization that receives communications and reports from all parts of the Netherlands; Channel and Net , national communications facility; Decoder , foreign office that decodes secret dispatches received from Netherlands embassies throughout the world; Associator , Dutch teaching institutions; Memory , libraries; Decider , the Queen and her government in The Hague; Encoder , governmental press secretary or speech writers; Output Transducer persons who speak officially for The Netherlands.

Figure 2.3(b): **Major subsystems for the country of Holland**

A more useful categorization of automated systems is as follows:

- On-line systems

- Real-time systems

- Decision-support systems

- Knowledge-based systems

We will examine each of these next.

2.4.1   On-Line Systems

In an earlier book ([Yourdon, 1972]), I defined on-line systems in the following way:

> An on-line system is one which accepts input directly from the area where it is created. It is also a system in which the output, or results of computation, are returned directly to where they are required.

This usually means that the computer system has a hardware architecture that looks like that in Figure 2.4.

A common characteristic of on-line systems is that data are entered into the computer system and received from the computer system *remotely.* That is, the users of the computer system typically interact with the computer from terminals[6] that may be located hundreds of miles from other terminals and from the computer itself.

Another characteristic of an on-line system is that its stored data, that is, its files or its database, are usually organized in such a way that individual pieces of data (such as an individual airline reservation record or an individual personnel record) can be retrieved and/or modified (1) quickly and (2) without necessarily accessing any other piece of data in the system. This is in stark contrast to the *batch* systems, which were more common in the 1960s and 1970s. In a batch computer system, information is usually retrieved on a sequential basis, which means that the computer system reads through *all* the records in its database, processing and updating those records for which there is some activity. The difference between a batch computer system and an on-line system is analogous to the difference between finding a specific musical selection on a tape cassette and a musical selection on an audio disk player; one involves sequential access through all the tracks, while the other allows "random" access to any one of the tracks without listening to the others.

---

6 The word terminal is so commonly used throughout society today that I'm not even sure it needs to be defined. However, you should be aware that there are many synonyms: "screen," "workstation," "keyboard," and "display unit" are among the more common ones. And there are common abbreviations used to describe the input/output device with which one communicates with the computer: "CRT" for "cathode ray tube," "VDU" for "visual display unit," and so on. These terms will be used interchangeably throughout the book.

Because an on-line system interacts directly with people (i.e., human users at terminals), it is important for the systems analyst to carefully plan the human-computer interface.[7] That is, the analyst must have a way of *modeling* all the possible messages that the human user can type on his or her terminal and all of the responses that the system can make—and all of the responses that the human can make to the computer's response, and so on. This is usually done by identifying all the *states* that the computer and the user can find themselves in and identifying all the state-changes. An example of a state that the computer in an automated bank-teller system might be in is "The user has inserted his credit card, and has identified himself, but has not yet told me his confidential password." An example of a state-change is, "He's told me his password, and now I can proceed to find out whether he wants to withdraw cash or display his current bank balance." Another state-change might be, "He has tried unsuccessfully three times to enter his password, and now I am going to sound the alarm." These states and changes of state are typically modeled with *state-transition diagrams,* which we will discuss in detail in Chapter 13.

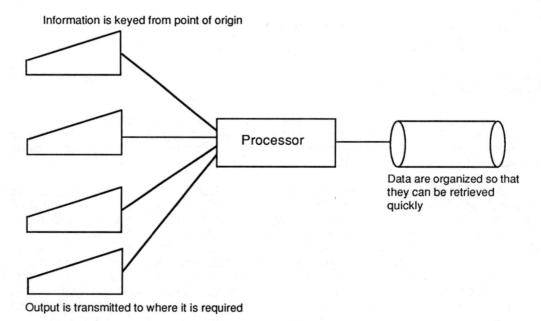

Information is keyed from point of origin

Processor

Data are organized so that they can be retrieved quickly

Output is transmitted to where it is required

Figure 2.4: **An on-line system**

Because on-line systems usually need to retrieve data quickly (in order to respond to inquiries and commands from on-line terminals), it is usually very important to design the files and databases as efficiently as possible. Indeed, it is often true that the *computations* performed by an on-line system are relatively trivial, while the *data*

---

7 This is sometimes referred to as the "man-machine dialogue," or the "man-machine interface." More and more systems development organizations are changing to "human-computer interface" or just "human interface" to avoid any unnecessary bias.

(especially the structure and organization of the data maintained by the on-line system) are rather complex. Hence the data modeling tools discussed in Chapter 12 are of great importance to the systems analyst and systems designer.

The decision to make a system on-line or not is, in the context of this book, an *implementation* decision, that is, not something that ought to be determined by the systems analyst, but rather by the people implementing the system. However, since the decision has such an obvious impact on the user (the presence or absence of computer terminals, and so on), it is an implementation decision in which the users will generally want to participate. Indeed, it is part of the *user implementation model,* which we will discuss in Chapter 21.

2.4.2   Real-Time Systems

A real-time system is considered by many to be a variant of an on-line system; indeed, many people use the terms interchangeably. However, it is important to distinguish between the two; we will use the following definition from [Martin, 1967]:

> A real-time computer system may be defined as one which controls an environment by receiving data, processing them, and returning the results sufficiently quickly to affect the environment at that time.

The term "sufficiently quickly" is, of course, subject to many interpretations. Certainly there are many on-line systems—banking systems, airline reservation systems, stock brokerage systems—that are expected to react within one or two seconds to a message typed on the terminal. However, in most real-time systems, the computer must react within *milliseconds* and sometimes within *microseconds* to inputs that it receives. This is characteristic of the following kinds of systems:

- *Process control systems*—the computer systems that are used to monitor and control oil refineries, chemical manufacturing processes, milling and machining operations are examples.

- *Automated teller systems*—the "cash machines" that many of us use for making simple deposits and withdrawals at a bank are examples.

- *High-speed data acquisition systems*—computer systems that receive high-speed telemetry data from orbiting satellites, or computers that capture massive amounts of data from laboratory experiments are examples.

- *Missile guidance systems*—computer systems that must track the trajectory of a missile and make continuous adjustments to the orientation and thrust of the missile engines.

- *Telephone switching systems*—computer systems that monitor voice and data transmissions over thousands of telephone calls, detecting phone numbers being dialed, on-hook and off-hook conditions, and all of the other many conditions of the typical telephone network.

- *Patient monitoring systems*—computer systems that monitor various patient "vital signs" (e.g., temperature and pulse) and either adjust medication or sound an alarm if those vital signs stray outside some predetermined conditions.

Besides speed, another characteristic differentiates real-time systems from on-line systems: on-line systems generally interact with *people,* while real-time systems interact with both people and an *environment* that is generally autonomous and often hostile. Indeed, the overriding concern of the real-time systems analyst is that, if the computer does not respond quickly enough, the environment will get out of control—incoming data may be irrevocably lost, or a missile may stray so far from its trajectory that it cannot be recovered, or a manufacturing process may blow up.[8] By contrast, an on-line system that does not respond quickly enough will generally do nothing more than make its users impatient and grumpy. People may "explode" or "blow up" in a figurative sense if they have to wait more than three seconds to get an answer from an on-line system, but not in a literal sense. This is illustrated in Figure 2.5.

Because of this concern with instant response to system inputs, a systems analyst working with real-time systems is generally very concerned with the *time-dependent behavior* of the system. We will discuss tools for modeling time-dependent system behavior in Chapter 13.

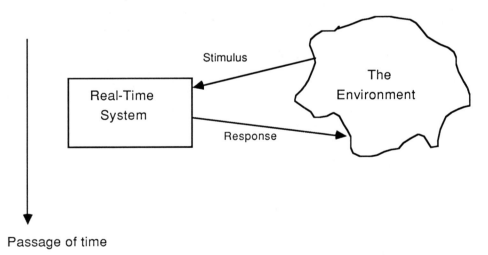

Passage of time

Figure 2.5: **A real-time system**

8 One of the more interesting examples of such a real-time situation involved a project team whose job was to attach a small computer to a nuclear bomb. When the bomb was detonated (as part of an underground testing program), the computer had only a very few microseconds to capture as much data as possible and transmit it to a remote computer system before the hardware and software vaporized as part of the explosion. Now *that* is a real-time processing requirement.

From an implementation point of view, real-time systems (as well as some on-line systems) are characterized by the following features:

- Many processing activities that are taking place simultaneously.

- Assignment of different priorities to different processing tasks: some need to be serviced immediately, while others can be delayed for reasonable periods of time.

- Interruption of one processing task before it is finished in order to begin servicing another, higher-priority task.

- Extensive communication between tasks, especially since many of the tasks are working on different aspects of an overall process like controlling a manufacturing process.

- Simultaneous access to common data, both in memory and on secondary storage, thus requiring elaborate "hand-shaking" and "semaphore" procedures to ensure that common data do not become corrupted.

- Dynamic use of and allocation of RAM memory in the computer system, since it is often uneconomical (even in today's world of cheap memory) to assign enough fixed memory to handle high-volume peak situations.

2.4.3   Decision-Support Systems and Strategic Planning Systems

Most of the automated information systems that have been built in the United States during the past 30 years have been *operational* systems that help carry out the details of an organization's day to day work. These systems, also known as *trans-action-processing* systems, include such familiar examples as payroll systems, order entry systems, accounting systems, and manufacturing systems. In organizations around the United States, these operational systems have been developed slowly, painfully, and at great cost; since many of them were initially developed more than 20 years ago, they are on the verge of collapse; thus, new operational systems are continuously being built in major organizations around the world.

But to the extent that today's operational systems continue to wobble along, many organizations are focusing their attention on a new kind of system: *decision-support.* As the term implies, these computer systems do not make decisions on their own, but instead help managers and other professional "knowledge workers" in an organization make intelligent, informed decisions about various aspects of the oper-ation. Typically, the decision-support systems are passive in the sense that they do not operate on a regular basis: instead, they are used on an *ad hoc* basis, whenever needed.

There are a number of simple examples of decision-support systems: spread-sheet programs (e.g., Lotus 1-2-3, Microsoft's Multiplan, Ashton-Tate's Framework), statistical analysis systems, marketing forecast programs, and others. Indeed, a com-mon characteristic of the decision-support systems is that they not only retrieve and display data, but also perform a variety of mathematical and statistical analyses of the data; decision-support systems also have the capability, in most cases, of presenting information in a variety of graphic forms (tables, charts, etc.) as well as conventional reports. Figure 2.6 shows a typical financial spreadsheet that a manager might use to evaluate the profitability of a division within the organization; Figure 2.7 shows a typical chart showing the division's revenues as compared to the industry average. Note that in both cases the output produced by this system does not "make" a decision, but rather provides relevant information in a useful format so that the manager can make the decision.

Some decision-support systems are useful for articulating and mechanizing the rules used to reach a business decision. One such system is a program called Lightyear, (from Lightyear, Inc.), which runs on IBM-compatible personal computers. It allows the user (or multiple users) to describe the details of a decision-oriented problem; an example might be the problem of deciding where to locate a new office facility. First, the user identifies the criteria that will be used to make the decision. For the problem of locating an office facility, this might include such things as "Must be accessible by public transport" and "Must not be in an earthquake zone." Some of the criteria are binary in the sense that failure to satisfy them will eliminate a candidate or cause the automatic selection of a candidate. Some of the criteria may be rankable on a numeric scale; for example, one of the criterion might be corporate income tax rate, which will take on different numerical values depending on the city and state where the new office is located. And the criteria themselves can be ranked in relationship to one another: perhaps a tax rate has a value of 5, on a 10-point scale, while convenient nearby shopping facilities has a value of 3. Having thus defined the criteria for making a decision, various candidates can be evaluated and analyzed; the best candidate will automatically be chosen by the Lightyear program. Figure 2.8 illustrates this process.

There is nothing magic about this: the program is merely applying, in a mechanistic way, the evaluation rules provided by the user. But the power of the system is more than just the mechanical calculation: it forces the user to articulate her or his criteria, which is often not done. It also provides a neutral facility for gathering the opinions of many users in situations where it is important to achieve a consensus. On an emotionally sensitive issue like choosing a new office location (e.g., relocating the families of those making the decision), it can be very useful to not only articulate the decision criteria but also to articulate each decision maker's ranking of the criteria. If two members of the office location committee are going to disagree, it should at least be clear to them what the basis of their disagreement is.

Strategic planning systems are used by senior management to evaluate and analyze the mission of the organization. Rather than providing advice about an isolated business decision, these systems provide broader, more general advice about the nature of the marketplace, the preferences of the customers, the behavior of competition, and so on. This is usually within the province of the Strategic Planning Department, or the Long Range Planning Department, though it may be a more informal activity carried out by one or two senior managers.

Strategic planning is a concept that became popular during World War II (though some organizations were obviously doing it long before that), and it is the subject of many books; see [Steiner, 1979], [Drucker, 1974], and [Ackoff, 1970]. Strategic planning systems are not computer programs per se; they are a complex combination of activities and procedures, much of it carried out by humans using information gleaned from outside sources (market surveys and the like) and internal data from the organization's operational systems and decision-support systems. Steiner points out that there can be many types of strategic planning systems, depending on the size and nature of the organization.

Two typical models are portrayed in Figures 2.9 and 2.10. The strategic planning system based on gap analysis tries to identify the discrepancy between an organization's current position (in terms of revenues, profits, etc.) and the position desired by senior management, stockholders, and others.

Strategic planning systems are a subject in itself, and we will not cover them in detail in this book. Our emphasis will be primarily on operational and decision-support systems.

Note the relationship between the three different kinds of systems discussed in this section. As shown in Figure 2.11, the operational systems represent the foundation upon which the decision-support systems and strategic planning systems rest. The operational systems *create* the data required by the higher-level systems, and they continue to update those data on a continuous basis.

Fribble Division Profit/Loss Projections

	1Q	2Q	3Q	4Q	TOTAL
Domestic sales	400	425	250	375	1450
International sales	100	150	200	125	575
License fee	25	60	50	25	160
Miscellaneous income	10	10	15	10	45
TOTAL REVENUE	535	645	515	535	2230
Cost of sales	123	148	118	123	513
Salaries	100	120	120	125	465
Other employment costs	15	18	18	19	70
Rent & occupancy	15	15	15	18	63
Telephone	20	20	20	20	80
Postage	5	6	5	7	23
Travel/entertainment	10	10	10	10	40
Legal/accounting	10	10	15	10	45
Depreciation	12	13	13	14	52
Miscellaneous expenses	5	5	5	5	20
TOTAL EXPENSES	315	365	339	351	1371
PROFIT/LOSS	220	280	176	184	859

Figure 2.6: **A typical spreadsheet**

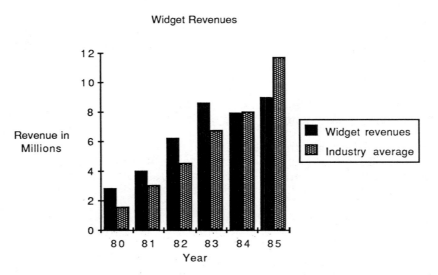

Figure 2.7: **A typical chart produced by a decision-support system**

The pyramid shape of Figure 2.11 represents another typical characteristic of information systems found in most organizations today: the *size* of the operational systems (measured in person-years, or millions of COBOL statements, etc.) vastly exceeds that of the decision-support systems and strategic planning systems. But we can expect this to change gradually over the next decade. As mentioned earlier, many organizations have spent the past thirty years building their operational systems: *for the most part, the job is done.*[9]   Much of the work now being done in some of these large organizations is the development of decision-support systems and strategic planning systems.

2.4.4   Knowledge-Based Systems

A relatively new term in the computer industry is that of "expert systems" or "knowledge-based systems." Such systems are associated with the field of artificial intelligence, defined in the following way by Elaine Rich [Rich, 1984]:

---

[9] There are some exceptions: smaller organizations that have not yet computerized much of their day-to-day operation; old operational systems developed by Fortune 500 companies in the 1960s that are on the verge of collapse; and new operational systems required by mergers, acquisitions, and forays into new markets and products; and the defense community has an apparently never-ending list of new operational systems to be built. Overall, though, the trend is that of a slow movement away from operational systems and toward the decision support systems.

The goal of computer scientists working in the field of artificial intelligence is to produce programs that imitate human performance in a wide variety of "intelligent" tasks. For some expert systems, that goal is close to being attained; for others, although we do not yet know how to construct programs that perform well on their own, we can begin to build programs that significantly assist people in their performance of a task.

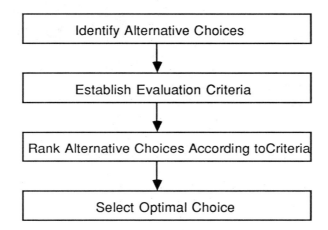

Figure 2.8: **The Lightyear decision-support system**

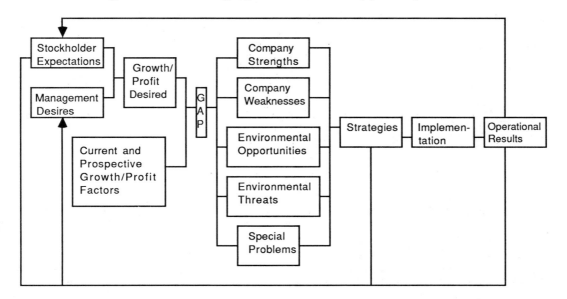

Figure 2.9: **A strategic planning model centered on gap analysis**

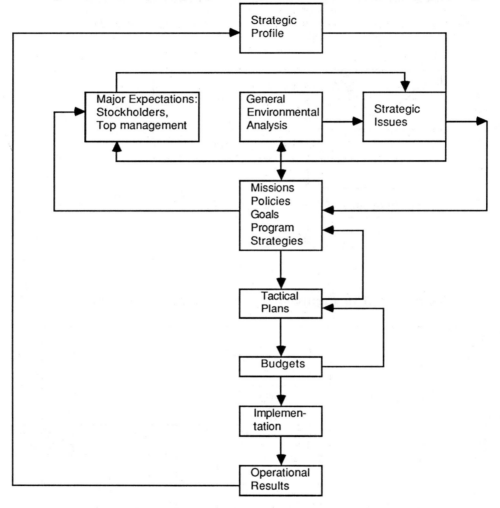

Figure 2.10: **A strategic planning model based on market strength**

Two eminent writers in the field of artificial intelligence, Feigenbaum and McCorduck describe knowledge-based systems and expert systems in [Feigenbaum and McCorduck, 1983] in the following way:

> Knowledge-based systems, to labor the obvious, contain large amounts of varied knowledge which they bring to bear on a given task. Expert systems are a species of knowledge-based system, though the two terms are often used interchangeably.

Just what is an expert system? It is a computer program that has built into it the knowledge and capability that will allow it to operate at the expert's level. Expert performance means, for example, the level of performance of M.D.'s doing diagnosis and therapeutics, or Ph.D.'s or very experienced people doing engineering, scientific, or managerial tasks. The expert system is a high-level intellectual support for the human expert, which explains its other name, intelligent assistant.

Expert systems are usually built to be able to explain the lines of reasoning that led to their decisions. Some of them can even explain why they rejected certain paths of reasoning and chose others. This transparency is a major feature of expert systems. Designers work hard to achieve it because they understand that the ultimate use of an expert system will depend on its credibility to the users, and the credibility will arise because the behavior is transparent, explainable.

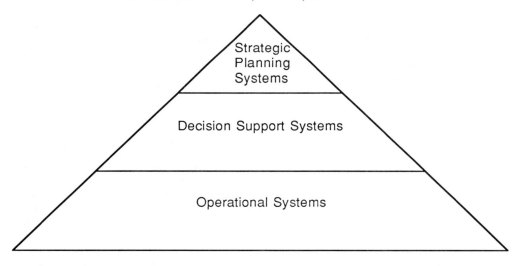

Figure 2.11: **The hierarchy of information processing systems**

Expert systems are still generally thought of as specialized systems, using special computer hardware, and such special programming languages as LISP and PRO-LOG. However, simple expert systems have begun appearing on standard-size personal computers, and expert system "shells"—software frameworks for developing specific expert system applications—have begun to appear in standard COBOL-based mainframe environments.

While expert systems are beyond the scope of this book, they will gradually become a more and more important component of the "typical" system that you work on as a systems analyst. Beginning in the late 1980s, researchers have begun studying the relationship between classical software development techniques and artificial intelligence; typical of this is [Jacob and Froscher, 1986]. Keller ([Keller, 1987]) foresees a time in the near future when AI and expert systems will be part of the "normal" activity of systems analysis; others, such as [Barstow, 1987] and [Lubars and Harandi, 1987] expect that artificial intelligence will be useful for helping systems analysts document user requirements by the mid-1990s. We will return to this point later.

2.5   GENERAL SYSTEMS PRINCIPLES

All the examples given above have one thing in common: they are all *systems.* While they may be different in many ways, they also share many common characteristics. The study of these "common characteristics" is known as *general systems theory,* and it is a fascinating topic to explore. For an initial glimpse of the subject, read [Weinberg, 1976]; for another, more formal view, consult [Bertalanffy, 1969]; and for a more humorous view of the often perverse nature of systems, read Gall's delightful *Systemantics* [Gall, 1977].

While the subject of general systems theory is beyond the scope of this book, there are a few "general" principles that are of particular interest to people building automated information systems. They include the following:

1.   *The more specialized a system is, the less able it is to adapt to different circumstances.* This is often used to describe biological systems (e.g., animals that have difficulty adapting to new environments), but it applies to computer systems, too. The more "general-purpose" a system is, the less "optimized" it is for any particular situation; but the more the system is optimized for a particular situation, the less adaptable it will be to new circumstances. This is a real problem for many real-time systems, which must be optimized in order to provide sufficiently fast responses to external stimuli; but the optimization process generally takes advantage of the idiosyncrasies of the special computer hardware and systems software used on the project, which means that it may be very difficult to transport the system to different hardware. This principle is also important for many business systems, which "mirror" the user's policies, which might also be extremely specialized. The more specialized the user's requirements for a payroll system, for example, the less likely that an off-the-shelf commercial package can be used.

2.   *The larger a system is, the more of its resources that must be devoted to its everyday maintenance.* Biology is, once again, the most familiar example of this principle: dinosaurs spent a major portion of their waking life stuffing food into their mouth in order to maintain their huge carcasses. But it applies to armies, companies, and a variety of other systems, too, including the automated systems that you will be studying in this book. A small "toy" system, the kind that you can develop in an afternoon, will usually involve very little "bureaucracy," whereas a large system will require *enormous* effort in such "unproductive" areas as error-checking, editing, backup, maintenance, security, and documentation.[10]

---

10 Users often don't appreciate this phenomenon, and it may be one of the reasons for the current fascination with fourth generation languages and prototyping tools. You can quickly build a system in a fourth generation language that does the main processing parts (and thus provide instant gratification for the user), but it takes a *lot* of work to put in the additional intelligence for error-checking, backup, maintenance, security, performance tuning, documentation, and so on. You must keep this point in mind or you are likely to be "railroaded" by the user into building a "quick and dirty" system that ultimately fails. To give you an idea of the extent of something as mundane as documentation, consider this statistic reported by Capers Jones in *Programming Productivity* (New York: McGraw-Hill, 1986): a large telecommunication system had 120 English words for each line of source code, totaling 30 million words

3.   *Systems are always part of larger systems, and they can always be partitioned into smaller systems.* This point is important for two reasons: first, it suggests an obvious way to organize a computer system that we are trying to develop—by partitioning it into smaller systems (we will see much of this in later chapters of this book). More important, though, it suggests that the *definition* of the system we are trying to develop is arbitrary—we could have chosen a slightly smaller system or a slightly larger system. Choosing the *scope* of a system and defining it carefully so that everyone knows what is inside the system and what is outside is an important activity; we discuss it in detail in Chapter 18. This is more difficult than it might seem: both users and systems analysts often think that the system boundary is fixed and immutable and that everything outside the boundary is not worth studying. I am indebted to Lavette Teague and Christopher Pidgeon ([Teague and Pidgeon, 1985]) for locating the following example of systems within systems, taken from [Eberhard, 1970]:

> One anxiety inherent in design methods is the hierarchical nature of complexity. This anxiety moves in two directions, escalation and infinite regression. I will use a story, "The Warning of the Doorknob," to illustrate the principle of escalation.
>
> This has been my experience in Washington when I had money to give away. If I gave a contract to a designer and said, "The doorknob to my office doesn't have much imagination, much design content. Will you design me a new doorknob?" He would say "Yes," and after we establish a price he goes away. A week later he comes back and says, "Mr. Eberhard, I've been thinking about that doorknob. First, we ought to ask ourselves whether a doorknob is the best way of opening and closing a door." I say, "Fine, I believe in imagination, go to it." He comes back later and says, "You know, I've been thinking about your problem, and the only reason you want a doorknob is you presume you want a door to your office. Are you *sure* that a door is the best way of controlling egress, exit, and privacy?" "No, I'm not sure at all." "Well I want to worry about that problem." He comes back a week later and says, "The only reason we have to worry about the aperture problem is that you insist on having four walls around your office. Are you sure that is the best way of organizing this space for the kind of work you do as a bureaucrat?" I say, "No, I'm not sure at all." Well, this escalates until (and this has literally happened in two contracts, although not through this exact process) our physical designer comes back with a very serious face. "Mr. Eberhard, we have to decide whether capitalistic democracy is the best way to organize our country before I can possibly attack your problem."
>
> On the other hand is the problem of infinite regression. If this man faced with the design of the doorknob had say, "Wait. Before I worry about the doorknob, I want to study the shape of man's hand and what man is capable of doing with it," I would say, "Fine." He would come back and say, "The more I thought about it, there's a *fit* problem. What I want to study first is how metal is

---

10 (cont.) and 60,000 pages; a large government system had 200 English words per line of source code, totaling 125 million words and *250,000 pages* of documentation.

formed, what the technologies are for making things with metal in order that I can know what the real parameters are for fitting the hand." "Fine." But then he says, "You know I've been looking at metal-forming and it all depends on metallurgical properties. I really want to spend three or four months looking at metallurgy so that I can understand the problem better." "Fine." After three months, he'll come back and say, "Mr. Eberhard, the more I look at metallurgy, the more I realize that it is atomic structure that's really at the heart of this problem." And so, our physical designer is in atomic physics from the doorknob. That is one of our anxieties, the hierarchical nature of complexity."

4. *Systems grow.* Of course, this could not really be true for *all* systems or it would violate a very familiar general systems principle, the law of conservation of energy. But many of the systems with which we are familiar *do* grow, and it is important to recognize this, because we often fail (as systems analysts and systems designers) to take it into account when we begin developing the system. A typical information system, for example, will grow to include more software than initially planned, more data, more functions, and more users. For example, Lientz and Swanson found in a classic survey of nearly 500 data processing organizations around the country ([Lientz and Swanson, 1980]), that the amount of code in an existing automated system increases by approximately 10% per year, and the size of the database increases by about 5% each year. You *cannot* assume that a system you build will remain static; the cost of expanding it over time should be included in your "cost-benefit" calculations, which we discuss in Chapter 5 and in Appendix C.

2.6   SUMMARY

Systems analysts in the data processing profession are often victims of the law of specialization discussed above: they become experts in their own field, without realizing that there are other kinds of "system builders" and that some general principles might apply. The primary purpose of this chapter has been to broaden your horizon and provide you with a larger perspective before we plunge more deeply into the study of automated information systems.

Obviously, you can't be an expert in living systems, physical systems, and all forms of man-made systems in addition to automated information systems. But since the systems you are likely to build almost always interact with these other forms of system, it is important for you to be aware of them. By understanding that other systems obey many of the same general principles as the computer system you're building, you're likely to be more successful at developing interfaces between your system and the external world.

REFERENCES

1. Edward Yourdon, *Design of On-Line Computer Systems.* Englewood Cliffs, N.J.: Prentice-Hall, 1972, page 4.

2. James Martin, *Design of Real-Time Computer Systems.* Englewood Cliffs, N.J.: Prentice-Hall, 1967.

3. James Grier Miller, *Living Systems.* New York: McGraw-Hill, 1978.

4. George Steiner, *Strategic Planning,.* New York: Free Press, 1979.

5. Peter Drucker, *Management: Tasks, Responsibilities, Practices.* New York: Harper & Row, 1974.

6. Russell L. Ackoff, *A Concept of Corporate Planning.* New York: Wiley, 1970.

7. Stafford Beer, *Brain of the Firm.* New York: Wiley, 1972.

8. Stafford Beer, *The Heart of Enterprise.* New York: Wiley, 1978.

9. Stephen Hall, "Biochips," *High Technology,* December 1983.

10. H. Garrett DeYoung, "Biosensors," *High Technology,* November 1983.

11. Nicholas Shrady, "Molecular Computing," *Forbes,* July 29, 1985.

12. David Olmos, "DOD Finances Case Western Biochip Research Center,"*Computerworld,* September 3, 1984.

13. Elaine Rich, "The Gradual Expansion of Artificial Intelligence," *IEEE Computer,* May 1984.

14. Edward Feigenbaum and Pamela McCorduck, *The Fifth Generation.* Reading, Mass.: Addison-Wesley, 1983.

15. R.J.K. Jacob and J.N. Froscher, "Software Engineering for Rule-Based Software Systems,"*Proceedings of the 1986 Fall Joint Computer Conference.* Washington, D.C.: IEEE Computer Society Press, 1986.

16. Robert E. Keller, *Expert Systems Technology: Development and Application.* Englewood Cliffs, N.J.: Prentice-Hall, 1987.

17. Robert Alloway and Judith Quillard, "User Managers' Systems Needs," CISR Working Paper 86. Cambridge, Mass.: MIT Sloan School Center for Information Systems Research, April 1982.

18. Ludwig von Bertalanffy, *General Systems Theory.* New York: George Braziller, 1969.

19. Gerald Weinberg, *An Introduction to General Systems Thinking.* New York: Wiley, 1976.

20. John Gall, *Systemantics.* New York: Quadrangle/The New York Times Book Company, 1977.

21. D. Barstow, "Artificial Intelligence and Software Engineering," *Proceedings of the 9th International Software Engineering Conference,* April 1987.

22. M.D. Lubars and M.T. Harandi, "Knowledge-Based Software Design Using Design Schemas," *Proceedings of the 9th International Software Engineering Conference,* April 1987.

23. Bennet P. Lientz and E. Burton Swanson, *Software Maintenance Management,* Reading, Mass.: Addison-Wesley, 1980.

24. Lavette Teague and Christopher Pidgeon, *Structured Analysis Methods for Computer Information Systems.* Chicago: Science Research Associates, 1985.

25. John P. Eberhard, "We Ought to Know the Difference," *Engineering Methods in Environmental Design and Planning,* Gary T. Moore, ed. Cambridge, Mass.: MIT Press, 1970, pp. 364-365.

QUESTIONS AND EXERCISES

1. Give two examples of each of the definitions of a system provided by Webster's dictionary in the beginning of Chapter 2.

2. Give five examples of systems that have lasted for at least 1 million years and that are still in existence today.

3. Give five examples of man-made systems that have lasted for more than 1000 years. For each case, give a brief description of why they have lasted and whether they can be expected to continue surviving over the next thousand years.

4. Give five examples of *non*-man-made systems that have failed in your lifetime. Why did they fail?

5. Give five examples of man-made systems that have failed in your lifetime. Why did they fail?

6. Research Project: read Miller's *Living Systems* and provide a book report.

7. Research Project: read Beers' *Brain of the Firm* and provide a book report for your colleagues.

8. Research Project: read Beers' *The Heart of Enterprise* and provide a book report for your colleagues.

9. From Section 2.3; give an example of a man-made system that, in your opinion, should *not* be automated. Why do you think it should not be automated? What would go wrong?

10. Give an example of a nonautomated system that, in your opinion, *should* be automated. Why do you think it should be automated? What would the benefits be? What would the costs be? How confident are you of the benefits and costs?

11. Give examples of Miller's 19 subsystems for the following kinds of automated systems: (a) payroll, (b) inventory control, (c) the telephone system.

12. Pick a small organization that you are relatively familiar with, or a department or division of a large organization. For the organization that you have chosen, conduct an inventory of the systems that it uses. How many of them are operational systems? How many are decision-support systems? How many are strategic planning systems? Are there any other useful categories of systems? To help you focus on this area, consult [Alloway and Quillard, 1982].

13. Give five examples from your own experience of (a) real-time systems, (b) on-line systems, (c) decision-support systems, (d) strategic planning systems, and (e) expert systems.

14. Figure 2.4 shows a typical hardware configuration for an on-line system. Draw a diagram for a reasonable *different* hardware configuration. Does it make sense to have some of the system's data physically located at the terminals? When, in the development of the system, should this be discussed with the user?

15. Give an example of a commercial system that is described either as an "artificial intelligence" or a "knowledge-based" system that, in your opinion, is not honestly or accurately described. Why do you think the description is misleading?

16. Could the stimulus-response model shown in Figure 2.5 apply to systems other than real-time systems? Don't *all* systems respond to stimuli? What is special about real-time systems?

17. Can a decision-support system actually make decisions? If not, why not? What could be done to change the typical decision-support system so that it *could* make decisions? Would this be desirable? What are the trade-offs?

3 PLAYERS IN THE SYSTEMS GAME

All the world's a stage,
And all the men and women merely players:
They have their exits and their entrances;
And one man in his time plays many parts,
Shakespeare,
As You Like It, II, vii

In this chapter, you will learn:

1. The categories of people with whom you will interact in a project.

2. The three main categories of users, by job category.

3. User reactions during a systems development project.

4. The difference between novice and expert users.

5. The role of management in a systems development project.

6. The role of the systems analyst in a systems development project.

7. Other roles in a systems development project.

As a systems analyst, you will work on systems development projects with a variety of other people. The cast of characters will change from project to project; the personalities will differ dramatically; and the *number* of people that you interact with will range from as few as one to as many as several dozen. However, the roles are fairly consistent, and you will see them over and over again.

To be a successful systems analyst requires more than an understanding of the technology of computers. Among other things, it requires interpersonal skills: you will be spending a great deal of your time working with other people, many of whom speak a very different "language" than you do, and many of whom will find your language of computer technology alien and frightening. Thus, it is important to know what expectations such people will have of you and what expectations you should have of them.

This chapter concentrates on the characteristics of the following major categories of "players" that you are likely to encounter in a typical systems development project:

- Users

- Management

- Auditors, quality assurance people, and "standards bearers"

- Systems analysts

- Systems designers

- Programmers

- Operations personnel

Each of these categories is described next.

3.1   USERS

The first, and by far the most important, player in the systems game is someone known to systems analysts as a *user*. The user is the person (or group of people) for whom the system is being built. He or she is the person whom you will interview, often in great detail, to learn what features the new system must have to be successful.

It should be emphasized that most users don't refer to *themselves* as "users"; after all, the word is often used in a different context to describe people addicted to drugs. In some organizations, the data processing organization avoids the problem by using the term *customer* or *owner* to identify the user. The user is the "owner" in the sense that he or she receives, or inherits—and thus owns—the system when it is finally built. And the user is the "customer" in at least two important respects: (1) as in so many other professions, "the customer is always right," regardless of how demanding, unpleasant, or irrational he or she may seem, and (2) the customer is ultimately the person paying for the system and usually has the right or ability to refuse to pay if he or she is unhappy with the product received.

In most cases, it is fairly easy to identify the user (or users): the user is typically the person who makes a formal request for a system. In a small organization, this is usually a very informal process; it may consist of the user picking up the phone and calling the Official Systems Analyst to say, "Hey, Joan! I need a new system to keep track of our new Widget marketing campaign!" In a large organization, the initiation of a systems development project is usually much more formalized. The "request for system survey and study," as it is sometimes called, usually goes through several levels of approval before the systems analyst gets involved. More on this in Chapter 5.

However, there are a number of situations where the identity of the real user is not known, or where the systems analyst has little or no opportunity to interact directly with the user. One common example is that of a system being developed by a consulting firm or software company: the interaction between the client organization and the consulting firm may take place between contract officers or other administrative agencies, sometimes with explicit provisos that the systems analyst may *not* talk directly to the user. Even if the system is being developed entirely within a single organization, the "real" user may nominate a spokesperson to work with the systems analyst because he or she is too busy with other work.[1]

Obviously, in situations like this there is a distinct possibility of miscommunication: whatever it is that the real user wants the system to do may not be communicated properly to the systems analyst, and whatever it is that the systems analyst thinks he or she is creating for the user may not be properly communicated—not until the entire system has been built, at which point it may be too late! There are two conclusions we can draw from this:

- Wherever possible, the systems analyst should try to establish direct contact with the user. Even if other people are involved as intermediaries (e.g., to deal with contract issues or administrative details), it is important to have regular, face-to-face meetings with the person who will ultimately inherit the system. Indeed, it is usually even better if the user is a full-time member of the project team. In many organizations, the user is the project manager; some even argue that the user should even *do* the project.

- If it is *not* possible to communicate directly with the user, then the documentation produced by the systems analyst becomes even more crucial. Part II of this book is devoted to modeling tools that can be used to describe the behavior of a system in a *rigorous, formal* way; it is essential to use tools of this kind to avoid costly misunderstandings.

3.1.1   The Heterogeneity of Users

One of the mistakes frequently made by people in the computer field—especially by computer programmers, and sometimes by systems analysts, too, is to as-

---

1 A common situation of this nature is the contracting officer in a governmental organization. In most cases, this person is not the user, and may not know very much about the real needs of the user, but he or she is the one designated to maintain all official communication with the person (or company) developing the system.

sume that all users are the same. "User" as a singular noun implies that the systems analyst will only have to interact with one person; even when it is obvious that more than one user is involved, there is a tendency to think of them as a formless, shapeless, homogeneous group of humans.

To say that one user is different from another is, of course, a trite statement: yes, they all have different personalities, different backgrounds, different interests, and so on. But there are some *important* differences that you must keep in mind in your work as a systems analyst. Here are two ways of categorizing users:

- Job category, or level of supervision.

- Level of experience with data processing.

3.1.2 Categorizing Users by Job Category

On a typical systems analysis project, you will spend a considerable amount of time interviewing users to determine system requirements. But which users? At which level? Naturally, this depends on the project and on the politics within your organization—but you can usually count on interacting with three main job categories: *operational* users, *supervisory* users, and *executive* users.[2]

Operational users are the clerical, operational, and administrative people most likely to have the most day-to-day contact with the new system (unless you are building a decision-support system, in which case you may have little or no contact with this group). Thus, in a typical large organization, you may find yourself interviewing secretaries, insurance agents, bookkeepers, shipping clerks, order entry personnel, and "assistants" of all sizes, shapes and colors. For a real-time system, you may be talking with operational users whose titles are engineer, physicist, factory worker, pilot, telephone operator, and so on. You should keep three things in mind when you work with operational-level users:

1. Operational users are very much concerned with the *functions* that the system will perform—but they are likely to be even more concerned with the *human interface* issues. Examples are: What kind of keyboard will I be using to communicate with the system; is it like the typewriter keyboard I've been using for so many years? What kind of on-line display screen will the system have; will there be a lot of glare, and will the characters be easy to read?[3] How will the system tell me if I've made a mistake; will I have to type everything all over again? What if I want to "undo" something that I typed a

---

2 There are variations on this terminology; [Teague and Pidgeon,1985], for example, refers also to the "beneficial user," the user who will receive the benefits of the new system. This person may not have any direct contact with the system, but will profit in some way from the improved service or functionality of the new system.

3 There are related issues that emphasize the fact that the new system is part of an even larger system: the user will ask, "Will I get back strain or tendonitis from sitting in front of a terminal all day?" "Do I have to worry about radiation leakage from the CRT screen?" "What if I don't know how to type?" And, most important, "What if this new system takes over my job and puts me out of work?"

few minutes ago? When the system produces a report for me, where will the information be on the page; can I get the date and time printed on the top of every page? And so on. These are issues that the operational-level user's supervisor may or may not be aware of or interested in; but, as you can imagine, they are crucial to the success of the system and they must be addressed.[4] This means that, as a systems analyst, you must either be allowed to communicate directly with the operational user, or (far less preferable) you must be *very* sure that the person who speaks on behalf of the operational user is knowledgeable about these issues. These issues are discussed in detail as part of the user implementation model in Chapter 21.

2.   Operational users tend to have a "local" view of the system; they tend to be knowledgeable about the specific job that they do and the people with whom they have immediate contact (customers, supervisors, colleagues, etc.). But they often are unfamiliar with the "big picture"; that is, they may have trouble describing how their activity fits into the overall organization or what the overall organization's charter really is. This is rarely because of stupidity, but it may reflect a lack of interest on their part. Or it may reflect the fact that the supervisory user has not told them anything about the "big picture" and prefers that they not know anything about it. A consequence of this situation is that the systems analyst must be able to develop system models that permit *both* local views (i.e., descriptions of a small, detailed part of the system, independently of other parts) *and* global views (i.e., high-level overviews of the entire system that avoid the detail).

3.   Operational users tend to think of systems in very physical terms, that is, in terms of the implementation technology currently used to implement the system or in terms of technology that they imagine *could* be used. Abstract discussions about "functions" and "data elements" may be difficult; hence, the systems analyst may find it necessary to talk with the user exclusively in familiar terms. Then, as a separate activity, the analyst can translate this physical description into an "essential model"—a model of what the system *must* do, regardless of the technology used to implement it. This is discussed further in Chapter 17.

Supervisory users are, as the term implies, employed in a supervisory capacity: they usually manage a group of operational users and are responsible for their performance (obviously, one can imagine more than one level of supervisory user in a large organization). They may have the title of supervisor, but it might also be shift leader, foreman, office manager, branch office executive, head engineer, or a variety of other titles. The significant things to remember about supervisory users are these:

•   Many of them are former operational users who have been promoted to their current position. Thus, they are generally familiar with the work done

---

4 In the extreme case, this also means that it is the operational user who can make or break a new system. They may seem passive, and they may not have the power or authority to approve a systems development project, but if they sabotage it or simply fail to use it, the new system will have failed.

by their operational subordinates, and they can usually be expected to sympathize with their needs, concerns, and perspectives. However, this is not always true. Because the marketplace and economy and technology have changed so much, the operational job today may be *very* different from what it was 20 years ago.

- One reason that the supervisory user may be perceived as out of touch with the operational user is that he or she is often measured and motivated by performance against a budget. Hence the supervisory user is often most interested in a new information system because of the possibility of increasing the volume of work done, reducing the cost of processing transactions, and reducing errors in the work. And it may occur to the supervisory user that a new system will provide an opportunity to monitor the performance (and even the minute-by-minute activity) of each individual operational user. Depending on how this is implemented, the operational users may or may not have the same perspective as the supervisory user.

- Because of this emphasis on operational efficiency, it is usually the supervisory user who thinks of a new system as a way of reducing the number of operational users (by layoffs or attrition) or avoiding further increases in their numbers as the volume of work increases. This is neither good nor bad, but it is often the focal point of heated political battles, in which the systems analyst is often caught in the middle.[5]

- For the same reasons, the supervisory user will often act as a middleman between the systems analyst and the operational user, arguing that the operational users are too busy to waste their time talking to the analyst. "After all," the supervisory user will argue, "it is precisely *because* we are so busy that we need a new computer system!" As you can imagine, this is a very dangerous position to find yourself in; after all, it is the operational user who will be most concerned about the human interface of the system, and it is unlikely that the supervisory user will be able to fully empathize with those needs.

- The supervisory user often thinks in the same physical terms as the operational user, and this perspective is often just as local as that of the operational user. Of course, one would expect that a management-level person would have a somewhat more global view; as a corollary, it may turn out that the supervisory user no longer remembers some of the detailed business policy carried out by the operational users.

- Finally, it is the supervisory user with whom you will have your primary day-to-day contact. He or she is the one who will typically define the re-

---

5 Note that this is a feature of an operational system (as we defined the term in Chapter 2), but generally not a feature of the decision-support systems. And note also that higher-level managers are generally more interested in systems that provide them with a competitive advantage than the system that reduces the operational staff by one or two people.

quirements and detailed business policy that your system must implement. He or she may be a passive member of the team (in the sense that he or she participates only when interviewed), a full-time member of the team, or even, as mentioned earlier, the project manager.

Executive-level users are generally not directly involved in a systems development project, unless the project is so large and so important that it has a major impact on the organization. For the normal project, though, the executive user is usually two or three levels above the action associated with the project. To the extent that you become involved with them, you will probably discover the following things about executive users:

- They may provide the initiative for the project, but are more likely to serve as the funding authority for project requests that originate at lower levels in the organization.

- They are usually*not* former operational users or, if they were, it was so long ago that whatever experience they had is obsolete. Thus, they are in no position to help define the requirements of the system for the people who will actually be using it on a day-to-day basis. An exception to this is the decision-support system discussed in Chapter 2; such a system would more commonly be used by the supervisory and executive users.

- Executive users are typically more concerned with strategic issues and long-term profit/loss. Hence, they are typically less concerned with such operational issues as reduced transaction costs or saving three clerical workers as they are with what Paul Strassman calls the "information payoff" in [Strassman, 1985]—that is, the new markets, new products, or new competitive advantage that they will gain from the new system.

- Executive-level users generally are more interested in a global view of the entire system; as a result, they are generally not interested in the details. As mentioned earlier, this means that we must use system modeling tools that allow us to provide an overview of the system to the executive users (and to anyone else who needs it) and detailed portions of the system to the operational users who are the "local experts."

- Similarly, executive-level users are generally able to work with abstract models of a system; indeed, they are already accustomed to working with such abstract models as *financial* models, *marketing* models, *organizational* models, and *engineering* models (of new products, factories, offices, etc.). Indeed, they will not be at all interested in "physical" models of the system and will wonder why you are bothering to show such things to them.

To summarize, then, you can expect to interact with three different types, or levels, of users, as shown in Figure 3.1. Keep in mind that they have different perspectives, different interests and priorities, and often different backgrounds. These three types of users can be characterized as shown in Table 3.1.

I have hinted in the previous discussion that the user is not always pleased at the prospect of a new system; indeed, sometimes they will actively oppose it. This is most often the case with the operational users (since they are the ones who will have to use it), but the resistance may also come from the supervisory user (since he or she may feel that it will have a negative impact on the efficiency or profitability of the area he or she is responsible for), or even the executive user. As Marjorie Leeson points out in [Leeson, 1981],

> The analyst who understands basic motivation, why people resist change, and how they resist change, may be able to overcome some of the resistance. Most management books make reference to psychologist A.H. Maslow's *hierarchy of needs.* The five categories, from lowest priority to highest, are:

	Need	**Example**
1.	Physiological	Food, clothing, and shelter
2.	Safety and security	Protection against danger and loss of job
3.	Social	Being able to identify with individuals and groups
4.	Egotistic	Recognition, status, and importance
5.	Self-fulfillment	Realizing one's fullest potential in creativity and self-development

Executive
User

Supervisory
User

Operational User

Figure 3.1: **The three types of user**

Thus, if you find some of the users resisting the idea of a new system, you should think about the possibility of one or more of these needs not being met. It is rare, of course, that a user would worry about the physiological level of need, but it is not at all surprising to find that a user is worried about the loss of his or her job. And it is also common for users (especially the operational users) to worry that a new system will lead to their *not* being able to identify with their familiar social groups; they fear that they will be confined to a CRT terminal all day and spend all of their time interacting with a computer rather than other humans. The operational user who has become an expert in performing an information-processing task on a manual basis may also feel that a new system will leave his or her "egotistic" needs unfulfilled; and the user who feels that the system will take away the creative aspects of his or her current work may also resist.

Table 3.1: Characteristics of different users

Operational user	Supervisory user	Executive user
Usually has a local view	May or may not have local view	Has a global view
Carries out the function of the system	Generally familiar with operation	Provides initiative for the project
Has a physical view of the system	Driven by budget consider-ations	No direct operat-ing experience
	Often acts as a middleman be-tween users and higher levels of management	Has strategic concerns

3.1.3   Categorizing Users by Level of Experience

It should be obvious that different users will have different levels of experience; unfortunately, it is common for systems analysts to assume that *all* users are blithering idiots when it comes to the subject of computers. Perhaps this was a safe assumption ten years ago, but it is likely to get you into a lot of trouble in most organizations today[6]: today, one can distinguish between rank amateurs, cocky novices, and a small (but rapidly growing) number of true computer experts.

The amateur user is the one who has never seen a computer and who exclaims loudly and frequently that he or she "doesn't understand all this computer stuff." Often,

---

6 Even if every user you encounter is unaware of and uninterested in computer technology, you should avoid the common mistake of treating them as a subhuman form of life. Young systems analysts and computer programmers, especially the "hackers" who began playing with computers when they were in elementary school, assume that *everyone* should be fascinated and facile with computers, and that those who are not are either (1) mentally deficient or (2) members of an older generation, and thus unworthy of any respect or consideration. Meanwhile, the world is full of users who don't like computers for a variety of legitimate reasons, *and there are users who are far too busy being an expert in their own profession or business to worry about being an expert in computers.* They have the same opinion of computer programmers and systems analysts that they have of electricians, carpenters, plumbers and auto mechanics: a healthy respect for the expertise and craftsmanship required of the job, but a total lack of interest in the details. Understanding this point will, in many cases, determine whether you succeed or fail on your first few projects as a systems analyst.

such a user is a middle-aged worker or business person who happily survived 16 years of education and another 10 or 20 years in a job *before* computers were introduced; however, it is also common to find younger users (those still in their twenties) who find computers boring, intimidating, or irrelevant to their lives. This presents a challenge to the systems analyst who loves to talk about "on-line access" and "menu-driven human-machine dialogues" or other such terminology—*but if the systems analyst does his or her job properly, there is no reason why the user should be interested in or knowledgeable about computers.*

Indeed, the real problem with the amateur user is somewhat more subtle: he or she may find it difficult to understand the "language" that the systems analyst uses to describe the features, functions and characteristics of the system to be built, even though that language avoids obvious computer-related terminology. As we will see in Parts II and III, the job of systems analysis involves the creation of a number of *models* of the system to be built. These models are formal and rigorous representations of a computer system, and at the same time they are *abstract* representations of the system. Most of the models involve graphics (pictures) supported by detailed text, and the overall representation (which is needed to ensure a formal, rigorous description) strikes some users as overwhelmingly mathematical and thus unreadable. These may be users who remember the difficulty of reading the complex graphical notation used in organic chemistry or the equally complex notation used in differential calculus and algebra. Whatever the reason, the result is the same: quite apart from understanding computer technology, if the user cannot understand the model of the system, there is little chance that he or she will be satisfied with the system when it is finally built.[7]

A second type of user is the one I like to call the "cocky novice," the person who has been involved in one or two systems development projects, or (even worse) the user who has a personal computer and who has written one or two (ugh) BASIC programs. This user often claims to know *exactly* what he or she wants the system to do and is prone to point out all the mistakes that the systems analyst made on the last project. This is all fine, except for one thing: *the user often becomes far too involved in discussions about the specific technology that will be used to implement the system.* Thus, the user may say to the systems analyst, "I need a new order processing system, and I'd like it to be built with a local area network connecting our IBM PCs, and I think we should either use dBASE-III or PC-FOCUS." These may *eventually* turn out to be the right technical choices, but it is premature to even consider the hardware, programming language, and database packages before the true requirements of the system have been documented. Indeed, in the extreme case, the user's "suggestion" about the appropriate hardware and software may turn out to be a "solution looking for a problem," that is, the discovery that there are underutilized hardware and software resources that can be put to some other use.

---

7 An analogy: if you were going to have a house built for you, you would begin by talking with an architect about the desired features of the house. After a great deal of discussion, the architect would retreat to his office and then eventually come back to you with a number of drawings and/or scale models of the house. If you refused to look at the drawings or objected that they were "too mathematical," the architect's chances of success would be small indeed. What you would probably do is take the architect to an *existing* house and say, "Build me one like that!" Unfortunately, we are not often in a position to do that in the computer field, though *prototyping* is sometimes a viable way of accomplishing the same thing.

There are, of course, some users who *really* understand systems analysis, as well as the underlying technology of computers (as well as their own business area, too!). It is a pleasure working with these people; indeed, the only problem may be that the user and the systems analyst derive so much pleasure talking about the tools and techniques of systems analysis that they forget that their true objective is to build a functioning system![8]

3.2   MANAGEMENT

Management is a rather loose term; indeed, the systems analyst is likely to come into contact with several different kinds of managers:

- *User managers*—managers in charge of several people in the operational area where the new system will be used. This was discussed above. These are usually middle-level managers who want systems that will produce a variety of internal reports and short-term trend analyses. The internal reports are usually financial reports, operational reports, exception reports, and the like.

- *EDP/MIS managers*—the person in charge of the systems development project itself, and the higher-level managers who are concerned with the overall management and allocation of resources of all the technical staff in the systems development organization.

- *General management*—top-level managers who are not directly involved in the EDP organization nor in the user organization. This might include the president and/or chairman of the organization, and/or the top financial management (the controller, vice president of finance, etc.). These managers are generally more interested in the strategic planning systems and decision-support systems that were discussed in Chapter 2. While top management does need internal financial reports, they usually don't need the level of detail (especially in the area of exception reports) that the user managers need. And they focus more attention on *external* information: government regulations, reports of competition in their marketplace, reports on new markets and products, and so on.

The primary interaction between the systems analyst and all these managers has to do with the *resources* that will be assigned to the project. It is the systems analyst's job to identify and document the user's requirements *and the constraints within which the system must be built.* These constraints usually consist of resources: people, time, and money. Thus, the systems analyst will eventually produce a document that says, "The new system must carry out functions X, Y, and Z, and it must

---

8 It is also encouraging to see that more and more of these "experts" are moving into top management positions in business organizations and top leadership positions in other parts of our society. Citibank and American Airlines, not to mention a number of computer companies and other high-tech organizations, are run by people who rose up through the ranks of data processing. And, as of the mid-1980s, there were approximately half a dozen members of Congress who are former programmers and systems analysts.

be developed within six months, with no more than three programmers from the EDP department, at a cost of no more than $100,000."

Obviously, management will want an ongoing assurance that the systems development project is staying within these constraints—it is not falling behind schedule or exceeding its budget. But these are issues of project management, not systems analysis.[9] And managers from several different functional areas often form a steering committee that helps prioritize potential development projects so that the most cost-effective projects get done first.

There are several points you should keep in mind about managers:

- The higher the level of manager, the less he or she is likely to know or care about computer technology. While this is a generalization, it is usually a fairly safe one with the current generation of senior managers. This should not affect you as a systems analyst (systems designers have a more difficult job!), but you should remember to concentrate on discussing the *essential* characteristics of a system when you talk with them.

- The goals and priorities of management may be in conflict with those of the users, especially the supervisory and operational users. Management may even impose a system on the users and force them to use it (e.g., if the user organization has been unprofitable or unable to respond to new changes in the marketplace).

- A variation on the above theme: management may not provide the resources, funding, or time that the users feel is necessary to build an effective system. It is convenient for the systems analyst and the user to respond to this by saying that management "doesn't understand," but it is often a conscious, calculated choice. For more about the politics of resource funding and scheduling, see Appendix B.

- The term management implies a homogeneous group of people who all think the same way; the truth, of course, is usually very different. Managers have different views and opinions, and they often have very different goals and objectives. They argue with each other and compete against each other. Hence, it may turn out that some members of management are very much in favor of the new system, while others are dead set against it. Even worse is the benign neglect that befalls some projects; they finally end after years of thrashing about.

- It is also convenient to assume that once management has made up its collective mind about a systems development project, it stays made up. But this is not necessarily so: external forces outside the organization may cause management to speed up the project schedule, or take resources away from it, or abandon it altogether. This often causes enormous

---

9 However, sometimes the systems analyst is very involved in project management. We will discuss this point in more detail in Chapter 16, as well as in Appendix B.

emotional distress to those working on the project—including you as the systems analyst!

The relationship between management and your systems development project may depend quite a lot on the overall management structure of your organization, especially the relationship of the systems development activities to the rest of the organization. The classical organizational structure is shown in Figure 3.2(a); note that the entire data processing organization reports to the head of finance and accounting. The reason for this is that most large organizations originally introduced computers to help automate their accounting activities (e.g., payroll, general ledger, and accounts receivable).

Beginning in the 1970s, some organizations began to realize that this was a rather lopsided organizational structure: it virtually guaranteed that the data processing function would be biased toward accounting applications and would have little interest or expertise in other parts of the organization. And as automated information processing began to permeate the organization (e.g., in manufacturing, marketing, and engineering), some organizations changed to the organization chart shown in Figure 3.2(b) . By having the data processing (or MIS, as it is sometimes called) group report directly to the president of the organization, it becomes clear to everyone that data processing is just as critical to the organization's survival as manufacturing, engineering, sales, and so on.

However, by the 1980s, some organizations had begun to find that the MIS department had become an "empire," with its own priorities and politics; user organizations, meanwhile, were finding that they had an ever-growing backlog of new systems waiting to be developed by the MIS department.[10] This coincided with the introduction and rapid proliferation of cheap, powerful personal computers; thus, some user departments began to feel that they could develop their own systems, without relying on a centralized MIS function. As a result, some organizations now have a structure like that shown in Figure 3.2(c); while there is still a central MIS department for such "classic" applications as payroll and general ledger, much of the departmental processing is done by system development groups *within the departments.*

If you work in an organization characterized by Figure 3.2(a), you may find that the systems analysts and the users in various other departments are not as good as they could be; indeed, you are likely to find that much of the systems development projects are the "transaction processing" type that one would find in an accounting department. If your organization looks more like the one shown in Figure 3.2(b), then there is a good chance that your systems development group has a reasonable amount of political "visibility" high in the organization; however, you may find that there is growing frustration about the backlog of new systems waiting to be developed. And if you are working in an organization characterized by Figure 3.2(c), you are likely to have *much* more direct contact with the users of your system; indeed, you may be reporting directly to them. And you are more likely to find yourself working on personal computers and other small networks of computer systems purchased directly by the user department.

---

10 We will discuss the backlog of applications in more detail in Chapter 6.

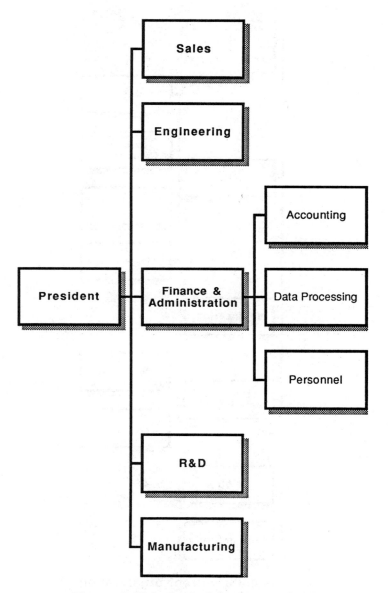

Figure 3.2(a): **A classical organization chart**

3.3   AUDITORS, QUALITY ASSURANCE, AND STANDARDS BEARERS

Depending on the size of your project and the nature of the organization **you** work in, you may or may not have auditors, quality assurance personnel, and/or members of the standards department participating in your project. I have grouped these people into a single category, because their objective and perspective **are** generally similar, if not the same.

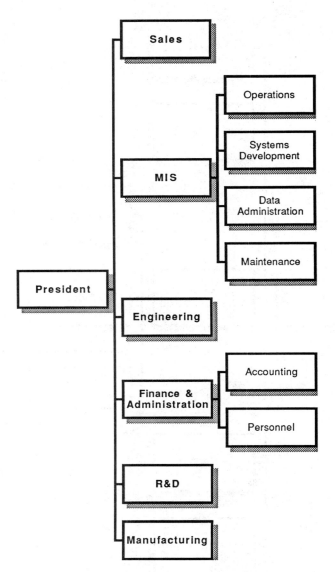

Figure 3.2(b): **A more current organization chart**

The general objective of this motley crew is to ensure that your system is developed in accordance with various *external* standards (external, that is, to your project): accounting standards developed by your organization's accounting firm; standards developed by other departments in your organization or by the customer/user who will inherit your system; and possibly standards imposed by various governmental regulatory agencies.

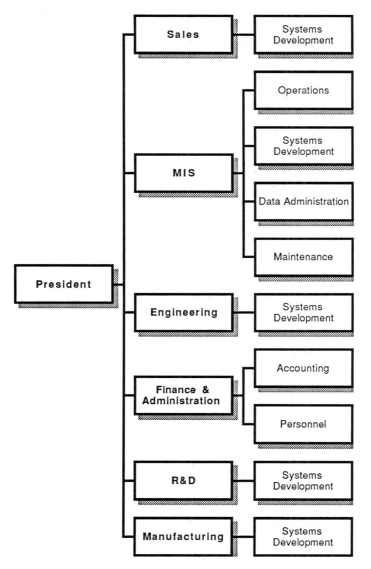

Figure 3.2(c): **Systems development within user organizations**

There are three problems that you should anticipate when working with auditors, quality assurance people, or members of the standards department:

1.   They often don't get involved in the project until the very end—after the
      systems analysis, design, and programming work have been finished, and
      the formal testing activity has commenced. At this point, of course, it is very
      difficult to make major changes to the system.

2.   They are often familiar with an older notation or format for documenting system requirements (e.g., flowcharts). Thus, it is usually very important to ensure that the system models that you develop (peek at Chapter 4 to see some examples!) are understandable.[11]

3.   Unfortunately, members of this group are often more interested in form than substance: if your documents are not *exactly* right, they may be rejected.

3.4   SYSTEMS ANALYST

This is *you!* The systems analyst is a key member of any systems development project, and the previous sections of this chapter have already given you several examples of how the systems analyst interacts with other players in the project.

In a broader sense, the systems analyst plays several roles:

*   *Archaeologist and scribe.* As a systems analyst, one of your main jobs is to uncover detail and to document business policy that may exist only as "tribal folklore," passed down from generation to generation of users.

*   *Innovator.* The systems analyst must separate the *symptoms* of the user's problem from the true *causes.* With his or her knowledge of computer technology, the analyst must help the user explore useful, new applications of computers—and new ways for the user to conduct business. While many early computer systems merely perpetuated the user's existing business at electronic speed, systems analysts are being challenged today to help the user find radically new, innovative products and markets made possible with the computer. Edward De Bono's *Lateral Thinking* ([De Bono, 1970]) may be worth reading for interesting new ways of thinking about problems.

*   *Mediator.* As mentioned earlier in this chapter, it is the systems analyst who often finds himself in the middle of users, managers, programmers, auditors, and various other players—all of whom frequently disagree with one another. There is a temptation for the systems analyst to try to impose his or her own view of what the system should look like or what functions it should contain. But the analyst's primary job is to achieve a consensus; that requires the delicate art of diplomacy and negotiation!

*   *Project leader.* This is not a universal role, but it happens often enough to mention it here. Since the systems analyst is usually more experienced than the programmers on the project, and since he is assigned to the project before the programmers begin working, there is a natural tendency to assign project management responsibilities to the analyst.

---

11 However, in at least a few cases, this is changing. For example, many of the Big 8 accounting firms in the United States are now quite familiar with the structured analysis documentation tools described in this chapter; hence they should have no problem participating in one of your projects as an auditor.

This means that, as a systems analyst, you need more than just the ability to draw flowcharts and other technical diagrams! You need *people skills* to interview users, mediate disagreements, and survive the inevitable political battles that surround all but the most trivial project. You need *application knowledge* to understand and appreciate the user's business. You need *computer skills* to understand the potential uses of computer hardware and software in the user's business. And (obviously!) you need a logical, organized mind: you must be able to view a system from many different perspectives; you must be able to partition it into levels of subsystems; and you must be able to think of a system in abstract terms as well as physical terms.[12]

Nobody ever said the job was easy!

3.5   SYSTEMS DESIGNERS

As we have implied in earlier discussions, the systems designer is the person (or group of people) who will receive the output of your systems analysis work: his or her job is to transform a technology-free statement of user requirements into a high-level architectural design that will provide the framework within which the programmers can work. The nature of this work is discussed in Chapter 22.

In many cases, the systems analyst and the systems designer are the same person, or members of the same unified group of people. Even if they are different people, it's important for the systems analyst and systems designer to stay in close touch throughout the project. The reason for this is the *feedback* that occurs between systems analysis and systems design: the systems analyst has to provide sufficiently detailed information for the systems designer to concoct a technologically superior design; and the systems designer has to provide sufficiently accurate information so that the systems analyst can tell whether the user requirements he or she is documenting are technologically feasible. Based on information received from the systems designer, the systems analyst may have to negotiate with the user to modify user requirements.

3.6   PROGRAMMERS

One could argue that in the best of all worlds there would be no contact between a systems analyst and a programmer. Particularly on large systems development projects, the systems designers are likely to be a "buffer" between the systems analysts and the programmers; that is, the systems analysts deliver their product (a technology-independent statement of the requirements of the system) to the system designers, and the system designers deliver *their* product (an architectural description of the hardware and software components that will be used to implement the system) to the programmer.

There is another reason why the systems analyst and the programmer may have little or no contact with each other: work is often performed in a strictly serial

---

12 Indeed, it is because of this requirement for expertise in *many* areas that most computer scientists feel that artificial intelligence and expert systems won't be able to be applied to systems analysis for several more years. More on this in Chapter 25.

sequence in many systems development projects.[13] Thus, the work of systems analysis takes place first *and is completely finished* before the work of programming begins. This means that the systems analyst has finished his or her work and has perhaps been reassigned to a new project before the programmer is even brought into the project.

However, there is likely to be *some* contact between programmers and systems analysts for the following reasons:

- On small projects, the roles of analysis, design, and programming are combined, so it may turn out that one person does the work of systems analysis *and* systems design, and then continues interacting with the programmer. Or it may turn out that one person does the work of systems design and programming.

- The analyst sometimes serves as the project manager, so even though she or he may have finished the work of specifying the requirements of the system, the analyst will still be involved in the project and will have some contact with the programmer.

- It is often the programmer who discovers errors and ambiguities in the "statement of requirements" produced by the systems analyst, for it is programming where, as my colleague Scott Guthery puts it, "the tire meets the road," where a wishy-washy statement of what the system has to do gets turned into a set of specific, detailed COBOL statements. If something is missing, wrong or confusing, the programmer has two choices: to ask the systems analyst for clarification, or to ask the user.[14]

- As mentioned in Chapter 2, many organizations are now finding it necessary to replace operational systems that were built 20 years ago. In the vast majority of these redevelopment projects, there is virtually no documentation that describes (1) how the system works, or (more importantly!!) (2) *what* the system is supposed to do. And since the systems are 20 years old, there is a whole new generation of users involved; the users who were initially involved in specifying the requirements of the system have retired or quit, and the new generation of users has little idea of the detailed policy requirements embodied in the

---

13 We will discuss some alternatives to this sequential approach, particularly those known as evolutionary development, or fast tracking, in Chapter 5. Indeed, for some projects systems analysis continues while programming is going on.

14 Indeed, direct contact between the programmer and the user is more common than you may think. In many cases, the systems analyst never gets around to describing the low-level details of the system, and the high-level users with whom the systems analyst communicates may be unaware of or uninterested in those details. Thus, it often turns out that the programmer *must* talk directly to the low-level user to find out *exactly* what the system is supposed to do. This is significant, because many organizations bemoan the fact that 50% of their systems development projects are spent on testing; in fact, it may well turn out that the work taking place under the official guise of testing is, in fact, systems analysis work that could have (and probably should have) taken place earlier in the project.

system. At this point, all eyes turn to the *maintenance programmer,* who has been keeping the system running for the past several years; this person, too, is likely to be a second- or third-generation worker, having had no contact with the designers and programmers who first constructed the system! As Nicholas Zvegintzov (author of the newsletter *Software Maintenance News*) points out,

> Up to now, the key computer professional was someone who could learn enough about the needs of organizations to express them in computer language. In the future, as our society becomes irrevocably computerized, the key professional [will be] someone who can learn enough about computerized systems to express them in human language. Without that someone, we [will] have lost control of our society. That someone is the reverse engineer. Software maintainers are the reverse engineers of society.

• Some organizations are beginning to change their project teams from a vertical structure to a horizontal structure. The typical assignment of duties (which is presumed throughout this book) involves *all* the duties of systems analysis being assigned to one person (or group of people); similarly, all the design activities are assigned to the designer, and all the programming activities are assigned to the programmer. To the extent that this approach is followed, it would certainly seem that systems analysts and programmers would have little contact with one another. But some organizations are beginning to realize that there is an inherent conflict with this approach: systems analysts are usually relatively senior, experienced people in the organization, and yet they are being asked to carry out not only the high-level conceptual statement of system requirements, but also the low-level "nitty-gritty" details of the user's requirements; a similar conflict exists with the programmers, who are typically more junior and less experienced. One solution is to give the senior technical personnel (whose title happens to be systems analyst) *all* the high-level activities: high-level systems analysis, high-level design, *and the coding of top-level modules in the system*; similarly, the junior-level technical people are given low-level, detailed assignments in the analysis area *and* in the design area, *and* in the programming area. To the extent that this approach is followed, systems analysts and programmers remain in close contact with one another throughout the project; indeed, each is doing some of the work formerly done by the other. This point is discussed again in Chapter 23.

3.7   OPERATIONS PERSONNEL

Just as one could argue that the systems analyst would never encounter a programmer, it could be argued that the systems analyst need never have any interactions with the *operations* personnel who are responsible for the computer center, telecommunications network, security of the computer hardware and data, as well as the actual running of computer programs, mounting of disk packs, and handling of output from computer printers. All this happens after a new system has not only been analyzed and designed, but has also been programmed and tested.

However, there is more to this than meets the eye: the systems analyst must have some understanding of the *constraints* imposed on a new system by the operations personnel, for this becomes part of the detailed specification produced by the systems analyst. That is, the systems analyst may produce a document that says, "The new order system must be capable of carrying out functions X, Y, and Z—*and, in order to conform to the requirements of the Operations Department, it must occupy no more than 16 megabytes of memory on the mainframe computer. The system must be implemented using standard IBM 3270 terminals connected to the company's XYZ telecommunications network.*"

In some cases, the operational details of the system may be a matter of negotiation between the user and the central computer operations group. This is especially common today, since users are often in a position to acquire their own personal computers or department-sized minicomputers. While many of these computers can be operated by clerical or administrative people in the user organization (thus not requiring the specialized talents of the operations personnel), and while many of the computers can operate in a normal office environment (thus not requiring the special wiring and air-conditioning equipment typical of large mainframe computers), it is still generally true that these small machines will have to communicate with the mainframe computer (e.g., to download part of a corporate database, or to upload the results of departmental computing), and it is often true that the small PCs and/or minicomputers have a need to communicate with one another through a local area network or some other telecommunications facility. All this usually involves interaction with the operations personnel; only a truly independent stand-alone system can be built without their assistance and approval.

These operational issues are documented in a part of the systems analysis effort known as the *user implementation model.* This is covered in detail in Chapter 21.

3.8   SUMMARY

As we have seen in this chapter, the systems analyst is an orchestrator, a communicator, and a facilitator. It will become evident in Parts II and III that the systems analyst does a great deal of work on his or her own, but even more work is done in harmony with the other players in the systems game. As a systems analyst, the more you know about the people you will be working with, the better off you will be.

All the players are people; and they have different goals, different priorities, and different perspectives. Though they may be publicly committed to its success, they may have hidden agendas that are opposed to one or more aspects of the project.

The questions and exercises at the end of this chapter are intended to make you think more about these issues. You may also wish to consult Block's excellent book on project politics ([Block, 1982]) or even Sun Tzu's classic book on the art of war [Tzu, 1983].

REFERENCES

1. Paul Strassman, *Information Payoff.* New York: Free Press, 1985.

2. Robert Block, *The Politics of Projects*. New York: YOURDON Press, 1982.

3. Alan Brill, *Building Controls into Structured Systems*. New York: YOURDON Press, 1982.

4. Sun Tzu, *The Art of War*. New York: Delacorte Press, 1983.

5. Edward De Bono, *Lateral Thinking*. New York: Penguin Books, 1970.

6. Marjorie Leeson, *Systems Analysis and Design*. Chicago: Science Research Associates, 1981.

7. Lavette C. Teague, Jr., and Christopher Pidgeon, *Structured Analysis Methods for Computer Information Systems*. Chicago: Science Research Associates, 1985.

QUESTIONS AND EXERCISES

1. List at least one additional player that you would expect to interact with in a systems development project.

2. Describe a project in which the systems analyst did not have direct contact with the real user. What were the advantages and disadvantages of this situation? What alternative arrangements could have been made?

3. Can you think of another term for user besides owner or customer?

4. Can you think of any situation where the systems analyst should *not* talk to the user?

5. What are the advantages and disadvantages of having the user be a full-time member of the systems development project team? Can you think of any specific projects where it makes particularly good sense to have a user on the project team?

6. What are the advantages and disadvantages of having the user be the manager of the systems development project team? Can you think of any specific projects where it would make particularly good sense to have the user manage the project?

7. What are the advantages and disadvantages of having the user develop an information system entirely by himself? Can you think of any projects where it makes particularly good sense to have the user be the analyst, designer, programmer, and manager?

8. How much should a user know about computers and software in order to participate in a project team during the systems analysis phase? How much should he or she know about the tools and techniques of systems analysis?

9. How much should a user know about computers and software in order to manage a systems development project team? How much should he or she know about systems analysis in order to be an effective manager?

10. How much should a user know about computers and software in order to accomplish a systems development project entirely by himself? How much should he or she know about systems analysis?

11. What special precautions would you take as a systems analyst if you did not have direct contact with the user? Do you think that the modeling tools described in this book would be sufficient?

12. Section 3.1.2 lists several concerns that an operational user might have about a new system. List three more likely concerns. Do you think these are reasonable concerns, or do they just reflect the typical user's unfamiliarity with computers?

13. What moral or ethical responsibility does the systems analyst have to the operational user if it she or he is convinced that it won't cause layoffs, but the user is concerned that it will? (See also question 19.)

14. Describe a scenario where the operational users could cause a new system to fail. Do you think your scenario is realistic? Couldn't the supervisory user simply *mandate* that the system be used?

15. When do you think the human interface issues should be discussed with the users? Early in the project? Late? What are the trade-offs? (You're allowed to peek ahead at Chapter 21 if you wish.)

16. Do you think it's unrealistic that operational users would have only a local view of the system in which they participate? Do you think it is safe for the systems analyst to take this for granted? Do you think this is a good situation? Should the systems analyst try to provide a global view—the "big picture"—to the operational users?

17. Give an example of a physical, or implementation-oriented, view of a system that an operational user might have. Do you see any problems with this?

18. What should the systems analyst do if the supervisory user won't let him or her talk directly to the operational users? How can the systems analyst deal with this situation?

19. What moral or ethical responsibility does the systems analyst have to the supervisory user if the operational users express concern about possible layoffs caused by the new system? (See also question 13.)

20. Give an example of a system where the supervisory user may not be familiar with the detailed business policy currently being carried out by the operational users.

21. Why are executive-level users typically *not* interested or concerned about the possible savings to be achieved by personnel reductions (e.g., through layoffs or attrition) made possible by a new system?

22. How closely involved should the executive-level users be in the development of a new information system?

23. What options does the systems analyst have if the user doesn't understand abstract, paper models?

24. How should the systems analyst deal with the "cocky novice" described in this chapter? What if the user *insists* on a particular choice of computer hardware or software for the new system?

25. How much responsibility should the systems analyst take for gaining consensus among the users? What if the analyst fails to do this?

26. What risks do you think the systems analyst faces from management, as discussed in Section 3.2? What can the systems analyst do to minimize the risks?

27. What should the systems analyst do if management's goals and priorities are in conflict with those of the user?

28. When do you think operations people should get involved in a project?

29. Should systems analysis and systems design (and programming, too) be done by the same person (or cohesive group of people)? What are the advantages and disadvantages?

4 TOOLS OF STRUCTURED ANALYSIS

Nature has ... some sort of arithmetical-geometrical coordinate system, because nature has all kinds of models. What we experience of nature is in models, and all of nature's models are so beautiful. It struck me that nature's system must be a real beauty, because in chemistry we find that the associations are always in beautiful whole numbers—there are no fractions.

R. Buckminster Fuller,
From "In the Outlaw Area: profile by Calvin
Tompkins," *The New Yorker,* January 8,1966

Man is a tool-using animal ... .Without tools he is nothing, with tools he is all.

Thomas Carlyle,
Sartor Resartus, Book I, Chapter 4

In this chapter, you will learn:

1. What a systems analyst uses modeling tools for.

2. The nature and components of a dataflow diagram.

3. The components of a data dictionary.

4. The components of a process specification.

5. How to model stored data and data relationships.

6. How to model the time-dependent behavior of a system.

7. How to model the structure of a computer program.

Much of the work that you will do as a systems analyst involves *modeling* the system that the user wants. As we will see in this chapter, and in more detail in Part II, there are many different kinds of models that we can build—just as there are many different models that an architect can build of a proposed new house. The systems analysis models discussed in this book are, for the most part, *paper* models of the system-to-be, that is, abstract representations of what will eventually become a combination of computer hardware and computer software.

The term model may sound rather formal and frightening to you, but it represents a concept that you have used for much of your life. Consider the following kinds of models:

- *Maps:* two-dimensional models of the world we live in.

- *Globes:* three-dimensional models of the world we live in.

- *Flowcharts:* schematic representations of the decisions and sequence of activities for carrying out some procedure.

- *Architect's drawings:* schematic representations of a building or a bridge.

- *Musical scores:* graphic/text representations of the musical notes and tempo of a piece of music.

Though you may not know how to read the architectural model shown in Figure 4.1, the *concept* of such a model ought not to frighten you; it is not too hard to imagine that you could learn how to read and understand such a model, even if you never intended to create one yourself. Similarly, you probably don't yet know how to read many of the models used by systems analysts, but you will know how to read them and create them by the end of this book. The users you work with will certainly be able to read the models (with a little initial assistance) and they may even be able to create them.

Why should we build models? Why not just build the system itself? The answer is that we can construct models in such a way as to highlight, or emphasize, certain critical features of a system, while simultaneously de-emphasizing other aspects of the system. This allows us to communicate with the user in a focused way, without being distracted by issues and system features that are irrelevant to us. And if we learn that our understanding of the user's requirements was incorrect (or that the user changed his mind about his requirements), we can change the model *or throw it away and build a new model, if necessary.* The alternative is to carry on some initial discussions with the user and then build the entire system; the risk, of course, is that the final product may be unacceptable, and it may be extraordinarily expensive to change at that point.

Thus, the systems analyst uses modeling tools to:

- Focus on important system features while downplaying less important features.

- Discuss changes and corrections to the user's requirements with low cost and minimal risk.

- Verify that the systems analyst correctly understands the user's environment and has documented it in such a way that the systems designers and programmers can build the system.

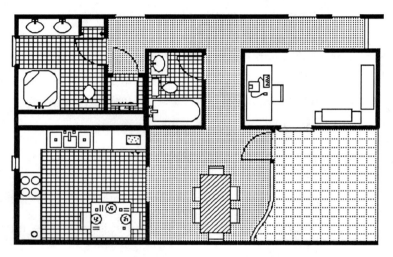

Figure 4.1: **A typical architectural model**

Not all modeling tools will accomplish these purposes: for example, a 500-page narrative description of the user's requirements (which is, in a crude sense, a model) could (1) thoroughly obscure *all* the system's features, (2) cost more to build than the system itself, and (3) fail to verify the system analyst's understanding of the user's true needs. In Chapter 8, we will explore in detail what characteristics a modeling tool must have in order to be useful to the systems analyst.

We will now introduce and briefly discuss three important systems modeling tools: the dataflow diagram, the entity-relationship diagram, and the state-transition diagram. The dataflow diagram illustrates the *functions* that the system must perform; the entity-relationship diagrams emphasize the *data relationships,* and the state-transition diagram focuses on the time-dependent behavior of the system. Chapters 9 to 16 explore these and other modeling tools in more detail. As we will see, all three of the major modeling tools consist of graphics (pictures) and supporting textual modeling tools. The graphics provide a vivid and easy-to-read way for the systems analyst to show the users the major *components* of the model, as well as the *connections* (or interfaces) between the components. The supporting textual modeling tools provide precise definitions of the *meaning* of the components and connections.

4.1   MODELING SYSTEM FUNCTIONS: THE DATAFLOW DIAGRAM

An old adage in the systems development profession emphasizes that a data processing system involves both data and processing, and that one cannot build a successful system without considering both components. The processing aspect of a system is certainly an important aspect to model and to verify with the user. The modeling that we are carrying out can be described in a number of ways:

- What functions must the system perform? What are the interactions between the functions?

- What transformations must the system carry out? What inputs are transformed into what outputs?

- What kind of work does the system do? Where does it get the information to do its work? Where does it deliver the results of its work?

The modeling tool that we use to describe the transformation of inputs into outputs is a *dataflow diagram*. A typical dataflow diagram is shown in Figure 4.2.

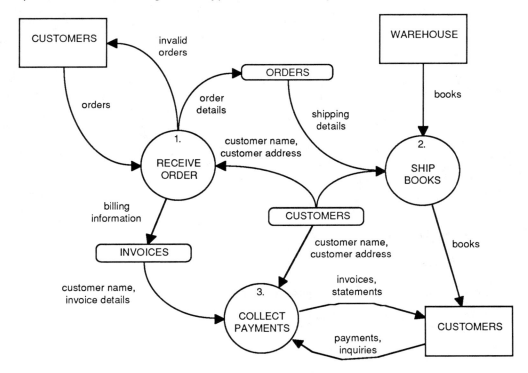

Figure 4.2: **A typical dataflow diagram**

Dataflow diagrams consist of processes, data stores, flows, and terminators:

- *Processes* are shown by the circles, or "bubbles," in the diagram. They represent the various individual functions that the system carries out. Functions transform inputs into outputs.

- *Flows* are shown by curved, directed arrows. They are the connections between the processes (system functions), and they represent the information that the processes require as input and/or the information they generate as output.

- *Data stores* are shown by two parallel lines, or by an ellipse. They show collections (aggregates) of data that the system must remember for a period of time. When the systems designers and programmers finish building the system, the stores will typically exist as files or databases.

- *Terminators* show the external entities with which the system communicates. Terminators are typically individuals, groups of people (e.g., another department or division within the organization), external computer systems, and external organizations.

The dataflow diagram is discussed in greater detail in Chapter 9. (In addition to processes, flows and stores, a dataflow diagram can also have *control flows, control processes,* and *control stores.* These are useful for modeling real-time systems and are discussed in more detail in Chapter 9.)

While the dataflow diagram provides a convenient overview of the major functional components of the system, it does not provide any detail about these components. To show the details of *what* information is transformed and *how* it is transformed, we need two supporting textual modeling tools: the *data dictionary* and the *process specification.* Figure 4.3 shows a typical data dictionary for the dataflow diagram that we saw in Figure 4.2. Similarly, Figure 4.4 shows a typical process specification for *one process* in the dataflow diagram that we saw in Figure 4.2.

name =	**courtesy-title + first-name + (middle-name)** **+ last-name**
courtesy-title =	[Mr. | Miss | Mrs. | Ms. | Dr. | Prof.]
first-name =	{legal-character}
last-name =	{legal-character}
legal-character =	[A-Z | a-z | ' | - | ⎵]

Figure 4.3: **A typical data dictionary**

1. **IF** the dollar amount of the invoice times the number of weeks overdue is greater than $10,000 **THEN**:

    a. Give a photocopy of the invoice to the appropriate salesperson who is to call the customer.
    b. Log on the back of the invoice that a copy has been given to the salesperson, with the date on which it was done.
    c. Refile the invoice in the file for examination two weeks from today.

2:     **OTHERWISE IF** more than four overdue notices have been sent **THEN**:

   a.   Give a photocopy of the invoice to the appropriate salesperson to call the customer.
   b.   Log on the back of the invoice that a copy has been given to the salesperson, with the date on which it was done.
   c.   Refile the invoice in the file to be examined one week from today.

3:     **OTHERWISE** (the situation has not yet reached serious proportions):
   a.   Add 1 to the overdue notice count on the back of the invoice (if no such count has been recorded, write "overdue notice count = 1").
   b.   **IF** the invoice in the file is illegible **THEN** type a new one.
   c.   Send the customer a photocopy of the invoice, stamped "Nth notice: invoice overdue. Please remit immediately," where N is the value of the overdue notice count.
   d.   Log on the back of the invoice the date on which the Nth overdue notice was sent.
   e.   Refile the invoice in the file for two weeks from today's date.

Figure 4.4: **A typical process specification**

There is much, *much* more to say about dataflow diagrams, data dictionaries, and process specifications; details are provided in Chapters 9 to11. We will see, for example, that most complex systems are modeled with more than one dataflow diagram; indeed, there may be dozens or even hundreds of diagrams, arranged in hierarchical levels. And we will see that there are conventions for labeling and numbering the items in the diagram, as well as a number of guidelines and rules that help distinguish between good diagrams and poor diagrams.

4.2   MODELING STORED DATA: THE ENTITY-RELATIONSHIP DIAGRAM

While the dataflow diagram is indeed a useful tool for modeling systems, it only emphasizes one major aspect of a system: its functions. The data store notation in the DFD show us the existence of one or more groups of stored data, but deliberately says very little about the details of the data.

All systems store and use information about the environment with which they interact; sometimes the information is minimal, but in most systems today it is quite complex. Not only do we want to know, in detail, what information is contained in each data store, we want to know what relationships exist *between* the data stores. This aspect of the system is not highlighted by the dataflow diagram, but is vividly portrayed by another modeling tool: the *entity-relationship* diagram. A typical entity-relationship diagram is shown in Figure 4.5.

The entity-relationship diagram consists of two major components:

1. *Object types* are shown by a rectangular box on the entity-relationship diagram. An object type represents a collection, or set, or objects (things) in the real world whose members play a role in the system being developed, can be identified uniquely, and can be described by one or more facts (attributes).

2. *Relationships* are shown by the diamond-shaped boxes on the diagram. A relationship represents a set of connections, or associations, between the object types connected by arrows to the relationship.

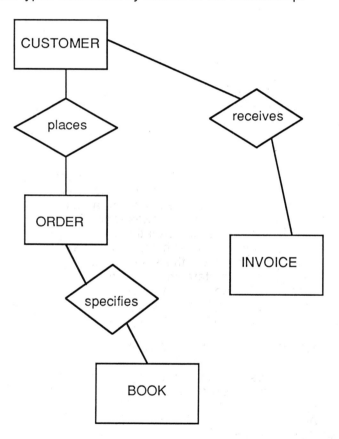

Figure 4.5: **An entity-relationship diagram**

As with the dataflow diagram, there is much more to say about the entity-relationship diagram; we will discuss it in much more detail in Chapter 12. We will see that there are certain specialized object types, as well as a number of guidelines for ensuring that the entity-relationship diagram is complete and consistent.

As with the dataflow diagram, we will find it necessary to augment the entity-relationship diagram with detailed textual information. The data dictionary, which we first saw in Figure 4.3, can also be used to maintain appropriate information about objects and relationships. This will be further explored in Chapters 10 and 12.

4.3   MODELING TIME-DEPENDENT BEHAVIOR: THE STATE-TRANSITION DIAGRAM

A third aspect of many complex systems is their time-dependent behavior, that is, the sequence in which data will be accessed and functions will be performed. For some business computer systems, this is not an important aspect to highlight, since the sequence is essentially trivial. Thus, in many batch computer systems (those which are neither on-line nor real-time), function N cannot carry out its work until it receives its required input; and its input is produced as an output of function N - 1; and so on.

However, many on-line systems and real-time systems, both in the business area and in the scientific/engineering area, have complex timing relationships that must be modeled just as carefully as the modeling of functions and data relationships. Many real-time systems, for example, must respond within a very brief period of time, perhaps only a few microseconds, to certain inputs that arrive from the external environment. And they must be prepared for various combinations and sequences of inputs to which appropriate responses must be made.

The modeling tool that we use to describe this aspect of a system's behavior is the *state-transition diagram,* sometimes abbreviated as STD. A typical diagram is shown in Figure 4.6; it models the behavior of a computer-controlled washing machine. In this diagram, the rectangular boxes represent *states* that the system can be in (i.e., recognizable "scenarios" or "situations"). Each state thus represents a period of time during which the system exhibits some observable behavior; the arrows connecting each rectangular box show the *state-change,* or transitions from one state to another. Associated with each state-change is one or more *conditions* (the events or circumstances that caused the change of state) and zero or more *actions* (the response, output, or activity that takes place as part of the change of state). We will examine the state transition diagram in more detail in Chapter 13.

4.4   MODELING PROGRAM STRUCTURE: THE STRUCTURE CHART

Though you will not use it much as a systems analyst, you should be aware that many additional modeling tools are used during the development of a complex system. For example, the system designers will usually take the dataflow diagram, data dictionary, process specifications, entity-relationship diagrams, and state transition diagrams created by the systems analyst and use them to create a software architecture, that is, a hierarchy of modules (sometimes referred to as subroutines or procedures) to implement the system requirements. One common graphical modeling tool used to represent such a software hierarchy is a *structure chart;* a typical structure chart is shown in Figure 4.7. In this diagram, each rectangular box represents a *module* (e.g., a FORTRAN subroutine, a Pascal procedure, a COBOL paragraph or subprogram). The arrows connecting the boxes represent module invocations (e.g., subroutine calls or procedure calls). The diagram also shows the input parameters passed to each module that is invoked, and the output parameters returned by the module when it finishes its job and returns control to its caller.

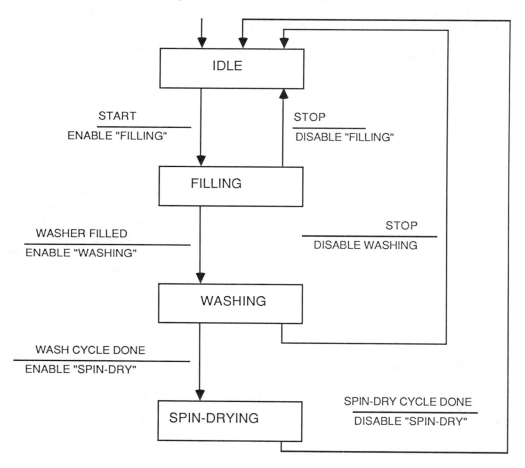

Figure 4.6: **A state-transition diagram**

While the structure chart is an excellent tool for system designers, it is not the sort of model one would normally show to the user, because it models an aspect of the *implementation* of the system, rather than the underlying requirements.[1] We will discuss structure charts again in Chapter 22.

----

1 As we pointed out in Chapter 3, some users are more knowledgeable about computers than others, and some users take a more active role in a systems development project than others. If you are working with a user who is a full-time member of the project team, or perhaps even the project leader, and if the user is somewhat knowledgeable about systems design, there is no reason why you should not show him or her a structure chart. However, if the user is only interested in describing *what* the system has to do, he or she will probably not be interested in looking at a diagram describing the organization of FORTRAN subroutines that will implement those requirements.

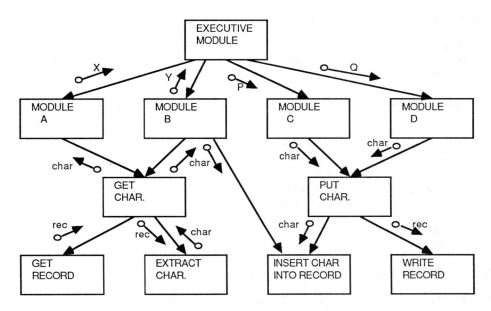

Figure 4.7: **A structure chart**

4.5   RELATIONSHIPS BETWEEN THE MODELS

As you can see, each graphic model described in this chapter focuses on a different aspect of a system: the DFD illustrates the functions, the ERD highlights the data relationships, and the STD emphasizes the time-dependent behavior of the system. Because there is so much complexity in a typical system, it is helpful to study each of these aspects in isolation; on the other hand, these three views of the system must be consistent and compatible with one another.

In Chapter 14, we will examine a number of consistency rules that ensure that the three major system models, together with the detailed textual models are indeed consistent. For example, we will see that each store on the DFD must correspond to an object or a relationship in the ERD.

4.6   SUMMARY

The models shown in this chapter are relatively simple and easy to read. Great care was taken to make them that way, for they are intended to be read and understood by users without a great deal of training or preparation. However, as we will see in Chapters 9 through 16, it requires a great deal of careful work to create the diagrams and ensure that they are complete, consistent, and accurate representations of the user requirements.

QUESTIONS AND EXERCISES

1. The introduction to Chapter 4 lists maps, globes, flowcharts, architectural drawings, and musical scores as examples of models. List three more examples of models in common use.

2. What is the dictionary definition of a model? Does it apply to information systems?

3. Why are models used in the development of information systems? List three reasons.

4. How would you respond if the user told you he thought models were a waste of time and that you should begin coding?

5. Do you think that a user's *verbal* description of his or her system requirements would be considered a model? Why or why not?

6. Why would it be useful to have more than one model for a system?

7. All the models discussed in Chapter 4 are paper models. Can you think of any other forms of models?

8. Most of the models discussed in Chapter 4 are graphical tools (i.e., pictures). What do you think are the advantages of using pictures as modeling tools?

9. Do you think graphical modeling tools are sufficient for representing the requirements of an information system? Why or why not?

10. Who should be responsible for creating the models needed to describe the requirements of an information system?

11. Should users be expected to create their own models? If so, under what circumstances?

12. What are the three main objectives of a dataflow diagram?

13. What are the four main components of a dataflow diagram?

14. Notice that the processes in a DFD are represented by circles and the terminators are represented by rectangles. Do you think this is significant? What if the processes were represented by rectangles and the terminators were represented by circles?

15. Notice that Figure 4.2 shows three different processes but does not indicate how many computers will be involved in the system. Do you think this is significant? What changes would be required if the project team decided to implement the system with one computer? With three computers?

16. Notice that Figure 4.2 shows several different dataflows between the processes, but does not indicate the physical medium that will be used to carry the data. Do you think this is significant? What if the system implementors decide to transmit data between the processes using telecommunication lines? What if they decide to transport the data from one process to another using magnetic tape?

17. What is the purpose of the data dictionary?

18. Who should be responsible for creating the data dictionary? Who should be responsible for keeping it up to date?

19. Figure 4.3 shows the data dictionary definition of a *name.* What do you think is the significance of the parentheses, ( ), in that definition?

20. What is the purpose of the process specification?

21. How many process specifications should we expect to see in a complete specification of user requirements?

22. Who should be responsible for creating the process specification? Who should keep it up to date?

23. Note that the process specification shown in the example in the chapter looks somewhat like program coding. What do you think of the idea of using pseudocode to write process specifications? What do you think of the notion of using a *real* programming language—such as Ada, as many people have suggested—for program specifications? Why would a real programming language be good or bad?

24. What is the purpose of an entity-relationship diagram?

25. What are the major components of an ERD?

26. How many object types are shown in Figure 4.5?

27. How many relationships are shown in Figure 4.5?

28. Does the ERD show the reader any information about the *functions* being carried out by the system?

29. Does the DFD show the reader any information about the object types or relationships between object types in the system?

30. Where should we describe the details of object types and relationships shown on the ERD?

31. What is the purpose of the state transition diagram?

32. What are the components of an STD?

33. Are STDs useful for modeling batch computer systems? Why or why not?

34. What is the purpose of a structure chart?

35. What are the graphical components of a structure chart?

36. Should the user be expected to read and understand a structure chart? Should the user be expected to be able to create one?

37. Describe the relationship that exists between an ERD and a DFD.

38. Is there a relationship between a DFD and a structure chart? If so, what is it?

5 THE PROJECT LIFE CYCLE

All human error is impatience, a premature renunciation of method, a delusive pinning down of a delusion.

Franz Kafka, *Letters*

In this chapter, you will learn:

1. The concept of a project life cycle.

2. The characteristics of the classical project life cycle.

3. The differences between classical and semistructured projects.

4. The components of the structured life cycle.

5. The differences between radical and conservative life cycles.

To be an effective systems analyst, we need more than just modeling tools; we need *methods.* In the systems development profession, the terms method, methodology, project life cycle, and systems development life cycle are used almost interchangeably. In Part III, we will look at the detailed methods for doing systems analysis, within the broader context of a method—known as a structured project life cycle—for carrying out the overall development of a new system.

Before introducing the structured project life cycle, it is important to examine the classical project life cycle discussed in many textbooks and used in many systems development organizations today, primarily to identify its limitations and weaknesses. This examination will be followed by a brief discussion of the *semistructured* life project life cycle: a project life cycle that includes some, but not all, of the elements of modern systems development. Next, we introduce the *structured* project life cycle, presenting an overview to show the major activities and how they fit together. Finally, we will examine briefly the *prototyping* life cycle popularized by Bernard Boar, James Martin, and several vendors of fourth-generation programming languages.

We will also explore the concept of *iterative* or *top-down* development. In particular, we will introduce the notion of *radical* top-down development and *conservative* top-down development. Depending on the nature of a systems development project, there may be valid reasons for adopting one approach rather than the other; indeed, some projects may call for a combination of the two.

5.1   THE CONCEPT OF A PROJECT LIFE CYCLE

As you might expect, small EDP organizations tend to be relatively informal: systems development projects are begun as the result of a verbal discussion between the user and the project manager (who may also be the systems analyst, programmer, computer operator, and janitor!), and the project proceeds from systems analysis through design and implementation without much fuss.

In the larger organizations, however, things are done on a much more formal basis. The various communications between users, management, and the project team tend to be documented in writing, and everyone understands that the project will go through several phases before it is complete. Even so, it is surprising to see the major differences between the way two project managers in the same organization will conduct their respective projects. Indeed, it is often left to the discretion of the individual project manager to determine what phases and activities her or his project will consist of and how these phases will be conducted.[1]

Recently, though, the approach taken to systems development has begun to change. More and more large *and* small organizations are adopting a single, uniform project life cycle—sometimes known as a project plan or systems development methodology or, simply, "the way we do things around here." Usually contained in a notebook as ponderous as the standards manual that sits (unread) on every analyst's and programmer's desk, the documented project life cycle provides a common way for everyone in the systems development organization to go about the business of developing a computer system.

The approach may be home-grown or, alternatively, the systems development organization may decide to purchase a project management package and then tailor it

---

1 This sounds as if anarchy prevails in most EDP organizations. However, there are two common situations that lead to this individualistic approach even in the most exemplary organization: (1) the highly decentralized organization, where every department has its own EDP group with its own local standards, and (2) the period of several years immediately after the last "official project life cycle" was deemed a failure and thrown out.

to company needs.[2] It seems apparent that, aside from providing employment for the people who create project life cycle manuals (and for those who write textbooks about them!), the project methodology is desirable. What then is the purpose of having a project life cycle? There are three primary objectives:

1. To define the activities to be carried out in a systems development project.

2. To introduce consistency among many systems development projects in the same organization.

3. To provide checkpoints for management control for go/no-go decisions.

The first objective is particularly important in a large organization in which new people are constantly entering the ranks of project management. The fledgling project manager may overlook or underestimate the significance of important project phases if he or she follows only intuition. Indeed, it can happen that junior programmers and systems analysts may not understand where and how their efforts fit into the overall project unless they are given a proper description of *all* the phases of the project.

The second objective is also important in a large organization. For higher levels of management, it can be extremely disconcerting to oversee a hundred different projects, each of which is being carried out in a different way. For example, if project A defines the systems analysis activity differently than does project B, and project B doesn't include a design phase, how is the second- or third-level manager to know which project is in trouble and which is proceeding on schedule?[3]

The third objective of a standard project life cycle pertains to management's need to control a project. On trivial projects, the sole checkpoint is likely to be the end of the project: Was it finished on time and within the specified budget? (Or even more simply: was it finished at all?) And did it accomplish the user's requirements? But for larger projects, management should have a number of intermediate checkpoints during the project, which provide it with opportunities to determine whether the project is behind schedule, and whether additional resources need to be procured. In

---

2 There are several such packages on the market, costing from $10,000 to $100,000 or more. Some of the better-known examples are Spectrum (from Spectrum International Corp.), SDM-70 (from AGS Software), and Method/1 (from Arthur Andersen). I won't comment on any specific project management package; I will only suggest that you keep the concepts presented in this book in mind if your organizations uses a vendor-supplied package.

3 Miller points out in [Miller, 1978] that this is a commonly observed phenomenon; indeed, he presents it as a general "hypothesis" applicable to all living systems:

> HYPOTHESIS 2-1: System components incapable of associating, or lacking experience which has formed such associations, must function according to rigid programming or highly standardized operating rules. It follows that as turnover of components rises above the rate at which the components can develop the associations necessary for operation, rigidity of programming increases.

addition, an intelligent user will also want checkpoints at several stages in the project so that he can determine whether he wants to continue funding it![4]

Having said all this, let me emphasize that the project life cycle definitely is not in charge of the project. It will not relieve the project manager of the difficult responsibility of making decisions, weighing alternatives, fighting political battles, negotiating with recalcitrant users, boosting the morale of dejected programmers, or any of the other project-related trials and tribulations. The project manager still has to *manage,* in every sense of the word. The only help that the project life cycle can provide is that it can *organize* the manager's activities, making it more likely that the right problems will be addressed at the right time.

5.2   THE CLASSICAL PROJECT LIFE CYCLE

The kind of project life cycle used in many organizations today differs from the one to which we'll be devoting most of our attention in Part III. The classical, or conventional, project life cycle is shown in Figure 5.1. Every project goes through some kind of systems analysis, design, and implementation, even if it's not done in exactly the way shown in the diagram. The project life cycle used in your organization, for example, might differ from the one shown in Figure 5.1 in one or all of the following ways:

- The survey phase and the analysis phase may be lumped together into a single phase (this is especially common in organizations in which anything the user wants is deemed at the outset to be feasible).

- There may not be a phase called hardware study if it can be taken for granted that any new system can be implemented on an existing computer without causing any major operational impact.

- The preliminary design and detail design phases may be lumped together in a single phase simply called design.

- Several of the testing phases may be grouped together into a single phase; indeed, they may even be included with coding.

Thus, an individual organization's project life cycle may have five phases, or seven phases, or twelve phases, but it is still likely to be of the classical variety.

What is it that really characterizes a project life cycle as being classical? Two features stand out: a strong tendency toward bottom-up implementation of the system, and an insistence on linear, sequential progression from one phase to the next.

---

4 In fact, the politics of most EDP projects are such that there is only one checkpoint at which the user has an obvious, clean way of backing out: at the end of the survey, or feasibility study, phase. In theory, though, the user should have the opportunity to cancel an EDP project at the end of any phase if he thinks he is wasting money.

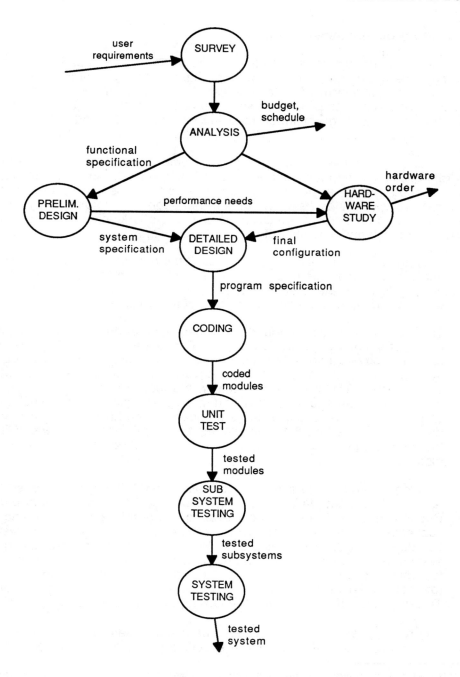

Figure 5.1(a): **The classical project life cycle**

5.2.1   Bottom-Up Implementation

The use of bottom-up implementation is one of the major weaknesses in the classical project life cycle. As you can see from Figure 5.1(a), the programmers are expected to carry out all their module testing first, then subsystem testing, and finally system testing. This approach is also known in the computer industry as the "waterfall life cycle," based on a diagram introduced in [Royce, 1970], and subsequently popularized by Barry Boehm in [Boehm, 1981]. It is shown in Figure 5.1(b).

It's not clear where this approach originally came from, but it may have been borrowed from assembly-line manufacturing industries. The bottom-up implementation approach is a good one for assembling automobiles on an assembly line, *but only after the prototype model has been thoroughly debugged!* [5] Unfortunately, many system development organizations are still producing one-of-a-kind systems, for which the bottom-up approach has a number of serious difficulties:

- Nothing is done until it's *all* done. Thus, if the project gets behind schedule and the deadline falls right in the middle of system testing, there will be nothing to show the user except an enormous pile of program listings—which, taken in their entirety, do nothing of any value for the user!

- The most trivial bugs are found at the beginning of the testing period, and the most serious bugs are found last. This is almost a tautology: Module testing uncovers relatively simple logic errors inside individual modules; system testing, on the other hand, uncovers major interface errors between subsystems. The point is that major interface errors are *not* what the programmer wants to find at the end of a development project; such bugs can lead to the recoding of large numbers of modules, and can have a devastating impact on the schedule, right at a time when everyone is likely to be somewhat tired and cranky from having worked so hard for so many months.

- Debugging tends to be extremely difficult during the final stages of system testing. Note that we distinguish here between *testing* and *debugging*. Debugging is the black art of discovering *where* a bug is located (and the subsequent determination of how to fix the bug) after the process of testing has determined that there *is* a bug. When a bug is discovered during the system-testing phase of a bottom-up project, it's often extremely difficult to tell which module contains the bug; it could be in any one of the hundreds (or thousands) of modules that have been combined for the first time. Tracking down the bug is often like looking for a needle in a haystack.

- The requirement for computer test time usually rises exponentially during the final stages of testing. More specifically, the project manager often

---

5 Many people feel that the bottom-up approach may also have come from the computer *hardware* industry, because many of the early computer programmers and programming managers in the 1950s and 1960s were electrical engineers who had previously been involved in the development of hardware.

finds that she or he needs large contiguous chunks of computer time for system testing, perhaps 12 hours of uninterrupted computer time per day. Since such a large amount of computer time is often difficult to obtain,[6] the project often falls seriously behind schedule.

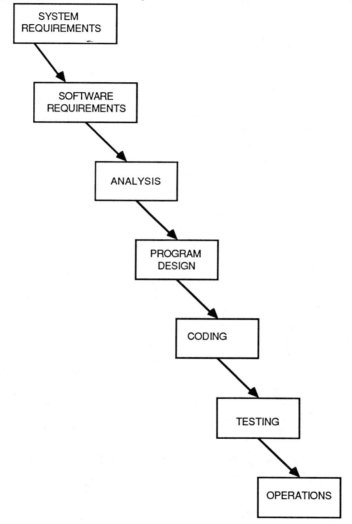

Figure 5.1(b): **The waterfall model of systems development**

---

6 I'm convinced that yet another of the Murphy-type laws applies in this regard: The larger and more critical the project, the more likely it is that its deadline will coincide with end-of-year processing and other organizational crises that gobble up all available computer time!

5.2.2   Sequential Progression

The second major weakness with the classical project life cycle is its insistence that the phases proceed sequentially from one to the next. There is a natural, human tendency to want this to be so: We want to be able to say that we have *finished* the systems analysis phase and that we'll never have to worry about that phase again. Indeed, many organizations formalize this notion with a ritual known as freezing the specification or freezing the design document.

The only problem with this desire for orderly progression is that it's completely unrealistic! In particular, the sequential approach doesn't allow for real-world phenomena having to do with personnel, company politics, or economics. For example, the person doing the work, such as the systems analyst or designer, may have made a mistake, and may have produced a flawed product. Indeed, as human beings, we rarely do a complex job right the first time, but we are very good at making repeated improvements to an imperfect job. Or the person reviewing the work, in particular, the user who reviews the work of the systems analyst, may have made a mistake. Or perhaps the person carrying out the work associated with each phase may not have enough time to finish, but may be unwilling to admit that fact. This is a polite way of saying that, on most complex projects, systems analysis and design (and system testing, too) finish when someone decides that you have run out of time, not when you want those activities to finish!

Other problems are commonly associated with the sequential, classical project life cycle: During the several months (or years) that it takes to develop the system, the user may change his or her mind about what the system should do. During the period that it takes to develop the system, certain aspects of the user's environment may change (e.g., the economy, the competition, or the government regulations that affect the user's activities).

An additional characteristic of the classical project life cycle is that it relies on outdated techniques. That is, it tends to make no use of structured design, structured programming, walkthroughs, or any of the other modern development techniques.[7] But because the classical project life *ignores* the existence of these techniques, there is nothing to prevent the project manager from using them. Unfortunately, many programmers, systems analysts, and first-level project leaders feel that the project life cycle is a statement of policy by top-level management; and if management doesn't say anything about the use of structured programming, then they, as mere project members and leaders, are not obliged to use nonclassical approaches.

5.3   THE SEMISTRUCTURED LIFE CYCLE

The comments in the previous section make it seem as if most EDP organizations are still living in the Dark Ages. Indeed, such a characterization is unfair: Not *every* organization uses the classical project life. Beginning in the late 1970s and early

---

7 We will summarize these modern development techniques in Chapter 7.

1980s, there has been a growing recognition that techniques like structured design, structured programming, and top-down implementation should be officially recognized in the project life cycle. This recognition has led to the semistructured project life cycle shown in Figure 5.2; it shows two obvious features not present in the classical approach:

1. The bottom-up sequence of coding, module testing, and system testing is replaced by top-down implementation, an approach where high-level modules are coded and tested first, followed by the lower-level, detailed modules. There is also a strong indication that structured programming is to be used as the method of actually coding the system.

2. Classical design is replaced by structured design, a formal systems design approach discussed in such books as [Yourdon and Constantine, 1989] and [Page-Jones, 1988].

Aside from these obvious differences, there are some subtle points about this modified life cycle. Consider, for example, that top-down implementation means that some coding and testing are taking place in parallel. That certainly represents a major departure from the sequential phases that we saw in the classical life cycle! In particular, it can mean *feedback* between the activity of coding and that of testing and debugging. When the programmer tests the top-level skeleton version of the system, he or she may be heard to mutter, "Jeez, I had no idea that the double-precision FRAMMIS instruction worked *that* way!" Naturally, you can be sure that subsequent use of the double-precision FRAMMIS instruction will be quite different.

Perhaps more important, the use of top-down implementation tempts the implementors (and the systems analysts, if they haven't abandoned the project by this time) to talk to the users *after* the specifications have been ceremoniously frozen. Thus, it is possible that the user will point out errors or misunderstandings in the specification; the user may even express a desire to *change* the specification, and if the conversation takes place directly between the user and the implementor, a change may actually be effected before the project manager knows what is happening. In short, top-down implementation often provides feedback between the implementation process and the analysis process—although this feedback exchange is not specifically shown on Figure 5.2, and although the user and the EDP project manager might well deny that it is taking place!

There is one final point about the semistructured life cycle: A significant part of the work that takes place under the heading of "structured design" is actually a manual effort to fix up bad narrative specifications. You can see this by looking at Figure 5.3, which depicts the details of structured design. (Note that this figure consists of the details of process 3 in Figure 5.2.)

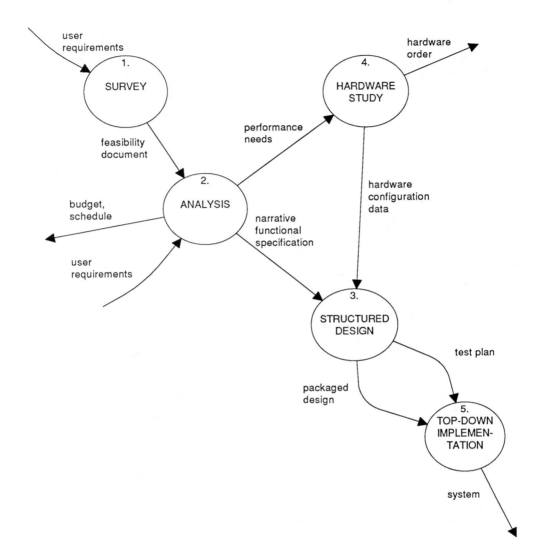

Figure 5.2: **The semistructured project life cycle**

In Figure 5.3, activity 3.1 (labeled CODIFY FUNCTIONAL SPECIFICATION) represents a task that designers have long had to do: translate a monolithic, ambiguous, redundant, narrative document into a useful, nonprocedural model to serve as the basis for deriving the hierarchy of modules that will implement the user's requirements. In other words, people practicing structured design have traditionally assumed that they would be given a classical specification; consequently, their first job, as they see it, is to transform that specification into a package of dataflow diagrams, data dictionaries, entity-relationship diagrams, and process specifications.

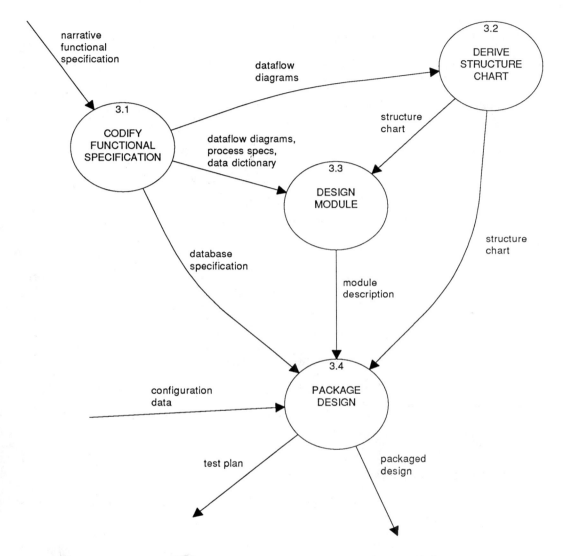

Figure 5.3: **Details of the design activity**

This is a more difficult job than you might imagine: Historically, it has been a task carried out in a vacuum. Designers generally had little contact with the systems analyst who wrote the long narrative specification, and they certainly had *no* contact with the user!

Obviously, such a situation is ripe for change. Introducing structured analysis—the kind of modern systems analysis approach presented in this book—into the picture, as well as expanding on the idea of feedback between one part of the project and another, creates an entirely different kind of project life cycle. This is the structured project life cycle, which we will discuss next.

5.4   THE STRUCTURED PROJECT LIFE CYCLE

Now that we have seen the classical project life cycle and the semistructured project life cycle, we are ready to examine the structured life cycle; it is shown in Figure 5.4.

We will briefly examine the project life cycle's nine activities and three terminators, as shown in Figure 5.4. The terminators consist of users, managers, and operations personnel; as you recall, we discussed their roles in Chapter 3. These are individuals or groups of individuals who provide input to the project team and who are the ultimate recipients of the system. They interact with the nine activities that we have shown in Figure 5.4. Each of the activities is summarized in the following sections.

5.4.1   Activity 1: The Survey

This activity is also known as the feasibility study or initial business study. Typically, it begins when a user requests that one or more portions of his or her business be automated. The major purposes of the survey activity are as follows:

- *Identify the responsible users and develop an initial "scope" of the system.* This may involve conducting a series of interviews to see which user(s) are involved in (or affected by) the proposed project and which are not.[8] It may also involve developing an initial *context* diagram—a simple dataflow diagram of the sort shown in Figure 4.2, in which the entire system is represented by a single process.[9]

- *Identify current deficiencies in the user's environment.* This will usually consist of a simple narrative list of functions that are missing or operating unacceptably in the current system. For example, this might include statements like the following:

  * The hardware for the current system is unreliable, and the vendor has just gone bankrupt.

  * The software for the current system is unmaintainable, and we can no longer hire maintenance programmers who are willing to maintain software in the programming language used to develop the current system.

---

8 Interviewing techniques are discussed in Appendix E.

9 The context diagram is part of the environmental model that we will discuss in detail in Chapter 18. Its major purpose, as indicated here, is to define the scope of the system (what is in the system and what is out of the system), as well as the various terminators (people, organizational units, other computer systems, etc.) with whom the system will interact.

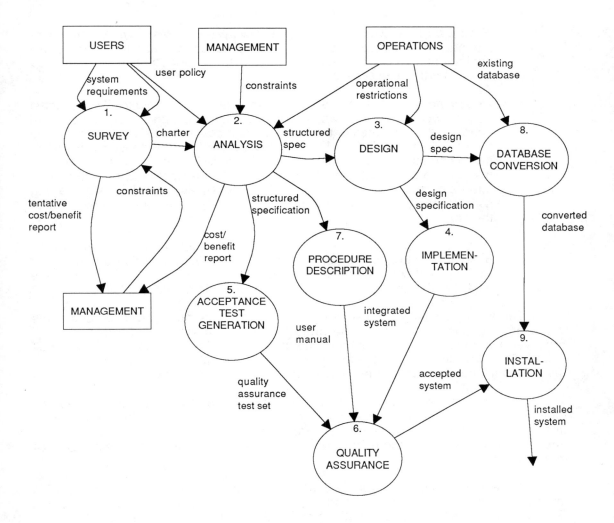

Figure 5.4: **The structured project life cycle**

* The response time for the current on-line order entry system is so bad that many customers hang up, in frustration, before they have entered their order.

* The current system is unable to produce the government reports required by last year's Tax Reform Act.

* The current system is unable to receive credit-limit reports from the accounting department and cannot produce reports of average order size for the marketing department.

- *Establish goals and objectives for a new system.* This may also be a simple narrative list consisting of existing functions that need to be re-implemented, new functions that need to be added, and performance criteria for the new system.

- *Determine whether it is feasible to automate the system and, if so, suggest some acceptable scenarios.* This will involve some very crude and approximate estimates of the schedule and cost to build a new system and the benefits to be derived;[10] it will also involve two or more scenarios (e.g., the mainframe scenario, the distributed processing scenario, etc.). Though management and the users will often want a precise, detailed estimate at this point, the systems analyst will be extremely lucky if she or he can estimate the time, resources, and costs to within ±50% at this early stage in the project.

- *Prepare a project charter that will be used to guide the remainder of the project.* The project charter will include all the information listed above, as well as identify the responsible project manager. It may also describe the details of the project life cycle that the rest of the project will follow.

The survey typically occupies only 5% to 10% of the time and resources of the entire project, and for small, simple projects it may not even be a formal activity. However, even though it may not consume much of the time or resources of the project, it is a critical activity: at the end of the survey, management may decide to cancel the project if it does not appear attractive from a cost-benefit point of view.

As a systems analyst, you may or may not be involved in the survey; the user, together with appropriate levels of management, may have done it before you even hear about the project. However, for large, complex projects, the survey involves enough detailed work that the user will often ask the systems analyst to be involved as early as possible.

We will not discuss the survey in any further detail in this book. If you become involved in this activity, you may find Appendixes E and C useful. For additional details, consult [Dickinson, 1981] [Gore and Stubbe, 1983] and [Yourdon, 1988].

5.4.2   Activity 2: Systems Analysis

The primary purpose of the analysis activity is to transform its two major inputs, user policy and project charter, into a structured specification. This involves modeling the user's environment with dataflow diagrams, entity-relationship diagrams, state-transition diagrams, and the other tools presented in Chapter 4; these tools are covered in detail in Part II.

---

10 Cost-benefit calculations are discussed in Appendix C.

The step-by-step *process* of systems analysis (i.e., the subactivities of the analysis activity in Figure 5.4) is discussed in Part III. As we will see, it involves the development of an *environmental model* (discussed in Chapter 18) and the development of a *behavioral model* (discussed in Chapters 19 and 20). These two models combine to form the *essential model* (discussed in Chapter 17), which represents a formal description of what the new system must do, independent of the nature of the technology that will be used to implement those requirements.

In addition to the system model describing user requirements, a more accurate, detailed set of budgets and cost-benefit calculations is generally prepared at the end of the analysis activity. This is discussed in more detail in Appendix C.

Obviously, as a systems analyst, this is where you will be spending the major part of your time. There is nothing more we need to say about the analysis activity at this point, since it is the subject of the rest of this book.

5.4.3   Activity 3: Design

The activity of design is concerned with allocating portions of the specification (otherwise known as the essential model) to appropriate processors (CPUs and/or humans) and to appropriate tasks (or jobs, or partitions, etc.) within each processor. Within each task, the design activity is concerned with the development of an appropriate hierarchy of program modules and interfaces between those modules to implement the specification created in activity 2. In addition, the design activity is concerned with the transformation of entity-relationship data models into a database design; see [Inmon, 1988] for more details.

Part of this activity will be of interest to you as a systems analyst: the development of something called the *user implementation model.* This model describes those implementation issues that the user feels strongly enough about that he or she is *not* willing to leave them to the discretion of the systems designers and programmers. The primary issues that the user is typically concerned about is the specification of the human-machine boundary and the specification of the human-machine interface. The human-machine boundary separates those parts of the essential model that are to be carried out by a person (as a manual activity) from the parts that are to be implemented on one or more computers. Similarly, the human-machine interface is a description of the format and sequence of *inputs* provided by human users to the computer (e.g., screen designs and the on-line dialogue between the user and the computer), as well as the format and sequence of *outputs* provided by the computer to the user. The user implementation model is described in Chapter 21.

An introduction to the process of systems design may be found in Chapter 22. Additional material may be found in [Yourdon and Constantine, 1989], [Page-Jones, 1988], [Jackson, 1975], and others.

5.4.4   Activity 4: Implementation

This activity includes both coding and the integration of modules into a progressively more complete skeleton of the ultimate system. Thus, activity 4 includes both structured programming and top-down implementation.

As you can imagine, this is typically an activity that the systems analyst is not involved with, though there are some projects (and some organizations) where systems analysis, design, and implementation are done by the same person. This topic is discussed in more detail in Chapter 23.

5.4.5   Activity 5: Acceptance Test Generation

The structured specification should contain all the information necessary to define an acceptable system from the user's point of view. Thus, once the specification has been generated, work can commence on the activity of generating a set of acceptance test cases from the structured specification.

Since the development of acceptance tests can take place in parallel with the activities of design and implementation, it is possible that you may be assigned to this task after you finish developing the essential model in activity 2. Testing is discussed in more detail in Chapter 23.

5.4.6   Activity 6: Quality Assurance

Quality assurance is also known as final testing or acceptance testing. This activity requires, as its input, acceptance test data generated in activity 5 and an integrated system produced by activity 4.

The systems analyst could conceivably be involved in the quality assurance activity, but typically is not. One or more members of the user organization may take responsibility, or it may be carried out by an independent testing group or Quality Assurance Department. Consequently, we will not discuss the quality assurance function in any further detail.

Note, by the way, that some people refer to this activity as quality control rather than quality assurance. Regardless of the terminology, we need an activity to *verify* that the system exhibits the appropriate level of quality; this is what we have called quality assurance in this book. Note also that it is important to carry out quality assurance activities throughout *each* of the earlier activities to ensure that they have been performed at an appropriate level of quality. Thus, one would expect a QA activity to be performed throughout the analysis, design, and programming activity to ensure that the analyst is developing high-quality specifications, the designer is producing a high-quality design, and the programmer is writing high-quality code. The quality assurance activity identified here is merely the *final* test of the system's quality.

5.4.7   Activity 7: Procedure Description

Throughout this book, we concern ourselves with the development of an *entire* system—not just the automated portion, but also the portion to be carried out by people. Thus, one of the important activities to be performed is the generation of a formal description of those portions of the new system that will be manual, as well as a description of how the users actually will interact with the automated portion of the new system. The output of activity 7 is a user's manual.

As you can imagine, this is also an activity in which you may become involved as a systems analyst. Though we do not discuss it further in this book, you may wish to consult books on technical writing for additional information on the writing of user manuals.

5.4.8   Activity 8: Database Conversion

In some projects, database conversion involved more work (and more strategic planning) than did the development of computer programs for the new system; in other cases, there might not have been any existing database to convert. In the general case, this activity requires, as input, the user's current database, as well as the design specification produced by activity 3.

Depending on the nature of the project, you may or may not become involved in the database conversion activity as a systems analyst. However, we do not discuss this activity in any greater detail in this book.

5.4.9   Activity 9: Installation

The final activity, of course, is installation; its inputs are the user's manual produced by activity 7, the converted database produced by activity 8, and the accepted system produced by activity 6. In some cases, however, installation may simply mean an overnight "cutover" to the new system, with no excitement or fanfare; in other cases, installation may be a gradual process, as one user group after another receives user's manuals, hardware, and training in the use of the new system and actually begin using it.

5.4.10   Summary of the Structured Project Life Cycle

It's important that you view Figure 5.4 for what it is: a *dataflow diagram*. It is *not* a flowchart; there is no implication that all of activity N must finish before activity N + 1 commences. On the contrary, the network of dataflows connecting activities strongly implies that several activities may be going on in parallel. It is because of this nonsequential aspect that we use the word *activity* in the structured project life cycle, rather than the more conventional word *phase*. The term phase has traditionally referred to a particular period of time in a project when one, and only one, activity was going on.

There is something else that must be emphasized about the use of a dataflow diagram to depict the project life cycle: A classical dataflow diagram, such as the one in Figure 5.4, does not explicitly show feedback, nor does it show control.[11] Virtually every one of the activities in Figure 5.4 can, and usually does, produce information that can provide suitable modifications to one or more of the preceding activities. Thus, the activity of design can produce information that may revise some of the cost-benefit decisions that take place in the analysis activity; indeed, knowledge gained in the design activity may even require revising earlier decisions about the basic feasibility of the project.

Indeed, in the extreme cases, certain events taking place in any activity could cause the entire project to terminate abruptly. The input of management is shown only for the analysis activity, because analysis is the only activity that requires *data* from management; it is assumed, however, that management exerts *control* over all of the activities.

In summary, then, Figure 5.4 only tells us the input(s) required by each activity and the output(s) produced. The sequence of activities can be implied only to the extent that the presence or absence of data makes it possible for an activity to commence.

5.5   RADICAL VERSUS CONSERVATIVE TOP-DOWN IMPLEMENTATION

In the previous section, I pointed out that the structured project life cycle allows more than one activity to take place at one time. Let me put it another way: In the most extreme situation, *all* the activities in the structured project life cycle could be taking place simultaneously. At the other extreme, the project manager could decide to adopt the sequential approach, finishing *all* of one activity before commencing on the next.

It is convenient to have some terminology to help talk about these extremes, as well as about compromises between the two extremes. A *radical* approach to the structured project life cycle is one in which activities 1 through 9 take place in parallel from the very beginning of the project; that is, coding begins on the first day of the project, and the survey and analysis continue until the last day of the project. By contrast, in a *conservative* approach to the structured project life cycle, all of activity N is completed before activity N + 1 begins.

Obviously, no project manager in his right mind would adopt either of these two extremes. The key to recognize is that the radical and conservative extremes defined above are the two endpoints in a range of choices; this is illustrated in Figure 5.5. There are an infinite number of choices between the radical and conservative extremes. A project manager might decide to finish 75% of the survey activity, followed by completion of 75% of systems analysis, and then 75% of design, in order to produce a reasonably complete skeleton version of a system whose details could

---

11 Actually, there are ways of showing feedback and control in dataflow diagrams, as we will see in Chapter 9. The additional notations (for control processes and control flows) are normally used for modeling real-time systems, and we have avoided their use in this model of the "system for building systems."

then be refined by a second pass through the entire project life cycle. Or, the manager might decide to finish *all* the survey and analysis activities, followed by completion of 50% of design and 50% of implementation. The possibilities are truly endless!

Figure 5.5: **Radical and conservative implementation choices**

How does a project manager decide whether to adopt a radical or conservative approach? Basically, there is no right answer; the decision is usually based on the following factors:

- How fickle is the user?

- What pressure is the project team under to produce immediate, tangible results?

- What pressure is the project manager under to produce an accurate schedule, budget, and estimate of people and other resources?

- What are the dangers of making a major technical blunder?

As you can appreciate, not one of these questions has a straight black-or-white answer. For example, one can't ask the user of the system, in casual conversation, "By the way, how fickle are you feeling today?" On the other hand, the project manager should be able to assess the situation, based on observation, especially if he or she is a veteran who has dealt with many users and many upper-level managers before.

If the project manager judges that he's dealing with a fickle user—one whose personality is such that he delays final decisions until he sees how the system is going to work—then the manager would probably opt for a more radical approach. The same is true if the manager is dealing with an inexperienced user, who has had very few systems built for him. Why spend years developing an absolutely perfect set of specifications only to discover that the user didn't understand the significance of the specifications?

If, however, the manager is dealing with a veteran user who is absolutely sure of what he wants, and if the user works in a business area that is stable and unlikely to change radically on a month-to-month basis, then the project can afford to take a more conservative approach. Of course, there are a lot of in-between situations: The user may be sure of *some* of the business functions to be performed, but may be somewhat unsure of the kinds of reports and management information he or she would like the system to provide. Or, if the user is familiar with batch computer systems, he or she may be unsure of the impact that an on-line system will have on the business.

Besides fickleness, there is a second factor to consider: the pressure to produce immediate, tangible results. If, due to politics or other external pressures, the project team simply *must* get a system up and running by a specific date, then a somewhat radical approach is warranted. The project manager still runs the risk that the system will be only 90% complete when the deadline arrives, but at least it will be a *working* 90% complete skeleton that can be demonstrated and perhaps even put into production. That's generally better than having finished all the systems analysis, all the design, and all the coding, but none of the testing.

Of course, *all* projects are under some pressure for tangible results; it's simply a question of degree. And it's an issue that can be rather dynamic: A project that begins in a low-key fashion with a comfortable schedule can suddenly become high-priority, and the deadline may be advanced six months or a year. One of the advantages of doing the systems analysis, design, coding, and implementation top-down is that one can stop an activity at any point and leave the remaining details for subsequent consideration; meanwhile, the top-level systems analysis that has been completed can be used to begin the top-level design, and so forth.

Yet another factor in project management is the ever present requirement, in most large organizations, to produce schedules, estimates, budgets, and the like. In some organizations, this tends to be done in a fairly informal fashion, typically because the projects are relatively small, and because management feels that any errors in estimating will have an insignificant impact on the whole organization. In such cases, one can adopt a radical approach, even though any attempts at estimating will have to be "gut-level" guesses. By contrast, most large projects require relatively detailed estimates of personnel requirements, computer resources, and so on; and this can only be done after a fairly detailed survey, analysis, and design have been completed. In other words, the more detailed and accurate the estimates have to be, the more likely the project is to follow a conservative approach.

Finally, the project manager must consider the danger of making a major technical blunder. For example, suppose that all his past experience as a project manager has been with a small batch-oriented IBM System/36 computer system. And now, all of a sudden, he finds himself in charge of developing an on-line, real-time, multiprocessing distributed database management information system that will process 2 million transactions a day from 5000 terminals scattered around the world. In such a situation, one of the dangers of a radical approach is discovering a major design flaw after a large portion of the top-level skeleton system has been implemented.

He may discover, for example, that in order for his whizbang system to work, a low-level module has to do its job in 19 microseconds—but his programmers suddenly tell him that there is no way on earth to code the module that efficiently—not in COBOL, not in C, not even in (ugh!) assembly language. So, he must be alert to the fact that following the radical approach requires his systems analysts and designers to pick a "top" to your system relatively early in the game, and there is always the danger of discovering, down toward the bottom, that they picked the wrong top!

However, consider another scenario: The project manager has decided to build an EDP system with new hardware, a new operating system, a new database management system (produced by someone other than the hardware vendor), and a new telecommunications package (produced by yet another vendor). All the vendors have impressive, glossy manuals describing their products, but the vendors have never interfaced their respective hardware and software products together. Who knows if they will work together at all? Who knows if the throughput promised by one vendor will be destroyed by the system resources used by one of the other vendors? Certainly, in a case like this, the project manager might elect a radical approach, so that a skeleton version of the system could be used to explore possible interface and interaction problems between the vendors' components.

If the project manager is in charge of a familiar kind of system, such as her 99th payroll system, then she probably has a very good idea of how realistic her goals are. She probably remembers, from the last project, what sort of modules she's going to need at the detailed level, and she probably remembers very clearly what the top-level system structure looked like. In such a case, she may be willing to accept the risks of making a mistake because of the other benefits that the radical approach will give her.

In summary, the radical approach is most suitable for thinly disguised research and development efforts, where nobody is quite sure what the final system is supposed to do. And it is good in environments in which something *must* be working on a specific date and in situations where the user's perception of what he wants the system to do is subject to change. The conservative approach, on the other hand, tends to be used on larger projects, in which massive amounts of money are being spent and for which careful analysis and design are required to prevent subsequent disasters. However, every project is different and requires its own special blend of radical and conservative top-down implementation. To deal with the individual nature of any project, the project manager must be prepared to modify his approach midstream, if necessary.

5.6   THE PROTOTYPING LIFE CYCLE

A variation on the top-down approach discussed above has become popular in the past few years. It is generally known as the *prototyping* approach and has been popularized by Bernard Boar, James Martin, and others. As Boar describes it in [Boar, 1984]:

> An alternative approach to requirements definition is to capture an initial set of needs and to implement quickly those needs with the stated intent of iteratively expanding and refining them as mutual user/developer understanding of the system grows. Definition of the system occurs through gradual and evolutionary discovery as opposed to omniscient foresight.... This kind of approach is called prototyping. It is also referred to as system modeling or heuristic development. It offers an attractive and workable alternative to prespecification methods to deal better with uncertainty, ambiguity, and fickleness of real-world projects.

In many ways, this sounds exactly like the radical top-down approach discussed in the section above. The primary difference is that the structured approach discussed throughout this book presumes that sooner or later, a complete *paper model* of the system will be built (i.e., a complete set of dataflow diagrams, entity-relationship diagrams, state-transition diagrams, process specifications, etc.). The model will be completed sooner with a conservative approach and later with a radical approach; but by the end of the project, there will be a formal set of documents that should live forever with the system as it undergoes maintenance and revision.

The prototyping approach, on the other hand, almost always assumes that the model will be a working model, that is, a collection of computer programs that will simulate some or all of the functions that the user wants. But since those computer programs are intended just as a model, there is also an assumption that, *when the modeling is finished, the programs will be thrown away and replaced with REAL programs.* Prototypers typically use the following kinds of software tools:

- An integrated data dictionary

- Screen generator

- Nonprocedural report writer

- Fourth generation programming language

- Nonprocedural query language

- Powerful database management facilities

The prototyping life cycle proposed by Boar is shown in Figure 5.6. It begins with a survey activity, similar to that proposed in this book; this is immediately followed by a determination of whether the project is a good candidate for a prototyping approach. Good candidates for a prototyping approach are projects that have the following characteristics:

- The user is unable (or unwilling) to examine abstract paper models like dataflow diagrams.

- The user is unable or unwilling to articulate (or "prespecify") his or her requirements in any form and can only determine the requirements through a process of trial and error. Or, as my colleague Bob Spurgeon puts it, this is the situation where the user says, "I don't know what I want, but I'll recognize it when I see it!"

- The system is intended to be on-line with full-screen terminal activities, as opposed to batch edit, update, and report systems. (Almost all prototyping software tools are oriented toward the on-line, database-driven, terminal-oriented approach; there are few vendor-supplied software tools to help build prototypes of batch systems.)

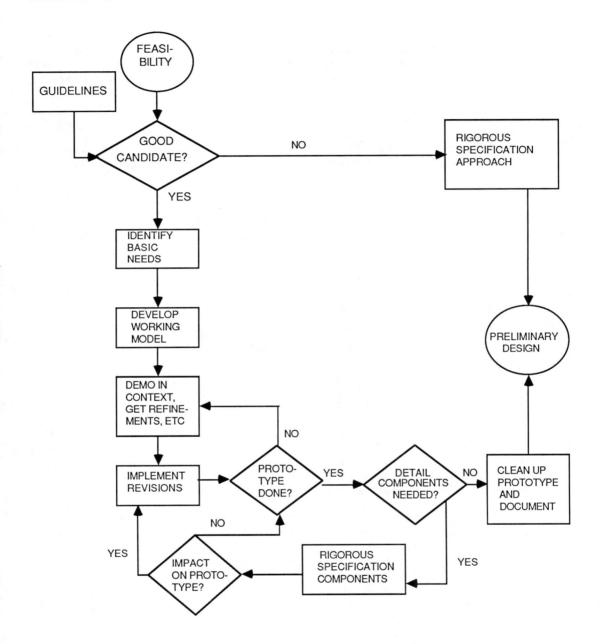

Figure 5.6: **The prototyping life cycle**

• The system does *not* require specification of large amounts of algorithmic detail, that is, the writing of many, many process specifications to describe the algorithms by which output results are created. Thus, decision support, ad hoc retrieval, and record management systems are good candidates for prototyping. Good candidates tend to be the systems in which the user is more concerned about the format and layout of the CRT data entry and output screens and error messages than about the underlying computations performed by the system.

It is significant to note that the prototyping life cycle shown in Figure 5.6 concludes by entering the design phase of a "traditional" structured life cycle of the sort described in this book. Specifically, this means that the prototype is *not* intended to be an operational system; it is intended solely as a means of modeling user requirements.

The prototyping approach certainly has merit in a number of situations. In some cases, the project manager may want to use the prototyping approach as an alternative to the structured analysis approach described in this book; in other cases, she or he may wish to use it *in conjunction with* the development of paper models such as dataflow diagrams. Keep in mind the following points:

- The top-down approach described in the previous section is another form of prototyping, but instead of using vendor-supplied tools, such as screen generators and fourth generation languages, the project team uses the system itself as its own prototype. That is, the various versions of a skeleton system provide the working model that the user can interact with to get a more realistic feeling of system functions than he or she might get from a paper model.

- The prototyping life cycle, as described above, involves the development of a working model that is then thrown away and replaced by a production system. There is a significant danger that either the user or the development team may try to turn the prototype itself into a production system. This usually turns out to be a disaster because the prototype cannot handle large volumes of transactions efficiently, and because it lacks such operational details as error recovery, audit trails, backup/restart facilities, user documentation, and conversion procedures.

- If the prototype is indeed thrown away and replaced by the production system, there is a real danger that the project may finish without having a permanent record of user requirements. This is likely to make maintenance increasingly difficult as time goes on (i.e., ten years after the system is built, it will be difficult for maintenance programmers to incorporate a change, because nobody, including the "second-generation" users who are now working with the system, will remember what it was supposed to do in the first place). The life cycle presented in this book is based on the idea that the paper models developed in the analysis activity will not only be input to the design activity, but will also be retained (and modified, as necessary) during ongoing maintenance. In fact, the models may survive the system that implements them and serve as a specification for the replacement system.

5.7   SUMMARY

The major purpose of this chapter has been to provide an overview of project life cycles in general. If you examine the formal project life cycle in any systems development organization, you should be able to tell whether it falls into the category of classical, semistructured, structured, or prototyping.

If your projects only allow one activity at a time, the discussion of radical top-down implementation and conservative top-down implementation in Section 5.6 may have disturbed you. This was my intent, as the major purpose of that section was to make you think about the *possibility* of overlapping some of the major activities in a systems development project. Obviously, it's more difficult to manage any project that has several activities taking place in parallel—but to some extent, that always happens in every project. Even if the project manager decides that his or her people will concentrate all their efforts on one major activity at a time, there will still be a number of subactivities taking place in parallel. Multiple systems analysts will be interviewing multiple users simultaneously; various pieces of the final product of systems analysis will be in various stages of progress throughout the analysis phase. One job of the project manager is to exercise sufficient control over those subactivities to ensure that they coordinate smoothly. And in virtually every EDP project, this same kind of parallel activity operated at a higher level, too; that is, despite what the organization's formal project life cycle may have recommended, the reality is that many of the major project activities do overlap to some extent. Nevertheless, if the project manager decides to insist on a strictly sequential progression of project activities, the project life cycle presented in this book will still work.

For more details on project life cycles, consult [Dickinson, 1981] and [Yourdon, 1988].The concept is also covered in a variety of software engineering textbooks and textbooks on project management.

REFERENCES

1.   Edward Yourdon and Larry L. Constantine, *Structured Design: Fundamentals and Applications in Software Engineering,* 2nd ed. Englewood Cliffs, N.J.: YOURDON Press, 1989.

2.   Meilir Page-Jones, *The Practical Guide to Structured Systems Design,* 2nd ed., Englewood Cliffs, N.J.: YOURDON Press, 1988.

3.   Bernard Boar, *Application Prototyping.* Reading, Mass.: Addison-Wesley, 1984.

4.   James Grier Miller, *Living Systems.* New York: McGraw-Hill, 1978.

5.   Brian Dickinson, *Developing Structured Systems.* New York: YOURDON Press, 1981.

6.   Edward Yourdon, *Managing the Systems Life Cycle,* 2nd ed. Englewood Cliffs, N.J.: Prentice-Hall, 1988.

7.   James Grier Miller, *Living Systems.* New York: McGraw-Hill, 1978.

8.   Michael Jackson, *Principles of Program Design.* New York: Academic Press, 1975.

9.   Winston W. Royce, "Managing the Development of Large Software Systems," *Proceedings, IEEE Wescon,* August 1970, pp. 1-9.

10.   Barry Boehm, *Software Engineering Economics.* Englewood Cliffs, N.J.: Prentice-Hall, 1981.

11.   Bill Inmon, *Information Engineering for the Practitioner: Putting Theory into Practice.* Englewood Cliffs, N.J.: Prentice-Hall, 1988.

12.   Marvin Gore and John Stubbe, *Elements of Systems Analysis,* 3rd ed. Dubuque, Iowa: William Brown, 1983.

QUESTIONS AND EXERCISES

1.   List two synonyms for methodology.

2.   What is the difference between a *tool,* as used in this book, and a *methodology*?

3.   What are the three major purposes of a project life cycle?

4.   Research Project: Find the price of three commercial methodology products offered by software vendors or consulting firms.

5.   Why do smaller data processing organizations typically *not* use formal methodologies?

6.   Why is a methodology useful for new managers?

7.   Why is it important to have a methodology in an organization with many different projects underway?

8.   Why is a methodology useful for controling projects?

9.   What are the major distinguishing characteristics of the classical life cycle?

10.   What does bottom-up implementation mean?

11.   What are the four major difficulties with the bottom-up implementation strategy?

12.   What kind of environment is suitable for a bottom-up implementation approach?

13. Why does it matter that "nothing is done until it's all done," which characterizes the bottom-up approach?

14. Why should trivial bugs be found first in the testing phase of a project?

15. What is the difference between testing and debugging?

16. Why is debugging difficult in a bottom-up implementation?

17. What is meant by the phrase sequential progression when describing a project life cycle?

18. What are the two major problems with sequential progression?

19. What are the main differences between the classical and the semistructured life cycle?

20. What are the two major consequences of the top-down implementation approach?

21. Why does the design activity in the semistructured life cycle often involve redundant work?

22. What are the major differences between the structured and semistructured life cycle?

23. List the nine activities of the structured project life cycle.

24. Who are the three types of people who provide primary input to the project life cycle?

25. What are the five major objectives of the survey activity?

26. What is a context diagram?

27. What is the major purpose of the analysis activity?

28. What are the types of *models* produced by the analysis activity?

29. What is the purpose of the design activity?

30. What are the two major issues that the user is typically concerned with in the design activity?

31. When can acceptance test generation (activity 5) begin?

32.   What is the purpose of the procedure description activity?

33.   Why has a DFD been used in Figure 5.4 to show the structured project life cycle?

34.   What is a possible synonym for activity?

35.   Why is feedback important in the structured project life cycle?

36.   What is the difference between the radical and conservative approach to the structured project life cycle?

37.   What are the four main criteria for choosing the radical approach versus the conservative approach?

38.   Can you think of any additional criteria that might be used for choosing a radical approach versus a conservative approach?

39.   What kind of approach (radical versus conservative) should a project manager choose if the user is likely to change his or her mind about the requirements of the system?

40.   What kind of approach (radical versus conservative) should a project manager choose if the project is under severe time pressure?

41.   What kind of approach (radical versus conservative) should a project manager choose if the project faces major technical risks?

42.   What is the difference between the prototyping life cycle and the radical life cycle?

43.   What characteristics does the ideal prototyping project have?

44.   What kind of tools are typically needed for a prototyping project?

45.   Why are batch systems generally not good candidates for prototyping projects?

46.   What are the dangers of the prototyping approach?

47.   How can the prototyping approach and the structured project life cycle be used together in a project?

6 MAJOR ISSUES IN SYSTEMS DEVELOPMENT

The dogmas of the quiet past are inadequate to the stormy present. The occasion is piled high with difficulty, and we must rise to the occasion. As our case is new, so we must think anew and act anew. We must disenthrall ourselves, and then we shall save our country.

Abraham Lincoln,
Second Annual Message to Congress

In this chapter, you will learn:

1. Why productivity is a major issue.

2. The common solutions to the productivity problem.

3. The number of errors in a typical system.

4. The relationship between age of a system and number of errors found.

As a systems analyst, you will be part of a team of people whose purpose is to develop a useful, high-quality information system that will meet the needs of the end user. As you carry out your work, you and your fellow project team members will undoubtedly find yourself influenced by the following major issues:

- Productivity

- Reliability

- Maintainability

Of course, everyone is in favor of productivity; it is a term used in the same manner as motherhood and loyalty to one's country. But a generation ago, when most of today's operational systems were being built, productivity was not something that anyone paid much attention to. Systems analysts and programmers in the 1960s worked long hours (though not always predictable hours!), but no one was ever sure how much work they would accomplish in a week, or how long it would take to build an entire system. The general feeling was that the systems development team would work Very Hard every day, and one day—voila! Magic!—the system would be finished.

Today, productivity is a much more serious issue. So is the issue of reliability: a system failure in a large, complex system is likely to have devastating consequences. And maintainability has become a major issue: it is now clear that many of the systems built today will have to last 20 years or longer before they can be rebuilt, and they will have to undergo constant revision and modification during their lifetime.

Each of these issues is explored in more detail in this chapter. Some, like the issue of maintenance, may appear to have little or nothing to do with systems analysis, but, as we will see, the systems analyst plays a crucial role in achieving improved productivity, increased reliability, and improved maintainability.

6.1   PRODUCTIVITY: THE APPLICATIONS BACKLOG

Perhaps the most visible problem facing the systems development profession today is that of *productivity.* Modern business and society seem to be demanding ever more: more systems, more sophistication, and everything more quickly. As a systems analyst, you will see two major aspects of this problem: one aspect is the backlog of new systems that need to be developed, and the other is the length of time needed to build any individual new system.

In almost any organization in the United States where there is a centralized group responsible for developing new systems, there is a backlog of several *years* of work waiting to be done;[1] indeed, many organizations have a backlog of four to seven years or more. The backlog consists of three different kinds of systems:

- *Visible* backlog: These are new systems that the users have officially re-quested and that have been approved and funded by appropriate management committees. However, the projects have not been started because there are not adequate resources (i.e., systems analysts, pro-grammers, etc.).

- *Invisible* backlog: These are new systems that the users know that they want, but have not bothered to ask for through "official" channels, because they are still waiting for projects in the visible backlog to be completed.

---

1 Informal discussions that I have had with EDP managers in Canada, Europe, Australia, South America, and various other parts of the world lead me to believe that this problem is by no means unique to the United States.

- *Unknown* backlog: These are new systems that the users do not even know that they want yet, but that will be identified as soon as any of the systems in the visible and invisible backlog are finished.

In a classic study of the backlog and demand for information systems (Alloway and Quillard, 1982]), MIT Sloan School researchers Robert Alloway and Judith Quillard found that the invisible backlog was typically 5.35 times larger than the visible backlog of new systems. This suggests that the backlog problem is very much like the proverbial iceberg: only a small portion is visible, with a large portion hidden under water. This is, of course, a major problem for the systems development organization that does its budgeting and planning based only on known, visible demands for its services.

A second aspect of the productivity problem is the length of time required to develop any individual system.[2] Obviously, if the average systems development project could be cut from three years to one year, the backlog problem would rapidly go away; but the point here is that users are generally concerned not only with the *global* problem of the backlog, but also the *local* productivity problem associated with an individual project. They worry that by the time the new system is built, business conditions will have changed so drastically that the original requirements will no longer be relevant.

Or, to put it another way, a new system is often associated with a business opportunity that the user perceives, and that business opportunity often has a window of opportunity, a time period after which the business opportunity will have disappeared and there will be no need for a new system.

There is a third reason for the productivity problem in some organizations: some projects turn out to be dismal failures and are canceled by management before they are ever finished. Indeed, various surveys have found that as many as 25% of all projects in large MIS organizations are never finished. There are many reasons, of course, why a project could fail: technical problems, managerial problems, an inexperienced staff, lack of time to do a proper job of systems analysis and design (which is usually a management problem), lack of involvement on the part of management or the users. For an excellent discussion of the reasons for project failures, see Robert Block's delightful *The Politics of Projects* [Block, 1980].

The productivity problem has existed in the systems development profession for a number of years, and many organizations are aggressively searching for ways to radically reduce their application backlog and cut the length of time required to develop a new system. Among the more commonly used techniques are these:

- *Hiring more programmers and systems analysts.* This is particularly common in new, growing organizations, (e.g., an organization created as a result of a merge, or a new organization formed to exploit new markets and

---

2 To give you an idea of the scope of this problem, Capers Jones found, in a survey of approximately 200 large U.S. organizations, that the typical project was one year late and 100% over budget. See [Jones, 1986]

new businesses).[3] For mature organizations, though, this approach has generally been shunned; indeed, many organizations feel that they have too many programmers and analysts already and that the real job is to make them more productive.[4]

- *Hiring more talented programmers and systems analysts, and giving them superior working conditions.* Rather than building a large army of mediocre systems developers, some organizations concentrate on creating a smaller group of highly talented, highly trained, well-supported (and presumably well paid!) professionals. This approach is based on the well-known disparity in performance among experienced computer programmers: a classic study in 1968 ([Sackman, Erickson, and Grant, 1968]) first documented the fact that some computer programmers are 25 times more productive than others. An extreme form of this concept is the "superprogrammer," or "chief programmer team," concept popularized by IBM in the 1970s (see [Aron, 1976], [Baker, 1972] and [Mills and Baker, 1973]), a project team of specialists (librarians, toolsmiths, language lawyers, etc.) supporting an extraordinarily talented professional who carried out both the systems analysis *and* the design *and* programming of the system. Of course, most organizations cannot build an entire systems development organization around a person ten times better than the average.[5] However, there is something to be said for building an organization with people twice as productive as the average analyst/programmer, even if those people have to be paid twice as much. And there is something to be said for making the existing staff as productive as possible by providing up-to-date training, modern software development tools (discussed in more detail later), and appropriate working conditions.[6]

- *Letting users develop their own systems.* It is interesting to note that many other technological developments interposed someone between the user

---

3 A good example of this occurred during the mid-1980s when several countries deregulated their banking and stock brokerage industries. Australia, Japan, and England are among the countries that suddenly found dozens of new foreign banks and stock brokerage companies opening their doors for business; of these, London was perhaps the most visible, with its Big Bang deregulation on October 27, 1986. These activities required the development of vast new information systems, which was generally accomplished by hiring as many new programmers and analysts as possible, in as short a time as possible.

4 This is in contrast to the dire predictions of a national *shortage* of programmers predicted by the U.S. Commerce Department and the National Science Foundation. For more details, see Chapter 28 of [Yourdon, 1986].

5 For a detailed discussion of why the superprogrammer concept is not practical for most organizations, see *Managing the Structured Techniques* ([Yourdon, 1988]).

6 One obvious interpretation of appropriate working conditions is to give each member of the systems development project a private office, or a two-person office, or a sound-buffered cubicle that affords privacy and concentration; this alone is likely to improve the productivity of the analyst/programmer by 10% or more, as compared to the analyst/programmer who works in a large, open area with Muzak blaring from the ceiling. Another interpretation is to let them work at home. For more on this concept, the "electronic cottage," see Chapter 3 of [Yourdon, 1986].

and the technological device itself: the automobile chauffeur and the telephone switchboard operator are two obvious examples. Of course, most of us don't have chauffeurs and most of us don't need a telephone operator to place our calls for us; the automobile and the telephone are sufficiently user friendly that we can operate them ourselves. Similarly, the combination of personal computers, information centers, and fourth generation programming languages, all introduced into many American organizations during the mid-1980s, has made it possible for many users (including, as we saw in Chapter 2, a generation of users who learned the fundamentals of computing in high school or college) to develop their own simple applications. Ad hoc reports, database inquiries, spreadsheet applications and certain maintenance changes to existing programs are among the projects that a computer-literate, motivated user can certainly do on her or his own.

- *Better programming languages.* Programming languages have gone through enormous change since the 1950s, when programmers created computer programs by laboriously coding the binary 0's and 1's that the hardware executes. This *first generation* of *machine* language gave way to a *second generation* of *assembly* language in the 1960s, and it is interesting to note that assembly language is still used on some projects today. However, *third generation procedural* languages began to prevail in the 1970s and remain the most common type of language today; examples are COBOL, FORTRAN, BASIC, Pascal, C, MODULA-2, and Ada. While the software industry continues to improve these languages (e.g., the version of FORTRAN available today is vastly better than the version of FORTRAN used by programmers in the early 1970s), most of the focus has shifted to a new, *fourth generation* of programming languages that eliminates the need for the programmer to worry about messy, time-consuming details of input editing and validation, report formatting, and file handling; examples of these languages are FOCUS, RAMIS, MAPPER, and MARK V (as well as languages like PC-FOCUS, dBASE-III and Rbase-5000 for personal computers). Many proponents argue that these new languages can increase the productivity of the programming activity by as much as a factor of ten; however, since programming typically represents only 10% to 15% of the overall systems development project, the overall productivity gain is often much less substantial.

- *Attacking the maintenance problem.* Maintenance is a major issue in the systems development field, as we will discuss in Section 6.4. However, most of the attention is currently focused (as one might expect) on the maintainability of *new* systems; meanwhile, as mentioned above, many organizations are devoting 50% to 75% of their resources to maintaining *old* systems. So the question becomes: what can be done to make these old systems easier to maintain, aside from the obvious idea of throwing the old systems away and building new replacements? One approach growing in popularity is that of *restructuring*—mechanically translating the old programs (whose program logic has been patched and changed so many times that it is often completely unintelligible) into new, well-organized, structured programs.[7] A related idea is the use of automated documentation packages that can produce cross-reference listings, data dictionaries, detailed flowcharts, structure charts, or system flowcharts directly from the program (this is referred to by some maintenance people as reverse engineering). Another approach, as mentioned above, is to encourage users to make their own maintenance changes.[8] Still another approach is to carefully document the specific nature of the maintenance work: it often turns out that as little as 5% of the code in an operational system is responsible for 50% or more of the maintenance work.

- *Software engineering disciplines.* Still another approach to improved productivity is a collection of tools, techniques, and disciplines generally known as software engineering or structured techniques. These include structured programming, structured design, and structured analysis,[9] as well as such related disciplines as software metrics, proofs of program correctness, and software quality assurance. In general, the structured techniques have had a modest impact, typically a 10% to 20% improvement, on the productivity of the systems development professionals *during the development phase of the project.* However, systems developed using structured techniques generally have substantially lower maintenance costs and substantially higher reliability, often as much as a factor of 10 or more. This tends to free up resources that would otherwise be used for maintenance or bugfixing, thus improving the productivity of the overall organization.

- *Automated tools for systems development.* Finally, we observe that one reason for the productivity problem is that much of the work of developing an automated information system is, ironically, carried out in a manual fashion. Just as the cobbler's children are the last to get shoes, programmers and systems analysts have traditionally been the last to get the benefits of automation for their own work. Of course, one could argue that a compiler is an automated tool for programming, just as testing packages and debugging aids provide some form of automation. But, until recently, there has been little automated assistance for the systems

---

7 Several commercial products exist in this area. Among the better known ones are *Superstructure* from Group Operations, Inc.; *Structured Retrofit,* marketed by Peat, Marwick; and *Recoder,* from Language Technology, Inc.

8 This is particularly relevant, because according to a study in [Lientz and Swanson, 1980], approximately 42% of the maintenance activity in a typical organization consists of "user enhancements," as compared to 12% for "emergency program fixes," 9% for "routine debugging, 6% for "accommodating hardware changes," etc. Of the portion spent on user enhancements, 40% was spent providing new additional reports, 27% was spent adding data to existing reports, 10% was spent reformatting reports without changing data content, 6% was spent consolidating data in existing reports, and fourth generation programming language, it is very likely that many (if not all!) of these data-related changes could be made directly by the user.

9 The systems analysis approach discussed in this book represents the current form of structured analysis. As we will see in Chapter 7, a number of changes have taken place since structured analysis was first introduced in textbooks in the late 1970s.

designer and almost nothing for the systems analyst. Now there are graphics workstations that can automate much of the drudgery of developing and maintaining dataflow diagrams, entity-relationship diagrams and other graphical models that we saw in Chapter 4; these automated tools also perform a variety of error-checking activities, thus ensuring that the specification produced by the systems analyst is complete, unambiguous, and internally consistent. And, in some cases, the automated tools can even generate code directly from the specification, thus eliminating the manual activity of programming altogether. Details of these automated tools for systems analysis are discussed in Appendix A.

Many of these productivity approaches can be used together, for they involve complementary concepts and techniques. Individually, each approach discussed above might lead to a 10% to 15% improvement; taken together, they can easily double the productivity of the organization and, in special cases, perhaps improve productivity by a factor of ten. An excellent discussion of the quantitative impact of these and a large number of productivity factors can be found in [Jones, 1986].

As a systems analyst, your reaction to all of this might be, "So what? Why is this relevant?" Indeed, it does seem that many of the productivity issues are in the province of programming, testing, and maintenance—none of which are in the province of systems analysis. Nevertheless, there are three reasons why you should be very sensitive to the issue of productivity as a systems analyst:

1.   The quality of work performed by the systems analyst can have a tremendous impact on the productivity of the systems designer and programmer; it can also have a tremendous effect on the amount of time spent testing, since 50% of the errors (and 75% of the cost of error removal) in a system are usually associated with errors of systems analysis. The programmers may get blamed for low productivity because of the amount of time they spend testing, but this is often an indication of low-quality work done by the systems analyst.

2.   Some of the productivity techniques—more people, better people, better working conditions, and especially automated tools—are of direct relevance to the systems analyst. It is worth your while to think about what could be done to make *you* and *your job* more productive.

3.   The productivity of systems analysis is a politically sensitive issue, because it often appears to the user (and sometimes to managers within the systems development group and in other parts of the organization) that very little is happening during the systems analysis phase; one often hears the comment, "So when are you people going to start writing the programs? We can't afford to sit around forever talking about the system, we need to get it implemented!" And the product of systems analysis, the functional specification, is not given much value by the users; the reaction to the specification will sometimes be, "What's the big deal with all these pictures and words? We told you what we want the system to do; why did you have to write all of this stuff?"

The fact of the matter is that you can't build a successful, high-quality, maintainable system if you don't know precisely, and in sufficient detail, what it is supposed to do. So, while some users and managers may complain that systems analysis is merely a period of "resting up" while getting ready for the *real* work of the project (programming), the fact is that it must be done carefully and rigorously. But it must also be done with as much efficiency and productivity as possible; so it behooves the systems analyst not to think that productivity is just a programming issue!

6.2   RELIABILITY

A second major problem facing systems developers is that of *reliability.* The enormous amount of time spent on testing and debugging, typically 50% of a systems development project, and the enormously low productivity (which many feel is related to the amount of time spent on testing) might be acceptable if the result were highly reliable, easily maintainable systems. The evidence of the past 30 years is just the opposite: the systems produced by organizations around the world are riddled with errors and are almost impossible to change.

"Riddled with errors" means different things to different people. On average, software developed in American organizations has between three and five errors for every hundred program statements—*after* the software has been tested and delivered to the customer; see [Jones, 1986]. A few exemplary software development projects have reported as few as three to five errors for every 10,000 program statements, dating back to IBM's superprogrammer project ([Baker, 1972]). And there have been pessimistic reports, such as [Sanger, 1985], suggesting that American software may have as many as three to five errors for every *ten* program statements!

Software errors range from the sublime to the ridiculous. A trivial error might consist of output (results) that are correct, but not printed or formatted quite as neatly and tidily as the user desires. A moderately serious software error might include a case where the system refuses to acknowledge certain kinds of inputs, but the end user can find some way to circumvent the problem. Serious errors are those that cause the entire program to stop working, with an associated major loss of money or human life. Examples of some serious software-related errors that have been documented over the years include the following assortment:

- In 1979, the SAC/NORAD (Strategic Air Command/North American Air Defense) system recorded fifty false alerts, including a simulated attack whose outputs accidentally triggered a live "scramble."

- An error in the F16 flight simulation program caused the plane to flip upside down whenever it crossed the equator.

- An F18 missile thrust while it was still clamped to the plane, causing the plane to lose 20,000 feet in altitude.

- The train doors on the computer-controlled San Francisco BART system sometimes open on long legs between stations.

- A NORAD alert from the Ballistic Missile Early Warning System (BMEWS) detected the moon as an incoming missile.

- The Vancouver Stock Index lost 574 points over a 22-month period because of roundoff errors (e.g., rounding off 3.14159 to 3.1416).

- On November 28, 1979, an Air New Zealand flight crashed into a mountain; later investigation showed that an error in computer course data had been observed and fixed, but the pilot had never been informed.

Unfortunately, the list goes on and on; see [Neumann, 1985] for examples. Many software others are never reported because the "guilty" individual or organization would rather not make a public admission. At the time this book was being written, there was widespread concern that software errors of this sort could lead to grievous consequences with the U.S. Defense Department's Star Wars program, or with some of the other major, complex software-controlled air defense systems; see [Jacky, 1985] and [Adams and Fischetti, 1985] for a discussion. Indeed, even if the reliability of the Star Wars software is 100 times better than that of average systems developed in the United States, it could still have 10,000 errors—hardly a reassuring prospect when any one of those errors could obliterate life on this planet!

In many cases, nobody is quite sure how many errors a system has because (1) some errors are never found before the system expires of old age, and (2) the process of documenting and recording errors is so slipshod that *half* of the errors that are found are not reported,[10] even within the systems development organization. In any case, the typical phenomenon of error discovery, over the period of several years of useful life of a software system usually takes the form shown in Figure 6.1.

The shape of this curve is influenced by a number of factors. For example, when the system is first released to the end users, they are often unable to put it into full-scale production; it takes them some period of time to convert their old system (which may have been a manual system) and to train their operational staff. Also, they are a little wary of the computer, and don't want to push it too hard, so not many errors are discovered. As they convert their old operation over to the new system, as their operational staff is better trained, and as they lose their feeling of intimidation, they begin to push the software much harder, and many more bugs are found.[11] Of course, if this continued indefinitely—more and more bugs found each day—the users would eventually stop using the software and throw it away. In most cases, the programmers are frantically fixing new bugs as users discover them. In most cases, there comes a time when the system begins to stabilize and the users find fewer and fewer bugs.

---

10 This is based on the survey conducted by Lientz and Swanson ([Lientz and Swanson, 1980]).

11 There are, of course, exceptions to the gradual phase-in, especially when a new system has to accept the full volume of work (transactions) of the old system all at once. For an interesting example of such a project, in which the nation-wide Danish bond-trading system was converted to a new system, see [Hansen, 1984].

There are three depressing aspects of Figure 6.1. First, the curve never returns to zero; that is, we almost never find a situation where time goes by without any new errors being discovered. Second, the area underneath the curve, which represents the total number of errors discovered over time, is atrociously high; it averages three to five errors for every hundred program statements. And third, the curve eventually begins rising again—usually after several years, but sometimes after only a few months. Eventually, all software systems reach such a state of crazyquilt patchwork that any effort to fix one error will introduce two new errors, and the changes required to fix those two errors will introduce four new errors, and so on.

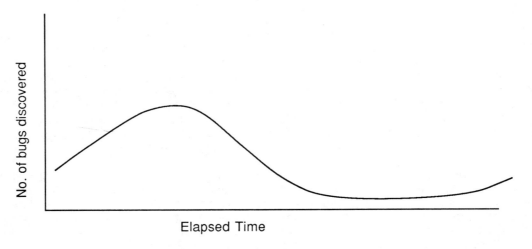

Figure 6.1 : **Errors discovered as a function of time**

There is one last problem to point out about software errors: they aren't easy to fix. When someone, either the programmer, the end user, or some other intermediary, discovers that the software is not working properly, two things must happen: (1) the programmer must identify the source and nature of the error, and (2) he or she must find a way of correcting the error (either by changing some existing program statements, removing some statements, or adding some new statements) without affecting any other aspect of the system's operation. This is not easy to do; in fact, the programmer has less than a 50% chance of success on the first attempt, and the odds drop rapidly if the programmer has to modify more than 10 to 20 program statements (see [Yourdon, 1986]).

6.3 MAINTAINABILITY

The correction of ongoing errors is one aspect of maintenance; Lientz and Swanson ([Lientz and Swanson, 1980]) found that it accounted for approximately 21% of the overall maintenance effort in American data processing organizations.[12] Maintenance also entails modification of a system to reflect changes in the hardware,

---

12 Because the computer industry represents approximately 8% to 10% of the U.S. GNP, this means that we are spending approximately $75 per capita *each year* for software maintenance.

modifications to speed up certain operational aspects of the system, or modifications to reflect a change in the end user's requirements of the system.

Software maintenance is a major problem for most organizations; between 50% and 80% of the work done in most systems development organizations is associated with the revision, modification, conversion, enhancement, or debugging of a computer program that someone else wrote long ago. And it is expensive work; in the early 1970s, the U.S. Defense Department reported that the cost of developing computer programs on one project averaged $75 per computer instruction; the cost of maintaining the system ran as high as $4000 per instruction.

To put this into even more vivid terms, consider the following examples from the U.S. Social Security Administration:

- Calculating the cost-of-living increase for 50 million recipients of Social Security benefits takes 20,000 hours of computer time on older computer systems within the Social Security System (see [Rochester and Gantz, 1983]).

- When the Social Security System upgraded its computer systems in 1981 from five-digit checks to six-digit checks, it required 20,000 person-hours of work and 2500 hours of computer time to modify 600 separate computer programs.

- The morale in the Social Security maintenance department was so bad at one point that one of the programmers was caught urinating on a disk pack in the computer room. While this is certainly a novel way of venting one's frustration, it's not very good for the disk pack.

The result, in more and more data processing organizations, is that existing systems that were built 10 or 20 years ago simply cannot be modified to meet the new demands of the government, or the economy, or the weather, or the fickle mood of the user. As our companies and our society become increasingly dependent on computers, we will find an interesting parallel: to the extent that the software stagnates, the company or society served by the software will stagnate.
The problem is even worse than this. If it were simply a case of the software being bad, we could consider throwing it away and replacing it. But many organizations have never capitalized their software (the costs are expensed each year), and their accounting and business policies make it prohibitively expensive to replace ancient systems. And there is an even more fundamental problem: in most organizations, there is no coherent description of what the systems are supposed to do. Whatever documentation exists is almost always obsolete and confusing. In any case, it provides, at best, some idea of *how* the software works, but not *what* its underlying purpose is or what business policy it is supposed to implement.

Thus, even though one could argue that maintainability is entirely a function of implementation (i.e., something for the programmers to worry about), it's impossible to maintain a system if there is no accurate, up-to-date model of system requirements. This, ultimately, is the job of the systems analyst; as we will see in Chapter 8, functional specifications developed by systems analysts have gradually progressed from absolutely unmaintainable Victorian novels (thousands of pages of narrative text) to hand-drawn graphical models of the system, to computer-generated and computer-maintained models. We will also discuss the issue of ongoing maintenance of system specifications in Chapter 24.

6.4   OTHER ISSUES

What does the systems analyst have to worry about besides productivity, reliability, and maintainability? Well, the list varies from organization to organization and from project to project, but it usually includes the following:

- *Efficiency.* A system must operate with an appropriate throughput (usually measured in transactions per second) and with an acceptable response time for on-line terminals. This is not usually an issue for the systems analyst to worry about, since the designers and programmers will have the most influence on the overall efficiency of the implemented system. Indeed, it is becoming less and less of an issue for modern systems, since computer hardware costs continue to decline each year, while the power and speed of computer hardware continues to increase steadily.[13]

- *Portability.* Most new systems are implemented on one brand of computer, but there may be a need to develop the system in such a way that it can be easily moved to different computers. Again, this is not usually an issue for the systems analyst to worry about, though she or he may need to *specify* the need for portability in the implementation model.

- *Security.* Since modern computer systems are more and more accessible (because they tend to be on-line), and since they are responsible for managing more and more sensitive assets of the organization, security is becoming a major issue for many systems development projects: the new system must prevent unauthorized access, as well as unauthorized updating or deletion of sensitive data.

6.5   SUMMARY

Various experts predict that computer hardware price/performance ratios will improve by a factor of 1000 and possibly by as much as a factor of 1 *million,* within the next 10 to15 years. Unfortunately, the history of software development over the past three decades would lead the average observer to conclude that software technology will only improve by a modest amount. Since software has now become the major cost and the "critical path" of most systems, such a modest improvement cannot be

---

13 There are some exceptions to this optimistic statement. For some critical applications (weather forecasting, nuclear research, modeling of the aerodynamic properties of airplanes and automobiles, etc.), current computer technology is not yet adequate (for a further discussion of this, see [Yourdon, 1986]). And for many real-time and embedded systems, current computer technology is adequate, but the system designers and programmers must work hard to achieve an acceptable level of efficiency. And in some cases hardware technology seems adequate, but new software (e.g., new fourth generation programming languages) turns out to be so inefficient that the overall system is not acceptably efficient.

considered acceptable. Throughout the computer industry, there is a massive, concerted effort to bring about order-of-magnitude improvements in the software development process.

The systems analysis techniques presented in this book are part of that effort. As we have seen, part of the effort is an issue of programming and systems design; but a good system specification is the foundation, the bedrock, on which design and programming must rest.

REFERENCES

1.   Robert Alloway and Judith Quillard, "User Managers' Systems Needs," CISR Working Paper 86. Cambridge, Mass.: MIT Sloan School for Information Systems Research, April 1982.

2.   Harold Sackman, W.J. Erickson, and E.E. Grant, "Exploratory Experimental Studies Comparing Online and Offline Programming Performance," *Communications of the ACM,* January 1968, pp. 3-11.

3.   J. Aron, "The Super-Programmer Project," *Software Engineering Concepts and Techniques.* eds. J.M. Buxton, P. Naur, and B. Randell. New York: Petrocelli/Charter, 1976, pages 188-190.

4.   F.T. Baker, "Chief Programmer Team Management of Production Programming," *IBM Systems Journal,* Volume 11, Number 1 (January 1972), pp. 56-73.

5.   H.D. Mills and F.T. Baker, "Chief Programmer Teams," *Datamation,* Volume 19, Number 12 (December 1973), pp. 58-61.

6.   Edward Yourdon, *Managing the Structured Techniques: Strategies for Software Development in the1990s,* 3rd ed. New York: YOURDON Press, 1986.

7.   Bennett P. Lientz and E. Burton Swanson, *Software Maintenance Management.* Reading, Mass: Addison-Wesley, 1980.

8.   T. Capers Jones, *Programming Productivity.* New York: McGraw-Hill, 1986.

9.   T. Capers Jones, "A Software Productivity Survey," speech at First National Conference on Software Quality and Productivity, Williamsburg, Virginia, March 1985.

10.   Edward Yourdon, *op cit.*

11.   F.T. Baker, *op cit.*

12.   David Sanger, "Software Fears on Star Wars," *New York Times,* July 4, 1985.

13.   Peter G. Neumann, "Some Computer-Related Disasters and Other Egregious Horrors," *ACM SIGSOFT Software Engineering Notes,* January 1985.

14.   Jonathan Jacky, "The Star Wars Defense Won't Compute," *Atlantic Monthly,* June 1985.

15.   John A. Adams and Mark A. Fischetti, "Star Wars—SDI: The Grand Experiment," *IEEE Spectrum,* September 1985, pp. 34-64.

16.   *New York Times* article around September 16, 1986 commenting on the number of errors in Star Wars.

17.   Dines Hansen, *Up and Running.* New York: YOURDON Press, 1984.

18.   Edward Yourdon, *op cit.*

19.   Bennett P. Lientz and E. Burton Swanson, *op cit.*

20.   Jack Rochester and John Gantz, *The Naked Computer.* New York: William Morrow, 1983.

21.   Edward Yourdon, *Nations at Risk.* New York: YOURDON Press, 1986.

22.   Robert Block, *The Politics of Projects.* New York: YOURDON Press, 1981.

QUESTIONS AND EXERCISES

1.   Examine the financial report for a large, publicly owned company to see if you can determine how much is spent on systems development. How much money would be saved if the productivity of the systems development organization could be doubled?

2.   Pick a large, publicly owned company that is obviously dependent on computers for their day-to-day operation. Estimate how many days, weeks, or months the organization could continue to function if its computer systems stopped working.

3.   What are the three major issues in systems development today?

4.   Why is productivity likely to be the most visible problem in systems development today?

5.   What are the three types of backlog that can be found in a typical organization?

6.   Research Project: Conduct a survey in your organization to find out how large the systems development backlog is. Is the figure well known among the users and managers in your organization?

7.   What is the difference between a visible and and invisible backlog?

8.   Why is there an unknown backlog?

9.   Why is the invisible backlog likely to be much larger than the visible backlog?

10.   What are the seven common solutions that organizations are pursuing to solve their productivity problems? Can you suggest any others?

11.   How do you think an organization should measure the productivity of its systems development organization?

12.   How practical is it to solve the productivity problem by hiring more programmers or systems analysts? What are the advantages and disadvantages?

13.   Do you think it is practical to solve the productivity problem by hiring more talented programmers or systems analysts? Why or why not?

14.   Suppose there was a programmer ten times more productive than an average programmer earning $25,000 per year. Do you think management in a typical organization would be willing to spend $250,000 per year for the talented programmer? Do you think they should be willing? Why or why not?

15.   How practical do you think it is to solve the productivity problem by letting users develop their own systems? What are the advantages and disadvantages?

16.   What type of system development projects are most appropriate for users to develop on their own? What percentage of projects do you think is likely to fall into this category in a typical organization?

17.   How practical do you think it is to use new programming languages, either third generation languages like Ada or fourth generation languages like Focus, RAMIS, and NOMAD, to solve the productivity problem? What are the advantages and disadvantages of this approach?

18.   Research Project: How much would productivity be improved in your organization during the next five years if the organization began using a new programming language? How is this affected by *existing* code and the existing "culture" of computer programmers and systems analysts?

19.   Why does a fourth generation programming language provide a productivity improvement over a conventional third generation programming language?

20.   How much would productivity in a typical organization be improved if maintenance could be reduced by a factor of ten?

21.   Research Project: Use a commercial "structuring engine" product to restructure an existing computer program in your organization, and measure the reduction in maintenance costs. What does this tell you about the potential benefits of a structuring engine?

22. Do you think that restructuring can turn bad programs into good programs? Why or why not? If your answer is no, then what is the purpose of restructuring programs?

23. Can users perform their own software maintenance? What is required to make this work? What percentage of software maintenance work do you think, realistically, users could actually do?

24. Why can software engineering improve productivity?

25. Why can automated software development tools improve productivity?

26. How can the work done by a systems analyst affect the productivity of a systems development project?

27. How much of a typical project is spent testing and debugging?

28. Research Project: What is the average number of errors in systems developed in your organization? What is the variance—the difference between the worst and the best?

29. Research Project: Find at least two documented examples within the past year of system failures that caused a loss of life or resulted in a cost of more than $1 million. How could these failures have been prevented?

30. Why do the number of errors in a system tend to *increase* after the system is first put into operation?

31. Why do the number of errors in a system tend to gradually increase after the system has been in operation for several years?

32. Research Project: What percentage of the resources in your systems development organization is spent carrying out maintenance? Is senior management in your organization aware of these figures?

33. What factors, besides productivity, quality and reliability, are important in the typical systems development organization today?

34. What role does the system analyst play in determining the efficiency of an information system today?

35. What role does the systems analyst play in determining the portability of an information system today?

36. What role does the systems analyst play in determining the security of an information system today?

7 CHANGES IN SYSTEMS ANALYSIS

New terms such as techno-stress and techno-shock have been coined to define the psychological manifestations of a public overwhelmed by everything from microwave ovens to home Pac-Man games. Unfortunately, these terms do not accurately describe progress within the data processing industry as it pertains to software development. For many data processing professionals, techno-stress is better defined as frustration with the slow pace of change in software development methods, in the face of ever-increasing demand for dp services.

While there is no question that some progress toward better systems development methods has been made during the last 30 years, there is equally no question that, overall, any process of change is slow and discontinuous. Speaking from an historical perspective, it seems that for true progress to be realized, there must be a periodic, collective rethinking of basic ideas. The periods between each great leap forward can be tens of years to hundreds of years.

F.J. Grant, "Twenty-First Century Software"
Datamation, April 1, 1985

In this chapter, you will learn:

1. The problems with classical systems analysis.

2. The changes that have taken place in classical structured analysis.

3. Why automated tools are important to the future of systems analysis.

4. Why problems in classical structured analysis have led to prototyping.

The systems analysis methods and tools presented in this book represent a state of the art approach that will be used in most systems development organizations for the remainder of the 1980s and early 1990s. By the mid-1990s, it is likely that systems analysis will have evolved substantially; Chapter 25 discusses the likely nature of that evolution.

But it is not enough for you to be aware of *today's* systems analysis techniques. You must also have an understanding of the changes that have taken place over the past five to ten years, changes that have led to the tools and techniques that we will explore in depth in Parts II and III. There are three reasons why you should be familiar with the evolution of systems analysis.

First, you may find that the systems development organization you work for has *not* evolved and that nobody has any intention of making any changes. Though the changes discussed in this chapter have occurred in approximately 80% of the data processing organizations in North America, Europe, and other parts of the world, there are still those backwater bastions of mediocrity that see no reason to change the way they were doing things 20 years ago. If you find yourself in this situation, the logical thing to do is to look for another job; or, if you are feeling brave, you might take on a leadership role and help bring your organization into the modern world of systems analysis.[1]

Second (and more likely), you may find that your organization has begun to implement some of the changes discussed in this chapter, but the process of change will continue for another few years. A good example of this is the development of automated tools for systems analysis. Almost all systems analysts will tell you that such PC-based tools are a good idea, and some EDP managers are beginning to support the concept. But the tools are relatively new; virtually none existed before 1984. And organizations are slow to change; at the end of 1987, it was estimated that less than 2% of the systems analysts in the United States had access to the kind of tools discussed in this book; by 1990, it is estimated that approximately 10% of the systems analysts will be using the tools, and a true saturation of the marketplace probably won't occur until the mid-1990s. Thus, even though you and the other members of your organization may know what kind of tools and techniques will be installed three years from now, *today's* approach to systems analysis may be somewhat different. It is important for you to know the approach that the organization was using previously and what kind of transition is underway.

Third, the notion of *transition* is important even if you work in one of the "leading edge" organizations that has completely implemented the systems analysis approach presented in this book. The field of systems analysis, like all other aspects of the computer field, is dynamic; the way we do systems analysis in 1995 will undoubtedly be different than the way we do it now. But to see what changes will take place during the middle and latter part of the 1990s, you need an appreciation of where the field came from and the *direction* it is heading in.

---

1 This is not a frivolous suggestion. If these organizations don't change, they will be out of business sometime during the 1990s.

7.1   THE MOVE TOWARD STRUCTURED ANALYSIS

Until the end of the 1970s, the overwhelming majority of systems development projects began with the creation of a "Victorian novel" statement of user requirements. That is, the systems analyst documented his or her understanding of the user's requirements in a massive document consisting primarily of narrative English. Early authors of "structured analysis" textbooks, especially [DeMarco, 1978], [Gane and Sarson, 1977], and [Weinberg, 1978]—pointed out that these ponderous tomes (often known as a functional specification) typically suffered from several major problems:

- They were *monolithic:* you had to read the functional specification in its entirety, from beginning to end, in order to understand it. Like a Victorian novel, if you didn't read the last page, you had little idea of how the story would end.[2] This is an important flaw, for there are many situations where the systems analyst or the user wants to read and comprehend one part of the specification without necessarily reading any other part.

- They were *redundant:* the same information was often repeated in several different parts of the document.[3] The problem with this is that if any aspect of the user's requirements change during the systems analysis phase (or, even worse, *after* the systems analysis phase has been declared finished), the change has to be reflected in several different parts of the document. This would be less of a problem today, since even the most primitive organization has ample access to word processing facilities; but in the 1960s and 1970s, most organizations created their functional specifications with nothing more sophisticated than an electric typewriter.[4]

---

2 Or to put it another way, there's never any sex until the last page.

3 There are several theories as to why redundancy was such a common characteristic. My own experience was that the functional specification served three different purposes in the organization (and thus the same information was presented in three different ways): *first,* it was the "official" statement of the user's requirements; *second,* it was an unofficial training manual, meant to explain how those "dumb" users would operate the system; and *third,* it was a politically oriented sales tool, meant to impress management that the system would be so glorious that it would be well worth the cost to build it.

4 Perhaps one of the best examples of this problem occurred in a major New York City bank's EDP organization in the mid-1970s. Embarked upon a typical "Mongolian horde" systems development project, the systems analysis group interviewed dozens of users throughout the bank and gradually developed a Victorian novel specification of mind-numbing size. Typing the document occupied the typing pool for two weeks, and all available Xerox machines were commandeered for several days in order to make enough copies to distribute to the users. The user community was given a week to read through the entire functional specification and indicate any desired changes or corrections; somewhat to their surprise (but to their immense relief!) the systems analysts received *no* comments from the users by the appointed deadline. So the functional specification was declared "frozen" and work commenced on design and programming. Three weeks later, six members of the user community announced that they had finally managed to read the entire specification—and, yes, they did have a few small changes. A small panic ensued: what should be done to the specification? After two angry meetings at which users and systems analysts insulted each other's heritage and intelligence in terms that cannot be repeated in a book like this, a decision was reached: the changes were *not* put into the typewritten specification (for that would be too difficult), but they *would* be incorporated into the system itself. Or, to put it another way: the project team found that it was easier to change COBOL than it was to change English.

Because it was so difficult to update and revise the document, the inherent redundancy led to a far worse problem: *inconsistency*. Just as a person with many watches is unlikely to know what time it *really* is, a functional specification with the same information repeated three or four times is likely to have the wrong information in several instances.

*   They were *ambiguous:* the detailed statement of user requirements could be (and often was) interpreted differently by user, systems analyst, systems designer, and programmer. Studies conducted in the late 1970s[5] found that 50% of the errors eventually found in an operational system and 75% of the cost of error removal could be traced to misunderstandings or errors in the functional specification.

*   They were *impossible to maintain:* for all the reasons described above, the functional specification was almost always obsolete by the end of the systems development process (i.e., by the time the system was put into operation), and often obsolete by the end of the systems analysis phase. This means that most of the systems developed during the 1960s and 1970s—systems that are now 20 years old or more—have no up-to-date statement of the business policy that they supposedly carry out. And since the original systems analysts and the original users have long since vanished, the awful reality is that *nobody knows what most of the major computer systems are doing today.*

While all these problems were being debated, a complementary set of ideas was already being adopted in the area of programming and design. These ideas, generally referred to as *structured programming* and *structured design,* promised great improvements in the organization, coding, testing, and maintenance of computer programs. And indeed structured programming and structured design have generally proved successful; but more and more EDP organizations gradually began to realize that there was no point writing brilliant computer programs and designing highly modular systems *if nobody really knew what the systems were supposed to do.* Indeed, it could be argued that structured programming and structured design allowed some project teams to arrive at a disaster more quickly than ever before—building a brilliant solution to the wrong problem!

As a result, there has been a gradual movement—gradual in the sense that it has taken the systems development profession nearly ten years to accept it—toward functional specifications that are:

*   *Graphic*—composed of a variety of diagrams, supported by detailed textual material that, in many cases, serves as reference material rather than the main body of the specification.

*   *Partitioned*—so that individual portions of the specification can be read independently of other pieces.

---

5 See James Martin, *An Information Systems Manifesto* (Englewood Cliffs, N.J.: Prentice-Hall, 1984).

- *Minimally redundant*—so that changes in the user requirements can usually be incorporated in just one part of the specification.

This approach, generally known as structured analysis, is now used in the majority of business-oriented systems development organizations, as well as a large number of engineering-oriented organizations. You will still find some organizations churning out Victorian novel specifications, but they are in the minority, and, like dinosaurs, they will eventually become extinct.

7.2   CHANGES IN CLASSICAL STRUCTURED ANALYSIS

As mentioned above, traditional systems analysis (characterized by Victorian novel specifications) began to change in the late 1970s. Most of the organizations now using structured analysis are basing their approach on the early textbooks of DeMarco, Gane and Sarson, Weinberg, and others, as well as the seminars, videotapes and other training materials based on those books.

However, several years of practical experience with classical structured analysis have pointed out a number of areas where changes or extensions need to be made. The major changes are these:

- The emphasis on building "current physical" and "current logical" models of the user's system has proven to be politically dangerous. The project team often spent so much time (sometimes as much as six months or a year or more) studying the user's *old* system, a system that everyone knew was to be thrown away and replaced with a new system, that the project was canceled by an impatient user before the project team could get on to the job of studying the proposed *new* system. This does not mean that we have decided to avoid modeling the user's current system in all cases, but merely that we recognize it as a politically dangerous activity, and one that will probably have to be minimized, if not eliminated in the real world. We will discuss this point again in Chapter 17.

- Classical structured analysis made a fuzzy, poorly defined distinction between physical models (models that make assumptions about, or are biased by, the implementation technology) and logical models (those that are entirely independent of implementation technology); indeed, even the terms logical and physical are confusing to many. Important ideas in this area were contributed by [McMenamin and Palmer, 1984] and even some of the terminology has changed: we now refer to essential models (models of the "essence" of a system) instead of logical models, and implementation models instead of physical models.

- More and more organizations are using structured analysis techniques to build *real-time* systems.[6] However, classical structured analysis has no way of modeling the time-dependent behavior of a system; it lacks the

_____

6 Recall the definition and examples of real-time systems in Chapter 2.

notation for showing interrupts and signals, and to show the synchronization and coordination of different processing tasks. Additional notation and a whole new modeling tool—control flows, control processes, and state-transition diagrams—have been added to solve this problem. This is discussed in more detail in Chapters 9 and 13.

* Classical structured analysis concentrated almost entirely on the modeling of the *functions* to be carried out in a system; the modeling of *data* was done in a primitive way[7] and often deemphasized or even ignored. Meanwhile, more and more organizations have found that their systems involve complex functions *and* complex data relationships *and* complex real-time characteristics. As we have seen, *state-transition diagrams* have been added to structured analysis to permit modeling of real-time systems; to permit modeling of systems with complex data relationships, *entity-relationship diagrams* have been added to structured analysis. More important than just the addition of one or two additional modeling tools is the fact that all three of the major modeling tools can be *integrated*, that is, used together so that each supports the other. Entity-relationship diagrams are discussed in Chapter 12, and the concept of integrated models is discussed in Chapter 14.

* The *process* of structured analysis has changed dramatically. Classical structured analysis assumed that the systems analyst would begin by drawing a context diagram, a dataflow diagram with a single bubble representing the entire system, and then partition the system into several functions and data stores in a strictly top-down fashion. Unfortunately, this has not worked well, for reasons discussed in Chapter 20; consequently, a new approach known as *event partitioning* has been added. The terminology and basic concept of event partitioning were introduced by [McMenamin and Palmer, 1984] and have been extended by [Ward and Mellor, 1985].

7.3   THE EMERGENCE OF AUTOMATED ANALYSIS TOOLS

As the graphical modeling techniques of structured analysis began to spread through systems development organizations in the late 1970s and early 1980s, systems analysts began to realize that there was a major problem: the artwork required to create dataflow diagrams, entity-relationship diagrams, structure charts, state-transition diagrams, and other graphic models was often overwhelming. The problem, in most cases, was not the initial creation of the diagrams, but rather their revision and maintenance; creating the initial diagram is time-consuming, but at least has the satisfaction of being a challenging, creative, intellectual activity. In a typical project, the

---

7 This is perhaps a bit unfair, as [DeMarco, 1978] and [Gane and Sarson, 1977] devote a chapter or more to the subject of data structures. But their notation ("data structure diagrams") is now generally considered obsolete; also, much of the emphasis in the early textbooks was on the conversion of an arbitrary set of data structures into third normal form, which is (1) simple enough that the process has been mechanized, and (2) more an issue of *implementation,* or design, rather than systems analysis.

systems analyst finds that he must redraw the graphical models several times before he and the user can reach an agreement on the requirements of the system.[8]

On a large system, there may be 50 to 100 or more dataflow diagrams, several entity-relationship diagrams, and potentially several state-transition diagrams; so the amount of artistic labor involved can be daunting indeed. The practical consequence of this, in many organizations, is that classical structured analysis was not as success-ful as it should have been. The following problems occurred:

- After the second or third revision made to a diagram, the systems analyst would grow increasingly hostile and reluctant to make any further changes. Thus, it was possible to find "frozen" diagrams that didn't truly reflect the user's system requirements.

- Because of the amount of work involved, the systems analyst would sometimes stop partitioning the system model into lower-level models— i.e., instead of developing a model consisting of five levels of dataflow diagrams, he would stop at the fourth level. The resulting model would contain "primitive" functions (i.e., the bubbles depicted at the fourth level) that were not very primitive at all; indeed, they would turn out to be so complex that the programmer would find it necessary to carry out additional systems analysis before he could write any programs.[9]

- Changes to the user requirements *after* the analysis phase of the project would often not be incorporated in the system model. Many of these changes took place during the design, programming, and testing phases of the project; still others took place after the system had been implemented. The result was an obsolete specification.

In addition to the work required to create and maintain the diagrams, classical structured analysis requires a great deal of work to *verify* the diagrams to ensure that they are complete and consistent; these rules are discussed in Chapter 14.[10] Throughout the 1970s and most of the 1980s, systems analysts have had to depend on manual verification techniques (i.e., visually inspecting the diagrams to spot errors). Because the work is labor intensive and boring, its tends to be error prone. Consequently, many of the specification errors that should have been found were not.

---

8 This may not be evident to you yet, for we have seen only a few structured analysis diagrams in Chapter 4. However, by the end of Part II it should be abundantly evident; if not, wait until the end of your first "real" structured analysis project!

9 As we will see in Chapter 11, there should be one process specification (usually written as a decision table, flowchart, or in a structured English format) for each bottom-level primitive bubble in the dataflow diagram. If the system has been properly partitioned, most process specifications should be less than a page long.

10 Examples of verification rules: all the dataflows in a DFD must be named, and the names must be defined in the data dictionary. All the entries in the data dictionary must correspond to dataflows or stores on the DFD. Each bubble in the DFD must have at least one incoming dataflow and at least one outgoing dataflow. And so on.

Many of these problems can be solved with proper automated support; this was well known even when classical structured analysis was first introduced, but the cost of automation was far higher than most organizations could afford. However, the development of powerful graphics workstations in the mid-1980s has led to a whole new industry known as CASE (an acronym meaning Computer-Aided Software Engineering); several dozen vendors offer products (usually PC-based) that will draw dataflow diagrams, and the like, as well as perform a variety of error-checking tasks. Features and examples of these tools are discussed in Appendix A.

As mentioned earlier, only 2% of the systems analysts in the United States had such tools available to them in 1987, and it is estimated that only 10% will have them in 1990. However, it is clearly the way of the future, and we can expect that all professional systems analysts will insist on such tools as time goes on. This will lead, primarily, to a higher level of quality in the systems models produced; secondarily, it will lead to more visually pleasing graphic models of the system. To the extent that the error-checking concepts discussed in Chapter 14 are automated, it may eliminate the need for systems analysts to learn the material in Chapter 14! And to the extent that the CASE tools eventually begin generating programs (in COBOL, Pascal, or perhaps a fourth generation language) *directly* from the specifications, it will even reduce the need for programmers!

7.4   THE USE OF PROTOTYPING

As we pointed out in Chapter 3, some users have a difficult time working with the graphic models of structured analysis; they prefer some other way of modeling the requirements and behavior of the system. Prototyping tools, which began to be widely available in the mid-1980s, have been seen by some as an alternative to structured analysis for such users.

There is another reason for the popularity of prototyping: classical structured analysis is regarded in some organizations as too time consuming; by the time the analysis phase is finished, the user will have forgotten why he wanted the system in the first place. This is usually the result of one of the following problems:

- The project team spent far too much time developing models of the user's *current* system and then had to spend even more time modeling the new system. As mentioned above, we now regard modeling of the current system as a politically dangerous activity.

- The organization previously invested little or no time doing *any* systems analysis, preferring to begin coding as soon as possible. In such an environment, the lengthy work of systems analysis, which appears to have no output except lots of pictures with circles and boxes on them, may appear unproductive.

- The first few projects using structured analysis may be more time-consuming than normal, because the systems analysts are learning new techniques and arguing with one another as to the best way of applying the techniques.

Prototyping tools (software tools that allow the systems analyst to build a "mockup" of the system) are thus seen as an effective solution to these problems. Note also that prototyping tends to concentrate on the human interface aspect of a systems development project.

Unfortunately, the prototyping tools are sometimes used to *avoid* the details of systems analysis and design altogether; an appropriate use of prototyping was shown in Section 5.6.

7.5   THE MARRIAGE OF SYSTEMS ANALYSIS AND DESIGN

As mentioned earlier in this chapter, improvements in the software engineering field began with structured programming and structured design; indeed, these two topics were the subject of considerable debate in systems development organizations throughout the early and mid-1970s. It was also during this period that the first textbooks on structured design began to appear (see [Myers, 1975] and [Yourdon and Constantine, 1975]); early books made no reference to structured analysis (since the concepts had not yet been developed), while later books such as [Page-Jones, 1980] included a brief overview of the subject. Work on structured analysis began in the mid-1970s, and the first textbooks began to appear in the late 1970s; *but there was little or no connection between the discussion of structured analysis and the discussion of structured design.* The main problem was that structured analysis dealt with the specification of large, complex *systems,* while structured design seemed more appropriate for the design of individual programs running on a single computer. The bridge between systems analysis and program design, that is, *systems* design, was missing.

This problem has been addressed by several consultants, authors, and systems development organizations in the 1980s. Recent books by [Ward and Mellor, 1985], as well as new editions of books by [Page-Jones, 1988] and [Yourdon and Constantine, 1989], now deal with the issues of systems design as well as program design.

7.6   SUMMARY

Like any field of science or engineering, systems analysis has undergone a series of evolutionary changes during the past 20 years. As indicated at the beginning of the chapter, it is important for you to know what those changes have been, because the software development industry is large enough and diverse enough that not everyone is practicing the same techniques at the same time. Your organization may be at the "leading edge" of technology, or it may be at the "bleeding edge."

You can expect the field of systems analysis to continue; the techniques presented in this book will have evolved even further within the next five to ten years. Chapter 25 discusses the likely nature of further evolutionary changes.

REFERENCES

1.   Tom DeMarco, *Structured Analysis and System Specification.* New York: YOURDON Press, 1978.

2. Chris Gane and Trish Sarson, *Structured Systems Analysis and Design.* New York: Improved Systems Technologies, Inc., 1977.

3. Victor Weinberg, *Structured Analysis.* New York: YOURDON Press, 1978.

4. Paul Ward and Steve Mellor, *Structured Development for Real-Time Systems.* Volumes 1-3. New York: YOURDON Press, 1985.

5. Steve McMenamin and John Palmer, *Essential Systems Analysis.* New York: YOURDON Press, 1984.

6. Glen Myers, *Reliable Systems through Composite Design.* New York: Petrocelli/Charter, 1975.

7. Edward Yourdon and Larry Constantine, *Structured Design,* 1st ed. New York: YOURDON Press, 1975.

8. Meilir Page-Jones, *The Practical Guide to Structured Systems Design,* 1st ed. New York: YOURDON Press, 1980.

9. Meilir Page-Jones, *The Practical Guide to Structured Systems Design,* 2nd ed. Englewood Cliffs, N.J.: Prentice-Hall, 1988.

10. Edward Yourdon and Larry Constantine,*Structured Design,* 2nd ed. Englewood Cliffs, N.J.: Prentice-Hall, 1989.

QUESTIONS AND EXERCISES

1. What are the three major reasons why you should be familiar with the evolution of systems analysis?

2. What do you think you should do if the organization you work for has not made the changes discussed in this chapter?

3. List four major problems with a classical narrative specification.

4. Why is it undesirable to have redundancy in a system specification? Is it possible to remove redundancy altogether from a specification?

5. Can you think of any reason why redundancy could be useful in a system specification?

6. What are the three common reasons that redundancy gets introduced into a classical specification?

7. What percentage of errors in an operational system can typically be traced back to errors that occurred during the systems analysis phase of the project?

8.   Research Project: What is the percentage of errors in *your* organization that can be traced back to errors that occurred during the systems analysis phase of the project?

9.   What are the consequences of a specification that is impossible to maintain?

10.   Give a brief description of structured programming.

11.   Give a brief description of structured design.

12.   Why have some organizations found that they are not successful when using structured programming and structured design?

13.   What are the three major characteristics of a structured specification?

14.   What are the five major changes that have taken place in classical structured analysis?

15.   What problems does classical structured analysis have when dealing with real-time systems?

16.   What are the dangers associated with modeling the user's current information system?   How long should one spend modeling the user's current system?

17.   What are the three major problems that the systems analyst is likely to encounter if he or she does not have automated support for his or her work?

18.   Is it important to have automated support for small information systems development projects? Why or why not?

19.   What problems are likely to be encountered if the systems analyst has to carry out error-checking activities on a manual basis?

20.   Why do you think that only 2% of the systems analysts in the United States had automated systems analysis workstations in 1987?

21.   What additional benefits can we expect to see from the introduction of a network of automated systems analysis tools? (Hint: One such benefit is electronic mail.)

22.   What are the three common problems that organizations have encountered when implementing classical structured analysis?

23.   What interface problems existed between structured analysis and structured design in the 1970s and early 1980s?

PART II: MODELING TOOLS

CHARACTERISTICS OF MODELING TOOLS

Anything is easy, if you can assimilate it to your collection of models.
Seymour Papert, *Mindstorms*

In this chapter, you will learn:

1. Why system modeling tools are usually graphical.

2. Why system modeling tools are top-down partitionable.

3. Why system modeling tools have minimal redundancy.

4. Why system modeling tools help model system behavior.

The next several chapters of this book describe the various modeling tools you will use as a systems analyst. Before we plunge into the details of dataflow diagrams, entity-relationship diagrams, and so on, there are some introductory points that we need to review.

You will recall from Chapter 4 that a model is an inexpensive facsimile of a complex system that we want to study. We build models of systems for three reasons:

1. To focus on important system features while downplaying less important features.

2.   To discuss changes and corrections to the user's requirements at a low cost and with minimal risk.

3.   To verify that we understand the user's environment and have documented it in such a way that systems designers and programmers can build the system.

But there are many different kinds of models that we could build for the user: narrative models, prototype models, various graphical models, and so on. Indeed, the final system that we build for the user may turn out to be a model—in the sense that it may represent, for the first time, a way for the user to visualize what it is that he or she wants.

In this book, we concentrate on *paper* models (or paper models produced by automated CASE systems). But here again, there is an enormous amount of variety: as we will see in more detail in the next several chapters, there are flowcharts, HIPO diagrams, decision tables, dataflow diagrams, systems flowcharts, state-transition diagrams, decision trees, entity-relationship diagrams, Ferstl diagrams, Hamilton-Zeldin diagrams, PAD diagrams, and an endless array of charts, tables, and graphs that we can present to the user. Which should we use?

The basic premise of this book is that you should use *any* model that works for you and for the situation you're in. Different users may require different modeling tools either because of past experience or because they find certain kinds of diagrams confusing and intimidating.[1] Different projects may require different modeling tools in order to comply with documentation standards imposed by external organizations. And different kinds of systems may require different models in order to properly highlight important characteristics.

To carry this last point further, most systems require *multiple* models: each model focuses on a limited number of aspects of the system, while downplaying (or ignoring altogether) other aspects of the system. This is especially true of many of the systems being built today, for they have complex *functional* characteristics, complex *data* structures, and complex *timing* considerations.

Any tool you use should have the following characteristics:

•   It should be graphical, with appropriate supporting textual detail.

•   It should allow the system to be viewed in a top-down, partitioned fashion.

•   It should have minimal redundancy.

---

1 A corollary to this is that good modeling tools will usually involve very simple notation, with very few rules, symbols, and new words for the user to have to learn. A purist might even argue that a good modeling tool requires *no* explanation or training; in any case, it should not be necessary to read through a 700-page book like this one in order to learn how to read and understand a model developed by the systems analyst.

- It should help the reader predict the system's behavior.

- It should be transparent to the reader.

We will elaborate on each of these points next.

8.1   GRAPHICAL MODELS

Most of the popular system models, and all of the ones used in this book, rely heavily on graphics. It is by no means *required* to use graphics in a system model, but the old adage that "a picture is worth a thousand words" is a good explanation for our preference for graphics over narrative text. A well-chosen picture can convey an enormous amount of information concisely and compactly.

This does not mean that a picture can necessarily describe *everything* about a system; to do so would usually mean a terribly cluttered mess that nobody would be willing to look at. In general, we use graphics to identify the *components* of a system and the *interfaces* between the components; all the other details (i.e., the answers to such questions as "How many?" and "In what sequence?", and so on) are presented in supporting textual documents. The supporting textual documents described in this book are the *process specification* and the *data dictionary.*

This does not mean that all systems analysts must use the particular set of graphic and text-oriented modeling tools presented in this book; the Great Systems Analyst in the sky will not strike you down with lightning bolts for failure to use dataflow diagrams. However, you probably should be struck down by lightning bolts if you choose either the extreme of *all* graphics (with no supporting text) or *all* text (with no graphics). And you should be zapped with at least a small lightning bolt if you make text the dominant part of the model, with graphics playing a minor, subordinate role. One or more graphics should be the primary document that the user turns to in order to understand the system; the textual documents should serve as reference material to be consulted when necessary.

8.2   TOP-DOWN PARTITIONABLE MODELS

A second important aspect of a good modeling tool is its ability to portray a system in a top-down partitioned fashion. This is not important for tiny systems, for we can say everything that needs to be said in one or two pages, and anyone who needs to know about any aspect of the system can learn about *all* of the system.

However, real projects in the real world are generally not tiny.[2] Indeed, most of the projects you are likely to become involved with will range from medium-sized to

---

2 Or to put this another way, more and more of the "tiny" projects are being developed by the users without any assistance from systems analysts or programmers. With the widespread availability of personal computers, spreadsheet packages, and fourth generation languages, many of the jobs that would have required a few days (or even weeks) of work by a professional computer person can now be done in a matter of minutes or hours by the user. However, there continue to be many information systems developed today that require more than 10 *million* program statements to carry out their required purpose.

enormous. Consequently, it will be impossible for anyone, whether they are users, systems analysts or programmers, to focus on the entire system at once. Nor will it be possible to present a graphical model of a large, complex system on a single sheet of paper—unless one wants to consider the ludicrous extreme of an 8-foot by 10-foot sheet of microfiche! So our modeling tools must allow us to portray individual parts of the system in a stand-alone fashion, *together with a straightforward way of getting from one part of the system model to another.*

However, we need even more than this: it would not be appropriate, for example, to create an enormous 100 foot by 100 foot graphical model and then cut it into 10,000 separate one foot by one foot pieces, with thousands of "off-page" connectors. That would be roughly equivalent to drawing a street map of the entire United States on a single (albeit large) sheet of paper and then cutting it into thousands of page-sized pieces.

Indeed, our experience with maps and atlases illustrates how we need to organize a model of a complex system. An atlas of the United States, for example, typically starts with a single one-page diagram of the entire country, as shown in Figure 8.1. That page shows the individual states, and may also show major interfaces between the states (rivers, interstate highways, train lines, airline routes, etc.). Subsequent pages are typically devoted to each individual state, with each page showing the individual towns and counties within a state, as well as the local state highways that would not have been shown on the country-level map. One could imagine lower-level maps that would provide details about each county, each city within a county, and each neighborhood within a city.

Figure 8.1: **A map of the United States**

A good model of a complex information system should proceed in the same top-down fashion. A high-level overview portion of the model should give the reader a good idea of the major high-level components and interfaces of the system.

Subsequent portions of the model should provide information about low-level detail components of the system. And just as an atlas provides a convenient mechanism for traversing the entire set of individual maps (i.e., getting from the country-level map down to the appropriate county-level map without a lot of confusion), so a good model of an information system provides a convenient mechanism for traversing smoothly from high level to low level.

8.3   MINIMALLY REDUNDANT MODELS

Models are a representation of some real-world system, and the system itself may be static (nonchanging) or dynamic. A map of the United States, for example, is a graphical representation of the country we live in. And while many aspects of our country are obviously very dynamic, one could argue that the aspects modeled by a map are relatively static: individual states don't appear or disappear very often, and the boundaries between states have been relatively constant for quite a long time. (By contrast, we wouldn't be able to say this about a map of the entire world!)

Why does this matter to the person building a model? Simply because it is desirable to *maintain* the model in an accurate and up-to-date form. If the system changes, then the model must be changed if we are to keep it up to date. Obviously, if only one local aspect of the system changes, we would prefer to change only one corresponding local aspect of the model; without being forced to change any other aspect. Indeed, if multiple changes *are* required, there is a good chance that they won't be made, or that they will be made haphazardly. And this means that the model will gradually become less and less accurate.

To illustrate this, consider our example of the atlas of the United States once again. We could imagine, in the simplest case, one page showing the entire country, and 50 subsequent pages showing the details of each state. Now imagine what would happen if the state of New Jersey were to disappear:[3] the country-level map would have to be redrawn to show the new 49-state country, and the former state-level map of New Jersey would be discarded.

But it would be a little more difficult with real atlases because, as is typical with many system models, there is some built-in redundancy. Each state-level map shows not only the state being described, but portions of the bordering states—information that is adequately provided in the country-level map, but that is convenient to have at the state level, too. So this means that if New Jersey were to disappear, we would probably have to redraw the maps of New York and Pennsylvania, and perhaps even Maryland and Delaware. What a nuisance!

Professional cartographers might object to this and argue that a certain amount of redundancy is necessary in order to make the atlas easy to read. But it should be evident that the more redundancy the model contains, the more difficult it is to maintain. Imagine, for example, that our mythical atlas shows the interstate highways on the country-level map and all the state-level maps. Imagine also that some

---

3 If you happen to live in New Jersey or have some other pathological connection to the state, feel free to use another state for this example. Apologies to Bruce Springsteen.

enterprising map maker has decided to show the overall length of each interstate highway *on each state map through which the highway travels.* Thus, Interstate 95, which runs from Maine to Florida, would appear on roughly a dozen state maps, each of which would be inscribed with the (redundant) fact that the entire highway is approximately 1700 miles long. Now what happens if we discover that this figure was wrong or that part of the highway was extended or rerouted? Obviously, a dozen different state-level maps will have to be changed.

8.4   TRANSPARENT MODELS

Finally, a good model should be so easy to read that the reader doesn't even stop to think that she or he is looking at a *representation* of a system, rather than the system itself. This is not always easy to accomplish, and it often does take some education and practice on the part of the reader. Think about a map, for example: how often do you think to yourself that you are looking at an abstract representation of the state of New Jersey rather than the real thing? On the other hand, observe a small child looking at a map as his parents or his teacher try to explain that New Jersey borders New York and that Newark is ten miles away from New York City. "No, it's not," the child will say, "Newark is only half an inch away from New York City."

As we grow older, though, we become more and more familiar with the concept of abstract representations *as long as they fit comfortably into our heads.* Scientists have studied the behavior and organization of the human brain and have found that the left side of the brain deals with sequential, one-thing-at-a-time processing; it is also the left side of the brain that deals with text, for example, the words that you are reading, one at a time, on this page of paper. The right side of the brain deals with pictures and with asynchronous, "lots of things going on at the same time" processing. This tells us that if we are trying to model something that is intrinsically linear and sequential, such as the flow of control in a computer program, we should use a textual modeling tool that fits comfortably into the left side of the brain that will be best at dealing with it. And if we are trying to model something that is intrinsically multidimensional, with lots of activities going on at the same time, we should use a graphical modeling tool.

8.5   SUMMARY

No doubt you will be so busy learning the modeling tools presented in this book that you won't think about the possibility of other modeling tools. However, they do exist, and we will briefly examine a variety of alternative tools in Chapter 15.

More importantly, you will be exposed to a variety of modeling tools in real-world projects. While the details (and shapes and forms) of these modeling tools may vary widely, you should check carefully to see that they follow the basic principles and guidelines presented in this chapter.

QUESTIONS AND EXERCISES

1.   What are the three major reasons for building system models?

2. Describe three different types of system models?

3. What are the major characteristics that a system modeling tool should have?

4. Why are graphical modeling tools generally preferred over textual modeling tools?

5. Is it *necessary* to use graphical modeling tools to develop an information system? Can you think of any situations where you would not want to use such tools?

6. What things do graphical models typically *not* show about a system?

7. Why is it important for a modeling tool to portray a system in a top-down fashion? Are there any situations where it doesn't matter?

8. Does a top-down *description* of a system require that the system be *designed* in a top-down fashion?

9. Describe a situation where it would be acceptable to include redundancy in a system model.

DATAFLOW DIAGRAMS

Form ever follows function.
Louis Henri Sullivan
"The Tall Office Building Artistically Considered,"
Lippincott's Magazine, March 1896

In this chapter, you will learn:

1. The components of a dataflow diagram.

2. How to draw a simple dataflow diagram.

3. Guidelines for drawing successful dataflow diagrams.

4. How to draw *leveled* dataflow diagrams.

In this chapter, we will explore one of the three major graphical modeling tools of structured analysis: the *dataflow diagram*. The dataflow diagram is a modeling tool that allows us to picture a system as a network of functional processes, connected to one another by "pipelines" and "holding tanks" of data. In the computer literature, and in your conversations with other systems analysts and users, you may use any of the following terms as synonyms for dataflow diagram:

- Bubble chart

- DFD (the abbreviation we will use throughout this book)

- Bubble diagram

- Process model

- Work flow diagram

- Function model

- "a picture of what's going on around here"

The dataflow diagram is one of the most commonly used systems-modeling tools, particularly for operational systems in which the *functions* of the system are of paramount importance and more complex than the data that the system manipulates. DFDs were first used in the software engineering field as a notation for studying systems design issues (e.g., in early structured design books and articles such as [Stevens, Myers, and Constantine. 1974], [Yourdon and Constantine, 1975], [Myers, 1975], et al.). In turn, the notation had been borrowed from earlier papers on graph theory, and it continues to be used as a convenient notation by software engineers concerned with direct implementation of models of user requirements.

This is interesting background, but is likely to be irrelevant to the users to whom you show DFD system models; indeed, probably the *worst* thing you can do is say, "Mr. User, I'd like to show you a top-down, partitioned, graph-theoretic model of your system." Actually, many users will be familiar with the underlying concept of DFDs, because the same kind of notation has been used by operations research scientists for nearly 70 years to build work-flow models of organizations. This is important to keep in mind: DFDs cannot only be used to model information-processing systems, but also as a way of modeling whole organizations, that is, as a tool for business planning and strategic planning.

We will begin our study of dataflow diagrams by examining the components of a typical dataflow diagram: the process, the flow, the store, and the terminator. We will use a fairly standard notation for DFDs, following the notation of such classic books as [DeMarco, 1978], [Gane and Sarson, 1977], and others. However, we will also include DFD notation for modeling real-time systems (i.e., control flows and control processes). This additional notation is generally not required for business-oriented systems, but is crucial when modeling a variety of engineering and scientific systems.

Next, we will review some guidelines for constructing dataflow diagrams so that we can minimize the chances of constructing a confusing, incorrect, or inconsistent DFD. Finally, we will discuss the concept of *leveled* DFDs as a method of modeling complex systems.

Keep in mind that the DFD is just one of the modeling tools available to the systems analyst and that it provides only one view of a system—the function-oriented view. If we are developing a system in which data relationships are more important than functions, we might de-emphasize the DFD (or conceivably not even bother developing one) and concentrate instead on developing a set of entity-relationship diagrams as discussed in Chapter 12. Alternatively, if the time-dependent behavior of the system dominated all other issues, we might concentrate instead on the state-transition diagram discussed in Chapter 13.

9.1   THE COMPONENTS OF A DFD

Figure 9.1 shows a typical DFD for a small system. Before we examine its components in detail, notice several things:

- It hardly needs to be explained at all; one can simply look at the diagram and understand it. The notation is simple and unobtrusive and, in a sense, intuitively obvious. This is particularly important when we remember who is supposed to be looking at Figure 9.1—not the systems analyst, but the user! If the user needs an encyclopedia in order to read and understand the model of his system, he or she probably won't bother to do either.

- The diagram fits easily onto one page. This means two things: (1) someone can look at the diagram without being overwhelmed, and (2) the system that is being modeled by the diagram is not very complex. What do we do if the system is intrinsically complex, for example, so complex that there would be literally hundreds of circles and lines in the diagram? We will discuss this in Section 9.4.

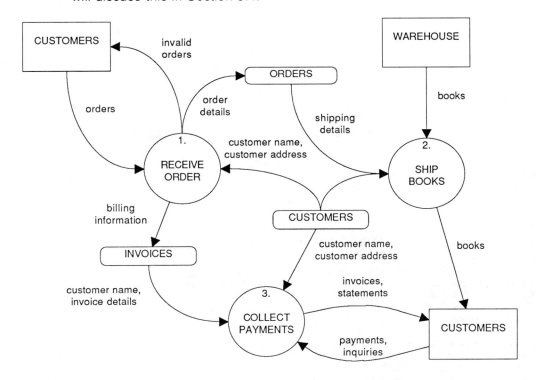

Figure 9.1: **A typical DFD**

- The diagram has been drawn by a computer. There is nothing wrong with a hand-drawn diagram, but Figure 9.1 and many of the other DFDs shown in this book have been drawn with the assistance of a Macintosh program called MacDraw. This means that the diagram is likely to be drawn more neatly and in a more standardized fashion than would normally be possible in a hand-drawn diagram. It also means that changes can be made and new versions produced in a matter of minutes.[1]

9.1.1　The Process

The first component of the DFD is known as a *process*. Common synonyms are a *bubble*, a *function*, or a *transformation*. The process shows a part of the system that transforms inputs into outputs; that is, it shows how one or more inputs are changed into outputs. The process is represented graphically as a circle, as shown in Figure 9.2(a). Some systems analysts prefer to use an oval or a rectangle with rounded edges, as shown in Figure 9.2(b); still others prefer to use a rectangle, as shown in Figure 9.2(c). The differences between these three shapes are purely cosmetic, though it is obviously important to use the same shape consistently to represent all the functions in the system. Throughout the rest of this book, we will use the circle or bubble.[2]

Figure 9.2(a): **An example of a process**

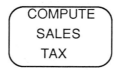

Figure 9.2(b): **An alternative representation of a process**

---

1 However, the disadvantage of MacDraw (and other generic programs like it) is that it does not know anything about the special nature of dataflow diagrams or other system models presented in this book. It knows only about primitive shapes such as rectangles, circles, and lines. The analyst toolkit products discussed in Appendix A are far more powerful, because they know a great deal about the subject matter of dataflow diagrams.

2 The shape that the systems analyst uses for the process is often associated with a particular "camp" of structured analysis. The circle is associated with the "Yourdon/DeMarco" camp, since it is used in various textbooks published by YOURDON Press, as well as the training and consulting activities of YOURDON Inc. Similarly, the oval shape is often associated with the "Gane/Sarson" camp, since it was introduced by Chris Gane and Trish Sarson in their book [Gane and Sarson, 1977], and has been used by McDonnell Douglas Automation Company (McAuto) and various other organizations. The rectangle shape is typically associated with the "SADT" camp, since it was popularized in various articles about Softech's Structured Analysis Design Technique (SADT); see, for example, [Ross and Schoman, 1977].

```
┌─────────────┐
│   COMPUTE   │
│    SALES    │
│     TAX     │
└─────────────┘
```

Figure 9.2(c): **Still another representation of a process**

Note that the process is named or described with a single word, phrase, or simple sentence. For most of the DFD models that we will discuss in this book, the process name will describe *what* the process does. In Section 9.2, we will say more about proper naming of process bubbles; for now, it is sufficient to say that a good name will generally consist of a verb-object phrase such as **VALIDATE INPUT** or **COMPUTE TAX RATE**.

In some cases, the process will contain the name of a person or a group of people (e.g., a department or a division of an organization), or a computer, or a mechanical device. That is, the process sometimes describes who or *what* is carrying out the process, rather than describing what the process is. We will discuss this in more detail in Chapter 17 when we discuss the concept of an *essential* model, and later in Part IV when we look at implementation models.

9.1.2   The Flow

A *flow* is represented graphically by an arrow into or out of a process; an example of flow is shown in Figure 9.3. The flow is used to describe the movement of chunks, or packets of information from one part of the system to another part. Thus, the flows represent data in motion, whereas the stores (described below in Section 9.1.3) represent data at rest.

CUSTOMER INQUIRY

Figure 9.3: **An example of a flow**

For most of the systems that you model as a systems analyst, the flows will indeed represent data, that is, bits, characters, messages, floating point numbers, and the various other kinds of information that computers can deal with. But DFDs can also be used to model systems other than automated, computerized systems; we may choose, for example, to use a DFD to model an assembly line in which there are no computerized components. In such a case, the packets or chunks carried by the flows will typically be *physical materials*; an example is shown in Figure 9.4. For many complex, real-world systems, the DFD will show the flow of materials *and* data.

Note that the flows in Figures 9.3 and 9.4 are *named*. The name represents the meaning of the packet that moves along the flow. A corollary of this is that the flow carries only one type of packet, as indicated by the flow name. The systems analyst should not name a dataflow **APPLES AND ORANGES AND WIDGETS AND VARIOUS OTHER THINGS**. However, we will see in Part III, that there are exceptions to this convention: it is sometimes useful to consolidate several elementary dataflows into a consolidated flow. Thus, one might see a single dataflow labeled **VEGETABLES** instead of several different dataflows labeled **POTATOES, BRUSSEL SPROUTS**, and **PEAS**. As we will see, this will require some explanation in the *data dictionary*, which is discussed in Chapter 10.

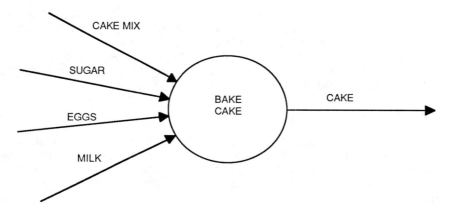

Figure 9.4: **A DFD with material flows**

While this may seem like an obvious point, keep in mind that the same content may have a different meaning in different parts of the system. For example, consider the fragment of a system shown in Figure 9.5.

The same chunk of data (e.g., 212-410-9955) has a different meaning when it travels along the flow labeled **PHONE-NUMBER** than it does when it travels along the flow labeled **VALID-PHONE-NUMBER**. In the first case, it means a telephone number that may or may not turn out to be valid; in the second case, it means a phone number that, within the context of this system, is known to be valid. Another way to think of it is that the flow labeled "phone number" is like a pipeline, undiscriminating enough to allow invalid phone numbers as well as valid phone numbers to travel along it; the flow labeled **VALID-PHONE-NUMBER** is narrower, or more discriminating, and allows a more narrowly defined set of data to move through it.

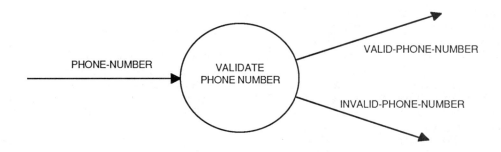

Figure 9.5: **A typical DFD**

Note also that the flows show *direction:* an arrowhead at either end of the flow (or possibly at both ends) indicates whether data (or material) are moving into or out of a process (or doing both). The flow shown in Figure 9.6(a), for example, clearly shows that a telephone number is being sent *into* the process labeled **VALIDATE PHONE NUMBER**. And the flow labeled **TRUCKER-DELIVERY-SCHEDULE** in Figure 9.6(b) is clearly an output flow generated by the process **GENERATE TRUCKER DELIVERY SCHEDULE**; data moving along that flow will either travel to another process (as an input) or to a store (as discussed in Section 9.1.3) or to a terminator (as discussed in Section 9.1.4). The double-headed flow shown in Figure 9.6(c) is a *dialogue*, a convenient packaging of two packets of data (an inquiry and response or a question and answer) on the same flow. In the case of a dialogue, the packets at either end of the arrow must be named, as illustrated by Figure 9.6(c).[3]

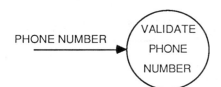

Figure 9.6(a): **An input flow**

Dataflows can diverge and converge in a DFD; conceptually, this is somewhat like a major river splitting into smaller tributaries, or tributaries joining together. However, this has a special meaning in a typical DFD in which packets of *data* are moving through the system: in the case of a diverging flow, it means that duplicate copies of a packet of data are being sent to different parts of the system, *or* that a

---

3 An acceptable alternative to the dialogue is to use two different flows, one showing the input (inquiry) to the process, and the other flow showing the output (response). This is, in fact, a better way to handle things if one input could conceivably lead to several entirely different actions (and responses) from the process. In the case of a simple inquiry-response situation, the use of one dialogue flow or separate input and output flows is a matter of choice. Most systems analysts prefer the dialogue notation because (1) it draws the reader's attention to the fact that the input and output are related to each other, and (2) it reduces the clutter on a DFD with several flows and processes and presents the reader with a cleaner, simpler diagram.

complex packet of data is being split into several more elementary data packets, each of which is being sent to different parts of the system, *or* that the dataflow pipeline carries items with different values (e.g., vegetables whose values may be "potato," "brussel sprout," or "lima bean") that are being separated. Conversely, in the case of a converging flow, it means that several elementary packets of data are joining together to form more complex, aggregate packets of data. For example, Figure 9.7(a) shows a DFD in which the flow labeled **ORDER-DETAILS** diverges and carries copies of the same packets to processes **GENERATE SHIPPING DOCUMENTS**, **UPDATE INVENTORY**, and **GENERATE INVOICE**. Figure 9.7(b) shows the flow labeled **CUSTOMER-ADDRESS** splitting into more elementary packets labeled **PHONE-NUMBER**, **ZIP-CODE**, and **STREET-ADDRESS**, which are sent to three different validation processes.[4]

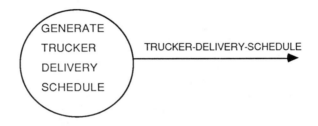

Figure 9.6(b): **An output flow**

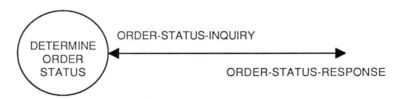

Figure 9.6(c): **A dialog flow**

Note that the flow doesn't answer a lot of procedural questions that you might have when looking at the DFD: it doesn't answer questions about input prompts, for example, and it doesn't answer questions about output flows. For example, Figure 9.8(a) shows the simple case of an input flow coming into the process labeled **PROCESS ORDER**. But how does this happen? Does **PROCESS ORDER** explicitly ask for the input; for example, does it prompt the user of an on-line system, indicating that it wants some input? Or do data packets move along the flow of their

---

4 Exactly how this duplication of data packets and/or decomposition of data packets takes place is considered an issue of *implementation*, that is, something that the systems designer will have to worry about, but not something that the systems analyst needs to show in the model of the system. It may eventually be accomplished by hardware or software, or manually, or by black magic. If the systems analyst is modeling a system that already exists, there may be some temptation to show the mechanism (i.e., the process) that carries out the duplication/decomposition of data. We will discuss this in more detail in Part III.

own volition, unasked for? Similarly, Figure 9.8(b) shows a simple output flow emanating from **GENERATE INVOICE REPORT**; do **INVOICE**s move along that flow when **GENERATE INVOICE REPORT** wants to send them, or when some other part of the system asks for the packet? Finally, consider the more common situation shown in Figure 9.8(c), in which there are multiple input flows and multiple output flows: in what *sequence* do the packets of data arrive, and in what sequence are the output packets generated? And is there a one-to-one ratio between the input packets and the output packets? That is, does process Q require exactly one packet from input flows A, B, and C in order to produce exactly one output packet for output flows X, Y, and Z? Or are there two A's for every three B's?

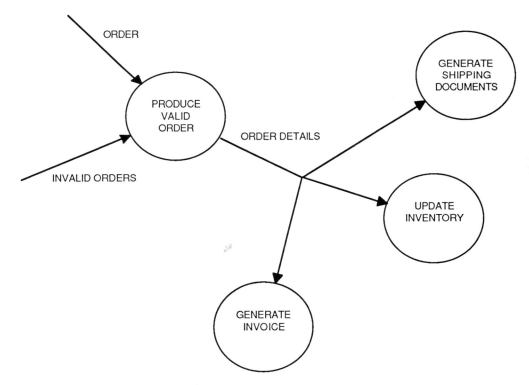

Figure 9.7(a): **A diverging flow**

The answer to all these questions is very simple: we don't know. All these questions involve *procedural* details, the sort of questions that would normally be modeled with a flowchart or some other *procedural* modeling tool. *The DFD simply doesn't attempt to address such issues.* If these questions do become important to you, then you will have to model the internal procedure of the various processes; tools for doing this job are discussed in Chapter 11.

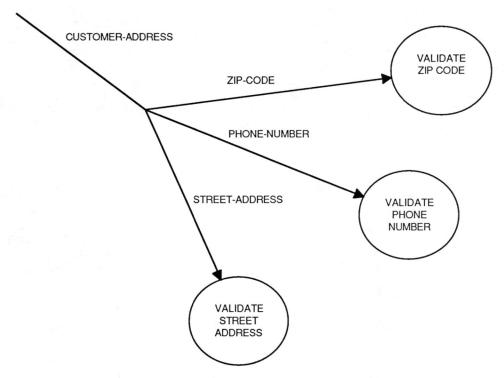

Figure 9.7(b): **Another example of a diverging flow**

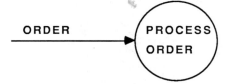

Figure 9.8(a): **An input flow**

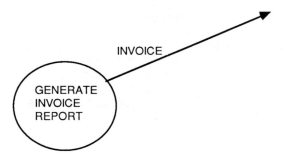

Figure 9.8(b): **An output flow**

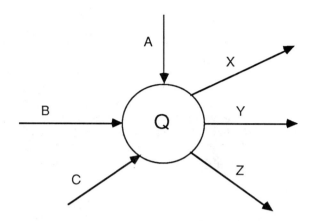

Figure 9.8(c): **A combination of input and output flows**

9.1.3   The Store

The *store* is used to model a collection of data packets at rest. The notation for a store is two parallel lines, as shown in Figure 9.9(a); an alternative notation is shown in Figure 9.9(b);[5] yet another notation, used in the case study in Appendix F, is shown in Figure 9.9(c). Typically, the name chosen to identify the store is the *plural* of the name of the packets that are carried by flows into and out of the store.

ORDERS

Figure 9.9(a): **Graphical representation of a store**

Figure 9.9(b): **An alternative notation for a store**

Figure 9.9(c): **The notation used in Appendix F**

5 The notation D1 in Figure 9.9(b) is simply a numbering scheme so that we can distinguish this store from other stores on the diagram. The convention followed in this book does *not* involve labeling or numbering the stores (simply because it hasn't seemed necessary or even useful), but (as we will see in Section 9.2), it *does* involve numbering the bubbles.

For the systems analyst with a data processing background, it is tempting to refer to the stores as *files* or *databases* (e.g., a magnetic tape file, or a disk file organized with IMS, DB2, ADABAS, IDMS, or some other well-known database management system). Indeed, this is how stores are often implemented in a computerized system; but a store can also be data stored on punched cards, microfilm, microfiche, or optical disk, or a variety of other electronic forms. And a store might also consist of 3-by-5 index cards in a card box, or names and addresses in an address book, or several file folders in a file cabinet, or a variety of other *non*computerized forms. Figure 9.9(d) shows a typical example of a "store" in an existing *manual* system. It is precisely because of the variety of possible *implementations* of a store that we deliberately choose a simple, abstract graphical notation and the term store rather than, for instance, database.[6]

Aside from the physical form that the store takes, there is also the question of its purpose: does the store exist because of a fundamental *user requirement*, or does it exist because of a convenient aspect of the *implementation* of the system? In the former case, the store exists as a necessary time-delayed storage area between two processes that occur at different times. For example, Figure 9.10 shows a fragment of a system in which, *as a matter of user policy* (independent of the technology that will be used to implement the system), the order entry process may operate at different times (or possibly at the same time) as the order inquiry process. The **ORDERS** store *must* exist in some form, whether on disk, tape, cards, or stone tablets.

Figure 9.9(d): **Another form of a store**

Figure 9.11(a) shows a different kind of store: the implementation store. We might imagine the systems designer interposing an **ORDERS** store between **ENTER ORDER** and **PROCESS ORDER** because:

- Both processes are expected to run on the same computer, but there isn't enough memory (or some other hardware resource) to fit both processes at the same time. Thus, the **ORDERS** store has been created as an intermediate file, because the available implementation technology has *forced* the processes to execute at different times.

---

6 It is also common to refer to one packet of information in the store as a record, and to refer to components of each packet as fields. There is nothing wrong with this terminology, but it is used so often in a computer-database context that it is likely to create the same kind of problems discussed above. For the time being, we will use the term packet to describe a single instance of a collection of related objects in the store.

- Either or both of the processes are expected to run on a computer hardware configuration that is somewhat unreliable. Thus, the **ORDERS** store has been created as a backup mechanism in case either process aborts.

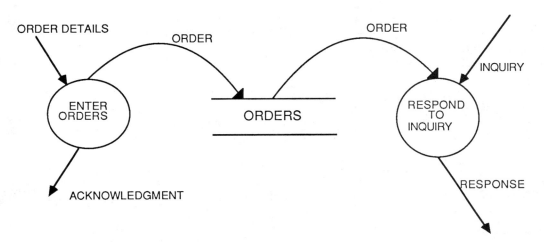

Figure 9.10: **A necessary store**

- The two processes are expected to be implemented by different programmers (or, in the more extreme case, different *groups* of programmers working in different geographical locations). Thus, the **ORDERS** store has been created as a testing and debugging facility so that, if the entire system doesn't work, both groups can look at the contents of the store to see where the problem lies.

- The systems analyst or the systems designer thought that the user might eventually want to access the **ORDERS** store for some other purpose, even though the user did not indicate any such interest. In this case, the store has been created in anticipation of future user needs (and since it will cost something to implement the system in this fashion, the user will end up paying for a system capability that was not asked for).

If we were to exclude the issues and model only the *essential* requirements of the system, there would be no need for the **ORDERS** store; we would instead have a DFD like the one shown in Fig. 9.11(b).

As we have seen in the examples thus far, stores are connected by flows to processes. Thus, the context in which a store is shown in a DFD is one (or both) of the following:

- A flow *from* a store

- A flow *to* a store

In most cases, the flows will be labeled as discussed in Section 9.1.3. However, many systems analysts do not bother labeling the flow if an *entire instance* of a packet flows into or out of the store.[7] For example, Figure 9.12 shows a typical fragment of a DFD.

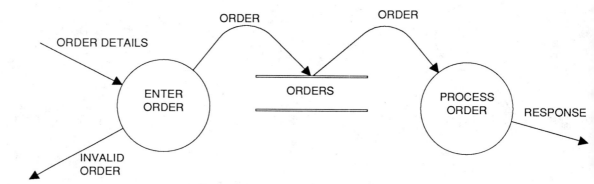

Figure 9.11(a): **An "implementation" store**

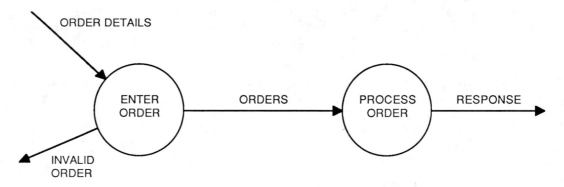

Figure 9.11(b): **The implementation store removed**

---

7 We will mention several such conventions in this chapter, as well as similar conventions concerning the other modeling tools. Your project manager, your organization's standards manual, or the CASE tool that you use for your project (see Appendix A) may force you to use one convention or another; but you should see that there is a certain amount of flexibility to the modeling tools and modeling notation presented here. The important thing is *consistency:* all the packet-bearing flows into or out of a store should either be consistently labeled or consistently unlabeled.

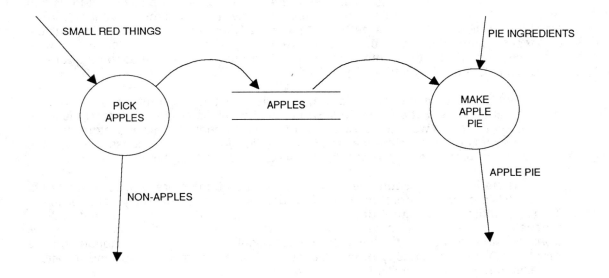

Figure 9.12: **Stores with unlabeled flows**

A flow from a store is normally interpreted as a read or an access to information in the store. Specifically, it can mean that:

- A single packet of data has been retrieved from the store; this is, in fact, the most common example of a flow from a store. Imagine, for example, a store called **CUSTOMERS**, where each packet contains name, address, and phone number information about individual customers. Thus, a typical flow from the store might involve the retrieval of a complete packet of information about one customer.

- More than one packet has been retrieved from the store. For example, the flow might retrieve packets of information about all the customers from New York City from the **CUSTOMERS** store.

- A portion of one packet from the store. In some cases, for example, only the phone number portion of information from one customer might be retrieved from the **CUSTOMERS** store.

- Portions of more than one packet from the store. For example, a flow might retrieve the zip-code portion of all customers living in the state of New York from the **CUSTOMERS** store.

As we noted earlier when we examined flows entering and leaving a process, we will have many *procedural* questions when we examine flows entering and leaving a store: does the flow represent a single packet, multiple packets, portions of a packet, or portions of several packets? In some cases, we can tell simply by looking at the label on the flow: if the flow is unlabeled, it means that an entire packet of information is being retrieved (as indicated above, this is simply a convenient convention); if the label on the flow is the same as that of the store, then an entire packet (or multiple instances of an entire packet) is being retrieved; and if the label on the flow is something other than the name of the store, then one or more components of one or more packets are being retrieved.[8]

While some of the procedural questions can thus be answered by looking carefully at the labels attached to a flow, not all the details will be evident. Indeed, to learn everything we want to know about the flow emanating from the store, we will have to examine the details—the *process specification*—of the process to which the flow is connected; process specifications are discussed in Chapter 11.

There is one procedural detail we can be sure of: the store is passive, and data will not travel from the store along the flow unless a process explicitly asks for them. There is another procedural detail that is assumed, by convention, for information-processing systems: *The store is not changed when a packet of information moves from the store along the flow.* A programmer might refer to this as a nondestructive read; in other words, a copy of the packet is retrieved from the store, and the store remains in its original condition.[9]

A flow *to* a store is often described as a write, an update, or possibly a delete. Specifically, it can mean any of the following things:

- One or more new packets are being put into the store. Depending on the nature of the system, the new packets may be *appended* (i.e., somehow arranged so that they are "after" the existing packets); or they may be placed somewhere between existing packets. This is often an implementation issue (i.e., controlled by the specific database management system) in which case the systems analyst ought not to worry about it. It may, however, be a matter of user policy.

- One or more packets are being deleted, or removed, from the store.

- One or more packets are being modified or changed. This may involve a change to *all* of a packet, or (more commonly) just a portion of a packet, or

---

8 How do we know that the labels on the flow have anything to do with the components of a packet of information in the store? How do we know, for example, that a flow labeled **PHONE-NUMBER** has anything to do with packets of information in the **CUSTOMERS** store? There is a temptation, especially in a real-world project where everyone is relatively familiar with the subject matter, to simply say, "Oh, that's intuitively obvious! *Of course* the phone number is a component of a customer packet." But to be sure, we need to see a rigorous definition of the composition of a **CUSTOMERS** packet. This is found in the data dictionary, which we will discuss in Chapter 10.

9 If you are using a DFD to model something other than a pure information processing system, this may not be true. For example, the store might contain physical items, and the flow might be a mechanism for conveying materials from the store to the process. In this case, a packet would be physically removed from the store, and the store would be depleted as a result. In a system model containing information stores and physical stores, it is important to annotate the DFD (or provide an explanation in the data dictionary) so that the reader will not be confused.

a portion of multiple packets. For example, suppose that a law enforcement agency maintains a store of suspected criminals and that each packet contains the suspect's name and address; the agency might offer a new "identity" to a cooperative suspect, in which case *all* the information pertaining to that suspect's packet would change. As an alternative, consider a **CUSTOMERS** store containing information about customers residing in Manhattan; if the Post Office decided to change the zip code for one area of Manhattan (as it did in 1983, when the area of Manhattan where I lived was changed from zip code 10028 to 10128), it would necessitate a change to one portion of several packets.

In all these cases, it is evident that the store is changed as a result of the flow entering the store. It is the process (or processes) connected to the other end of the flow that is responsible for making the change to the store.

One point that should be evident from all the examples shown thus far: flows connected to a store can only carry packets of information that the store is capable of holding. Thus, a flow connected to a **CUSTOMERS** store can only carry customer-related information that the store contains; it cannot carry inventory packets or manufacturing packets or astronomical data.

9.1.4　　The Terminator

The next component of the DFD is a *terminator;* it is graphically represented as a rectangle, as shown in Figure 9.13. Terminators represent external entities with which the system communicates. Typically, a terminator is a person or a group of people, for example, an outside organization or government agency, or a group or department that is *within* the same company or organization, but *outside* the control of the system being modeled. In some cases, a terminator may be another system, for example, some other computer system with which your system will communicate.

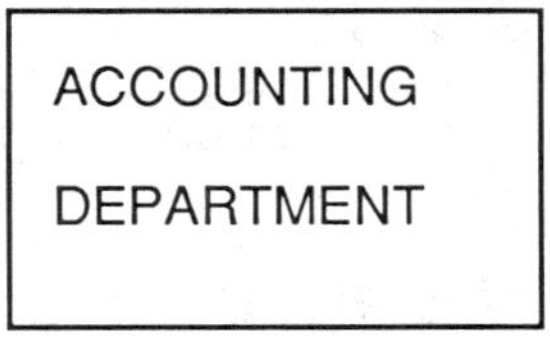

```
┌──────────────────┐
│                  │
│  ACCOUNTING      │
│                  │
│  DEPARTMENT      │
│                  │
└──────────────────┘
```

Figure 9.13: **Graphical representation of a terminator**

It is usually very easy to identify the terminators in the system being modeled. Sometimes the terminator is the user; that is, in your discussions with the user, she will say, "I intend to provide data items X, Y, and Z to your system, and I expect the system to provide me with data items A, B, and C." In other cases, the user considers herself part of the system and will help you identify the relevant terminators; for example, she will say to you, "We have to be ready to receive Type 321 forms from the Accounting Department, and we have to send weekly Budget Reports to the Finance Committee." In this last case, it is evident that the Accounting Department and the Finance Committee are separate terminators with which the system communicates.

There are three important things that we must remember about terminators:

1.   They are *outside* the system we are modeling; the flows connecting the terminators to various processes (or stores) in our system represent the *interface* between our system and the outside world.

2.   As a consequence, it is evident that neither the systems analyst nor the systems designer are in a position to change the contents of a terminator or the way the terminator works.   In the language of several classic textbooks on structured analysis, the terminator is outside the domain of change.   What this means is that the systems analyst is modeling a system with the intention of allowing the systems designer a considerable amount of flexibility and freedom to choose the best (or most efficient, or most reliable, etc.) implementation possible. The systems designer may implement the system in a considerably different way than it is currently implemented; the systems analyst may choose to model the requirements of the system in such a way that it looks considerably different than the way the user mentally imagines the system now (more on this in Section 9.4 and Part III). *But the systems analyst cannot change the contents, or organization, or internal procedures associated with the terminators.*

3.   Any relationship that exists *between* terminators will not be shown in the DFD model. There may indeed be several such relationships, but, by definition, those relationships are not part of the system we are studying. Conversely, if there *are* relationships between the terminators, and if it is essential for the systems analyst to model those requirements in order to properly document the requirements of the system, then, by definition, the terminators are actually part of the system and should be modeled as processes.

In the simple examples discussed thus far, we have seen only one or two terminators.   In a typical real-world system, there may be literally dozens of different terminators interacting with the system. Identifying the terminators and their interaction with the system is part of the process of building the environmental model, which we will discuss in Chapter 17.

9.2   GUIDELINES FOR CONSTRUCTING DFDs

In the preceding section, we saw that dataflow diagrams are composed of four simple components: processes (bubbles), flows, stores, and terminators. Armed with these tools, you can now begin interviewing users and constructing DFD models of systems.

However, there are a number of additional guidelines that you need in order to use DFDs successfully. Some of these guidelines will help you avoid constructing DFDs that are, quite simply, *wrong* (i.e., incomplete or logically inconsistent). And some of the guidelines are intended to help you draw a DFD that will be pleasing to the eye, and therefore more likely to be read carefully by the user.

The guidelines include the following:

1. Choose meaningful names for processes, flows, stores, and terminators.

2. Number the processes.

3. Redraw the DFD as many times as necessary for esthetics.

4. Avoid overly complex DFDs.

5. Make sure the DFD is internally consistent and consistent with any associated DFDs.

9.2.1   Choose Meaningful Names for Processes, Flows, Stores, and Terminators

As we have already seen, a process in a DFD may represent a *function* that is being carried out, or it may indicate *how* the function is being carried out, by identifying the person, group, or mechanism involved. In the latter case, it is obviously important to accurately label the process so that the people reading the DFD, especially the users, will be able to confirm that it is an accurate model. However, if the process is carried out by an individual person, I recommend that you identify the *role* that the person is carrying out, rather than the person's name or identity. Thus, rather than drawing a process like the one shown in Figure 9.14(a), with Fred's name immortalized for all to see, we suggest that you represent the process as shown in Figure 9.14(b). The reason for this is threefold:

1. Fred may be replaced next week by Mary or John. Why invite obsolescence in the model?

2. Fred may be carrying out several different jobs in the system. Rather than drawing three different bubbles, each labeled Fred but meaning something different, it's better to indicate the actual job that is being done—or at least the role that Fred is playing at the moment (as modeled in each of their bubbles).

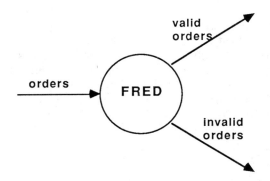

Figure 9.14(a): **An inappropriate process name**

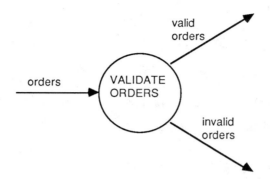

Figure 9.14(b): **A more appropriate process name**

3.   Identifying Fred is likely to draw attention to the way Fred happens to carry out the job at hand. As we will see in Part III, we will generally want to concentrate on the underlying *business policy* that must be carried out, without reference to the procedures (which may be based on customs and history no longer relevant) used to carry out that policy.

If we are lucky enough to avoid names of people (or groups) and political roles altogether, we can label the processes in such a way as to identify the *functions* that the system is carrying out. A good discipline to use for process names is a *verb* and an *object.* That is, choose an active verb (a transitive verb, one that takes an object) and an appropriate object to form a descriptive phrase for your process. Examples of process names are:

- CALCULATE MISSILE TRAJECTORY

- PRODUCE INVENTORY REPORT

- VALIDATE PHONE NUMBER

- ASSIGN STUDENTS TO CLASS

You will find, in carrying out this guideline, that it is considerably easier to use specific verbs and objects if the process itself is relatively simple and well defined. Even in the simple cases, though, there is a temptation to use wishy-washy names like DO, HANDLE, and PROCESS. When such "elastic" verbs are used (verbs whose meaning can be stretched to cover almost any situation), it often means that the systems analyst is not sure what function is being performed or that several functions have been grouped together but don't really belong together. Here are some examples of poor process names:

- DO STUFF

- MISCELLANEOUS FUNCTIONS

- HANDLE INPUT

- TAKE CARE OF CUSTOMERS

- PROCESS DATA

- GENERAL EDIT

The names chosen for the process names (as well as flow names and terminator names) should come from a vocabulary that is meaningful to the user. This will happen quite naturally if the DFD is drawn as a result of a series of interviews with the users *and* if the systems analyst has some minimal understanding of the underlying subject matter of the application. But two cautions must be kept in mind:

1.   There is a natural tendency for users to use the specific abbreviation and acronyms that they are familiar with; this is true for both the processes and the flows that they describe. Unfortunately, this usually results in a DFD that is very heavily oriented to the way things happen to be done now. Thus, the user might say, "Well, we get a copy of Form 107—it's the pink copy, you know—and we send it over to Joe where it gets frogulated." A good way to avoid such excessively idiosyncratic terms is to choose verbs (like "frogulate") and objects (like "Form 107") that would be meaningful to someone in the same industry or application, but working in a different company or organization. If you're building a banking system, the process names and flow names should, ideally, be understandable to someone in a different bank.

2.   If the DFD is being drawn by someone with a programming background, there will be a tendency to use such programming-oriented terminology as "ROUTINE," "PROCEDURE," "SUBSYSTEM," and "FUNCTION," even though such terms may be utterly meaningless in the user's world. Unless you hear the users using these words in their own conversation, avoid them in your DFD.

9.2.2   Number the Processes

As a convenient way of referencing the processes in a DFD, most systems analysts number each bubble. It doesn't matter very much how you go about doing this— left to right, top to bottom, or any other convenient pattern will do—*as long as you are consistent in how you apply the numbers*.

The only thing that you must keep in mind is that the numbering scheme will imply, to some casual readers of your DFD, a certain *sequence* of execution. That is, when you show the DFD to a user, he may ask, "Oh, does this mean that bubble 1 is performed first, and then bubble 2, and then bubble 3?" Indeed, you may get the same question from other systems analysts and programmers; anyone who is familiar with a flowchart may make the mistake of assuming that numbers attached to bubbles imply a sequence.

This is not the case at all. The DFD model is a network of communicating, asynchronous processes, which is, in fact, an accurate representation of the way most systems actually operate. Some sequence may be implied by the presence or absence of data (e.g., it may turn out that bubble 2 cannot carry out its function until it receives data from bubble 1), but the numbering scheme has nothing to do with this.

So why do we number the bubbles at all? Partly, as indicated above, as a convenient way of referring to the processes; it's much easier in a lively discussion about a DFD to say "bubble 1" rather than "EDIT TRANSACTION AND REPORT ERRORS." But more importantly, the numbers become the basis for a *hierarchical* numbering scheme when we introduce *leveled* dataflow diagrams in Section 9.3.

9.2.3   Avoid Overly Complex DFDs

The purpose of a DFD is to accurately model the functions that a system has to carry out and the interactions between those functions. But another purpose of the DFD is to be read and understood, not only by the systems analyst who constructed the model, but by the users who are the experts in the subject matter. This means that the DFD should be readily understood, easily absorbed, and pleasing to the eye.

We will discuss a number of esthetic guidelines in the next subsection, but there is one overriding guideline to keep in mind: *don't create a DFD with too many processes, flows, stores, and terminators.* In most cases, this means that you shouldn't have more than half a dozen processes and related stores, flows, and terminators on a single diagram.[10] Another way of saying this is that the DFD should fit comfortably onto a standard 8.5- by 11-inch sheet of paper.

There is one major exception to this, as we will discuss in Chapter 18: a special DFD known as a *context diagram* that represents an entire system as a single process and highlights the interfaces between the system and the outside terminators. Figure 9.15 shows a typical context diagram, and you can see that it is enough to scare away many systems analysts, not to mention the unwary user! Typically, context diagrams like the one shown in Figure 9.15 cannot be simplified, for they are depicting, even at the highest level of detail, a reality that is intrinsically complex.[11]

---

10 This guideline comes from "The Magical Number Seven, Plus or Minus Two," by George Miller, *Psychology Review,* 1956.

11 Actually, there are a few things that we can do: if there are several different dataflows between a terminator and the single system bubble, they can be consolidated into a single dataflow. The data dictionary, discussed in Chapter 10, will be used to explain the composition and meaning of the aggregate dataflow. And if the context diagram is being shown to several disparate audiences (e.g., different user groups with different interests), different context diagrams can be drawn to highlight only those terminators and flows that a particular user group in interested in. But, in most cases, there is no escaping the bottom line: if the overall system is intrinsically complex, the context diagram will be, too. More on this in Chapter 18.

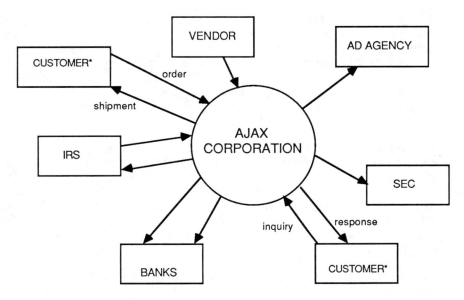

Figure 9.15: **A typical context diagram**

9.2.4   Redraw the DFD as Many Times as Necessary

In a real-world systems analysis project, the DFD that we have discussed in this chapter will have to be drawn, redrawn, and redrawn again, often as many as ten times or more, before it is (1) technically correct, (2) acceptable to the user, and (3) neatly enough drawn that you wouldn't be embarrassed to show it to the board of directors in your organization. This may seem like a lot of work, but it is well worth the effort to develop an accurate, consistent, esthetically pleasing model of the requirements of your system. The same is true of any other engineering discipline: would you want to fly in an airplane designed by engineers who got bored with their engineering drawings after the second iteration?[12]

What makes a dataflow diagram esthetically pleasing? This is obviously a matter of personal taste and opinion, and it may be determined by standards set by your organization or by the idiosyncratic features of any automated workstation-based diagramming package that you use. And the user's opinion may be somewhat different from yours; within reason, whatever the user finds esthetically pleasing should determine the way you draw your diagram. Some of the issues that will typically come up for discussion in this area are the following:

---

12 Lest you think that airplanes are different from automated information systems or that they are more critical, keep in mind that computer systems now control most of the planes that you fly on; a typical large passenger airplane may have a dozen or more complex computer systems, which in turn interface with such complex real-time systems as the the the one used by the Federal Aviation Administration to monitor the airspace around airports.

- *Size and shape of bubbles.* Some organizations draw dataflow diagrams with rectangles or ovals instead of circles; this is obviously a matter of esthetics. Also, some users become quite upset if the bubbles in the DFD are not all the same size: they think that if one bubble is bigger than another, it means that that part of the system is more important or is different in some other significant way. (In fact, it usually happens only because the bubble's name was so long that the systems analyst had to draw a larger bubble just to encompass the name!)

- *Curved dataflows versus straight dataflows.* To illustrate this issue, consider the DFDs in Figure 9.16(a) and (b). Which one is more esthetically pleasing? Many observers will shrug their shoulders and say, "They're really both the same." But others—and this is the point!—will choose one and violently reject the other. It's obviously a good idea to know in advance which choice will be accepted and which will be rejected. In roughly the same category is the issue of crossed arrows; are they allowed or not allowed?

- *Hand-drawn diagrams versus machine-generated diagrams.* Within a few years, virtually all dataflow diagrams and related system models will be drawn on graphic computer systems; today, though, many of the diagrams are still hand drawn because the systems analysts don't have access to such tools. The issue here, though, is the *user's* reaction to these diagrams: some have a strong preference for the machine-generated diagrams because they're "neater," while others prefer handdrawn pictures because it gives them the feeling that the diagram hasn't been finalized or "frozen" yet, and that they can still make changes.

9.2.5   Make Sure That Your DFD Is Logically Consistent

As we will see in Chapter 14, a number of rules and guidelines that help ensure the dataflow diagram is consistent with the *other* system models—the entity-relationship diagram, the state-transition diagram, the data dictionary, and the process specification. However, there are some guidelines that we use now to ensure that the DFD *itself* is consistent. The major consistency guidelines are these:

- *Avoid infinite sinks*, bubbles that have inputs but no outputs. These are also known by systems analysts as "black holes," in an analogy to stars whose gravitational field is so strong that not even light can escape. An example of an infinite sink is shown in Figure 9.17.

- *Avoid spontaneous generation bubbles;* bubbles that have outputs but no inputs are suspicious, and generally incorrect. One plausible example of an output-only bubble is a random-number generator, but it is hard to imagine any other reasonable example. A typical output-only bubble is shown in Figure 9.18.

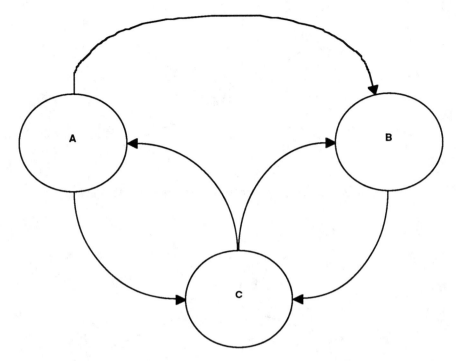

Figure 9.16(a): **One version of a DFD**

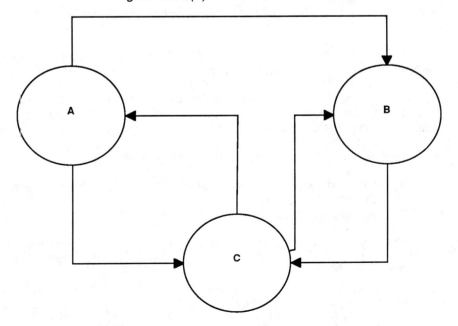

Figure 9.16(b): **A different version of the DFD**

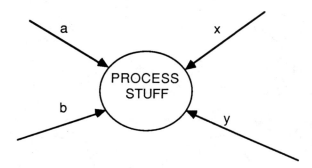

Figure 9.17: **An example of an infinite sink**

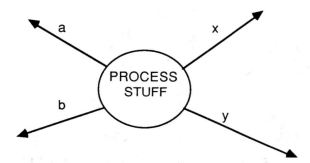

Figure 9.18: **An example of an output-only bubble**

- *Beware of unlabeled flows and unlabeled processes.* This is usually an indication of sloppiness, but it may mask an even deeper error: sometimes the systems analyst neglects to label a flow or a process because he or she simply cannot think of a reasonable name. In the case of an unlabeled flow, it may mean that several unrelated elementary data items have been arbitrarily packaged together; in the case of an unlabeled process, it may mean that the systems analyst was so confused that he or she drew a disguised flowchart instead of a dataflow diagram.[13]

- *Beware of read-only or write-only stores.* This guideline is analogous to the guideline about input-only and output-only processes; a typical store should have both inputs *and* outputs.[14] The only exception to this guideline

---

13 There is one idiomatic convention that violates this guideline, which we discussed in section 9.1.3: an unlabeled flow into or out of a store is, by convention, an indication that one entire instance (or record) is being put into or taken out of the store.

14 Sometimes it may not be immediately evident whether the store has both inputs and outputs. As we will see in the next section, DFDs are often partitioned into pieces; thus, we may find ourselves looking at one piece of the system that appears to have read-only (or write-only) stores. Some other piece of the system, documented on a separate DFD, may have the compensating write-only (or read-only) activity. Very tedious consistency checking is required to verify that *some* part of the system reads the store, and

is the external store, a store that serves as an interface between the system and some external terminator. Figure 9.19 shows an example of a stock market system with a legitimate write-only store.

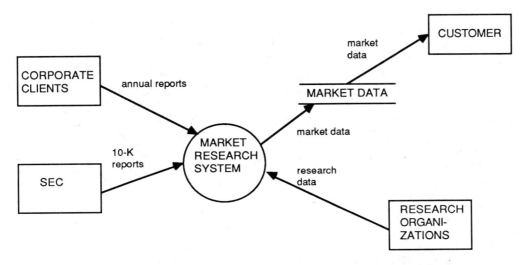

Figure 9.19: **A legitimate case of a write-only store**

9.3   LEVELED DFDs

Thus far in this chapter, the only complete dataflow diagrams we have seen are the simple three-bubble system shown in Figure 9.1 and the one-bubble system shown in Figure 9.19. But DFDs that we will see on *real* projects are considerably larger and more complex. Consider, for example, the DFD shown in Figure 9.20. Can you imagine showing this to a typical user?

Section 9.2.3 already suggested that we should avoid diagrams such as the one depicted in Figure 9.20. But how? If the system is intrinsically complex and has dozens or even hundreds of functions to model, how can we avoid the kind of DFD shown in Figure 9.20?

The answer is to organize the overall DFD in a series of *levels* so that each level provides successively more detail about a portion of the level above it. This is analogous to the organization of maps in an atlas, as we discussed in Chapter 8: we would expect to see an overview map that shows us an entire country, or perhaps even the entire world; subsequent maps would show us the details of individual countries, individual states within countries, and so on. In the case of DFDs, the organization of levels is shown conceptually in Figure 9.21.

---

14 (cont.) that some part of the system writes it; this is an area where the automated systems analysis packages discussed in Appendix A are extremely valuable.

The top-level DFD consists of only one bubble, representing the entire system; the dataflows show the interfaces between the system and the external terminators (together with any external stores that may be present, as illustrated by Figure 9.19). This special DFD is known as a *context diagram* and is discussed in Chapter 18.

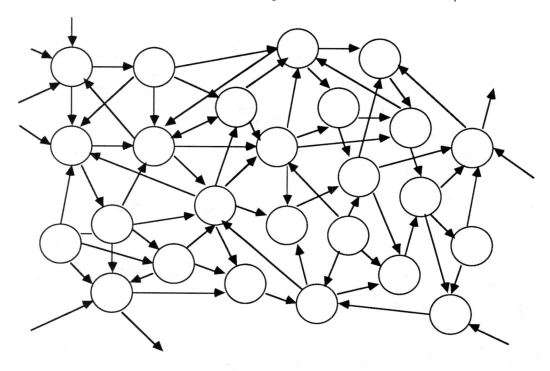

Figure 9.20: **A complex DFD**

The DFD immediately beneath the context diagram is known as Figure 0. It represents the highest-level view of the major functions within the system, as well as the major interfaces between those functions. As discussed in Section 9.2.2, each of these bubbles should be numbered for convenient reference.

The numbers also serve as a convenient way of relating a bubble to the next lower level DFD which more fully describes that bubble. For example:

- Bubble 2 in Figure 0 is associated with a lower-level DFD known as Figure 2. The bubbles within Figure 2 are numbered 2.1, 2.2, 2.3, and so on.

- Bubble 3 in Figure 0 is associated with a lower-level DFD known as Figure 3. The bubbles within Figure 3 are numbered 3.1, 3.2, 3.3, and so on.

- Bubble 2.2 in Figure 2 is associated with a lower-level DFD known as Figure 2.2. The bubbles within Figure 2.2 are numbered 2.2.1, 2.2.2, 2.2.3, and so on.

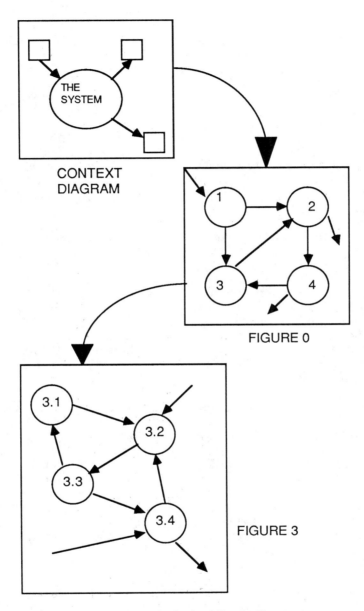

CONTEXT
DIAGRAM

FIGURE 0

FIGURE 3

Figure 9.21: **Leveled dataflow diagrams**

- If a bubble has a name (which indeed it should have!), then that name is carried down to the next lower level figure. Thus, if bubble 2.2 is named **COMPUTE SALES TAX**, then Figure 2.2, which partitions bubble 2.2 into more detail, should be labeled "**Figure 2.2: COMPUTE SALES TAX.**"

As you can see, this is a fairly straightforward way of organizing a potentially enormous dataflow diagram into a group of manageable pieces. But there are several things we must add to this description of leveling:

1. *How do you know how many levels you should have in a DFD?* The answer to this was suggested in Section 9.2.3: each DFD figure should have no more than half a dozen bubbles and related stores. Thus, if you have partitioned a large system into three levels, but your bottom-level DFDs still contain 50 bubbles each, you have at least one more level to go. An alternative checkpoint is provided in Chapter 11, when we discuss process specifications for the bubbles in the bottom-level DFDs: if we can't write a reasonable process specification for a bubble in about one page, then it probably is too complex, and it should be partitioned into a lower level DFD before we try to write the process specification.

2. *Are there any guidelines about the number of levels one should expect in a typical system?* In a simple system, one would probably find two to three levels; a medium-size system will typically have three to six levels; and a large system will have five to eight levels. You should be extremely wary of anyone who tells you that all systems can be modeled in exactly three levels; such a person will also try to sell you the Brooklyn Bridge. On the other hand, remember that the total number of bubbles increases exponentially as we go from one level to the next lower level. If, for example, each figure has seven bubbles, then there will be 343 bubbles at the third level, 16,807 bubbles at the fifth level, and 40,353,607 bubbles at the ninth level.

3. *Must all parts of the system be partitioned to the same level of detail?* For example, if bubble 2 in Figure 0 requires three more levels of detail, is it necessary for bubble 3 to also have three more levels of detail: that is, a Figure 3; a set of figures labeled Figure 3.1, Figure 3.2, ...; and a set of figures labeled 3.1.1, 3.1.2, ..., 3.2.1, 3.2.2, and so on. The answer is "No." Some parts of a system may be more complex than others and may require one or two more levels of partitioning. On the other hand, if bubble 2, which exists in the top-level Figure 0, turns out to be primitive, while bubble 3 requires seven levels of further partitioning, then the overall system model is skewed and has probably been poorly organized. In this case, some portions of bubble 3 should be split out into a separate bubble or perhaps reassigned to bubble 2.

4. *How do you show these levels to the user?* Many users will only want to look at *one* diagram: a high-level executive user may only want to look at the context diagram or perhaps at Figure 0; an operational-level user may only want to look at the figure that describes the area of the system in which she or he is interested. But if someone wants to look at a large part of the system or perhaps the entire system, then it makes sense to present the diagrams in a top-down fashion: begin with the context diagram and work your way down to lower levels of detail. It is often handy to have two diagrams side by side on the desk (or displayed with an overhead

projector) when you do this: the diagram that you are particularly interested in looking at, plus the parent diagram that provides a high-level context.

5. *How do you ensure that the levels of DFDs are consistent with each other?* The issue of consistency turns out to be critically important, because the various levels of DFDs are typically developed by *different people* in a real-world project; a senior systems analyst may concentrate on the context diagram and Figure 0, while several junior systems analysts work on Figure 1, Figure 2, and so on. To ensure that each figure is consistent with its higher-level figure, we follow a simple rule: *the dataflows coming into and going out of a bubble at one level must correspond to the dataflows coming into and going out of an entire figure at the next lower level which describes that bubble.* Figure 9.22(a) shows an example of a balanced dataflow diagram; Figure 9.22(b) shows two levels of a DFD that are out of balance.

6. *How do you show stores at the various levels?* This is one area where redundancy is deliberately introduced into the model. The guideline is as follows: *show a store at the highest level where it first serves as an interface between two or more bubbles; then show it again in EVERY lower-level diagram that further describes (or partitions) those interface bubbles.* Thus, Figure 9.23 shows a store that is shared by two high-level processes, **A** and **B**; the store would be shown again on the lower-level figures that further describe **A** and **B**. The corollary to this is that *local* stores, which are used only by bubbles in a lower-level figure, will *not* be shown at the higher levels, as they will be subsumed into a process at the next higher level.

7. *How do you actually DO the leveling of DFDs?* The discussion thus far has been misleading in a rather subtle way: while it is true that the DFDs should be *presented* to a user audience in a top-down fashion, it is not necessarily true that the systems analyst should *develop* the DFDs in a top-down fashion. The top-down approach is intuitively very appealing: one can imagine beginning with the context diagram, and then developing Figure 0, and then methodically working down to the lower levels of detail.[15] However, we will see in Chapter 17 that there are problems with this approach; a more successful approach is to first identify the external *events* to which the system must respond, and to use those events to create a rough, "first-cut" DFD. In Chapter 20, we will see that this first-cut DFD may have to be partitioned *upward* (to create higher-level DFDs) and *downward* (to create lower-level DFDs). For now, it is sufficient that you simply realize that the organization and presentation of a leveled set of DFDs does not necessarily correspond to the strategy for developing those levels in the first place.

---

15 It's very appealing to project managers, also. A project manager on one large project was heard saying to her project team, "I want all of you to *bubble on down* to the next level of detail by the end of this week!"

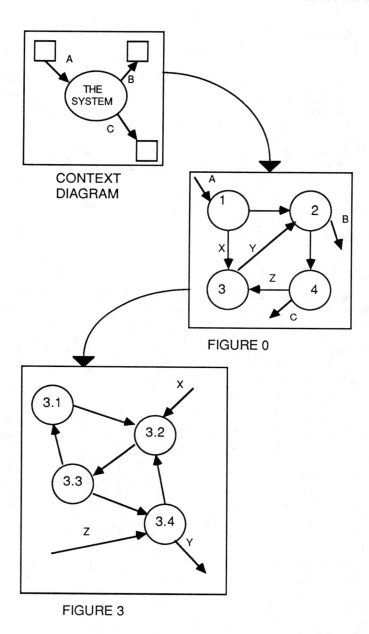

CONTEXT DIAGRAM

FIGURE 0

FIGURE 3

Figure 9.22(a): **A balanced DFD fragment**

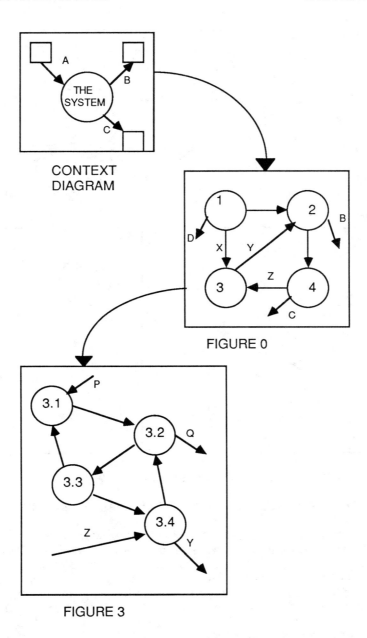

CONTEXT
DIAGRAM

FIGURE 0

FIGURE 3

Figure 9.22 (b): **A DFD fragment that is out of balance**

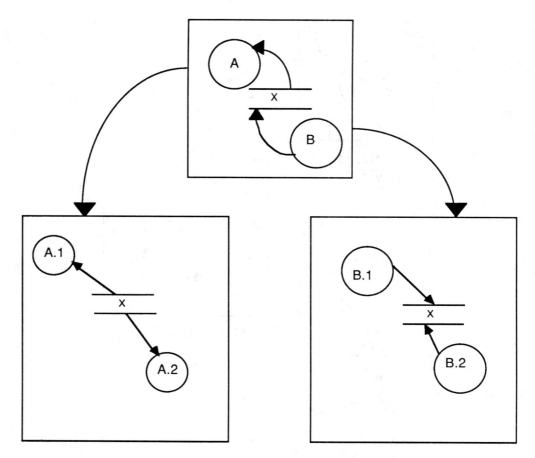

Figure 9.23: **Showing stores at lower levels**

9.4   EXTENSIONS TO THE DFD FOR REAL-TIME SYSTEMS

The flows discussed throughout this chapter are *data* flows; they are pipelines along which packets of *data* travel between processes and stores. Similarly, the bubbles in the DFDs we have seen up to now could be considered processors of data. For a very large class of systems, particularly business systems, these are the only kind of flows that we need in our system model. But for another class of systems, the *real-time* systems, we need a way of modeling *control flows* (i.e., signals or interrupts). And we need a way to show *control processes*—(.e., bubbles whose only job is to coordinate and synchronize the activities of other bubbles in the DFD).[16] These are shown graphically with dashed lines on the DFD, as illustrated in Figure 9.24.

---

[16] In some cases, it may even be appropriate to include *control stores* or *event stores*. These are analogous to the concept of semaphores first introduced by Dijkstra in [Dijkstra, 1968]. For additional details, see [Ward and Mellor, 1985].

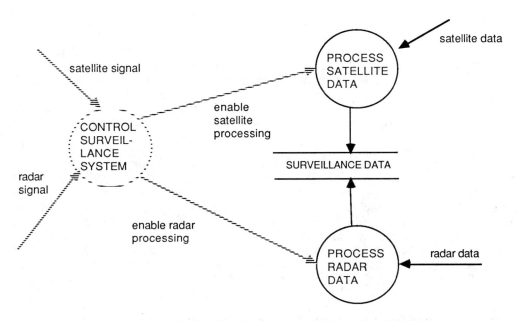

Figure 9.24: **A DFD with control flows and control processes**

A control flow may be thought of as a pipeline that can carry a binary signal (i.e., it is either on or off). Unlike the other flows discussed in this chapter, the control flow does not carry value-bearing data. The control flow is sent from one process to another (or from some external terminator to a process) as a way of saying, "Wake up! It's time to do your job." The implication, of course, is that the process has been dormant, or idle, prior to the arrival of the control flow.

A control *process* may be thought of as a supervisor or executive bubble whose job is to coordinate the activities of the other bubbles in the diagram; its inputs and outputs consist *only* of control flows. The outgoing control flows from the control process are used to wake up other bubbles; the incoming control flows generally indicate that one of the bubbles has finished carrying out some task, or that some extraordinary situation has arisen, which the control bubble needs to be informed about. There is typically only one such control process in a single DFD.

As indicated above, a control flow is used to wake up a normal process; once awakened, the normal process proceeds to carry out its job as described by a process specification (see Chapter 11). The internal behavior of a control process is different, though: this is where the time-dependent behavior of the system is modeled in detail. The *inside* of a control process is modeled with a *state-transition diagram,* which shows the various states that the entire system can be in and the circumstances that lead to a change of state. State-transition diagrams are discussed in Chapter 13.

9.5   SUMMARY

As we have seen in this chapter, the dataflow diagram is a simple but powerful tool for modeling the functions in a system. The material in Sections 9.1, 9.2, and 9.3 should be sufficient for modeling most classical business-oriented information systems. If you are working on a real-time system (e.g., process control, missile guidance, or telephone switching), the real-time extensions discussed in Section 9.4 will be important; for more detail on real-time issues, consult [Ward and Mellor, 1985]

Unfortunately, many systems analysts think that dataflow diagrams are all they need to know about structured analysis. If you ask one of your colleagues if he is familiar with structured analysis, he is likely to remark, "Oh, yeah, I learned about all those bubbles and stuff." On the one hand, this is a tribute to the power of dataflow diagrams—it is often the only thing that a systems analyst remembers after reading a book or taking a course on structured analysis! On the other hand, it is a dangerous situation: without the additional modeling tools presented in the following chapters, the dataflow diagrams are worthless. Even if the data relationships and time-dependent behavior of the system are trivial (which is unlikely), it is still necessary to combine DFDs with the data dictionary (discussed in Chapter 10) and the process specification (discussed in Chapter 11).

So don't put the book down yet! There's more to learn!

REFERENCES

1.   Wayne Stevens, Glen Myers, and Larry Constantine, "Structured Design," *IBM Systems Journal,* May 1974.

2.   Ed Yourdon and Larry Constantine, *Structured Design.* New York: YOURDON Press, 1975.

3.   Glen Myers, *Reliable Software through Composite Design.* New York: Petrocelli/Charter, 1975.

4.   Tom DeMarco, *Structured Analysis and Systems Specification.* Englewood Cliffs, N.J.: Prentice-Hall, 1979.

5.   Chris Gane and Trish Sarson, *Structured Systems Analysis: Tools and Techniques,* Englewood Cliffs, N.J.: Prentice-Hall, 1978.

6.   Doug Ross and Ken Schoman, Jr., "Structured Analysis for Requirements Definition," *IEEE Transactions on Software Engineering,* January 1977, pp. 41-48. Also reprinted in Ed Yourdon, *Classics in Software Engineering.* New York: YOURDON Press, 1979.

7.   Paul Ward and Steve Mellor, *Structured Development of Real-Time Systems,* Volumes 1-3. New York: YOURDON Press, 1986.

8. Edsger W. Dijkstra, "Cooperating Sequential Processes," *Programming Languages,* F. Genuys (editor). New York: Academic Press, 1968.

9. Paul Ward, "The Transformation Schema: An Extension of the Dataflow Diagram to Represent Control and Timing," *IEEE Transactions on Software Engineering*, February 1986, pp.198-210.

10. Derek Hatley, "The Use of Structured Methods in the Development of Large Software-Based Avionics Systems," *AIAA/IEEE 6th Digital Avionics Conference*, Baltimore, 1984.

11. M. Webb and Paul Ward, "Executable Dataflow Diagrams: An Experimental Implementation," *Structured Development Forum*, Seattle, August 1986.

12. E. Reilly and J. Brackett, "An Experimental System for Executing Real-Time Structured Analysis Models," *Proceedings of the 12th Structured Methods Conference*, Chicago, August 1987.

QUESTIONS AND EXERCISES

1. Give a brief description of a dataflow diagram. What is the difference between a DFD and a flowchart?

2. List six synonyms for dataflow diagram.

3. What can DFDs be used for besides modeling information systems?

4. What are the four major components of a DFD?

5. What are three common synonyms for process in a DFD?

6. Is there any significance to the choice of a circle for a process? Would it be better to use a triangle or a hexagon? Why or why not?

7. What is wrong with the following process?

8.   What is wrong with the following process?

9.   What is wrong with the following process?

10.   What is wrong with the following process?

11.   What is wrong with the following process?

12.   Why would a systems analyst draw a DFD with a process consisting of the name of a person or organizational group?

13.   Are flows on a DFD restricted to just showing the movement of information? Could they show the movement of anything else?

14. What is wrong with this DFD?

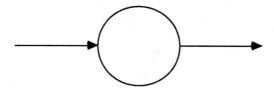

15. What is wrong with this DFD?

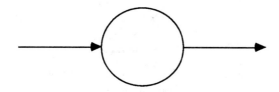

16. How can the same chunk of data have different meanings in a DFD? Draw an example of such a situation.

17. What is the significance of the following DFD?

18. Is there any limit to the number of inputs and outputs that a process can have in a DFD? What would your reaction be if you saw a process with 100 inputs and 100 outputs?

19. What is wrong with the following DFD?

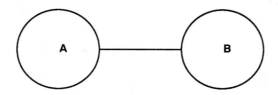

20. What is wrong with the following DFD?

21. What is wrong with the following DFDs?

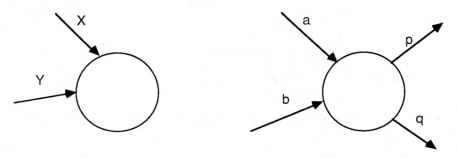

22. What is wrong with the following DFD?

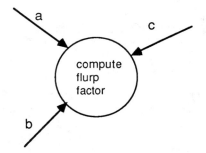

23. What is wrong with the following DFD?

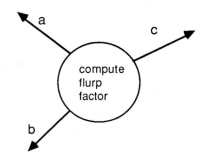

24. Give a description of a dialogue flow.

25. Is the following DFD valid? Is there any other way to draw it?

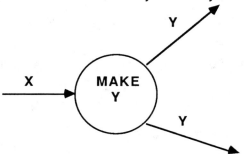

26. Is the following DFD valid? Is there any other way to draw it?

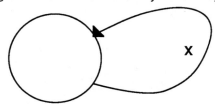

27. Under what circumstances would you expect to see duplicate copies of an output flow from a process?

28. Why do DFDs avoid showing procedural details?

29. In the diagram below, how many x and how many y elements are required to produce one z output?

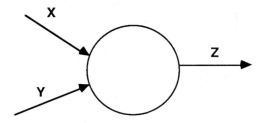

30. What does a *store* show in a DFD?

31. What is the convention for naming stores in a DFD?

32. What are alternative names for a store? Is it acceptable to use the term file? Why or why not?

33. What names are commonly used to describe packets of information in a store?

34. What are the four common reasons for showing implementation stores in a DFD?

35. Do you think implementation stores should be allowed in a DFD? Why or why not?

36. What is the meaning of an unlabeled flow into or out of a store?

37. Is there any limit to the *number* of flows into or out of a store? If so, state what the limit is.

38. What is wrong with the following DFDs?

(a)

(b)

(c)

(d)

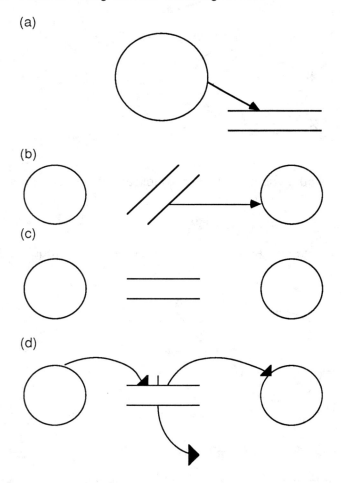

(e)

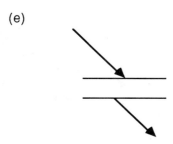

39. What are the four possible interpretations of a dataflow from a store into a process?

40. Does the following DFD make sense? Why or why not?

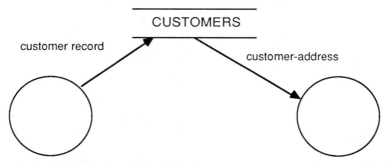

41. Give an example of a situation where a process might extract portions of more than one record from a store in a single logical access.

42. Give an example of a situation where a process might extract more than one packet of information from a store in a single logical access.

43. Can you tell from looking only at the diagrams whether the following DFDs are correct?

(a)

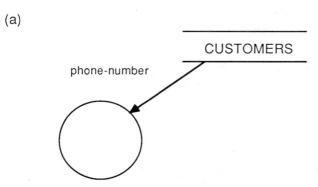

(b)

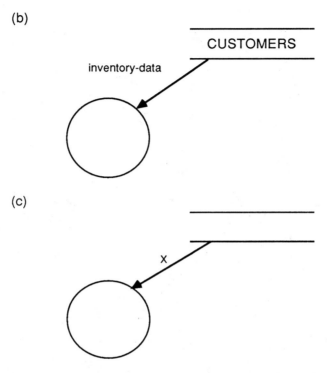

CUSTOMERS

inventory-data

(c)

X

44. What happens to a store after data have moved from the store, along a flow, to a process? Is this true of all types of systems or just information systems?

45. What are the three possible interpretations of a flow *into* a store?

46. How do we show packets of data being *deleted* from a store?

47. What is wrong with the following DFD?

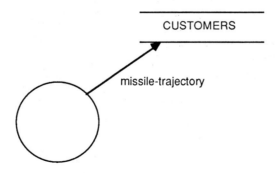

CUSTOMERS

missile-trajectory

48. What is the purpose of showing a terminator on a DFD?

49. How should the systems analyst identify the terminators?

50. What do the flows between terminators and processes represent?

51. What is wrong with the following DFDs?

(a)

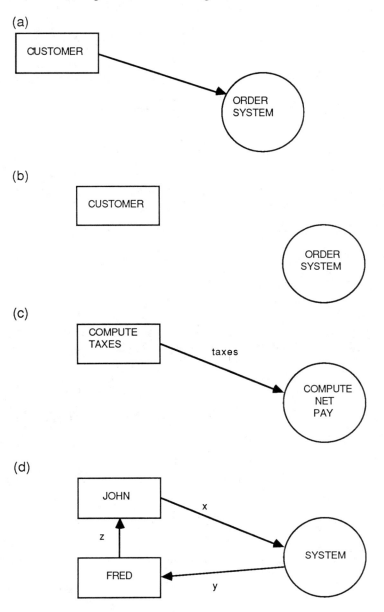

(b)

(c)

(d)

52. Is the systems analyst allowed to change the contents or organization of a ter-
     minator as part of her project? What if she feels strongly that it should be
     changed?

53. Why should a process *not* show the name of the person currently performing that function?

54. What is a good guideline for naming the processes in a DFD?

55. Give five examples of process names that you would *not* like to see in a DFD.

56. How can you tell whether the name chosen for a process is likely to be meaningful?

57. What is the misinterpretation that a user is likely to make of bubble numbers in a DFD?

58. How can you tell whether a DFD is likely to be too complex for the user to comprehend?

59. How rigidly enforced should the complexity guideline be? Should any exceptions be allowed? Why or why not?

60. Why is it often necessary to redraw a DFD many times?

61. What are the major issues that determine whether a DFD is esthetically pleasing? Do you think that these issues can be expressed as standards?

62. Do your colleagues prefer bubbles or ovals for processes? Which do you prefer?

63. Do you think the dataflows between processes should be shown as curved lines or straight lines? Can you think of any advantage or disadvantage of either approach? Is it an important issue?

64. What is an infinite sink? Why should it be considered an error in a typical DFD?

65. What are spontaneous generation bubbles in a DFD? Why should they be avoided in a typical DFD?

66. Why are unlabeled flows and processes dangerous?

67. Why are read-only stores and write-only stores typically an error in a DFD?

68. Why are leveled DFDs important in a system model?

69. How many levels of DFD should the systems analyst expect to see in a typical large system? Can you suggest an upper limit on the number of levels in a DFD?

70. In a leveled DFD:

    (a)   What would we call the "children" bubbles below bubble 2.3?

(b)   What would be the *figure* name of the figure in which bubble 2.3 appears?

(c)   How many *higher*-level figures are there above the figure in which bubble 2.3 appears? What are they called?

71.   Is it necessary for all parts of a system to be partitioned to the same level of detail? Why or why not?

72.   Suppose someone showed you a DFD in which bubble 1 was partitioned into 2 lower levels, and bubble 2 was partitioned into 17 lower levels. What would your reaction be? What recommendations, if any, would you make?

73.   What does balancing mean, in the context of this chapter? How can you tell whether a DFD is balanced?

74.   Why is Figure 9.22(b) in this chapter out of balance?

75.   What is the guideline for showing stores at different levels of a DFD?

76.   What is a local store? What are the guidelines for showing a local store in a leveled DFD?

77.   Research Project: What is the relationship between the guideline for showing local stores and the concept of object-oriented design? To pursue this further, read Chapters 19 and 20.

78.   What problems might be associated with *developing* a set of leveled DFDs in a top-down fashion (as compared to *reading* an already developed set of DFDs in a top-down fashion)?

79.   What is a control flow? Why is it different from a dataflow?

80.   What is a control process? Why is it different from a normal process in a DFD?

81.   What is a control store? Why is it different from a normal store in a DFD?

82.   Draw a dataflow diagram to model the following recipe for *Fruits de Mer au Riz* (mixed shellfish with rice), taken from *The New York Times 60-Minute Gourmet*, by Pierre Franey (New York: TIMES Books, 1979).

"1.   To begin, prepare and measure out all the ingredients for the rice. To save time, chop an extra cup of onions and 2 extra cloves of garlic for the seafood mixture. Set these aside.

2.   Heat the 2 tablespoons of oil for the rice in a saucepan and add 1/4 cup of onion, green pepper, and 1 clove of garlic and cook until wilted. Add the saffron and cook about 2 minutes longer.

3.   Add the rice, water, salt, and pepper and cover closely. Cook about 17 minutes or just until the rice is tender. As the rice cooks, prepare the seafood. Remember that when the rice is cooked, remove it from the heat. It can stand several minutes, covered, without damage.

4. In a kettle, heat the 1/4 cup oil and add the 1 cup of onions and 2 cloves of garlic. Stir and cook until wilted. Add the red pepper, tomatoes, wine, and oregano. Add salt and pepper. Cover and cook for 10 minutes.

5. Add the clams and mussels to the kettle and cover again. Cook about 3 minutes and add the shrimp, scallops, salt and pepper to taste. Cover and cook about 5 minutes."

83. Draw a dataflow diagram for the following recipe for *Coquille St. Jacques Meuniere* (scallops quick-fried in butter), taken from *The New York Times 60-Minute Gourmet,* by Pierre Franey (New York: TIMES Books, 1979):

"A point to be made a hundred times is organization. Before you cook, chop what has to be chopped and measure what has to be measured. Bring out such pots and pans as are necessary for cooking—in this case two skillets (one for the scallops, one for the tomatoes) and a saucepan (for the potatoes).

1. Empty the scallops into a bowl and add the milk, stirring to coat. Let stand briefly.

2. Place the flour in a dish and add salt and pepper to taste. Blend well. Drain the scallops. Dredge them in flour and add them to a large sieve. Shake to remove excess flour. Scatter them onto a sheet of foil or wax paper so that they do not touch or they might stick together.

3. The scallops must be cooked over high heat without crowding. Heat 3 tablespoons of the oil and 1 tablespoon of butter in a large skillet. When the mixture is quite hot but not smoking, add half of the scallops, shaking and tossing them in the skillet so that they cook quickly and evenly until golden brown on all sides.

4. Use a slotted spoon and transfer the scallops to a hot platter. Add remaining 2 tablespoons of oil to the skillet and when it is quite hot, add the remaining scallops, shaking and tossing them in the skillet as before. When brown, transfer them to the platter with the other scallops. Wipe out the skillet, add the remaining butter and cook until lightly browned or the color of hazelnuts. Sprinkle over the scallops. Then sprinkle scallops with the lemon juice and chopped parsley."

84. Draw a dataflow diagram for the following recipe for *Omelette Pavillon* (omelet with chicken, tomato, and cheese), taken from *The New York Times 60-Minute Gourmet,* by Pierre Franey (New York: TIMES Books, 1979):

"Just before you start cooking the omelets, break three eggs for each omelet into as many individual bowls as needed for the number of omelets to be made. Add salt and pepper to taste and about two teaspoons of heavy cream. You may also beat the eggs to expedite making the omelets.

1. Heat 2 tablespoons of butter in a saucepan and add the flour. Stir with a wire whisk until blended. Add the chicken broth and cook, stirring vigorously with the whisk. Add the cream and bring to the boil. Simmer for about 10 minutes.

2. Meanwhile, heat another tablespoon of butter in a saucepan and add the onion. Cook, stirring, until wilted, and add the tomatoes, thyme, bay leaf, salt and pepper. Simmer, stirring occasionally, about 10 minutes.

3. Heat another tablespoon of butter and add the chicken. Cook, stirring about 30 seconds. Add 3 tablespoons of the cream sauce. Bring to the boil and remove from the heat. Set aside.

4. To the remaining cream sauce add the egg yolk and stir to blend. Add salt and pepper to taste and the grated Swiss cheese. Heat, stirring, just until the cheese melts. Set aside.

5.   Beat the eggs with salt and pepper. Add 6 tablespoons of the tomato sauce. Heat the remaining 3 tablespoons of butter in an omelet pan or a Teflon skillet, and when it is hot, add the eggs. Cook, stirring, until the omelet is set on the bottom but moist and runny in the center. Spoon creamed chicken down on the center of the omelet and add the remaining tomato sauce. Quickly turn the omelet out into a baking dish.

6.   Spoon the remaining cream sauce over the omelet and sprinkle with grated Parmesan cheese. Run the dish under the broiler until golden brown."

10 THE DATA DICTIONARY

In this chapter, you will learn:

1. Why we need a data dictionary in a systems development project.

2. The notation for data dictionary definitions.

3. How a data dictionary should be presented to the user.

4. How to implement a data dictionary.

The second important modeling tool that we will discuss is the *data dictionary.* Though it doesn't have the glamour and graphical appeal of dataflow diagrams, entity-relationship diagrams, and state-transition diagrams, the data dictionary is crucial. Without it, your model of the user's requirements cannot possibly be considered complete; all you will have is a rough sketch, an "artist's rendering" of the system.

The importance of a data dictionary is often lost on many adults, for they have not used a dictionary for 10 or 20 years. Try to think back to your elementary school days, when you were constantly besieged with new words in your schoolwork. Think back also to your foreign language courses, particularly the ones that required you to read books and magazines. Without a dictionary, you would have been lost. The same is true of a data dictionary in systems analysis: without it, you will be lost, and the user won't be sure you have understood the details of the application.

The phrase data dictionary is almost self-defining. The data dictionary is an organized listing of all the data elements that are pertinent to the system, with precise, rigorous definitions so that both user and systems analyst will have a common understanding of all inputs, outputs, components of stores, and intermediate calculations. The data dictionary defines the data elements by doing the following:

- Describing the *meaning* of the flows and stores shown in the dataflow diagrams.

- Describing the *composition* of aggregate packets of data moving along the flows, that is, complex packets (such as a customer address) that can be broken into more elementary items (such as city, state, and postal code).

- Describing the *composition* of packets of data in stores.

- Specifying the relevant *values* and *units* of elementary chunks of information in the dataflows and data stores.

- Describing the details of *relationships* between stores that are highlighted in an entity-relationship diagram. This aspect of the data dictionary will be discussed in more detail in Chapter 12 after we have introduced the entity-relationship notation.

10.1   THE NEED FOR DATA DICTIONARY NOTATION

In most real-world systems that you will work on, the packets, or data elements, will be sufficiently complex that you will need to describe them in terms of other things. Complex data elements are defined in terms of simpler data elements, and simple data elements are defined in terms of the legitimate units and values they can take on.

Think, for example, about the way you would respond to the following question from a Martian (which is the way many users think of systems analysts!) about the meaning of a person's **name**:

Martian: "So what is this thing called a name?"

You (shrugging impatiently): "Well, you know, it's just a name. I mean, like, well, it's what we call each other."

Martian (puzzled): "Does that mean you can call them something different when you're angry than when you're happy?"

You (slightly amazed at the ignorance of this alien): "No, of course not. A name is the same all the time. A person's name is what we use to distinguish him or her from other people."

Martian (suddenly understanding): "Ahh, now I understand. We do the same thing on my planet. My name is 3.141592653589793238462643."

You (incredulous): "But that's a number, not a name."

Martian: "And a very good name it is, too. I'm proud of it. Nobody has anything close."

You: "But what about your first name? Or is your first name 3, and your last name 1415926535?"

Martian: "What's this about first name and last name? I don't understand. I have only one name, and it's always the same."

You: "Well, that's not the way it works here. We have a first name, and a last name, and sometimes we have a middle name too."

Martian: "Does that mean you could be called 23 45 99?"

You: "No, we don't allow numbers in our names. You can only use the alphabetic characters A through Z."

As you can imagine, the conversation could continue for a very long time. You might think the example is contrived, because we rarely run into Martians who have no concept of the meaning of a name. But it is not too far from the discussions that take place (or should take place) between a systems analyst and a user, in which the following questions might be raised:

- Must everyone have a first name? What about the character "Mr. T" on the popular TV series, "The A Team"?

- What about punctuation characters in a person's last name, for example, "D'Arcy"?

- Are abbreviated middle names allowed, for example, "John X James"?

- Is there a *minimal* length required of a person's name? For example, is the name "X Y" legal? (One could imagine that it would wreak havoc with many computer systems throughout the country, but is there any legal/business reason why a person couldn't give himself a first name of X and a last name of Y?)

- How should we treat the suffixes that sometimes follow a last name? For example, the name "John Jones, Jr." is presumably legitimate, but is the Jr. to be considered part of the last name or a special new category? And if it is a new category, shouldn't we allow numeric digits, too; for example, Sam Smith 3rd?

Note, by the way, that none of these questions has anything to do with the way we will eventually store the information on a computer; we are simply trying to determine, as a matter of business policy, what constitutes a valid name.[1]

---

1 On the other hand, it is likely that the business policy presently in place has been strongly influenced by

As you can imagine, it gets rather tedious describing the composition of data elements in a rambling narrative form. We need a concise, compact notation, just as a standard dictionary like Webster's has a compact, concise notation for defining the meaning of ordinary words.

10.2   DATA DICTIONARY NOTATION

There are many common notational schemes used by systems analyst. The one shown below is among the more common, and it uses a number of simple symbols:

=	is composed of
+	and
()	optional (may be present or absent)
{}	iteration
[]	select one of several alternative choices
**	comment
@	identifier (key field) for a store
|	separates alternative choices in the [] construct

As an example, we might define **name** for our friendly Martian as follows:

name =   **courtesy-title + first-name + (middle-name) + last-name**

courtesy-title =   [Mr. | Miss | Mrs. | Ms. | Dr. | Professor]

first-name =   {**legal-character**}

middle-name =   {**legal-character**}

last-name =   {**legal-character**}

legal-character = [A-Z|a-z|0-9|'|-| |]

As you can see, the symbols look rather mathematical; you may be worried that it's far too complicated to understand. As we will soon see, though, the notation is quite easy to read. The experience of several thousands of DP projects and several tens of thousands of users has shown us that the notation is also quite understandable to almost all users *if it is presented properly;* we will discuss this in Section 10.3.

---

1 (cont.) the computer systems that the organization has been using for the past 30 years. Fifty years ago, someone might have been considered eccentric if he decided to call himself "Fre5d Smi7th" but it probably would have been accepted by most organizations, because names were transcribed onto pieces of paper by human hands. Early computer systems (and most of the ones in place today) have a lot more trouble with such nonstandard names.

10.2.1   Definitions

A *definition* of a data element is introduced with the symbol "="; in this context, the "=" is read as "is defined as," or "is composed of," or simply "means." Thus, the notation

A = B + C

could be read in any of the following ways:

- Whenever we say **A**, we mean a **B** and a **C**

- **A** is composed of **B** and **C**

- **A** is defined as **B** and **C**

To completely define a data element, our definition will include the following:

- The *meaning* of the data element within the context of this user's application. This is usually provided as a comment, using the "*" notation.

- The *composition* of the data element, if it is composed of meaningful elementary components.

- The *values* that the data element can take on, if it is an elementary data element that cannot be decomposed any further.

Thus, if we were building a medical system that kept track of patients, we might define the terms **weight** and **height** in the following way:

weight =   * patient's weight upon admission to the hospital*
                * units: kilograms; range: 1-200*

height =   * patient's height upon admission to the hospital*
                * units: centimeters; range: 20-200*

Note that we have described the relevant *units* and the relevant *range* within matching "*" characters. Again, this is a notational convention that many organizations find convenient, but it can be changed if necessary.

In addition to the units and range, you may also need to specify the accuracy or precision with which the data element is measured. For a data element like **price,** for example, it is important to indicate whether the values will be expressed in whole dollars, to the nearest penny, and so on. And in many engineering and scientific applications, it is important to indicate the number of significant digits in the value of data elements.

10.2.2   Elementary Data Elements

Elementary data elements are those for which there is no meaningful decomposition in the context of the user's environment. This is often a matter of interpretation and one that you must explore carefully with the user. For example, we have seen in the discussion above that the term **name** could be decomposed into **last-name**, **first-name**, **middle-name**, and **courtesy-title**. But perhaps in some user environments no such decomposition is necessary, relevant, or even meaningful (i.e.,*where the terms* **last-name**, *etc., have no meaning to the user).*

When we have identified elementary data items, they must be entered in the data dictionary. As indicated above, the data dictionary should provide a brief narrative comment, enclosed within "*" characters, describing the *meaning* of the term within the user's context. Of course, there will be some terms that are self-defining, that is, terms whose meaning is universally the same for all information systems, or where the systems analyst might agree that no further elaboration is necessary. For example, the following might be considered self-defining terms in a system that maintains information about people:

> **current-height**
> **current-weight**
> **date-of-birth**
> **sex**
> **home-phone-number**

In these cases, no narrative comment is necessary; many systems analysts will use the notation "**" to indicate a "null comment" when the data element is self-defining. However, it *is* important to specify the values and units of measure that the elementary data item can take on. For example:

current-height =
> **
> "units: pounds; range: 1-400*

current-weight =
> **
> *units: inches; range: 1-96*

date-of-birth =
> **
> *units: days since Jan 1, 1900; range: 0-36500*

sex   =
> *values: [M | F]*

10.2.3   Optional Data Elements

An optional data element, as the phrase implies, is one that may or may not be present as a component of a composite data element. There are many examples of optional data elements in information systems:

- A customer's name may or may not include a middle name.

- A customer's street address may or may not include such secondary information as an apartment number.

- A customer's order may contain a billing address, a shipping address, or possibly both.

Situations like the last one must be carefully verified with the user and must be accurately documented in the data dictionary. For example, the notation

customer-address = (shipping-address) + (billing-address)

means, quite literally, that the customer-address might consist of:

- just a shipping-address

or

- just a billing-address

or

- a shipping-address *and* a billing-address

or

- *neither* a shipping-address *nor* a billing-address

This last possibility is rather dubious. It is far more likely that the user *really* means that the customer-address must consist of a shipping-address *or* a billing-address *or both*. This could be expressed in the following way:

**customer-address =   [shipping-address | billing-address |
shipping-address + billing-address]**

One could also argue that, in a mail-order business, one *always* needs a shipping address to where the customer's order will be sent; a separate billing address (e.g., the customer's accounting department) is optional. Thus, it is possible that the user's *real* business policy is better expressed by

customer-address =   shipping-address + (billing-address)

But of course the only way to know this is to ask the user and to carefully explain the implications of the different notations shown above.[2]

---

2 There is one possibility that might explain the absence of both shipping address and billing address in a customer order: the walk-in customer who wishes to purchase an item and carry it away with him. It is likely that we would want to explicitly identify such a customer (by defining a new data element called **walk-in** that could have a value of true or false) because (1) walk-in customers may need to be treated differently (for example, their orders won't have any shipping charges), and (2) it's a good way to double-check and ensure that the missing **shipping-address** or **billing-address** was not a mistake.

10.2.4   Iteration

The iteration notation is used to indicate the *repeated* occurrence of a component of a data element. It is read as "zero or more occurrences of." Thus, the notation

order = customer-name + shipping-address + { item }

means that an order must *always* contain a customer-name, and must *always* contain a shipping-address, and will also contain *zero or more occurrences of* an **item**. Thus, we may be dealing with a customer who places an order involving only one item or two items, or someone on a shopping binge who decides to order 397 different items.[3]

In many real-world situations, the user will want to specify upper and lower limits to the iteration. For instance, in the example above, the user will probably point out that it does not make sense for a customer to place an order with zero items; there must be at least one item in the order. And the user may want to specify an upper limit; perhaps 10 items is the most that will be allowed. We can indicate upper and lower limits in the following way:

order = customer-name + shipping-address + 1{item}10

It's okay to specify *just* a lower limit, or *just* an upper limit, or *both* or *neither*. Thus, all of the following are allowable:

a = 1{b}

a = {b}10

a = 1{b}10

a = {b}

10.2.5   Selection

The *selection* notation indicates that a data element consists of exactly *one* of a set of alternative choices. The choices are enclosed by the square brackets "[" and "]" and separated by the vertical bar "|" character. Typical examples are:

sex = [Male | Female]

---

3 Keep in mind once again that we are defining the intrinsic *business* meaning of a data element without regard to the technology that will eventually be used to implement it. Eventually, for example, our systems designers are likely to ask for a reasonable upper limit on the number of different items that can be contained in a single order. "In order to make things work efficiently with our SUPERWHIZ database management system, we'll have to restrict the number of items to 64. It's unlikely that anyone would want to order more than 64 different items anyway, and if they do, they can simply place multiple orders." And the user may have his own limitations, based on the paper forms or printed reports that he deals with; this is part of the *user implementation model*, which we will discuss in Chapter 21.

customer-type = [Government | Industry | University | Other]

It is important to review the selection choices with the user to ensure that all possibilities have been identified. In the last example, the user might tend to concentrate her or his attention on the "government," "industry" and "university" customers, and might require some prodding to remember that some customers fall into the "none of the above" category.

10.2.6 Aliases

An *alias*, as the term implies, is an alternative name for a data element. It is a common occurrence when dealing with a diverse group of users, often in different departments or different geographical locations (and sometimes with different nationalities and different languages), who insist on using different names to mean the same thing. The alias is included in the data dictionary for completeness, and it is cross-referenced to the primary or official data name. For example:

client   =
                 alias for customer

Note that the definition of client does *not* show the composition (i.e., it does not show that a client consists of a name, address, telephone number, etc.). All this detail should be provided *only* for the primary data name, in order to minimize the redundancy in the model.[4]

Even though the data dictionary correctly cross-references the aliases to the primary data name, your should avoid using aliases whenever possible. This is because the data names are usually first seen, and are most visible to all users, on the dataflow diagrams, *where it may not be obvious that* **customer***and* **client***are aliases for one another*. It is far better, if at all possible, to get the users to agree on one common name.[5]

10.3 SHOWING THE DATA DICTIONARY TO THE USER

The data dictionary is created by the systems analyst during the development of the system model, but the user must be capable of reading and understanding the data dictionary in order to verify the model. This raises some obvious questions:

•   Will the users be able to understand the data dictionary notation?

---

4 You may wish to ignore this advice if you are using a computerized data dictionary package that can manage and control the redundancy; however, this is fairly uncommon. The crucial thing to remember is that if we change the definition of a primary data element (e.g., if we decide that the definition of a customer should no longer include the phone-number) then the change must apply to all the aliases as well.

5 An alternative is to annotate the flow *on the dataflow diagram* to indicate that it is an alias for something else; an asterisk, for example, could be appended to the end of alias names. For example, the notation **client*** could be used to indicate that client is an alias for something else. But even this is cumbersome.

- How should the users verify that the dictionary is complete and correct?

- How is the dictionary created?

The question of user acceptance of the dictionary notation is a "red herring" in most cases. Yes, the dictionary notation looks somewhat mathematical; but, as we have seen, the number of symbols that the user has to learn are very few. Users are accustomed to a variety of formal notations in their work and personal life; consider, for example, the notation for musical scores, which is far more complex.

Figure 10.1: **Musical score notation**

Similarly, the notation for bridge, chess, and a variety of other activities is at least as complex as that of the data dictionary notation shown in this chapter.

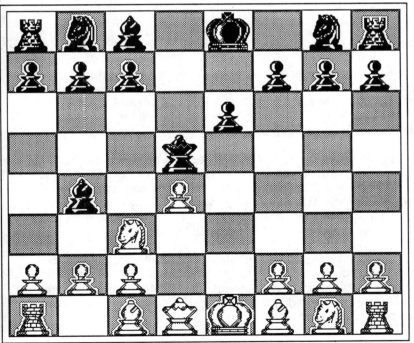
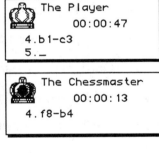

Figure 10.2: **Chess notation**

The question of user verification of the data dictionary usually leads to this question: "Should the users read through the entire dictionary, item by item, to ensure that it is correct?" It is difficult to imagine that any user would be willing to do this! It is more likely that the user will verify the correctness of the data dictionary *in conjunction with the dataflow diagram, entity-relationship diagram, state-transition diagram, or process specification* that he or she is reading.

There are a number of "correctness" issues that the systems analyst can carry out on his own, without the assistance of the user: he can ensure that the dictionary is complete, consistent, and non-contradictory. Thus, he can examine the dictionary on his own and ask the following questions:

- Has every flow on the dataflow diagram been defined in the data diction-ary?

- Have all the components of composite data elements been defined?

- Has any data element been defined more than once?

- Has the correct notation been used for all data dictionary definitions?

- Are there any data elements in the data dictionary that are *not* referenced in the dataflow diagrams, entity-relationship diagrams, or state-transition diagrams?

10.4   IMPLEMENTATION OF THE DATA DICTIONARY

On a medium- or large-sized system, the data dictionary can represent a formidable amount of work. It is not uncommon to see a data dictionary with several thousand entries, and even a relatively simple system will have several hundred entries. Thus, some thought must be given to the way the dictionary will be developed, or the task is likely to overwhelm the systems analyst.

The easiest approach is to make use of an automated (computerized) facility to enter dictionary definitions, check them for completeness and consistency, and produce appropriate reports. If your organization is using any modern database management system (e.g., IMS, ADABAS, TOTAL, IDMS), a dictionary facility is already available. In this case, you should take advantage of the facility and use it to build your data dictionary. However, beware of the following potential limitations:

- You may be forced to limit your data names to a certain length (e.g., 15 or 32 characters). This probably won't be a major problem, but you may find that your user may *insist* on a name such as **destination-of-customer-shipment** and that your data dictionary package forces you to abbreviate the name to **dest-of-cust-ship**.

- Other artificial limitations may be placed on the name. For example, the hyphen character "-" may not be allowed, and you may be forced to use the underscore "_" character instead. Or you may be forced to prefix (or suffix) all your names with a project code indicating the name of the systems development project, leading to such names as

acct.pay.GHZ345P14.vendor_phone_number.

- You may be forced to assign *physical* attributes (e.g., the number of bytes, or blocks of disk storage, or such data representations as packed decimal) to an item of data, even though it is not a matter of user policy. The data dictionary discussed in this chapter should be an *analysis* dictionary and should not require unnecessary or irrelevant implementation decisions.

Some systems analysts are also beginning to use automated toolkit packages that include graphic facilities for dataflow diagrams, and the like, *as well as* data dictionary capabilities. Again, if such a facility exists, you should make use of it. Automated toolkits are discussed in more detail in Appendix A.

If you have no automated facility for building the data dictionary, you should at least be able to use a conventional word-processing system to build a text file of data dictionary definitions. Or, if you have access to a personal computer, you can use any of the common file-management and database management programs (e.g., dBASE-III, Rbase-5000, PFS-File, Microsoft File on the Apple Macintosh) to construct and manage your data dictionary.

Only in the most extreme case should you resort to a manual data dictionary, that is, separate, 3-by-5 index cards for each dictionary entry. This was often necessary in the 1970s and even in the 1980s; despite the popularity of personal computers and word processing facilities, it is discouraging to see how many organizations have kept their programmers and systems analysts in the Dark Ages. The cobbler's children, as the saying goes, are usually the last to get shoes. But today, it is unforgivable; if you are working on a project where you do not have access to a data dictionary package *or* an automated analyst's toolkit *or* a personal computer *or* a word processing system, then you should (1) quit and find a better job, or (2) get your own personal computer, or (3) both of the above.

10.5   SUMMARY

Building a data dictionary is one of the more tedious, time-consuming aspects of systems analysis. But it is also one of the more important aspects: without a formal dictionary that defines the meaning of all the terms, there can be no hope for precision.

In the next chapter, we will see how to use the data dictionary and the dataflow diagram to build *process specifications* for each of the bottom-level processes.

REFERENCES

1. J.D. Lomax, *Data Dictionary Systems.* Rochelle Park, N.J.: NCC Publications, 1977.

2. Tom DeMarco, *Structured Analysis and Systems Specification*. New York: YOURDON Press, 1979.

3. D. Kroenke, *Database Processing*. Chicago: Science Research Associates, 1977.

4. Shaku Atre, *Data Base: Structured Techniques for Design, Performance, and Management*. New York: Wiley, 1980.

QUESTIONS AND EXERCISES

1. Give a definition of data dictionary.

2. Why is a data dictionary important in systems analysis?

3. What information does a data dictionary provide about a data element?

4. What is the meaning of the "=" notation in a data dictionary?

5. What is the meaning of the "+" notation in a data dictionary?

6. What is the meaning of the "()" notation in a data dictionary?

7. What is the meaning of the "{}" notation in a data dictionary?

8. What is the meaning of the "[| |]" notation in a data dictionary?

9. Do you think the users you work with can understand the standard data diction-ary notation provided in this chapter? If not, can you suggest an alternative?

10. Give an example of an elementary data item.

11. Give three examples of optional data elements.

12. What are the possible meanings of the following:

     (a)   **address = (city) + (state)**

     (b)   **address = street-address + city + (state) + (zipcode)**

13. Give an example of the use of the iteration {} notation.

14. What is the meaning of each of the following notations:

     (a)   a = 1{b}
     (b)   a = {b}10
     (c)   a = 1{b}10
     (d)   a = 10{b}10

15. Does it make sense to have an **order** defined in the following way?

order = customer-name + shipping-address + 6{item}

Why or why not?

16. Give an example of the selection ("[ ] ") construct.

17. What is the meaning of an alias in a data dictionary?

18. Why should the use of aliases be minimized wherever possible?

19. What kind of annotation can be used on a DFD to indicate that a data element is an alias?

20. What are the three major issues when a user looks at a data dictionary?

21. Do you think the users in your organization will be able to understand data dictionary notation?

22. Do you think that the data dictionary notation shown in this chapter is more complex or less complex than musical notation?

23. What are the three error-checking activities that the systems analyst can carry out on a data dictionary *without* the user?

24. What are the likely limitations of an automated data dictionary package?

25. Give a data dictionary definition of **customer-name** based on the following verbal specification from a user: "When we record a customer's name, we're very careful to include a courtesy title. This can be either "Mr.," "Miss," "Ms.," "Mrs.," or "Dr." (There are lots of other titles like "Professor,"" "Sir," etc., but we don't bother with them.) Every one of our customers has a first name, but we allow a single initial if they prefer. Middle names are optional. And of course, the last name is required; we allow a pretty broad range of last names, including names that have hyphens ("Smith-Frisby," for example) and apostrophes ("D'Arcy") and so forth. We even allow an optional suffix, to allow for things like "Tom Smith, Jr." or "Harvey Shmrdlu 3rd."

26. What is wrong with the following data dictionary definitions:

    (a)   a = b c d

    (b)   a = b + + c

    (c)   a = {b

    (d)   a = 4{b}3

    (e)   a = {x)

(f) $x = ((y))$

(g) $p = 4\{6\{y\}8\}6$

27.   In the hospital example of Section 9.2, what are the implications of the definition of **height** and **weight**? Comment: It would imply that we are only measuring in integral units and are not keeping track of fractional centimeters, and so on.

28.   Write a data dictionary definition of the information contained on your driver's license. If you don't have a driver's license, find a friend who does.

29.   Write a data dictionary definition of the information contained on a typical bank credit card (e.g., MasterCard or Visa).

30.   Write a data dictionary definition of the information contained in a passport.

31.   Write a data dictionary definition of the information contained in a lottery ticket.

11 PROCESS SPECIFICATIONS

Our little systems have their day.
Alfred, Lord Tennyson
In Memoriam,1850

In this chapter, you will learn:

1. How to write structured English process specifications.

2. How to write process specifications with pre/post conditions.

3. How to use decision tables to write process specifications.

4. When to use alternative specification tools.

In this chapter, we explore the *process specification*, the description of what's happening inside each bottom-level, primitive bubble in a dataflow diagram. Various textbooks, including [DeMarco, 1978], [Gane and Sarson, 1977], and [Weinberg, 1978] also use the term minispec (as an abbreviation for miniature specification) as an alternative for process specification. Regardless of its name, the purpose of a process specification is quite straightforward: it defines what must be done in order to transform inputs into outputs. It is a detailed description of the user's business policy that each bubble carries out.

As we will see in this chapter, there is a variety of tools that we can use to produce a process specification: decision tables, structured English, pre/post conditions, flowcharts, Nassi-Shneiderman diagrams, and so on. While most systems analysts favor structured English, you should remember that *any* method can be used, as long as it satisfies two crucial requirements:

- *The process specification must be expressed in a form that can be verified by the user and the systems analyst.* It is precisely for this reason that we avoid narrative English as a specification tool: it is notoriously ambiguous, especially when describing alternative actions (decisions) and repetitive actions (loops). By its nature, it also tends to cause great confusion when expressing compound Boolean conditions (i.e., combinations of the Boolean operators AND, OR, and NOT).

- *The process specification must be expressed in a form that can be effectively communicated to the various audiences involved.* While it will typically be the systems analyst who *writes* the process specification, it will usually be a diverse audience of users, managers, auditors, quality assurance personnel, and others who must read the process specification. A process specification could perhaps be expressed in predicate calculus, or in Pascal, or in a formal diagramming approach such as Higher Order Software's USE-IT[1]; but if the user community refuses to look at such specifications, they are worthless. The same may turn out to be true of decision tables, structured English or other specification tools, too; it is very much a function of the personality, background, and attitude of the users you deal with.

As mentioned above, most systems analysts use structured English as their preferred method of writing process specifications. It is perhaps more important to point out that most systems analysts, and most organizations, use *one* tool for writing *all* of their specifications.[2] This is, in my opinion, a major mistake: you should feel free to use a *combination* of specification tools, depending on (a) the user's preference, (b) your own preferences, and (c) the idiosyncratic nature of the various processes.

A good process specification tool should have a third characteristic, too: it should not impose (or imply) arbitrary design and implementation decisions. This is often very difficult, because the user, on whom we must depend for a statement of the "policy" carried out by each bubble in the DFD, is prone to describe the policy *in terms of the way he carries it out today.* It is your job as a systems analyst to distill from this presentation the essence of *what* the policy is, not *how* the policy is carried out today.

Consider the following example: the systems analyst is discussing a small fragment of a system, as illustrated by Figure 11.1. He wants to develop a process specification for the bubble labeled **COMPUTE WIDGET FACTOR**. Since the systems analyst is entirely unfamiliar with the application, he has interviewed the user and has learned that the policy for computing widget factors for any value of the input data element, **x**, is as follows:

---

1 For more information on USE-IT, see James Martin and Carma McClure's *Structured Techniques for Computing.* (Englewood Cliffs, N.J.: Prentice-Hall, 1986).

2 This is often caused by the introduction of an entire set of structured analysis *standards* in the organization. While the standards are an admirable effort to combat sloth, ignorance, and total anarchy, they often go too far and prescribe a rigidly regimented solution to all problems. As a common saying goes, "If your only tool is a hammer, all the world looks like a nail."

1. The widget factor is not produced as the result of a single calculation. In fact, we have to begin by making a guess. The user has told us that he is particularly fond of 14 as a first guess.

2. Then we make another guess. We do this by dividing our current guess into the number, **x**, that we started with.

3. We then take the result of this calculation and subtract it from the current guess.

4. We then take the result of step 3, and divide it in half. This becomes our new guess.

5. If the new guess and the current guess are pretty close to each other, say, within 0.0001, then we can stop; the new guess is the **widget factor**. Otherwise, go back to step 2 and do it all over again.

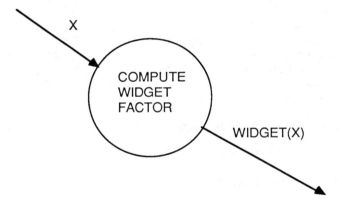

Figure 11.1: **Computation of widget factor**

You might argue that this process specification is difficult to read and understand because it is written in narrative English. Indeed, the following description is much more compact (note that the vertical bars "|" in the **UNTIL** clause mean "absolute value of" the enclosed expression):

$$\text{widget-factor}_0 = 14$$

REPEAT for $N = 0$ in steps of 1

$$\text{widget-factor}_{N+1} = (\text{widget-factor}_N - (X/\text{widget-factor}_N))/2$$

UNTIL $|\text{widget-factor}_{N+1} - \text{widget-factor}_N| < 0.0001$

However, even this is flawed: it describes the policy in terms of a particular procedural implementation. The policy, as may have been evident (but equally likely, may *not* have been evident), is the Newton-Raphson algorithm for approximating a square root.[3] The following process specification describes the same policy, but leaves the designer/programmer complete freedom to choose her own algorithm:

> PRECONDITION
> There exists a number **X** that is nonnegative.

> POSTCONDITION
> A **widget-factor** is produced such that
> **X = widget-factor * widget-factor**

The programmer may indeed choose to use the user's algorithm for calculating the square root, but she should not be constrained to do so by the systems analyst. Indeed, the extravagant attention to the procedural algorithm, especially in the first version of the specification above, entirely obscured what the process really was!

Before we explore the various process specification tools, we should emphasize one point: process specifications are *only* developed for the *bottom-level* processes in a leveled set of dataflow diagrams. As we can see in Figure 11.2, all the higher-level processes are defined by the next lower-level network of processes. In other words, the process specification for a higher-level bubble *is* the lower-level DFD. To write an additional process specification in structured English would not only be superfluous, it would be redundant; that is, it would create a specification that would be more difficult to keep up to date.[4]

We will concentrate on three major process specification tools in this chapter:

- Structured English

- Pre/post conditions

- Decision tables

We will also comment briefly on a number of other less commonly used specification tools: narrative English, flowcharts, and Nassi–Shneiderman diagrams.

11.1   STRUCTURED ENGLISH

Structured English, as the name implies, is "English with structure." That is, it is a subset of the full English language with some major restrictions on the kind of

---

3 Try the algorithm out on a couple of test cases. You'll find that it converges fairly quickly.

4 Notwithstanding this warning, we should point out that you will sometimes be *required*, as a systems analyst, to produce a written process specification for higher-level processes. This will happen if the user decides that he wants to show the specification to his boss and is concerned that the boss won't tolerate the idea of leveled DFDs. Thus, the user will say to you, "Look, I know that you don't need a process specification for these top-level bubbles, but I'd appreciate it if you would write them anyway so that the boss can understand what the system is all about." You'll have to deal with this problem with the same diplomatic skills that you use to solve all other political problems in your project.

sentences that can be used and the manner in which sentences can be put together. It is also known by such names as PDL (for program design language) and PSL (for problem statement language or problem specification language). Its purpose is to strike a reasonable balance between the precision of a formal programming language and the casual informality and readability of the English language.

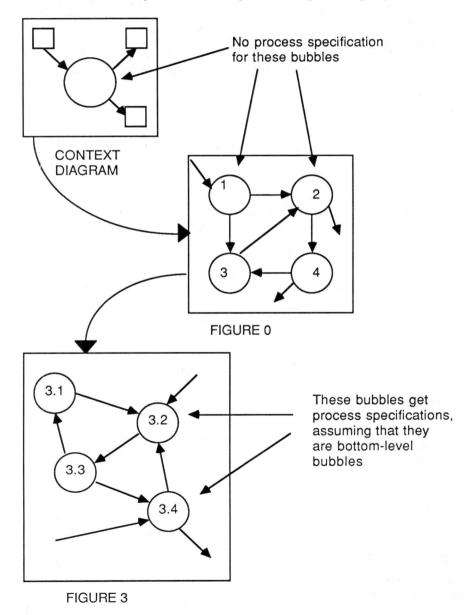

Figure 11.2: **Process specifications for bottom-level bubbles**

A *sentence* in structured English may consist of an algebraic equation, for example,

$$X = (Y*Z)/(Q+14)$$

or a simple imperative sentence consisting of a verb and an object. Note that this sentence does not have the semicolon that terminates a programming statement in many different programming languages; it may or may not terminate with a period ("."), depending on your taste in such things. Also, note that sentences describing computations can be prefixed with the verbs COMPUTE, ADD, SET, and so on; thus, we could have written the above example as

$$COMPUTE\ X = (Y*Z)/(Q+14)$$

and we can have structured English computations like the following ones:

        SET TAX-RATE TO 13
        ADD 3 TO X
        MULTIPLY UNIT-PRICE BY QUANTITY
        DIVIDE CURRENT-ASSETS BY CURRENT-LIABILITIES.

Verbs should be chosen from a small set of action-oriented verbs such as:

        GET (or ACCEPT or READ)
        PUT (or DISPLAY or WRITE)
        FIND (or SEARCH or LOCATE)
        ADD
        SUBTRACT
        MULTIPLY
        DIVIDE
        COMPUTE
        DELETE
        FIND
        VALIDATE
        MOVE
        REPLACE
        SET
        SORT

Most organizations find that 40 to 50 verbs are sufficient to describe any policy in any process specification.

Objects (the subject of the simple imperative sentences) should consist only of data elements that have been defined in the data dictionary or local terms. Local terms are terms (words) that are explicitly defined within an individual process specification; they are only known, relevant, and meaningful within that process specification. A typical example of a local term is an intermediate calculation, which is used to produce the final output of the process.[5] For example, the structured English process specification below examines a series of order records in an ORDERS store to compute a daily total:

daily-total = 0
DO WHILE there are more **orders** in **ORDERS** with **Invoice-date** = today's date
    READ next **order** in **ORDERS** with **Invoice-date** = today's date
    DISPLAY to Accounting **invoice-number**, **customer-name**,
  total-amount
    daily-total = daily-total + **total-amount**
ENDDO
DISPLAY to Accounting daily-total

Finally, structured English allows sentences to be combined in a few limited ways; these are taken from the familiar structured programming constructs.[6]

- The **IF-THEN-ELSE** construct is used to describe alternative sentences that are to be carried out based on the result of a binary decision. The **IF-THEN-ELSE** construct can take either of the following two forms:

  IF condition-1
    sentence-1
  ENDIF

  or

  IF condition-1
    sentence-1
  ELSE
    sentence-2
  ENDIF

  Thus, the systems analyst may write:

  IF customer lives in New York
    add **customer** to **MARKETING-PROSPECTS**
  ENDIF

  or

  IF customer-age greater than 65

---

5 Local terms are defined within the process specification where they occur and are *not* defined in the data dictionary. They are often *derived* (directly calculated) from terms that are already in the data dictionary, so it would be redundant to add the local terms. Also, by definition, the local terms are only known within a *local* context (i.e., *inside* a bubble in a dataflow diagram). They should not appear as a flow on the DFD, and they are usually not part of the normal vocabulary of application-oriented words used by the user.

6 If you are not familiar with structured programming, consult any of the standard texts on the subject, or see some of the early papers on the subject collected in [Yourdon, 1979].

```
    set billing-rate to senior-citizen-rate
ELSE
    set billing-rate to normal-rate
ENDIF
```

- The **CASE** construct is used to describe alternative sentences to be carried out based on the results of a multivalued decision (as compared to the *binary* decision that takes place with an **IF-THEN** construct). The CASE construct takes the general form:

```
DO  CASE
CASE variable = value-1
   sentence-1
   .
   .
   .

CASE variable = value-n
   sentence-n
OTHERWISE
   sentence-n+1
ENDCASE
```

Thus, the systems analyst might write:

```
DO  CASE
CASE customer-age < 13
   set billing-rate to child-rate
CASE customer-age > 12 and customer-age < 20
   set billing-rate to teenage-rate
CASE   customer-age > 19  and customer-age < 65
   set billing-rate to adult-rate
OTHERWISE
   set billing-rate to senior-citizen-rate
END  CASE
```

Or, as another example, consider the following portion of a structured English process specification:

```
DO  CASE
CASE state = "NY"
   set salestax to 0.0825
CASE state = "NJ"
   set salestax to 0.07
CASE state = "CA"
   set salestax to 0.05
OTHERWISE
   set salestax to 0
END  CASE
```

Note that the **OTHERWISE** clause is often used to catch situations that the user forgets to specify and that the systems analyst forgets to ask about; it will often prompt some discussions between user and systems analyst that would otherwise not take place until after the system had been put in operation. Consider the following example:

DO CASE
CASE payment-type = "cash"
  set **discount-rate** to 0.05
CASE payment-type = "credit-card"
  set **discount-rate** to 0.01
OTHERWISE
  set **discount-rate** to 0
END CASE

The user might question this process specification and ask why the systems analyst included the **OTHERWISE** clause; the systems analyst might respond by asking about payments by check, traveler's check, gold coins, and barter.

The **DO-WHILE** construct is used to describe a sentence that is to be carried out repetitively until some Boolean condition is true. It takes the general form:

DO WHILE condition-1
  sentence-1
ENDDO

The test ("condition-1" in the example above) is made *before* sentence-1 is carried out; thus, if the condition is not satisfied, it is possible that sentence-1 will be carried out *zero* times.

For example, the systems analyst might write:

DO WHILE there are more items in the customer-order
        extended-price = unit-price*unit-quantity
ENDDO

Many organizations include another structure that carries out a specified sentence *at least once* before making a test to see if it should be repeated. This variation, usually known as the **REPEAT-UNTIL** construct, has the following form:

REPEAT
  sentence-1
UNTIL condition-1

Compound sentences can be built from combinations of simple sentences and the simple structures presented above, according to the following rules:

1. A linear sequence of simple sentences is equivalent (structurally) to a simple sentence. Thus, the sequence

        sentence-1
        sentence-2
        .
        .
        .
        sentence-n

    is structurally equivalent to a single, simple sentence *and can be substituted wherever a simple sentence is expected.* This allows us to build structures like this:

        IF condition-1
              sentence-1
              sentence-2
        ELSE
              sentence-3
              sentence-4
              sentence-5
        ENDIF

    or

        DO WHILE condition-1
              sentence-1
              sentence-2
              sentence-3
        ENDDO

2. A simple **IF-THEN-ELSE** construct is considered structurally equivalent to a single, simple sentence. This allows **IF-THEN-ELSE** structures to be *nested* within other **IF-THEN-ELSE** structures, or within **DO-WHILE** structures, or within **CASE** structures. For example:

        IF condition-1
              sentence-1
              IF condition-2
                    sentence-2
                    sentence-3
              ELSE
                    sentence-4
                    sentence-5
              ENDIF
              sentence-6
        ELSE

```
            sentence-7
        IF condition-3
                sentence-8
        ENDIF
            sentence-9
    ENDIF
```

3. A simple **DO-WHILE** structure is considered structurally equivalent to a simple, single sentence. This allows **DO-WHILE** structures to be nested within other **DO-WHILE** structures, or within **IF-THEN-ELSE** structures, or within **CASE** structures. Thus, we might have a structured English specification of the following nature:

```
    grand-total = 0
    DO WHILE there are more orders to process
        invoice-total = 0
        READ next order from ORDERS
        DO WHILE there are more items in the order
            invoice-total = invoice-total + item-amount
        ENDDO
        DISPLAY invoice-number, invoice-total
        grand-total = grand-total + invoice-total
    ENDDO
    DISPLAY grand-total
```

4. A simple **CASE** structure is considered structurally equivalent to a simple, single sentence. This allows **CASE** structures to be nested within other **CASE** structures, or within **IF-THEN-ELSE** structures, or within **DO-WHILE** structures.

As you can see, this allows us to construct arbitrarily complex descriptions of business policy, while maintaining strict control over the vocabulary, organization and structure of the description. However, this arbitrary complexity is also the major disadvantage of structured English: if the systems analyst composes a process specification that is too complex for the user to understand and verify, he has failed. This can usually be prevented by adhering to the following three guidelines:

1. Restrict the structured English process specification to a single page of text (e.g., 8-by-11 sheet of paper, 66 lines of text on a word processing system). If the specification takes more than one page, then the systems analyst (with the help of the user) should think of an entirely different way of formulating the policy (i.e., pick a different, simpler algorithm). If that cannot be done, then it is possible that the process itself (i.e., the bubble within the DFD) is too complex and should be split into a network of lower-level, simpler processes.

2. Don't allow more than three levels of nesting (i.e., three levels of nested **IF-THEN-ELSE** structures, or three levels of **CASE** structures, etc.). Particularly in the case of **IF-THEN-ELSE** structures, more than even two

levels of nesting is a strong indication that a *decision table* specification would be preferable; this is discussed in Section 11.3.

3.   Avoid confusion about levels of nesting by using indentation, as shown in the examples above. This can be accomplished and controlled very easily if you are using any kind of automated support to develop the process specifications (even something as simple as a standard word processing system). If the process specifications are being typed manually by a clerical person who is not familiar with structured programming or structured analysis, you will have to explain very carefully what kind of indentation you want; you should also proofread the resulting text very carefully to see if it is correct.

Many systems analysts ask whether the user can be expected to read and understand a process specification written in structured English. My experience has been almost uniformly positive in this area: users *can* read structured English, with the following provisos:

1.   You will have to walk through the document once or twice to ensure that they understand the format and the various constructs. On the first reading, it may well look like a legal document, especially if you have "highlighted" the **IF-THEN-ELSE** construct, and the like.

2.   Don't refer to the process specification as "structured English." If necessary, refer to it as "a formal description of your business policy for carrying out this activity."

3.   Pay careful attention to the overall format and layout of the document; the indentation of nested blocks of logic is especially important. Some users prefer an outline style of indentation, that is, where indented levels are numbered 1.1, 1.1.1, 1.1.1.1, and so on.

Several examples of structured English process specifications are shown in the case study in Appendix F.

11.2   PRE/POST CONDITIONS

Pre/post conditions is a convenient way of describing the *function* that must be carried out by a process, without saying very much at all about the *algorithm* or *procedure* that will be used. It is a particularly useful approach when:

(1)   The user has a tendency to express the policy carried out by a bubble in terms of a particular, idiosyncratic algorithm that he or she has been using for decades.

(2)   The systems analyst is reasonably sure that there are *many* different algorithms that could be used.

(3)   The systems analyst wants to let the programmer explore several such algorithms, but does not want to get involved in such details himself, and *especially* does not want to engage in arguments with the user about the relative merits of such algorithms.

An example of a process specification written with the pre/post condition approach is shown in Figure 11.3:

PROCESS SPECIFICATION 3.5: COMPUTE SALES TAX

Precondition 1
     SALE-DATA occurs with **ITEM-TYPE** matching an
     ITEM-CATEGORY in **TAX-CATEGORIES**
Postcondition 1
     SALES-TAX is set to **SALE-AMOUNT * TAX-RATE**

Precondition 2
     SALE-DATA occurs with **ITEM-TYPE** that does not
     match an **ITEM-CATEGORY** in **TAX-CATEGORIES**
Postcondition 2
     ERROR-MESSAGE is generated

Figure 11.3: **A pre/post condition specification**

As you can see, there are two main parts of the specification: *pre* conditions and *post* conditions. In addition, such specifications can contain *local terms,* as defined in Section 11.1 (see also footnote 5).

Preconditions describe all the things (if any) that must be true before the process begins operating. It's sometimes convenient to think of the process as a "sleeping princess," and the pre-conditions represent the "magic kiss" that will awaken the process and set it to work. Alternatively, you can think of the preconditions as a guarantee from the user: "I guarantee that when this process is activated the following things will be true." Typically, the preconditions will describe the following:

- *What inputs must be available.* These inputs will arrive via a flow connected to the process, as shown on the dataflow diagram. Note that there may be cases where there are several flows coming into a process, but only one of the flows is a necessary precondition to activate the process. For example, if we saw a specification that began with

     Precondition
     data element **X** occurs

associated with the dataflow diagram shown in Figure 11.4, we would interpret it as follows: the arrival of data element **X** is the activating stimulus that makes the process begin its work. As part of its work, it seeks input from dataflow **Y** or **Z**, or both, *but Y and Z are not necessary for the process to begin doing its work.*

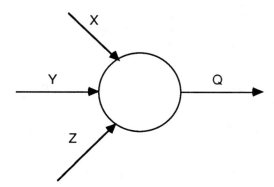

Figure 11.4: **A DFD with inputs X,Y, and Z**

- *What relationships must exist between inputs or within inputs.* Quite often a precondition will specify that two inputs with matching fields must arrive (e.g., order details and shipping details with the same account number). Or the precondition may specify that one component of an input data element be within a certain range (e.g., "an order with a delivery date more than 60 days in the future occurs").

- *What relationships must exist between inputs and data stores.* A precondition might stipulate that there be a record within a store that matches some aspect of an input data element (e.g., the precondition might say, "There is a customer-order with customer-account-number matching a customer-account-number in the customers store").

- *What relationships must exist between different stores or within a single store.* Thus, the precondition might say, "There is an order in the orders store whose customer-account-number matches the customer-account-number in the customers store." Or the precondition might say, "There is an order within the orders store with a shipping-date equal to the current date."

Similarly, the *postconditions* describe what must be true when the process has finished doing its job. Again, this can be thought of as a guarantee: "I guarantee that when the process is finished the following will be true." Postconditions typically describe the following:

- *The outputs that will be generated or produced by the process.* This is the most common form of postcondition (e.g., "An invoice will be produced").

- *The relationships that will exist between output values and the original input values.* This is common for the situation where an output is a direct mathematical function of an input value. Thus, a postcondition might say, "The **invoice-total** will be calculated as the sum of **unit-item-price**s plus **shipping-charge**s."

- *The relationships that will exist between output values and values in one or more stores.* This is common when information is to be retrieved from a store and used as part of an output of the process. For example, a process specification might have as a postcondition the following statement: "The **on-hand-balance** in the **INVENTORY** store will be increased by **amount-received**, and the new **on-hand balance** will be produced as output from this process."

- *The changes that will have been made to stores:* new items added, existing items modified, or existing items deleted. Thus, we might see statements like "The **order** will be appended to the **ORDERS** store" or "The **customer** record will be deleted from the **CUSTOMERS** store."

When building a pre/post condition specification, begin by describing the normal processing situations first. There may be several different normal situations (e.g., unique combinations of valid input/storage relationships) each of which is expressed as a distinct, separate precondition. For each such precondition, you should then describe the condition of the process bubble when the outputs have been produced and the stores have been modified. After the normal processing situations have been described, you should include appropriate preconditions and postconditions for error cases and abnormal cases. Consider the pre/post condition specification shown in Figure 11.5(b) that would be developed for a new system from the narrative specification in Figure 11.5(a).

If a customer tells me that he's a "charge" customer when he comes to the cash register to check out, I look up his account in my file. If I can find his account, and if it's not marked "suspended" or "canceled," then I write up the charge slip with the account number and the amount of the sale. Otherwise, I tell the customer that he'll have to pay cash or talk to the manager.

Figure 11.5(a): **An example of narrative specifications**
Precondition 1
Customer arrives with **account-number** matching an account number in **ACCOUNTS**, whose **status-code** is set to "valid."

Postcondition 1
Invoice is produced containing **account-number** and **amount-of-sale**.

Precondition 2
Precondition 1 fails for any reason (**account-number** can't be found on **ACCOUNTS** or **status-code** is not equal to "valid").

Postcondition 2
Error message is produced.

Figure 11.5(b): **An example of pre/post conditions**

Though the pre/post condition approach is quite useful and has a number of advantages, there are times when it may not be appropriate. The lack of intermediate steps between the inputs (preconditions) and the outputs (postconditions) is deliberate and conscious—but it may make the specification hard to understand if the reader cannot visualize some kind of procedure that will lead from inputs to outputs. Also, if there are complex relationships between inputs and outputs, it may be easier to write the specification using structured English. An example of a precondition/postcondition specification that is probably too complicated is shown in Figure 11.6.

DETERMINE LOAN RATE BASED ON CUSTOMER FACTORS

Precondition 1

loan-application occurs
and **years-employed** > 5 or **net-worth** > **loan-amount**
and **monthly-expenses** < 0.25 * **loan-amount**
or **collateral-guarantee** > 2 * **loan-amount** and **age** > 25
or **collateral-guarantee** > **loan-amount** and **age** > 30
or **years-employed** > 2 and **net-worth** > 2* **loan-amount**
    and **age** > 21 and **monthly-expenses** < 0.5 * **loan-amount**

Postcondition 1

approved-amount = **loan-amount**

Figure 11.6: **An overly complicated pre/post condition specification**

As with all the forms of process specification, you should let your own judgment and the user's reactions guide you; if the user finds it difficult to read the precondition/postcondition specification, choose another format. The precondition-/postcondition approach are shown in the case study in Appendix G; the alternative structured English approach is used in the case study in Appendix F. Look carefully at both case studies to determine the suitability of these two process specification tools.

11.3   DECISION TABLES

There are situations where neither structured English nor pre/post conditions are appropriate for writing process specifications. This is particularly true if the process must produce some output or take some actions based on *complex decisions*. If the decisions are based on several different variables (e.g., input data elements), and if those variables can take on many different values, then the logic expressed by structured English or pre/post conditions is likely to be so complex that the user won't understand it. A decision table is likely to be the preferred approach.

As shown in Figure 11.7, a decision table is created by listing all the relevant variables (sometimes known as *conditions* or *inputs*) and all the relevant actions on the left side of the table; note that the variables and actions have been conveniently separated by a heavy horizontal line. In this example, each variable is a *logical* variable, meaning that it can take on the value of true or false.

In many applications, it is easy (and preferable) to express the variables as binary (true-false) variables, but decision tables can also be built from multivalued variables; for example, one could build a decision table with a variable called "customer-age" whose relevant values are "less than 10," "between 10 and 30," and "greater than 30."

	1	2	3	4	5	6	7	8
Age > 21	Y	Y	Y	Y	N	N	N	N
Sex	M	M	F	F	M	M	F	F
Weight > 150	Y	N	Y	N	Y	N	Y	N
Medication 1	X				X			X
Medication 2		X			X			
Medication 3			X			X		X
No medication				X			X	

Figure 11.7: **A typical decision table**

Next, every possible combination of values of the variables is listed in a separate column; each column is typically called a *rule*. A rule describes the action (or actions) that should be carried out for a specific combination of values of the variables. At least one action needs to be specified for each rule (i.e., for each vertical column in the decision table), or the behavior of the system for that situation will be unspecified.

If there are N variables with binary (true-false) values, then there will be 2^N distinct rules; thus, if there are 3 conditions, there will be 8 rules, and if there are 7 conditions, there will be 128 rules. Enumerating all the rules is a fairly straightforward process: by treating the Yes (or T) as a binary zero, and the No (or F) as a binary one, it is easy to generate a sequence of 000, 001, 010, 011, 100, 101, and so forth until all 2^N combinations have been generated.[7]

You must discuss *each* rule with the user to ensure that you have identified the correct action, or actions, for each combination of variables. It is quite common, when doing this, to find that the user has never thought about certain combinations of variables or that they have never occurred in his or her experience.[8] The advantage of the decision table approach is that you can concentrate on one rule at a time.

---

7 Of course, there will be situations where the decision table conditions are not binary in nature, but are capable of taking on several values (e.g., an insurance application might involve **customer-age** and might use the values "under 18 years," "18 through 64," and "65 or over"). To determine the total number of rules in such a decision table, we must multiply the number of values that variable 1 can take on by the number of values that variable 2 can take on by ... the number of values that variable N can take on. Thus, if we have an application where variable 1 can take on 3 values, variable 2 can take on 5 values, and variable 3 can take on 4 values, we will need 3 x 5 x 4 = 60 distinct rules.

8 There are guidelines for simplifying decision tables and combining several rules into composite rules, but we will not cover them in this book. See [Yourdon, 1976] for details.

Another advantage of the decision table approach is that it does not imply any particular form of implementation. That is, when the systems analyst delivers the decision table (along with the DFDs, etc.) to the designer/programmer, there is a tremendous freedom of choice in terms of implementation strategy: the decision table can be programmed with nested IF statements, with a CASE construct or a GO TO DE-PENDING ON construct in COBOL; in the extreme case, a decision table code generator can *automatically* generate code from the decision table. Thus, decision tables are often referred to as a *nonprocedural* system modeling tool, for they do not specify any specific procedural algorithm to carry out the required actions.

To summarize, we must go through the following steps to create a decision table for a process specification:

1. Identify all the conditions, or variables, in the specification. Identify all the values that each variable can take on.

2. Calculate the number of combinations of conditions. If all the conditions are binary, then there are 2^N combinations of N variables.

3. Identify each possible action that is called for in the specification.

4. Create an "empty" decision table by listing all the conditions and actions along the left side and numbering the combinations of conditions along the top of the table.

5. List all the combinations of conditions, one for each vertical column in the table.

6. Examine each vertical column (known as a rule) and identify the appropriate action(s) to be taken.

7. Identify any omissions, contradictions, or ambiguities in the specification (e.g., rules in the decision table for which the specification does not indicate that actions should be taken).

8. Discuss the omissions, contradictions, and ambiguities with the user.

11.4   OTHER PROCESS SPECIFICATION TOOLS

11.4.1   Graphs and Charts

In some cases, it may be appropriate to express a process specification as a graph or a chart. Indeed, the user may *already* have a graph or a chart that is currently used to carry out that part of the application. If so, use it! There is no need for the systems analyst to translate a graph into structured English; instead, let the *programmer* translate the graph directly into COBOL, FORTRAN, or some other programming language when it is time to implement the system.

Consider, for example, a process specification that determines a customer's insurance premium as a function of age. The user has told us that the current business policy is to determine the premium from the graph shown in Figure 11.8.

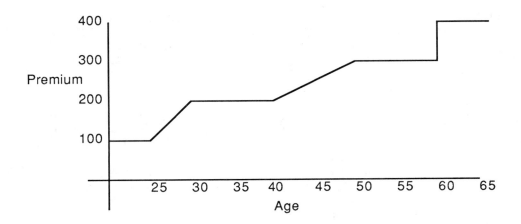

Figure 11.8: **Insurance premium as a function of age**

Assuming that the policy is not going to change when a new system is built, and assuming that the insurance premium is *only* a function of age, there is no need for the systems analyst to do any further work. Figure 11.8 *is* the process specification.

11.4.2   Narrative English

As we have implied several times in this chapter, narrative English is not a recommended tool for writing process specifications. This is because:

- An unrestricted vocabulary (i.e., indiscriminate use of nouns, verbs, and adjectives) makes it likely that the process description will include terms that are not in the data dictionary and whose meaning is not clear.

- Alternative actions (i.e., decisions) are often expressed in a clumsy, ambiguous fashion. This becomes even more dangerous when *nested* decisions are expressed.

- Repetitive actions (i.e., loops) are also expressed in a clumsy, ambiguous fashion. Nested loops are extremely dangerous when expressed in colloquial English.

- The concept of block structures can only be expressed with indentation or an outline-style presentation; if one is willing to go this far, one might as well use the formal structured English notation.

If, for some reason, you are *forced* to use narrative English, you should at least maintain some of the advantages of the highly partitioned structured analysis approach that we have discussed throughout this book. That is, under *no* circumstances should you allow yourself to be forced into the position of writing a 2000 page monolithic Victorian novel specification. At the very least, you should partition the specification into small pieces, so that you can write 2000 independent "short stories."

11.4.3   Flowcharts

We have avoided the use of flowcharts thus far in our discussion, but that is a reflection of current disinterest in flowcharts rather than an indictment of them.[9] Much of the criticism of flowcharts has resulted from their *misuse* in the following two areas:

1. As a high-level *systems* modeling tool, flowcharts suffer badly. A flowchart shows sequential, procedural logic; as we have seen in Chapter 9, a dataflow diagram is a more appropriate tool for modeling a network of asynchronous, communicating processes.

2. There is nothing to prevent the systems analyst from creating an arbitrarily complex, unstructured flowchart of the sort shown in Figure 11.9.

However, *if* the flowchart is only used to describe detailed logic, and *if* the systems analyst restricts himself to flowcharting symbols equivalent to the structured English constructs described in Section 11.1, then there is nothing wrong with their use. To create a structured flowchart, the systems analyst must organize his or her logic with nested combinations of the flowchart symbols shown in Figure 11.10.[10]

An alternative is the use of Nassi-Shneiderman diagrams, discussed in Section 11.4.4. However, it should be pointed out that *very few* systems analysts use flowcharts for process specifications (nor, for that matter, are they frequently used for program design either). Though the automated tools described in Appendix A could be used to create and maintain flowcharts, the simple truth is structured English, decision tables, and pre/post condition specifications are easier to create and maintain.

---

9 However, it is interesting to note that flowcharts may be about to experience a rebirth. Recent work by David Scanlan at California State University in Sacramento has shown that programming students *strongly* prefer flowcharts as the preferred method of learning about algorithms. If this is true for programming students, maybe it will be true for users, too. For more on this, see Scanlan's paper entitled "A Niche for Structured Flowcharts,"*Proceedings of the 1987 ACM Computer Science Conference.*

10 For more information on structured flowcharts, see the classic paper [Böhm and Jacopini, 1966].

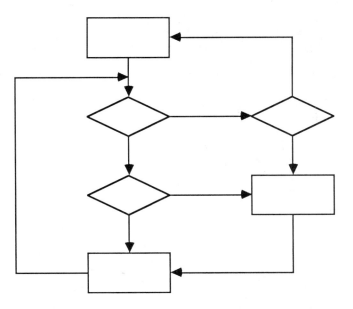

Figure 11.9: **An unstructured flowchart**

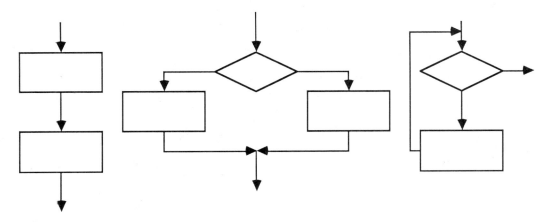

Figure 11.10: **The Böhm-Jacopini structured flowchart symbols**

11.4.4   Nassi-Shneiderman Diagrams

When structured programming first became popular in the mid-1970s, Nassi-Shneiderman diagrams were introduced as a structured flowcharting technique; see [Nassi and Shneiderman, 1973] and [Chapin, 1974]. A typical Nassi-Shneiderman diagram has the form shown in Figure 11.11.

Note that a simple imperative statement is represented by a rectangle, as shown in Figure 11.12(a); the rectangle can also be used to represent a *block* of sequential statements. The binary **IF-THEN-ELSE** construct is represented by the graphic notation shown in Figure 11.12(b); and the repetitive **DO-WHILE** construct is represented by the graphic notation shown in Figure 11.12(c).

The Nassi-Shneiderman diagrams are generally more organized, more structured, and more comprehensible than the typical flowchart; for that reason, they are sometimes preferred as a tool for creating process specifications. However, they *do* still require a nontrivial amount of graphics, and it is not clear that the graphics add that much value. As many systems analysts have been heard to mutter after spending an hour creating a Nassi-Shneiderman diagram, "This is just structured English with some boxes drawn around the statements!"

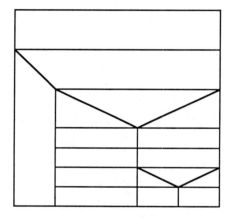

Figure 11.11: **A typical Nassi-Shneiderman diagram**

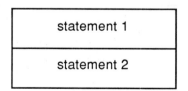

Figure 11.12(a): **Representation of a sequential statement**

The Nassi-Shneiderman diagrams are generally more organized, more structured, and more comprehensible than the typical flowchart; for that reason, they are sometimes preferred as a tool for creating process specifications. However, they *do* still require a non-trivial amount of graphics, and it is not clear that the graphics add that much value. As many systems analysts have been heard to mutter after spending an hour creating a Nassi-Shneiderman diagram, "This is just structured English with some boxes drawn around the statements!"

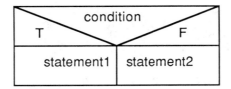

Figure 11.12(b): **Representation of an IF-THEN-ELSE construct**

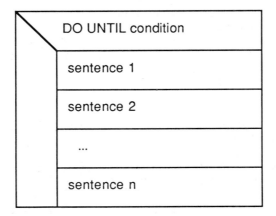

Figure 11.12(c): **Representation of a DO-WHILE construct**

On the other hand, recent research conducted by David Scanlan at California State University ([Scanlan, 1987]) shows that 75% to 80% of computer science students *strongly* prefer Nassi-Shneiderman diagrams over pseudocode when learning about complex algorithms; although this does not agree with the typical negative reaction of experienced programmers toward flowcharts, Scanlan's conclusions are based on careful factor-analytic studies of several hundred students. While end users do not necessarily have the same preferences as computer science students, there is at least the possibility that they would prefer a graphical representation of a process specification than a narrative/textual represenation.

11.5   SUMMARY

The purpose of this chapter has been to show you that there are many different ways to describe the detailed user policy inside each primitive bubble in a dataflow diagram. While structured English is the most commonly used technique at the present time, you should consider the use of decision tables, flowcharts, pre/post conditions, or any other approach that can be verified and communicated easily to your users.

Keep in mind that the process specifications represent the largest amount of detailed work in building a system model; there may be hundreds or even thousands of process specifications, and each one may be a page in length. Because of the amount of work involved, you may want to consider the top-down implementation approach discussed in Chapter 5: begin the design and implementation phase of your project before all the process specifications have been finished.

Keep in mind also that the activity of writing process specifications serves as a "sanity test" of the dataflow diagrams that have already been developed. You may discover that the process specification needs additional input dataflows or that it produces additional output dataflows (i.e., flows that were not shown on the DFD). And as you write the process specification, you may find that additional functions are needed; for example, as you write the process specification for a function that adds a new record to the **CUSTOMERS** store, you may notice that the DFD does not have a bubble that modifies or deletes a record from that store. Thus, you should expect that changes, revisions, and corrections to the DFD model will be required based on the detailed work of writing the process specifications.

REFERENCES

1.   Tom DeMarco, *Structured Analysis and Systems Specification.* Englewood Cliffs, N.J.: Prentice-Hall, 1979.

2.   Chris Gane and Trish Sarson, *Structured Systems Analysis: Tools and Techniques.* Englewood Cliffs, N.J.: Prentice-Hall, 1978.

3.   Edward Yourdon, *Techniques of Program Structure and Design*, 2nd ed. Englewood Cliffs, N.J.: Prentice-Hall,1988.

4.   James Martin and Carma McClure, *Diagramming Techniques for Software Engineering.* Englewood Cliffs, N.J.: Prentice-Hall, 1985.

5.   Victor Weinberg, *Structured Analysis.* Englewood Cliffs, N.J.: Prentice-Hall, 1978.

6.   Edward Yourdon, *Classics in Software Engineering.* New York: YOURDON Press, 1979.

7.   Corrado Böhm and Guiseppe Jacopini, "Flow Diagrams, Turing Machines, and Languages with Only Two Formation Rules," *Communications of the ACM,* Volume 9, Number 5 (May 1966), pp. 366-371. Also reprinted in *Classics in Software Engineering* (op. cit.).

8.   I. Nassi and B. Shneiderman, "Flowchart Techniques for Structured Programming," *ACM SIGPLAN Notices,* Volume 8, Number 8 (August, 1973), pp.12-26.

9.   Ned Chapin, "New Format for Flowcharts," *Software—Practice and Experience,* Volume 4, Number 4 (October-December 1974), pp. 341-357.

10.   H. McDaniel, editor, *Application of Decision Tables.* Princeton, N.J.:, Brandon Systems Press, 1970.

11.   S. Pollack, H. Hicks, and W. Harrison, *Decision Tables—Theory and Practice.* New York: Wiley, 1971.

12.   T.R. Gildersleeve, *Decision Tables and Their Practical Applications in Data Processing.* Englewood Cliffs, N.J.: Prentice-Hall, 1970.

13.   David Scanlan, "Cognitive Factors in the Preference for Structured Flowcharts: A Factor Analytic Study," presented at the First Annual YOURDON Press Author's Conference, New York, December 5, 1987.

QUESTIONS AND EXERCISES

1.   Consider the following specification, provided to you in a *narrative* form. Which of the specification tools presented in this chapter do you think would be the most appropriate? Why?

> When I get a purchase order, my job is to pick a supplier from our file of available suppliers. Of course, some suppliers get eliminated right away because their price is too high, or because they've been temporarily "blacklisted" because of poor quality. But the real work that I do is to pick the optimal supplier from those that qualify—the one that will deliver our order in the shortest amount of time. My boss had a system for estimating delivery time, and he taught it to me, but at this point I just look at the supplier's location, the quantity of items being ordered, and the date that we need the goods, and I *know* which supplier will be the best one....I'm not even sure how I do it any more.

2.   What is a process specification? What are its objectives?

3.   What are five common tools for modeling process specifications?

4.   What are the three requirements that a process specification should satisfy?

5.   Should a systems development project use *one* tool for process specifications? Why or why not?

6.   Research Project: Which specification tools are used in your organization? Are there restrictions on which tools are used? Do you think the *right* tools are in use?

7.   Which bubbles in a DFD require process specifications?

8.   What are the consequences of writing process specifications for nonatomic (nonprimitive) bubbles?

9.   How should the systems analyst determine what the process specifications for a bubble should be?

10.   How does it happen that process specifications sometimes impose arbitrary design and implementation decisions? What are the consequences of this?

11.   Research Project: Find an example of a process specification in your organization that exhibits arbitrary design or implementation decisions. How would you rewrite it to avoid this problem?

12.   Give a definition of the term structured English? What are some synonyms for this term?

13.   How many verbs are needed to form structured English sentences? Suggest a list of 20 verbs.

14.   Why are algebraic equations usually necessary in a structured English process specification?

15.   What characteristics should the *objects* in a structured English process specification have?

16.   What are local terms?

17.   Should local terms be included in a data dictionary? Why or why not?

18.   Do local terms appear as flows on DFDs?

19.   Give a specific example of a local term.

20.   What structured programming constructs are used in structured English?

21.   What is the purpose of the **OTHERWISE** clause in structured English?

22.   What is the difference between a **DO-WHILE** construct and a **REPEAT-UNTIL** construct in structured English?

23.   What is a compound sentence?

24.   Is the **CASE** construct necessary in structured English? What are the advantages and disadvantages of the **CASE** construct?

25.   What are the four components of a compound sentence?

26.   What is the difference between (a) and (b)?

(a)   **IF A THEN**
              IF B THEN
                     sentence-1
              ELSE
                     sentence-2
       ELSE
              sentence-2.

(b)   **IF A AND B THEN**

           sentence-1
    ELSE
           sentence-2.

    Which of these two examples do you think is easiest to understand? Why?

27. Research Project: Construct several examples similar to that in question 26, and conduct a survey among your users to see which version they prefer.

28. What three guidelines should be followed to ensure that a structured English specification will be readable?

29. Do you think that three levels of nested **IF** constructs in a structured English specification are OK? Why or why not?

30. Research Project: Make up several examples of structured English process specifications involving two, three, and four levels of nested IF constructs. Conduct a survey to determine, on average, how many levels the users in your organization are willing to accept.

31. What is the purpose of indentation in a structured English process specification?

32. Why is it important to conduct walkthroughs of a structured English process specification with the appropriate user?

33. What is the purpose of using outline-style numbering in a structured English process specification?

34. Give a definition of the precondition/postcondition specification technique.

35. What is the difference between the structured English specification technique and the precondition/postcondition technique?

36. Under what conditions is the precondition/postcondition specification technique a good one for the systems analyst to use?

37. Give a definition of a precondition.

38. What are the four things that a precondition typically describes?

39. What is the relationship between preconditions in a process specification and input flows on a DFD?

40. What happens if the preconditions of a process specification are *not* satisfied?

41. Give a definition of a postcondition.

42. What are the four things that a postcondition typically describes?

43.   What is the relationship between postconditions and output flows on a DFD?

44.   If a process specification has four sets of preconditions, how many sets of postconditions should it have?

45.   What is the minimum number of preconditions that a process specification could have?

46.   What are the potential disadvantages of the precondition/postcondition approach?

47.   Research Project: Find an example of a real-world process specification that would *not* be well suited to the precondition/postcondition specification approach. Why is it not well suited?

48.   Look at Figure 11.6. What would be a better modeling tool for creating a process specification for this situation?

49.   Research Project: Find an example of a real-world process specification that *would* be well suited to the precondition/postcondition approach. Why is it well suited?

50.   What is a decision table? What are the components of a decision table?

51.   Under what conditions is a decision table a good modeling tool for process specifications?

52.   What is wrong with the following decision table?

Age greater than 21	T	F	F
Sex is MALE	T	T	F
Medication 1	X		
Medication 2		X	

53.   What is wrong with the following decision table?

Height greater than 6 ft	T	T	F	F
Weight greater than 200	T	F	T	F
Insurance premium = $100	X		X	
Insurance premium = $200		X		X
Insurance premium = $300				

54. What is wrong with the following decision table?

Height greater than 6 ft	T	T	F	F
Weight greater than 200	T	F	T	F
Insurance premium = $100	X	X		X
Insurance premium = $200			X	
Insurance premium = $300		X		

55. What is the difference between a decision table with binary variables and a decision table with multivalued variables?

56. If a decision table has N binary-valued variables, how many rules should it have?

57. Under what conditions should the systems analyst use a graph for a process specification?

58. What are the advantages of a graph over structured English as a modeling tool for process specifications?

59. What are the four major disadvantages of narrative English as a modeling tool for process specifications?

60. What guidelines should be followed if narrative English *must* be used as a modeling tool for process specifications?

61. What are the two common criticisms of flowcharts as a modeling tool?

62. What are the three components of a *structured* flowchart?

63. Research Project: Show the same specification to a user in the form of structured English and a flowchart. Which approach is preferred? For more information on this see [Scanlan, 1987].

64. What is a Nassi-Shneiderman diagram? What is the difference between a flowchart and a Nassi-Shneiderman diagram?

65. From *Structured Analysis* by Victor Weinberg (New York: YOURDON Press, 1978): Write a decision table for the following narrative specification, and indicate any omissions, ambiguities, or contradictions that you find:

> "The Swell Store employs a number of salesmen to sell a variety of items. Most of these salesmen earn their income from a commission, paid on the items they sell, but a few are salary-plus-commission employees; that is, they receive a fixed salary, regardless of the quantity or type of items they sell, plus a commission on certain items. The Swell Store sells several different lines of merchandise, some of which are known as standard items (a can of tomato soup, for example) because they are widespread and do not require any creative sales techniques; in addition, there are bonus items that are highly profitable but difficult to sell (a gold-plated, diamond-studded Cadillac, perhaps). The standard and bonus items generally represent the low and high ends of the price spectrum, sandwiching a greater number of items in the middle of the spectrum.
>
> Customers, also, are categorized. Some are known as regulars, because they do business so often that no creative selling is required. Most of the customers, however, do a small amount of business at the Swell Store, and are likely to walk in right off the street, buy something, and then disappear forever.
>
> The management's commission policy is as follows: If a nonsalaried employee sells an item that is neither standard nor bonus to someone other than a regular customer, he receives a 10 percent commission, unless the item costs more than $10,000, in which case the commission is 5 percent. For all salesmen, if a standard item is sold, or if any item is sold to a regular customer, no commission is given. If a salaried salesman sells a bonus item, he receives a 5 percent commission, unless the item sells for more than $1,000, in which case he receives a flat $25 commission. If a nonsalaried salesman sells a bonus item to someone other than a regular customer, he receives a 10% commission, unless the item sells for more than $1,000, in which case he receives a flat commission of $75."

12 ENTITY-RELATIONSHIP DIAGRAMS

Obviously, a man's judgment cannot be better than the information on which he has based it. Give him the truth and he may still go wrong when he has the chance to be right, but give him no news or present him only with distorted and incomplete data, with ignorant, sloppy or biased reporting, with propaganda and deliberate falsehoods, and you destroy his whole reasoning processes, and make him something less than a man.

Arthur Hays Sulzberger
Address, New York State Publisher's Association, 1948

In this chapter, you will learn:

1. Why data models are useful in systems analysis.

2. The components of an entity-relationship diagram.

3. How to draw an entity-relationship diagram.

4. How to refine an initial entity-relationship diagram.

In this chapter, we explore a graphical notation for modeling data. The *entity relationship diagram* (also known as an ERD, or E-R diagram) is a network model that describes the stored data layout of a system at a high level of abstraction. It is quite different from the dataflow diagram, which models the *functions* performed by a system; and it is different from the *state-transition diagram,* which models the time-dependent behavior of a system.

Why should we be interested in a data model of a system? Primarily because the data structures and relationships may be so complex that we want to highlight them and examine them *independently* of the processing that will take place. Indeed, this is particularly true when we show our system model to higher-level executive users in an organization (e.g., vice-presidents or department managers who may not be interested in the day-to-day operational details of the system). Such users are often more concerned with the data: What data do we need to run our business? How are the data related to other data? Who owns the data? Who is allowed to access the data?

Some of these questions, access to data, and ownership of data, for example, may be the responsibility of a dedicated group within the organization. The *data administration* group (or DA group) is often responsible for managing and controlling the essential information of the business; whenever you begin building a new information system, you will need to talk with these people so that you can coordinate your system's information with their global, corporate-wide information model. *The entity-relationship diagram is a useful modeling tool for carrying out this conversation.*

There is often another group within the organization with a similar name: the *database administration group* (sometimes known as the DBA group). The group is usually located within the DP department (while the data administration group is not necessarily so located), and its job is to ensure that computerized databases are organized, managed, and controlled effectively. Thus, they are often the implementation team responsible for taking an essential model (one that is independent of a specific technology) and translating it into an effective, efficient *physical* database design for IMS, ADABAS, IDMS, TOTAL, or some other database management system. *The entity-relationship diagram is an effective modeling tool for communicating with the DBA group.* Based on the information presented by the ERD, the database administration group can begin to see what kind of keys or indexes or pointers they will need to access database records efficiently.

For the systems analyst, the ERD has a major benefit, too: it highlights relationships between data stores on the DFD that would otherwise be seen only in the process specification. For example, a typical ERD is shown in Figure 12.1. Each of the rectangular boxes corresponds to a data store on a DFD (a correspondence that we will explore further in Chapter 14), and you can see that there are relationships (connections) that one would normally not see on a DFD. This is because the DFD focuses the attention of the reader on the *functions* that the system is performing, not the data that it needs.

Indeed, consider an extreme case: what if there are no functions to be performed? What if the purpose of the system you are building is not to *do* anything, but merely to be the repository of a large amount of interesting information? Such a system might be called an ad hoc inquiry system, or a decision support system. In such a system, we might concentrate entirely on the data model, and not even bother building the function-oriented DFD model. Of course, this is indeed a rare situation: most systems do have functions to carry out; often we find that building the data model first makes it easier to discover what the required functions are.

Of course, the notation of the ERD in Figure 12.1 is quite mysterious at this point. In the following sections, we will examine the structure and components of an ERD; we will then discuss guidelines for drawing a well-structured ERD. The notation presented in this chapter is derived from [Flavin, 1981] and is similar to notation developed by [Chen, 1976], [Martin, 1982], [Date, 1986], and others.

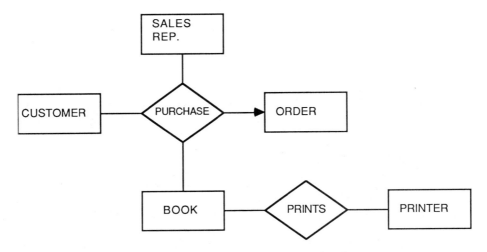

Figure 12.1: **A typical entity-relationship diagram**

12.1   THE COMPONENTS OF AN ERD

There are four major components of an entity-relationship diagram:

1.   Object types

2.   Relationships

3.   Associative object type indicators

4.   Supertype/subtype indicators

12.1.1   Object Types

An object type is represented by a rectangular box on an entity-relationship diagram; an example is shown in Figure 12.2. It represents a collection or set of *objects* (things) in the real world whose individual members (or instances) have the following characteristics:

- *Each can be identified uniquely in some fashion.* There is some way of differentiating between individual instances of the object type. For example, if we have an object type known as **CUSTOMER**, we must be able to distinguish one customer from another (perhaps by an account number, by last name, or by Social Security number). If all customers are the same (if we are operating a business where customers are just nameless, faceless blobs who come into our store to buy things), then **CUSTOMER** would not be a meaningful object type.

```
┌─────────────────────────┐
│                         │
│                         │
│       CUSTOMER          │
│                         │
│                         │
└─────────────────────────┘
```

Figure 12.2: **An object type**

- *Each plays a necessary role in the system we are building.* That is, for the object type to be legitimate, we must be able to say that *the system could not operate without access to its members.* If we are building an order entry system for our store, for example, it might occur to us that in addition to customers, the store has a staff of janitors, each of whom is individually identified by name. While janitors presumably play a useful role in the store, the order entry system can happily function without them; therefore, they do not deserve a role as an object type in our system model. Obviously, this is something that you must verify with the users as you build your model.

- *Each can be described by one or more data elements.* Thus, a **CUSTOMER** can be described by such data elements as name, address, credit limit, and phone number. Many database textbooks describe this as attributing data elements to an object type. Note that the attributes must apply to *each instance* of the object type; for example, *each* customer must have a name, address, credit limit, phone number, and so on.

In many of the systems you develop, object types will be the system's representation of a *material thing* in the real world. Thus, typical objects are customers, inventory items, employees, manufactured parts, and the like. The *object* is the material thing in the real world, and the *object type* is the system representation. However, an object may also be something nonmaterial: schedules, plans, standards, strategies, and maps are but a few examples.

Since *people* are often object types in a system, keep something else in mind, too: a person (or, for that matter, any other material thing) could be several different object types in different data models *or even within the same data model.* John Smith, for example, may be an **EMPLOYEE** in one data model and a **CUSTOMER** in a different data model; he could also be an **EMPLOYEE** and a **CUSTOMER** within the same data model.

Note that in all the examples of an object, we have used the singular form of a noun (e.g., employee, customer). This is not required, but it is a useful convention; as we will see in Chapter 14, there is a correspondence between objects in the ERD and stores in the DFD; thus, if there is a **CUSTOMER** object in the ERD, there should be a **CUSTOMERS** store on the DFD.

12.1.2   Relationships

Objects are connected to one another by *relationships*. A relationship represents a set of connections between objects and is represented by a diamond. Figure 12.3 shows a simple relationship that could exist between two or more objects.

Figure 12.3: **A relationship**

It is important to recognize that the relationship represents a *set* of connections. Each instance of the relationship represents an association between zero or more occurrences of one object and zero or more occurrences of the other object. Thus, in Figure 12.3, the relationship labeled **PURCHASES** might contain the following individual instances:

- instance 1:   customer 1 purchases item 1

- instance 2:   customer 2 purchases items 2 and 3

- instance 3:   customer 3 purchases item 4

- instance 4:   customer 4 purchases items 5, 6, and 7

- instance 5:   customer 5 purchases *no* items

- instance 6:   customers 6 and 7 purchase item 8

- instance 7:   customers 8, 9, and 10 purchase items 9, 10, and 11

- etc.

As you can see, then, a relationship can connect two or more instances of the same object.

Note that the relationship represents something that must be *remembered* by the system—something that could not be calculated or derived mechanically. Thus, our data model in Figure 12.3 indicates that there is some important user-related reason for remembering the fact that customer 1 purchases item 1, and so on. And the relationship also indicates that there is nothing *a priori* that would have allowed us to determine that customer 1 purchased item 1 and no other items. *The relationship represents system memory.*[1] (An object represents system memory, too, of course.)

Note also that there can be more than one relationship between two objects. Figure 12.4, for example, shows two different relationships between a **PATIENT** and a **DOCTOR**. At first glance, you might think this is belaboring the obvious: every time the doctor treats a patient, he invoices the patient. But Figure 12.4 suggests that the situation might be different: it may turn out, for example, that there are several different instances of a "treatment" between a doctor and the same patient (i.e., an initial treatment, follow-up treatments, etc.).   And Figure 12.4 implies that the invoicing relationship is entirely separate from the treatment relationship: perhaps some patients are invoiced only for their first treatment, while others are invoiced for every treatment, and still others are not invoiced at all.

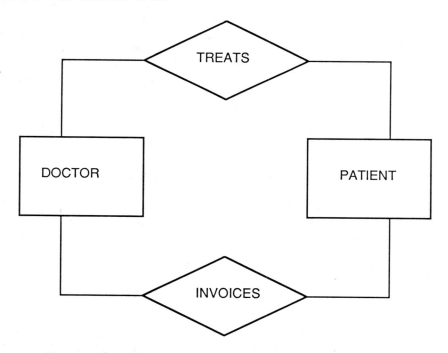

Figure 12.4: **Multiple relationships between objects**

---

1 Other relationships may exist between the objects that will not be shown on the ERD. Since the ERD is a *stored data model,* relationships that can be calculated, or derived, will not be shown. For example, consider the object **DRIVER** and the object **LICENSE**. There might be a renewal date relationship between the two, which is calculated as a function of the driver's birthday (e.g., the driver must renew her license each year on her birthday). Such a relationship would not be shown on the ERD, because it is not a stored data relationship. However, if the renewal date were randomly chosen, then it would probably have to be remembered by the system.

A more common situation is to see multiple relationships between multiple objects. Figure 12.5 shows the relationship that typically exists between a buyer, a seller, a real estate agent, the buyer's attorney and the seller's attorney, for the sale and purchase of a house.

With a complex diagram like the one in Figure 12.5 (which is typical of, if not simpler than, the ERDs you are likely to find in a real project), the relationship and its connected object types should be read as a unit. The relationship can be described from the perspective of *any* of the participating object types, and *all* such perspectives are valid. Indeed, it is the set of all such viewpoints that completely describes the relationship. For example, in Figure 12.5, we can read the negotiates price relationship in any of the following three ways:

1.　Real estate agent negotiates price between buyer and seller.

2.　Buyer negotiates price with seller, through real estate agent.

3.　Seller negotiates price with buyer, through real estate agent.

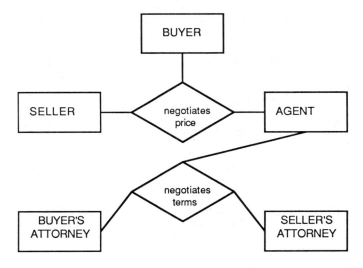

Figure 12.5: **Multiple relationships between multiple objects**

Note that, in some cases, we can have relationships between different instances of the same object type. For example, imagine a system being developed for a university, in which **COURSE, STUDENT,** and **TEACHER** are object types. Most of the relationships that we will concentrate on are between instances of different object types (e.g., the relationships "enrolls in," "teaches," etc.). However, we might need to model the relationship "is a prerequisite for" between one instance of **COURSE** and another instance of **COURSE.**

12.1.3   Alternative Notation for Relationships

As we have seen in Section 12.1.2, relationships in the E-R diagram are *multidirectional*; they can be read from any direction. Also, we have seen that the E-R diagrams do not show *cardinality*; that is, they do not show the number of objects participating in a relationship. This is quite conscious and deliberate: we prefer to bury such details in the data dictionary. This is discussed further in Section 12.3.

An alternative notation used by some systems analysts shows both *cardinality* and *ordinality*. For example, Figure 12.6(a) shows a relationship between **CUSTOMER** and **ITEM** in which the additional notation indicates that

(1)   The **CUSTOMER** is the anchor point, the primary object from whose viewpoint the relationship should be read.[2]

(2)   The relationship consists of one customer connected to N items. That is, an individual customer can purchase 0, 1, 2, ... or N items. However, the relationship indicates that only *one* customer can be involved in each instance of a relationship. This would preclude, for example, the case where multiple customers are involved in the purchase of a single item.

Figure 12.6(a): **Anchor point notation for E-R diagrams**

Another common notation is shown in Figure 12.6(b); the double-headed arrow is used to show the one-to-many relationship, while a single-headed arrow is used to show a one-to-one relationship between objects.

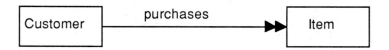

Figure 12.6(b): **Alternative notation for one-to-many relationships**

Such annotated E-R diagrams are discussed in detail in [Chen, 1976], [Martin, 1982], and [Date, 1986]. However, I prefer *not* to include such detail, for it can easily be included in the data dictionary (as discussed in Section 12.4), and it tends to distract from the major purpose of the E-R diagram, which is to give an *overview* of the components of and interfaces between the elements of data in a system. Though there is nothing intrinsically wrong with procedural annotations on the diagram, my experience has been that systems analysts often carry a good idea too far and clutter up the diagram with far more information than is appropriate.

_____

2 The term anchor point was introduced in [Flavin, 1981].

12.1.4   Associative Object Type Indicators

A special notation on the E-R diagram is the *associative object type indicator;* this represents something that functions both as an object *and* a relationship. Another way of thinking about the associative object type is that it represents *a relationship about which we wish to maintain some information.*[3]

Consider, for example, the simple case of a customer purchasing an item (or items), which we illustrated in Figure 12.6. Regardless of whether we include the procedural annotation or not, the main point is that *the relationship of* **PURCHASE** *does nothing more than associate a* **CUSTOMER** *and one or more* **ITEM**s. But suppose that there is some *data* that we wish to remember about *each* instance of a purchase (e.g., the time of day when it took place). Where could we store this information? "Time of day" is certainly not an attribute of **CUSTOMER**, nor is it an attribute of **ITEM**. Instead, we attribute "time of day" to the purchase itself and show it in a diagram as illustrated by Figure 12.7.

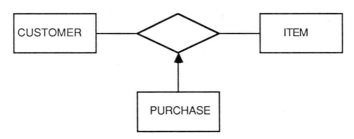

Figure 12.7: **An associative object type indicator**

Notice that **PURCHASE** is now written inside a rectangular box and that it is connected, via a directed line, to an unnamed relationship diamond. This is meant to indicate that **PURCHASE** functions as:

- *An object type*, something about which we wish to store information. In this case, we want to remember the time at which the purchase took place and the discount offered to the customer. (Again, this assumes that such information could not be derived, after the fact, by the system.)

- *A relationship* connecting the two object types of **CUSTOMER** and **ITEM**. The significant thing here is that **CUSTOMER** and **ITEM** stand on their own. *They would exist whether or not there was a purchase.*[4]

---

3 This is referred to as intersection data in several database textbooks.

4 A purist might argue that this is not true in the long run. If there were no **ITEM**s for several days in a row, the **CUSTOMER**s would disappear from the scene and take their business elsewhere. And if there were no **CUSTOMER**s, the shop would eventually go out of business and the **ITEM**s would disappear. But in the short term steady-state situation, it is obvious that customers and items can happily coexist without necessarily having anything to do with one another.

A **PURCHASE**, on the other hand, obviously depends for its very existence on the **CUSTOMER** and the **ITEM**. It comes into existence *only as the result of a relationship between the other objects to which it is connected.*

The relationship in Figure 12.7 is deliberately unnamed. This is because the associative object type indicator (**PURCHASE**) is *also* the name of the relationship.

12.1.5   Subtype/Supertype Indicators

The subtype/supertype object types consist of an object type and one or more subcategories, connected by a relationship. Figure 12.8 shows a typical subtype/supertype: the general category is **EMPLOYEE** and the subcategories are **SALARIED EMPLOYEE** and **HOURLY EMPLOYEE**. Note the subtypes are connected to the supertype via an unnamed relationship; note also that the supertype is connected to the relationship with a line containing a crossbar.

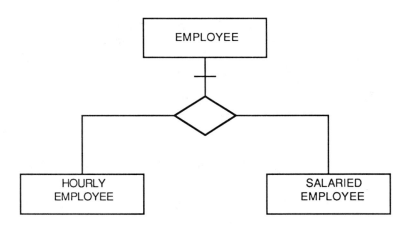

Figure 12.8: **A supertype/subtype indicator**

In this notation, the supertype is described by data elements that apply to *all* the subtypes. For example, in Figure 12.8, we could imagine that all employees are described by such facts as:

- Name

- Years of service

- Home address

- Name of supervisor

However, each subtype is described by *different* data elements; otherwise, there would be no point distinguishing between them. For example, we could imagine that a **SALARIED EMPLOYEE** is described by such things as:

   • Monthly salary

   • Annual bonus percentage

   • Amount allowed for company car

And the **HOURLY EMPLOYEE** might be described by such things as:

   • Hourly pay

   • Overtime rate

   • Starting time

12.2   GUIDELINES FOR CONSTRUCTING ENTITY-RELATIONSHIP DIAGRAMS

The notation shown in the previous section is sufficient to build arbitrarily complex entity-relationship diagrams. However, you may be thinking to yourself at this point, "How do I discover what the objects and relationships are in the first place?" Your initial model of object types and relationships will usually be derived from (1) your understanding of the user's application, (2) interviews with the user, and (3) any other research and data gathering that you can use. (Interviewing and data gathering techniques are discussed in Appendix E.)

You should not expect that the first E-R diagram you draw will be a final one that you will review with the user community or deliver to the system designers. Like dataflow diagrams and all the other systems modeling tools, E-R diagrams should be revised and improved several times; the first version will typically be nothing more than a crude beginning, and subsequent versions will be produced using a series of refinement guidelines presented in this section. Some of the refinement guidelines will lead to the creation of additional object types, while other refinement guidelines will lead to the removal of object types and/or relationships.

12.2.1   Adding Additional Object Types

As indicated above, your first-cut ERD will typically be created from initial interviews with the user and from your knowledge of the subject matter of the user's business. This will, of course, give you a strong clue as to the identity of the major objects and relationships.[5]

---

5 However, it will probably not identify *all* the relationships between the objects. Given a system with N objects, the number of possible relationships is proportional to N!, which is typically an *enormous* number. Many of the (theoretically) possible relationships will turn out to have either (1) no legitimate meaning whatsoever within the system, or (2) no relevance within the context of the system being modeled. One could imagine, for example, a system in which the primary relationship between customers and salespeople is that of **SELLS**. It may also turn out that a customer and a salesperson are married to one another; or that the salesperson is the daughter of the customer; or that the customer and the salesperson are classmates at school. All this may be very interesting, but it is not going to be represented in the system model unless it is *relevant* to the system model.

After the first-cut ERD has been developed, the next step that you should carry out is that of attributing the data elements in the system to the various object types. This assumes, of course, that you know what the data elements are! This may happen in any one of three ways:

1. If the process model (DFD) has already been developed or is being developed in parallel with the data model, then a data dictionary will already exist. It may not be complete at this point, but it will be enough to begin the process of attribution.

2. If the process model has *not* been developed (or, in the extreme case, if you don't intend to develop one at all), then you may have to begin by interviewing all the appropriate users to build up an exhaustive list of (and definitions of) data elements. As you do this, you can attribute the data elements to the objects in the E-R diagram. (However, note that this is a time-consuming, bottom-up process that may cause some delays and frustration.)

3. If you are working with an active data administration group, there is a good chance that a data dictionary will already exist. This may be given to you at a fairly early stage in your project, at which point you can begin the process of attribution.

The attribution process may provide one of three reasons for creating new object types:

1. You may discover data elements that can be attributed to some instances of an object type, but not to others.

2. You may discover some data elements that are applicable to all instances of two different objects.

3. You may discover that some data elements describe relationships between other object types.

If, during the process of attributing data elements to object types, you find that some data elements *cannot* apply to all instances of an object type, then you will need to create a set of subtypes beneath the object type you have been working with and assign the unique data elements to appropriate subtypes.

Suppose, for example, you are developing a personnel system, and you have identified (with extraordinary brilliance and creativity!) an object type called **EMPLOYEE**. While reviewing the available data elements, you find that many of them (**age**, **height**, **date-employed**, etc.) are applicable to all instances of an employee. However, you then discover a data element called **number-of-pregnancies**; it is obviously a relevant data element for female employees but not for male employees. This would prompt you to create **MALE-EMPLOYEE** and **FEMALE-EMPLOYEE** as subtypes of the general category of employee.

Obviously, I am not suggesting that all personnel systems should keep track of the number of pregnancies that each employee has had; the example was chosen merely because there is general agreement that male employees *cannot* be pregnant. Compare this, however, to the data element **spouse's-name**: there are several instances of **EMPLOYEE** for whom spouse's-name *may* not apply (because they are not currently married), but that is a very different situation from that of a data element that *cannot* apply.[6]

In most cases, this process of creating new subtypes and assigning data elements appropriately is very straightforward. However, keep one exceptional situation in mind: it may turn out that *all* the relevant data elements are attributed to one of the subtypes, and that *none* of the data elements can be attributed to the supertype object; that is, it may turn out that the data elements are mutually exclusive, belonging to one subtype or another subtype, but not both. Suppose, for example, that the *only* data elements that we can attribute to employees are **number-of-pregnancies** and **years-of-experience-playing-on-New-York-Knicks-basketball-team**. We might well decide (after wondering what kind of lunatic user was responsible for such a system!) that the general supertype of **EMPLOYEE** did not apply.

The opposite situation can occur, too: data elements may describe instances of two (or more) different object types in the same way. If this occurs, then you should create a new supertype and assign the common data elements to the supertype. For example, we may have identified **CASH-CUSTOMER** and **CREDIT-CARD-CUSTOMER** as two distinct object types when first creating an ERD for an order entry system (perhaps because the user told us that these were two distinct categories). However, it might quickly become apparent that the data elements **customer-name** and **customer-address** describe both types of customer in the same way; this would argue for the creation of a supertype, as shown in Figure 12.9.

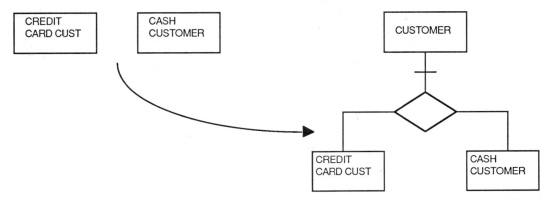

Figure 12.9: **Creation of a new supertype/subtype object**

---

6 Throughout this example, we are obviously ignoring a number of obscure exceptions. We ignore, for example, the case of the female employee who had three pregnancies and then had a sex change operation. And, in the case of spouse's names, we are assuming that none of the employees are underage children, for whom marriage is presumably an impossibility.

Similarly, if a data element describes the *interaction* of two or more object types, then we should replace the "naked" relationship between the two objects with an associative object type. For example, look at the first-cut ERD shown in Figure 12.10(a) in which there is a **PURCHASES** relationship between **CUSTOMER** and **ITEM**. During the attribution of data elements, we might find that there is a data element called date-of-purchase that (1) seems to belong to the **PURCHASE** relationship, and (2) obviously describes, *or provides data about,* the interaction of a **CUSTOMER** and an **ITEM**. This suggests that we should replace the relationship **PURCHASES** with an associative object type, as shown in Figure 12.10(b).

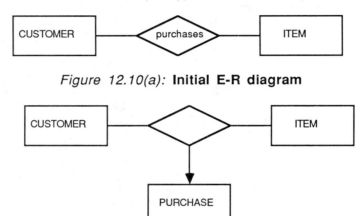

Figure 12.10(a): **Initial E-R diagram**

Figure 12.10(b): **Replacing a relationship with an associative object type**

Sometimes the initial E-R diagram will contain an object type that, on closer analysis, clearly deserves to be an associative object type. For example, Figure 12.11(a) shows an E-R diagram with three related objects: **CUSTOMER**, **ORDER**, and **PRODUCT**. During the process of attributing data elements to the various objects, we find that **date-of-delivery** most sensibly belongs to the object **ORDER**; after all, customers don't get "delivered," and products get delivered only as the result of an order. Indeed, thinking about this makes it evident that the **ORDER** itself is a relationship between **CUSTOMER** and **PRODUCT**, as well as an object about which we wish to remember some facts. This leads to Figure 12.11(b).

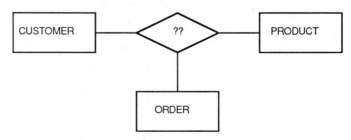

Figure 12.11(a): **An initial E-R diagram**

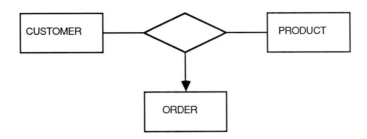

Figure 12.11(b): **An object transformed into an associative object**

Finally, we have the case of repeating groups. Consider, for example, the object type **EMPLOYEE**, with such obvious data elements as name and home address. Now suppose that we find additional data elements **child's-name, child's-age,** and **child's-sex**. It could obviously be argued that **child's-name, child's-age,** and **child's-sex** are ways of describing a new object type called **CHILD,** which has inadvertently been previously embedded within **EMPLOYEE**. It could also be argued that there are (potentially) multiple instances of child-related information associated with each instance of an employee, and that each instance of child-related information is uniquely identified by the **child's-name**. In this case, the object type that we initially thought of in the form shown in Figure 12.12(a) should be transformed into *two* object types, connected by a new relationship, as shown in Figure 12.12(b).

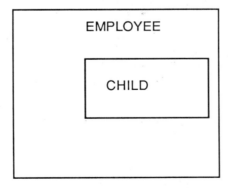

Figure 12.12(a): **Initial view of an object**

This process of removing embedded objects is part of a more comprehensive refinement activity often described as *normalization.* The objective of normalization is to produce object types in which each instance (or member) consists of a primary key value that identifies some entity, together with a set of mutually independent attribute values that describe that entity in some way. The process of normalization is described in detail in Chapter 14 of [Date, 1986] and in Chapter 19 of [DeMarco, 1978].

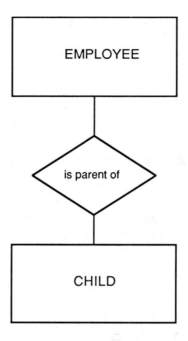

Figure 12.12(b): **Revised E-R diagram**

12.2.2   Removing Object Types

The previous section dealt with ERD refinements that created additional objects and/or relationships. However, there are also a number of situations where refinement of the ERD will lead to the removal of redundant or erroneous object types and relationships. We will examine four common situations:

1. Object types that consist of only an identifier

2. Object types for which there is only a single instance

3. Dangling associative object types

4. Derived relationships

If we have an E-R diagram in which one of the object types has only an *identifier* assigned to it as a data element, there *may* be an opportunity to eliminate the object type and assign the identifier as a data element in a related object type. For example, let us imagine that we have constructed an initial E-R diagram as shown in Figure 12.13(a) for a personnel system:

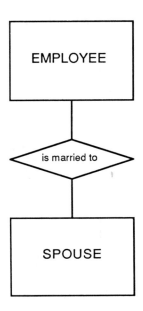

Figure 12.13(a): **An initial E-R diagram**

During the process of attributing data elements to the various objects, though, we may find that the *only* information that the personnel system keeps about a spouse is his or her name (i.e., the identifier that distinguishes one spouse from any other spouse in the system). In this case, an obvious refinement is to eliminate **SPOUSE** as an object type and instead include spouse-name as a data element within the object **EMPLOYEE**.

Note that this refinement only makes sense when there is a one-to-one correspondence between instances of the about-to-be-deleted object and instances of the related object. The example immediately above, for instance, makes sense because modern society presumes that a person will have, at most, one spouse. This leads to the reduced E-R diagram shown in Figure 12.13(b).

Figure 12.13(b): **A reduced E-R diagram**

An even greater reduction can be made if we find that our initial E-R diagram contains an object for which our only fact is the identifier *and* that is a single-instance object. Consider the initial E-R diagram shown in Figure 12.14(a).

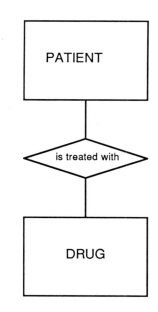

Figure 12.14(a): **An initial E-R diagram**

At first glance, this seems like a reasonable way of showing the relationship between patients and drugs (medicinal, of course!) in a hospital. But suppose the only information that we keep about the drug is its name (identifier); and suppose that the hospital only administers one type of drug (e.g., aspirin). In this case, the drug is a constant and does not even have to be shown on the diagram. (Note that this also means that our system would not have a data store called drugs). Our reduced diagram would look like Figure 12.14(b).

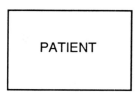

Figure 12.14(b): **Reduced E-R diagram**

Because of the situation above, it is possible to create a dangling associative object type. Consider the following variation on the previous hospital example, as shown in Figure 12.15(a). If, as suggested above, it turns out that **DRUG** is a single-instance, identifier-only object, then it would be deleted. This would result in the reduced diagram shown in Figure 12.15(b); note that **TREATMENT** is still an associative object type, even though it is connected to only one other object type. This is known as a dangling associative object type and is quite legal (though somewhat unusual) in an ERD.

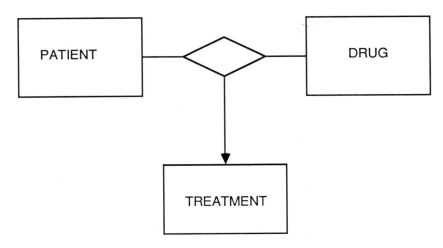

Figure 12.15(a): **An initial E-R diagram**

Finally, relationships that can be *derived,* or calculated, should be removed from the initial E-R diagram. As mentioned earlier in the chapter, the ERD should show the requirements for *stored data.* Thus, in Figure 12.16(a), if the **renews** relationship between **DRIVER** and **LICENSE** can be derived (based on the driver's birthday, or on the first letter of his last name, or on a variety of other schemes often used by Motor Vehicle Bureaus throughout the United States), then it should be eliminated. This leads to Figure 12.16(b), in which the object types are *unconnected.* This is quite legal in an ERD; it is not necessary for all object types to be connected to one another.

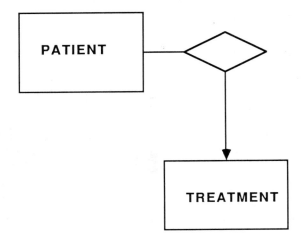

Figure 12.15(b): **The reduced E-R diagram**

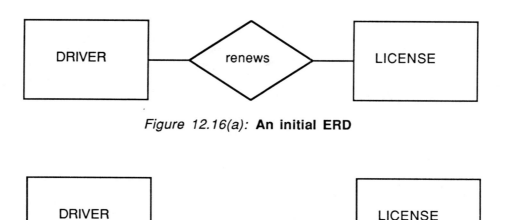

Figure 12.16(a): **An initial ERD**

Figure 12.16(b): **The reduced ERD**

12.3   EXTENSIONS TO THE DATA DICTIONARY FOR E-R DIAGRAMS

Finally, we observe that the data dictionary discussed in Chapter 10 needs to be extended to provide for the ERD notation discussed in this chapter. In general, *objects* on the ERD correspond to *stores* on the DFD; more about this will be discussed in Chapter 14. This means that in the data dictionary definition below, **CUSTOMER** is both the definition of the object type and an instance of the store **CUSTOMERS**:

CUSTOMERS = {CUSTOMER}

CUSTOMER = @customer-name + address + phone-number

Note also that the definition of a **CUSTOMER** includes a specification of the *key field,* which is the data element (or attribute) that differentiates one instance of a customer from any other. The "at" sign (@) is used to indicate the key field(s).[7]

However, we also need to include in the data dictionary a definition of all the *relationships* shown in the ERD. The relationship definition should include a description of the *meaning* of the relationship, within the context of the application; and it should indicate the objects that form the association. Appropriate upper and lower limits should be specified to indicate whether the association is a one-to-one association, a one-to-many association, or a many-to-many association. For example, the relationship **purchases** shown in Figure 12.10(a) might be defined in the data dictionary in the following way:

---

7 Some textbooks use the convention of underlining the key field(s). Thus, we could define customer as

CUSTOMER = <u>customer-name</u> + address + phone-number

purchases =   *the association of a customer and one or more items*
@**customer-id** + 1{@**item-id** + **quantity-purchased**}

12.4   SUMMARY

For any system with multiple stores (objects) and complex data relationships, the ERD can be a valuable tool. As we have seen in this chapter, it focuses entirely on the data relationships, without providing any information about the *functions* that create or use the data.

While we have used the ERD in this book as the graphic modeling tool for showing data relationships, you should be aware that a variety of other modeling tools are used for the same purpose; [Martin, 1982] and [Date, 1986] show many examples of alternative modeling tools.

At this point, many students ask whether the DFD model should be developed first and then the ERD, or whether it is better to develop the ERD first and then the DFD. Indeed, some students even ask whether it is really necessary to develop *both* models, when *either* the DFD or the ERD provides so much interesting information. The answer to the first question is simple: it doesn't matter which model gets developed first. Depending on your own preferences or the preferences of the user, or the nature of the system itself (i.e., whether it is function-rich or data-rich), one of the models will often cry out to be developed first. In other cases, though, you may find that both models are developed concurrently; this is particularly common when the project team contains a distinct database design group, or when the EDP organization has a data administration group that develops corporate data models.

The second question is more important: Is it really important to develop two different models of a system (and, as we will see in Chapter 13, a third model of the time-dependent behavior of the system)? The answer is that it depends on the kind of system you are developing. Many of the classic business data processing systems developed in the 1960s and 1970s appeared (at least superficially) to consist of many complex functions, but relatively trivial data structures; hence the DFD model was emphasized, and the ERD model was often ignored. Conversely, many of the decision-support systems and ad hoc database inquiry systems built in the 1980s appeared (at least superficially) to consist of complex data relationships, but almost no functional activities; hence the ERD model was emphasized, and the DFD model was downplayed. And the timing characteristics of real-time systems built in the 1960s and 1970s appeared (at least superficially) to dominate any consideration of functions and data relationships; in such systems, the state-transition model (discussed in Chapter 13) was often emphasized to the exclusion of DFDs and ERDs.

The systems of the late 1980s and 1990s, however, tend to be far more complex than the special-purpose systems of a decade or two ago; indeed, many of them are between 100 times and 1000 times larger and more complex. Many of these large, complex systems have incredibly complex functions *and* complex data relationships *and* complex time-dependent behavior; consider, for example, the Star Wars system, which is estimated to require 100 *million* computer instructions, and which will have a real-time behavior of mind-boggling complexity. For any such complex system, it is obvious that all three of the modeling tools discussed in this book will be critically important. On the other hand, if you do become involved in a simple, one-dimensional system, you may find that you can concentrate on the modeling tool that illuminates and highlights the one important aspect of the system.

In Chapter 14, we will see how the ERD, the DFD, the state-transition diagram, the process specification, and the data dictionary can all be checked against each other in order to produce a *complete* system model that is internally consistent.

REFERENCES

1. Matt Flavin, *Fundamental Concepts of Information Modeling.* New York: YOURDON Press, 1981.

2. Peter Chen, "The Entity-Relationship Model—Toward A Unified View of Data," *ACM Transactions on Database Systems,* Volume 1, Number 1 (March 1976), pp. 9-36.

3. Peter Chen, *The Entity-Relationship Approach to Logical Database Design.* Wellesley, Mass.: Q.E.D. Information Sciences, 1977.

4. D. C. Tsichritzis and F.H. Lochovsky, *Data Models.* Englewood Cliffs, N.J.: Prentice-Hall, 1982.

5. James Martin, *Computer Database Organization.* Englewood Cliffs, N.J.: Prentice-Hall, 1982.

6. *Proceedings of the International Conference on Data Engineering.* Washington, D.C.: IEEE Press, 1984.

7. C.J. Date, *An Introduction to Database Systems,* 4th ed. Reading, Mass.: Addison-Wesley, 1986.

8. Sally Shlaer and Stephen Mellor, *Object-Oriented Systems Analysis: Modeling the World in Data.* Englewood Cliffs, N.J.: YOURDON Press, 1988.

9. R. Veryard, *Pragmatic Data Analysis.* Oxford, U.K.: Blackwell Scientific Publications, 1984.

10. Jeffrey Ullman, *Principles of Database Systems.* Potomac, Md.: Computer Science Press, 1982.

11. Tom DeMarco, *Structured Analysis and System Specification.* New York: YOURDON Press, 1978.

QUESTIONS AND EXERCISES

1. What is an entity-relationship diagram? What is its purpose?

2. Why is an ERD different from a dataflow diagram?

3. Why are people interested in data models?

4. Which group besides systems analysts are likely to create data models in an organization?

5. Why is the DBA group in an organization typically interested in a data model?

6. What are the four major components of an entity-relationship diagram?

7. What is the definition of an object type?

8. What is the difference between an object and an object type?

9. What are the three criteria that an object type must satisfy?

10. Which of the following are likely to be reasonable object types in a typical business system? For those that you do *not* think are reasonable object types, indicate why.

    (a) "customer"
    (b) "compute sales tax"
    (c) "height"
    (d) "product"
    (e) "tomato"
    (f) "religion"
    (g) "temperature"
    (h) "edit transaction"
    (i) "manufactured part"
    (j) "map"
    (k) "ASCII character"

11. What is the definition of a relation?

12. How many object types can be connected by a relation?

13. Which of the following are likely to be relationships in an ERD and which are not? Why or why not?

    (a) "purchases"
    (b) "customer"
    (c) "belongs to"
    (d) "weight"
    (e) "produces"
    (f) "sales tax computation"

14. What is the difference between a *derived* relationship and a *remembered* relationship? Which one is shown on an ERD?

15. Give two examples of a derived relationship between two objects.

16. How many relationships can exist between two objects in an ERD?

17. Consider the ERD shown.

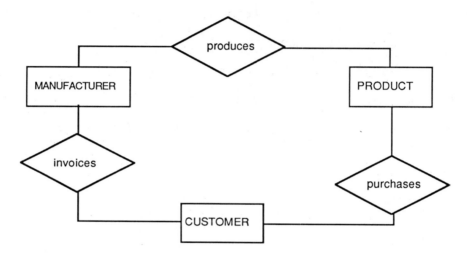

(a) Write a narrative description of the objects and relationships.

(b) How many invoices can exist between an instance of **manufacturer** and an instance of **customer**?

(c) How many **products** can a **customer** purchase in one instance of the **purchases** relationship?

18. Do ERDs show cardinality?

19. Use the notation in Figure 12.6 to show a reasonable version of the diagram in Figure 12.5.

20. What arguments are there *against* showing ordinality and cardinality in an ERD?

21. What is an alternative notation for ERDs that shows both ordinality and cardinality?

22. Draw an ERD diagram to represent the following situation for an airline:

"XYZ airline has three major resources: airplanes, pilots, and crew members. Pilots and crew members have respective home bases, which they return at the end of an assigned flight. A flight must have at least one pilot and one or more crew members attached to an airplane. Each airplane has a maintenance base."

23. Draw an ERD to describe the following situation for a publisher:

"ABC Press works with several different authors who write the books it publishes. Some authors have written only one book, while others have written many; also, some books are coauthored by multiple authors. ABC also works with multiple printers; each book, though, is printed by only one printer. An editor at ABC Press works with several authors at a time, editing and producing their book projects; it is the editor's job to turn over the final camera-ready copy to the printer when the manuscript has been copyedited and typeset."

24. Draw an ERD for the following situation for a management consulting organization:

"Each sales representative works with several different clients and has access to several different consultants in the organization. A consulting engagement with a client may involve several different consultants. During the engagement, the salesperson is uninvolved and the consultants report directly to the client."

25. Draw an ERD for the following situation:

"A teacher can teach several different classes, as long as he or she is qualified to teach the material. Each class must have one teacher, but it can be attended by several different students. At the beginning of each semester, classes are assigned to individual classrooms, where the class meets on a regular basis."

26. What is an associative object type? What is the difference between an associative object type and a relationship?

27. What is an anchor point?

28. Give three examples of an associative object type.

29. Look at Figure 12.7. Suppose that there are *no* data about the purchase that the system needs to remember. How does this change the diagram?

30. What is a subtype/supertype in an ERD?

31. Give three examples of a subtype/supertype.

32. Why do we bother having subtype/supertypes in an ERD? Why don't we just have "ordinary" object types?

33. What refinements should the systems analyst expect to make after drawing a first-cut ERD?

34. What are the three ways that the systems analyst is likely to use to discover the data elements in a data model?

35. What does attribution mean in the context of this chapter?

36. How should the systems analyst proceed with an ERD if the DFD has already been developed?

37. What are the three reasons for creating additional object types in an ERD after the first-cut model is done?

38. What should the systems analyst do if she or he discovers data elements that can be attributed to some instances of an object type, but not to others?

39. What should the systems analyst do if she or he discovers data elements that are applicable to all instances of two different object types?

40. What should the systems analyst do if she or he discovers data elements that describe relationships between other object types?

41. What should the systems analyst do if she or he discovers repeated sets within an object type?

42. Describe what it means to have repeating sets in an object type. Give an example.

43. What are the four common reasons for removing an object type from a first-cut ERD?

44. What is a dangling associative object type?

45. What should the systems analyst do if she or he discovers in a first-cut ERD an object type consisting of only an identifier?

46. What should the systems analyst do if she or he discovers in a first-cut ERD an object type of which there is only one instance?

47. What should the systems analyst do if she or he discovers in a first-cut ERD a derived relationship?

48. What extensions must be made to the data dictionary to support the ERD?

49. What does the notation @ mean in a data dictionary entry?

13 STATE-TRANSITION DIAGRAMS

> Every body continues in its state of rest, or of uniform motion in a right line,
> unless it is compelled to change that state by forces impressed upon it.
>
> Sir Isaac Newton,
> *Philosophiae Naturalis Principia Mathematica,*
> *Laws of Motion, I* , 1687

In this chapter, you will learn:

1. The notation for state-transition diagrams.

2. How to draw partitioned state-transition diagrams.

3. How to build a successful state-transition diagram.

4. The relationship between STDs and other models.

In the previous chapters, we have seen modeling tools that highlight the *functions* that a system performs, as well as the *stored data* that a system must remember. Now we look at a third kind of modeling tool, the *state-transition diagram* (also known as STD), which highlights the time-dependent behavior of a system.

Until recently, models of a system's time-dependent behavior were important only for a special category of systems known as real-time systems. Examples of these systems (which we discussed very briefly in Chapter 2) are process control, telephone switching systems, high-speed data acquisition systems, and military command and control systems. Some of these systems are passive, in the sense that they do not seek to control the surrounding environment, but rather to react to it or capture data about it. Many high-speed data acquisition systems fall into this category (e.g., a system capturing high-speed scientific data from a satellite). Other real-time systems are more active, in the sense that they seek to maintain control over some aspect of the surrounding environment. Process control systems and a variety of embedded systems fall into this category.

As you might imagine, systems of this kind deal with high-speed external sources of data, and they must provide responses and output data quickly enough to deal with the external environment. An important part of specifying such systems is the description of *what* happens *when*.

For business-oriented systems, this issue has generally not been so important. Inputs may arrive in the system from many different sources and at relatively high speeds, but the inputs can usually be delayed if the system is busy doing something else. A payroll system, for example, does not have to worry about interrupts and signals from external radar units. Typically, the only timing issues that we see in such systems are specifications of response time, which is included in the user implementation model, which we discuss in Chapter 21.

However, we are beginning to see some large, complex business-oriented systems that *do* have aspects of real-time behavior. If the system is dealing with inputs from thousands of terminals, as well as high-speed inputs from other computer systems or satellite communication facilities, then it may have the same kind of time-dependent issues that a classical real-time system has. Hence, though you may not have to deal with such problems in every system you build, you should be familiar with the modeling tools for time-dependent behavior

13.1   STATE-TRANSITION DIAGRAM NOTATION

A typical state-transition diagram is shown in Figure 13.1(a) (though it is somewhat simpler than the diagrams we will see later in this chapter). This diagram shows the behavior of a typical telephone answering machine.

The major components of the diagram are *states* and arrows representing *state changes.* There are a variety of alternative notations for state-transition diagrams; one common one is shown in Figure 13.1(b). While it is equivalent in content to Figure 13.1(a) it has the disadvantage of looking too much like a dataflow diagram. To avoid confusion, we will use the notation of Figure 13.1(a) throughout this book.

13.1.1   System States

Each rectangular box represents a *state* that the system can be in. Webster's *New World Dictionary* defines a "state" in the following way:

> A set of circumstances or attributes characterizing a person or thing at a
> given time; way or form of being; condition.

Thus, typical system states might be any of the following:

- Waiting for user to enter password

- Heating chemical mixture

- Waiting for next command

- Accelerating engine

- Mixing ingredients

- Waiting for instrument data

- Filling tank

- Idle

Note that many of these examples involve the system *waiting* for something to occur and are not expressed in terms of the computer *doing* something. This is because our state-transition diagram is being used to develop an essential model of the system,[1] a model of how the system would behave if we had perfect technology. One aspect of perfect technology is that our computer operates infinitely quickly, so any processing or computation that the system has to do, or any action that it has to take, will be done in zero time. Thus, any observable state that the system is in can only correspond to periods of time when (1) it is waiting for something in the external environment to occur, or (2) it is waiting for a current activity in the environment (mixing, washing, filling, accelerating, etc.) to change to some other activity.

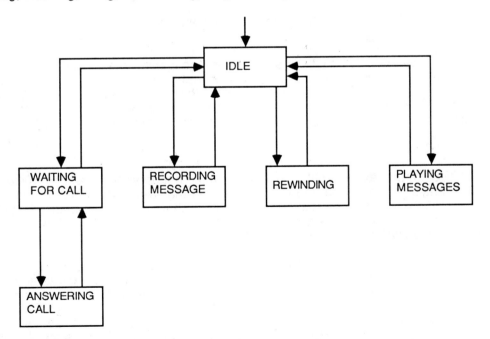

Figure 13.1:(a) **A typical state-transition diagram**

1 We will discuss the concept of an essential model in more detail in Chapter 17.

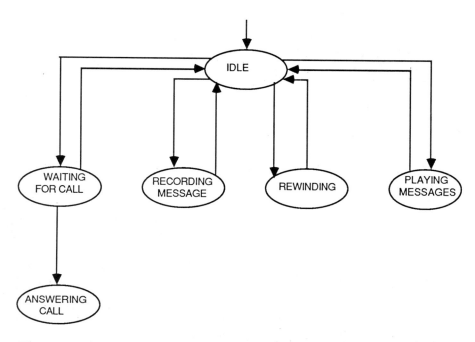

Figure 13.1(b): **An alternative state-transition diagram notation**

This does not mean that our systems are incapable of taking action or that we do not intend to show those actions. It's just that actions, which happen instantaneously in our perfect technology model, are not the same as states, which represent observable conditions that the system can be in. Thus, a state represents some behavior of the system that is observable and that lasts for some finite period of time.

13.1.2   Changes of State

A system that existed in only one state would not be very interesting to study: it would be static. Indeed, the information systems that we typically model may have dozens of different states. But how does a system change from one state to another? If the system has orderly rules governing its behavior, then typically only certain kinds of state changes will be meaningful and valid.

We show the valid state changes on our STD by connecting the relevant pairs of states with an arrow. Thus, Figure 13.2 shows that the system can change from state 1 to state 2; it also shows that when the system is in state 2, it can change to either state 3 or back to state 1. However, according to this STD, the system cannot change from state 1*directly* to state 3. On the other hand, the diagram tells us that the system *can* change directly from state 3 back to state 1. Note that state 2 has two successor states. This is quite common in STDs; indeed, any one state might lead to an arbitrary number of successor states.

While Figure 13.2 gives us some interesting information about the time-dependent behavior of a system, it does not tell us something that may turn out to be very important: what the system's *initial* and *final* states are. Indeed, Figure 13.2 is a steady-state model of a system that has been active forever and will continue to be active forever. Most systems do have a recognizable initial state and a recognizable final state; this is shown in Figure 13.3.

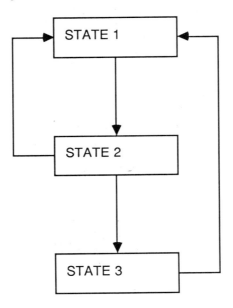

Figure 13.2: **Changes of state**

The initial state is typically the one drawn at the top of the diagram, though this is not mandatory; what really identifies state 1 in Figure 13.3 as the initial state is the "naked" arrow that is not connected to any other state. Similarly, the final state is often the one drawn at the bottom of the diagram, but this is not mandatory. What really identifies state 5 as the final state is the absence of an arrow leading out of state 5. In other words, once you get to state 5, you aren't going anywhere!

Common sense tells us that a system can have only one initial state; however, it can have multiple final states; the various final states are mutually exclusive, meaning that only one of them can occur during any one execution of the system. Figure 13.4 shows an example in which the possible final states are states 4 and 6.

Since we are using STDs to build an essential model, we also assume that state changes occur instantaneously; that is, it requires no observable time for the system to change from one state into another state. When the designers and programmers begin to build an *implementation model,* this will be a real issue: it typically *does* take a few microseconds for a computer to switch from one processing activity to another, and they must ensure that it happens quickly enough that the environment does not get out of control.

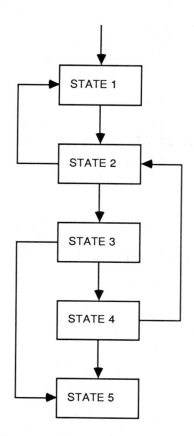

Figure 13.3: **Initial and final states**

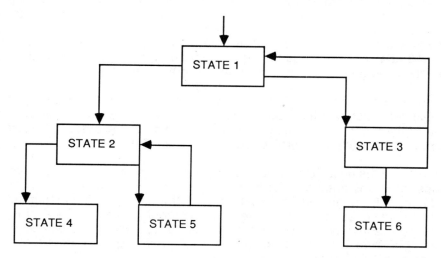

Figure 13.4: **Multiple final states of a system**

13.1.3   Conditions and Actions

To make our state-transition diagram complete, we need to add two more things: the *conditions* that cause a change of state, and the *actions* that the system takes when it changes state. As Figure 13.5 illustrates, the conditions and actions are shown next to the arrow connecting two related states.

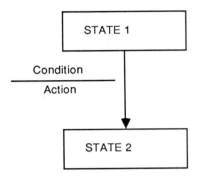

Figure 13.5: **Showing conditions and actions**

A condition is some event in the external environment that the system is capable of detecting; it will typically be a signal, an interrupt, or the arrival of a packet of data. This will typically cause the system to change from a state of waiting for X to a new state of waiting for Y, or carrying out activity X to carrying out activity Y.

But as part of the change of state, the system will typically take one or more actions: it will produce an output, display a message on the user's terminal, carry out a calculation, and so on. Thus, actions shown on the STD are either responses sent back to the external environment, or they are calculations whose results are remembered by the system (typically in a data store shown on the dataflow diagram) in order to respond to some future event.[2]

13.2   PARTITIONED DIAGRAMS

In a complex system, there may be dozens of distinct system states; trying to show them all on a single diagram would be difficult, if not impossible. Thus, just as we used leveling or partitioning with dataflow diagrams, we can use partitioning with STDs. Figure 13.6(a) shows an example of two levels of state-transition diagrams for a complex system.

Note that in this case, any individual state of a higher-level diagram can become the *initial* state for a lower-level diagram that further describes that higher-

---

2 Note that to carry out an action the system may require additional inputs from the external environment. Thus, we can say that each *condition* corresponds to an external event to which the system must respond, and that those external events will usually be recognized by the system when some incoming dataflow arrives. However, it is not necessarily true that every incoming dataflow to the system is an event corresponding to a condition on the STD.

level state; and the final state(s) in a lower-level diagram correspond to the exit conditions in the associated higher-level state. In other cases, the systems analyst may need to show, explicitly, how a low-level STD diagram exits to an appropriate place in the higher-level diagram.

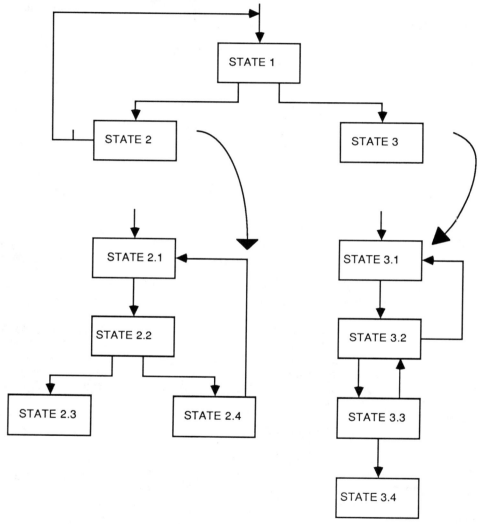

Figure 13.6(a): **Two levels of STD**

An example of the need for a partitioned state-transition diagram might be the automated teller machine now found in most banks; an STD for this application is shown in Figure 13.6(b).

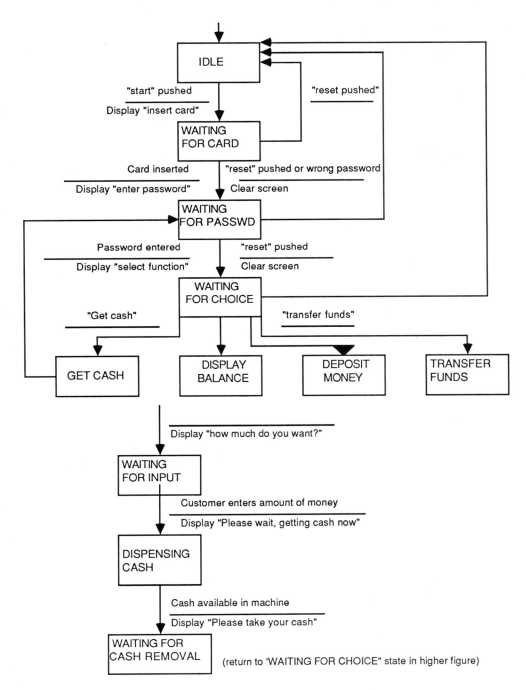

Figure 13.6(b): **A partitioned STD for an ATM machine**

13.3   BUILDING THE STATE-TRANSITION DIAGRAM

Now that we have seen the notation for state-transition diagrams, we briefly discuss the steps in building one. You can follow either of two approaches:

1.   You can begin by identifying all possible system states, representing each one as a separate box on a sheet of paper. Then you can explore all meaningful connections, (i.e., state changes) between the boxes.

2.   Alternatively, you can begin with the initial state, and then methodically trace your way to the next state(s); and then from the secondary state(s) to the tertiary state(s); and so on.

Your approach will be dictated, in many cases, by the user with whom you are working, particularly if the user is the only one familiar with the time-dependent behavior of the system.

When you have finished building the preliminary STD, you should carry out the following consistency checking guidelines:

•   *Have all states been defined?* Look at the system closely to see if there is any other observable behavior or any other condition that the system could be in besides the ones you have identified.

•   *Can you reach all the states?*   Have you defined any states that do not have paths leading into them?

•   *Can you exit from all the states?*   As mentioned above, the system may have one or more final states with multiple entrances into them; but all other states must have a successor state.

•   *In each state, does the system respond properly to all possible conditions?* This is the most common error when building a state-transition diagram: the systems analyst identifies the state changes when normal conditions occur, but fails to specify the behavior of the system for unexpected conditions. Suppose the analyst has modeled the behavior of a system as shown in Figure 13.7; she expects that the user will press a function key on his terminal to cause a change from state 1 to state 2 and a *different* function key to change from state 2 to state 3. But what if the user presses the same function key twice in a row? Or some other key? If the system behavior is not specified, there is a good chance that the designers and programmers will not program for it either, and the system will exhibit unpredictable behavior under a variety of circumstances.

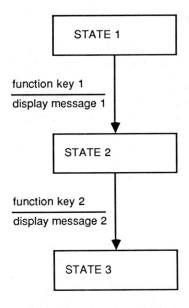

Figure 13.7: **An incomplete STD**

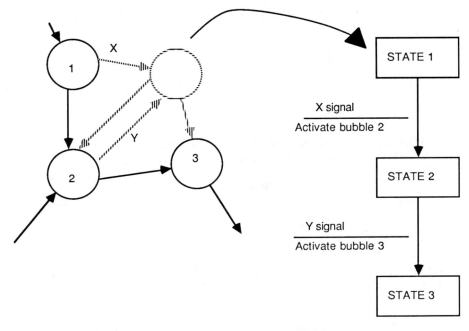

Figure 13.8: **Relationship between DFD and STD**

13.4   THE RELATIONSHIP TO OTHER MODEL COMPONENTS

The state-transition diagram can be used as a modeling tool by itself. However, it can be, and usually should be, used in conjunction with those other tools.

In most cases, the state-transition diagram represents a process specification for a control bubble in a dataflow diagram. This is illustrated in Figure 13.8; note that the *conditions* in the STD correspond to *incoming* control flows on the DFD, and the *actions* on the STD correspond to *outgoing* control flows on the DFD. As a high-level modeling tool, the state-transition diagram can even serve as a process specification for the entire system. Thus, if we represent the *entire system* with a one-bubble dataflow diagram,[3] we can use a state-transition diagram to show the sequence of activities within the system.

13.5   SUMMARY

The state-transition diagram is a powerful modeling tool for describing the required behavior of real-time systems, as well as the human interface portion of many on-line systems. Though it is not as widely known or used in the development of business-oriented information systems, it is a tool that you should become familiar with, because, in the future, we can expect that more and more systems, whether business-oriented or scientific/engineering in nature, will take on real-time overtones.

REFERENCES

1. *Webster's New World Dictionary,* Second College Edition. New York: Simon & Schuster, 1980.

QUESTIONS AND EXERCISES

1. What is a state-transition diagram? What is its purpose?

2. What kind of system is most likely to use an STD as a modeling tool?

3. Are STDs important tools for describing the requirements of a typical business-oriented information system? Why or why not?

4. Are STDs important tools for describing the design/implementation of a typical business-oriented information system? Why or why not? If so, what kind of business systems?

5. What are the two major components of an STD?

6. Show an alternative notation for an STD, that is, one different than the standard diagrams shown in this chapter and throughout the book.

---

3 Such a diagram is known as a context diagram. We will discuss the context diagram in more detail in Chapter 18.

7.   What is the definition of a state?

8.   Give three examples of a state.

9.   What is a change of state? How is it shown on an STD?

10. What is a successor state?

11. What is the initial state of a system? How many initial states may there be in a system?

12. What is the final state of a system? How many final states may there be in a system?

13. What are conditions in an STD? How are they shown?

14. What are actions in an STD? How are they shown?

15. How many conditions can there be in a state-transition diagram?

16. How many actions can be associated with each conditions in a state-transition diagram?

17. Which of the following sound like reasonable states? For those that do *not* sound like reasonable states, indicate why:

   (a) Compute sales tax
   (b) Monitoring reagent mixture
   (c) Customer-billing-address
   (d) Product-file
   (e) Elevator rising
   (f) Reagent temperature out of range
   (g) Update invoice total
   (h) Stop elevator
   (i) Interrupt key pressed
   (j) Processing data

18. What is a partitioned state-transition diagram?

19. What is the relationship between initial states and final states in a partitioned STD?

20. How many levels can there be in a partitioned STD?

21. What are the two common approaches for building an STD?

22. What are the four guidelines for determining whether an STD is consistent?

23. What is the relationship between an STD and a DFD?

24.   What is wrong with the following STD?

STATE

25.   What is wrong with the following STD?

STATE1

STATE2

26.   What is wrong with the following STD?

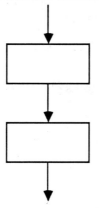

27.   What is wrong with the following STD?

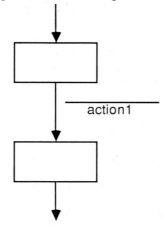

28. What is wrong with the following STD?

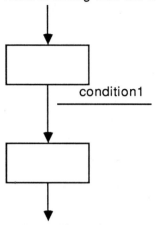

condition1

29. What is wrong with the following STD?

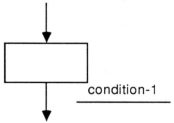

STATE1

30. What is wrong with the following STD?

STATE1

condition-1
action-1

31. What is wrong with the following STD? If you do not think anything is wrong with
it, describe what might be happening in the system being modeled by this STD.

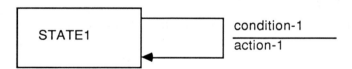

condition-1

32. What is wrong with the following STD?

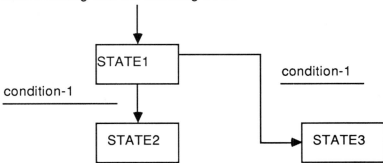

33. In a complex system, should the systems analyst begin by drawing a set of DFDs for the system, or begin with ERDs, or begin with STDs?

34. Where should the details of STD conditions and actions be described in a system model?

35. Draw a state-transition diagram for a simple tape recorder or cassette tape player.

36. Draw a state-transition diagram for your bank's automated teller machine.

37. Draw a state-transition diagram for a digital wristwatch (most digital watches these days have a "normal" mode, as well as an alarm clock and a chronograph).

38. Draw a state-transition diagram for a microwave oven.

39. Draw a state-transition diagram for the human interface menu for Lotus 1-2-3.

14 BALANCING THE MODELS

All men are liable to error; and most men are, in many points, by passion
or interest, under temptation to it.

John Locke,
*Essay Concerning Human Understanding,*1690

In this chapter, you will learn:

1. How to balance a dataflow diagram against the data dictionary.

2. How to balance a dataflow diagram against a process specification.

3. How to balance a process specification against the data dictionary.

4. How to balance an ERD against the DFD and process specification.

5. How to balance an ERD against the data dictionary.

6. How to balance a dataflow diagram against the state-transition diagram.

In the past five chapters, we have examined several important modeling tools for structured analysis:

- Dataflow diagram

- Data dictionary

- Process specification

- Entity-relationship diagram

- State-transition diagram

Each of these tools, as we have seen, focuses on one critical aspect of the system being modeled. It is important to keep this in mind, for it means that the person *reading* the model is also focusing on one critical aspect, that is, the aspect to which his or her attention is being drawn by the modeling tool itself. Because the underlying system has so many different dimensions of complexity, we want the dataflow diagram to focus the reader's attention on the system *functions* without letting data relationships distract his attention; and we want the entity-relationship diagram to focus attention on the *data* relationships without letting the functional characteristics distract his or her attention; and we want the state-transition diagram to focus attention on the *timing* characteristics of the system without the distractions of functions or data.

But there comes a time for pulling all the modeling tools together, and that is what this chapter is all about. The situation faced by the systems modeler is somewhat analogous to the ancient fable of the three blind wise men in India who stumbled up against an elephant. As Figure 14.1 illustrates, they came to three different opinions about the "reality" they were dealing with after touching different parts of the elephant:

Figure 14.1: **Three blind men touching an elephant**

- One blind man touched the sharp end of one of the elephant's long tusks. "Aha," he said, "what we have here is a bull. I can feel its horns."

- The second blind man touched the bristly hide of the elephant. "Without a doubt," he said, "this is a ... what? A porcupine? Yes, indeed—a porcupine!"

- The third blind man felt one of the elephant's thick legs and said, "This must be a tree that we're dealing with."

Similarly, when modeling three different aspects of a system (functions, data, and timing), as well as modeling detailed characteristics of the system in a data dictionary and set of process specifications, it is easy to develop several different *inconsistent* interpretations of that one reality. This is a particularly serious danger on large projects, where various people and various special interest groups are likely to be involved. It is also a danger whenever the project team (and/or the user community) involves people with very different backgrounds.

There is another reason for focusing on model consistency: whatever errors exist will eventually be found, but they become increasingly difficult and expensive later in the project. Indeed, any errors that are introduced into the requirements model during the systems analysis phase are likely to be propagated and magnified during the design and implementation phases of the project. This is a particularly serious danger on large projects where the systems analysis is often done by different people (or even different companies!) than the design and implementation. Thus, Martin points out that 50% of the errors that are detected in a system and 75% of the cost of error removal are associated with errors in the systems analysis phase. And studies in [Boehm, 1981] have shown that the cost of correcting an error goes up exponentially in later stages of a project; it is ten times cheaper to fix a systems analysis error *during* the systems analysis phase of the project than it is to fix the same error during the design phase.

Some of these errors are, of course, simple errors in each individual model (e.g., a dataflow diagram with an infinite sink). And some of the errors can be characterized as *wrong* interpretations of what the user really wanted. But many of the more difficult and insidious errors are intermodel errors, that is, inconsistencies between one model and another. A structured specification in which all the modeling tools have been cross-checked against each other for consistency is said to be *balanced*.

The most common balancing error involves a *missing* definition: something defined (or described) in one model is not appropriately defined in another model. We will see several examples of this in the following sections (e.g., a data store shown on the DFD but not defined in the data dictionary, or an object in the ERD not shown as a corresponding data store on the DFD). The second common type of error is one of *inconsistency:* the same "reality" is described in different, contradictory ways in two different models.

We will examine several major aspects of balancing:

- Balancing the dataflow diagram against the data dictionary.

- Balancing the dataflow diagram against the process specifications.

- Balancing the process specifications against the data dictionary.

- Balancing the ERD against the DFD and process specifications.

- Balancing the ERD against the data dictionary.

- Balancing the DFD against the state-transition diagram.

As we will see, the balancing rules are all very straightforward; they require very little intelligence or creativity to carry out. But they *must* be carried out, and carried out diligently.

14.1   BALANCING THE DFD AGAINST THE DD

The rules for balancing the dataflow diagram against the data dictionary are as follows:

- Every dataflow (i.e., an arrow on the DFD) and every data store must be defined in the data dictionary. If it is missing in the data dictionary, the dataflow or data store is considered to be *undefined*.

- Conversely, every data element and every data store defined in the data dictionary must appear someplace on a DFD. If it does not appear, the offending data element or data store is a "ghost"—something defined but not "used" in the system. This can happen if the data elements are defined to correspond with an early version of the DFD; the danger is that the DFD may be changed (i.e., a dataflow or data store may be deleted) without a corresponding change to the data dictionary.

This means, of course, that the systems analyst must painstakingly review both the DFDs and the data dictionary to ensure that they are balanced. It doesn't matter which model is examined first, though most analysts begin with the DFD to ensure that all the elements are defined in the data dictionary. Like all the other balancing activities in this chapter, it is a tedious chore and one that is well suited to automated support.

14.2   BALANCING THE DFD AGAINST THE PROCESS SPECIFICATION

Here are the rules for balancing the DFD against the process specifications:

- Every bubble in the DFD must be associated with a lower-level DFD *or* a process specification, but not both. Thus, if the DFD shows a bubble that is identified as 1.4.2, then there must either be a corresponding *figure* identified as Figure 1.4.2 whose bubbles are identified as 1.4.2.1, 1.4.2.2, and so on, *or* the structured specification must contain a process specification for bubble 1.4.2. If *both* exist, the model is unnecessarily (and dangerously) redundant.

- Every process specification must have an associated bottom-level bubble in the DFD. Since the process specification does require a lot of work, one would think it highly unlikely that there would be "tramp" process specifications floating around a system. But it can happen: the process specification may have been written for a preliminary version of the DFD, after which a revision process might eliminate some of the DFD bubbles.

- Inputs and outputs must match. The DFD will show incoming and outgoing flows for each bubble, as well as connections to stores. These should be evident in the process specification, too: thus, we should expect to see a READ statement (or GET, or INPUT, or ACCEPT, or some other similar verb) corresponding to each incoming dataflow and a WRITE (or PUT, or DISPLAY, etc.) for each outgoing dataflow.

Note that these comments apply specifically to *processing* bubbles. For the *control* bubbles in a DFD, there are correspondences between the bubbles and associated state-transition diagrams, as discussed in Section 14.6.

14.3   BALANCING THE PROCESS SPECS AGAINST THE DFD AND DD

The rules for balancing the process specifications against the dataflow diagram and data dictionary can be described as follows: Each data reference in the process specification (typically a noun) must satisfy one of the following rules:

- It matches the name of a dataflow or data store connected to the bubble described by the process specification, *or*

- It is a local term, explicitly defined in the process specification, *or*

- It appears as a *component* in a data dictionary entry for a dataflow or data store connected to the bubble. Thus, the data elements X and Y appear in the process specification shown in Figure 14.2, but do not appear as a connected dataflow in the DFD shown in Figure 14.3. However, the data dictionary, a fragment of which is shown in Figure 14.4, indicates that X and Y are components of Z; and in Figure 14.3 we see that Z is indeed a dataflow connected to the bubble, so we conclude that the model is balanced.[1]

---

[1] However, it may be worth doing some further checking at this point: if X is the *only* component of Z that is used in the process specification, we could seriously question why Z was shown as an input in the first place. That is, the remaining components of Z may be "tramp data" that "float" through the bubble without being used. This often reflects a model of an arbitrary *implementation* of a system, rather than a model of the *essential* behavior of the system.

PROCESS SPECIFICATION 3.5: COMPUTE WIDGET FACTOR

* P AND Q ARE LOCAL TERMS USED FOR INTERMEDIATE RESULTS *

P = 3.14156 * X

.
.

Q = 2.78128 * Y - 13

.

WIDGET-FACTOR = P * Q + 2

Figure 14.2: A process specification component of a system model

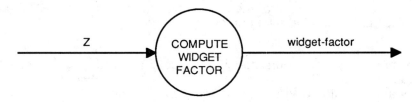

Figure 14.3: A DFD component of a system model

.
.
X =   * horizontal component of frammis factor *
        * units: centimeters; range: 0 - 100 *

.

.
Y =   * vertical component of frammis factor *
        * units: centimeters; range: 0 - 10 *

.
.

.
Z =   * frammis factor, as defined by Dr. Frammis *
        X + Y

Figure 14.4: A data dictionary component of a system model

14.4   BALANCING THE DATA DICTIONARY AGAINST THE DFD AND PROCESS SPECIFICATIONS

From the discussion above, it can be seen that the data dictionary is consistent with the rest of the model if it obeys the following rule:

- Each entry in the data dictionary must be referenced by a process specification, or a DFD, or another data dictionary entry.

This assumes, of course, that we are modeling the *essential* behavior of a system. A complex, exhaustive data dictionary of an existing *implementation* of a system may contain some data elements that are no longer used.

One could also argue that the data dictionary might be planned in such a way that it permits future expansion; that is, it contains elements that are not needed today, but might be useful in the future. A good example of this is a data dictionary that contains elements that may be useful for ad hoc inquiry. The project team, perhaps in concert with the user, can determine whether this kind of unbalanced model is indeed an appropriate thing to do. However, it *is* important to at least be aware of the occurrence of such deliberate decisions.

14.5 BALANCING THE ERD AGAINST THE DFD AND PROCESS SPECIFICATIONS

The entity-relationship diagram, as we saw in Chapter 12, presented a very different view of a system than did the dataflow diagram. However, there are some relationships that must hold in order for the overall system model to be complete, correct, and consistent:

- Every store on the DFD must correspond to an object type, or a relationship, or a combination of an object type and relationship (i.e., an associative object type) on the ERD. If there is a store on the DFD that does not appear on the ERD, something is wrong; and if there is an object or relationship on the ERD that does not appear on the DFD, something is wrong.

- Object names on the ERD and data store names on the DFD must match. As we saw in Chapters 9 and 12, the convention in this book is to use the *plural* form (e.g., **CUSTOMERS**) on the DFD and the *singular* form on the ERD.

- The data dictionary entries must apply to *both* the DFD model and the ERD model. Thus the data dictionary entry for the above example should include definitions for both the object on the ERD and the store on the ERD. This would imply a data dictionary definition such as the following:

CUSTOMERS = {CUSTOMER}

CUSTOMER = name + address + phone-number + ...

The data dictionary entries for the singular form (e.g., **CUSTOMER**) must provide the meaning and composition of a single instance of the *set* of objects referred to (in the singular) in the ERD and (in the plural) in the data store of a DFD. The data dictionary entries for the plural form (e.g., **CUSTOMERS**) provide the meaning and the composition of the *set* of instances.

Similarly, there are rules for ensuring that the ERD is consistent with the process specification portion of the function-oriented model (keep in mind that the process specifications are the detailed components of the model whose graphical "incarnation" is the DFD). The rules are that the combined set of all process specifications must, in their entirety:

- *Create and delete* instances of each object type and relationship and relationship shown in the ERD. This can be understood by looking at the DFD shown in Figure 14.5: as we know, the **CUSTOMERS** store corresponds to the **CUSTOMER** object. Something must be capable of creating and deleting instances of a *customer*, which means that some bubble within the DFD must have a dataflow connected to the **CUSTOMERS** store. But the actual *work* of writing to the store (i.e., creating or deleting an instance of the related **CUSTOMER** object in the ERD) must take place *inside* the bubble, which means that it must be documented by the process specification associated with the bubble.[2]

- Some DFD bubble *sets values* for each data element attributed to each instance of each object type, and some DFD process uses (or reads) values of each data element.

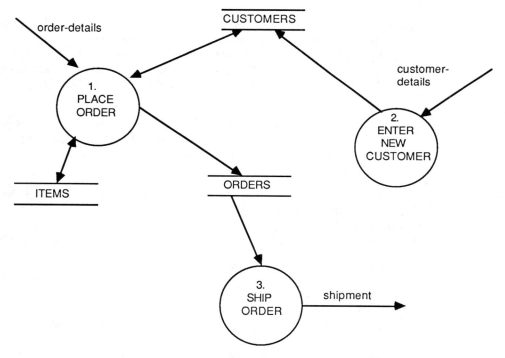

Figure 14.5: **Creating and deleting ERD instances**

---

2 Note that the situation may be somewhat more complicated: the bubble shown on the DFD may not be a bottom-level bubble. Thus, it is possible that the bubble labeled **ENTER-NEW-CUSTOMER** in Figure 14.5 may be described by a *lower-level dataflow diagram*, not by a process specification. If this is the case, then one of the lower-level bubbles (perhaps not one level, but *several* levels below) will be a primitive and will access the store directly. Recall from Chapter 9 that our convention on the DFD is that the store is shown at the *highest* level where it is an interface between two bubbles, and it is repeated in *every* lower-level diagram.

14.6   BALANCING THE DFD AGAINST THE STATE-TRANSITION DIAGRAM

The state condition can be considered balanced against the dataflow diagram if the following rules are met:

- Every control bubble in the DFD has associated with it a state-transition diagram as its process specification. Similarly, every state-transition diagram in the overall system model must be associated with a control process (bubble) in the DFD.

- Every *condition* in the state-transition diagram must correspond to an *incoming* control flow into the control process associated with the state-transition diagram. Similarly, every incoming control flow on the control bubble must be associated with an appropriate condition on the corresponding state-transition diagram.

- Every *action* in the state-transition diagram must correspond to an *outgoing* control flow in the control process associated with the state-transition diagram. Similarly, every outgoing control flow on the control bubble must be associated with an appropriate action on the corresponding state-transition diagram.

These correspondences are illustrated in Figure 14.6.

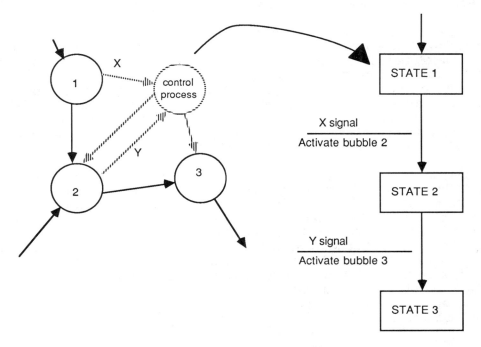

Figure 14.6: **Correspondences between the DFD and STD**

14.7   SUMMARY

Note that all the balancing rules presented in this chapter have been presented as if you were going to *personally* examine all the components of a system model to spot potential errors and inconsistencies. This would imply that you should lay out, on the floor or on a very large bulletin board, all the DFDs, process specifications, ERDs, STDs, and data dictionary, and then walk from one to the other, carefully checking that everything is in place.

As this book is being prepared, in 1987, that is *precisely* what you would have to do in 98% of the systems development organizations in the world. If you are lucky enough to be reading this book in the 1990 time frame, that figure may have dropped to 90%. And if you are still reading this book in 1995 (by which time my editor should have forced me to produce a new edition in which this entire section will be deleted), the figure might be 50%. The point is that the balancing rules we have presented in this chapter can be automated, and there are already a number of PC-based workstation tools that will carry out some or all of the error-checking mechanically.

But we have seen exactly the same phenomenon in a number of other fields. One could argue that the proliferation of cheap word-processing systems has obviated the need for learning script writing; indeed, one might argue that the availability of spelling checkers has even obviated the need for learning how to spell. And the universal availability of pocket calculators has obviated the need to learn how to do long division. And the ubiquitous presence of automatic-shift cars has obviated the need to learn how to drive stick-shift cars.

Indeed, I can't think of any compelling reason for teaching someone in North America how to drive a stick-shift car as we approach the end of the 20th century. Nor can I think of any reason for emphasizing the art of calligraphy and handwriting (except, perhaps, as an art form) in an age where word-processing systems are about to be replaced by voice-recognition systems. But I can appreciate the need for learning the basic principles of long division, even if one is supremely confident that one will never be without a pocket calculator; if nothing else, as Joshua Schwartz of Harvard University points out, it helps us to know whether the answer we have produced with our calculator has the decimal point in the right place.

One could even argue the merits of learning script handwriting in 1987, when (1) less than half of the privileged children in the United States have a personal computer at home; (2) only about 3% of the U.S. population overall has a personal computer at home; (3) only about 10% of the American teachers have their own PC; and (4) only a tiny percentage of U.S. schools are prepared to teach the mechanical skills of typing. Script handwriting is *technologically* obsolete, and it is painful for computer-literate parents (not to mention computer-literate children!) to be forced to learn this ancient, primitive communication skill; but it is probably still a necessary skill in today's society. After all, it was only a few years ago that most parents stopped teaching their children how to replace the spark plugs, change the oil, and fix a flat tire on their automobile.

Similarly, I am convinced that a professional systems analyst needs to understand the *principles* of balancing presented in this chapter. As a systems analyst, chances are that you will have no alternative but to carry out these error-checking rules mechanically for the next few years until proper software engineering tools are widely distributed. The manual error-checking process will normally be validated in a *walkthrough* environment; walkthroughs are discussed in Appendix D.

REFERENCES

1. James Martin, *An Information Systems Manifesto.* Englewood Cliffs, N.J.: Prentice-Hall, 1984.

2. Barry Boehm, *Software Engineering Economics.* Englewood Cliffs, N.J.: Prentice-Hall, 1981.

QUESTIONS AND EXERCISES

1. Why is it important to balance the models of a system specification? What are the dangers of an unbalanced specification?

2. Why is it important to find errors in a system model as early as possible?

3. What percentage of the cost of error removal is associated with the systems analysis phase of a project?

4. What are the two most common forms of balancing errors?

5. What parts of the system model must the DFD be balanced against?

6. What parts of the system model must the ERD be balanced against?

7. What parts of the system model must the STD be balanced against?

8. What parts of the system model must the data dictionary be balanced against?

9. What parts of the system model must the process specification be balanced against?

10. Are there are any other components of the system model that must be balanced?

11. What are the rules for balancing the DFD against the data dictionary?

12. Under what conditions could an item be defined in the data dictionary without appearing somewhere on a DFD?

13. What are the rules for balancing the DFD against the process specifications?

14. What would happen if a process specification were written for a nonprimitive (or nonatomic) bubble in the DFD?

15. Should there be a process specification for control processes in the DFD? If so, should it take the same form as a process specification for a normal process?

16. What are the rules for balancing the process specification against the DFD and data dictionary?

17. What are "tramp data"?

18. Under what conditions is it acceptable for a term (or data reference) in the process specification to *not* be defined in the data dictionary?

19. What are the rules for balancing the data dictionary against the DFD and process specification?

20. Under what conditions is it possible that the project team might *deliberately* put items into the data dictionary that are not in the DFD?

21. What are the rules for balancing the ERD against the DFD?

22. What is the convention for matching names in the ERD with stores in the DFD?

23. What are the rules for balancing the ERD against the process specification?

24. What are the rules for balancing the STD against the DFD?

25. Under what conditions is it valid *not* to have an STD in a system model?

26. How should the balancing rules presented in this chapter be carried out in a typical systems development project? Who should be responsible for seeing that it gets done?

27. If you have an automated systems analysis workstation, is it necessary to learn the balancing rules presented in this chapter? Why or why not?

28. If the system models have been balanced, can we be confident that they are correct? Why or why not?

29. Point out three balancing errors in the following system model.

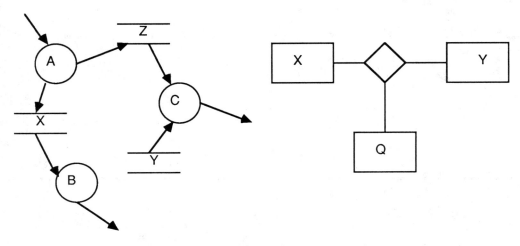

30. Should the STD be balanced against the ERD? Why or why not?

15 ADDITIONAL MODELING TOOLS

> The need to discover inefficiency early makes it important to *externalize* (that is, make visible) an evolving design at each stage. Engineering blueprints, for instance, serve this purpose and are useful not only for a designer by calling his attention to trouble spots and potential inconsistencies, but also for a team or an entire organization developing a product. Blueprints are the major medium of communication, criticism, and collective refinement. Moreover, representation methods must be relatively simple and direct in bridging the gap between reality and the program; and they must be efficient during the multiple iterative steps.
> L.A. Belady, foreword to *Software Design,* [Peters, 1981]

In this chapter, you will learn:

1. How to identify several variations on flowcharts.

2. How to draw HIPO diagrams and structure charts.

3. How to identify several variations on DFD diagrams.

4. How to identify several variations on ERD diagrams.

The modeling tools presented in the last several chapters should be sufficient for any project that you work on. However, you should also be familiar with some additional modeling tools; even if you don't use them, you may encounter them in your work, and you should at least know how to read and interpret them.

The additional modeling tools that we will discuss in this chapter include the following:

- Flowcharts and their variants

- System flowcharts

- HIPO diagrams and structure charts

- Variations on dataflow diagrams

- Variations on entity-relationship diagrams

The purpose of this chapter is not to make you an expert in any of these modeling tools, but merely to show you that they exist as possible alternatives. Additional details on each modeling tool can be found in the references at the end of the chapter.

15.1   FLOWCHARTS AND THEIR VARIANTS

15.1.1   The Classic Flowchart

One of the earliest and best known modeling tools is the classic flowchart; a typical flowchart is shown in Figure 15.1.

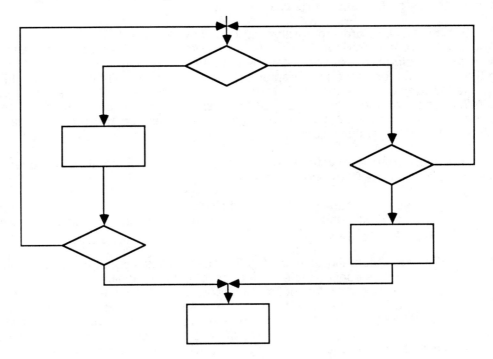

Figure 15.1: **A typical flowchart**

If you have been exposed to computers, or programming, or data processing in any form, chances are that you have had at least some informal exposure to flowcharts. We will not discuss them in detail in this book and will only look at a subset of the diagramming notation. For details on flowchart notation, refer to [Chapin, 1970].

The notation shown in Figure 15.1 has only three components:

- The rectangular box represents an executable computer instruction *or a contiguous sequence of instructions.*

- The diamond-shaped box represents a decision; in the simple case, it represents a *binary* decision.

- The arrows connecting the boxes represent the flow of control. There can be only one arrow flowing *out* of a rectangular box; that is, when a computer instruction finishes its execution, it can proceed to any one single *next* instruction or decision. Similarly, there can be only two arrows emanating from a decision.

As you can see, the flowchart allows us to graphically represent the procedural logic of a computer program. And that is where flowcharts are used most, though the introduction of high-level programming languages in the 1960s and 1970s has eliminated much of the need for detailed flowcharts.

But if flowcharts are a programming tool, why discuss them in this book? The answer may have occurred to you already: some systems analysts use flowcharts as a way of documenting process specifications (i.e., as an alternative to structured English and the other tools presented in Chapter 11). As you may recall from Chapter 11, my feeling is that *any documentation technique that accurately describes the user's policy and effectively communicates that policy is acceptable.* Thus, if the user enjoys reading flowcharts and if the flowcharts accurately describe the policy carried out within a bubble in a dataflow diagram, they can be used.

However, very few systems analysts actually do use detailed flowcharts for process specifications. There are several reasons for this:

- Unless great care is taken, the flowchart can become incredibly complicated and difficult to read.[1] An example of a typical unstructured flowchart is shown in Figure 15.2.

- Though automated support (on PC-based workstations) is now available, it still requires considerable work to develop the graphics of a flowchart. And if the user's detailed policy changes, or if the systems analyst has to change it several times before he has something that the user will accept as correct, it will be time consuming and tedious to redraw the flowchart each time. If the process specification has been represented in some textual form that can be manipulated with a word processor, changes are usually much easier.

---

1 As a consequence of this, a *specification* developed with flowcharts would be enormously larger than a specification developed with the other modeling tools discussed in this book.

- Graphical models are usually most effective as a way of illustrating a *multi*dimensional reality. Dataflow diagrams, for example, vividly illustrate the fact that all the bubbles in the system can be active at the same time. But the flow of control in a program or an individual process specification can be described in a *one*-dimensional form; that is, the logic can be arranged so that it flows uniformly from "top to bottom".[2] Because of this, graphics are unnecessary.

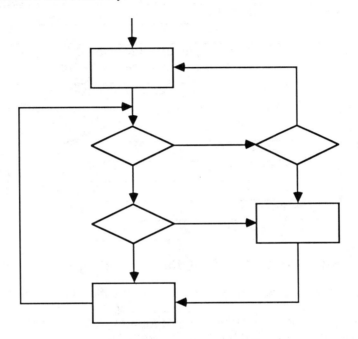

Figure 15.2: **An unstructured flowchart**

15.1.2   Variations on Flowcharts

While the classic flowcharts are the ones most commonly used—when they are used at all!—there are some variations that you should be aware of. We will mention four:

1. Nassi-Shneiderman diagrams
2. Ferstl diagrams
3. Hamilton-Zeldin diagrams
4. Problem analysis diagrams

---

2 The fact that any arbitrary flowchart logic can be rearranged into an equivalent top-to-bottom flow is the basis of *structured programming.* Böhm and Jacopini[2] first proved that this could be done in flowchart terms; in programming terms, it means that any program can be written in a Pascal-like language without **GOTO** statements.

Nassi-Shneiderman diagrams (sometimes referred to as Chapin charts) were introduced in the 1970s (see [Nassi and Shneiderman, 1973] and [Chapin, 1974]) as a way of enforcing a strict structured programming approach. A typical Nassi-Shneiderman diagram is shown in Figure 15.3. As you can see, the diagram is easy to read. However, one could argue that Nassi-Shneiderman diagrams are just structured English statements with boxes drawn around them.

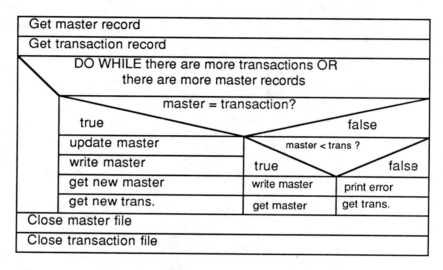

Figure 15.3: **A typical Nassi-Shneiderman diagram.**

Ferstl diagrams are another variation on the classic flowchart; a full description is provided in [Ferstl, 1978]. A typical Ferstl diagram is shown in Figure 15.4(a). In addition to showing normal, sequential program logic, the Ferstl diagram can also be used to show parallel processing; the Ferstl notation for parallel processing is shown in Figure 15.4(b).

Hamilton-Zeldin diagrams were developed as part of the software development activities for NASA's Space Shuttle project; see [Hamilton and Zeldin, 1972]. A typical Hamilton-Zeldin diagram, sometimes referred to as a structured design diagram, is shown in Figure 15.5. In Hamilton-Zeldin diagrams, the rectangular boxes have the same meaning as a rectangular box in an ANSI flowchart: an executable statement or contiguous group of executable statements. An elongated pentagon is used to show both IF statements and DO-WHILE/REPEAT-UNTIL iterations. Control normally flows from top to bottom of the diagram, except in the case of IF tests and iterations (DOs and REPEATs), which proceed from left to right.

Problem analysis diagrams (PAD), developed at the Hitachi Corporation (see [Futamura, Kawai, Horikoshi, and Tsutsumi, 1981]), are a two-dimensional, tree-structured representation of program logic. The components of a PAD diagram are shown in Figure 15.6(a). As with the Hamilton-Zeldin diagrams, PAD diagrams are read from top to bottom, with IF constructs and iterations being shown left to right; an example is shown in Figure 15.6(b).

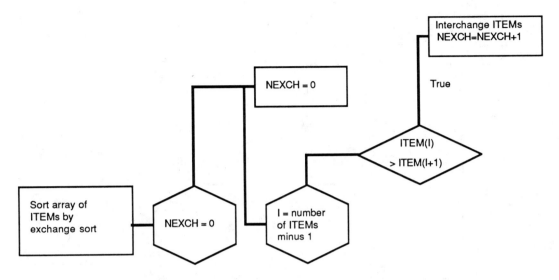

Figure 15.4(a): **A typical Ferstl diagram**

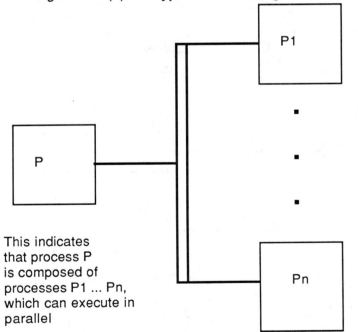

This indicates
that process P
is composed of
processes P1 ... Pn,
which can execute in
parallel

Figure 15.4(b): **Parallel processing notation in Ferstl diagrams**

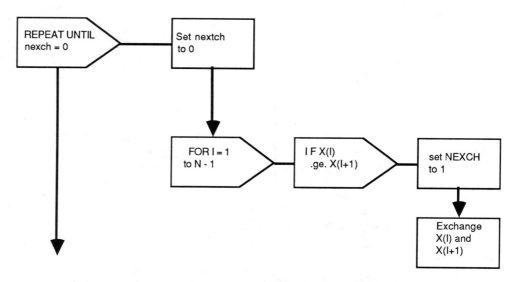

Figure 15.5: **A typical Hamilton-Zeldin diagram**

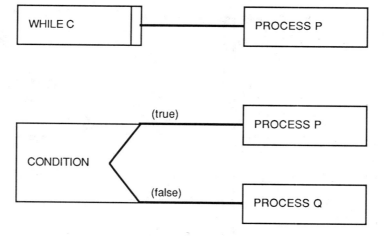

Figure 15.6(a): **Components of a PAD diagram**

Like the Ferstl diagrams, a PAD diagram can show parallel processing; it also uses a combination of vertical display of sequential flow with a horizontal display of nesting levels (e.g., loops within loops within loops) that is similar to the Hamilton-Zeldin diagrams.

15.2   SYSTEM FLOWCHARTS

The various flowchart approaches in the previous section are useful for showing detailed logic, either within a computer program or within a process specification for an individual bubble in a DFD. However, a high-level view of the organization of a system can be shown by another kind of flowchart: the *system flowchart*. A typical system flowchart is shown in Figure 15.7.

Note that the rectangular boxes represent operational *aggregates* of computer software (e.g., computer programs, job steps, runs, or other units of computer software). The system flowchart also shows various kinds of physical files (e.g., magnetic tape files or disk files). And it may show the presence of on-line terminals and telecommunication links.

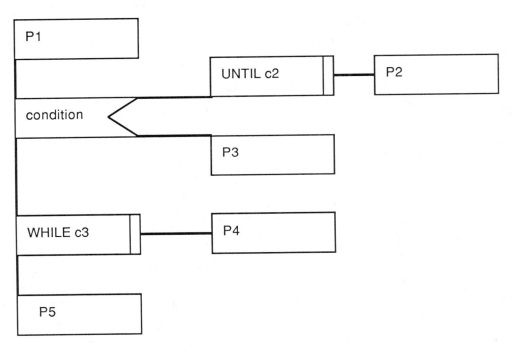

Figure 15.6(b): **A typical PAD diagram**

The system flowchart is often a very useful diagram for the systems designers who must develop an overall systems architecture of hardware and software to implement the user requirements. However, I feel that it is not an appropriate modeling tool for systems analysis, for the simple reason that it emphasizes *physical* implementation details that the user and systems analyst should not be discussing. Rather than talking about a disk file, for example, the systems analyst and user should be discussing the *content* of the file; rather than talking about individual computer programs, they should be talking about the *functions* to be carried out.

There is one situation where the system flowchart could be a useful modeling tool: at the end of the systems analysis activity, when the *user implementation model* is being developed. At this point, the user, the systems analyst, and the implementation team (designers and programmers) discuss those implementation constraints that must be imposed upon the system; these include such things as the determination of the automation boundary (what parts of the system will be automated and what parts will be manual) and the human interface (details of the interaction between the system and its human users).

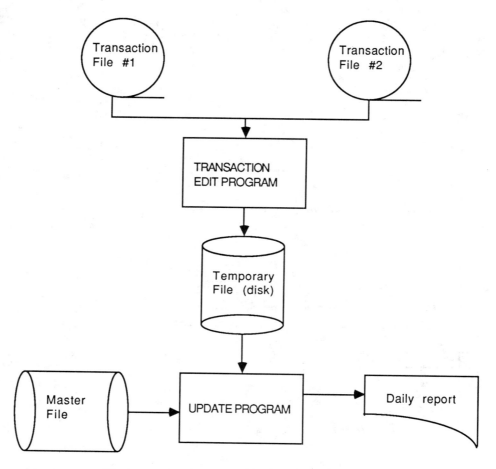

Figure 15.7: **A typical system flowchart**

15.3   HIPO DIAGRAMS

HIPO diagrams were developed by IBM in the 1970s (see [HIPO, 1974] and [Katzan, 1976]) and have been used by some systems analysts to present a high-level view of the functions performed by a system, as well as the decomposition of functions into subfunctions, and so on. A typical HIPO diagram is shown in Figure 15.8.

In some user environments, HIPO diagrams can be useful modeling tools, because they look like the familiar organization chart that describes the hierarchy of managers, submanagers, and so on. However, the diagram does not show the data used by, or produced by the system; while it is understandable that one might want to de-emphasize data relationships in a model, I don't feel that it helps to eliminate *all* information about the data.

Actually, there is a second component of the HIPO diagram that does show the data. The diagram shown in Figure 15.8 is known as a VTOC, or visual table of contents. Each function represented by a rectangular box can be described in further detail in an IPO (or input-process-output) diagram; a typical IPO diagram is shown in Figure 15.9.

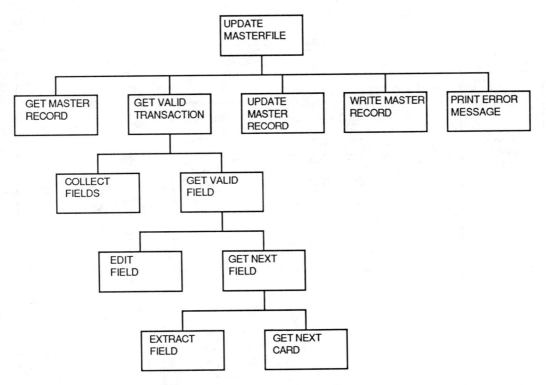

Figure 15.8: **A typical HIPO diagram**

While the details of the data are indeed shown at this level, they are not shown on the high-level VTOC diagram. Thus, anyone looking at an overview of the system has no easy way of seeing the interfaces between the various system components.

15.4   STRUCTURE CHARTS

A variation on HIPO diagrams that is in wide use is the *structure chart.* A typical structure chart is shown in Figure 15.10; notice that in addition to showing the functional hierarchy, it also shows the *data* interfaces between the components.

Unlike many of the previous diagrams, the rectangular box in a structure chart does not represent a single computational statement or a contiguous group of statements; instead, it represents a *module.* (Common examples of modules are FORTRAN subroutines, Pascal procedures, COBOL subprograms, and SECTIONs.) The arrows connecting the modules do not represent GOTO statements, but instead represent subroutine calls; the notation implies that a subroutine will exit, or return, to its caller when it has finished carrying out its function.

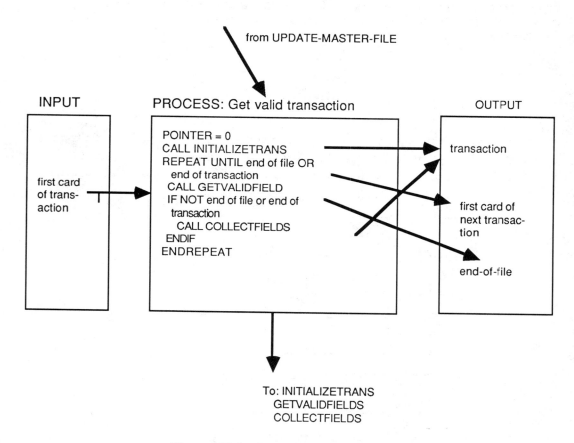

Figure 15.9: **A typical IPO diagram**

While the structure chart is generally preferred over the HIPO diagram, it still has no real use in the area of systems analysis. Why? Because it is used as a design tool to model a *synchronous hierarchy of modules* in a system; by synchronous, we mean that only one module is executing at any given time, which is an accurate representation of the way things work on most common computers today. The systems analyst, on the other hand, needs a modeling tool that allows him or her to show a *hierarchy of asynchronous networks* of processes; this is effectively accomplished with the leveled set of dataflow diagrams.

The structure chart is extensively used in program design; we will discuss it in more detail in Chapter 22.

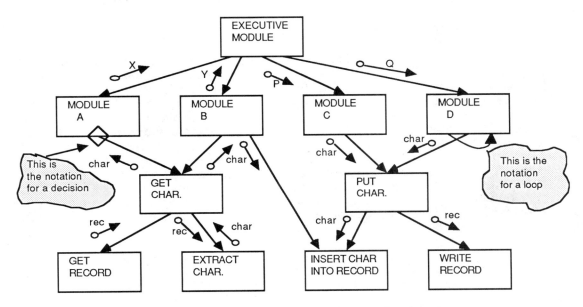

Figure 15.10: **A typical structure chart**

15.5   VARIATIONS ON DATAFLOW DIAGRAMS

As mentioned in Chapter 9, there are various "cosmetic" differences between the dataflow diagrams in this book and the dataflow diagrams shown in other textbooks. The primary differences usually involve such things as the use of a rectangle or oval instead of a bubble to show the functions carried out by a system; dataflow diagrams drawn with ovals are frequently referred to as Gane-Sarson diagrams.

However, there is at least one significant variation on the classic dataflow diagram; it is known as the SADT diagram and was developed at Softech (see [Ross and Schoman, 1977]).   Figure 15.11 shows a typical SADT diagram.

While similar in nature to the dataflow diagrams presented in this book, the SADT diagrams distinguish between *dataflow* and *control* flow by the placement of the arrows on the rectangular boxes. While this can certainly be done, it does place some topological constraints on the diagram, which many systems analysts find awkward.

15.6   VARIATIONS ON ENTITY-RELATIONSHIP DIAGRAMS

The entity-relationship diagrams presented in Chapter 12 are considered by most systems analysts to be the most general, abstract way of representing data relationships. However, there are at least three other popular data structure notations:

- Bachman diagram

- DeMarco's data structure diagrams

- Jackson's data structure diagrams

One of the more common forms of data model is the Bachman diagram, first developed by Charles Bachman in the 1960s. A typical Bachman diagram is shown in Figure 15.12. Note that it is similar to the entity-relationship diagram discussed in Chapter 12, but does not explicitly show the relationship between objects. Note also the double-headed arrow: this indicates a one-to-many relationship (e.g., a customer can own more than one home, but (in this model) a home can only be owned by one customer).

The DeMarco data structure diagrams have achieved considerable popularity during the past ten years; a typical data structure diagram is shown in Figure 15.13. Note that in addition to showing each object in the data model, the diagram shows the *key field;* as you will recall, the convention used in this book is to show the key field in the data dictionary.

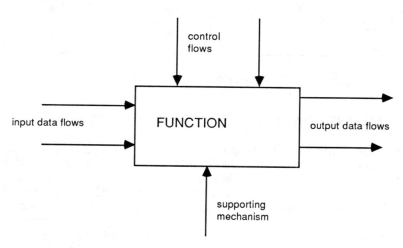

Figure 15.11: **A typical SADT diagram**

Though Jackson's data structure diagrams are not widely used in the United States at the present time, they are quite popular in England, Europe, and other parts of the world; Jean-Dominique Warnier, [Warnier, 1976] and Ken Orr, [Orr, 1977[have developed similar data models, which are somewhat more popular in the United States. Rather than concentrating on the relationship between different objects in a system, the Jackson diagrams provide a graphical means of showing the hierarchical structure of a single object. The components of a Jackson diagram are shown in Figure 15.14(a); note that this same hierarchical structure can also be documented directly in a data dictionary using the notation presented in Chapter 11, as shown in Figure 15.14(b).

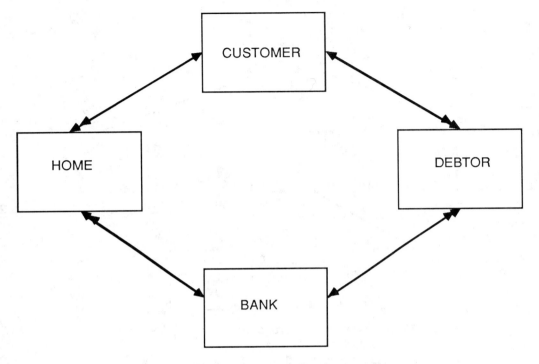

Figure 15.12: **A typical Bachman diagram**

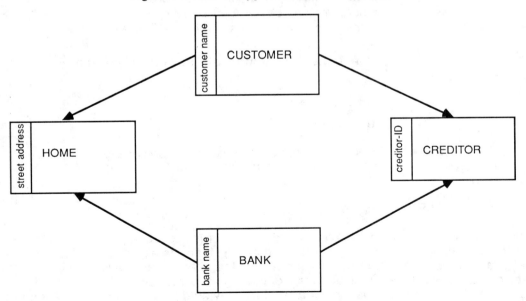

Figure 15.13: **A typical DeMarco data structure diagram**

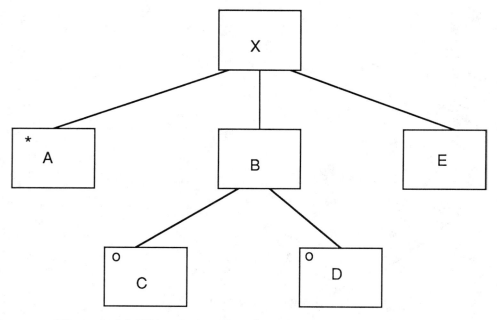

The asterisk "" is used to show iteration, and the "o" is used to show an "either-or."*

Thus, this model indicates that data element (or object) X consists of zero or more occurrences of A, followed by a B, followed by an E. Data element B consists of either a C or a D.

Figure 15.14(a): **A typical Jackson data structure diagram**

$$X = \{A\} + B + E$$

$$B = [C \mid D]$$

Figure 15.14(b): **Data dictionary notation corresponding to the Jackson data structure of Fig. 15.14(a)**

15.7 SUMMARY

The list of modeling tools shown in this chapter is not a complete one, nor have any of these alternative modeling tools been discussed in detail; to find out more, you will have to consult the references at the end of the chapter. However, keep in mind that you may never see any of these diagrams in a real project (with the likely exception of the ubiquitous flowchart); thus, I would advise against becoming intimately familiar with Hamilton-Zeldin diagrams, PAD diagrams, Ferstl diagrams, and so on, unless you find yourself working on a project where they are required.

Keep in mind also that you may be exposed to some entirely idiosyncratic diagramming techniques that are not discussed in this book (and possibly not described in *any* book!). This should not concern you: there is nothing particularly sacred about the modeling tools used in this book. However, there is a difference between *good* modeling tools and *bad* modeling tools; if you are faced with new diagramming techniques, reread Chapter 8 to identify the criteria for good modeling tools.

REFERENCES

1. Ned Chapin, "Flowcharting with the ANSI Standard: A Tutorial," *ACM Computing Surveys*, Volume 2, Number 2 (June 1970), pp. 119-146.

2. Corrado Böhm and Guiseppe Jacopini, "Flow Diagrams, Turing Machines and Languages with Only Two Formation Rules," *Communications of the ACM*, Volume 9, Number 5 (May 1966), pp. 366-371. Also published in *Classics in Software Engineering*, E. Yourdon (editor). New York: YOURDON Press, 1979.

3. I. Nassi and B. Shneiderman, "Flowchart Techniques for Structured Programming," *ACM SIGPLAN Notices*, Volume 8, Number 8 (August 1973), pp.12-26.

4. Ned Chapin, "New Format for Flowcharts," *Software—Practice and Experience*, Volume 4, Number 4 (October-December 1974), pp. 341-357.

5. O. Ferstl, "Flowcharting by Stepwise Refinement," *ACM SIGPLAN Notices*, Volume 13, Number 1 (January 1978), pp. 34-42.

6. M. Hamilton and S. Zeldin, *Top-Down, Bottom-Up, Structured Programming, and Program Structuring, Charles Stark Draper Laboratory*, Document E-2728. Cambridge, Mass: Massachusetts Institute of Technology, December 1972.

7. Y. Futamura, and others, "Development of Computer Programs by PAD (Problem Analysis Diagram)," *Proceedings of the Fifth International Software Engineering Conference*. New York: IEEE Computer Society, 1981, pp. 325-332.

8. *HIPO—A Design Aid and Documentation Technique*, IBM Corp., Manual No. GC20-1851-0. White Plains, N.Y.: IBM Data Processing Div., October 1974.

9. Harry Katzan, Jr., *Systems Design and Documentation: An Introduction to the HIPO Method*. New York: Van Nostrand Reinhold, 1976.

10. Doug Ross and Ken Schoman, "Structured Analysis for Requirements Definition," *IEEE Transactions on Software Engineering*, Volume SE-3, Number 1, January 1977, pp. 6-15. Also reprinted in *Classics in Software Engineering*, E. Yourdon (editor). New York: YOURDON Press, 1979.

11. C.W. Bachman, "Data Structure Diagrams," *Data Base, The Quarterly Newsletter of the Special Interest Group on Business Data Processing of the ACM*, Volume 1, Number 2 (Summer 1969), pp. 4-10.

12. Tom DeMarco, *Structured Analysis and Systems Specification*. New York: YOURDON Press, 1978.

13. Michael Jackson, *Principles of Program Design*. London: Academic Press, 1975.

14. Larry Peters, *Software Design: Methods and Techniques*. New York: YOURDON Press, 1981.

15. Ken Orr, *Structured Systems Development*. New York: YOURDON Press, 1977.

16. Jean-Dominique Warnier, *Logical Construction of Programs*, 3rd ed., translated by B. Flanagan. New York: Van Nostrand Reinhold, 1976.

QUESTIONS AND EXERCISES

1. Why is it important to be familiar with modeling tools other than the DFD, ERD and STD?

2. What are the three major components of a flowchart?

3. Research Project: What additional icons are sometimes used in flowcharts. Consult Chapin [Chapin, 1970] for more information?

4. How many arrows can emanate from a process box in a flowchart?

5. What is the difference between a flowchart and a dataflow diagram?

6. Draw a flowchart for a binary search algorithm.

7. Draw a flowchart for a simple interchange sort algorithm.

8. Draw a flowchart for Newton-Raphson approximation for computing the square root.

9. What are the three major reasons why flowcharts aren't used?

10. What are the four major variations on flowcharts?

11. What is a Nassi-Shneiderman diagram? What is a common synonym for the Nassi-Shneiderman diagram?

12. Draw a Nassi-Shneiderman diagram for a binary search algorithm.

13. Draw a Nassi-Shneiderman diagram for a simple interchange sort.

14. Draw a Nassi-Shneiderman diagram for the Newton-Raphson method for approximating the square root function.

15. What is a Ferstl diagram?

16. Draw a Ferstl diagram for a binary search algorithm.

17. Draw a Ferstl diagram for a simple interchange sort.

18. Draw a Ferstl diagram for the Newton-Raphson method for approximating a square root.

19. Why is a Ferstl diagram different from a flowchart? What can it show that a flowchart cannot?

20. What is a Hamilton-Zeldin diagram? What is a synonym for a Hamilton-Zeldin diagram? Where was it developed?

21. Draw a Hamilton-Zeldin diagram for a binary search algorithm.

22. Draw a Hamilton-Zeldin diagram for a simple interchange sort.

23. Draw a Hamilton-Zeldin diagram for the Newton-Raphson method for approximating a square root.

24. What is a PAD diagram? Where was it developed?

25. Draw a PAD diagram for a binary search algorithm.

26. Draw a PAD diagram for a simple interchange sort.

27. Draw a PAD diagram for the Newton-Raphson method for approximating a square root.

28. What features do Ferstl diagrams and PAD diagrams have in common?

29. What is a system flowchart? What is it used for?

30. At what stage in the development of an information system is a system flowchart likely to be used?

31. What is a HIPO diagram? Where was it developed?

32. Draw a HIPO diagram showing the design of a program to play tic-tac-toe.

33. What is an input-process-output (IPO) diagram. What is the relationship between an IPO diagram and the HIPO concept?

34. Draw an IPO diagram for a binary search algorithm.

35. Draw an IPO diagram for a simple interchange sort.

36. Draw an IPO diagram for the Newton-Raphson method for approximating a square root.

37. What is a structure chart?

38. What is the difference between a structure chart and a HIPO diagram?

39. Draw a structure chart for a simple program that plays tic-tac-toe.

40. Why is a structure chart usually insufficient as a systems analysis modeling tool?

41. What is an SADT diagram? What is the difference between an SADT diagram and a dataflow diagram?

42. What is a Bachman diagram? What is the difference between a Bachman diagram and an entity-relationship diagram?

43. What is a DeMarco data structure diagram? What is the difference between a DeMarco data structure diagram and an entity-relationship diagram?

44. What is a Jackson data structure diagram? What is the difference between a Jackson data structure diagram and an entity-relationship diagram?

16 MODELING TOOLS FOR PROJECT MANAGEMENT

> For the sake of persons of ... different types, scientific truth should be presented in different forms, and should be regarded as equally scientific, whether it appears in the robust form and the vivid coloring of a physical illustration, or in the tenuity and paleness of a symbolic expression.
>
> James Clerk Maxwell
> *Address to the Mathematics and Physics Section,*
> *British Association for the Advancement of Science,1870*

In this chapter, you will learn:

1. Why management needs its own modeling tools.

2. How to draw PERT charts.

3. How to draw Gantt charts.

4. The relationships between management tools and other modeling tools.

16.1   INTRODUCTION

Though this is not a book on project management, it is appropriate to pause here, in this last chapter on modeling tools, to present some modeling tools that are useful for managing a systems development project; we will focus primarily on modeling tools known as *PERT charts* and *Gantt charts*.

Why should you be concerned with management modeling tools? There are several possible reasons:

- In addition to your role as systems analyst, you may be the project manager; junior-level systems analysts, as well as programmers, may report directly to you for the duration of the project. Thus, you may develop management models yourself for presentation to higher levels of management; or you may ask one of your subordinates to develop them for you.

- As the senior technical person on the staff, the project manager may ask you to develop management models for her or him. In this scenario, you may be the apprentice project manager, to whom the project manager turns for assistance and advice on various issues that are both managerial and technical in nature.

- Even if you aren't responsible for developing the models, they are important to know about, for they reflect management's perception of how work on the project should be proceeding. You can draw your own conclusions about the project's likely success or failure by comparing the models with your own perception of reality.

- The organization of work and the assignment of people to various activities, often known as the work breakdown of the project, will usually parallel the *technical* breakdown of the system. Since you will be intimately involved in the decomposition of the system into its component functions and data objects, you may have some influence on the way the project is organized.[1]

In the rest of this chapter, we will examine the most commonly used management modeling tools and see how they address the major issues faced by project managers. We will also see how the project management tools are related to the other system modeling tools discussed in the last several chapters.

16.2   WHY DOES MANAGEMENT NEED MODELS?

There are three primary reasons why project management needs models associated with a systems development project:

1. To estimate the money, time, and people required to develop the project.

2. To update and revise those estimates as the project continues.

3. To manage the tasks and activities of the people working on the project.

Budget and estimates are, of course, a major activity of managers in any project; they are all the more difficult in many systems development projects because each project is (or at least seems to be) unique. Appendix B discusses a number of formulas and methods for estimating the amount of work to be done on a project, and

---

1 Sometimes it is just the opposite. As IBM consultant George Mealy has said of some projects, "The structure of the system is isomorphic to the structure of the organization that builds it."

the number of people that will be required. However, management still needs models—and graphical models are desirable, for the same reasons that graphical models are useful in other aspects of systems analysis—to see when the people are available to carry out tasks in the project, what will happen if those people are not available, and so forth. We will examine this in more detail in Section 16.5

Even the best plan, though, is likely to fail if it is implemented blindly. Circumstances change continuously during the project: critical resources may not be available at exactly the time they are needed; important staff members may get sick or may leave the project; the original estimate of the amount of work to be done may turn out to be inaccurate; the user may suddenly announce that he needs the system to be operational a month earlier than originally anticipated; the manager may see that the work is being done more slowly than originally expected. Thus, it is important for the project manager to have models that can let her or him explore the consequences of changes in the plan.

And finally, the project manager must not only manage *tasks,* he or she must manage *people.* The manager must ensure that all the systems analysts, programmers, systems designers, and other personnel are doing *what* they should be doing, *when* they should be doing it. Thus, the manager needs modeling tools that will focus on the people, in addition to modeling tools that focus on the tasks

16.3   PERT CHARTS

PERT is an acronym that stands for **P**rogram **E**valuation **R**eview **T**echnique. It was originally developed in the 1960s as a management tool for the U.S. Navy's Polaris submarine project; Booz Allen (the consulting firm), Lockheed Aircraft, and the Navy are generally credited with developing the concept. PERT charts have been used widely in industry and government projects since then; many people now refer to them as activity diagrams.

Figure 16.1 shows a typical PERT chart for a hypothetical project. Each rectangular box represents a *task* or an *activity* (i.e., a recognizable chunk of work that needs to be done). The boxes with rounded corners are known as milestones, and they have an obvious meaning within the context of a typical project. The lines connecting the boxes show *dependencies*; that is, they show which activities must be finished prior to the commencement of some other activity. The heaviest, dark lines that form a contiguous path from the beginning to the end of the project represent the critical path, those activities whose delay would force a delay in the overall project (activities *not* on the critical path have "slack time" available; they can be started later than the scheduled date up to the amount of slack time available, if desirable, without affecting the overall project).

Note that it is the project manager (or a subordinate) who determines which tasks are dependent on which other tasks. In many cases, the dependency is data related: activity N + 1 requires, as its input, something that is produced as an output by activity N. In other cases, the dependency represents a checkpoint in the project (e.g., milestone N might be a management review meeting that must approve the work that has been done up to this point, before activity N + 1 is allowed to begin).

Note that that the example of Figure 16.1 is truly a trivial one: it contains only ten activities and ends when the systems analysis activity has been finished. A typical project, of course, continues on after the systems analysis work has been done and spends a considerable amount of time in the area of design, coding, testing, and so on. Indeed, a typical project is likely to have several *hundred* activities that would be shown on a PERT chart. This may fit on the wall of the project manager's office, but it certainly would not fit conveniently in this book!

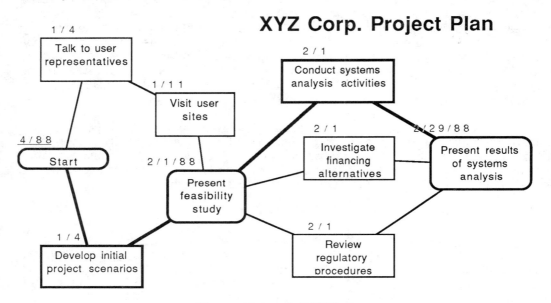

Figure 16.1: **A PERT chart**

More importantly, most projects identify major activities, which are then broken into smaller ones. For example, Figure 16.1 shows an activity labeled "Conduct systems analysis activities." As we have seen throughout this book, there are many, many things that fall under the heading of "conducting" systems analysis; indeed, we might expect to see a large PERT chart that elaborates on those subactivities. Thus, just as we saw the concept of leveled dataflow diagrams in Chapter 9, we could imagine the concept of leveled PERT charts to help organize the complexity of many hundreds, or even thousands, of tasks in a large project.

Note, by the way, that the PERT chart focuses on the activities and interdependencies between activities, but it says little or nothing about many other aspects of a project that are of interest to a manager. It does not indicate, for example, which person or group of people is supposed to carry out the various activities; nor does it say anything explicitly about the length of time (or number of person-days) that each activity requires. And it does not show what products or outputs are produced by each activity. Some of this information, however, is highlighted in the other management models discussed next.

Finally, note that the PERT chart appears to make the assumption that every-thing moves in a forward direction, as indicated by the left-to-right sequence of the activities. In fact, it is often necessary to cycle back and redo some of the earlier activities if problems are found at a later stage. This kind of iterative activity is not shown well on a typical PERT chart.

On the other hand, the PERT chart *does* show, quite vividly, the fact that many activities can take place in parallel in a real-world project. This is important, because many of the other project models strongly imply that activities must take place in sequence (see, for example, Figure 5.1). Project managers generally want to take advantage of as much "parallelism" as possible, since it can help reduce the calendar time required for the project.

16.4   GANTT CHARTS

A second kind of project management model is the *Gantt* chart, sometimes known as a task timeline. Figure 16.2 shows a Gantt chart for the same hypothetical project used in Figure 16.1. Note that each activity is shown, with an indication of when it begins and when it ends; the shaded area indicates slack time, while those activities in white rectangles are critical path activities.

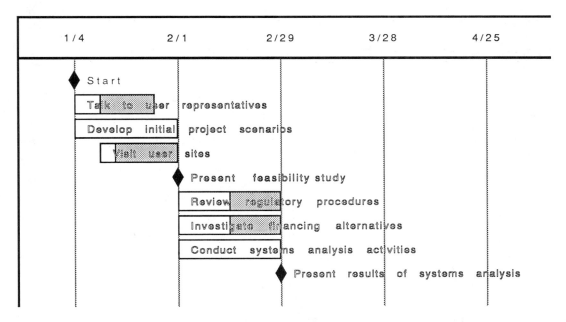

Figure 16.2: **A Gantt Chart**

As you can see, the Gantt chart presents much the same kind of information as the PERT chart; its primary different is the fact that it shows the duration of each activity,[2] which the PERT chart does not. Because it is somewhat more of a tabular representation of the project, it can often be used to present a large amount of information in a relatively compact form.

16.5   ADDITIONAL MANAGEMENT MODELING TOOLS

In addition to the two primary modeling tools discussed above, project managers often like to use additional charts and tables to help them keep track of their work. For example, instead of showing the *tasks* as we did in Figure 16.2, we could easily produce a chart showing the activity of each *resource* in the project.[3] Figure 16.3 shows a resource listing for the same hypothetical project; obviously, this would be useful for keeping track of the various activities that each project member is responsible for. Similarly, we may decide that it would be convenient to have a tabular listing of the various activities in the project, perhaps with an indication of the earliest date that each activity can begin and the latest date that it could begin without disrupting other tasks and delaying the final completion of the project.

It should be evident that the information in Figure 16.4 is yet another view of the management aspects of the project; it should be compatible with the other views, just as the various DFD, ERD, and STD models of an information system are compatible with each other. Indeed, having created any one of the project management models, we should be able to derive the others in a mechanical fashion; we will return to this point in Section 16.7.

16.6   RELATIONSHIP BETWEEN PROJECT MANAGEMENT
AND OTHER SYSTEM MODELING TOOLS

What is the relationship between PERT charts, Gantt charts, and the various system models (DFDs, ERDs, STDs, etc.) that we have discussed throughout this book? The strongest relationship seems to exist between the PERT chart and the dataflow diagram: both show activities (or functions) being carried out, and both show something about the interaction between those functions. However, the DFD shows absolutely *nothing* about the sequence in which functions are carried out, while the PERT chart does indeed show which activities can take place concurrently and which must take place in a sequential fashion. Also, we saw that the PERT chart does not show the output produced by each activity, nor does it indicate the inputs required by each activity.

As we saw in Chapter 5, DFDs can be used to show activities in a project, as well as inputs and outputs; hence, it could conceivably be used as a modeling tool in

---

2 We have not indicated here exactly how the project manager determines the duration of each task. In the simple case, he may be able to estimate it himself, or he may ask the *people* doing the work to perform their own estimates. If the task is large or complex, it will generally be broken into smaller subactivities. Formulas for estimating the time and resources for programming and the like are given in Appendix B.

3 In most projects, the resources that we are most interested in managing are people; but a resource might also be a machine, a conference room, or anything else that is (1) needed by the project at one time or another, and (2) in sufficiently scarce supply that it must be managed.

place of the PERT chart. However, most project managers would want the diagram to be annotated to show the critical path; and they would need additional information, such as the duration of each activity and the people working on each activity. Hence, it is more common to see the combination of the classical PERT chart, together with the Gantt chart and the resource timeline that we discussed earlier.

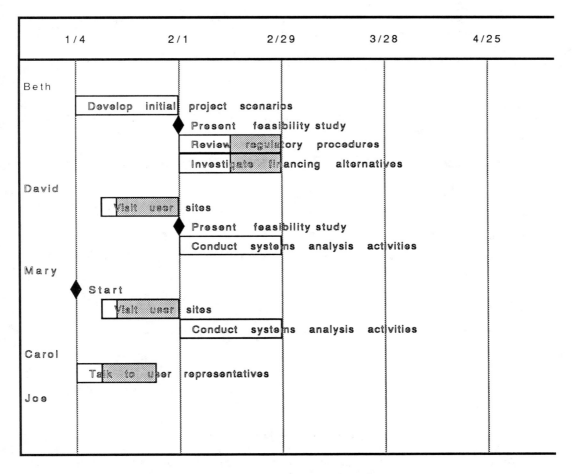

Figure 16.3: **A resource listing**

More significant is the fact that the activities shown in the typical PERT chart will be the various activities of drawing DFDs, ERDs, and so on. Thus, while Figure 16.1 showed a high-level activity of "conduct systems analysis," a realistic PERT chart would probably show a list of activities like these:

- Draw dataflow diagrams for new system

- Draw entity-relationship diagrams for new system

- Draw state-transition diagrams for new system

- Develop data dictionary for new system

- Write process specifications for bottom-level bubbles

- Balance the models

- Carry out cost-benefit calculations

- And so on

	Task	Days	Earliest Start	Earliest Finish	Latest Start	Latest Finish
1	Start	0	1/4/88	1/4/88	1/4/88	1/4/88
2	Talk to user repre-sentatives	5	1/4/88	1/11/88	1/19/88	1/26/88
3	Develop initial scenarios	20	1/4/88	2/1/88	1/4/88	2/1/88
4	Visit user sites	4	1/11/88	1/15/88	1/26/88	2/1/88
5	Present feasibility study	0	2/1/88	2/1/88	2/1/88	2/1/88
6	Review regulatory procedures	10	2/1/88	2/15/88	2/15/88	2/29/88
7	Investigate financing alternatives	10	2/1/88	2/15/88	2/15/88	2/29/88
8	Conduct systems analysis activities	20	2/1/88	2/29/88	2/1/88	2/29/88
9	Present results	0	2/29/88	2/29/88	2/29/88	2/29/88

Figure 16.4: **A task listing**

As we will see in Part IV, the modeling tools of dataflow diagrams and the like are used to build a series of different models of the new system. Thus, we are likely to find the following high-level activities:

- Develop environmental model

- Develop first-cut behavioral model

- Refine behavioral model

- Develop user implementation model

At this point, none of these terms will make much sense to you; we will discuss the environmental model in Chapter 18, the behavioral model in Chapters 19 and 20, and the user implementation model in Chapter 21.

The major point to keep in mind is that the activities that we show in the PERT chart and Gantt charts correspond to the model-building activities that we have discussed throughout this book. Of course, a real PERT chart for a project, encompassing the entire life cycle, must also show the activities of design, programming, testing, database conversion, and installation.

16.7   THE ISSUE OF AUTOMATION

Three things should now be evident from the brief discussion of project management tools in this chapter:

1.   Several of the modeling tools involve graphics; thus, to make them work, someone or some*thing* has to draw pictures.

2.   For a large, real-world project, the models become immense. And as things change (as they inevitably do during a project), the models have to be redrawn. This involves a tremendous amount of work.

3.   The models are all related to one another; so, with enough information about the project, one should be able to create either a PERT chart *or* a Gantt chart, *or* a resource timeline, as well as the appropriate narrative support.

This leads to a very obvious conclusion: it would be tremendously helpful if the project management modeling tools could be computerized. And indeed they have been; there are now a variety of project management packages available on personal computers, as well as on mini and mainframe computers.[4] Indeed, a project manager in the late 1980s would be foolish to manage anything other than a truly trivial project without such automated tools. In addition to the simple modeling activities discussed in this chapter, the computerized tools generally have the following features:

•   An ability to specify the *cost* of each resource in the project. This is enormously helpful in budgeting activities.

•   An ability to describe the calendar within which the project must work (e.g., holidays, normal working hours, etc.). Indeed, some programs allow each resource to have his/her/its own calendar, thus accounting for the fact that different people have different vacation schedules, and the like.

•   An ability to schedule forward or backward. In a normal project, the start date is known and the objective is to estimate when the project will be finished. But in other cases, the finish date is known (because a deadline

---

4 The diagrams shown in this chapter were created using MacProject on the Apple Macintosh computer. There is a somewhat larger selection of project management packages available for the IBM PC.

has been externally imposed on the project), and the objective is to determine the latest start date for each of the activities.[5]

- An ability to provide a variety of reports in a variety of formats.

- An ability to interface with various other programs (e.g., spreadsheet programs and graphics programs).

- An ability to show actual versus estimated performance so that the manager can see how accurate his or her estimates are and perhaps use this as a means of revising future estimates.

For small- or medium-sized projects, a PC-based project management package is usually quite adequate; among the more popular project management packages for the PC are Microsoft Project, Timeline, and the Harvard Project Manager. For large projects with thousands of tasks and hundreds of resources to manage, a larger computer may be required. Also, many large organizations integrate the plans of individual projects into *aggregate* models and budgets; so it is important that everyone use a compatible PC-based modeling system or that they share a larger, mainframe-based system.

16.8   SUMMARY

Obviously, there is more to project management than just drawing PERT charts. The typical project manager is involved in hiring and firing, in negotiating, motivating, communicating with, and cajoling programmers, systems analysts, users, and higher levels of management. But without modeling tools of the nature described in this chapter, it is almost impossible for the project manager to keep track of the activities, costs, and resources involved.

REFERENCES

1. Philip Metzger, *Managing a Programming Project,* 2nd ed. Englewood Cliffs, N.J.: Prentice-Hall, 1983.

2. Tom Gildersleeve, *Successful Data Processing Systems Analysis,* 2nd ed. Englewood Cliffs, N.J.: Prentice-Hall, 1985.

3. Marvin Gore and John Stubbe, *Elements of Systems Analysis,* 3rd ed. Dubuque, Iowa: William C. Brown, 1983.

QUESTIONS AND EXERCISES

1. Give three reasons why project managers need models associated with a systems development project.

2. What is PERT an acronym for?

---

5 Tom DeMarco is fond of referring to this as "backward wishful thinking."

3.   Give a brief definition of a PERT chart.

4.   What is a critical path in a PERT chart? Why is it important?

5.   What information does a PERT chart *not* show about a project?

6.   Give a brief definition of a Gantt chart. What is a synonym for a Gantt chart?

7.   What information does a Gantt chart show that a PERT chart does not?

8.   Give a brief definition of a resource listing?

9.   What is the relationship between PERT charts, Gantt charts, and DFD models of a system?

10. Why is it useful to have automated tools for producing PERT charts and Gantt charts?

PART III: THE ANALYSIS PROCESS

17 THE ESSENTIAL MODEL

> Look to the essence of a thing, whether it be a point of doctrine, of prac-
> ice, or of interpretation.
>
> Marcus Aurelius, *Meditations VIII*

In this chapter, you will learn:

1. The four major system models in the life cycle.

2. Why modeling the user's current system is dangerous.

3. The distinction between essential and implementation models.

4. How to "logicalize" an implementation model.

In the previous section (Chapters 9 through 16), we examined a number of modeling *tools* that every systems analyst should have at his or her disposal. However, given these tools, what *kind* of models should we build? Should we build a model of the user's current implementation of a system? Should we build a model of the proposed new implementation? Or a model that is independent of the implementation technology? Or all three? These questions are addressed in the next several chapters.

We begin by examining the classical structured analysis approach to developing system models; as we will see, there are major problems with this approach. We will then discuss the *essential* model, which is the primary systems analysis model that we recommend building. Finally, we discuss some guidelines for constructing an essential model from an existing implementation model.

17.1   THE CLASSICAL MODELING APPROACH
AND WHY IT DIDN'T WORK

17.1.1   The Four System Models

When structured analysis was first introduced, it was commonly argued that the systems analyst should develop four distinct models. These are shown in Figure 17.1.

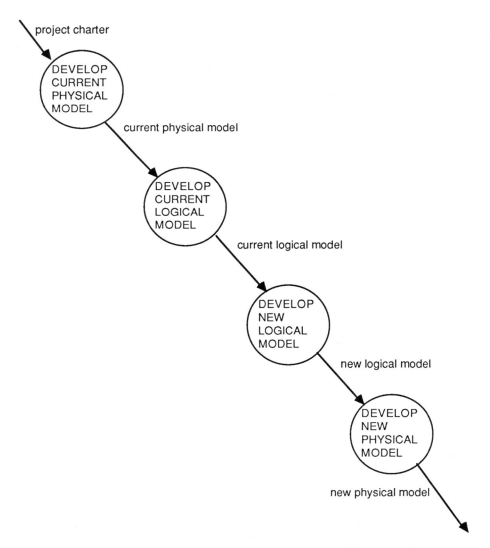

Figure 17.1: **The four system models**

The *current physical* model is a model of the actual system that the user is presently using. It may be a manual system, an automated system, or a mixture of the two. Typically, the processes (bubbles) in the dataflow diagram for the current physical system are named for the names of people, or organizational units, or computer systems that do the work of transforming inputs into outputs. An example is shown in Figure 17.2. Note also that the dataflows typically show physical forms of data being transported from bubble to bubble; also, the data stores may be represented by file folders, magnetic tape files, or some other technology.

The *new logical* model is a model of the pure or essential requirements of the *new* system that the user wants. In the ideal case (from the systems analysts' point of view), it is the same as the *current logical* model; that is, it contains the same functions and the same data. This situation could occur if the user was completely satisfied with the functionality of the current system, but was dissatisfied with its implementation.[1] In most cases, though, the user will ask for additional functions: "While you're at it, could you add another transaction to take care of the following situation...." Or the user may ask that the system keep track of a new form of data. Thus, while 80% to 90% of the new logical model may be identical to the current logical model, there are likely to be at least a few changes and additions.

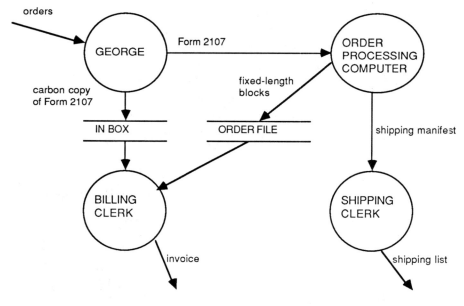

Figure 17.2: **A current physical model**

---

1 There are many possible reasons for this. The system may be implemented on computer hardware that is now obsolete or on hardware whose manufacturer has gone out of business. Or the system's performance or response time may be inadequate. Or the user may ask that some manually maintained data (e.g., paper files) be computerized. Or, as is increasingly common these days, the software may be so poorly documented that it can no longer be maintained or modified.

The *current logical* model is a model of the pure or essential requirements being carried out by the user's current system. Thus, arbitrary implementation details are removed, and the resulting model shows what the system would do if perfect technology were available.[2] An example of a current logical model is shown in Figure 17.3.

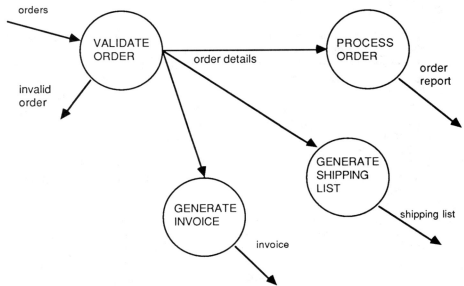

Figure 17.3: **The current logical model**

The *new physical* model is a model showing the implementation *constraints* imposed by the user. One of the most important such constraints is the determination of the *automation boundary* (i.e., the determination of which functions in the new system will be automated and which will be performed manually). The new physical model corresponds to what we now call the *user implementation* model, which we discuss in more detail in Chapter 21.

17.1.2   Why The Classical Approach Didn't Work

The classical approach described above was based on three major assumptions:

1. The systems analyst may not be very familiar with the application or business area: he may be an expert in computer technology, but only superficially knowledgeable about banking, insurance, inventory control,

---

2 Perfect technology can be interpreted as computer hardware that costs no money, takes up no space, consumes no power and generates no heat, runs at infinite speeds (i.e., carries out any computation in zero time), stores an infinite amount of data, any or all of which can be retrieved in zero time, and the computer never, ever breaks down and never makes mistakes.

or whatever area the user is working in. Because of this, it is important for the systems analyst to begin with a current physical model as a way of educating himself. The model he draws will be relatively easy to verify, because it will contain a number of physical landmarks that can be observed in the user's current physical environment. Once having gathered this background information, the systems analyst can continue by transforming the physical model into a logical model.

2. The user may be unwilling or unable to work with a new logical model at the beginning of a project. The most common reason for this is suspicion of the systems analyst's ability to develop a logical model of the new system. Even if the systems analyst thinks that he is an expert in the user's business area, the user may not agree. "Why should I trust you to design a new system for me," she will ask, "when you don't even understand how my business works now?" Also, some users find it difficult to look at an abstract system model with no recognizable landmarks; they may need a model of the current physical system as a way of familiarizing themselves with the process of structured analysis and assuring themselves that the analyst hasn't overlooked anything. (An alternative is the prototyping approach discussed in Chapter 5.)

3. The transformation of a current logical model into a new logical model does not require much work and, in particular, does not require much *wasted* work. As indicated above, the user will typically add some new functions, or new data, to the system she already has, but most (if not all) of the existing *logical* (or essential) system remains intact.

These assumptions have indeed turned out to be correct in many projects. However, they ignore a much larger danger: *the process of developing a model of the current system may require so much time and effort that the user will become frustrated and impatient, and ultimately cancel the project.* To appreciate this, you must keep in mind that:

• Some users (and some managers and some programmer-analysts) regard *any* form of systems analysis as a waste of time—as a way of "resting up" until the *real* work of the project (i.e., coding) begins.

• Many users are understandably dubious about the merits of carefully modeling a system *that, by definition, will be superseded and replaced as a result of the development of the new system*.

The problem occurs most often because the systems analyst gets carried away with the task of modeling the current system and begins to think of it as an end in itself. Thus, instead of drawing just the dataflow diagram(s) and documenting a few key process specifications, the systems analyst often draws *every* dataflow diagram, documenting *every* process specification, and developing a *complete* data dictionary.

Unfortunately, this approach almost always involves a great deal of wasted time. Indeed, you can normally expect that as much as 75% of the physical model will be thrown away in the transition from current physical to current logical; or to put it another way, the current physical model is typically three to four times as large as the current logical model. This is because of redundancy (the same function being carried out in several different parts of the current system, and several data elements being duplicated or triplicated), and because of verification, validation, and error-checking that are appropriate in the current physical system but not appropriate in the current logical system.[3]

All this may seem rather obvious to the casual reader. However, in project after project, systems analysts have been observed getting so involved in the *process* of modeling that they have forgotten the user's ultimate objective: to produce a working system. As Steve McMenamin (co-author of [McMenamin and Palmer, 1984]) points out, "Bubbles don't compile."[4]

Consequently, this book recommends that the systems analyst should *avoid* modeling the user's current system if at all possible. The modeling tools discussed in Part II should be used to begin, *as quickly as possible,* to develop a model of the *new* system that the user wants. This new system, referred to in classical structured analysis textbooks as the new logical system, is referred to here as the *essential model* of the system.

There will occasionally be a situation where the systems analyst *must* build a model of the user's current system; this is true, for example, if the systems analyst needs to model the current physical system in order to discover what the essential processes really are. This situation is discussed further in Section 17.3.

17.2   THE ESSENTIAL MODEL

17.2.1   What It Is

The essential system model is a model of *what* the system must do in order to satisfy the user's requirements, with as little as possible (and ideally *nothing*) said about *how* the system will be implemented. As mentioned earlier, this means that our system model assumes that we have perfect technology available and that it can be readily obtained at zero cost.

---

3 Regardless of whether we are building a logical (essential) or physical (implementation) model, it is usually appropriate to perform some error-checking of data *that come into the system from the external world.* However, as data are transmitted from place to place *within* the system, the logical (essential) model does *no* error-checking, because it assumes that the system will be implemented with perfect technology. In the physical (implementation) model, *especially* a model of the *current* physical system, the error-checking is vital because (1) some of the processing is error prone, especially if carried out by humans, (2) the transportation of data from one process to another may be error prone, depending on the communications medium used, and (3) the storage and retrieval of data from physical data stores may be an error prone activity.

4 Eventually, bubbles *will* compile. That is, the combination of dataflow diagrams, data dictionary, and rigorous process specifications can become input to a code generator that will produce executable programs. However, even in this case, the effort to produce a complete, detailed *physical* model is a waste of time. Nobody wants a computerized replica of the current system.

Specifically, this means that when the systems analyst talks with the user about the requirements of the system, the analyst should avoid describing specific implementations of processes (bubbles in the dataflow diagram) in the system; that is, he or she should not show the system functions being carried out by humans or an existing computer system. As illustrated by Figure 17.4(a) and (b), these are arbitrary choices of how the system *might* be implemented; but this is a decision that should be delayed until the systems design activity has begun.[5] Figure 17.4(c) shows a more appropriate essential model of what the system function must carry out regardless of its eventual implementation.

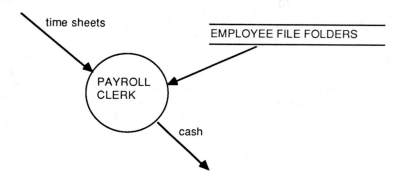

Figure 17.4(a): **A model of *how* a system function will perform its job**

The same is true of dataflows and data stores: the essential model should describe the *content* of dataflows and data stores, without describing the medium (e.g., disk or tape) or physical organization of the data.

17.2.2   Difficulties in Building an Essential Model

While the guidelines above may seem simple and obvious, it often turns out to be very difficult to completely eliminate all implementation details from the essential model. The most common examples of implementation details are:

- *Arbitrary sequencing of activities in a dataflow model.* The only sequencing on the dataflow diagram should be that required by *data* (e.g., bubble 2 may require a data element produced by bubble 1 and thus cannot begin its work until bubble 1 has finished) or by the sequencing of events external to the system.

- *Unnecessary files*, data stores that would not be required given perfect technology. Temporary files (or intermediate files) are required in an

---

5 A popular term for this is "constructive procrastination." My colleague Steve Weiss prefers "safe deferral," which is less perjorative, and is indeed the principle upon which the top-down approach is based.

implementation model because processes are scheduled to do their work at different times (e.g., an overnight batch program produces a file used by the daytime, on-line system); they are also introduced in implementation models for backup and recovery purposes, because the implementation technology is error prone, as are the people who operate the computers.

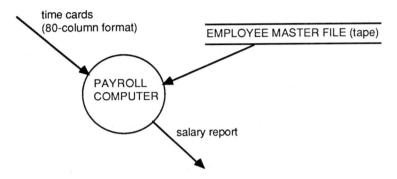

Figure 17.4(b): **Another model of how the system function will be performed**

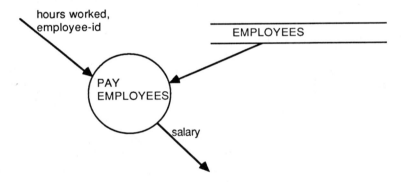

Figure 17.4(c): **A model of *what* the system function is**

- *Unnecessary error-checking and validation of data and processes inside the system.* Such validation activities are necessary in an implementation model, because one must work with error prone processes (e.g., some functions are carried out by humans, who are notoriously error prone) and noisy paths of data between processes.

- *Redundant or derived data.* Redundant data elements are sometimes included in data stores for the sake of efficiency; while this is usually a reasonable thing to do, it should be done during the design phase of the project, not during the modeling of essential functions and data. Also, the systems analyst may inadvertently include data elements that can be *derived,* or computed, from values of other data elements.

17.2.3   Components of the Essential Model

The essential model consists of two major components:

1. Environmental model

2. Behavioral model

The environmental model defines the *boundary* between the system and the rest of the world (i.e., the environment in which the system exists). It is discussed in more detail in Chapter 19; as we will see, it consists of a context diagram, an event list, and a short description of the purpose of the system.

The behavioral model describes the required behavior of the insides of the system necessary to interact successfully with the environment. Chapters 20 and 21 describe a strategy for deriving the behavioral model; the model consists of the familiar dataflow diagrams, entity-relationship diagrams, state-transition diagrams, data dictionary entries, and process specifications that we have discussed earlier in the book.

17.3   WHAT TO DO IF YOU *MUST* BUILD AN IMPLEMENTATION MODEL

As mentioned earlier in this chapter, there are circumstances where you may find it necessary or desirable to build an implementation model before you build the essential model of the system. Typically, this will happen because the user is not convinced that you understand the business well enough to model a new system, or because you have decided on your own that you need to study the current environment before proposing a new system.

If you decide to proceed in this fashion, the primary thing you must remember is that your main objective is to get a general understanding and a general overview of the existing system. *It is not your objective to document the current system in minute detail.* Thus, it will probably be useful and appropriate to create one or more levels of dataflow diagrams for the current system; and it will probably be appropriate to generate an entity-relationship diagram. And it *might* be useful to write process specifications for a few of the more critical (or obscure) functions in the system; it *might* be useful to collect some of the physical documents that would represent a physical data dictionary. But you should *not* try to write process specifications for all the functions, nor should you try to develop a complete data dictionary for the existing system.

When you have finished developing the model of the current implementation, your next job is to logicalize it (i.e., to remove as many implementation-oriented details as possible). This will usually include the following steps:

- *Look for essential flows that have been arbitrarily packaged together in the same medium and separate them.* For example, you may find that in the current system, several data elements are being transmitted together from one computer to another computer via a common telecommunications link; or you may find that several unrelated data elements are being copied onto a paper form to be transmitted to various functions.

• *Look for aggregate or packaged flows that are sent to bubbles (representing people, computers, etc.) that don't need all the data in those flows.* Thus, Figure 17.5(a) shows a process, **COMPUTE FRAMMIS FACTOR**, that requires only data element **X**; meanwhile, another process, **COMPUTE WIDGET FACTOR**, requires only data element **Y**. For convenience, the current implementation has packaged **X** and **Y** into an aggregate data element **Z**; logicalizing this model would result in the dataflow diagram shown in Figure 17.5(b).

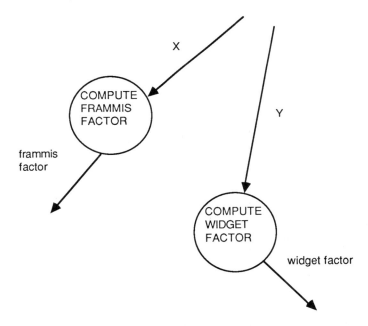

Figure 17.5(a): **A physical model**

• *Distinguish between the essential work done by a process and the iden-tification of the processor shown in the implementation model.* The processor might be a person or a computer or some other form of tech-nology; and an individual processor might be carrying out fragments of one or more essential processes or, in their entirety, carrying out multiple essential processes. As we will see in Chapter 20, the essential processes should be grouped together if they are triggered by the same external event.

• *Eliminate processes whose only purpose is to transport data from one place to another within the system.* Also, eliminate the bubbles responsible for physical input and output between the system and the external environment. A physical model of a system might show, for instance, a courier or messenger function; it should be eliminated in the essential model. And many physical DFDs have processes with names like "obtain input from user" or "print report"; these, too, should be eliminated.

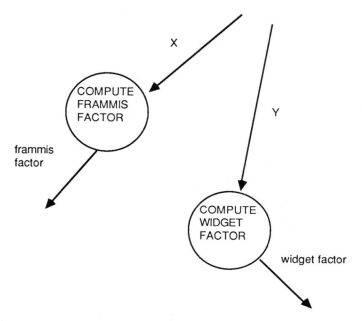

Figure 17.5(b): **The logicalized version**

- *Eliminate processes whose job is to verify data that are both produced inside the system and used inside the system.* Since we are assuming perfect technology in the essential model, such internal verification and cross-checking is not necessary. It is appropriate, though, to provide error-checking for data brought into the system from the external environment. Thus, any processes whose names are "double check ..." or "verify..." or "validate..." or "edit..." should be regarded with suspicion, unless they exist at the boundary of the system and are dealing with external inputs.

- *Look for situations where essential stores have been packaged together into the same implementation store* (e.g., disk files, tape files, or paper files); this is very common in second-generation systems and in systems that have been optimized over a period of years to handle large volumes of data efficiently. Separate the content of the store from the medium of storage.

- *Remove any data elements from stores if they are not used by any process;* also, remove data elements from stores if they can be computed, or derived, directly from other data elements. (Note that derived data elements and redundant copies of data elements may be reinserted later when the *implementation* model is developed during systems design.)

- *Finally, remove any data stores that exist only as an implementation-dependent time delay between processes.* These include intermediate files, report files, spooling files, and the like.

17.4   SUMMARY

The concept of an essential model seems quite natural, but it is not as easy to achieve on real-world projects as you might think. Most users are so involved in the implementation details of their current system that it is hard for them to focus on the "perfect technology" view of a system. And it is equally difficult for many veteran systems analysts, for they have spent so many years building systems that it is difficult for them to avoid making implementation assumptions as they describe a system.

Remember that it is critically important to develop the essential model of a system, for (as noted several times throughout this book) most large information systems have a lifetime of 10 to 20 years. During that period of time, we can expect computer hardware technology to improve by at least a factor of a thousand, and probably closer to a factor of a *million* or more. A computer that is a million times faster, smaller, and cheaper than today's computer is indeed close to perfect technology; we must begin *today* modeling our systems as if we had that technology available to us.

REFERENCES

1. Tom DeMarco, *Structured Analysis and Systems Specification.* New York: YOURDON Press, 1978.

2. Chris Gane and Trish Sarson,*Structured Systems Analysis: Tools and Techniques.* Englewood Cliffs, N.J.: Prentice-Hall, 1978.

3. Edward Yourdon, *Managing the Systems Life Cycle.* New York: YOURDON Press, 1982.

4. Victor Weinberg, *Structured Analysis.* New York: YOURDON Press, 1978.

5. Steve McMenamin and John Palmer, *Essential Systems Analysis.* New York: YOURDON Press, 1984.

QUESTIONS AND EXERCISES

1. What are the four models recommended by classical systems analysis textbooks?

2. What is a current physical model?

3. Give three examples of physical processes (bubbles).

4. Give three examples of physical stores.

5. Give three examples of physical dataflows.

6. What is a current logical model?

7. What is the difference between a current physical model and a current logical model?

8. What is perfect technology in the context of this chapter?

9. What is a new logical model?

10. What is the difference between a current logical model and a new logical model?

11. Under what circumstances could the current logical model and the new logical model for a system be the same?

12. What degree of overlap should the systems analyst expect to see between the current logical and new logical model of a system?

13. What is a new physical model?

14. What is another name for the new physical model?

15. What is the major constraint that the new physical model describes?

16. What are the three major assumptions that the classical approach to structured analysis is based on?

17. Research Project: In your organization, what percentage of projects have systems analysts who are not intimately familiar with the user's business area? Is this a reasonable percentage in your opinion? Is it changing?

18. What are the two major reasons why a user might have trouble reading and understanding a logical model?

19. What is the major problem with the classical approach to structured analysis?

20. Why are some users dubious about the merits of modeling their current system?

21. How much of the current physical model is likely to be thrown away in the transition to a current logical model?

22. What are the reasons that the current physical model is so much larger than the current logical model of a system?

23. What is a synonym for new logical model?

24. What kind of error-checking is appropriate in a logical model? What kind is inappropriate? Why?

25. Give a definition of the essential model of a system.

26. What does constructive procrastination mean in the context of this chapter?

27. When, in a systems development project, should the decision be made about implementing a function (i.e., a process in the DFD) with a person versus a computer?

28. What are the four common errors or mistakes typically made by systems analysts when trying to create an essential model?

29. Why should temporary files not be shown in an essential model?

30. When *should* temporary files be shown in a system model? Why?

31. When should redundant data be shown in a system model?

32. When should derived data be shown in a system model?

33. What are the two components of the essential model of a system?

34. What is the purpose of the environmental model of a system?

35. What is the purpose of the behavioral model of a system?

36. If you have to document the current implementation of a system, what should you be careful to avoid?

37. Is it a good idea to document all the dataflows in the current implementation of a system? Why or why not?

38. Is it a good idea to document all the process specifications in the current implementation of a system? Why or why not?

39. Is it a good idea to document all the elements of the data dictionary in the current implementation of a system? Why or why not?

40. When logicalizing a current physical model, what should you do with essential flows that have been packaged in the same medium?

41. When logicalizing a current physical model, what should you do with packaged flows sent to processes that don't need all the data?

42. When logicalizing a current physical model, what should you do with processes whose only purpose is to transport data from one place to another?

43. When logicalizing a current physical model, what should you do with bubbles whose only purpose is to verify data that are created *within* the system?

44. When logicalizing a current physical model, what should you do with essential stores that have been packaged in the same medium?

45. When logicalizing a current physical model, what should you do with data elements that exist in stores but are not used anywhere in the system?

46. When logicalizing a current physical model, what should you do with temporary files that are found in the current physical system?

18 THE ENVIRONMENTAL MODEL

The stability of the *internal medium* is a primary condition for the freedom and independence of certain living bodies in relation to the environment surrounding them.

Claude Bernard, *Lecons sur les Phenomenes de la Vie Communs aux Animaux et aux Vegetaux*, 1875-1879

In this chapter, you will learn:

1. Why the system boundary is arbitrary but critical.

2. How to draw a context diagram for a system.

3. How to produce an event list for a system.

4. How to use the context diagram and event list to build the environmental model.

For the systems analyst, the most difficult job in specifying a system is often that of determining what *is* part of that system and what *is not*. Whatever system you develop, no matter how ambitious, no matter how grandiose, it will be part of an even larger system. As we saw in Chapter 2, virtually all systems with which we have human experience are merely subsystems of even larger systems: even if our job were to "design the world," we would have to recognize that the world is only a part of the solar system, which is part of a small, obscure galaxy, which is (ultimately) part of the universe.

Thus, the first major model that you must develop as a systems analyst is one that does nothing more than define the *interfaces* between the system and the rest of the universe, that is, the *environment*. For obvious reasons, this model is known as the *environmental model*. It models the *outside* of the system; the model of the *inside* of the system, known as the *behavioral* model, is discussed in Chapters 20 and 21.

In addition to determining what is *inside* the system and what is *outside* the system (which we accomplish by defining the *boundary* between the system and the environment), it is also critically important to define the *interfaces* between the system and the environment. We need to know what information comes into the system from the external environment, and we must know what information the system produces as an output to be delivered to the external environment.

Of course, inputs and outputs are not produced at random: no information system gobbles up all available data from the universe, nor does any realistic system spew output at random for consumption by the external environment. The systems we build are rational, purposeful systems; specifically, they produce outputs as a *response* to an *event,* or a *stimulus*, in the environment. Thus, another critical aspect of the environmental model is that of identifying *the events occurring in the environment to which the system must respond.* Not all events—after all, the environment, in its totality, generates an infinite number of events! We are only concerned w th those events which (1) occur in the external environment, and (2) require a response from the system.

Note that the boundary between a system and its environment, as illustrated in Figure 18.1, is *arbitrary*. It may be made by management decree, or as the result of political negotiation, or simply by accident. *And it is something that the systems analyst usually has some opportunity to influence.*

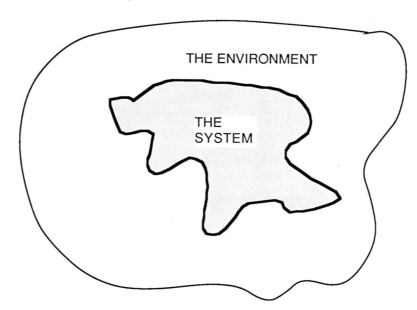

Figure 18.1: **The boundary between the system and the environment**

Generally, the user will have a fairly good idea of the *general* boundary between the system and the environment. But, as illustrated in Figure 18.2, there is often a "gray area" that is open for negotiation, an area that the user (1) isn't sure about, (2) hadn't thought about, (3) had some preconceived ideas about which he or she is willing to rethink, or (4) all the above.

Thus, for example, the user may ask the systems analyst to develop an accounts receivable system. While this may represent a well-defined, firm boundary between the system (known as the A/R system) and the environment, the systems analyst should certainly consider the "gray area," as illustrated by Figure 18.3, of accounts payable, inventory control, cash management, invoicing, and order entry as a somewhat larger scope.

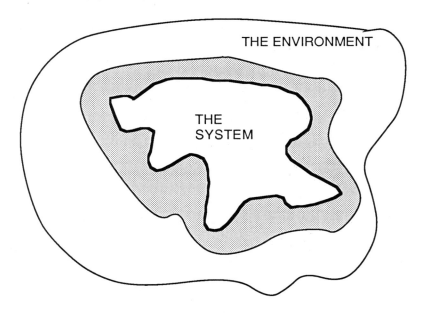

Figure 18.2: **The gray area between the system and the environment**

If the systems analyst chooses too *small* a scope for a project, he is doomed to failure, for the user may have unwittingly identified the *symptom* of the problem (e.g., "our accounts receivable are out of control") rather than the *cause* of the problem. And if the systems analyst, through overconfidence, naivete, or exuberance, chooses too *large* a scope for the project, he is doomed to failure, for he will be dealing with a vastly more complex political situation, and will be attempting to develop a system that is probably too large to develop under any circumstances. And he may be dealing with issues that the user doesn't care about or which cannot be changed at all. Thus, it is important to spend sufficient time and to get sufficient user concurrence with the choice of an appropriate system boundary.

In a large system, a number of factors may be taken into account when the scope of the project is being chosen. Among the more important factors are these:

* *The user's desire to achieve a certain share of the market for the product or to increase it beyond its current level.* This might be done by offering a new product or increased functionality in an existing product (e.g., increased functionality offered by automated teller systems and on-line home banking systems). Or the user might try to increase market share by offering a better, faster service to the marketplace (e.g., "All of our orders are shipped within 24 hours, and we have a sophisticated system that tracks your order so we can tell where it is at all times").

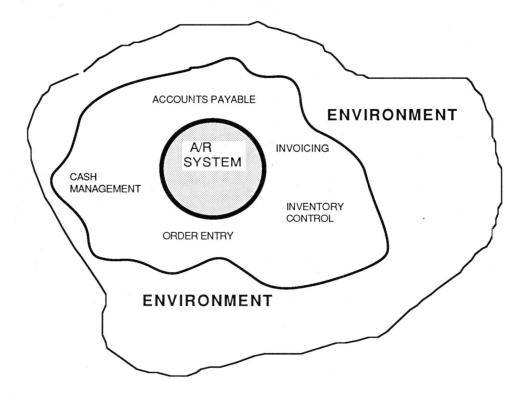

Figure 18.3: **The gray area surrounding accounts receivable systems**

* *Legislation enacted by city, state, or federal government(s).* The majority of such systems are reporting systems, for example, systems that report the employment (or unemployment) of workers based on age, sex, nationality, and so on. Or a new system might have to be built to accommodate changes in the tax laws.

* *A desire by the user to minimize operational expenses for some area of his or her business.* This was particularly common in large companies in the 1960s and is true for many small businesses that are installing their first computer today. But most organizations that have had computers installed

for ten years or more have already taken advantage of the obvious opportunities to reduce clerical overhead.

• *A desire by the user to gain some strategic advantage for the product line or business area that he is operating.* The user might attempt to do this by organizing and managing information about the marketplace so that he can produce goods in a more timely and economic fashion. A good example of this is the airline industry (as well as many other recently deregulated industries) where better information about market trends and customer preferences can lead to more efficient airline schedules and fares.

The area inside the system boundary is sometimes referred to as the *domain of change.* By this, we mean simply that everything inside the system boundary is subject to change (e.g., reorganization and/or automation), while everything outside the boundary is to be left in its current form and not investigated by the systems analyst.

To see two examples of system boundaries, examine the case studies in Appendix F and Appendix G. In the case of the YOURDON Press Information System (Appendix F), the system boundary is somewhat larger than one might have expected: it includes invoicing and handling of cash receipts that would typically be part of the Accounting Department (and thus outside the system boundary). Similarly, the elevator controller in Appendix G has a boundary somewhat smaller than one might have wanted: a very different system could have been developed if the elevator control panels had been considered part of the system rather than part of the environment. In both cases, the choices were arbitrary.

18.1   TOOLS USED TO DEFINE THE ENVIRONMENT

The environmental model consists of three components:

1.   Statement of purpose

2.   Context diagram

3.   Event list

Each of these is discussed next.

18.1.1   The Statement of Purpose

The first component of the environmental model is a brief, concise textual statement of the *purpose* of the system. It is intended for top management, user management, and others who are not directly involved in the development of the system.

An example of a typical statement of purpose is:

The purpose of the Ajax Book Processing System is to handle all of the details of customer orders for books, as well as shipping, invoicing, and back-billing of customers with overdue invoices. Information about book orders should be available for other systems, such as marketing, sales, and accounting.

The statement of purpose can be one, two, or several sentences long. However, it should not be more than a single paragraph, as *it is not intended to give a comprehensive, detailed description of the system.* Such an effort would be self-defeating: it is the purpose of the rest of the environmental model and the behavioral model to fill in all the details.

As a result, the statement of purpose will be deliberately vague about many details. In the Ajax example above, we might ask such questions as:

- Exactly what *kind* of information is provided to accounting, sales, and marketing by the book order system?

- How does the book order system determine whether a customer is credit worthy? Is this determined by the system itself or by means of advice from the accounting department?

- How does the system become aware that new books have been published and are now available for sale?

These detailed questions can only be answered by looking at the behavioral model, which we discuss in Chapters 19 and 20.

While the detailed behavioral questions are not answered by the statement of purpose document, it is generally sufficient to answer a series of high-level questions:

- Is the book order system responsible for payroll activities? *No;* virtually anyone reading the material above would agree that payroll is outside the scope of the system and is probably included in the accounting system.

- Is the book order system responsible for sending invoices to customers who order books? *Yes;* the statement of purpose says so. One could imagine this to be a subject of some debate between the book order department and the accounting department. So, it is appropriate that it be mentioned in the statement of purpose.

- Is the book order system responsible for inventory control, that is, for determining when to reorder books that are about to become out of stock? *No.* The statement of purpose makes no such statement. It is highly conceivable that inventory control is one of the many other systems (or departments) that will make use of information about book orders, as produced by the book order system.

Many systems analysts also feel that the statement of purpose should summarize the tangible, quantifiable benefits that will be achieved by the new system; for example, "the purpose of the system is to reduce the amount of time required to process an order from three days to one day." While this can be quite useful in small, highly focused projects, it is not easy to accomplish on larger projects. Instead, a separate cost-benefit analysis is usually required.

18.1.2   The Context Diagram

The next part of the environmental model begins to answer some of the questions raised by the statement of purpose. The *context diagram* is a special case of the dataflow diagram, in which a single bubble represents the entire system. A context diagram for the book order system is shown in Figure 18.4. Examples of context diagrams for two real systems are provided in Appendixes F and G.

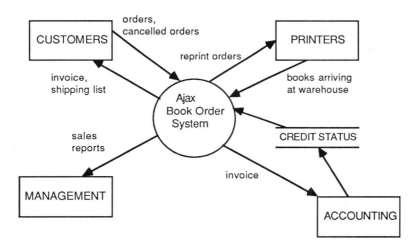

Figure 18.4: **A context diagram**

The context diagram highlights several important characteristics of the system:

*   The people, organizations, or systems with which our system communicates. These are known as *terminators*.

*   The data that our system receives from the outside world and that must be processed in some way.

*   The data produced by our system and sent to the outside world.

*   The data stores that are shared between our system and the terminators. These data stores are either created outside the system and used by our system or created by our system and used outside the system.

*   The boundary between our system and the rest of the world.

Techniques for constructing the context diagram are discussed in Section 18.2.

18.1.3   The Event List

The event list is a narrative list of the "stimuli" that occur in the outside world *and to which our system must respond.* An event list for the book order system is shown in Figure 18.5:

> 1. Customer places order. (F)
> 2. Customer cancels order. (F)
> 3. Management requires sales report. (T)
> 4. Book reprint order arrives at warehouse. (C)

Figure 18.5: **An event list**

Note that each event is labeled with either an F, a T, or a C. This is to show whether the event is a *flow-oriented* event, a *temporal* event, or a *control* event. A flow-oriented event is one associated with a dataflow; that is, the system becomes aware that the event has occurred when a piece of data (or possibly several pieces of data) has arrived. As you can imagine, this will correspond to a dataflow on the context diagram.

However, not every dataflow on the context diagram is necessarily a flow-oriented event. Consider, for example, the partial context diagram shown in Figure 18.6.

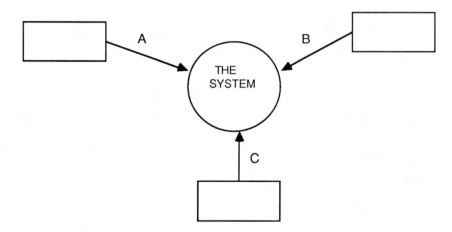

Figure 18.6: **A partial context diagram**

At first glance, one might be tempted to conclude that dataflows A, B, and C are all indicators of separate, discrete events. However, it may turn out that only dataflow A is associated with an event (e.g., the flow of data is initiated by the terminator). In order to process the event, it may turn out that the system *explicitly* asks other terminators for inputs along dataflow B and C pursuant to producing some system response.

Thus, there is not necessarily a one-to-one correspondence between dataflows on the context diagram and events in the event list. In general, each dataflow is *either* an event (or, more precisely, the indication that the event has occurred) *or* is required by the system in order to process an event.

In addition to flow-oriented events, a system may also have *temporal* events. As the name implies, temporal events are triggered by the arrival of a point in time. Thus, examples of temporal events might be the following:

* A daily report of all book orders is required at 9:00 AM.

* Invoices must be generated at 3:00 PM.

* Management reports must be generated once an hour.

Note that the temporal events are not triggered by incoming dataflows; one might imagine that the system has an internal clock with which it can determine the passage of time. However, keep in mind also that a temporal event may require the system to ask for inputs from one or more terminators. Thus, one or more dataflows may be associated with a temporal event, though the dataflows, themselves, do not represent the event itself.

Control events could be considered a special case of a temporal event: an external stimulus that occurs at some unpredictable point in time. Unlike a normal temporal event, the control event is not associated with the regular passage of time, so the system cannot anticipate it by using an internal clock. And unlike a normal flow-oriented event, the control event does not make its presence known by the arrival of data. As shown in Figure 18.7, a control event is associated with a *control flow* on the context diagram.

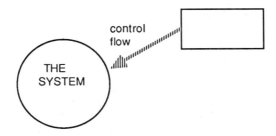

Figure 18.7: **A control flow associated with a control event**

The control flow could be regarded as a binary dataflow: it is either on or off, and it can switch from one state to the other at any point in time, thereby signaling the system that it needs to take some *immediate* action. Business-oriented information systems typically have *no* control flows on their context diagrams; the YOURDON Press Information System described in Appendix F, for example, has none. But control flows are quite common in real-time systems; for an example of this, look at the context diagram for the elevator control system in Appendix G.

18.1.4   Additional Components of the Environmental Model

In most projects, the event list, context diagram, and statement of purpose are sufficient. However, two additional components may be useful, depending on the nature and complexity of the system:

- Initial data dictionary, defining external flows and stores

- Entity-relationship model of the external stores

Even a medium-sized system will typically have a few dozen incoming and out-going dataflows; a large system may literally have hundreds. While these dataflows will eventually be defined in great detail in the behavioral model (discussed in Chapter 20), it may be useful to begin the construction of the data dictionary *now*. This can be important if the interfaces between the system and the various terminators are subject to change and negotiation; the earlier one begins formally defining those interfaces (by defining the composition and meaning of the stores), the earlier they can be finalized.

Similarly, an entity-relationship diagram can be constructed of the external stores (if there are any). This can help expose relationships between the stores that otherwise would not become evident until the behavioral model was being developed. By concentrating on these relationships at this early stage, we have a way of double-checking the interactions between the terminators (who typically include the end users of the system) and the system itself.

18.2   CONSTRUCTING THE ENVIRONMENTAL MODEL

The discussion above probably makes the environmental model seem rather simple and straightforward: after all, there is only one process, a few dataflows and terminators, a short narrative description of the system's purpose, and a list of events. While this is true, it often turns out that the environmental model requires a great deal of work; also, it is usually developed as a series of iterative refinements, with additional details being filled in and refined.

One important reason why so many refinements and revisions are usually necessary is that *no one person usually understands the full scope of the system as it is initially being defined.* If the project involves a new system that will replace an existing system, it is possible to talk to the users who are currently carrying out the system's functions; in a sense, they have the perspective of people on the inside looking out, as illustrated by Figure 18.8. However, even in this case, the various individual inside users are generally familiar only with a portion of the system, and their various views sometimes conflict. Even worse, your initial interviews with the user community may omit one or two important users whose interactions with the termi-nators outside the system must be modeled.[1]

---

1 Such users may not be important in terms of the organizational hierarchy; they may be regarded as humble clerks, secretaries, or administrators. Nevertheless, the *functions* they perform may be vital, and it may be crucial to accurately model the inputs they receive from the external world and the outputs they send to the outside world. The reason that the systems analyst often forgets to talk to these people is very

Figure 18.8: **The user's view of the system**

It is important to spend a great deal of time and energy on the environmental model, for it is often the focal point of a number of important meetings and presentations early in the life of a systems development project. Indeed, it is often the *only* part of the overall system model that many high-level users and managers (the ones with the money to continue funding the project and the power to cancel the project!) will ever see. After it has been constructed and approved, you will find it pinned to several walls and bulletin boards—so it is important that it be correct.

18.2.1   Constructing the Context Diagram

The context diagram, as we have seen, consists of terminators, dataflows and control flows, data stores, and a single process representing the entire system. We will discuss each in turn next.

The easiest part of the context diagram is the process; as we have seen, it consists of a single bubble. The name inside the process is typically the name of the entire system or an agreed-upon acronym for the system. Examples are shown in Figure 18.9(a) and (b).

Figure 18.9(a): **A typical process name for a context diagram**

---

1 (cont.) simple: a higher-level user (i.e., the boss) will tell the systems analyst who to talk to. "Don't bother any of my people," the boss will say to the analyst, "they're all too busy—hat's why we need the new system. I'll tell you everything you need to know about the system." As we discussed in Chapter 3, there may not be any diplomatic way of avoiding this; but it is crucial to check the environmental model carefully to ensure that nothing is missing.

Figure 18.9(b): **Another typical process name**

Note that, in the extreme case, the new system may represent an entire organization; in this case, the process name would typically be that of the organization itself, as shown in Figure 18.9(c).[2]

Figure 18.9(c): **A process name representing an entire organization**

The terminators, as we have seen, are represented by a rectangular box on the context diagram. Terminators communicate directly with the system through dataflows or control flows, as shown in Figure 18.10(a), or through external data stores, as shown in Figure 18.10(b).

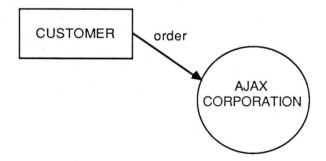

Figure 18.10(a): **Direct communication between terminator and system**

---

2 This is an unlikely scenario for a typical systems development project, but it is beginning to happen more and more often as people use dataflow diagrams and other modeling tools described in this book to build *enterprise* models. This may be done without any intention of computerizing the entire enterprise, but simply to understand what already exists—especially to understand the *data* that the organization needs to carry out its purpose. The subject of enterprise models is discussed in William Inmon's *Information Engineering for the Practitioner* (Englewood Cliffs, N.J.: Prentice-Hall, 1987), and James Martin's *Strategic Data Base Modeling* (Englewood Cliffs, N.J.: Prentice-Hall, 1985).

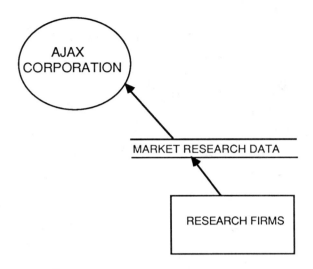

Figure 18.10(b): **Communication through an external store**

Note that terminators do *not* communicate directly with one another; thus, the context diagram shown in Figure 18.11 is incorrect. Actually, terminators *do* communicate with one another, but since, by definition, the terminators are *external* to the system, the nature and content of any terminator-to-terminator interactions are irrelevant to the system. If, during your discussions with the users, you find that it is essential to know when, why, or how one terminator communicates with another, *then the terminators are part of the system, and they should be buried within the process bubble of the context diagram.*

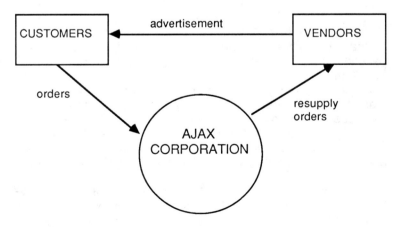

Figure 18.11: **An incorrect context diagram**

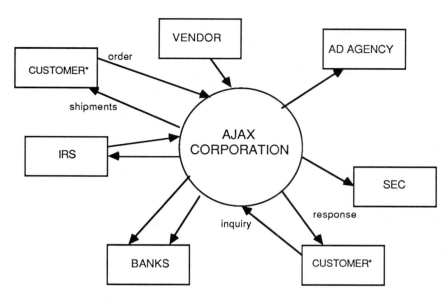

Figure 18.12(a): **Duplicated terminators on the context diagram**

Three other points should be made about the terminators:

1. Some terminators may have a large number of inputs and outputs. To avoid an unnecessarily cluttered diagram, it may be convenient to draw the terminator more than once, as shown in Figure 18.12(a). Note that the duplicated terminators are marked with an asterisk; an alternative convention is to represent the duplicated terminators with a diagonal cross-hatch, as shown in Figure 18.12(b).

2. When the terminator is an individual person, it is generally preferable to indicate the *role* that the person is playing, rather than indicating the person's identity; thus, Figure 18.13(a) is preferred over Figure 18.13(b). There are two reasons for this: first, the person carrying out the role may change over time, and it is desirable that the context diagram remain stable and accurate even if there are personnel changes. And, second, an individual person may play several different roles in the system; rather than showing one terminator labeled "John Smith" with several unrelated incoming and outgoing flows, it is more meaningful to show the various roles that John Smith plays, each as a separate terminator.

3. Because we are primarily interested in developing an *essential* model of the system, it is important to distinguish between *sources* and *handlers* when we draw terminators on the context diagram. A handler is a mechanism, device, or physical medium used to transport data into or out of the system. Because such handlers are often familiar and visible to users of the current implementation of a system, there is often a tendency to show the handler, rather than the true source of data. However, since

the new system will generally have the option of *changing the technology by which data are brought into and sent out of the system*, the handler should not be shown. Thus, the context diagram shown in Figure 18.14(a) is preferred to the one shown in Figure 18.14(b).

As a compromise, particularly if the user insists, one can label a terminator to show both the true source *and* the handler that conveys data into or out of the system; this is illustrated in Figure 18.14(c).

The *flows* shown on the context diagram model data coming into the system and data transported out of the system, as well as control signals received by the system or generated by the system. Dataflows are included on the context diagram if they are needed to detect an event in the environment to which the system must respond, or if they are needed (as data) in order to produce a response. Dataflows may also appear on the context diagram to illustrate data that are being transported between terminators by the system. Finally, dataflows are shown on the context diagram when data are produced by the system to respond to an event.

As we have already noted, the context diagram of an essential model avoids (wherever possible) showing the implementation-oriented handlers that transport data into and out of the system. Furthermore, we want to avoid showing the implementation-oriented prompts and handshaking by which the system and the terminators tell each other that they are ready for input or output. Thus, we want to avoid drawing context diagrams like the one shown in Figure 18.15(a) because it incorporates implementation assumptions that may be drastically changed when the new system is implemented.

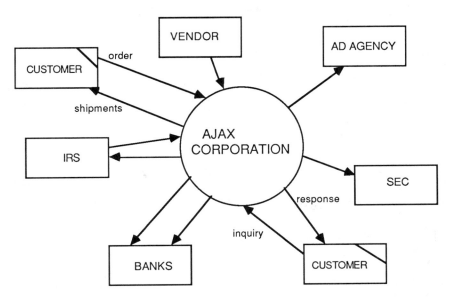

Figure 18.12(b): **An alternative way of showing duplicated terminators**

SHIPPING CLERK

Figure 18.13(a): **A preferred way of showing a terminator**

FRED QUIMBY

Figure 18.13(b): **A less preferred way of showing a terminator**

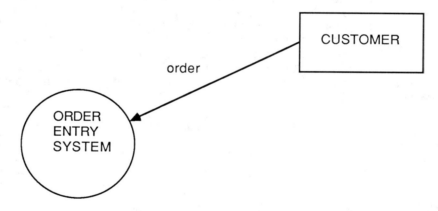

Figure 18.14(a): **A terminator showing the true source of data**

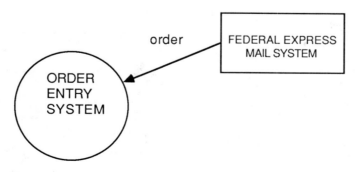

Figure 18.14(b): **A terminator that acts as a handler**

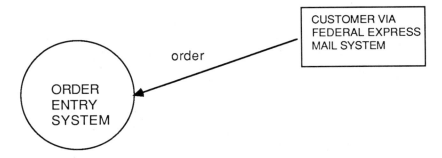

Figure 18.14(c): **A terminator that combines both source and handler**

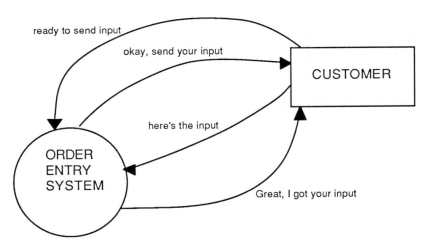

Figure 18.15(a): **A context diagram with unnecessary prompts**

Instead, we should draw the context diagram on the assumption that inputs are caused by *and initiated by* the terminators, and that outputs are caused by *and initiated by* the system. By avoiding the extraneous prompts and implementation-oriented inputs and outputs, we model only the *net* flow of data.

However, there will be occasions when a terminator does not initiate input, because, even given perfect technology, the terminator does not know that the system requires its input. Similarly, there are occasions when the system does not initiate the generation of output, because it does not know that the terminator needs or wants the output. In both these cases, a prompt is an *essential* part of the system, and it must be shown on the context diagram; an example is shown in Figure 18.15(b). It is sometimes convenient to show the prompt and the corresponding input or output flow with a dialogue flow (a double-headed arrow), as shown in Figure 18.15(c).[3]

---

3 It's not *required* that you use a dialogue flow, but it does make the context diagram more readable by packaging the associated input and output together so they are immediately visible to the reader. Also, using one arrow to show that the dialogue, as opposed to two separate arrows, creates a less cluttered

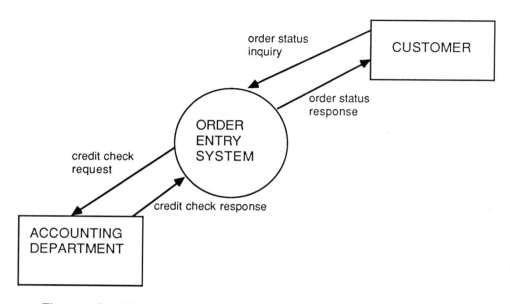

Figure 18.15(b): **Dialogue flows to show essential prompts**

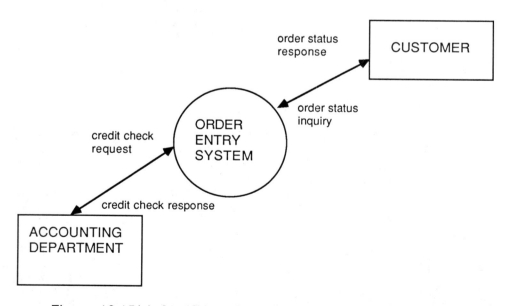

Figure 18.15(c): **An alternative way to show dialogue flows**

3 (cont.) context diagram. This is important on large systems, where there may be as many as a hundred or more different interactions with external terminators.

18.2.2   Constructing the Event List

The event list, as we have seen, is a simple textual listing of the events in the environment to which the system must respond. When building the event list, make sure that you distinguish between an event and an event-related flow. For example, the following is probably *not* an event:

"Customer order is received by the system."

Instead, this is probably the incoming dataflow by which the system becomes aware that the event has occurred. A more appropriate name for the event might be

"Customer places order."

This may seem like an exercise in semantics, but it's not. If we describe the event from the system's point of view (i.e., from the inside looking out), we might mistakenly identify incoming flows that are *not* events on their own, but that are required to process some other event. Thus, we always want to describe the events from the environment's point of view (i.e., from the outside looking in).

In most cases, the easiest way to identify the relevant events for a system is to visualize the system in action: we examine each terminator and ask ourselves what effect the terminator's actions can have on the system. This is usually done in concert with the system's users, who may be playing the role(s) of the terminators themselves. However, we must be careful to distinguish between discrete events that have been accidentally "packaged" together as if they were a single event; this happens quite often with flow-oriented events. We must examine the candidate event and ask ourselves whether all instances of the event involve the same data; if data are present in some instances and absent in others, we may actually have two distinct events. For example, if we look closely at the event "customer places order," we may find that some instances of the event include the data element "salesperson-ID" and others do not; and we may find that the system's response is different if a salesperson is involved than if there is no salesperson. Thus, it might be more appropriate to have two separate events: "customer places order," and "salesperson places customer order."

Also, keep in mind that the event list must include not only normal interactions between the system and its terminators, but also failure mode situations as well. Since we are creating an essential model, we do not have to worry about failures of our system; but we do have to take into account possible failures or errors caused by the terminators. As Paul Ward and Stephen Mellor point out in *Structured Development for Real-Time Systems* (New York: YOURDON Press, 1985),

> Since the terminators are by definition outside the bounds of the system-building effort represented by the model, the implementors cannot modify the terminator technology at will to improve its reliability. Instead, they must build responses to terminator problems into the essential model of the system. A useful approach to modeling responses to terminator problems is to build a list of "normal" events and then to ask, for each event, "Does the system need to respond if this event fails to occur as expected?

For example, our event list for the Ajax Book Order System (Figure 18.5) included an event "Book reprint order arrives at warehouse." But what if it does not arrive in a timely fashion (e.g., within a week of the date promised by the printer)? What should the system do? We probably need an additional system-initiated event to cause the system to follow up with the printer and see why there is a delay.

18.2.3   Which Comes First, the Context Diagram or the Event List?

You can begin with *either* the event list or the context diagram. It really doesn't matter, as long as you eventually produce both components of the environmental model *and check to see that they are consistent with each other.*

You may also find yourself talking with people who are aware of all the things that come into the system and go out of the system; some users may be able to provide you with this information, or the maintenance programmers in charge of maintaining a current version of the system might be knowledgeable in this area. This will provide you with the pieces of the context diagram as a starting point. You can then discuss the transactions that the users send to the system and the responses they expect the system to make. This allows you to create the event list from the context diagram.

However, you may find yourself in a situation where the context diagram is not available. This is particularly common at the beginning of some systems development projects: it may not be easy to immediately identify the terminators and the various flows into and out of the system. *In this case, it is often more practical to begin with an ERD diagram that shows the objects and relationships.* Candidate events can then be found by looking for activities or operations that cause instances of a relationship to be created or deleted. Creation of the event list can then lead to the development of the context diagram; this is illustrated in Figure 18.16.

For example, suppose we had identified the objects **CUSTOMER** and **BOOK** in a publishing system; our user might also tell us that there is a relationship, "orders," between **CUSTOMER** and **BOOK**. A likely event, then, would be an action that creates an instance of the orders relationship; another event would an action that deletes an instance of the relationship. This would lead us to identify "Customer orders book," and "Customer cancels book order" as events in our event list. It should not require too much investigation to realize that "customer" is a terminator for the system (while "book" is not); we could then begin to draw the the context diagram.

When we have finished both components of the environmental model, we should be able to confirm the following:

- Each input flow on the context diagram should be needed by the system to recognize that an event has occurred, or it should be needed by the system in order to produce a response to an event, or both.

- Each output flow should be a response to an event.

- Each nontemporal event on the event list should have input from which the system can detect that the event has occurred.

- Each event should either produce an immediate output as its response, or it should store data to be output later (as a response or part of a response to some other event), or it should cause the system to change its state (as indicated on a state-transition diagram).

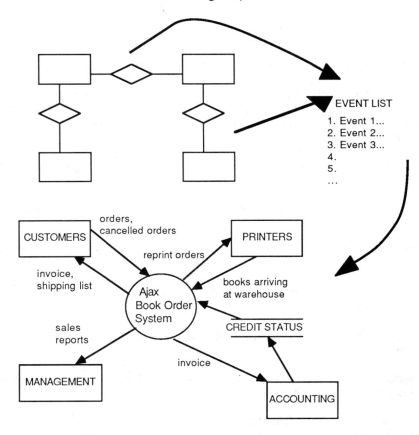

Figure 18.16: **Creation of the context diagram from an ERD**

18.3   SUMMARY

Building the environmental model is the first and most important part of building a complete model of user requirements for a new system. At this point, it may seem like an easy job; after all, the context diagram consists of only a single bubble, and the event list looks like a simple list of transactions. But on a large project, a great deal of work can be involved: the single bubble in the context diagram may be interacting with dozens of external terminators and may have over a hundred incoming and outgoing dataflows. And the event list is also a major effort on large systems; there can easily be over a hundred events that the system has to deal with, and they all need to be identified. Also, it may be difficult to come up with an agreed-upon simple statement of why the system is to exist.

Once you have built the environmental model, it should be carefully reviewed by all the key user representatives, as well as by the project team. Then you are ready to start building the behavioral model, the model of the inside of the system. This is discussed in Chapters 19 and 20.

QUESTIONS AND EXERCISES

1. What are the three things that are defined by the essential model?

2. What kind of events must be modeled in an essential model?

3. How is the boundary between the system and the environment determined by the systems analyst?

4. What is the likely consequence if the systems analyst chooses too small a scope for the project?

5. What is the likely consequence if the systems analyst chooses too large a scope for the project?

6. What factors should be taken into account when choosing the scope for a project?

7. How does the user's desire to achieve a certain share of the market affect the scope of a system?

8. How does legislation enacted by various governmental bodies affect the scope of a system?

9. How does the user's desire to minimize (or reduce) operational expenses affect the scope of a system?

10. How does the user's desire to gain some strategic advantage against competition affect the scope of a project?

11. Research Project: Investigate a project in your own organization. Which factor do you think was most influential in choosing the scope? Do you think the user, the systems analyst, and the project team were aware of this and were in agreement with it?

12. In general, what do you think are likely to be the key factors for systems developed in the 1990s? For example, will minimization of operational expenses be more important than changes caused by government legislation?

13. What are the three major components of the environmental model?

14. Approximately how long should the statement of purpose document be?

15. What five characteristics of a system does a context diagram show?

16. What are the components of a context diagram?

17. What is an event list?

18. What are the three types of events that must be modeled in a context diagram?

19. What is the relationship between flows and events on the context diagram?

20. What is a temporal event?

21. What additional components may be found in an environmental model besides the context diagram, the event list, and the statement of purpose?

22. Why is it usually necessary to make many revisions and refinements to the environmental model?

23. Why is it important to ensure that the environmental model is correct?

24. What kind of name should be put inside the bubble of a context diagram?

25. What is an enterprise model?

26. How do terminators communicate with the system?

27. Do terminators communicate with each other in a system model? Why or why not?

28. Under what conditions would a terminator be drawn more than once on a context diagram? How would it be shown?

29. If a terminator is an individual person, how should he or she be shown on the context diagram?

30. How can the systems analyst be sure that he or she has identified all the terminators in the context diagram?

31. What is a handler? What is the difference between a source and a handler?

32. Why should sources rather than handlers be shown on a context diagram?

33. What should the systems analyst do if the user insists on showing handlers on a context diagram?

34. Under what conditions are flows shown on a DFD?

35. Why should prompts and handshaking generally not be shown on a context diagram?

36. What does the term net flow of data mean?

37. Under what conditions does a terminator *not* initiate input into a system?

38. Under what conditions does the system *not* initiate output to a terminator?

39. Which should be developed first, the context diagram or the event list? Why?

40. What four things should be checked to ensure that the environmental model is correct?

41. What is wrong with the following context diagram?

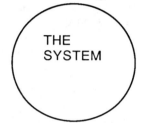

42. What is wrong with the following context diagram?

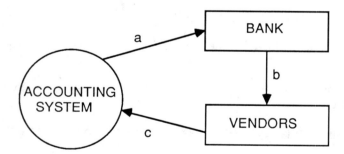

43. What is wrong with the following context diagram?

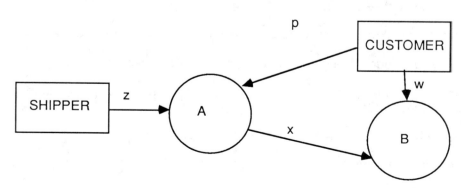

44. What is wrong with the following context diagram?

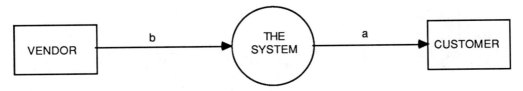

EVENT LIST

1. Customer needs an "a"
2. Vendor needs invoice.
3. Vendor makes a shipment.
4. Customer places order.

19 BUILDING A PRELIMINARY BEHAVIORAL MODEL

> Things are always at their best in their beginning.
> Blaise Pascal, *Lettres Provinciales, 1656-1657, no. 4*

In this chapter, you will learn:

1. Why a pure top-down approach to the behavioral model is difficult.

2. How to develop a preliminary behavioral model using event partitioning.

3. How to develop the initial ERD data model.

In the previous chapter, we saw how to develop the environmental model for a system. If you were working on a real project at this point, you would have finished the context diagram, the event list, and a statement of purpose. In addition, you should have begun constructing the data dictionary, with at least a definition of the data elements that represent interfaces between the external terminators and the system.

Our task now is to begin building the behavioral model, that is, the model of what the internal *behavior* of the system must be in order to deal successfully with the environment. This will involve the development of a preliminary dataflow diagram and entity-relationship diagram, as well as an elaboration of the initial data dictionary entries.

Basically, this approach involves drawing a first-cut dataflow diagram, with one process (bubble) for the system response to each event that we have identified in our event list. We then draw stores on our first-cut DFD to model the data that must be remembered between asynchronous events. Finally, we connect appropriate input flows and output flows to the bubbles and check our set of DFDs against the context diagram for consistency.

Once having done this, we will go through a clean-up process, described in Chapter 20, to produce a well-organized process model and data model for presentation to the end user. This approach was given the name event partitioning in [McMenamin and Palmer, 1984].

We begin by comparing this approach to the classical top-down approach.

19.1   THE CLASSICAL APPROACH

The approach suggested in this chapter is substantially different from the top-down approach described in such classical textbooks as DeMarco [DeMarco, 1979], Gane [Gane and Sarson, 1979], and others. The classical approach assumes that you have already drawn your context diagram; but it assumes that you will proceed *directly* from the single bubble in the context diagram to a high-level DFD (known as Figure 0), in which each of the bubbles represents a major subsystem. Each bubble in Figure 0 is then partitioned into lower-level figures, and each bubble in the lower-level figures is partitioned further, and so on, until you have reached the level of an "atomic" bubble that requires no further decomposition. This is illustrated by Figure 19.1.

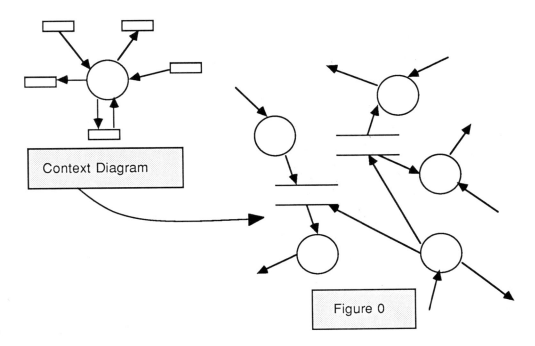

Figure 19.1: **The top-down development of the behavioral model**

Though this top-down approach is different than the one presented in this book, I am not opposed to its approach,....*if it works.* However, you should be aware that many systems analysts encounter the following problems when attempting to follow a top-down approach:

- *Analysis paralysis.* In many large, complex systems, there simply isn't a clue to guide the systems analyst in drawing an appropriate Figure 0 from the context diagram. So the analyst sits at her desk, staring at the context diagram, waiting for divine inspiration, or for someone to tell her that the project has run out of time for systems analysis and that it's time to begin coding.

- *The six-analyst phenomenon.* On a large, complex system, there is often more than one systems analyst staring at the context diagram. In order to divide up the work equally and not get in each other's way, they arbitrarily create a Figure 0 with one bubble for each systems analyst. Thus, if there are six systems analysts, Figure 0 will consist of six bubbles. Needless to say, this may not be the optimal partitioning of the system. What happens, for example, if the same system is specified by three systems analysts? Nine analysts? One analyst?

- *An arbitrary physical partitioning.* In many cases, a new system is based on an existing system, or it represents the computerization of an existing organization. The top-level partitioning of the current system (e.g., the current organizational units or the existing computer systems) is often used as the rationale for developing the partitioning of the new system. Thus, if the existing system is represented by a Purchasing Department and a Quality Assurance Department, the new system will often have a Purchasing Subsystem and a Quality Assurance Subsystem even though those might not be (and often are not) the best partitioning (from a functional point of view) of the system.

The approach described in this chapter is not a pure top-down approach; neither is it a pure bottom-up approach. It is, in a sense, a "middle-out" approach; after the initial DFD is developed, some *upward* leveling is required, and some further *downward* partitioning may be necessary.

19.2   IDENTIFYING EVENT RESPONSES

The event partitioning approach involves the following four steps:

1. A bubble, or process, is drawn for each event in the event list.

2. The bubble is named by describing the response that the system should make to the associated event.

3. Appropriate inputs and outputs are drawn so that the bubble will be able to make its required response, and stores are drawn, as appropriate, for communication between bubbles.

4.   The resulting first-cut DFD is checked against the context diagram and event list for completeness and consistency.

The first step is straightforward, indeed almost mechanical in nature. If there are 25 events in the event list, you should draw 25 bubbles. For convenient reference, you should number the bubble to match the associated event. Thus, event 13 corresponds to bubble 13. (Later, as we will see in Chapter 20, we will renumber the bubbles appropriately.)

The second step is also straightforward and mechanical: each bubble is given an appropriate name based on its required response. This means that you should examine the event and ask yourself, "What response is the system supposed to make to this event?" Remember, though, that you should choose names that are as specific as possible. Thus, if an event is CUSTOMER MAKES PAYMENT, an appropriate bubble name might be UPDATE ACCOUNTS RECEIVABLE (if that is the only required response from the system), rather than PROCESS CUSTOMER PAYMENT (which tells us nothing about the nature of the response).

The third step is definitely not mechanical, but it is usually fairly straightforward. For each bubble that you have drawn, you must identify the inputs that the bubble requires to do its work; you must identify the outputs (if any) that the bubble produces; and you must identify the stores that the bubble must access. This is normally done by interviewing the appropriate user(s) and concentrating on each event and its associated bubble. "What does this bubble need to do its job?" you will ask the user, and "What outputs does it generate?"

In many cases, the event is flow-driven; this means that the system becomes aware of the occurrence of the event because of the arrival of some data from an external terminator. Obviously, this means that the appropriate dataflow must be attached to the process required to respond to that event. But, as shown in Figures 19.2(a) and (b), additional inputs (from other terminators and possibly from data stores) may be required in order for the process to be able to produce its required output.

Similarly, you must draw in the appropriate outputs produced by the process as part of the response. In many cases, this will involve outputs being sent back to the terminators outside the system; however, it may involve outputs that are sent to data stores, to be used as inputs by other processes. This is illustrated by Figures 19.3(a) and (b).

Finally, the fourth step is a consistency-checking activity similar to the balancing steps described in Chapter 14. You must verify that every input shown on the context diagram is associated with an input on one of the processes in the preliminary DFD; and you must verify that every output produced by a process in the preliminary DFD is either sent to a store or is an external output shown on the context diagram.

There are two special cases: (1) single events that cause multiple responses and (2) multiple events that cause the same response. In the first case, a single event may cause multiple responses, *each* of which is modeled with its own bubble in the preliminary DFD. This is illustrated in Figure 19.4. This is appropriate only if all the responses use the same incoming dataflow, and only if all the responses are independent of one another. No output from one part of the overall response should be needed as input by another part of the overall response.

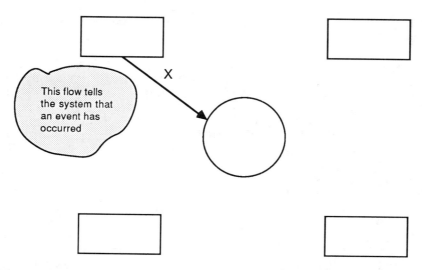

Figure 19.2(a): **A dataflow signalling the occurrence of an event**

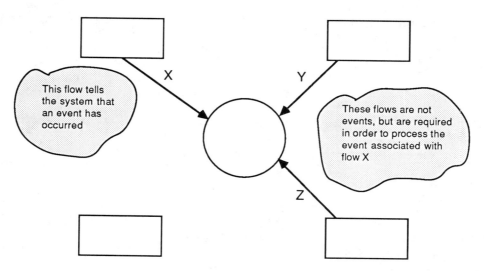

Figure 19.2(b): **Additional inputs required to produce the response**

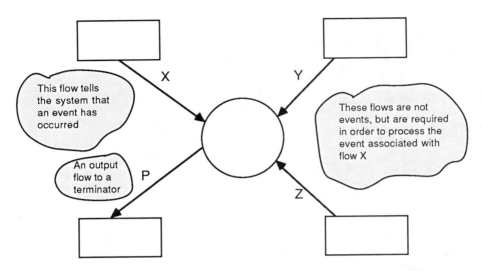

Figure 19.3(a): **An output sent from a process to a terminator**

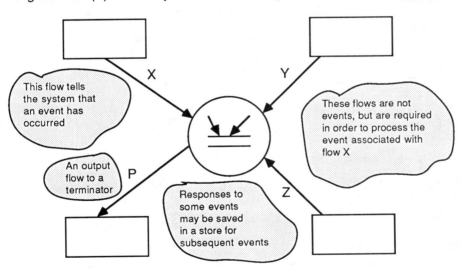

Figure 19.3(b): **An output being sent from a process to a store**

Conversely, there will be occasional situations where one process is associated with more than one event; this is illustrated by Figure 19.5. This is valid and appropriate only if the response made by the bubble is *identical* for the various events, and only if the input data and output data are identical for the various event responses.

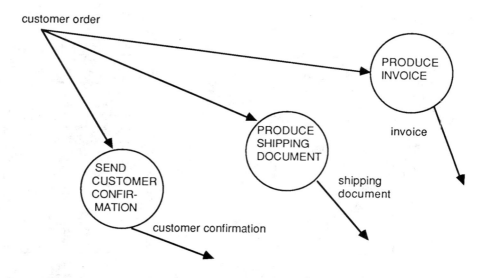

Figure 19.4 : **Multiple responses from the same event**

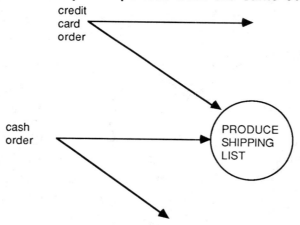

Figure 19.5: **Multiple events with the same response**

19.3   CONNECTING EVENT RESPONSES

Note that in the previous examples, none of the processes in the preliminary dataflow diagram are connected to each other: *bubbles do not talk directly to other bubbles.* Instead bubbles communicate with each other through data stores.

Why is this? Simply because the bubbles in the preliminary DFD represent *responses to an event,* and events that occur in the external environment are, in the general case, asynchronous. That is, we have no way of guaranteeing that two events will occur at the same instant, or within two seconds of one another, or within any other specified period of time. Events happen in the external environment whenever the environment feels like making them happen.

And since:

- the response to one event may require data produced by some other event, and

- we have no way of knowing when the events will occur in time, and

- we have to assume, in an essential model, that each process will perform its work infinitely quickly, and

- each dataflow acts as a pipeline that can transmit data elements at infinite speed,

it follows that the only way we can synchronize multiple interdependent events is through a store. Note that this is an *essential* store: a store required, not because of time delays associated with imperfect technology, but because of timing considerations in the environment.

Thus, you should not see a preliminary dataflow diagram like the one shown in Figure 19.6(a); since the associated events are asynchronous, Figure 19.6(a) could only work if a time-delayed storage of data was hidden within one of the processes or the dataflow itself. Thus, Figure 19.6(b) is the proper way of showing the communication between processes.

19.4   DEVELOPING THE INITIAL DATA MODEL

As we have seen, the procedure of sketching the initial DFD involves drawing data stores between asynchronous processes. In most cases, the nature of these stores will be obvious, and the names can be chosen from your understanding of the subject matter of the project.

Meanwhile, however, you or one of your colleagues should have begun working on the initial version of the entity-relationship diagram *as an independent activity, in parallel with the development of the initial DFD.* This should be done using the techniques described in Chapter 12.

As the ERD and DFD are being developed in parallel, they can be used to cross-check each other. Thus, *stores* that have been tentatively defined in the preliminary DFD can be used to suggest *objects* in the preliminary ERD; and *objects* that have been tentatively identified in the preliminary ERD can be used to help choose appropriate *stores* in the preliminary DFD. Neither model should be considered the dominant model that controls the other; each is on an equal footing and can provide invaluable assistance to the other.

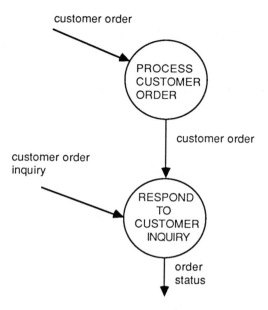

Figure 19.6(a): **Improper model of time-delayed communication between processes**

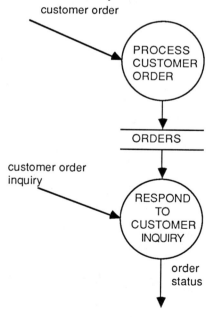

Figure 19.6(b): **Proper model of time-delayed communication between processes**

You may also find that the *event list* is as useful for creating the initial ERD as it is for creating the initial DFD. *Nouns* in the event list will often turn out to be objects in the ERD; for example, if an event is "Customer places order," we would immediately identify **customer** and **order** as tentative objects. Similarly, we can use the event list as a means of cross-checking the initial ERD: all the object types in the ERD should correspond to nouns in the event list.

19.5   SUMMARY

The most important thing to realize from this chapter is that you will *not* produce a behavioral model that is ready to be shown to the user. It is not finished; it is not pretty; it is not simple enough or well-organized enough to be understood in its entirety. You can see an example of this by looking at the case study in Appendix F.

So what is it? What is the point of carrying out the steps described in Section 19.3? Very simply, it is a beginning, a *framework* upon which you can base the development of the finished, final version of the essential model.

You should not be concerned at this point about the organization of the behavioral model, or its complexity, or its understandability. You should resolutely resist the temptation to reorganize, package, decompose, or "recompose" any of the bubbles in the preliminary DFD. All you should care about at this point is the underlying *correctness* of the model: Does it have a process for each event? Does it show the necessary inputs and outputs for each event? And does it show the necessary connections between events?

Once you have established this, then you can begin working on a reorganization of the model. This is discussed in more detail in Chapter 20.

REFERENCES

1. Tom DeMarco, *Structured Analysis and Systems Specification.* Englewood Cliffs, N.J.: Prentice-Hall, 1979.

2. Chris Gane and Trish Sarson, *Structured Systems Analysis: Tools and Techniques.* Englewood Cliffs, N.J.: Prentice-Hall, 1979.

3. Steve McMenamin and John Palmer, *Essential Systems Analysis.* New York: YOURDON Press, 1984.

QUESTIONS AND EXERCISES

1. What is a behavioral model of a system? What is its purpose?

2. What are the three major components of the *preliminary* behavioral model?

3. What is the classical approach to building a behavioral model? Why is it characterized as a top-down approach?

4. What are the three major problems typically faced by systems analysts when trying to follow the classical top-down approach to building a behavioral model of an information system?

5. Why do you think that some systems analysts suffer paralysis, or "writer's block," when trying to develop a Figure 0 DFD from the context diagram?

6. Why does the behavioral model in some projects exhibit an arbitrary physical partitioning?

7. What does the term event partitioning mean?

8. What are the four steps in event partitioning?

9. If the systems analyst has discovered 13 events in the environmental model, how many processes (bubbles) should be in the first-cut behavioral model?

10. What kind of numbering scheme is used to number the bubbles in the first-cut DFD of the behavioral model?

11. What rationale is used to give a name to each bubble in the first-cut DFD of the behavioral model?

12. How should the systems analyst determine the inputs, outputs, and stores required by each bubble in the first-cut DFD?

13. If an event is flow-driven, how many input dataflows must the bubble processing that event receive?

14. What are the consistency-checking guidelines that the systems analyst must go through when drawing the first-cut DFD of the behavioral model?

15. How should the first-cut DFD be drawn for the case of an event that produces multiple responses?

16. Under what conditions could a single bubble in the first-cut DFD be associated with more than one event?

17. In the first-cut DFD, how do bubbles communicate with one another? That is, how does an output produced by one bubble become input to another bubble?

18. How does the first-cut DFD show the synchronization of multiple, asynchronous, interdependent events?

19. Which should be developed first: the first-cut DFD or a first-cut data model (ERD)? Why?

20. What should the systems analyst do with the first-cut DFD and first-cut ERD after he or she has finished them?

21. When the first-cut DFD has been finished, should it be reviewed with the user? Why or why not?

22. What is wrong with the following first-cut DFD?

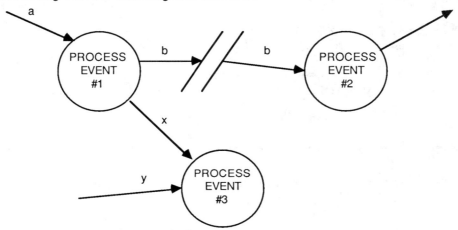

23. What's wrong with the following first-cut DFD?

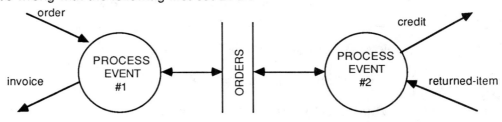

EVENT LIST (from environmental model)

1. Customer orders item.
2. Customer returns an item.
3. Customer makes payment.

20 FINISHING THE BEHAVIORAL MODEL

Give us the tools, and we will finish the job.
Winston Churchill, *radio broadcast*, 1941

In this chapter, you will learn:

1. How to level an initial DFD *upward.*

2. How to hide local data stores.

3. When and how to partition initial DFD bubbles *downward.*

4. How to complete the initial data dictionary.

5. How to complete the process specifications.

6. How to complete the data model.

7. How to complete the state-transition diagram.

In the previous chapter, I presented a strategy for developing an initial version of the behavioral model. However, it should be evident that this model cannot be presented to the user for verification. Why not? Primarily because it is too complicated. As we saw in Chapter 19, the preliminary DFD will have one process for each event that we identified in the environmental model; hence, it may have as many as 40 or 50 bubbles, or possibly more. Similarly, the initial version of the ERD is probably too rough to review with the users; as we discussed in Chapter 12, refinement is necessary to eliminate unnecessary objects and/or to add new objects.

There is a second problem with the model: it consists largely of graphics, with little or no textual support. While the dataflow diagram and entity-relationship diagram are excellent vehicles for presenting an overview of the system to the user, they need the support of a full data dictionary and complete set of process specifications.

20.1   FINISHING THE PROCESS MODEL

20.1.1   Leveling The DFD

The first order of business is to reorganize the DFD that we developed in Chapter 19. As we have seen, it consists of a single level, with far too many bubbles on it. Hence, we need *upward* leveling of the preliminary DFD. This means that we want to group *related* processes together into meaningful aggregates, each of which will represent a bubble in a higher-level diagram. This is illustrated in Figure 20.1.

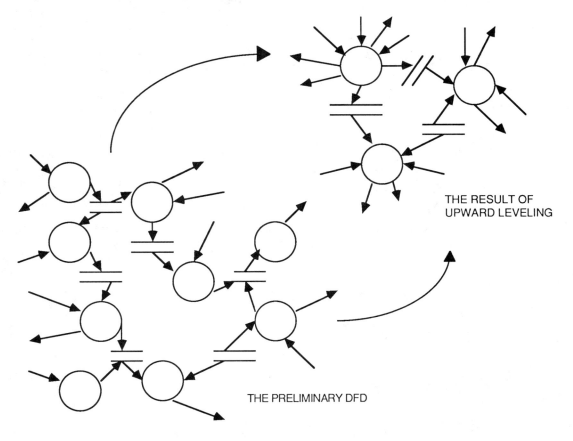

THE RESULT OF
UPWARD LEVELING

THE PRELIMINARY DFD

Figure 20.1: **Upward leveling of the DFD**

There are three guidelines that you should keep in mind as you do this:

1. Each grouping of processes should involve closely related responses (remember that each bubble in the preliminary DFD is named for the response to an event in the event list). This usually means that the processes are dealing with closely related *data*.

2. Look for opportunities to hide, or "bury," stored data that appear at the lower level. Thus, if you see a group of processes in the preliminary DFD that refer to a common store,*and no other processes in the preliminary DFD refer to that store*, then you can create a higher level bubble that hides the store. This is illustrated in Figure 20.2.

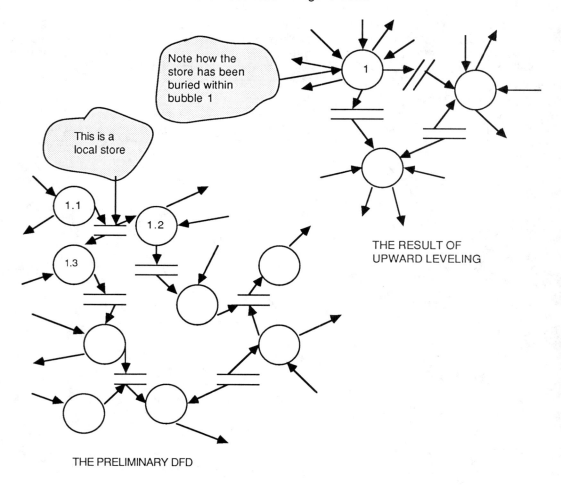

THE RESULT OF
UPWARD LEVELING

THE PRELIMINARY DFD

Figure 20.2: **Hiding a local store at the upper level**

3.   Keep in mind that the person who looks at your dataflow diagrams, whether it is a user or another systems analyst, will not want to look at too much at one time. Thus, you should create aggregates or groups from the preliminary DFD consisting of roughly 7 plus or minus 2 chunks of information, where a process (and its related flows) or a store could be considered a chunk.[1]

Of course, this means we may need several upward leveling efforts. For example, if we began with a preliminary DFD that had (for the sake of argument) 98 processes in it, and if we organized the diagram into groups of 7 bubbles (ignoring, for the sake of simplicity, all the stores), then we would create a higher-level diagram with 14 bubbles, each of which represents an "abstraction" of seven of the lower-level bubbles. But 14 bubbles is too much to deal with and too much to show the user at one time; so we would probably be inclined, as illustrated in Figure 20.3, to create an even higher-level diagram with only two bubbles on it.

Note that this example involves entirely artificial numbers. You should *not* conduct your leveling activity in order to ensure that each diagram has exactly seven bubbles! Indeed, the first two guidelines mentioned above, grouping bubbles around common data and looking for opportunities to conceal local stores, should be your primary rationale for upward leveling, not some arithmetic rule.

Note also that you may also need some *downward* leveling. That is, the processes identified in the preliminary DFD may not turn out to be primitive processes and may require downward partitioning into lower-level DFDs. This means only that the initial processes, each of which is responsible for producing the response to an event, may turn out to be too complex to describe accurately in a one-page process specification. Often, this will become evident as soon as you look closely at the process, or when you ask the user for an explanation of what the bubble must do. If the user thinks for a moment, takes a deep breath, and says, "Well, it's a long story, but it goes something like this..." you have a strong clue that your preliminary bubble probably needs to be partitioned!

In other cases, it may not become evident that downward leveling is required until you actually try to write the process specification; if you find that you've written three pages of material about a preliminary bubble and there is much, much more to say, once again you have a strong clue that downward partitioning is necessary.

Here are some guidelines for carrying out downward leveling:

•   In some cases, a pure functional decomposition approach is appropriate. That is, if you find a process bubble that is carrying out a complex function, try to identify subfunctions, each of which could be carried out by a lower-

---

1 This seemingly arbitrary number (seven plus or minus two) is a guideline for controlling complexity in a variety of problem-solving situations. It is based on the work of George Miller, who first observed peoples' difficulty dealing with multiple chunks of information in a classic paper entitled "The Magical Number Seven, Plus or Minus Two: Some Limits on Our Capacity for Processing Information," published in *Psychological Review,* Volume 63 (1956), pp.81-97.

level bubble. For example, suppose that we had a process called "Adjust missile trajectory"; this might be the bubble that is responsible for handling a temporal event in a real-time missile guidance system. The overall function of adjusting the missile trajectory might be decomposed into several subfunctions:

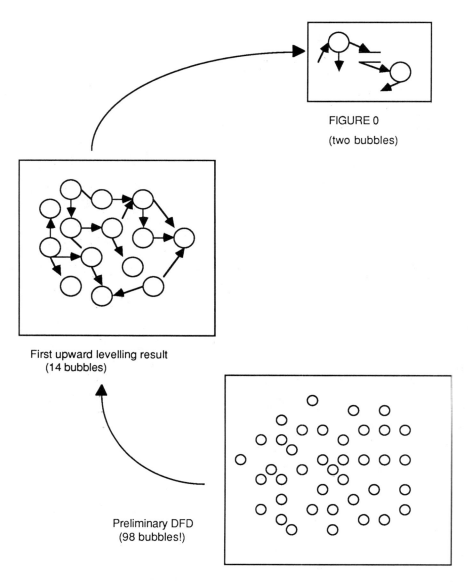

FIGURE 0

(two bubbles)

First upward levelling result
(14 bubbles)

Preliminary DFD
(98 bubbles!)

Figure 20.3: **Multiple upward leveling of a DFD**

- Calculate x-coordinate variance.

- Calculate y-coordinate variance.

- Calculate z-coordinate variance.

- Calculate new atmospheric "drag" factor.

- Calculate new wind velocity.

- Compute x-coordinate thrust impulse.

- Compute y-coordinate thrust impulse.

- etc.

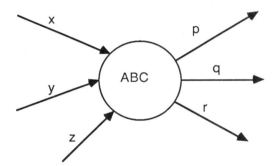

Figure 20.4: **Downward leveling of a complex bubble**

- In other cases, the bubble's incoming dataflows and outgoing dataflows will provide the best guidance for downward leveling. For example, supposed we had a bubble like the one shown in Figure 20.4. It is likely that a lower-level DFD could be created with the general form shown in Figure 20.5. Obviously, more than one bubble might be needed for combining or aggregating individual data elements, but the idea is the same: *let the data be the guide.*

Keep in mind as you go through this activity of upward and downward leveling that *balancing* is important. That is (as we discussed in Chapter 14), you must ensure that the net inputs and outputs shown for a high-level bubble correspond to the net inputs and outputs shown for the lower-level diagram. To see an example of the upward leveling activity, look at the YOURDON Press Information System case study in Appendix F. In this case, we began with a preliminary DFD containing 40 bubbles; one level of upward leveling was required, leading to a Figure 0 DFD diagram with nine bubbles on it.

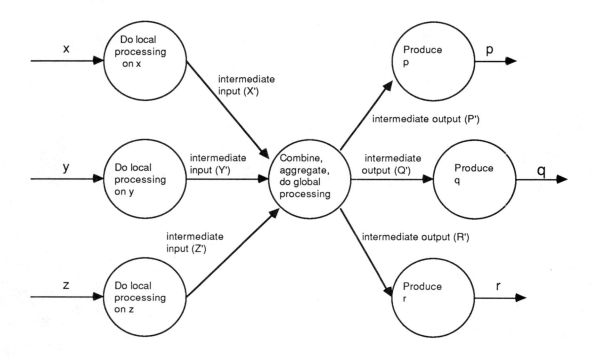

Figure 20.5: **The lower-level DFD**

20.1.2   Completing the Data Dictionary

As you began developing the preliminary DFD in Chapter 19, you should have begun developing the data dictionary; indeed, it is quite common to begin the data dictionary when the context diagram is being developed. However, it is by no means complete at this point. Typically, it will be necessary to fill in the description of the *meaning* of each data item; it may also be appropriate to break complex data items into subitems for clarity.

As the data dictionary becomes more complete, you should also begin checking it for consistency and completeness. Check to make sure that the dictionary is internally consistent (e.g., that one part of the dictionary doesn't contradict another part). Also, check to ensure that the dictionary is balanced against the leveled dataflow diagram and the entity-relationship diagram and the process specifications.

20.1.3   Completing the Process Specifications

When you develop the preliminary dataflow diagram, using the event-partitioning approach shown in Chapter 19, chances are that you will not have written *any* process specifications. There may be a few cases where an individual process specification will be sketched out because of particular interest on your part or the user's part, but your primary concern will simply be to organize the DFD itself.

Indeed, it is often a *bad* idea to devote any time to the writing of process specifications until the preliminary DFD has been finished, because the initial development of the DFD is subject to many changes, corrections, and revisions. Bubbles may appear, disappear, and be moved around and renamed. When the preliminary DFD begins to settle down, and when it has stood the test of upward leveling (i.e., if that activity does not uncover any major flaws in the model), *then* you can begin writing the process specifications.

This will often be a lengthy, time-consuming effort, because *each* of the bottom-level bubbles in the DFD set requires a process specification. Thus, it may be possible for a group of two or three systems analysts to draw a few dozen DFDs; but it may take a larger group of analysts to complete all the process specifications in a timely fashion.

As the process specifications are completed, they should be balanced and cross-checked against the data dictionary and ERD, using the guidelines presented in Chapter 14.

20.2   FINISHING THE DATA MODEL

As we pointed out in Chapter 12, the ERD is developed in a fashion somewhat similar to what we have described for the DFD: a rough ERD is developed, and then it is refined and improved. Much of this improvement can take place simply by assigning or attributing data elements to the appropriate object types; this will usually help us identify new object types or unnecessary object types.

However, keep in mind that the ERD is often being developed at roughly the same time as the DFD. It is very common to find one person (or a small group) within the project team working on the ERD, while another person (or a small group) works on the DFD. Or the DFD might be developed by the project team, while the ERD is developed by a centralized data administration group within the EDP organization. In any case, if the ERD and DFD are being developed at approximately the same time, then the knowledge gained from the DFD (e.g., the existence of stores, dataflows, etc.) can often be used to refine and cross-check the ERD.[2]

20.3   FINISHING THE STATE-TRANSITION DIAGRAM

If your system has real-time characteristics, you will be developing a state-transition diagram in addition to the DFD and entity-relationship diagram. Detailed knowledge of the behavior of the system should help you refine this model. As we pointed out in Chapter 13, you should examine the initial state-transition diagram to look for the following common types of errors:

- Have all the states been defined?

- Can you reach all the states?

---

2 Ideally, the DFD and ERD models should be developed by the same group, working together. This prevents communication problems, and it also tends to ensure that equal emphasis will be given to both models. Unfortunately, it rarely happens in the real world.

- Can you exit from all the states?

- In each state, does the system respond properly to all possible conditions?

20.4   SUMMARY

Having gotten this far, we have reached the end of the essential model. If you have followed all the steps in Chapters 18, 19, and this chapter, you should have a complete, detailed, formal, rigorous model of everything that the system must do to meet the user's requirements. It will contain all of the following items:

- Context diagram

- Event list

- Statement of purpose

- Complete set of leveled dataflow diagrams

- Complete, finished entity-relationship diagram

- Complete set of state-transition diagrams

- Complete data dictionary (for the analysis phase of the project)

- Complete set of process specifications, with one such specification for each bottom-level process

Assuming that you have reviewed the components of the specification to ensure that they are complete and consistent, and assuming the user has reviewed and approved the document, you should be through. You should be able to wrap a nice red ribbon around the entire package and deliver it to the design/programming team whose job will be to *build* the system. Then you can retire to the cozy comfort of your office until the next project comes along.

But wait! There is one last step. Everything that we have developed in this, the essential model, has assumed the existence of perfect technology, but has also assumed that the user would have no implementation constraints to impose on the system. Perfect technology is a figment of our imagination, but we can leave it to the implementation team to decide how best to strike a reasonable compromise with existing technology.

Assuming that the user will ignore all implementation constraints is also a figment of our imagination and one that we must deal with before we turn over the final version of the specification to the implementation team. This final activity, which must be done with the collaboration of users, systems analysts, *and some members of the implementation team*, is the development of the *user implementation model*. This is discussed in the next chapter.

QUESTIONS AND EXERCISES

1. Why can't the initial, first-cut behavioral model be presented to the user?

2. Is the first-cut behavioral model complete? If not, what elements are missing?

3. What does upward leveling mean in the context of this chapter?

4. What rationale should the systems analyst use for grouping bubbles together in a DFD?

5. What are the three guidelines that the systems analyst should keep in mind as she or he carries out upward leveling?

6. What does the concept of hiding stored data mean in the context of this chapter?

7. How many levels of higher-level DFDs should be created from a single first-cut DFD? Is there a mathematical formula that can be used to give an approximation of the number of levels required?

8. Under what conditions will downward leveling of a DFD be necessary?

9. Is it possible that the systems analyst will have to carry out both upward *and* downward leveling of the DFD? Why or why not?

10. Why does the data dictionary typically have to be completed during this stage of development of the behavioral model?

11. What kind of error-checking should be done on the data dictionary during this period of the project?

12. Why is it often a bad idea for the systems analyst to spend time writing process specifications before the preliminary DFD is completed? Under what conditions might it make sense to write at least a few process specifications?

13. What are the eight major components of the finished model of user's requirements?

21 THE USER IMPLEMENTATION MODEL

In this chapter, you will learn:

1. How to choose the automation boundary for a system.

2. How to select input devices and output devices for the user.

3. How to develop input formats and output formats.

4. How to design forms for the system.

5. How to develop coding schemes for system inputs.

6. How to identify manual support activities.

7. How to describe the system's operational constraints.

At the end of the last chapter, we had finished the development of the essential model of an information system. This model contains a complete description of *what* the system must do in order to satisfy the user. Specifically, the essential model describes:

- The essential policy, or logic, of the functions that need to be performed.

- The essential content of the data that are stored by the system and that move through the system.

- The essential time-dependent behavior that the system must exhibit in order to deal with signals and interrupts from the external environment.

In the best of all worlds (from the viewpoint of the systems analyst and the implementation team), this would be sufficient information for the designers and programmers: we would simply give them the essential model and let them choose the best hardware, best operating system, best database management system, and best programming language, within the overall project constraints of time, money, and people resources. However, it's not as simple as this: in virtually every systems development project, the user will insist on providing some additional information.

This additional information involves *implementation* issues—but implementation issues that are sufficiently important, that have sufficient impact on the user's ability to use the system, that they need to be specified now. The most obvious implementation issue of interest to the user is the automation boundary, that is, which parts of the essential model are going to be implemented on a computer, and which parts are going to be performed manually by people in the user organization? The systems analyst may have an opinion about this, and the designer/programmer group may also want to voice an opinion, but it is obviously an issue about which the user has the final say.

Similarly, the *format* of system inputs and outputs (sometimes known as the human interface) is of enormous interest to the user—often, it seems, of more interest than the system functions! Ever since computer systems began generating paper reports, users have had strong opinions about the organization and layout of the information in the report. Where should the page numbers be? Where should the page headers be? How should each line of information be arranged for maximum readability? Should there be a summary or subtotal at the end of each page or only at the end of the entire report? And so on.

With the advent of on-line systems in the 1970s, this issue expanded to include the user's interest in formatting input screens on a CRT terminal. Where should the input prompts be displayed on the screen? What kind of error messages should be displayed? What color should the error messages be? How should the user be allowed to move from one screen to another screen?

More recently, a number of other options and possibilities have increased the importance of these user implementation issues:

- End users are often given the opportunity to use personal computers (PCs) as a part of a distributed network of computers (e.g., they are given PCs that connect to the organization's mainframe computer). This raises a series of questions: Which parts of the essential model will be assigned to the PC (under the user's control) and which to the mainframe? Which part of the *data* will be assigned to the PC and which part to the mainframe? What will be the format of input that the user provides to the PC? What additional support activities must be provided to ensure that the user does not inadvertently damage the data on the PC or the mainframe?

- End users have more and more opportunities today to write their own programs in fourth-generation languages like FOCUS, NOMAD and IDEAL on mainframe computers, or dBASE-III, and Rbase-5000 on PCs. To the extent that they get involved in such implementation issues, they need to specify the formats of inputs and outputs to the system. More importantly, they may want to decide which parts of the system will be implemented using fourth generation languages and which parts will be implemented with conventional third generation languages.[1]

- In many situations today, the user and systems analyst may decide to prototype portions of the system, using either a high-level fourth generation language or an application generator package. The prototyping may be done because the user is unsure of the detailed policy that will eventually have to be written into process specifications in the essential model; but more often the prototyping activity is concerned with exploration and experimentation with input formats, on-line dialogues, and output formats for screens or reports.

- For many business applications, one option available to the user is the selection and purchase of a software package, that is, an existing software product that can be licensed or purchased from a vendor. In this case, the same kind of implementation issues are important to the user: Which parts of the essential functions will be implemented by the vendor-supplied package and which parts will have to be done by the user (or implemented by the user's MIS department as a separate system)? Which parts of the essential data will be maintained by the vendor-supplied package and which parts will have to be maintained by the user? What will be the form and sequence of inputs required by the vendor-supplied system and will this be acceptable?[2]

These issues should be addressed as part of the *user implementation model*. It can be created by augmenting, annotating, and revising the essential model, as we will see in subsequent sections of this chapter. However, I recommend that you always keep a copy of the original essential model intact; this will allow you to explore alternative user implementation models in the future.

---

1 This illustrates the need for good communication between the users and the implementation team, as well as systems analysts. While the users might be quite interested in using fourth generation languages, the implementation team may need to investigate the performance of the language. Systems with large volumes of input and output may find that the fourth generation languages are too inefficient. We will discuss this further in Chapter 23.

2 A *very* important assumption is being made here: the essential model should be developed first, *before* the vendor-supplied package is evaluated. Many organizations do just the opposite: they first evaluate the package and then try to derive a model of essential requirements from the features of the package.

Generally speaking, the user implementation model will cover the following four issues:

1. Allocation of the essential model to people versus machines.

2. Details of the human-machine interaction.

3. Additional manual activities that may be needed.

4. Operational constraints that the user wishes to impose on the system.

Each of these is discussed in more detail next.

21.1   DETERMINING THE AUTOMATION BOUNDARY

Remember that the system model we are working with at this point identifies all the essential activities (functions) and all the essential data. The question at this point is: Which functions and which data will be handled manually, and which will be automated? While there may have been a preliminary, tentative choice of the automation boundary during the feasibility study, we should not regard it as frozen. Indeed, the automation boundary is almost irrelevant in the essential model, because, while the user obviously wants us to develop an automated system, he or she also needs a well-described statement of requirements for the functions and data that will be just outside the automation boundary.

There are three extreme cases that we mention briefly:

*   *The user may not care where the automation boundary is.* This is unlikely to ever happen, but it is a theoretical possibility. Effectively, the user is saying to the implementation team, "You tell me whether it makes more sense for portions of the system to be manual or automated." Aside from the fact that the user normally has strong feelings about this issue, the systems analyst is usually expected to produce (as a by-product of his or her work) a revised cost-benefit analysis for the entire project. This will usually require at least some preliminary decision as to which parts of the essential model will be automated and which will be manual.

*   *The user may opt for a fully automated system.* This is a more common situation, particularly if the system you are developing is a replacement for an existing system *and the system boundary is not changing.* Thus, the manual activities carried out by the user may already be outside the system boundary—represented on the context diagram as the terminators with which the system communicates.

*   *The user may opt for a fully manual system.* This is a rather uncommon option, particularly in this age of automation, because the systems analyst usually has a vested interest in computerizing as much as possible. However, it can happen in situations where the user's express intention is

not to computerize anything, but simply to reorganize the way activities are currently being carried out in an organization.

Normally, these extreme options won't occur; based on interactions between the user, the systems analyst, and the implementation team, some compromise will be chosen. That is, *some* of the essential model activities will be automated, and *some* will be identified as manual functions; similarly, some of the essential data will be identified as an obvious candidate for computerization (thus presumably putting it under the control of an MIS organization) and some will be left under the user's direct control. Unless the user makes an immediate, arbitrary choice by fiat, it is a good idea for all three parties (the user, the systems analyst and the implementation team) to explore several options. As Figures 21.1(a), (b), and (c) illustrate, there might be several reasonable alternatives for drawing the automation boundary. Each will have different costs (which the implementation team must help estimate, since they will have the knowledge about implementation technology possibilities) and different organizational ramifications in the user's area.

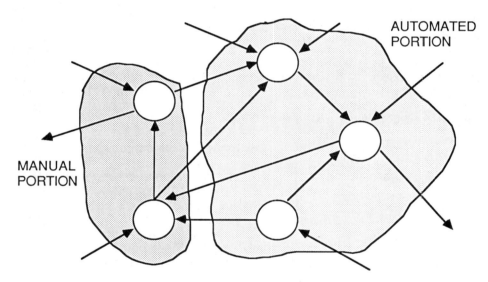

Figure 21.1.(a): **One choice for the automation boundary**

It is neither the systems analyst's job nor the implementation team's job to choose the automation boundary; it is ultimately the user's responsibility, and this book does not provide any guidelines for determining what kind of choice would be best. But note how the essential model serves as a useful tool for both the user and the implementation team to explore various choices. Once the automation boundary has been chosen, the systems analyst may think he has the luxury of eliminating manual processes and manual data (i.e., those bubbles and stores that will not be automated) from any further consideration. But this is generally not true. In the simplest case, the manual activities and data may have to be moved back into the terminators surrounding the system, as shown in Figure 21.2(a) and (b).

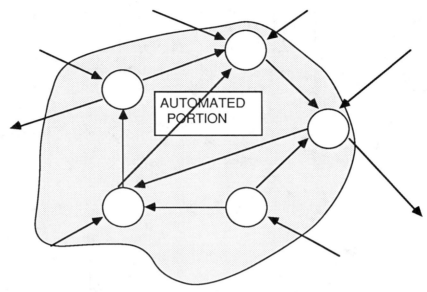

Figure 21.1(b): **Another choice for the automation boundary**

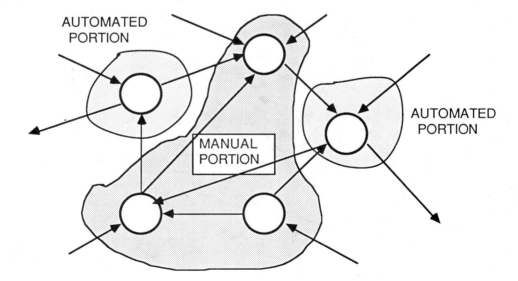

Figure 21.1(c): **A third choice for the automation boundary**

But, in the general case, the systems analyst must recognize that even the manual activities *are part of the new system.* Thus, the analyst may have to write user procedures so that members of the user community will know how to

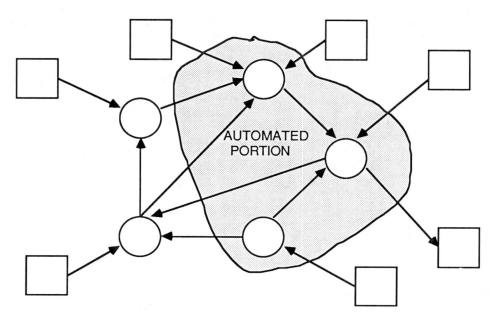

Figure 21.2(a): **An essential model with a automation boundary**

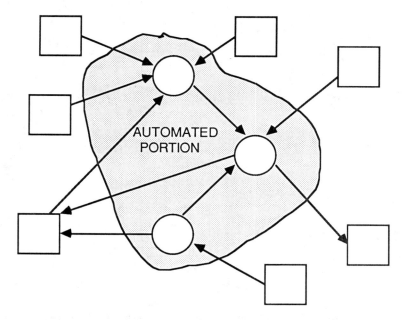

Figure 21.2(b): **Manual activities have been buried within the terminators**

carry out the required functions. And the analyst may have to provide some guidance on the organization of stores that are not going to be automated.[3] Note that this aspect of the user implementation model merely requires that we annotate the DFD and ERD to indicate manual versus automated activities and data.

Note that when the automation boundary is chosen it may be important to consider a number of environmental issues: noise level, radiation, lighting, ergonomics of the CRT terminal and work space, and so on. Quite often, the new system will disrupt the user's normal working environment (e.g., it will cause a CRT terminal to be placed on the user's desk where there had never been one before.)[4] Or it may bring information processing activities to an environment where there had never been any such activities before (e.g., a factory floor in a manufacturing environment). Thus, it is important to ensure that these human factors have been carefully studied before making a final determination of the automation boundary. The user will often have some strong feelings to express on this issue, but if she or he has no prior experience with information systems, the user may not be able to predict in advance what the problems will be. You should get advice from other systems professionals who have developed and installed similar systems in similar environmental conditions.

Finally, note that once the automation boundary has been chosen, it may be necessary to augment the essential model to show how the system is started up and shut down; the essential model shows only the steady-state behavior of the system, and assumes that the system has been running forever and will continue running forever. Thus, we may need to include additional processes (bubbles in the DFD), dataflows, and stores to show system initialization activities and system shut-down activities; this might include reports to management (or to the users or to the operations department) on the operational characteristics of the system.

21.2   DETERMINING THE HUMAN INTERFACE

Probably the most time-consuming activity, and the one that the user will be most interested in, is the specification of the human interface. This involves four related issues:

1.   The choice of input and output devices (e.g., CRT terminals, OCR devices, punched cards, etc., for input, and paper reports, CRT displays, or flashing lights for output).

---

[3] The user procedures for manual processes can be based on the process specification for those processes. Indeed, in the simplest case, the process specification *is* the user procedure; however, since the process specifications have been carefully written to avoid any unnecessary implementation bias, they may need to be expanded or rewritten to provide guidance to the users.

[4] Think for a moment about the kind of problems that can be encountered by simply putting a terminal on the user's desk. First, there may not be room for it: the user may need all the available workspace for other things that he or she is doing. Second, there may not be enough electrical outlets to plug in the CRT terminal, the printer, the modem, and the other paraphernalia. Third, the desk may be the proper height for reading and writing, but perhaps not for typing. Fourth, the surrounding office light may cause so much glare that it is hard to read the information on the CRT display. Fifth, the noise caused by the user's typing on the terminal may prove bothersome to other users in the same area.

2.   The format of all the inputs flowing from terminators into the system.

3.   The format of all the outputs flowing from the system back out to the terminators.

4.   The *sequence* and timing of inputs and outputs in an on-line system.

21.2.1   Input and Output Devices

The choice of input and output devices may be dictated by the terminators outside the system; for example, if the system produces output reports to be sent to the government, there may be no choice other than producing the reports on paper. Devices typically used for providing input to a system[5] include the following:

- *Punched cards.* Punched cards used to be the most common form of system input, but are seldom used today except on a few very large batch computer systems. One advantage of the punched card is that it can be used as a source document by the external user (e.g., think of the checks produced by some government systems; they are negotiable documents, but they are also used as direct input to a computer system). The major disadvantages of punched cards are their bulky size, limited data storage capacity, "one-time-only" usability, and susceptibility to operator errors.

- *Magnetic tape.* Magnetic tape may be an appropriate form of input from other systems; it can also be an appropriate input medium if the user has a key-to-tape data entry device. The primary advantage of this approach, of course, is that a much larger volume of input data can be stored on a tape than on a card; the disadvantage is that the data cannot be easily manipulated once they are recorded on the tape. The punched card, on the other hand, is more primitive, but it does offer the user the flexibility of rearranging the cards or deleting some of them (by throwing them away) before submitting them to the system.

- *Floppy disks.* With the advent of personal computers in the early 1980s, floppy disks have become a popular form of input medium. Data are normally recorded on the floppy disk by off-line interaction with a personal computer (by off-line we mean that the activity is not connected to the information system under development). A typical floppy disk can store between 360,000 characters and 1.2 million characters; this is not as much as a magnetic tape, but it is adequate for many medium-volume applications.

- *Terminals and personal computers.* Terminals, or CRTs, have become one of the most common forms of input media during the past ten years as the price has dropped from $3000 (or more) to $300 (or less). It is

---

5 Note that we are discussing inputs provided by the user. Many systems (especially real-time systems) must deal with devices that provide input independent of any humans (e.g., radar units, data recorders, and satellite signals).

important to distinguish between dumb terminals that provide nothing more than a keyboard and screen, intelligent terminals that provide a variety of local editing features and a local storage capacity, and personal computers, which have much more local storage and all the computational powers of a general-purpose computer. Intelligent terminals and PCs make it possible for the user to make changes and correct trivial errors instantly, rather than waiting for the delay of sending the input through telecommunication lines to the main computer; the local storage capability makes it possible for the user to enter a great deal of input even if the main computer system is not operational all the time.

- *Optical readers and bar-code readers.* Optical readers and bar-code readers can read information printed or encoded on various types of documents; this is particularly advantageous for applications like the checkout counter at a store, where the user needs to enter the product code and other relevant data about a purchase. To the extent that these devices can read data *directly,* it eliminates the need for the user to manually type the data on a terminal. Some optical readers can read ordinary typewritten documents, and a few can read handwritten documents. The major disadvantage of this type of input medium is its cost; another disadvantage is its error-prone tendency.

- *Telephone.* For some applications, the Touch-Tone telephone can be an appropriate input medium.[6] This is particularly advantageous for systems that must deal with the general public; few people have a terminal or PC in their home, but approximately 98% of the U.S. population has at least one phone in their home. Since the Touch-Tone telephone only provides numeric input, its applications are somewhat limited; it is convenient for situations where the user needs to provide such things as an account number, but would not be practical for situations requiring text entry.

- *Voice input.* Finally, some systems may use the human voice as an input medium. Voice input technology in the late 1980s is capable of recognizing a vocabulary of a few hundred words for an individual user; it must be retrained for each new user. The advantages of such an input medium are obvious; the disadvantages, at the present time, are (1) the cost of the device, (2) its limited vocabulary, (3) the slow response time, and (4) real problems if the user's voice changes significantly because of a cold or other cause.

Just as the user has a choice of several different input media for his or her system, there are several possible output media. The most common media used for output are the following:

---

6 Note that we are distinguishing here between the use of the telephone instrument (handset) and the telecommunications line. Many terminals are connected, via a modem, to a telephone line; but here we are talking about the telephone "handset" itself as an input medium.

- *Printed output.* By far the most common form of output on computer systems today is printed output. This can be produced on a variety of devices: dot matrix printers (often attached to the terminal used for input), high-speed line printers, high-speed laser printers, personal laser printers, personal daisy wheel printers, and so on. The principal advantage of printed output is that it is a permanent document, and it can be used in a variety of applications outside the system. The disadvantages of printed reports are their bulkiness, the likelihood that more information (or more copies of information) will be printed than is really needed, and the relatively slow speed with which the information is produced.

- *Punched cards.* Just as punched cards can serve as an input medium, they can serve as an output medium. As noted earlier, punched cards can be used as legal documents; as Marjorie Leeson points out [Leeson, 1981], punched cards can serve as a "turnaround document" (i.e., a document that is sent *out* of the system to an external terminator and that later becomes input to the system from the same terminator). But, in general, punched cards are bulky, and they cannot hold much information; hence they are not used for most information systems today.

- *Terminal.* On-line systems that use terminals as an input medium typically use terminals as an output medium, too. The advantage of the terminal is that it can display a substantial amount of information at a high rate; with modern terminals, combinations of text and graphics can be conveniently displayed. The major disadvantage of the terminal is that it does not represent hard-copy output; the output is transient and is lost when the next display is shown.

- *Voice output.* For some applications, voice output is a suitable output medium. This is true in applications where the telephone is used as an input medium (see above); the same telephone can be used to convey voice output to the user. Some terminals are also equipped with voice output devices, though this is somewhat rare. The main advantage of the voice output medium is that it can be used to convey fairly brief output messages in an environment (e.g., a manufacturing facility) where the user might not have the opportunity to read printed output.

- *Plotter.* A plotter is normally used to produce large, intricate diagrams and drawings (e.g., architectural drawings and blueprints). Drawings that would fit onto a normal-sized page of paper can usually be produced today by laser printers or dot-matrix printers, but plotters often produce output measuring two or three feet wide by several feet long. The disadvantage of this output medium is its cost, its physical bulkiness, and the length of time required to produce the output.

- *Magnetic tape or disk.* Obviously, just as magnetic tape and disk can be used for input, it can be used for output. This is normally practical only in cases where the output is going to be sent to other computer systems (i.e., where the system terminator is not a person, but a computer).

- *COM.* COM is an acronym for Computer Output Microform. COM output is normally reserved for archival output (e.g., voluminous reference material that would be too expensive and too bulky to be produced as normal printed reports). Examples of COM are rolls of microfilm (used, for example, by banks to keep copies of canceled checks) or microfiche cards.

21.2.2   Input/Output Formats

Once the input/output devices have been chosen, the next step is to determine the *formats* of system inputs and outputs. In some cases, the formats of inputs and outputs may not be a matter of negotiation, but simply a matter of the user informing the systems analyst of "the way things have gotta be." This is particularly true if the new system must communicate with other computer systems or with people (or groups of people) *external* to the organization building the new system. External organizations or other external computer systems may supply data to the new system in a prescribed physical format that cannot be changed. And they may require output from the system in an equally rigidly prescribed format.

If the human-machine dialog has not been entirely fixed, what is there to negotiate about? Not the internal representation of data within the computer system; the user won't care about and should not even be aware of this information. And not such things as the legal values and ranges of input data elements, for this should have been specified as part of the essential model. However, this *is* a place to negotiate reasonable *implementation* constraints on various aspects of the data elements. Some examples follow:

- The essential model may have identified the data element **CUSTOMER-LAST-NAME**. As a matter of *essential* policy, there may be no limit to the length (number of characters) of this data element. After all, what's wrong with a last name that happens to be 357 characters long? While it doesn't happen often, some members of European nobility may wish to demonstrate their lineage by including the names of all their ancestral forebears in their last name. This is interesting and may be of some historical significance, but the user and the systems analyst may nonetheless agree to restrict **CUSTOMER-LAST-NAME** to 25 characters. Note, by the way, that this will require a change to the appropriate process specification(s) that deal with the inputting of **CUSTOMER-LAST-NAME** to ensure that it is valid according to this implementation constraint.

- In an order entry system, a **CUSTOMER-ORDER** might be defined in the following way: **CUSTOMER-ORDER = NAME + ADDRESS + {ORDER-ITEM}.** In the essential model, there might be no reason at all to limit the number of different items that a customer might purchase in one order. From the user's implementation perspective, though, there might be several reasons: (1) as a manual support activity (discussed further in Section 21.3, the user might want the sales clerk to write the order on a preprinted form that only has room for, say, eight different items; (2) the user might be concerned that the sales clerk will make a mistake if he or she tries to deal with more than a limited number of items in each order; (3) the user might be concerned that spending an inordinate amount of time servicing one customer with his or her 597 different items might annoy other customers waiting to be serviced. And so on. Hence there might be a number of good reasons to put a user-defined implementation constraint on this data element.

Note that user implementation issues of this sort primarily involve extra notations in the data dictionary, as well as additional logic (if appropriate) in the process specifications that deal with validation of input data elements. But there is one other aspect of the human-machine dialogue that requires something more than data dictionary notations: the *sequence* of inputs and outputs, especially in an on-line system, can be conveniently modeled using a state-transition diagram. Figure 21.3 shows a typical example of a state-transition diagram used to model the sequence of CRT screens that the end user will use to communicate with the system.

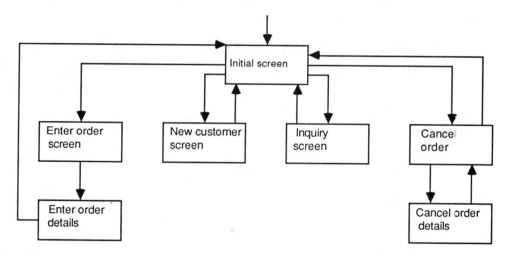

Figure 21.3: **A state-transition diagram for modeling CRT screens**

This is particularly useful for dealing with questions like, "Can I get back to the main menu screen from screen 12?" and "What are all the ways of getting to the order-entry screen?" Other major input/output issues include the physical arrangement of input data elements on a CRT screen, the nature of the error messages if an input error is made; and the physical arrangement of output data elements on display screens and reports. With today's vast array of fourth-generation languages, prototyping tools, and PCs, I recommend that you give the user an opportunity to play with several variations of input screens, output displays, and the like.[7] Once you have gotten agreement from the user, you should attach a copy of the screen displays, report

_____

7 Indeed, you might need to use fifth-generation AI tools as well in order to experiment with natural-language input, voice input, graphical output, and so on.

formats, and appropriate state-transition diagrams to the essential model, with appropriate cross-references to the essential data elements in the data dictionary.

Of course, in many cases the user won't have any major suggestions to make because he or she has no previous experience working with a computer system; this is somewhat analogous to someone who has lived in an apartment all his life, but now wants to specify the details of his first custom-built, split-level ranch-style home. In the case of computerized information systems, the following guidelines will help you develop a user-friendly human interface in most cases:

1.   *Your system should request inputs and produce outputs in a consistent fashion.* This is particularly true for on-line systems where the user can enter one of several different transactions and/or receive one of several different displays. For example, suppose that your system asks the user for the date whenever a transaction is entered; it would be a disaster if one type of transaction requires the date in the form 12/23/87 while another transaction requires the date in the form 87/12/23. And it would be a disaster if one part of the system required the user to specify the state as a two-character code (e.g., NY for New York), while another part of the system required the state to be spelled out. Similarly, if one part of the system requires the user to provide an area code when she or he enters a telephone number, then *all* parts of the system should require an area code when the telephone number is entered.

2.   *Ask for information in a logical sequence.* In many cases, this depends on the nature of the application and will require careful discussions with the user. For example, suppose you are developing an order entry system, and you want the user to specify the customer's name. Whether the information is entered on punched cards or (more likely) from a CRT terminal, you will have to specify the sequence in which you want the components of "customer name" entered. One logical sequence would be to ask the user to provide the information in the following sequence:

   title (Mr./Ms., etc.)

   first name

   middle initial

   last name

But the user may find this quite awkward; suppose the user has obtained the customer name from some external source like a telephone book? In this case, it would be far more convenient for the user to enter

   last name

   first name

middle initial

title

About the only thing we can be sure of is that the following sequence would *definitely* be unpopular with the user:

middle initial

first name

title

last name

3.   *Make it obvious to the user what kind of error he or she has committed and where it is.* In many systems, the user provides a substantial amount of information to the system for each event or transaction. In an order entry system, for example, the user may specify the customer's name, address, and phone number, as well as information about the items being ordered, the applicable discount, shipping instructions, and sales tax. All this information may be entered in a single CRT screen of information before it is sent to the system; and, of course, the system may then determine that some or all of the input is erroneous. The important thing is to make sure that the user understands the kind of error that has been committed and where the error is located; it is *not* acceptable for the system to simply beep once and display the message BAD INPUT. *Each* error (assuming there is more than one) should be identified, either with a descriptive message or (in the case of an on-line system) by highlighting or color-coding the erroneous data. Depending on the nature of the system and the user's level of sophistication, it may also be important to display an explanatory message; this is discussed in more detail in item 5.

4.   *Distinguish between field edits and screen edits.* In many cases, your system will be able to determine whether a data element provided by the user is correct or incorrect, without reference to any other data elements. For example, if the user enters a two-character code for a state, the system should be able to immediately determine whether the two characters represent one of the fifty states, or one of the Canadian provinces, and so on. But if the user were to enter a postal code as an individual data element, there is only a limited amount of field editing the system could do without additional inputs; we would need both the postal code *and* the state code to determine whether the postal code should be a five-digit (or nine-digit) zip code or a six-character Canadian postal code. The system could also compare the state code and zip code to see if the zip code is in the right range (e.g., if the state code is NY then the zip code should begin with the digit 1). The relationship between data elements may be obvious to the systems analyst; however, it may require intimate, detailed knowledge of the application that can only be obtained from the user.

5. *Make the editing and error-checking user dependent.* As indicated above, it is usually a good idea for the system to display an explanatory message when an error is detected. But this is only true if the user is unable to determine, on his own, what he did wrong. If the user typed a three-digit zip code, for example, it would not be necessary for the system to display an elaborate message about the length of zip codes; however, it *would* be appropriate if the user typed a five-digit zip code and the system was expecting one of the new nine-digit zip codes. Note also that (a) some users are more expert than others and may become annoyed even more quickly if they have to look at long, turgid error messages, and (b) after repetitive use, even the novice user becomes expert at some parts of the system. So it is often important to make the error messages flexible and perhaps even changeable by the user; the easiest compromise is a combination of short error messages (which may consist of nothing more than highlighting the erroneous input and ringing a bell to get the user's attention) and long error messages (with explanatory text and a reference to the appropriate part of the user's training manual). See also item 7 for more on this concept.

6. *Provide a way for the user to (a) cancel part of a transaction and (b) cancel all of a transaction.* It is unwise to assume that the user will always finish entering an entire transaction without getting interrupted. With a batch computer system, this is not an issue; the system typically does not see *anything* from the user until several individual transactions have been composed.[8] But for on-line systems, it is an important issue: the user may have entered a customer's name and address before discovering that she was working with the wrong customer; she wants to be able to delete what she has typed and start over. Or the user may have finished entering most of the customer information and then happen to notice that she misspelled the customer's first name; she wants to be able to go back to that data element and correct it without losing all the other information she has typed.

7. *Provide a convenient "help" mechanism.* For on-line systems, it is more and more important to provide the user with a convenient mechanism for obtaining information about how to use the system. In some cases, the "help" facility will simply provide an explanation if the user commits an error; in other cases, it might be used to explain the details of various commands or transactions available to the user. There are many ways of implementing such a facility, and both you and the user should investigate several typical examples (most of the software packages available on the IBM PC and the Apple Macintosh have "help" facilities; this is a good place to start) before making a decision.

---

8 But even with a batch system, the user may find that she has entered some data into the system by mistake. It will almost always be necessary to provide the user with a facility to undo or reverse anything that she has entered. But this should have been discovered during your interviews with the user, and it should already be evident in the DFD and process specifications for the system.

8. *Distinguish between menu-driven and command-driven systems; if appropriate, give the user a choice.* A menu-driven system is one that presents the user with a list of alternative choices (or functions, or transactions, etc.); once he has chosen one, he may be given another submenu, which could lead to even lower-level sub-menus before the system finally carries out some action. A command-driven system, on the other hand, expects the user to provide a detailed (and often lengthy) command indicating what he wants the system to do for him. Menu-driven systems are considered more user friendly, since they display *all* the available choices for the user; hence the menu-driven approach is often considered preferable for new users or if the system has to interact with a wide variety of users with different backgrounds and skill levels. But the menu-driven system is considered tedious by the experienced user, for it often requires two or three separate interactions with the system (each with some time delay) before it finally knows what the user wants; the experienced user generally prefers a command-driven system, so that he can accomplish what he wants as quickly as possible.

9. *If your system is engaged in lengthy processing, display a message to the user so that he won't think the system has crashed.* If your system has to carry out extensive calculations or if it is likely to be delayed periodically because of voluminous inputs, it is important to display an appropriate message to the user; otherwise, he is likely to think that his terminal has "frozen" or "hung," or that the computer has crashed, or that there has been a power failure. At the very least, your system should flash a message (e.g., SYSTEM WORKING - PLEASE WAIT) at regular intervals. Even better would be a series of messages telling the user how much of the work has been finished and approximately how much longer it will take to completion.

10. *Provide defaults for standard inputs.* In many cases, the system can make a good guess about the likely value of an input provided by the user; by making it a default, it can save the user a considerable amount of time and typing activity. This approach is valid for all types of systems, but it is especially apparent with on-line systems, where the user may not be a professional typist. One example of a default value is the date: in many applications, the most likely date that the user will enter is today's date. Or suppose that you are building an order entry system, and the user tells you that 95% of the customers live in the local area; then when you ask the user to provide the customer's telephone number, the system should assume that the default area code is your local area code.

11. *Take advantage of color and sound, but don't overdo it.* Modern on-line terminals have a variety of colors and sound effects; these can be quite useful for emphasizing different kinds of input or drawing the user's attention to important aspects of the human interface. Thus, you might use the color green for all material displayed by the system, blue for all input data provided by the user, and red for all error messages. However, you should not get carried away: most users will get annoyed if their display

screen looks like a Christmas tree. The same is true of sound effects; an occasional bell or beep is useful, but the user doesn't want the terminal to produce all the sound effects from a Star Wars movie.

21.2.3   Forms Design

Designing the formats of system inputs and outputs has traditionally been referred to as forms design, because most systems in the 1960s and 1970s required the user to encode inputs on paper forms that were then transcribed onto punched cards before being entered into a batch computer system. But even in today's on-line systems, there may be some forms design to be done; consider, for example, the common situation where the system input originates with an external customer. The customer may provide the required input by filling out a paper form and mailing it to the users who interact with the system; an example of a real-world form is shown in Figure 21.4. ·Thus, some attention must be given to the design of the form.

In some cases, the systems analyst can turn to an in-house graphics department or to an external forms manufacturer for help with the design of a form; alternatively, the user may already have forms associated with the existing system that she or he will want to continue using in the new system. But there are also many situations where the systems analyst and the user must design a new form for a new system. While there are many different styles for a form, they should all contain the following basic information:

- *Title,* to distinguish this form from any other forms. The title is usually printed in large, bold letters at the top of the form so that the user knows that this is an "order form" or a "trouble report form."

- *Instructions,* to tell the user how to fill out the required information on the form. General instructions are usually placed at the beginning of the form near the top; specific instructions are typically given next to, or beneath, each item of data that needs to be filled in.

- *Body,* the main part of the form, in which the data are entered. This may be organized in an open style, a boxed style, or a combination of both. The boxed style is typically used for information that is binary (e.g., "check this box if you want your name added to our mailing list for future product announcements") or fixed-format (e.g., a telephone number or zip code). The open style is typically used for variable-length information such as a name or address.

Deciding exactly how the form should be laid out is an art unto itself and is best done by people who are experienced in form design. One of the most common mistakes of the novice forms designer, for example, is that of not leaving adequate space for the user to fill in required information. This is particularly true of forms that require handwritten information.[9]

---

9 Leave at least half an inch of vertical space for each line of handwritten information on a form. Leave at least 1/3 inch and some multiple of 1/6 inch for each line of typewritten information on a form. Make sure that the typist does not have to realign the typewriter for each line of information.

ORDERS
800/228-8910
Good anywhere in U.S.
408/625-0465

MAIL ORDERS
P.O. BOX 911 • Dept. CT077 • Monterey, CA 93942

DATE OF ORDER

___/___/___
MO DAY YR

BILL TO: (Please Print)

NAME
ATTENTION:
COMPANY
ADDRESS
CITY
STATE ZIP
( ) ( )
DAYTIME PHONE HOME PHONE

SHIP TO: (If different than Bill To)

CUSTOMER ID NUMBER (as it appears on mailing label)
NAME
COMPANY (if applicable)
ADDRESS (no P.O. Box, please)
CITY
STATE ZIP
( ) ( )
DAYTIME PHONE HOME PHONE

G[illegible]1

ITEMS ORDERED

STOCK NO.	DESCRIPTION	QTY	UNIT PRICE	SHIP	TOTAL	OFFICE

SUBTOTAL		
6% SALES TAX (CA residents only)		
SHIPPING/ HANDLING	$3.00	

SHIPPING/HANDLING CHARGES

All shipping/handling charges calculated by weight. To figure the delivery charge for an order shipped UPS Ground or U.S. mail, simply add the shipping charge listed in parentheses ( ) directly after the price for each item ordered and add $3.00 to the total. **Priority service available; call for charges.**

Outside the continental United States:
If you require delivery outside the continental United States, please add one of these special charges to your order instead of using the table at left.
Hawaii: call for charges.
Canada: add 8%, $15 minimum.
Foreign Orders: add 21%, $35 minimum.
All payments must be in U.S. dollars.
Note: Foreign orders subject to FTC restrictions; call for details.

TOTAL		

Icon Review does not guarantee machine compatibility; please be sure to check product requirements.

METHOD OF PAYMENT

☐ CHECK ☐ MONEY ORDER ☐ MASTER CARD ☐ VISA ☐ PO NUMBER ________
Purchase orders must be attached and are subject to credit approval.

ACCOUNT NO. (FOR CHARGE CARD) EXP DATE

SIGNATURE

Figure 21.4: **An example of a typical form**

Depending on the application, the systems analyst may design either *cut forms* or *speciality forms.* Cut forms are usually printed on single sheets of paper and are suitable for the vast majority of situations; with the widespread availability of desktop publishing systems and forms design programs, the user and systems analyst can easily design their own forms.

Specialty forms are more complex, and should be designed with the assistance of an experienced forms designer (typically associated with a forms manufacturer). The most common example of a specialty form is a multipart form, which may use sheets of carbon paper between the copies or special carbonless paper. The common types of specialty forms are:

- Forms bound into books (e.g., sales order books).

- Detachable multipart forms, with an original and multiple copies that can be separated (e.g., credit card charge forms).

- Continuous forms, either manually filled out or computer generated.

- Mailers: preprinted forms already inserted into an envelope, attached together as a continuous form. The computer can then print standard information such as a customer's name and address and (through the judicious placement of carbon paper) it will be printed on both the envelope and the letter inside.

Specialty forms are, as one might expect, far more expensive than single-sheet cut forms; thus, some care must be taken to ensure that they do not represent a major system cost. The specialty forms should be produced in a reasonable quantity to keep the unit cost down: the cost of printing 10,000 copies of a specialty form is often only 10% to 20% more than the cost of printing 5000 copies. Standard-size forms should be used so that the printer does not have to carry out expensive cutting and trimming; most standard-size forms are either 8.5 inches by 11 inches or 5.5 inches by 8.5 inches.

21.2.4   Input and Output Codes

As part of the job of specifying input and output formats, the systems analyst must often specify *codes,* that is, abbreviations for information that would be awkward and time-consuming to describe in detail. Examples of codes are Social Security Numbers, zip codes, ISBN numbers for published books, and Employer Identification Numbers (EINs) that the IRS assigns to companies that file tax returns.

The examples above represent *external codes* for most of us; that is, regardless of the kind of system, we have to use the coding schemes developed by the IRS, the U.S. Post Office, and the Social Security Administration. But there are often many situations where we need to design new codes associated with the system itself (e.g., customer account numbers, part numbers, form numbers, product codes, color codes, and airline flight numbers). Just as forms design is an art, so coding techniques are a specialized area of expertise; as Gore and Stubbe point out in [Gore and Stubbe, 1983, a coding method must be:

- "•   Expandable—The code must provide space for additional entries that may be required.

- Precise—The code must identify the specific item.

- Concise—The code must be brief and yet adequately describe the item.

- Convenient—The code must be easy to encode and decode.

- Meaningful—The code must be useful to the people dealing with it. If possible, it should indicate some of the characteristics of the item.

- Operable—The code should be compatible with present and anticipated methods of data processing—manual or machine."

In some cases, it may not be necessary, desirable, or practical for the code to have any obvious relationship to the item it describes. A good example is a customer number, account number, or employee number in many systems: the code is simply a number, chosen in sequence. However, it is also common for the coding technique to reserve *blocks* of numbers (or letters) for items that fall into a common category; for example, an order entry system might use a four-digit number as a *product number,* with the numbers 1 to 500 reserved for standard items, and the numbers 501 to 999 reserved for specialty items.

Even more common is a *classification code,* which uses groups of digits (or letters) within the code to identify major, intermediate, and minor classifications within the item being described. For example, to call my office in London, I dial the following digits:

011-44-1-637-2182

The first three digits identify the phone number as an international number (as compared to a call within North America). The next two digits are the country code, with 44 as the code for the United Kingdom. The next digit is the area code for London, analogous to the three-digit area code used throughout the United States. The next three digits represent a telephone exchange and will often give the astute user a good idea of the neighborhood in London where the phone is located. And, finally, the last four digits identify a specific telephone.

Alphabetic codes are also commonly used for information systems. Most alphabetic codes are attempts at mnemonics, or memory aids, that the user will be able to remember easily.[10] Whether the attempt is successful or not depends on the brevity of the code (i.e., two characters versus ten characters), the diversity and disparity of the data elements themselves, and the user's familiarity with the data elements. For example, consider the two-letter codes used to identify different airlines; most U.S. citizens would immediately recognize that AA stands for American Airlines, and UA stands for United Airlines. But how many would know that HW stands for Havasu Airlines, or that AQ stands for Aloha Airlines? With three-letter codes, we have a somewhat better chance at choosing mnemonic codes, as illustrated by the codes used to identify airports. Almost everyone would know that JFK stands for John F.

---

10 Some other alphabetic coding schemes appear to be just the opposite of mnemonic; these are the codes that are derived from one or more of the attributes of the data element. An example is the code that one finds on the mailing label for most magazines; this subscriber code usually consists of a portion of the subscriber's last name, his or her street address, zip code, the subscription expiration date, and other details. As such, it is certainly not mnemonic: there is no way that anyone would remember a code that is often 20 or 30 characters in length. However, once the code is given to the computer system, the subscriber's record can be retrieved very quickly, which may be very important for a subscriber data base of several million records. For more information about such derived codes, see IBM Form GF20-8093, *Data Processing Techniques: Coding Methods.*

Kennedy airport in New York and SFO stands for San Francisco airport. But even here we have trouble unless the user has memorized many codes that are less than mnemonic (e.g., ORD for O'Hare, and YYZ for the airport in Toronto!).

Finally, some codes are *self-checking*; that is, they contain additional (redundant) information that can be used to ensure that the code was entered correctly. A common example of a self-checking code is one that contains a check digit, which is usually appended to the end of a numerical code. The check digit can be calculated in a variety of ways, one of which is given below:

check-digit = 0
FOR each digit in the numeric code
        sum = digit multiplied by its position number
        checkdigit = checkdigit + sum
END

DO WHILE there is more than one digit in check-digit
        checkdigit = the sum of all the digits in **check-digit**
ENDDO

For example, if we had a numeric code of 9876, the check digit would be computed as (9*1) + (8*2) + (7*3) + (6*4), which results in 70. Adding together the digit 7 and 0 would yield a final result of 7 as the check digit. The objective here is *not* to make the user go through this calculation, but rather to use a code that contains an embedded check digit (e.g., 9876-7). Then, when the user enters the code into the system, the computer can automatically recalculate the expected check digit (using the algorithm described above) and compare it to the actual check digit. If there is an error, it will usually mean that one of the digits was transposed by the user when she or he entered it.

21.3   IDENTIFYING ADDITIONAL MANUAL SUPPORT ACTIVITIES

In the essential model, we assume the existence of perfect technology—which means, among other things, that we assume that our implementation technology will never break down and never make mistakes. Users may not be willing to accept this, and who can blame them? Also, the user may decide that certain portions of the automated system will be under his own operational control (e.g., a PC or minicomputer in his work area) and he may be concerned about possible operational errors that his own people could commit. In addition, he may be working with financial data, in which case there may be legal requirements (or requirements imposed by the auditors) to ensure the integrity of the inputs, outputs, and system files. In most cases, these additional support activities will be represented by new processes in the behavioral model DFD. An example is shown in Figure 21.5.

In general, we have to be concerned about the possibility of faulty technology in four major areas, as illustrated by Figure 21.6.

     •   *Getting input into the system.* If the input data are provided by CRT terminals connected to the main computers via telecommunication lines, then it is possible for some or all of a transaction to be lost or scrambled. The same can happen with almost any other form of input; for example, one or two input cards might be dropped by the computer operator or one of a set of floppy disks might not be read into the system).

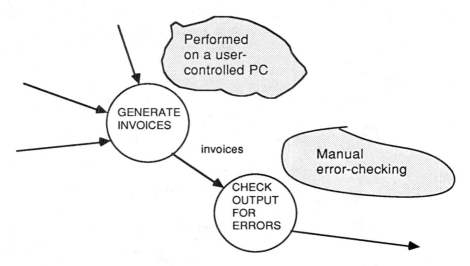

Figure 21.5: **A manual support error-checking activity**

- *Carrying out the computations.* Once the input data get into the system, there is the remote possibility that the computer itself might malfunction, and the much larger (!) possibility that an error in the computer programs might produce an incorrect result. Computer hardware errors could occur within an individual CPU or in the interface between the various CPUs in the system configuration.

- *Long-term data storage.* Most systems retain data for long periods of time on magnetic disk, magnetic tape, floppy disk, and the like. It is possible for some (or all) of this data to be lost or destroyed because of computer hardware errors and/or computer software errors. The hardware errors could consist of problems in the storage device itself or problems in the connection between the CPU and the storage device. Software errors could occur either in the application programs developed by the project team or in vendor-supplied database management software.

- *Getting output out of the system.* The potential problems here are analogous to the problems of getting input into the system. In some cases, output must be transmitted via telecommunication lines, often to the same CRT display unit that is used for input. In other cases, output is produced on magnetic tape or on paper reports. In all cases, it is possible for output information to be lost or incorrectly altered as a result of hardware and/or software errors.

What should be done about these possible areas of faulty technology? Obviously, this depends very much on (1) the estimated level of reliability of the hardware and software being used, (2) the nature of the user's application, and (3) the costs or penalties associated with faulty inputs or outputs. Obviously, this calls for a detailed discussion between the user, the systems analysts, and the implementation team; they may decide to add any of the following items to the essential model to deal with faulty technology:

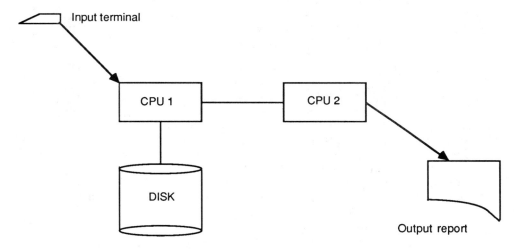

Figure 21.6: **Possible areas of faulty technology**

- *Redundant inputs and/or outputs.* In the most extreme case, duplicate copies of inputs could be provided from two different sources (e.g., from two different users at different CRT displays). And the system could produce duplicate outputs (e.g., two different copies of an output report printed on different printers). This is an unusual approach, but may have to be considered for extremely sensitive applications.

- *Redundant processor technology.* Data maintained by the system could be stored, in duplicate, on two different disks or magnetic tapes. And the computations carried out by the system could be done, in duplicate, on two different CPUs. Indeed, even more redundancy may be required: while a second CPU or a second disk unit allows the system to continue if the first unit breaks down completely, it does not protect against subtle errors. What if CPU 1 and CPU2 carry out the same calculation (e.g., the calculation of interest on a savings account or the computation of a missile trajectory for a flight to the moon) and produce different answers? Which CPU is correct? In the extreme case, then, we could even insist on triplicate processors and triplicate data storage, with majority voting logic to determine which two computers have the right answer. But what if all three computers disagree?

- *Internal redundancy.* A more common way to deal with faulty technology is to provide partial redundancy. For example, a bank teller who provides data about a deposit in an on-line banking system might be asked to provide both the account number *and* the name of the depositor. While the account number would normally be sufficient to identify the customer's record in the system, there is always the possibility that the teller will enter it incorrectly, or that the account number might be altered because of a telecommunications error, or an error in the CRT terminal, or an error in the CPU. Alternatively, the system might require the bank teller to enter only the account number and might verify that it is correct by displaying the customer's name after the record has been retrieved.

- *Batch controls.* This is an approach that was first introduced in second-generation batch computer systems, but it is still relevant in many of today's systems. It requires that the user keep a count of the transactions that she or he inputs to the system, as well as a cumulative total of any important data items within those transactions; in a financial system, the obvious thing to count would be the dollar amount of each transaction. Meanwhile, the system maintains its own count as it receives transactions; periodically, the system and the user compare their counts to ensure that nothing has been lost or altered. The same approach can be used with outputs: the system can maintain its own count of the number of transactions it has outputted, and this can be compared with a manual count provided by the user.

- *Sequence checks.* Related to the concept of batch controls is the sequence check approach. The user can assign a sequence number or transaction number for each input, and the system can verify, as it processes those inputs, that they are all in sequence and that no transaction has been lost. Similarly, the system can attach a sequence number to each output it produces, and the user can manually verify that no outputs have been lost.

21.4 SPECIFYING OPERATIONAL CONSTRAINTS

Ultimately, the implementation team will have to decide what combination of hardware, operating system, telecommunication facilities, programming language, and design strategy will best implement the requirements. But this will be difficult to achieve without some statement of operational constraints, which the essential model deliberately avoids. The major issues are typically such things as:

- *Volumes of data.* The user needs to specify volumes of input transactions and the required size of data stores. This is particularly important if there are any major variations in transaction volumes (e.g., during busy times of the day or busy seasons of the year). Thus, the user may say to you, "We normally process 2000 orders a day, but the volume jumps to 4000 orders per day during the month of December." In addition, the user needs to estimate the increase of transaction rates and storage requirements over the estimated useful life of the system. Thus, the user might say, "The INVENTORY store needs to be able to handle on-hand balances of 4000 different parts now, and we expect that we'll be dealing with about 6000 parts within the next five years." In general, you can expect the amount of data stored by an information system to increase by approximately 10% per year.[11]

- *Response time to various inputs.* This may be stated in absolute terms, but is more realistically stated as a probability: "90% of all transactions must have a response time of less than 2 seconds." In some cases, this may be stated in terms of deadlines: "The XYZ report must be produced no later than 8:00 AM every morning," or "all deposit transactions must be processed by midnight each night so that customers can determine their current balance from their home banking systems."

- *Political constraints on implementation choices.* The user may, for rational or irrational reasons, specify the brand of hardware to be used (or the brand of hardware to be avoided), the programming language to be used ("It's gotta be programmed in Ada"), the vendor of telecommunication facilities that will be used, and so on. This is to be avoided wherever possible, but you should expect at least some pressures of this sort. Note that implementation constraints are more likely to be imposed by the organization's operations department; that is, you're likely to hear something like, "Well, this new system sounds fine, but of course it's got to run on the corporate mainframe. So make sure that it doesn't take up more than 8 megabytes; we'll allocate a couple of disks for you."

- *Environmental constraints.* Temperature, humidity, electrical (RFI) interference, power consumption, limitations on weight, size or electrical emissions, vibration, pollution, noise, radiation, and other environmental constraints may be imposed by the user on the implementation team. Sometimes the user won't mention this explicitly; he'll just assume that the new system will operate satisfactorily within his normal environment (e.g., in an oil refinery, on a factory floor, or in an open office environment). Thus, it may be necessary for you to document the relevant features of the user's environment for the benefit of the implementation team. Or you may wish to simply indicate in the user implementation model that the system must operate in the user's environment, and let the implementation team figure out for themselves what that means.

- *Security and reliability constraints.* The user may specify mean time between failures (MTBF) and mean time to repair (MTTR) for the system. The required system reliability may also be expressed in terms of availability; for example, the user may say, "We can't afford anything less than 99.5% uptime for this system."

---

11 This estimate is based on a survey of approximately 500 U.S. computer installations, as documented by Lientz and Swanson in *Software Maintenance Management* (Reading, Mass.: Addison-Wesley, 1980).

- *Security constraints.* The user may specify a variety of constraints intended to minimize unauthorized use of the system. This may include a provision for account numbers and passwords (so that individual users will have to identify themselves). It may also include mechanisms to prevent unauthorized access to confidential data; some users may be allowed to read records in various stores, while other users may be allowed to modify (or delete) existing data, and still others may be allowed to append new records. And the user may request mechanisms to prevent unauthorized users from carrying out certain functions in the system (e.g., not everyone should be able to run the payroll system). Various security measures may be imposed on data coming into the system and leaving the system; this could include, for example, encryption of data transmitted over tele-communication lines.[12] And, for security purposes, the system might be required to produce an *audit trail:* a complete listing of all the transactions entered into the system, all the outputs produced, and perhaps even a record of all the changes made to the system's files.

21.5   SUMMARY

The user implementation model is often described as the "twilight zone" between structured analysis and structured design. It *cannot* be done by the systems analyst alone, and it is dangerous for the analyst and the user to develop the user implementation model without the participation of the designers and programmers who will ultimately build the system. While the functions, data, and time-dependent behavior are ultimately the most important characteristics of an information system, the human interface is often the area that causes the most emotional reactions from the user. Awkward input formats, confusing error messages, and a slow response time can make even the most elegant system functions unacceptable to the user. And it should also be remembered that implementation constraints imposed by the user (usually in an innocent fashion) can torpedo even the best-managed project: it may simply not be possible to implement the system within the user's constraints.

When the user implementation model has been built and reviewed by users, systems analysts, and the designer/programmer group, the business of systems analysis is done. At this point, it is usually necessary to present the results of the entire systems analysis phase of the project to management in order to get approval to continue on with the design and implementation of the system. The presentation should include the following information:

1.   The current status of the existing system (assuming there is one).

2.   Problems (weaknesses, missing functions, etc.) that were identified in the current system during the initial survey or feasibility study.

3.   Alternative solutions that were identified.

---

12 Computer security is a major subject in itself and is not discussed in any detail in this book. For more information, consult textbooks on computer security and computer crime; also, contact the Computer Security Institute.

4. An overview of the essential model and user implementation model, with as much detail as management wants to see. Typically, the high-level DFD model is presented and the detailed components of the model are made available to management for their subsequent perusal.

5. Projected costs and benefits of the new system.[13]

6. Cost, schedule, and resource (work hours) estimates for the remaining phases of the project.

7. Recommendations of the project team or the systems analyst.

Assuming that management approval is forthcoming, the project itself is just beginning: there is still a great deal of design, programming and testing to be done before the user finally receives the system he or she wanted. These areas are discussed in the following chapters.

REFERENCES

1. Marjorie Leeson, *Systems Analysis and Design.* Chicago: Science Research Associates, 1981.

2. Tom Gilb and Gerald Weinberg, *Humanized Input.* Cambridge, Mass.: Winthrop Publishers, 1977.

3. James Martin, *Design of Man-machine Dialogues.* Englewood Cliffs, N.J.: Prentice-Hall, 1973.

4. Marvin Gore and John Stubbe, *Elements of Systems Analysis,* 3rd ed. Dubuque, Iowa: William C. Brown Co., 1983.

5. *Data Processing Techniques: Coding Methods,* Form GF20-8093. White Plains, N.Y.: IBM Technical Publications Department.

QUESTIONS AND EXERCISES

1. What are the three major things that the essential model of a system describes?

2. Why is the essential model usually not enough information for the systems designers and programmers to begin implementing the system?

3. What additional information needs to be added to the essential model?

4. What is a user implementation model? What are its major components?

5. What are the two major implementation issues that users generally have strong feelings about in an information systems project?

13 Cost-benefit calculations are discussed in Appendix C.

6. Give a definition of the automation boundary of a system. What other term or synonym could be used instead of automation boundary?

7. Why do users often have strong feelings about the format of inputs and outputs of an information system?

8. Give four examples of formatting issues (involving either inputs, outputs or both) that a user might want to specify as part of the user implementation model.

9. Give three examples of formatting issues associated with on-line systems that a user might want to specify as part of the user implementation model.

10. How has the introduction of personal computers affected the work that the systems analyst must do to develop the user implementation model?

11. Give three examples of questions that will need to be answered in the user implementation model if user-controlled PCs are part of the implementation of the system.

12. How does the introduction of fourth generation programming languages in many organizations affect the work that the systems analyst must do to develop the user implementation model?

13. How does the concept of *prototyping* affect the development of the user implementation model in a typical systems development project?

14. How does the possible purchase of a vendor-supplied software package affect the development of the user implementation model in a typical systems development project?

15. What mistake do many organizations make when developing an essential model in a situation where they expect to user a vendor-supplied software package?

16. What are the three extreme cases that might occur when the automation boundary is being determined for an information system?

17. Under what conditions is the user likely to have no strong feelings about the placement of the automation boundary in a systems development project? How likely do you think this is in a typical organization?

18. Under what conditions is the user likely to opt for a fully automated system when the automation boundary is being determined, with all functions carried out by computers and all data stored in a computerized form?

19. Under what conditions is the user likely to opt for a fully manual system when the automation boundary is being determined? How likely do you think this is?

20. How many alternative automation boundaries do you think the project team should explore with the users before finally settling on one? Give a justification for your answer.

21. From the systems analyst's point of view, what is the simplest thing that could happen to processes and data that have been placed *outside* the automation boundary when the automation boundary has been determined?

22. What is the more likely thing that the systems analyst will have to do with manual processes and manual data after the automation boundary has been determined?

23. What are the three major issues that need to be addressed when defining the automation boundary in the user implementation model?

24. Where should the systems analyst document the details of most automation boundary issues that are discussed with the user?

25. Give two examples of implementation constraints on a data element that might be determined as part of the automation boundary.

26. How can the state-transition diagram be effectively used during the development of the user implementation model?

27. What kind of manual support activities might need to be specified during the development of the user implementation model?

28. What are the five major types of operational constraints on a system that usually need to be specified in the user implementation model?

29. Why is it important to specify in the user implementation model the volume of data that the system must handle?

30. Give three examples of political constraints that might be imposed on a system as part of the user implementation model.

31. Is your bank's automated teller system a menu-driven system or a command-driven system? What are the advantages and disadvantages of the approach taken by the system?

PART IV   FOLLOW-ON ISSUES

22   MOVING INTO DESIGN

For close designs and crooked counsels fit,
Sagacious, bold, and turbulent of wit,
Restless, unfix'd in principles and place,
In power unpleas'd, impatient of disgrace;
A fiery soul, which working out its way,
Fretted the pygmy-body to decay....
John Dryden, *Absalom and Achitophel,* 1680

In this chapter, you will learn:

1. The three levels of systems design.

2. The three major criteria for evaluating a systems design.

3. How to draw a structure chart.

4. How to use coupling and cohesion to evaluate a design.

When the user implementation model has been completed, the job of systems analysis is officially over. Everything past that point becomes a matter of implementation. The visible part of this work is programming and testing, which we will discuss in Chapter 23. However, programming should be preceded by a higher-level activity: *design*.

As a systems analyst, you may not feel that you are interested in the details of systems design or program design; however, as we saw in the previous chapter, the work of the systems analyst and the work of the designer cannot always be separated. Especially in the area of the user implementation model, the analyst must make sure that she or he understands the user's requirements, while the designer must ensure that those requirements can be realistically implemented with current computer technology. Thus, it is important for you to have some understanding of the process that the designer goes through when your job is finished.

There is another reason for being interested in systems design: you may find yourself doing the job! Especially on small- and medium-sized systems, the same individual is often expected to document the user requirements and also develop the design. Thus, you may be expected to decide the best way of mapping the model of user requirements onto a configuration of different CPUs; you may have to decide how the logical data model (which was documented with ERDs) can best be implemented by a database management system; and you may have to decide how the system functions should be allocated to different tasks within each processor.

It is not the purpose of this book to discuss the activities of systems design in great detail; this is better accomplished in books devoted to the subject, such as [Page-Jones, 1988], [Yourdon and Constantine, 1989], [Ward and Mellor, 1985], [Jackson, 1975], [Orr, 1977], and others. However, we will briefly examine the major stages of design and some of the more important objectives that a system designer should try to achieve. Since systems design and program design are indeed subjects unto themselves, you should definitely examine the references at the end of this chapter if you need additional information.

22.1   THE STAGES OF DESIGN

The activity of design involves developing a series of *models,* in much the same way that the systems analyst develops models during the systems analysis phase of a project. The specific design models and their relationship to the systems analysis models discussed in this book are illustrated in Figure 22.1.

The most important models for the designer are the *systems implementation model* and the *program implementation model.* The systems implementation model is further divided into a *processor* model and a *task* model.

22.1.1   The Processor Model

The first job that the systems designer faces is deciding how the essential model (or, to be more accurate, the automated portion of the user implementation model) will be allocated to major pieces of hardware and system software technology. At the level of the processor model, the systems designer is primarily trying to decide how the essential model should be allocated to different processors (CPUs) and how those processors should communicate with one another. There are typically a variety of choices:

- The entire essential model can be allocated to a single processor. This is often referred to as the mainframe solution.

- Each bubble in the essential model's Figure 0 DFD can be allocated to a different CPU (typically a mini or micro computer).[1] This is often referred to as the distributed solution.

---

1 Note that this is unrealistic, given the computer technology of the late 1980s, for anything other than a trivial system. If a system had 500 bottom-level bubbles in its essential model DFD, would it be realistic to consider implementing the system with 500 separate CPUs? This will change by the mid-1990s.

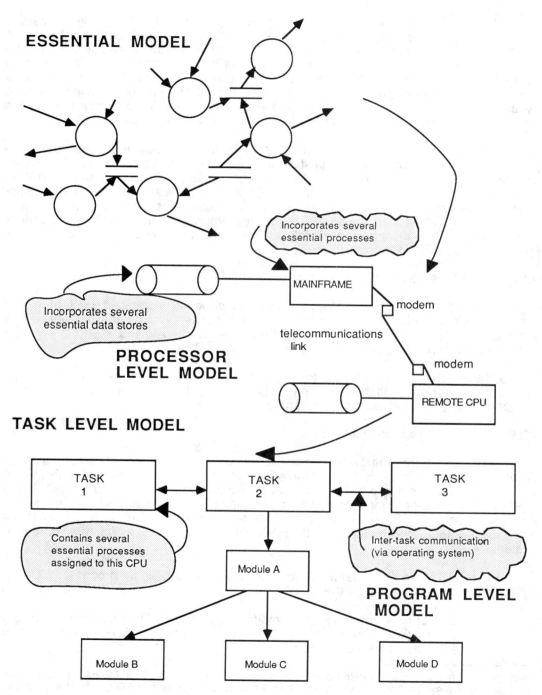

ESSENTIAL MODEL

Incorporates several essential processes

Incorporates several essential data stores

MAINFRAME

modem

telecommunications link

modem

PROCESSOR LEVEL MODEL

REMOTE CPU

TASK LEVEL MODEL

TASK 1

TASK 2

TASK 3

Contains several essential processes assigned to this CPU

Inter-task communication (via operating system)

Module A

PROGRAM LEVEL MODEL

Module B

Module C

Module D

Figure 22.1: **Analysis models and design models**

- A combination of mainframes, minis, and micros can be chosen to mini-mize costs, maximize reliability, or achieve some other objective.

Just as *processes* must be assigned to appropriate hardware components, *data stores* must be similarly allocated. Thus, the designer must decide whether a store will be implemented as a database on processor 1 or processor 2. Since most stores are shared by many processes, the designer may also have to decide whether duplicate copies of the store need to be assigned to different processors. The activity of allocating processes and stores to processors is illustrated in Figure 22.2.

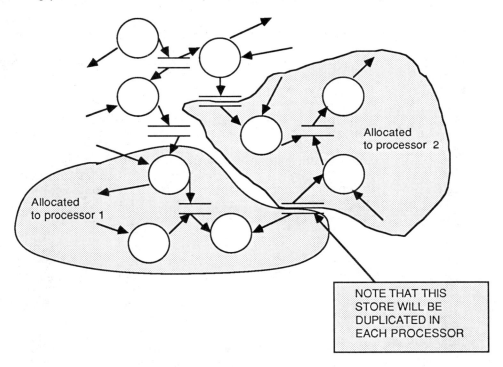

Allocated
to processor 2

Allocated
to processor 1

NOTE THAT THIS
STORE WILL BE
DUPLICATED IN
EACH PROCESSOR

Figure 22.2: **Allocating processes and stores to processors**

Notice that anything other than a single-processor implementation will involve some mechanism for *communicating* between processors; what we have traditionally shown as dataflows must now be specified in physical terms. Some of the choices available to the systems designer for processor-to-processor communication are:

- A direct connection between the processors. This could be implemented by connecting the processors with a cable, or a channel, or a local area network. This kind of communication will generally permit data to be transmitted from one processor to another at speeds ranging from 50,000 bits per second (often abbreviated as 50KB) to several million bits per second.

- A telecommunications link between the processors. This is especially common if the processors are physically separated by more than a few hundred feet. Depending on the nature of the telecommunications link, data will typically be transmitted between the processors at speeds ranging from 300 bits per second to as high as 50,000 bits per second.

- An indirect link between the processors. Data may be written onto magnetic tape, floppy disk, punched cards, or some other storage medium on one processor and then physically carried to another processor to be used as input.

The last case (sometimes known as the "sneaker interface") is somewhat extreme, but it illustrates an important point: processor-to-processor communication is generally much, much slower than communication between processes (bubbles) within the same processor. Thus, the systems designer will generally try to group processes and stores that have a high volume of communication within the same processor.

A variety of factors must be taken into account by the systems designer as he or she makes these allocations. Typically, the major issues are these:

- *Cost.* Depending on the nature of the system, a single-processor implementation may be the cheapest, or it may not be. For some applications, a group of low-cost microcomputers might be the most economical solution; for others, implementation on the organization's existing mainframe computer might be the most practical and economical.[2]

- *Efficiency.* The systems designer is generally concerned with response time for on-line systems and turn-around time for batch computer systems. Thus, the designer must choose processors and data storage devices that are fast enough and powerful enough to meet the performance requirements specified in the user implementation model. In some cases, the designer may choose a multiple-processor implementation so that different parts of the system can be carried out in parallel, thus speeding up overall response time. At the same time, the designer must be concerned about the *in*efficiency of processor-to-processor communication, as discussed earlier.

For example, suppose that the designer sees that the system contains an edit function and a process function, as shown in Figure 22.3. By putting each function in a separate processor, the designer knows that the system will be able to edit one transaction while simultaneously carrying out the processing for another transaction, thus presumably improving the efficiency of the overall system. On the other hand, the edited transactions

---

2 Keep in mind that there is a budget for the entire project, which should have been determined as part of the analysis process (see Chapter 5). Thus, the designer must choose the most efficient system that fits within the budget. However, keep in mind also the fact that budgets can change: the budgets developed during the analysis phase of the project were only estimates and may be subject to revision if the designer can show that more money needs to be spent for an acceptable implementation.

will have to be sent from one CPU to another; this may be very efficient if it can be done through a direct hardware connection, or it may be very inefficient if the communication takes place via slow telecommunication lines.

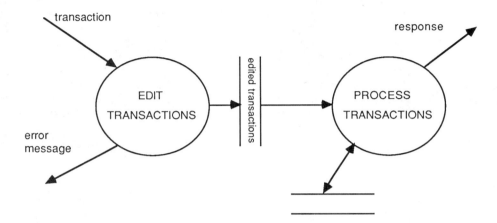

Figure 22.3: **Processor-to-processor communication**

- *Security.* The end user may have security requirements that dictate the placement of some (or all) processors and/or sensitive data in protected locations. Security requirements may also dictate the nature of (or the absence of) processor-to-processor communication; for example, the designer may be precluded from transmitting data from one processor to another over ordinary telephone lines if the information is confidential.

- *Reliability.* The end user will typically specify reliability requirements for a new system; these requirements may be expressed in terms of mean time between failure (MTBF) or mean time to repair (MTTR), or system availability.[3] In any case, this can have a dramatic influence on the kind of processor configuration chosen by the designer: he or she may decide to separate the system processes into several different processors so that some portion of the system will be available even if other parts are rendered inoperable because of a hardware failure. Alternatively, the designer may decide to implement redundant copies of processes and/or data on multiple processors, perhaps even with spare processors that can take over in the event of a failure. This is shown in Figure 22.4; even if the processing CPU should fail (which is perhaps more likely, because it is a large, complex mainframe computer), the individual edit CPUs can

---

3 System availability is usually defined as the percentage of time that the system is available for use. It can be calculated based on MTBF and MTTR as follows:

$$availability = MTBF/(MTBF+MTTR)$$

continue operating—collecting transactions, editing them, and storing them for later processing. Similarly, if one of the edit CPUs breaks down, the others can presumably continue operating.

- *Political and operational constraints.* The hardware configuration may also be influenced by political constraints imposed directly by the end user, by other levels of management in the organization, or by the operations department in charge of maintaining and operating all computer systems. This may lead to a specific choice of hardware configuration, or it may preclude the choice of certain vendors. Similarly, environmental constraints (e.g., temperature, humidity, radiation exposure, dust/dirt, vibration) may be imposed upon the designer, and this can have an enormous influence on the processor configuration that he or she chooses.

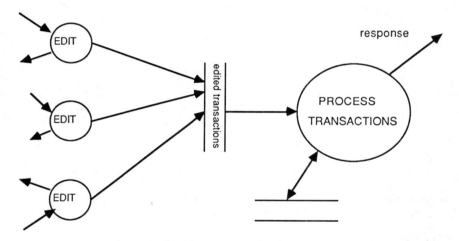

Figure 22.4: **Multiple processors for reliability**

22.1.2   The Task Model

Once the processes and stores have been allocated to processors, the designer must, on a processor by processor basis, assign processes and data stores to individual tasks within each processor. The notion of a task is common to virtually every brand of computer hardware, though the terminology may differ from vendor to vendor: some vendors will use the term partition, while others use the terms job step, overlay, or control point. Regardless of the term, Figure 22.5 shows how a typical processor divides its available storage into separate areas, each managed by a central operating system. The systems designer generally has to accept the vendor's operating system as a given (though she or he may be able to choose between several different operating systems for a given computer), but the designer *does* have the freedom to decide which portions of the essential model assigned to that processor should be allocated to individual tasks within the processor.

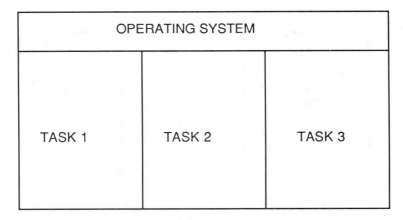

Figure 22.5: **Organization of tasks within a processor**

Note that processes within the same processor may need to communicate through some form of intertask communication protocol. The mechanism for doing this varies from one vendor to another, but it is almost universally true that the communication takes place through the vendor's operating system, as illustrated by Figure 22.6. Just as transmission of data from one processor to another processor is relatively slow and inefficient, the communication of data (or control signals) from one task to another task within the same processor is also inefficient. Communication between processes in the same task is usually much more efficient. Thus, the systems designer will generally try to keep within the same task those processes that have a high volume of communication.

Within an individual processor, it is not always clear whether activities are occurring synchronously or asynchronously; that is, it isn't always clear whether only one thing can be happening at a time or multiple things at a time. Typically, each individual processor only has a single CPU, which can only be executing instructions for one process at a time; however, if one process is waiting for some input or output from a storage device (e.g., disk, tape, CRT terminal, etc.), the processor's operating system can switch control to another task. Thus, the systems designer can often pretend that each task is an independent, asynchronous activity.

22.1.3   The Program Implementation Model

Finally, we reach the level of an individual task; at this point, the systems designer has already accomplished two levels of process and data storage allocation. Within an individual task, the computer operates in a *synchronous* fashion: only one activity at a time can take place. The most common model for organizing the activity within a single, synchronous unit is the *structure chart,* which shows the hierarchical organization of modules within one task. The major components of a structure chart are shown in Figure 22.7.

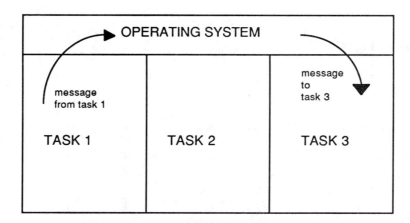

Figure 22.6: **Intertask communication within a processor**

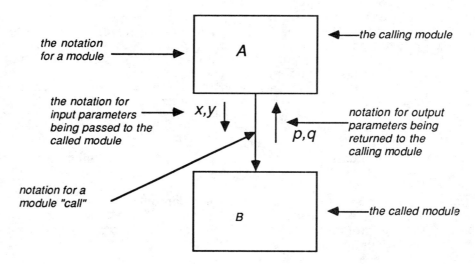

Figure 22.7: **Components of a structure chart**

You would read this small structure chart in the following way:

- Module A is the top-level executive module of the system consisting of modules A and B. The reason that A is identified as the top-level (superordinate) module is *not* because it is topologically above module B, but rather because no other module calls it. Module B, on the other hand, is said to be *subordinate* to module A. (Module A is presumed to be called or invoked by the operating system of the computer.)

- Module A contains one or more executable instructions, including a call to module B. This call may be implemented as a CALL statement in languages like FORTRAN; or a PERFORM statement or CALL USING statement in COBOL; or simply by invoking the name of B in other languages. The structure chart deliberately avoids describing how many times module A actually calls module B; that depends on the internal program logic within module A. Thus, there may be a statement of the following kind in module A:

> **IF** nuclear-war-begins
> > CALL Module-B
>
> **ELSE**
> > ...

in which case module B may never be called. But there might also be a program statement in module A of the following kind:

> **DO WHILE** there are more orders in ORDERS file
> > CALL Module-B
>
> **ENDDO**

in which case module B may be called several thousand times.

- When module B is called, module A's execution is suspended. Module B begins executing at its first executable statement; when it finishes, it exits or returns to module A. Module A then resumes its execution at the point where it left off.

- Module A may or may not pass input parameters to module B as part of its call, and module B may or may not return output parameters when it returns to module A. In the example shown in Figure 22.7, module A passes parameters X and Y to module B, and module B returns parameters P and Q. Detailed definitions of X, Y, P, and Q would normally be found in a data dictionary. The actual mechanics of transmitting the parameters will vary from one programming language to another.

An example of a complete structure chart is shown in Figure 22.8. Note that it contains four levels of modules; this would normally represent a program of about 500 to 1000 program statements, assuming that each module represents about 50 to 100 program statements.[4]

There is an obvious question at this point: How does the systems designer transform a network model of processes in a dataflow diagram into the synchronous model represented by a structure chart? Several books on systems design, including [Page-Jones, 1988] and [Yourdon and Constantine, 1989], discuss this question in great detail. As Figure 22.9 illustrates, there is a cookbook strategy for transforming the network dataflow model into a synchronous structure chart model; indeed, the strategy

---

4 Of course, a module called EXTRACT CHARACTER does not sound as if it would require 50 to 100 statements; it might only require two to three statements in a typical high-level programming language. In a lower-level machine-oriented language, though, many more statements would typically be required.

is generally referred to as transform-centered design. Transform-centered design is only one of several strategies for converting a network dataflow model into a synchronous, hierarchical model; [Page-Jones, 1988], [Yourdon and Constantine, 1989], and [Ward and Mellor, 1985] discuss a variety of such strategies. Note that each process bubble in the dataflow diagram shown in Figure 22.9 becomes a module in the derived structure chart; this is a realistic situation if the processes are relatively small and simple (e.g., if the process specification is less than a page of structured English). In addition to the module that implements the dataflow processes, it is evident that the structure chart also contains modules to coordinate and manage the overall activity, as well as modules concerned with bringing input into the system and getting output out of the system.

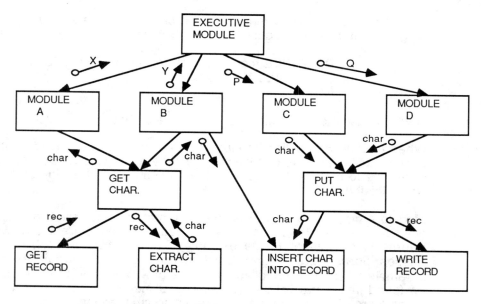

Figure 22.8: **An example of a structure chart**

Other design strategies use the entity-relationship diagram or other forms of data-structure diagrams as a starting point in deriving the appropriate structure chart; see [Jackson, 1975] and [Orr, 1977] for more information about such design strategies.

22.2   DESIGN GOALS AND OBJECTIVES

In addition to achieving the design objectives specified in the user implementation model, the designer is also concerned with overall quality of the design. The ultimate ability of the programmers to implement a high-quality, error-free system depends very much on the nature of the design created by the designer; similarly, the ability of the maintenance programmers to make changes to the system after it has been put into operation depends on the quality of the design.

The field of structured design contains a number of detailed guidelines that help the designer determine which modules, and which interconnections between the modules will best implement the requirements specified by the systems analyst; all the books listed at the end of this chapter elaborate on those guidelines. The two most important guidelines are coupling and cohesion; these as well as some other common guidelines are discussed next.

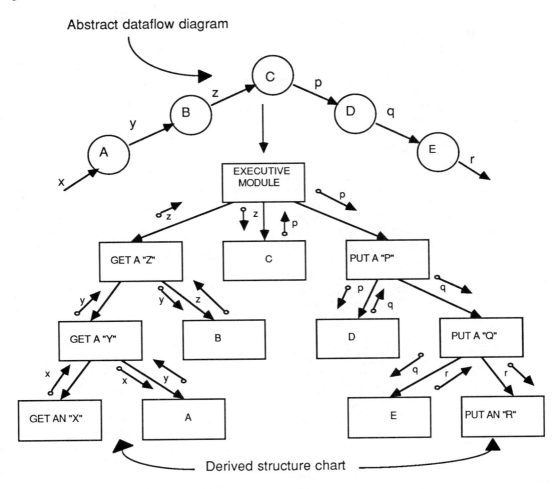

Figure 22.9: **Transform-centered design strategy**

- *Cohesion.* The degree to which the components of a module (typically the individual computer instructions that make up the module) are necessary and sufficient to carry out one, single, well-defined function. In practice, this means that the systems designer must ensure that she or he does not split essential processes into fragmented modules; and the designer must ensure that she or he does not gather together unrelated processes (represented as bubbles on the DFD) into meaningless modules. The best modules are those that are *functionally cohesive* (i.e., modules in which every program statement is necessary in order to carry out a single, well-defined task). The worst modules are those that are *coincidentally cohesive* (i.e., modules whose program statements have no meaningful relationship to one another at all).[5]

- *Coupling.* The degree to which modules are interconnected with or related to one another. The stronger the coupling between modules in a system, the more difficult it is to implement and maintain the system, because a modification to one module will then necessitate careful study, as well as possible changes and modifications, to one or more other modules. In practice, this means that each module should have simple, clean interfaces with other modules, and that the minimum number of data elements should be shared between modules. And it means that one module should not modify the *internal* logic or data of another module; this is known as a pathological connection. (The dreaded ALTER statement in COBOL is a preeminent example.)

- *Module size.* If possible, each module should be small enough that its program listing will fit on one page (or, alternatively, so that it can be displayed on one screen of a CRT). Of course, sometimes it is not possible to determine how large a module will be until the actual program statements have been written; but initial design activities will often give the designer a strong clue that the module is going to be large and complex. If this is the case, the large complex module should be broken into one or more levels of submodules. (On rare occasions, designers create modules that are overly trivial, for example, modules consisting of two to three lines of code. In this case, several such modules can be aggregated together into a larger supermodule.)

- *Span of control.* The number of immediate subordinates that can be called by a manager module is known as the span of control. A module should not call more than approximately half a dozen lower-level modules. The reason for this is to avoid complexity: if a module has, say, 25 lower-level modules, then it will probably contain so much complex program logic (in the form of nested **IF** statements, nested **DO-WHILE** iterations, etc.) that nobody will be able to understand it. The solution to such a situation is to introduce an intermediate level of manager modules, just as a manager in a human organization would do if he found that he was trying to directly supervise 25 immediate subordinates.[6]

- *Scope of effect/scope of control.* This guideline suggests that any module affected by the outcome of a decision should be subordinate (though not necessarily immediately subordinate) to the module that makes the

---

5 Examples of functionally cohesive modules are CALCULATE-SQUARE-ROOT, COMPUTE-NET-SALARY, and VALIDATE-CUSTOMER-ADDRESS. An example of a coincidentally cohesive module is MISCELLANEOUS-FUNCTIONS

6 There is an exception to this, known as a transaction center. If the manager module makes one simple decision in order to invoke only one of the immediate subordinates, then the program logic within that manager module will probably be fairly simple. In this case, we do not have to worry about the manager's span of control.

decision. It is somewhat analogous to a management guideline that says that any employee affected by the outcome of a manager's decision (i.e., within the scope of effect of the decision) should be within the manager's scope of control (i.e., working somewhere in the hierarchy of people that reports to the manager). Violating this guideline in a structured design environment usually leads to unnecessary passing of flags and switches (which increases the coupling between modules), or redundant decision making, or (worst of all) pathological connections between modules.

22.3 SUMMARY

There is much more to learn about design, but with this introduction you should understand the process that the system designer goes through. As we have seen, the first step is to map the essential model of user requirements onto a configuration of processors. Then, within each processor, the designer must decide how to allocate processes and data to different tasks. Finally, we must organize the processes within each task into a hierarchy of modules, using the structure chart as our modeling tool.

Note also that additional processes and data repositories will probably have to be added to the implementation model to accommodate the specific features of the implementation technology. For example, additional processes may be needed for error-checking, editing, and validation activities that were not shown in the essential model; other processes may be necessary for transporting dataflows between CPUs. Once this is accomplished, programming can begin. The subjects of programming and testing are discussed in Chapter 23.

REFERENCES

1. Meilir Page-Jones, *The Practical Guide to Structured Systems Design,* 2nd ed. Englewood Cliffs, N.J.: Prentice-Hall, 1988.

2. Edward Yourdon and Larry L. Constantine, *Structured Design: Fundamentals of a Discipline of Computer Program and Systems Design.* Englewood Cliffs, N.J.: Prentice-Hall, 1989.

3. Paul Ward and Steve Mellor, *Structured Development for Real-Time Systems, Volume 3.* New York: YOURDON Press, 1986.

4. Michael Jackson, *Principles of Program Design.* New York: Academic Press, 1975.

5. Ken Orr, *Structured Systems Development.* New York: YOURDON Press, 1977.

QUESTIONS AND EXERCISES

1. What activity follows the development of the user implementation model in a typical systems development project?

2. What are the three major stages of design in a typical systems development project? What models are developed during these three stages?

3. Why are models important during the design phase of a project?

4. What is the major purpose of the processor model during the design activity?

5. Give three examples of how the processes in an essential model could be mapped onto CPUs in an implementation model.

6. What decisions must be made during the processor modeling activity about data stores that were identified in the essential model?

7. List three common methods for interprocessor communication.

8. What factors should the designer take into account when choosing one of these three methods? Which of these factors do you think is most important?

9. If you are working on a systems development project where *reliability* is a high priority, how would this affect your decision about allocating essential processes and essential stores to different processors?

10. Give an example of how political constraints could influence the allocation of essential tasks and essential stores to different processors.

11. What is a task model in the context of this chapter? What are its components?

12. Give three common synonyms for task.

13. Under what circumstances could different tasks be operating at the same time?

14. Research Project: Pick a common computer and operating system. Describe how different tasks operating under the control of the operating system can communicate with each other. What is the typical overhead (in terms of CPU time, memory utilization, and any other significant hardware resources) for such intertask communication?

15. Give a definition of the program implementation model. What are its components?

16. How should the designer transform an asynchronous, network-oriented DFD essential model into a synchronous, hierarchical model?

17. Under what conditions does each bubble in the essential model become a module in the program implementation model?

18. List two common design strategies. Give a brief description of each.

19. What is the primary objective that the designer is trying to achieve when he or she translates the essential model into an implementation model?

20. What other objectives does the designer usually try to achieve when he or she creates an implementation model?

23 PROGRAMMING AND TESTING

It is impossible to dissociate language from science or science from language, because every natural science always involves three things: the sequence of phenomena on which the science is based; the abstract concepts which call these phenomena to mind; and the words in which the concepts are expressed. To call forth a concept a word is needed; to portray a phenomenon, a concept is needed. All three mirror one and the same reality.

Antoine Laurent Lavoisier
Traite Elementair de Chimie, 1789

What we have to do is to be forever curiously testing new opinions and courting new impressions.

Walter Pater, *The Renaissance,* 1873

In this chapter, you will learn:

1. The role of the systems analyst in programming and testing.

2. Why fast-tracking is advantageous during programming and testing.

3. What the systems analyst should look for when examining a program.

4. The major forms of testing that should be carried out.

Programming and testing normally commence, as you might expect, when the design activity is finished. The programming, or implementation phase of a typical project involves the writing of statements in COBOL, Pascal, or in some other programming language to implement what the systems analyst has specified and what the designer has organized into modules. And testing, as the name implies, involves exercising the system to ensure that it produces the proper outputs and exhibits the proper behavior for a wide range of inputs.

Why should this be of any interest to you as a systems analyst? Isn't it true that you will be uninvolved in the project at this point? No, not necessarily. For various reasons, the work that the programmers and testers do may influence your work, and the way you organize *your* work may influence the way they do theirs. This interrelationship between systems analysis and programming/testing is the subject of this chapter.

23.1   THE ROLE OF THE ANALYST IN PROGRAMMING AND TESTING

In the extreme case, the systems analyst will finish his or her job of specifying the system, and then spend some time with the design team as the user implementation model is developed and as the early stages of design take place. But by the time programming begins, the systems analyst may have moved on to another project. But here are some reasons why you, as a systems analyst, may need to remain involved in the project as the programming activity commences:

- *A simple reason.* You're the project leader, and you're in charge of the programmers. Obviously, you can't abandon them. You'll be involved with the project until the final testing, acceptance, and delivery to the end user. Thus, it will be important for you to know if the programmers have written high-quality code, and it will be equally important to know whether they have tested their programs adequately.

- *Another simple reason.* You are a junior systems analyst, and your title is programmer/analyst or analyst/programmer. So, in addition to developing the specifications for the system, you are also involved in writing the computer programs.

- *A more interesting reason.* You are part of the group writing test cases that will be used to exercise the programs being written by the programmers. In many projects, you may be joined by one or more users in this activity, on the theory that the users are the people best able to think of unusual and exceptional test cases. Development of test data can begin as soon as the specification is finished (indeed, even before it is completely finished); as Tom DeMarco says, "The specification *is* the test of the system." Since you only know the logical content of the inputs and outputs at this point, you will probably have to wait until the user implementation model is finished before you can determine the physical format of the inputs and outputs. You will also need the user implementation model to know what operational constraints (response time, volumes, etc.) need to be tested. But this activity can easily keep you occupied right through the end of the project; after all, if the programs fail your test cases, you will need to work with the programmers to see whether your test case is wrong or whether their code is wrong.

- *A less obvious reason.* You may be involved in developing user manuals, training the users, planning for installation of the new system and conversion of data from the old system. In most cases, this can take place in parallel with the programming and testing of the new system. As the systems analyst involved in the new project from the beginning, you will often be seen as the ideal candidate for doing this work.

- *A discouraging reason.* The programmers may not understand your specification. Or your specification may be incomplete, inconsistent, or contradictory. Tsk! Tsk! But these things do happen, and you may find that the programmers need to come back to you periodically to review and clarify the specification as they translate it into a programming language. Another variation on this theme: the programmers may ask you to *change* the specification because it is difficult to implement. In this case, of course, you will have to be the mediator (as well as interpreter) between the programmers and the other systems analysts.

- *Another discouraging reason.* The users may have begun to change their mind about their requirements, even as the programmers are implementing the requirements they said they wanted. Aside from the fact that some users are ornery and do this just for the fun of it, there are very good reasons for this phenomenon; users live in a dynamic world and they must often react to changing policies imposed upon them by government legislation, customer requirements, or general marketplace conditions. So you may find that you are changing the specification even as the programmers are implementing the specification, something that won't make anyone happy, but may have to be done anyway. This is discussed further in Section 23.4.

23.2 THE IMPACT OF ANALYSIS, PROGRAMMING, AND TESTING ON ORGANIZATIONAL STRUCTURE

Throughout this book, it has been evident that structured analysis involves a steady progression from high-level modeling aspects (e.g., top-level dataflow diagrams) to low-level modeling issues, such as the development of process specifications and a complete, detailed data dictionary. Similarly, the process of design involves the development of design models ranging from high-level structure charts to such low-level forms as pseudocode or flowcharts. Programming must follow this same pattern: programs have to be written for high-level executive modules, and will eventually be developed for the bottom-level modules that carry out detailed calculations, validate input data elements, and so on.

What we have not talked about is the relationship between levels of the *system* and the levels of the *organization* that builds the system. But you probably got the impression after reading through most of this book that people having the title of systems analyst would be responsible for doing *all* the work of systems analysis, people with the title of systems designer would be responsible for the job of design, and people with the title of programmer would be responsible for the job of writing computer programs.

But there is a problem with this approach—actually, two related problems. First, people with the title of systems analyst are usually relatively senior people with several years of experience. While such senior people generally enjoy the work of drawing dataflow diagrams and entity-relationship diagrams, it is hard for them to get excited at the prospect of writing hundreds of process specifications and defining thousands of data elements.

And then there is the other side of this problem: if the senior people actually *do* carry out all this detailed work, what is there for the programmers to do? Their work becomes almost mechanical in nature, translating carefully thought out process specifications into COBOL or FORTRAN. Whatever creativity they thought they had in their job seems to have disappeared.[1]

One solution to this apparent dilemma is to let senior people do *all* the high-level activities in a project and let the junior people do *all* the low-level detailed activities. This would mean, for instance, that the senior-level people (the ones with the title of senior systems analyst or something else equally impressive) would not only carry out the high-level activities of systems analysis (drawing dataflow diagrams and the like) but would also do the high-level activities of systems design, and would even (gasp! shudder!) write high-level code. The junior people, meanwhile, would be involved in the project from the beginning (or as soon as the senior people had completed the high-level aspects of analysis) and would be involved in the job of writing process and module specifications, developing data dictionary entries, and writing the code for low-level modules.

The advantage of this scheme for the programmers is that they get to do the creative work of writing process specifications and then have the pleasure of turning their own process specifications into code. It gets them involved in the process of systems analysis at an earlier stage in their career than might otherwise be possible. And it also has the advantage of keeping the senior people somewhat in touch with technology by forcing them to continue to do some design and programming work.

Not all senior systems analyst think this is a good idea, though they will admit that they don't enjoy the drudgery of writing all the detailed process specifications as part of their job. In any case, there is growing agreement that the job of programming, *if preceded by careful, detailed systems analysis of the sort described in this book*, is becoming a menial, clerical job and may disappear entirely as we develop intelligent code generators that can compile process specifications directly. Thus, we can expect that organizations will gradually change their work assignments over the next 5 to 10 years to conform with the ideas discussed above.

---

[1] Actually, things could be even worse, and they might be a little better. The worst situation (from the programmer's point of view) is that we might not need any programmers at all! If the process specification is written in a sufficiently formal language, it can be compiled without any human intervention at all! This is already happening in isolated cases (e.g., process specifications being written in the Ada language and then compiled directly). On the other hand, there is the possibility that the programmer will still have a lot of creative work to do if the systems analyst wrote the process specification using the precondition/postcondition approach discussed in Chapter 11. In this case, the analyst will have specified the inputs and outputs for each module, but will have left the designer and, ultimately, the programmer the job of determining the best algorithm.

23.3   FAST-TRACKING AND TOP-DOWN IMPLEMENTATION

There is another impression you may have gotten from reading the material in this book: that the activities of systems analysis must be carried out *and completed* before the activities of design and programming can begin. While many projects do indeed work this way, it is not strictly necessary. Systems analysis, design, and programming can proceed in parallel with one another.

The concept of parallel development of the specification, design, and code for a system is sometimes known as fast-tracking and is referred to in some books (see, for example, [Yourdon, 1988]) as top-down implementation. It is not unique to the computer field. We discussed the idea briefly in Chapter 5; you may wish to review the concept of top-down implementation as part of the overall systems development life cycle that was discussed in that chapter.

The construction industry and many engineering disciplines follow this approach on many projects. As many construction project managers have been heard to exclaim, "You don't need to know the number of doorknobs in a building before you lay the foundation." In the case of developing an information system, this means that the high-level products of systems analysis, the framework documents of dataflow diagrams, entity-relationship diagrams, and state-transition diagrams, can be used as the basis for high-level design. And the high-level design can be used as the foundation for writing high-level code *even before the details of systems analysis have been finished*.

There is a great deal of flexibility in this approach; one can finish 80% of the systems analysis work before beginning the design and programming, or one can finish only 10%. A project plan that calls for nearly complete systems analysis before the beginning of systems design is usually referred to as a conservative approach; a project plan that calls for the almost immediate overlap of systems analysis, design, and programming is known as a radical approach. Every project manager can decide just how radical or conservative he wants his project to be, and he can change his mind dynamically during the project.

Why would the project manager consider a radical approach? Why would anyone want to begin the work of systems design and programming before the systems analysis is complete? There are many reasons, of which the following are the most important:

- Because the work of systems analysis, design, and programming is being done concurrently, there is usually an opportunity to *dramatically* shorten the *elapsed time* of a project. In some environments, this can be crucially important, for example, if a system absolutely, positively *must* be finished by a certain date.

- The concurrent development work can be used as a form of prototyping: it allows the project team to show a skeleton version of the system to the user before all the detailed work of systems analysis has been finished. This can help avoid major misunderstandings between user and systems analyst that might otherwise take place even with the most carefully developed structured specification.

- Beginning the programming work at an earlier point in the project often smooths out various resource demands, such as computer time, that would otherwise become a bottleneck. For example, the conservative approach often required enormous amounts of computer test time during the final stages of testing, and this can be a major problem.

Whether or not the project decides to follow a conservative or radical approach is beyond the scope of this book; some project environments may favor a conservative approach, and others will call for a highly radical approach. The main thing to be aware of is that the structured analysis approach described in this book does not preclude either approach, nor does it insist on either approach.

23.4   PROGRAMMING AND PROGRAMMING LANGUAGES

If you are still involved in the project during the implementation stage, you should have at least a general understanding of the issues and techniques of programming. In this section, we will discuss:

- Four generations of programming languages

- Important issues in programming

- Things you should look for if you examine the programmers' coding

23.4.1   The Four Generations of Programming Languages

People have been writing computer programs since general-purpose computers were first developed nearly 40 years ago. Programs are written in programming *languages,* of which BASIC, COBOL, and FORTRAN are common examples. It is convenient to group all the different programming languages (there are several *hundred* different languages in use around the world) into four distinct generations:

- *First generation languages:* First generation programming languages were the machine languages used in the 1950s; programmers wishing to make a computer do something useful would code their instructions in binary ones and zeroes. There are still times today when a faulty computer system disgorges pages of mind-numbing digits; and there are still a few misguided youths who think that machine language is the best way of playing with personal computers. But the rest of the world stopped thinking about machine language some 25 years ago.

- *Second generation languages:* Second-generation languages are the successor to machine language; they are generally known as assembly languages or assembler. Second generation languages are low-level languages in the sense that the programmer has to write one statement for each machine instruction. Thus, while she might conceptually think in terms of the statement X = Y + Z, she would have to translate the following statements into assembly language:

```
CLEAR ACCUMULATOR
LOAD Y INTO ACCUMULATOR
ADD Z TO CONTENTS OF ACCUMULATOR
STORE ACCUMULATOR IN X
```

Even this tiny example shows the major disadvantage of assembly language. Rather than being able to think in terms of the problem she wants to solve, the programmer must think in terms of the machine. Starting around 1960, more powerful languages began to be introduced; most sane programmers have long since abandoned assembly language. Unfortunately, there are still a few situations where such languages are needed. Most of them involve very small, low-powered computers (which can be manufactured very cheaply and which are small enough to fit, say, into a digital watch) that do not have the capacity to tolerate the overhead associated with higher-level languages.

- *Third generation languages:* Third generation languages are the norm today; they include BASIC, COBOL, FORTRAN, Pascal, C, Ada, and many others. They are high-level in the sense that a single statement (such as "MOVE A TO B" in COBOL) usually represents five or ten assembly language statements (and sometimes as many as a hundred statements); they are high-level in the more important sense that they allow the programmer to express thoughts in a form that is somewhat more compatible with the problem area in which she is working. However, they are low-level in some important respects. They require the programmer to become intimately involved in the tedious business of formatting the layout of computer reports, as well as editing and validating the input to the program. Often the programmer will think to herself, "This report should have the standard heading at the top of each page, with a page number on the right and the date on the left, just like all the other reports around here," but she may have to write 20 or 30 COBOL statements to accomplish it.

Third generation languages are also characterized as *procedural* languages. They require the programmer to think carefully about the sequence of computations, or the procedure, necessary to accomplish some action. In a scientific application, for example, the programmer may know that she wants to add array A to array B; however, she may be forced to write the detailed procedural steps to add each of the elements of the two arrays, rather than simply saying, "Add these two arrays" without having to worry about the procedural steps.

- *Fourth generation languages:* Fourth generation languages, or 4GLs, are the current rage and are considered by some computer consultants to be the most important development in the software field in the past 20 years. Some of them have been in existence for nearly a decade, but they have only become popular in the past few years. Examples of 4GLs are

FOCUS, IDEAL, MARK IV, RAMIS, MANTIS, MAPPER, dBASE-III Plus, and Rbase-5000. Most of these languages have the structured programming features that the older third generation languages lack, but they have other features, too. In particular, most of the tedious programming details associated with getting data into the computer (via a terminal) are hidden from the programmer; with one simple command, the programmer can specify that the computer should accept a specified kind of data from the keyboard, validate it, and store it in a designated data element. The same job might require 10 or 20 statements in a third generation programming language or 100 to 200 statements in a second generation programming language.

Similarly, many of the tedious programming details associated with producing an output report (e.g., an inventory listing, paychecks, invoices, or a summary of the day's orders) are handled automatically by the fourth generation languages. If the precise placement of information on the computer printout is relatively unimportant (as is often the case), the programmer does not even have to specify it; otherwise (as in the case of a computer-produced paycheck, where dollar amounts must be printed in a precise location), the details are easily specified in a few 4GL instructions.

23.4.2 Important Issues in Programming

Regardless of the programming language used, there are common issues that face all programmers. As a systems analyst, you should be familiar with these issues; the most common ones are itemized next:

- *Productivity:* Probably the most important issue in programming today is that of productivity: getting more software written more quickly than ever before. The major reason for this is the enormous backlog of unwritten systems and applications in large organizations: the typical large organization has a backlog of between four and seven years of new work to be done.[2] Thus, programming languages and programming techniques that promote productivity are to be highly encouraged; except in rare cases, productivity is considered more important today than efficiency.

- *Efficiency:* In some applications, efficiency is still important. This is true for many real-time systems, and it may be true for other types of systems that process large volumes of data (e.g., most of the systems running at the Social Security Agency, as well as other equally enormous systems running in banks, airline reservation operations, stock brokerage companies, and insurance companies). For these applications, it is usually important to minimize the amount the amount of CPU time required by the program; it may also be important to minimize memory utilization as well as the utilization of other resources such as the disk. Note that the goal of efficiency is usually in conflict with the other goals discussed in this

---

2 This does not mean four to seven years of work for a single person, but rather four to seven years of work for the entire MIS organization. For more information on this, see [Yourdon, 1986].

section: if one spends more time developing an efficient program, it is likely to be less maintainable and less portable, it is more likely to have subtle residual errors, and it is likely to decrease the productivity of the person who wrote the program.

- *Correctness:* Ultimately, one could argue that this is the most important issue. After all, if a program does not work correctly, it does not matter how efficient it is. Programming languages like Ada and Pascal are considered preferable if correctness is a critical concern (as it would be, for example, if one was working on the Star Wars system or building a control system for a nuclear reactor) because they are "strongly typed": the programmer is required to declare the nature of his or her variables (i.e., whether they are integer, character, floating point, etc.) and the language checks carefully to prevent illegal data references, and the like.

- *Portability:* In some environments, portability is important; the user may want to run the same system on several different types of computers. Some programming languages are more portable than others; ironically, this is more true of third generation programming languages (C, Pascal, FORTRAN, COBOL, etc.) than fourth generation languages. However, there is no such thing as a universally portable language; there are always ways for the programmer to take advantage of the special features of a specific computer or operating system. Thus, in addition to the programming *language,* we must also be concerned with the *style* of programming if portability is an important factor.

- *Maintainability:* Finally, we must remember that systems live for a long time, and the computer software must be maintained. Maintenance is discussed in more detail in Chapter 24.

23.4.3   Things to Watch For

As a systems analyst, you may have occasion to watch the work done by the programmers on the project; indeed, you may be their supervisor. As indicated above, you should be aware that productivity, efficiency, correctness, portability, and maintainability are likely to be important issues. But how are these goals to be achieved? You should consult other textbooks, such as [Yourdon, 1976] and [Kernighan and Plaugher, 1975], for detailed discussions of programming techniques; however, the following are key programming issues:

- *Structured programming:* Assuming that the programs are being written in a third or fourth generation language, a structured programming approach should be followed. This organizes all the program logic (decisions and loops) into nested combinations of IF-THEN-ELSE and DO-WHILE constructs. Almost all modern programming textbooks teach a structured programming approach; see, for example, [Wells, 1986], [Benton and Weekes, 1985], [Yourdon, Gane, and Sarson, 1976], and [Yourdon and Lister, 1977].

- *Small modules:* It is essential that programs be organized into small modules so that the programming logic will fit onto one page of a program listing. It is important to remember that the complexity of a program does not increase linearly with the size of the program: a 100-statement program will almost always be *more* than twice as complex as a 50-statement program. As we saw in Chapter 22, this is primarily under the control of the designer; but the designer might not be able to tell how large a module will be, especially if he is not familiar with the programming language that will be used on the project. Thus, the programmer may have to continue the design activity, breaking a module into lower-level submodules so that each one represents no more than about 50 programming statements.

- *Simplicity of style:* Many programming textbooks, such as [Yourdon, 1976] and [Kernighan and Plauger, 1975], have detailed guidelines for writing simple programs—programs that the average programmer can understand and that can be passed on to the maintenance programmer; among these guidelines is the suggestion that the programmer should try to avoid programming statements with compound Boolean expressions, for example,

IF A AND B OR NOT C AND D THEN ADD 3 TO X.

It is interesting to note that several mathematical models of program complexity have been developed during the past ten years; one of the more popular is McCabe's cyclomatic complexity model (see [McCabe, 1976]), which provides a quantitative measure of the intrinsic complexity of a program.[3] Some organizations are now insisting that all new programs be run through an automated complexity checker to ensure that they are not too complex.

23.5   TESTING

The process of testing is likely to take as much as half of the development schedule for your system, depending on how carefully the initial activities of analysis, design, and programming has been done. Even if a *perfect* job of systems analysis, design, and programming have been done, some effort must be done to verify that there are no errors. If, on the other hand, an imperfect job was done (as is almost always the case!), then the testing becomes iterative: the first round of testing exposes the presence of errors, and subsequent rounds of testing check to see if the corrected programs are now operating correctly.

What do you need to know about testing as a systems analyst? This will depend, of course, on how deeply involved you are in the process. In many cases, the systems analyst works closely with the user to develop a thorough, comprehensive set of test cases *based on the essential model and user implementation model of the system.* This process of developing acceptance test cases can be carried out in

---

3 For third generation languages like COBOL, the cyclomatic complexity is approximately equal to the number of IF statements in the program. For more on this, see [DeMarco, 1982].

parallel with the implementation activities of designing and programming, so that, when the programmers have finished writing their programs and carrying out their own local testing, the user/analyst team will be ready with their own test cases.

In addition to this basic concept (that the description of user requirements forms the basis of the final test cases), you should be familiar with different types of testing, as well as some concepts closely related to testing. These are discussed next.

23.5.1   Types of Testing

At this point, it might not have occurred to you that there is more than one type of testing: What more could be involved than just thinking of test cases and then checking to see if the system performs properly?

The first thing to realize is that there are different *strategies* of testing; the two most common strategies are known as bottom-up testing and top-down testing. The bottom-up approach begins by testing small, individual modules in a stand-alone fashion; this is often called unit testing, module testing, or program testing. Then individual modules are combined together into larger and larger units to be tested en masse; this is often referred to as subsystem testing. Finally, all the components of the system are combined together for testing; this is known as system testing, and it is often followed by acceptance testing, where the user is allowed to submit his own test cases to verify that the system is working properly.

The top-down testing approach begins with a skeleton of the system; that is, the testing strategy assumes that the top-level executive modules of the system have been developed, but that the lower-level modules exist only as dummy modules or stubs.[4] Because most of the detailed system functions have not been implemented, the initial tests are very limited; the purpose is simply to begin exercising the interfaces between major subsystems. Subsequent tests then become more and more comprehensive, exercising more and more detailed aspects of the system. The top-down approach to testing is generally considered a preferable approach for most systems today; for more details, see [Yourdon, 1986].

In addition to these basic concepts, you should be familiar with the following types of testing:

- *Functional testing:* This is the most common form of testing; its purpose is to ensure that the system performs its normal functions properly. Thus, test cases will be developed and entered into the system; the outputs (and the results of updated files) will be examined for correctness.

---

4 An example of a stub is a module that does no processing at all, but simply exits as soon as it is called; another example is a module that returns the same output parameters, regardless of the input parameters passed to it when it is invoked. Thus, the initial top-down testing of a payroll system might involve stub modules that pay everyone $100 per week, regardless of their job classification; the stub module for tax calculations might always deduct $10 in taxes from everyone's paycheck. The objective of the initial top-down test would be to simply determine whether the system can run at all and whether it is indeed capable of generating a series of $100 paychecks.

- *Recovery testing:* The purpose of this kind of testing is to ensure that the system can recover properly from various types of failures. This is particularly important on large on-line systems, as well as various types of real-time systems that may be controlling physical devices and/or manufacturing processes. Recovery testing may require the project team to simulate (or bring about) hardware failures, power failures, failures in the vendor operating system, and so on.

- *Performance testing:* The purpose of this kind of testing is to ensure that the system can handle the volume of data and incoming transactions specified in the user implementation model, as well as ensuring that it provides the response time required. This may require the project team to simulate a large network of on-line terminals, so that the system will be fooled into thinking that it is operating under a heavy load.

There is one last concept that you should be aware of: the notion of exhaustive testing. In the ideal project, we would generate test cases to cover every possible input and every possible combination of situations the system could ever face; we would then exhaustively test the system to ensure that its behavior would be perfect. There is only one problem with this: it doesn't work! The number of test cases for a typical large, complex system is so staggeringly large, often on the order of 10^{100} distinct test cases or more, that even if we could conduct one test every millisecond, it would take longer than the age of the universe to finish all the tests! Consequently, *nobody carries out truly exhaustive tests on anything other than a trivial system;* at best, the system developers can hope to create test cases that will exercise (or cover) a large percentage of the different decision paths that the system can take.[5] This makes it all the more important to ensure that the model of user requirements and the various implementation models are as correct as possible.

Suppose, for example, that one wanted to develop test cases for a portion of a system that calculates an employee's net pay, as shown in Figure 23.1. Assume that **gross pay** is defined in the data dictionary as an integer (i.e., a salary expressed in whole dollars) ranging from 0 to 10,000. Then it would appear that a truly exhaustive test would consist of specifying what the proper **net pay** *should* be for each of the 10,000 possibly **gross pay** amounts. Presumably, if our implementation team then carried out those 10,000 test cases and verified that the proper **net pay** was, in fact produced, we would be confident that the process was operating correctly.

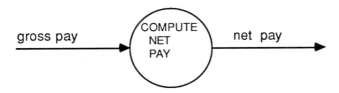

Figure 23.1: **A small portion of a system**

---

5 Detailed discussions of test coverage is provided by [Dunn, 1984] and [Myers, 1979].

But wait! What about potentially incorrect values of gross pay? What if the user provides a negative **gross pay**? What if he provides a **gross pay** of 100,000? Since there are potentially an infinite number of potential values of **gross pay**,[6] and since we have no knowledge of the internal behavior of the program that implements **COMPUTE NET PAY**, we are faced with an apparently infinite number of test cases. If the test cases are developed at the end of the analysis phase of the project, using the data dictionary and the process specification, then there is no way that we can know how the program will eventually work when the programmer writes the code; thus, we are forced to carry out a black box test.

If we *do* know the internal logic and structure of the program (i.e., after the programmer has written the code), then we can base the test cases on the existing program logic and carry out what is often called "glass box" or "white box" testing. We can generally demonstrate, for example, that if the program correctly identifies one value of **gross pay** less than zero, it will correctly identify all such negative **gross pays**. In general, we should be able to demonstrate that the program will exhibit consistent behavior for various *ranges* of gross pay, and thus reduce the number of required test cases to a manageable number. While this does not constitute exhaustive testing, we could presumably achieve a fairly high level of confidence that we had developed test cases for all of the significant paths that the program could take.

But wait! **COMPUTE NET PAY** is only one process, one bubble out of hundreds, or even thousands, in a large system. If it requires, say, 1000 test cases to verify that COMPUTE NET PAY is operating correctly (in terms of functional correctness), then it might well require 1000 tests for each of the other, say, 1000 processes in the system. The total number of distinct test cases, then, could be 1000 * 1000 = 1,000,000. And even this is conservative! (And it doesn't take into account the added dimension of complexity caused by throughput testing, recovery testing, etc.).

Thus, we must admit from the outset that exhaustive testing is impossible. But it is possible, as noted above, to choose test cases judiciously, in order to exercise as many logic paths as possible in the system. Even so, we must be prepared for a large, if not enormous, volume of testing. To carry out such testing effectively, the systems development team needs three things: test plans, test descriptions, and test procedures. A *test plan* is exactly what it sounds like, an organized document describing some testing activity. A typical test plan document will contain the following information:

- *Purpose of the test:* what the objective of the test is, and what part of the system is being tested.

- *Location and schedule of the test:* where and when it will be done.

---

6 Actually, the number of test cases is not infinite, because of the limited precision of numbers stored in the computer's memory. If a number is stored as an integer, a typical computer will allow a number as large as 2^{32}, or possibly 2^{64}, to be stored. If the number is stored as a floating point number, we may be able to represent numbers as large as 10^{100} or larger, but we will usually have only eight or nine significant digits of precision. So, this does not represent infinity, but it is a very, very large number nonetheless.

- *Test descriptions:* a description of the inputs that will be provided to the system, and the anticipated outputs and results. Descriptions of test inputs will usually be given in the data dictionary format discussed in Chapter 10.

- *Test procedures:* a description of how the test data are to be prepared and submitted to the system, how the output results are to be captured, how the test results will be analyzed, and any other operational procedures that must be observed.

23.5.2   Related Concepts

Though most organizations carry out testing in the manner discussed above, there are some related concepts that can be used to augment the standard process of testing. These include the following:

- Walkthroughs

- Inspections

- Proofs of correctness

Walkthroughs, which are discussed in Appendix D, are a form of peer-group review of technical products; they are widely used in the data processing industry to review dataflow diagrams (and other products of systems analysis), structure charts (and other products of design), as well as computer programs. While different from testing, their objective is the same: to discover possible errors in the system.

Inspections are similar to walkthroughs, but with a more formalized agenda of items that must be examined in the program (or in the specification or design, depending on the type of inspection) before it can be approved. To draw an analogy, consider what happens each year when your automobile is inspected: the auto mechanic has a specific checklist of features—brakes, headlights, exhaust emissions, and so on—that must be examined before he can put the appropriate sticker on your car.

Finally, there are a limited number of cases where formal *proofs of correctness* will be developed for a computer program; the process here is somewhat analogous to the process of developing geometry proofs that you once studied in high school. Unfortunately, it is extremely difficult and time consuming to develop a rigorous proof of correctness for computer programs, and it has rarely been done for anything larger than a few hundred program statements. However, at least one U.S. government project has developed a computer-assisted proof of correctness for a system involving approximately 10,000 program statements; while it cost nearly $500,000 and took 6 months of work, it could be justified for certain high-risk or high-security systems. For a discussion of proofs of correctness, see Chapter 6 of [Dunn, 1984] or the surveys in [Elspas et al, 1972], and [Dunlop and Basili, 1982].

23.6   MAINTAINING THE SPECIFICATION WHILE PROGRAMMING: A PRELUDE TO CHAPTER 24

As mentioned above, it is possible for the structured specification to change during the programming process. This may happen as a result of the fast-tracking strategy described above, or because the original specifications were wrong, or simply because the users change their mind about their requirement. In any case, it is a reality, and it highlights one important point: the system specification cannot be considered frozen after the systems analysis phase has been declared over. It must be considered a living document that will require ongoing maintenance *even before the system itself has entered the maintenance phase.* Chapter 24 discusses this issue in more detail.

23.7   WHAT HAPPENS AFTER TESTING?

You might think that your work is completely done when you have finished testing the system. Unfortunately, there is more to do, though you may not be involved in your role as systems analyst. However, someone (and often a large group of "someones") must carry out the final activities in a systems development project:

- Conversion

- Installation

- Training

Conversion is the task of translating the user's current files, forms, and databases to the format required by the new system. In some rare cases, this may not be a relevant activity, for there may not be any existing data. However, if the user is replacing a current system with a new system, this is likely to be a delicate and difficult task. A conversion plan needs to be developed, preferably as soon as the user implementation model is complete, to cover the following issues:

- If the user already has existing data associated with an existing system, he will probably want to use it until the last possible moment before "cutting over" to the new system. Thus, it is difficult to consider the existing data as static.

- There may be such a large volume of existing data that it will be impractical to considering converting it all at once. Files and records may have to be converted on an incremental, as needed basis. This will obviously require careful coordination and planning.

- The conversion should be carried out in an automated fashion; this can only be done if the current files and data exist in some automated form. If so, it should be relatively straightforward to write a computer program (or to use an existing vendor-supplied package) to translate the current files into the format required for the new system. However, it sometimes turns out to be rather difficult to convert the data in an automated form, especially if the existing files are located on several different computers, in different formats, and so on. Indeed, developing the conversion software can turn out to be a major systems development project of its own!

*   The existing data may contain errors; indeed, if the existing data were created manually and have been maintained manually, you can be virtually *certain* that there will be errors. Thus, part of the process of conversion is that of error detection and error correction, which can make the process even more difficult and time consuming. Some existing files and records may turn out to be illegible or incomprehensible; in other cases, it may be obvious that the existing data are wrong, but it may not be clear what the correct values are.

*   In addition to converting existing files, it may be necessary to convert existing programs and procedures. In some cases, existing programs and procedures can be used in their present form; in other cases, they will have to be thrown away and completely replaced.

Installation of the new system may be an instantaneous affair, but it is often a major task. Usually, the following things must be done:

*   Computer site preparation must precede the installation of the new system, usually by several months. This involves building or leasing a computer facility with appropriate power, space, lighting, and environmental controls (temperature, humidity, dust, static electricity, etc.). This is often done in conjunction with the computer hardware vendor or with the organization's computer operations department.

*   User site preparation may also be required, especially in the case of on-line systems that have terminals and printers in the user's work area. In the simple case, terminals can be distributed to the user's work area just before the system is installed; in some cases, though, an entirely new workspace environment may have to be constructed (consider, for example, an airline reservation terminal at an airport).

*   Hardware installation, assuming that the new system requires its own computer hardware, is usually carried out by the hardware vendor; multiple vendors are sometimes involved, especially in the case of on-line and real-time systems. In the case of a simple system developed for a personal computer, installation may be as simple as taking the computer out of a box and plugging it in.

*   Software installation, which involves loading all the computer programs that were written for the new system onto the appropriate computer(s) and making them ready for operation.

Keep in mind that the scenario described above presumes that there is only one installation at a single site. But this is often not the case; for a large, distributed system, there may be a single, centralized computer site and dozens or even hundreds of user sites. Thus, it may be necessary to install the system in stages, with specially trained installation teams visiting each user site according to a prearranged schedule. In this case, installation and "cutover" to the new system cannot take place in one fell swoop, but must instead be phased in over a period of days, weeks, or even months.

Training is the final task of the systems development team: training of the users (obviously!), as well as training of the operations personnel, maintenance programmers, and various levels of management. A training plan should be developed early in the project, for there is a great deal of work to be done, and it needs to be ready at the same time (if not earlier than) the system is ready to go into operation. The training plan should deal with the following issues:

- How will the training be carried out? Most systems development projects rely on *user manuals* and *reference guides* to provide written documentation for the users. However, live classes and seminars may be appropriate, as well as orientation briefings for managers and others who need to be aware of the system even though they will not interact with it every day. And, with current technology, there is a wide range of choices for training media: videotape and videodisk training, computer-based training, and even mock-up versions of the actual system so that users can try entering transactions and learn how to interact with the system.

  In the extreme case, the training may consist of extremely sophisticated help facilities built into the system itself. This is becoming more and more popular with the proliferation of personal computers, but it is not very practical for large systems that interact with a large, diverse user community; on the other hand, it can be used to augment and reinforce other forms of training.

- Who will do the training? In some cases, members of the systems development team participate in the training process, especially since they are presumed to be the best experts on how the system works. However, keep in mind that the best programmer (or systems analyst) is not always the best trainer; indeed, the developers often behave in a very defensive fashion if the users begin asking what they consider to be hostile questions. Also, the developers are (almost by definition) terribly busy with the designing, coding, and testing of the system until the very last minute; the systems analysts may have more time available after the essential model and user implementation model have been finished.

- Who will be trained and on what schedule? Obviously, the users need training before they can begin using the system; on the other hand, it is not effective to train them six months before they will see the new system. So the training must be done in a fairly condensed period of time; but this, in turn, will often interfere with the normal day-to-day work that the users are trying to accomplish. A careful schedule of training activities must therefore be negotiated with the users.

23.8 SUMMARY

This chapter has covered a wide range of topics: programming, testing, conversion, installation, and training. Space does not provide the opportunity for a detailed coverage of these topics, but the brief coverage provided in this chapter should give the systems analyst an overview of these final activities in the systems development project. Additional details can be found in the many references at the end of the chapter.

REFERENCES

1. Edward Yourdon, *Managing the Systems Life Cycle,* 2nd ed. Englewood Cliffs, N.J.: Prentice-Hall, 1988.

2. Edward Yourdon, *Nations at Risk.* New York: YOURDON Press, 1986.

3. Edward Yourdon, *Techniques of Program Structure and Design, 2nd ed.* Englewood Cliffs, N.J.: Prentice-Hall, 1976.

4. Brian Kernighan and P.J. Plauger, *The Elements of Programming Style.* Reading, Mass.: Addison-Wesley, 1975.

5. Timothy Wells, *Structured Systems Development in COBOL.* New York: YOURDON Press, 1986.

6. Timothy Wells, *Structured Systems Development in BASIC.* New York: YOURDON Press, 1985.

7. Timothy Wells, *Structured Systems Development in Pascal.* New York: YOURDON Press, 1986.

8. Stan Benton and Leonard Weekes, *Program It Right: Structured Programming in BASIC.* New York: YOURDON Press, 1985.

9. Edward Yourdon, Chris Gane, and Trish Sarson, *Learning to Program in Structured COBOL, Part I.* New York: YOURDON Press, 1976.

10. Edward Yourdon and Timothy Lister, *Learning to Program in Structured COBOL, Part II.* New York: YOURDON Press, 1977.

11. Tom DeMarco, *Controlling Software Projects.* New York: YOURDON Press, 1982.

12. Glenford Myers, *The Art of Software Testing.* New York: Wiley, 1979.

13. Tom McCabe, "A Complexity Measure," *IEEE Transactions on Software Engineering,* Volume SE-2, Number 12 (December 1976), pp. 308-320.

14. Edward Yourdon, *Managing the Structured Techniques,* 3rd ed. New York: YOURDON Press, 1986.

15. Robert Dunn, *Software Defect Removal.* New York: McGraw-Hill, 1984.

16. B. Elspas and others, "An Assessment of Techniques for Proving Program Correctness," *ACM Computing Surveys,* Vol. 4 (June 1972), pp. 97-147.

17. D. Dunlop and V. Basili, "A Comparative Analysis of Functional Correctness," *ACM Computing Surveys,* Vol. 14 (June 1982), pp. 229-244.

QUESTIONS AND EXERCISES

1. What activities in a systems development project commence when design has finished?

2. What are the six reasons why the systems analyst may need to remain involved with a project during the programming and testing activities?

3. If the systems analyst is also the project leader, do you think it is important for him or her to be familiar with programming techniques and testing strategies? Why or why not?

4. In your organization, are systems analysts also expected to participate in the design and programming activities? Do you think this is a good idea? Why or why not?

5. Why is the systems analyst likely to be involved in the development of test data for a system? Who else is likely to be involved?

6. What should the systems analyst do if the programmers ask to change the system specification during the programming phase of the project?

7. What should the systems analyst do if the users ask to change the requirements of the system after the programmers have begun implementing the system? How likely a situation do you think this is?

8. Why is it possible that a user will want to change the system requirements after the analysis phase of the project has ended?

9. What difficulties can be expected if a senior systems analyst is expected to carry out *all* the work of systems analysis in a project?

10. What kind of negative reaction might be expected from programmers in an organization if systems analysts carry out all of the detailed specification activities discussed throughout this book?

11. What kind of organizational structure could be set up to accommodate the combination of senior people/junior people and high-level/low-level technical activities in a project?

12. If systems analysis and systems design activities have been carried out completely and in detail, can the programming aspects be automated? Why or why not? Do you think this situation is likely to change in the next 5 to 10 years?

13. Is it necessary to carry out all the systems analysis activities *to completion* before the work of programming begins? Why or why not?

14. What does fast tracking mean?

15. In what other industries besides the systems development industry is fast-tracking practiced?

16. What is a conservative approach to implementing a system? What is a radical approach?

17. What are the three major reasons why a project manager might adopt a radical approach to systems implementation?

18. Why can't the system specification be considered frozen at the end of the systems analysis phase of the project?

24 MAINTAINING THE SPECIFICATION

Up to now, the key computer professional was someone who could learn enough about the needs of organizations to express them in computer language. In the future, as our society becomes irrevocably computerized, the key professional [will be] someone who can learn enough about computerized systems to express them in human language. Without that someone, we [will] have lost control of our society. That someone is the reverse engineer. Software maintainers are the reverse engineers of society.

Nicholas Zvegintzov, publisher,
Software Maintenance News

In this chapter, you will learn:

1. Why it is important to keep a specification up to date.

2. What kind of changes need to be made to a specification.

For many systems analysts, the project is over when the structured specification has been finished and accepted by the user. At this point, the specification is delivered to an implementation team of designers and programmers who will build a system from the specification.

Of course, some systems analysts remain with the project through the design and implementation phases. Sometimes the systems analyst serves as a project manager, guiding and directing the efforts of the implementation team. Sometimes the systems analyst remains with the project to continue doing systems analysis, that is, to continue serving as an intermediary between the user and the implementation team. And the systems analyst may also be involved in the development of user manuals, acceptance test data, installation planning, and a variety of other complementary activities that can take place concurrently with the implementation process.

However, almost all systems analysts leave the project after development has been completed and the new system is put into operation. Some programmers will remain to carry out maintenance activities, but when the development phase finishes, the party is over, and most of the systems analysts, designers, and programmers will move on to new projects (and often new companies, where they can get a larger salary than their current employer will pay!).

But the work done by the systems analyst (all the work discussed throughout this book) continues to be important. Just as the computer *programs* must be maintained during the 5, 10, or 20 years of the operational life of the system, so the *specification* must be maintained as well. Or, to put it another way, various aspects of the *implementation* of the system will be changed during the system's lifetime, and for each of those changes an appropriate, corresponding change must be made to the specification.

Though the original systems analyst may not remain with the project during its operational lifetime, it is important for him or her to leave behind a legacy that *can* be maintained. This chapter discusses the maintenance of the system specification.

24.1   WHY IT'S IMPORTANT

At this point, you may be rather puzzled; after all, you may be thinking, it's perfectly obvious that the system specification be kept up to date. Why would anyone do things differently? Unfortunately, the history of the systems development field suggests otherwise: the vast majority, probably more than 80%, of systems currently in operation do not have an accurate, up-to-date statement of the user requirements that the system is carrying out.

This is not a phenomenon unique to the computer field. How many century-old houses have up-to-date documents describing the wiring, plumbing, heating, and other architectural details? The simple truth is that it's often a lot easier to make a "quick-and-dirty" correction, improvement, or change to an existing system than it is to begin by changing the requirements document and then propagating that change through the design document and the implementation itself. This is especially true if the change needs to be made to fix an immediate, pressing, urgent problem.[1] "We'll get around to changing the documentation later," the maintenance person will say, "but first we have to fix the problem itself." Documentation is the last thing that anyone wants to do, and often it never gets done at all.

Information systems have an important characteristic when it comes to maintenance: they last longer than the developers or the users who were involved in the original development of the system. This is true of houses, too; neither the architect nor the end user of a Victorian townhouse built in the 1880s is available for consultation today. And it is true of many information systems, too; after 10 or 20 years, the system is being used by third-generation users (some of whom may have no idea why the system was developed in the first place) and is being maintained by

---

[1] A survey in [Lientz and Swanson, 1980] showed that approximately 9% of all maintenance work consists of "emergency program fixes."

third-generation maintenance programmers (some of whom may have no idea why the original developers adopted a particular design strategy).[2] This is why Nicholas Zvegintzov describes maintenance programmers as the "reverse engineers of society."

There is something else important about information systems: they tend to be complex from the outset, and they grow increasingly complex as they undergo years of maintenance. If a system were simple (e.g., 250 Pascal statements), then it could be maintained easily even if it had no documentation. But a typical system has at least 100,000 program statements; many of the larger systems presently being maintained have well over 500,000 statements; and some have over one million statements. No one person can understand the complexity of such a system, *especially* if (1) he or she was not involved in the development of the original system, and (2) the requirements and design of the original system were not documented. And yet that is exactly what we ask most of our maintenance programmers to do.[3]

There are dozens, if not hundreds, of examples of organizations with severe maintenance problems of the sort described above. Virtually every major organization that began computerizing 20 years ago is now faced with 20-year-old systems whose implementation is a mystery and, far worse, whose user requirements are a mystery.

The only solution to this crisis in the future is to maintain accurate, up-to-date documentation for as long as the system itself survives. But how do we do this?

24.2   NECESSARY PREREQUISITES

We can't keep a system and its associated documentation up to date if the documentation isn't accurate to begin with. So this is the starting point: we *must* ensure that when a new system is put into operation, all the related documents are complete, consistent, accurate, and up-to-date.

Throughout this book, we have discussed the characteristics of an accurate model of user requirements, as well as guidelines for ensuring that the system model is complete and internally consistent. In order for ongoing maintenance to be successful, these guidelines must be enforced, and an independent person or group must certify that the documentation is accurate before the system is put into operation.

In addition to certifying that the documents themselves are accurate, we must ensure that there is a mechanism for making ongoing changes to the documents. It will do us no good if the structured specification has been permanently enscribed with

---

2 A study by the British computer manufacturer ICL in the 1970s indicated that the typical system was maintained by *seven generations* of maintenance programmers before it was finally scrapped. This suggests that much of what we call maintenance programming would be more accurately described as archaeology.

3 One of the more extreme examples of a large, complex system with ongoing maintenance requirements is the Space Station project currently under development by NASA. Its charter: to colonize and industrialize the nearby solar system. Its development schedule: 30 years. And it will need *permanent* maintenance.

a stainless steel stylus on stone tablets as a permanent record for future generations; the specification must be seen as a living document, subject to constant, though controlled, change.

24.3   HOW TO DO IT

The first and most fundamental rule of systems maintenance is this: *any* proposed change to the existing operational system must, in all cases, begin with an examination of the impact on the system's specification of requirements. This must be done in *all* of the cases illustrated next, together with any other proposed system change:

- The user decides that she or he would like a new function added to the current system.

- The user is unhappy with the way some current function is carried out and wants to change it.

- The user wants a new output report in addition to those he already has.

- The user wants to modify the format or organization of an existing output report.

- The maintenance programmers wish to recode a module in order to make it more efficient.

- The operations department has announced that they plan to upgrade the organization's computer systems and that certain programming changes will be necessary.

- The user complains that the system produces incorrect output for a certain combination of inputs.

- The systems development organization has decided that Ada will be adopted as the new, standard programming language. Plans are being made to convert all existing software to Ada.

- The system is required to send output reports to a new government agency, one that did not exist when the system was originally developed.

Any such change must be illustrated, documented, and verified with the user by making the appropriate changes on the system model. This is usually done by filling out a form known as a system change request. The maintenance change may involve any or all of the following:

- New terminators may need to be added to the context diagram, or old terminators may need to be eliminated. Dataflows between the system and the terminators may need be added, deleted, or changed. Functions carried out previously by terminators may now be carried out within the system; conversely, functions carried out by the system may now be considered outside the system and within the domain of a terminator.

- New events may need to be added to the event list, or existing events may need to be deleted.

- If the change is substantial, the statement of purpose in the environmental model may need to be changed.

- The dataflow models, entity-relationship models, and/or state-transition models may need to be modified.

- The process specifications and the data dictionary may need to be refined or modified.

- Various aspects of the user implementation model, involving the person-machine interface, the implementation constraints dealing with response time, and so on, may need to be changed.

Any such change will not be free. It is possible that some changes will be minimal and will require only a few minutes of work to incorporate—only a few minutes to make the necessary changes to the specification *and* the existing computer programs. However, the person or group making the change has an obligation to go through the exercise of writing an *impact statement:* a precise and detailed statement of the changes that will need to be made to the system specification in order to implement the proposed change. Along with this, there should be an economic impact statement: a statement of the cost of making the change and the estimated benefit to be derived from the change. This is particularly important if the maintenance activity will change the *scope* of the system.

Of course, there will be some changes that have *no* impact on the system specification: a programming correction to fix a bug, a coding change to enhance the readability or efficiency of the existing system, or a change of the existing computer hardware or systems software (compiler, operating system, database management system, etc.). However, even in these cases, an economic impact statement should be generated so that the user and the systems development organization will understand the costs and benefits associated with the change.

Any change in the system will typically result in a change to the software and/or the hardware of the system; it may also result in a change to the user manuals, operating procedures, and various other components of the system. *But by far the most important document to keep up to date is the statement of user requirements!* Without it, future changes and modifications will become more and more difficult to make; and the change to an altogether new system will be infinitely more expensive, time consuming, and painful than it should be.

No doubt this plea for an up-to-date system specification would be viewed with a jaundiced eye by a veteran systems analyst with 20 years experience. After all, the process of systems analysis has been so difficult for so many years, and the task of developing an accurate system specification has been so difficult, that the notion of keeping it permanently up to date seems almost ludicrous.

The answer, in the long run, will be automation. Automated systems analysis workstations of the sort described in Appendix A are now available at affordable costs, and they represent a dramatic improvement over the technology used by most systems analysts today, just as word processing systems represent a dramatic improvement over the electric typewriter of the 1960s. More ambitious plans are underway to develop all-encompassing, integrated software engineering environments that will serve as a central repository for *all* the documents associated with the development of a system. However, such advanced technology will probably not be fully developed until the mid-1990s.

However, there is much to be done even with the technology available today. There is simply no excuse for making a change to an existing system without making the corresponding change to the system specification. To make this work, though, requires strong, disciplined management within the MIS organization.

24.4   SUMMARY

There is a growing body of literature on the subject of software maintenance, as well as at least one professional society (the Software Maintenance Association) concerned with issues of maintenance. However, most current emphasis is on the management and refurbishing of existing programs; there is also some emphasis on the use of good design techniques to create maintainable programs. But the systems development industry is only now beginning to realize that without maintainable *specifications* we will never have maintainable software.

REFERENCES

1. Bennet Lientz and B. Swanson, *Software Maintenance Management*. Reading, Mass.: Addison-Wesley, 1980.

2. James Martin and Carma McClure, *Software Maintenance: The Problem and Its Solution*. Englewood Cliffs, N.J.: Prentice-Hall, 1983.

3. Girish Parikh, editor, *Techniques of Program and Systems Maintenance*. Lincoln, Neb.: Ethnotech, Inc., 1980.

4. Carma McClure, *Managing Software Development and Maintenance*. New York: Van Nostrand Reinhold, 1981.

5. Robert Glass and R.A. Noiseux, *Software Maintenance Guidebook*. Englewood Cliffs, N.J.: Prentice-Hall, 1981.

6. Ned Chapin, "Software Maintenance with fourth-generation Languages," *ACM Software Engineering Notes*, Volume 9, Number 1, January 1984, pp. 41-42.

7. R.N. Britcher and J.J. Craig, "Using Modern Design Practices to Upgrade Aging Software Systems," *IEEE Software*, Volume 3, Number 3, May 1986, pp. 16-24.

8. Salah Bendifallah and Walt Scacchi, "Understanding Maintenance Work," *IEEE Transactions on Software Engineering,* Volume SE-13, Number 3, March 1987.

QUESTIONS AND EXERCISES

1. Why is it necessary to maintain a system specification even after the system has been fully developed?

2. Why are maintenance programmers tempted to make changes to an operational system without updating the associated specification documents?

3. Research Project: Find out the average age of the systems currently in operation in your organization. Even more interesting, find out how much longer they are expected to continue operating before they are replaced with new systems.

4. Research Project: Find out how many of the systems currently in operation have up-to-date specifications. Are the users and managers in your organization aware of these statistics?

5. What difficulties are caused if a system is being used by users and maintained by programmers who were not involved in the original system development ?

6. Give six examples of the kind of changes that a user might want to make to an operational system.

7. Why is it possible that new terminators might have to be added to the context diagram during maintenance of a system?

8. Why is it possible that new events might have to be added to the event list during maintenance of a system?

9. Under what conditions might the statement of purpose for a system have to be changed during maintenance?

10. What is an impact statement? Why is it important?

11. Why has it been difficult to keep the systems analysis documents (the essential model of the system) up to date in most organizations?

12. What kind of technological development is likely to be needed in order to ensure that systems analysis documents *will* be kept up to date?

25 THE FUTURE OF
STRUCTURED ANALYSIS

> All attempts to predict the future in any detail appear ludicrous within a
> few years. This book has a more realistic, yet at the same time, more
> ambitious, aim. It does not try to describe *the* future, but to define the
> boundaries within which possible futures must lie. If we regard the ages
> that stretch ahead of us as an unmapped and unexplored country, what I
> am attempting to do is to survey its frontiers and to get some idea of its
> extent. The detailed geography of the interior must remain unknown—
> until we reach it.
>
> Arthur C. Clarke, *Profiles of the Future*

Throughout this book, we have seen an evolution of ideas and techniques in
the field of systems analysis. They fall into three broad periods of time:

1. Conventional systems analysis, prior to the mid-1970s, characterized (if it
    was done at all) by narrative Victorian novel specifications that were hard
    to read, hard to understand, and virtually impossible to maintain.

2. Classical structured analysis, from the mid-1970s to the mid-1980s, as
    described in [DeMarco, 1978], [Gane and Sarson, 1977], and others. This
    was characterized by early versions of graphical models, and an emphasis
    on the modeling of current implementations of a system before modeling
    the new system.

3. Modern structured analysis, as described in this book and recent books
    such as [Ward and Mellor, 1985] and [McMenamin and Palmer, 1984].

This chapter summarizes some of the major changes that have taken place
since the introduction of classical structured analysis in the late 1970s, and to use this
as a starting point for discussing likely changes over the next 5 to 10 years.

25.1   WHAT HAS CHANGED

Several aspects of structured analysis have gradually changed over the past
ten years. The major areas of change include the following:

- *Terminology changes.* We now use the term environmental model as a way of describing what used to be called just a context diagram. This is because classical structured analysis did not include an event list as part of the formal system model. Also, we now use the term *essential* instead of *logical* to describe a model which concentrates on *what* the system has to do, and the term *implementation* instead of *physical* to describe a model that concentrates on *how* the system will be developed. These are obviously minor changes, but they have helped reduce confusion when talking with users who wonder whether the opposite of a logical system is an illogical system.

- *Event partitioning.* One of the more significant developments in structured analysis, which we discussed in Chapters 20 and 21, is the use of an event list to guide the initial development of the behavioral model. This replaces the approach of strict top-down partitioning of the context diagram to a top-level dataflow diagram (Figure 0), and from Figure 0 to lower levels, and so on. While the top-down approach is not wrong in any sense of the word, it has been difficult for many systems analysts to practice; the event partitioning approach, which is a middle-out approach, has proved more successful in many analysis projects.

- *De-emphasis of current physical modeling.* As Chapter 17 pointed out, there are a number of reasons why the systems analyst might be tempted to model the current implementation of a system. But time and again we have found that it is a dangerous temptation and that the systems analyst spends far more time engaged in this activity than it warrants. While we don't outlaw the current physical model, we do discourage and de-emphasize it. Modern structured analysis emphasizes the development, as early as possible, of an essential model of the user's *new* system.

- *Real-time modeling tools.* Classical structured analysis was primarily intended for the development of straightforward business systems; it made no provision for interrupts, signals, or timing issues. However, many of today's complex systems do include a variety of real-time issues, and the structured analysis modeling tools have been extended accordingly. Control flows and control processes have been used to augment dataflow diagrams; and *state-transition diagrams* have been introduced as a new modeling tool to illuminate the time-dependent requirements of a system.

- *Closer integration of process modeling and data modeling.* Classical structured analysis used *data structure diagrams* to model the relationships between stores on the dataflow diagram. However, the relationships were often obscured by the notation, and the notation tended to foster intense discussions and debates about the design and implementation of the *physical* data base. The entity-relationship diagram presented in this book provides a more logical or conceptual model of the data required by the system, and it allows the relationships between data entities to be described rigorously and in detail. Also, the balancing rules discussed in Chapter 14 ensure that the data model (documented with ERDs) is fully consistent and compatible with the process model (documented with DFDs and process specifications).

It is important for you to be familiar with these changes, for you may find yourself working for an organization that has *not* yet incorporated the changes into their standards; in 1987, when this book was being written, many large organizations that I visited throughout the United States were still using systems development methods that were at least 10 years old.

25.2   FUTURE DEVELOPMENTS IN STRUCTURED ANALYSIS

No one can profess to know the future in any detail; the most we can hope for, as Arthur C. Clarke points out in the introduction to this chapter, is to find some signposts to the future. Recent developments suggest a number of trends that are likely to continue well into the next decade. They include the following:

25.2.1   More Widespread Awareness of Systems Analysis

Computers, as we all know, are becoming a ubiquitous part of everyone's life. Consequently, we are finding that a larger and larger part of society is learning to use computers and talk about computers; more importantly (in the context of this book), many people are becoming increasingly familiar with structured analysis and other aspects of software engineering. I am especially interested in the future impact of structured analysis on three groups: top management in our business and government organizations, children, and computer professionals in Third World countries.

In most large organizations, one typically finds that the top levels of management are people in their late 40's, or 50's, or 60's. This means that they received their education and spent the formative years of their career 20 or 30 or even 40 years ago. Computers certainly existed 20 years ago (even 30 years ago!), but they were not widely available and they were not part of the technology or culture that people grew up with. But that is beginning to change; we are beginning to see senior levels of management who either (1) began their career in the data processing or MIS organization,[1] or (2) began their career in some other part of the organization (e.g., accounting, sales, or manufacturing) whose day-to-day operation was dramatically affected by computer technology. This means that you can expect, as a systems analyst, that top management will be increasingly aware of the strategic importance of information processing systems in their organization, and they will be increasingly interested in seeing high-level models of major new systems. If you tried to show a dataflow diagram to the CEO of your organization today, chances are that he would not understand it and would not understand why he *should* understand it. Within the next 5 years, I believe that top management will come to realize that it is just as important to be able to read (and critique) a system model as it is to read and critique a balance sheet or profit and loss statement.

---

[1] Three examples of this are John Reed, the current Chairman of Citicorp; Richard Crandall, head of American Airlines; and Frank Lautenberg, formerly Chairman of ADP (the payroll services company) and presently one of the two U.S. Senators from New Jersey. There are also several former programmers and systems analysts who are members of Congress.

Children will also become more and more familiar with structured analysis over the next several years. Already structured programming and structured design are being taught at the high school level in some parts of the United States. Structured analysis, once the subject of graduate level seminars, is now being taught at the third year and fourth year of undergraduate computer science and business school curricula, and will soon be part of a standard first-year college subject. Long division was once a college subject and is now taught regularly to young children; similarly, structured analysis will be a topic that children learn during their normal educational process.

It has been estimated that a child born in 1980 will graduate from secondary school toward the end of this century having written 10,000 lines of code; this is equivalent to roughly two years of full-time programming experience for today's adult programmer. Along with all this programming experience, we can expect that the current generation children will have more and more experience with systems design and systems analysis. Not all this generation will end up choosing a career as a programmer or systems analyst; indeed, only a small fraction will choose such a career path. But the rest of today's children, whether they choose to be accountants or engineers, salespeople, teachers, or politicians, will form a community of *intelligent end users* of information systems; users will know much more about what to expect from a systems analyst and what to ask of a systems analyst. Much of our present work, predicated, it seems, on the difficulty of dealing with ignorant users, may be superfluous in the future.

There is one other aspect of the growing awareness of structured analysis that we should mention: the impact on Third World software industries. Over the past decade, international competition in a variety of manufacturing industries has become more and more intense, and American industries have often lost competitive ground (or gone out of business) when faced with Japanese, Korean, Chinese, or Brazilian industries offering a high-quality product at a competitive price. *The same phenomenon is beginning to happen in the systems development industry.* Software engineering techniques, including the structured analysis techniques discussed in this book, can help the competitive organization develop systems with a productivity ten times higher than that of many American organizations and with a level of quality (expressed in mean time between failure or number of bugs) *one hundred times higher* than that of comparative American organizations.[2] And since, to a larger and larger degree, *all* our products and *all* our services depend on computer-based information systems, this has profound implications for all of American industry.

25.2.2   Proliferation of Automated Tools

Throughout this book, we have mentioned the possibility of using workstation-based tools to automate various aspects of structured analysis, especially the labor-intensive activities of creating graphical system models and checking them for completeness and correctness.

---

2 For a discussion of this, see D. Tajima and T. Matsubara, "The Computer Industry in Japan," *Computer,* Volume 14, No. 5 (May 1981), pp.89-96.

Appendix A describes the features of many such analyst toolkits that were available on the market in the 1987 timeframe, as well as the features that are likely to be added to commercial products over the next few years. The point is that these products exist *now,* and they will become increasingly powerful over the next decade.

But few systems analysts are using these tools today. In 1987, it was estimated that less than 2% of the systems analysts in North America and Europe had convenient personal access to an appropriate automated tool. This means that the typical systems development organization has one or two workstation units to draw dataflow diagrams, entity-relationship diagrams, and so on. These workstations may be shared by the entire organization of a hundred or more people, but are more often used by an isolated project team that had the luck, tenacity, or foresight to invest in this technology.

By 1990, it is estimated that approximately 10% of the systems analysts in North America and Europe (and other civilized parts of the world, too) will have their own personal workstations. And by the middle of the 1990s it is reasonable to expect that at least 50% of the analysts will have their own workstations. When we have reached this critical mass it will be reasonable to argue that our approach to systems analysis will have fundamentally changed, because the majority of practicing systems analysts will have powerful new tools. To draw an analogy: it is interesting to talk about the improvements that can be achieved in the field of carpentry by using a power saw instead of a hand saw, but the issue is moot if only 1% of the carpenters have electricity. And the power of the tool does indeed affect the way we work with the world around us; Craig Brod made this point very eloquently in a classic book called *Technostress* ([Brod, 1984]):

> Tools have always set in motion great changes within human societies. Tools create us as much as we create them. The spear, for example, did much more than extend a hunter's reach; it changed the hunter's gait and use of his arms. It encouraged better eye-hand coordination; it led to social organizations for tracking, killing and retrieving large prey. It widened the gap between the unskilled hunter and the skilled hunter and made pooling of information more important as hunting excursions became more complex. There were other, less obvious effects: changes in the diets of hunting societies led to sharing of food and the formation of new social relationships. The value of craftsmanship increased. People began to plan ahead, storing weapons for reuse. All of these new tool-related demands, in turn, spurred greater development of the brain. Brain complexity led to new tools, and new tools made yet more complex brains advantageous to the survival of the species.

It seems evident at this point that the technology of automated tools will continue to advance during the next 10 years. The analyst's toolkit of the mid-1990s will almost certainly have sophisticated error-checking features, as well as the ability to generate code and even suggest (using artificial intelligence techniques) possibilities for reusing code from software libraries.

25.2.3   The Impact of Maintenance Disasters

In the previous chapter, we discussed the user of the structured analysis model to facilitate ongoing maintenance and modification of systems. But this is an issue that often seems abstract, philosophical, and *politically unimportant* during the development phase of a project, when the primary emphasis seems to be getting the system delivered to the user. Preferably a working system; hopefully the system the user wanted. But, failing that, *any* system that appears to work and appears to satisfy at least some of the user requirements. The simple political reality is this: the importance of structured analysis and formal, rigorous system models has not been fully appreciated by many senior managers in our organizations. Even within the ranks of EDP management, structured analysis doesn't have the same "gut-level" sense of urgency as the political necessity of delivering a working (or allegedly working) system on time to the user.

As I suggested above, this situation may change as the user population becomes more familiar with computer technology and as competition from Third World countries becomes more intense. But there is another phenomenon that will dramatically highlight the need for current, up-to-date system models that are maintained as diligently as the source code: *maintenance disasters that that will cause current systems to collapse.*

In the extreme case, this may happen because an existing system—a large, complex, undocumented system—aborts or comes to a standstill, with no one able to figure out how to repair it. But this is unlikely; it is more likely that the *cause* of the failure will be identified and simply outlawed. The word will go out, "You can't enter a type X25 transaction into the system any more because it causes problems."

No, the likely cause of a major maintenance disaster will be the *total impossibility of making a necessary, urgent modification to an existing system.* Such changes are often mandated by new legislation or government policy; but they may also be required because of changes to the business environment or competitive situation.

Already many organizations are faced with this problem; many of their systems designed in the late 1960s or early 1970s are on the verge of collapse, and one day they *will* collapse. Part of the problem will be related to the *implementation* of the system, that is, coding that has been patched and repatched so many times that it is no longer possible to determine accurately *how* the system operates.

But the larger problem, in my opinion, is that nobody knows or remembers *what* these systems are really supposed to do. Third-generation maintenance programmers are now interacting with third-generation users to discuss potential changes to a system whose original requirements are a mystery to both. In this environment, it is inevitable that the maintenance programmers will eventually throw up their hands and refuse to make any more changes.

When faced with a problem like this, top management is likely to have a "knee-jerk" reaction: committees will be formed, standards will be imposed, and new procedures will be promulgated. Just as we have seen government leaders react to problems of toxic waste, oil spills, corruption, and a number of other problems only *after* a major disaster occurs, I believe that a number of top business and government managers will react to the problem of nonexistent system models only after a major maintenance problem occurs.

25.2.4   The Marriage of Structured Analysis and Artificial Intelligence

As this book is being written, an enormous amount of attention is being devoted throughout business, government, and the computer industry to artificial intelligence (AI): expert systems, natural language systems, robotics, and many related fields. Though AI was once considered an academic subject with little practical application, and though it was once implemented on exotic hardware with unfamiliar programming languages like LISP and PROLOG, it is now becoming more and more of a mainstream topic—particularly the area of expert systems, those systems that can replicate the behavior of human experts in certain narrowly defined fields.

More and more AI software packages and textbooks are available for COBOL-based environments and PC-based environments (see, for example, [Taylor, 1985], [Derfler, 1985], [Webster, 1985], [Keller, 1986], and [Rose, 1985]). More and more AI applications, ranging from medical diagnosis to oil exploration to stock portfolio evaluation to tax planning, are finding their way into the mainstream business world.[3]

What does this have to do with structured analysis? The connection between artificial intelligence and expert systems works in both directions: structured analysis can help in the process of building an expert system, and expert system technology can help in the process of doing structured analysis.

When building an expert system, three aspects of the system are often dominant: the person-machine interface, the knowledge representation, and the inference engine that evaluates and interrogates the knowledge base. The person-machine interface may involve natural-language (English, French, German, etc.) input and a combination of graphics, text, and sound for output. The knowledge base may be expressed as a series of **IF-THEN-ELSE** rules or as a series of frames.[4] And the inference engine may be based on a forward-chaining or backward-chaining approach and may be implemented with a vendor-supplied "expert shell."

But the significant thing about all this is that the expert system components are now becoming just a part of a larger system, for example, an operational system that feeds and updates the knowledge base or that uses the output of the expert system component to carry on other system functions. Thus, the modeling tools of structured analysis may be used to help model the overall system. But more important, it means that during the next 5 to 10 years, you will have to become familiar with the technology of expert systems and artificial systems in order to be a successful systems analyst. Keller's book ([Keller, 1986]) is a good place to start, for it shows many of the interactions between structured analysis and expert systems.

---

3 A large amount of artificial work is still carried out on specialized computer hardware, using specialized programming languages such as Lisp and Prolog. However, (1) most companies would prefer to integrate their AI applications with the other applications that they run on their standard IBM mainframe hardware, (2) most programmers would rather use such familiar languages as COBOL than such esoteric languages as Prolog, and (3) the business-oriented AI applications will have to tap into the knowledge base, *which already exists on the mainframe computer.*

4 See [Keller, 1986] for a description of frames.

In a reverse sense, AI can assist the *process* of structured analysis by acting as a tutor to guide a junior analyst through the various steps and processes described in this book. One could easily imagine, for instance, an "analyst's assistant" that would ask a series of questions of the human analyst and then produce a proposed context diagram or event list. Just think: can you remember, now that you have reached the end of this book, all of the rules and guidelines of the past several hundred pages? Do you think you'll remember them all a year from now? Wouldn't it be nice to have an expert system available in a PC that could remind you how to draw DFDs, ERDs, and STDs that are all properly balanced.

While all this sounds very exciting, you should not be concerned that expert systems are doing to do away with human systems analysts. Researchers in this field point out that all the successful expert systems, ranging from medical diagnosis to portfolio analysis, have succeeded because they have concentrated on a very limited domain of expertise. A successful systems analyst, though, really needs to be an expert in several different areas: he must understand the technology of structured analysis presented in this book; he must understand the user's application area; he should know a lot about accounting, so that he can produce accurate cost-benefit calculations; he should be an expert in communications and cognitive psychology, so that he can communicate effectively with the user; and he should also be well-versed in computer hardware and software, so that he can communicate effectively with designers and programmers. Current estimates (see, for example, [Barstow, 1987]) are that expert systems will be able to help do the job of systems analyst on simple systems by the mid-1990s, but it will be well past the end of the century before expert systems technology will be able to do systems analysis on large systems.

25.2.5   The Impact of New Generations of Computer Hardware

Enormous sums of money are being expended today by private companies, universities, research organizations, military organizations, and governments around the world, all with the objective of producing dramatically more powerful computer *hardware* during the next 10 to 15 years. One recent estimate, provided in a keynote speech at the 1986 Fall Joint Computer Conference by Gordon Bell of the National Science Foundation, is that hardware technology will improve by a factor of 10 within the next 5 years; and then another factor of 10 within the next 5 years after that; and yet another factor of 10 in the succeeding 5 years. At the same conference, Nobel prize laureate and physicist Ken Wilson made an even more optimistic prediction: a factor of 100 improvement in the next 5 years, followed by another factor of 100 in the following 5 years, followed by yet another factor of 100 in the subsequent 5 years. Thus, these two eminent scientists suggest that within the next 10 to 15 years we can expect computer hardware between 10^3 and 10^6 times more powerful than today's computers.

What has this to do with systems analysis? Simply this: the business of defining user requirements for an information system has to be done within the context of what the user and the systems analyst think is *possible* with available technology. But what we think is possible is based largely on what we know *now* about computer technology. It could well be argued that most end users and most systems analysts do not even begin to make use of existing computer hardware technology, so what are they going to do with technology one million times more powerful?

Past experience with other technological advances, for example, in the field of communication (from smoke signals to telegraph to telephone, etc.) and transportation (from walking to horses to cars to airplanes, etc.) gives us a clue; our first reaction to radically improved technology is to continue doing the same kind of things we did before, but a little faster and more easily (and more economically, in many cases). Only later do we begin to see entirely new applications for the new technology.

As an example, consider the field of transportation, with which we are all familiar; while airplane travel is relatively new (compared to the history of the human race), it has been with us all our lives, and it has an important impact on our assumptions, both conscious and unconscious, explicit and implicit, about the way we can live our lives. Suppose someone told you tomorrow, though, that a supersonic underground train was available to carry you from the East Coast of the United States to the West Coast at speeds of 3000 miles per hour.[5] What would this do to your business life? To your social life? What kind of changes would you begin making *today* if you were reasonably certain that this advanced technology would be available to you within the next 3 to 5 years?

And that is exactly the position that we will find ourselves in as systems analysts for the rest of this century; each time we are given dramatically more powerful computer technology, our first reaction (and the reaction of the end users, too) will be to reimplement existing applications somewhat more efficiently. *The challenge will be to find entirely new applications—entirely new, radically different uses of computer technology—than the applications currently being developed.*

25.3   CONCLUSION

It is important that you have a future-oriented perspective as you finish this book and begin practicing structured analysis in the real world. While the modeling, iterative problem solving, top-down partitioning, and other concepts discussed in this book will almost certainly be valid for the foreseeable future, many of the details (e.g., the technology available to support structured analysis, and even such specific techniques as event partitioning) may change or be replaced.

You should not expect that the material you have learned in this book is constant, permanent, impervious to change. Like all science, and especially like all other aspects of *computer* science, the field of systems analysis is destined to continue changing, evolving, and (hopefully) improving well into the next century and beyond. For some, it is frightening to realize that half of what one learns in this technical field is obsolete within 5 years. For others, and I hope that you will include yourself in this category, it is a source of constant renewal and excitement.

And on that note we come to the end of this book. You are not yet a veteran systems analyst, but you should have enough tools and techniques to enter the profession without fear of falling flat on your face. May you enjoy the practice of structured analysis on information systems that will benefit society. And may you return in less than 5 years to see what has changed. *Ciao!*

---

5 This is not science fiction. Serious engineering proposals for such a supersonic train have been drawn up at MIT.

REFERENCES

1. Tom DeMarco, *Structured Analysis and Systems Specification.* Englewood Cliffs, N.J.: Prentice-Hall, 1979.

2. Chris Gane and Trish Sarson, *Structured Systems Analysis: Tools and Techniques.* Englewood Cliffs, N.J.: Prentice-Hall, 1978.

3. Arthur C. Clarke, *Profiles of the Future.* New York: Holt, Rinehart, and Winston, 1984.

4. Jared Taylor, "Lightyear's Ahead of Paper," *PC Magazine,* April 16, 1985.

5. Frank Derfler, "Expert-Ease Makes Its Own Rules," *PC Magazine,* April 16, 1985.

6. Robin Webster, "M.1 Makes a Direct Hit," *PC Magazine,* April 16, 1985.

7. Robert E. Keller, *Expert System Technology: Development and Application.* Englewood Cliffs, N.J.: YOURDON Press, 1986.

8. Frank Rose, *Into the Heart of the Mind.* New York: Harper & Row, 1985.

9. D. Barstow, "Artificial Intelligence and Software Engineering," *Proceedings of the 9th International Conference on Software Engineering.* Washington, D.C.: IEEE Computer Society Press, March 1987.

10. Paul Ward and Steve Mellor, *Structured Development of Real-Time Systems.* New York: YOURDON Press, 1986.

11. Steve McMenamin and John Palmer, *Essential Systems Analysis.* New York: YOURDON Press, 1984.

12. Craig Brod, *Technostress.* New York: John Wiley, 1984.

QUESTIONS AND EXERCISES

1. What are the three broad evolutionary stages of systems analysis that have taken place over the last 20 years?

2. What are the five major changes that have taken place in the field of systems analysis during the past 10 years?

3. What do the terms logical and physical mean in the context of this chapter?

4. What is event partitioning? What has it replaced in the field of systems analysis?

5. Why has current physical modeling been de-emphasized in systems analysis?

6. What additional tools have been added to the field of systems analysis to help model real-time systems?

7. What is a data structure diagram? What has it been replaced by in the field of systems analysis?

8. How are computers beginning to affect the jobs and activities of senior management in organizations?

9. Why will the teaching of structured analysis and structured design to children in the coming years have an impact on systems development projects?

10. Why is structured analysis likely to be a factor in international competition between the United States, Europe, and many Third World countries?

11. Research Project: What percentage of the programmers and systems analysts have analyst toolkit workstations available to them in your organization?

12. Why are automated tools important for systems analysis?

13. Why will maintenance disasters have an impact on structured analysis in the future?

14. What relationship are we likely to see between artificial intelligence and structured analysis in the future?

15. By what percentage, or multiple, is computer hardware expected to improve over the next 10 to 15 years?

16. Why will continued improvements in computer hardware have an impact on the way systems analysis is done?

APPENDIX

 AUTOMATED TOOLS

A.1   THE BACKGROUND OF AUTOMATED TOOLS

An automated tool can be defined as anything that replaces manual work on the part of the computer programmer, the systems analyst, or even the end user who must somehow communicate his or her requirements to the computer professionals. Thus, there are many things that could be regarded as tools:

- *High-level programming languages,* ranging from COBOL and Pascal, to the current fourth generation languages that allow the programmer to use high-level, English-like statements that are automatically translated into the low-level, primitive instructions that the computer understands.

- *Cross-reference listings, "pretty-print" programs,* and other utility programs that provide the programmer with ancillary, static information about his or her program.

- *Testing tools, debugging tools, simulators, and the like,* that provide the programmer with information about the dynamic behavior of his or her program *as it is running*. Testing tools help the programmer create a wide variety of test cases to ensure that a program is well-tested. Debugging tools help the programmer track down errors once he or she knows that something has gone wrong. Simulators provide the programmer with a more visual, graphic representation of the execution of the program, for example, by showing the program as a flowchart on a CRT screen, and simulating the behavior of the program as it executes by showing the flow of control through the flowchart.

- *Time-sharing terminals* that replace batch development environments. This battle was fought and won 15 years ago in most software organizations, but it is important to realize that the time-sharing terminal is a tool. In the 1960s and early 1970s, programmers had to write their programs, manually, on large coding pads; the program statements were then keypunched on cards (remember punched cards?) and then fed into the computer in the middle of the night. If something was wrong (because the programmer wrote a syntactically incorrect statement or because the keypunch operator mispunched something), an error report would be waiting for the the programmer the next morning. And the cycle would begin anew. That all disappeared by the mid-1970s in most organizations: a programmer now types his or her program directly into a time-sharing terminal, shared with hundreds of other programmers and/or end users. The program can be checked for syntactic correctness on the spot, and he can test and debug his program on the spot. Today, it is hard to imagine any other environment. But that is partly because dumb terminals can be acquired for less than $500. Ten years ago, the cost was typically $3000 or more, and nobody was quite sure whether a programmer merited that much of a capital investment.

- *Personal computers that allow off-line program development.* Today, the $3000 investment is a personal computer. Dumb terminals are OK, but only if the mainframe computer to which they are connected can provide sufficiently consistent, fast response time to allow the programmers to work productively. Many of them simply cannot; they often provide a 5-second response to the most trivial input, and 10-second response to significant inputs. An attractive alternative is a dedicated personal computer the programmer can use to compose a computer program and make appropriate corrections and revisions using a standard word-processing program, compile the program to see if there are any syntax errors that the mainframe computer would reject, and carry out some limited off-line testing.

- *Source code control packages* that prevent the programmer from making unauthorized changes to official versions of a program in the middle of the night. In a large programming project, one of the difficulties is configuration management: making sure that there is a firm control over the various pieces of the final system. Each programmer works on her or his own piece and may need dozens of revisions to that piece before it is finished. But that piece interacts with similar pieces being worked on by a dozen other programmers. Unless everyone knows which version of which piece is to be considered the official version, anarchy prevails. A source code control package is like an automated librarian: it prevents unauthorized withdrawal of or tampering with official documents.

- *Systems analysis and design workbenches.* The tools described above are concerned primarily with the job of writing programs (i.e., deciding what COBOL statements or FORTRAN statements are required to solve a well-defined problem). But that is not where we have the major difficulty in building a software system. The real problem is in the early stages of systems analysis (figuring out *what* the system should do) and design (figuring out what the overall architecture of the system should be). Now we are beginning to see tools that provide assistance to the systems analysts and systems designers.

Most of the tools described above have been available for the past 10 to 15 years and many are widely used in MIS organizations. The workbenches, on the other hand, are very new and have barely begun to permeate the software industry as of 1987. *It is these tools, in my opinion, that have the potential of saving the American software industry.*

As we have seen throughout this book, successful systems analysis relies heavily on *models* of a system that is to be computerized. The analyst workbench and designer workbench tools are primarily concerned with the effective development of those models, for example, they help the systems analyst construct graphical diagrams that enable the end user to understand what the system will do for him. The workbenches also help the analyst and designer ensure that the model is complete, accurate, and consistent, so the errors discovered downstream in the programming phase will be *only* programming errors, and not a reflection of an ongoing misunderstanding between the end user and the systems analyst.[1] And, finally, the workbenches may assist the programmer in translating the model into a working program. In the future, we may expect the workbenches to *completely* automate this process.

The software industry has been talking about tools like this for 5 years or more; however, nothing much was done about it. This was partly because the technology of software engineering had not yet permeated the industry, but it was more a question of economics. As I indicated earlier, it was not until the mid-1970s that most MIS organizations accepted the notion that every programmer should have a dumb terminal on his or her desk, and it took another 5 years for many organizations to actually purchase the terminals and provide a separate mainframe computer for the systems development staff. (In the interim, two or three programmers often had to share one terminal, much like two or three people having to share the same phone in an office,[2] and the entire systems development staff had to share the mainframe computer with hundreds of end users trying to accomplish useful work on *their* terminals.)

Meanwhile, personal computers and workstations were gradually beginning to appear in the consumer marketplace. In the late 1970s and early 1980s, most programmers ignored the machines, for they were not very powerful, not by the mainframe standards by which they judged computer power. A sufficiently high-power workstation capable of helping the analyst/designer with his or her software engineering models would have cost $50,000 to $100,000 in the 1980-1981 timeframe, and that was simply out of the question for most MIS organizations. Only a very few organizations with enormous projects and enormous budgets could even consider such an expenditure; and then the most one could hope for was *one* workstation for an entire

---

1 This is important, because we know that 50% of the errors in a typical systems development project today are due to misunderstandings between the end user and the systems analyst; 75% of the cost of error removal in an operational system is associated with errors that originated in the systems analysis phase.

2 In the opinion of most programmers, it's more like two or three people sharing the same toothbrush.

department of hundreds of people. Some early workstations were developed in aerospace companies, defense contractors, and manufacturers of sophisticated computer graphics workstations, but the mainstream MIS community studiously ignored the concept.

By 1983, things had begun to change. Powerful personal computers, with high-resolution graphics and adequate storage capacity, had dropped below a magical price barrier of $10,000.[3] Some of these were engineering-oriented workstations made by aggressive new computer companies like Apollo Computer and Sun Computer; some turned out to be a "flash in a pan," like Apple's Lisa computer.

Most, though, turned out to be customized configurations of IBM's immensely popular personal computer. By providing an open architecture, IBM made it possible for anyone to build a special-purpose configuration to suit his or her own needs. Thus, the software tool industry could construct a powerful workstation consisting of an IBM PC chassis, a graphics board from vendor A, additional memory from vendor B, and a high-resolution display screen from vendor C.

This ability to construct a powerful workstation that says IBM on the front is crucially important in the marketplace. The political reality is that in business organizations—banks, insurance agencies, and the nonmilitary government agencies—the personal computer *must* say IBM on the front panel; this is, unfortunately, more important than technological superiority of the hardware. Engineering and scientific organizations don't care as much whose computer they use (though many of them would prefer that any personal computer they buy look like a DEC VAX computer), and defense contractors don't care what kind of computer they use, as long as its cost can be included in the government contract.

There are now several dozen companies in the United States and Europe building software products and hardware workstations to assist the systems analyst and designer. A representative list of the vendors and products that were available in 1987 is shown in Table A.1. One of the driving forces behind this cadre of companies is the belief that within the next 5 to 10 years virtually every white-collar worker in the United States, and *especially* every programmer, systems analyst, systems designer, and end user of computer systems, will have a powerful personal computer on his or her desk. The hardware power will be there; now all we need to do is augment that power with a few additional hardware gadgets and some very powerful software.

---

3 $10,000 is magical because it is the level at which higher levels of authorization are required before spending corporate funds. A project manager can often see the practical benefits of a software engineering workstation and can often provide realistic cost-benefit figures. But if the decision involves $20,000, it will escalate up to the level of an assistant vice-president who has spent weeks trying to stay awake long enough to do something useful in the organization. Now he can organize a committee, develop standards, survey the industry, and write memos to dozens of other equally sleepy assistant vice-presidents. While all this high-level decision making is taking place, the project manager shrugs his shoulders, tries to forget that he ever submitted the requisition in the first place, and goes back to using his tried-and-true Stone Age techniques for building systems. As you can tell, I am entirely objective and have absolutely no emotional feelings about this subject.

Table A.1: Analyst Workstation Vendors

Vendor	Product
AIMS Plus, Inc. 1701 Directors Blvd. Austin, TX 75234	Aims Plus
Cadre Technologies Inc. 222 Richmond Street Providence, RI 02903	Teamwork/SA
Cap Gemini Software 2350 Valley View, #420 Dallas, TX 75234	Multi Pro
CGI Systems Inc. One Blue Hill Plaza P.O. Box 1645 Pearl River, NY 10965	Pacbase
Computer Corp. of America Four Cambridge Center Cambridge, MA 02142	PC/Workshop
Cortex Corp. 128 Roberts Road Waltham, MA 02154	CorVision
DBMS, Inc. 1717 Park Street Naperville, IL 60540	Developer Workstation
Iconix Software Engineering, Inc. 1037 Third Street, Suite 105 Santa Monica, CA 90403	Iconix
Index Technology 101 Main Street Cambridge, MA 02142	Excelerator
Ken Orr & Associates 1725 Gage Blvd. Topeka, KS 66604	The Design Machine
Knowledgeware 3340 Peachtree Road NE Atlanta, GA 30326	Information Engineering Workbench

Meta Systems   Structured Architect
315 E. Eisenhower Parkway
Suite 200
Ann Arbor, MI 48104

Nastec Corp.   DesignAid
24681 Northeastern Highway
Southfield, MI 48075

Promod Inc.   ProMod
22981 Alcade Drive
Laguna Hills, CA 92653

StarSys, Inc.   MacBubbles
11113 Norlee Drive
Silver Spring, MD 20902-3619

Tektronix   CASE
P.O. Box 500, Station Y3-314
Beaverton, OR 97077

Yourdon Inc.   Analyst/Designer Toolkit
1501 Broadway
New York, NY 10036

Most of the products run on IBM PCs, though a few of the vendors have chosen the Apple Macintosh or the more powerful Apollo or VAX computers. Virtually all the products provide the user with a palette of icons (shapes that can be used to create drawings) and a "mouse" with which to select the icons. This may be familiar to you if you have used such graphics programs as MacPaint or MacDraw on the Macintosh or PC-Draw or EGA-Paint on IBM PCs. However, the analyst workstation products are far more; they understand the subject matter of the drawings. And, as we will see below, they have many features not found on simple drawing programs.

A.2   IMPORTANT FEATURES IN AUTOMATED TOOLS

It is easy to think of automated workbenches for systems analysts and designers as nothing more than "electronic etch-a-sketch" products. It is certainly true that the graphics capability of these products is the most visible and the most "sexy," but it is only one of the important features. The workbenches must provide the following features to be of significant use in the development of a complex system:

- Graphics support for multiple types of models

- Error-checking features to ensure model accuracy

- Cross-checking of different models

- Additional software engineering support

A.2.1   Graphics Support

As we have seen throughout this book, structured analysis models rely on various forms of information: text, data dictionaries, and graphical diagrams. Text and data dictionaries can be automated using word-processing systems and conventional mainframe computers; it is the graphics support that has always been lacking. The systems analyst needs a workstation that will allow him to compose, revise, and store the following kinds of diagrams:

- Dataflow diagrams (DFD)

- Structure charts (SC)

- Flowcharts (FC)

- Entity-relationship diagrams (ERD)

- State-transition diagrams (STD)

Thus, an analyst workbench might allow the systems analyst to compose the DFD shown in Figure A.1(a).

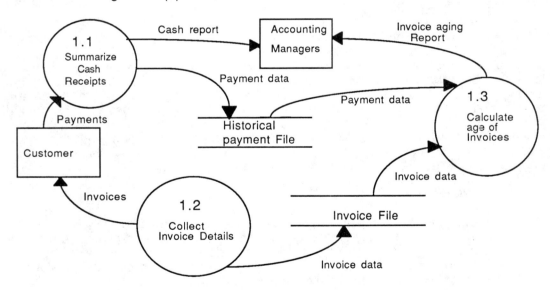

Figure A.1(a): **A typical DFD**

The CRT screen that the systems analyst looks at while composing such a diagram is shown in Figure A.1(b).

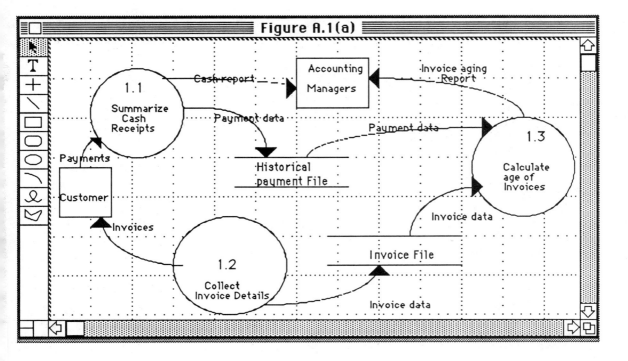

Figure A.1(b): **A typical analyst workstation screen**

I should point out that I composed this diagram using a simple drawing program called MacDraw on the Apple Macintosh computer that I am using to write this book.[4] It took me 15 minutes to compose the diagram and another 30 seconds to copy it directly into the text of this chapter. I could have drawn the diagram by hand in 3 minutes, and I could have pasted it into the chapter, using scissors and tape, in about 30 seconds. The benefit of graphics support clearly does not come from the initial drawing of the diagram; it comes instead from the ease of modification.

In a typical systems development project, a diagram like Figure A.1 might be modified a dozen times. Indeed, one systems analyst at Tektronix told me that he and the end user had modified a DFD like Figure A.1 *over a hundred times* before they finally agreed that it was an accurate model of the user's requirements.[5] Nobody in his right mind would consider redrawing a diagram manually a hundred times; however, making a small change to a diagram on the computer display screen usually takes

---

4 Most software developers use CASE products that run on IBM PC computers, but the diagrams in this book are not from such products. To use them, I would have had to figure out how to merge the diagrams the text file for this book, which I am writing on a Macintosh.

5 It was obviously a more complicated diagram than the one shown in Figure A.1. Indeed, most real-world dataflow diagrams are; they have seven or eight bubbles, three or four data stores, a dozen or more dataflows, and several external terminators.

only a minute or so. Some early results from the Hartford Insurance Group, which has over 600 workstations installed, indicate as much as a 40% improvement in productivity just because of the automated graphics support (see [Crawford, 1985]).

I should also emphasize that general-purpose graphics programs like MacDraw or MacPaint (on the Macintosh) or PC Draw or EGAPaint (on the IBM PC) are not really adequate for the software engineer. To build formal software engineering models, we must first decide what icons, or graphical symbols, will be allowed. We must then define rules that define the properties of the icons and the legal connections between icons. Figure A.1, for example, uses the four icons associated with a standard DFD: a circle, a rectangle, a notation for a data store, and a line showing the flow of data from one place to another. MacDraw, however, would have happily allowed me to include triangles, hexagons, and any other graphic representation on the diagram. And MacDraw doesn't know that once a dataflow has been connected to a bubble the two objects should thereafter be treated as a group or composite object.[6] On a simpler level, I had a difficult time creating bubbles (circles) that were the same size, and it took forever to put arrowheads at the end of the lines.

A.2.2   Error-Checking Features

Though graphics support is clearly necessary, it is by no means enough to justify the expense of a $10,000 computer workstation. An analyst workbench must examine the model created by the systems analyst or designer to ensure that it is complete and internally consistent. Figure A.1, for example, could be analyzed in the following way:

- Are all the icons connected? Are there any free-standing data stores or process bubbles floating around on the diagram, with no inputs and no outputs?

- Does each process bubble have at least one output? If not, it is a suspicious black hole that gobbles up data but never produces any output.

- Are all the dataflows (the named lines connecting the boxes and bubbles) named? Do all the names exist in a data dictionary?

- Do all the processes (the bubbles) have unique names?

Similar error-checking can be done on SCs, FCs, ERDs, and STDs. And the error-checking can be extended to different *levels* of modeling. Figure A.1, for example, might be a low-level subsystem represented by a single bubble (bubble number 1) in a higher-level accounting system modeled in Figure A.2.

---

6 Actually, you can tell MacDraw that certain objects in the drawing should be grouped together, so that they can be moved en masse; but this doesn't guarantee that the result, after being moved, will look the way you want it to. More sophisticated drawing packages, like Design, from Meta Software (55 Wheeler Street, Cambridge, MA 02138) are more sophisticated in the way they handle objects and connectors. But no matter how sophisticated the drawing package is, it's not much use without all the error-checking rules discussed in Section A.1.2.

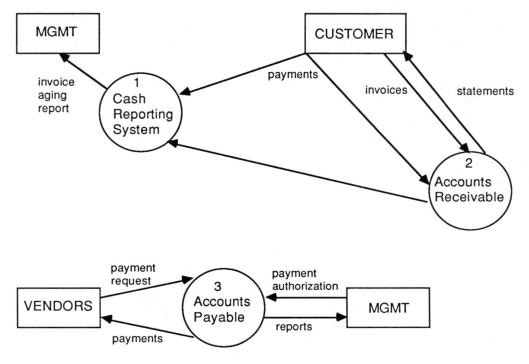

Figure A.2: **A higher-level DFD**

The analyst workbench should ensure that the inputs and outputs shown in Figure A.1 match those shown for bubble 1 in Figure A.2. If they do not match, the model is inconsistent, and there will be hell to pay weeks later (or months later) when someone tries to translate the graphical model into COBOL. The same kind of balancing can be applied to several other graphical models that provide a top-down view of a system.

A.2.3   Cross-Checking of Different Models

The most important feature of an analyst/designer workbench is its ability to cross-check the consistency of several different types of models of a system. There are two aspects of this: cross-checking different models in one phase of a project and cross-checking different models at different phases of a project.

In the systems analysis phase of a project, for example, the primary objective is to determine *what* the user wants from the system, with little or no reference to the particular computer technology that will be used to implement those requirements. To do this, we need DFDs to highlight the division of those requirements into separate *functions* and the interface between the functions. We need ERDs to highlight the *objects* of stored data in the system and the relationship between the objects. And we need STDs to highlight the *states* in which the system may find itself and the time-dependent behavior of the system. In addition, we use a data dictionary to maintain a definition of all the data elements in the system and some form of textual description to define the formal business policy for each bottom-level function in the system.

The key point is that *all these models must be consistent with one another.* If the DFD refers to a data element that is not in the data dictionary, something is wrong; if the data dictionary defines data elements that do not appear in any other model, something is wrong. If the DFD shows data stores that are not defined in the ERD, there is an inconsistency; and if the ERD shows objects that are not defined in the data dictionary and not shown in a DFD, there is an inconsistency. As we discussed in Chapter 14, all this cross-checking could be done manually, but it is a tedious, error-prone process at best. My several years of experience with software engineering in typical MIS environments allows me to say with some confidence (unfortunately) that it will *not* be done manually, despite the exhortations of project managers and the best intentions of the technicians.

In addition to consistency checking between models in one phase of a project, it is important to compare the models developed during *different* phases. For example, the models developed during the analysis phase should be compared with the models developed during the design phase. This comparison should demonstrate a one-to-one correspondence between the two: every requirement described in the analysis model (i.e., the DFDs, ERDs, etc.) should be represented somewhere in the design model (i.e., the SCs, etc.), and every feature described in the design model should correspond to a requirement described somewhere in the analysis model. The most common problem, of course, is that a requirement in the analysis model gets dropped and doesn't show up anywhere in the design model.

This is particularly common when the systems analysis model is developed by one group of people, and the design model (and subsequent coding and testing) is developed by a separate group. In the extreme case (which often occurs on government projects), the two groups may work for different companies. In any case, the two groups often represent different interests and perspectives, and they may not communicate well with each other on any level. Hence a requirement that the analysis team thought was perfectly clear may not be understandable to the design team.

Sometimes the problem is just the opposite of the above: the design team decides to introduce features that were never requested by the user and never documented in the analysis model. This may happen innocently, but it usually occurs when someone on the design team says, "Even though they didn't ask for it, I'll bet the users will really love this feature." Or the veteran, slightly cynical, designer says, "Even though the users didn't request feature X today, I know from past experience that they'll want it next week. It's easier to put it in now than to wait for them to ask for it." Whether or not this is reasonable is beside the point. The important thing is to get this discussion out in the open, rather than letting the designer make a unilateral decision.

In the same way, the design model should be compared against the actual code. Again, there should be a one-to-one relationship between components of the code (the actual implementation of the analysis and design models) and components of the design model.

A.3   FUTURE TECHNOLOGY OF AUTOMATED TOOLS

Many of the features described above exist in the analyst/designer work-benches in the market today. Some of the features are implemented in a somewhat primitive form, but the products are being improved on almost a daily basis. Nevertheless, *all* the products must be regarded as first-generation tools; they represent just the beginning of a series of developments that will take place over the next 5 to 10 years.

The timetable for second-generation and third-generation automated development tools is somewhat unclear. Some of it is dependent on the resources of the companies building the tools; some of it is dependent on the continued development of hardware technology that will provide more and more power in the personal workstations. And much of it is dependent on the technology transfer issue. Large organizations are just beginning to experiment with one or two workstations in the mid-1980s, and it will take several years for even the first-generation technology to permeate the software development industry.

However, I am hopeful that if you visit a large, professional MIS organization in 1995, you will find that every programmer (if there are any programmers left by then) and every systems analyst and every end user and every project manager will have a workstation on his desk that is between 10 and 100 times more powerful than today's workstation. It will provide the following features:

- Networks for project-wide use

- Customized software engineering methodology support

- Document control

- Project management facilities

- Productivity statistics and software metrics

- Early checking for excessive complexity

- Automated testing and simulation

- Computer-assisted proof of correctness

- Code generation

- AI support of reusable code

- Project team "blackboards"

A.3.1   Networks for Project-Wide Use

Automated tools are useful even on small, one-person projects; so is software engineering. But a small project has the advantage that the work can be done over and over again until it is right so that the use of formal models and formal tools does not have much of a sense of urgency.

Automated tools will be of most use on the large, multiperson, multiyear, multimillion dollar software development project. In projects of this kind, there are several systems analysts (often a dozen or more), several end users (often in different geographical locations), and several designers and programmers. In this kind of environment, it is important not only that the work of each systems analyst be internally consistent, but also that the work of analyst A and analyst B be consistent with one another.

This means that there has to be a level of intelligence above that of the individual systems analyst or programmer. Though there are many ways of implementing this, one of the more attractive architectures is shown in Figure A.3. Many of the vendors listed in Table A.1 are working to provide this kind of network, typically with Wang or DEC VAX minicomputers.

The project-level minicomputer should have enough storage capacity and enough processing power to carry out project-wide consistency checking. It should also have enough power to perform additional functions. It should allow the programmers to connect directly to the organization's mainframe for testing and other normal duties. And it is the obvious place to put the intelligence associated with many of the functions described next.

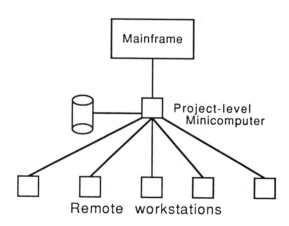

Figure A.3: **A project-level analyst/designer workbench**

The addition of such a minicomputer, together with associated disk storage, communication channels, and so on, obviously increases the cost of automated support. In 1985 dollars, the cost of an appropriately configured stand-alone workstation is between $8000 and $15,000; with the hardware and software for the project-level minicomputer, the price could easily double. It is a price well worth paying, but it probably cannot be funded out of a single year's operating budget for a large MIS staff; it would cost millions of dollars for an organization with a few hundred system developers. It must be recognized as part of a capital investment in the effort to make the staff more productive and more professional.

A.3.2   Customized Software Engineering Methodology Support

The automated tool usually supports a specific form of software engineering notation and procedures. The diagrams in this appendix, for example, as well as the earlier ones throughout this book, use the notation described in several YOURDON Press textbooks. Surprise! But several CASE products also support other popular software engineering methodologies, such as the Gane/Sarson notation as well as the Warnier/Orr notation. Several of the other automated support tools currently available also support more than one brand of software engineering methodology.

But there is something much more important than just supporting the methodology of vendor A or vendor B: the automated tool should allow for a *customized* methodology. An MIS organization will almost always find that *any* of the popular software engineering methodologies fails to provide an adequate notation or adequate set of guidelines for the peculiar kind of system it is developing. Perhaps, for example, the MIS organization feels strongly that it wants to use triangles to emphasize inputs and outputs from Martians and Captain Kirk's Star Trek explorers (most of us don't have to worry about such inputs and outputs, so it's never occurred to us to ask for triangles on our automated tool). And maybe the MIS organization has decided to pass an edict that no dataflow diagram will have more that 13 (a baker's dozen) bubbles on it; another organization may decide that no system should have more than three *levels* of dataflow diagram. And so forth.

Clearly, this kind of customization *must* be allowed or the tool will gradually fall into disuse as system developers find that it does not meet their needs. Most of the current automated tools do not have this facility; virtually all second-generation products will have such a feature or they will disappear from the marketplace.

A.3.3   Document Control

As we have seen, structured analysis relies on a number of formal graphical models, supported by such textual materials as data dictionaries and process specifications; the workstations automate the development and maintenance of these documents. However, they permit something else: the *control* of the documents. While this may seem straightforward, it is a radical concept for most MIS organizations. Many of them have only recently begun to control the source code that is produced in the programming phase of the project.

But just as it is disastrous to allow a programmer to make a "teeny-weeny" change to an operational computer program in the middle of the night, so it is equally disastrous to allow a systems analyst to make a "teeny-weeny" change to a DFD or ERD in the middle of the systems analysis phase of a project, unless that change has been authorized and approved.

To make this work, we must distinguish between the private libraries that each project member maintains on his or her stand-alone workstation and the project file maintained on the project-level minicomputer shown in Figure A.3. It is the project file that we want to control. Once a systems analyst or designer has indicated that he has finished a model (or diagram) and is ready to submit it to the project file, the analyst is no longer the unilateral owner of the material.

A.3.4   Project Management

Document control is one aspect of another feature that can be provided by a project-level minicomputer: *project management.* The project manager can have his or her own workstation and can use the facilities of the minicomputer to coordinate and supervise the activities of the project team. With appropriate software support, he can make sure that he knows when analyst A finishes the DFD he was working on; he can instruct the minicomputer to send that DFD to analyst B for review and comments; he can then assign another piece of work to analyst A. He can use all of this material to update his project schedule and budget; and since the minicomputer keeps its own neutral record of when analyst A began and finished his DFD, he is likely to get much more accurate, unbiased input for his project scheduling activities. The project manager can use the electronic mail capabilities that will almost certainly be provided by the architecture of Figure A.3 to communicate with his staff. It may be difficult to provide a hard estimate of the value of such a facility, but most project teams will find that it is a feature that they cannot live without once it is given to them.

A.3.5   Productivity Statistics and Software Metrics

As mentioned above, the project minicomputer can keep its own record of the starting date and ending date of each piece of work (the development of a DFD, the revision of the DFD, the walkthrough of the DFD, etc.) that a systems analyst or designer or programmer carries out. Thus, productivity measures can be generated almost invisibly, which will hopefully lessen the impact of the Heisenberg uncertainty principle.[7] Compare this to the typical software development project today, where programmers and systems analysts spend an hour or so each week recording information about how they spent their time. There is a barely disguised tendency to fill out the form to make it look the way the boss wants it to (programmers may be rascals and charlatans, but they are not entirely out of touch with reality!). Also, if the recording process takes an hour, then it is interfering with the work itself; this is a form of what nuclear physicists call the Heisenberg uncertainty principle.

Almost any other software metrics that the project team decides to keep track of can be carried out by the project level minicomputer. Thus, the project team may decide that it is important to know how many DFDs are required for the system, or how many data elements, or how many functional primitives, or how many revisions were required of a DFD before it was finally accepted by the user. This information may be useful for future projects; it may also be useful for estimates of project size and cost.

---

7 Though the Heisenberg uncertainty principle is usually associated with the field of nuclear physics, it applies here as well: very simply, the principle says that you can't measure a phenomenon without changing the phenomenon. If a worker has to spend 10% of his time measuring his own work, then his productivity goes down by at least 10%—and the fact that he knows that he is being measured (by virtue of measurements that he captures himself) is likely to alter his behavior.

A.3.6   Early Checking for Excessive Complexity

One of the most useful metrics in the long term is that of *complexity*. There are mathematical models of program complexity that can be used to predict the difficulty of testing and maintaining a computer program.[8] If the mathematical models are applied *automatically* to every module or program in the system being developed, then the developers and the project manager will have an early warning of potentially dangerous portions of the system; alternative designs can then be explored.

A.3.7   Computer-Assisted Testing and Simulation

As mentioned earlier in this appendix, there are already computer-assisted testing packages and animators that provide the programmer with a graphical representation of the execution of her or his program. There is no reason why that intelligence could not be put into the remote workstation or the project-level minicomputer.

Indeed, almost all the conventional program support tools listed at the beginning of this appendix could be incorporated into the automated workbench. As personal workstations become more powerful, it should be possible for the programmer to follow up the modeling process with actual writing of code (if it can't be generated automatically), as well as compilation and testing. Only when the program is finished should the programmer need to upload it to the project-level minicomputer.

A.3.8   Computer-Assisted Proof of Correctness

As we discussed in Chapter 23, the field of computer-assisted proofs of correctness is still not developed to the point where average programmers and systems analysts can make use of it. But there is a wide spectrum between *informal* consistency checking and *formal* proofs of correctness. With automated support tools, we will gradually find that we move further and further away from informal consistency checking and closer and closer to complete, formal proofs of correctness. To accomplish this will require a higher level of training and sophistication on the part of the programmer than can be expected today. Hence, we should not expect to see this feature in most business-oriented workstations for another 5 years.

A.3.9   Code Generation

A major goal of many tool builders is the *automated* generation of COBOL or FORTRAN code by the workbenches. Thus, nobody would ever have to look at the code, just as today hardly anyone looks at the binary 1s and 0s that the computer hardware actually understands. In this context, we would be dealing with computable specifications, developed by the end user and the systems analyst.

We may never be able to achieve this for *all* systems, nor will we be able to insist on the necessary level of formal, rigorous specification from *all* end users. But by

---

8 As we discussed in Chapter 23, one of the more popular models is the McCabe cyclomatic complexity measure. For more about this and other models, see Tom DeMarco's *Controlling Software Projects* (New York: YOURDON Press, 1982).

putting more and more emphasis on the analysis and design activities, we can easily reduce programming to a simple clerical activity. Even if we can't completely automate it, we can arrange for it to be carried out by junior clerks, rather than Computer Science graduates earning $40,000 per year.

A.3.10   AI Support of Reusable Code

Far more appealing than the concept of automated code generation is the concept of *reusable code.* In the vast majority of projects (business-oriented and scientific/engineering-oriented) most of the software we intend to develop has already been done before. This year's brand-new system is, in fact, almost like last year's system, and not too different than the one before that. And most of the bottom-level functional primitives have been programmed before hundreds of times and exist *free* as library routines supplied as part of the vendor's operating system. The only thing that distinguishes this year's brand-new system as unique is the particular combination of those previously implemented functions, or some parameters that can be fed into the program when it begins running. For example, this year's payroll system is basically the same as last year's, but the FICA tax rate has changed.

This suggests that the systems analyst (and even more so the systems designer) should *not* look upon each new project as a grand experiment in scientific exploration, but rather a scavenger hunt to see which *existing* library modules, subroutines, and programs can be connected together to satisfy the user's needs.

This is where artificial intelligence could come in handy. By matching the characteristics of a function identified by the systems analyst (e.g., number of inputs, nature of outputs, and transformation specifications or the rules that describe how inputs are turned into outputs, etc.) with an existing library of implemented functions, an expert system could suggest to the designer a number of potential candidates to be used to implement the system. And it could interact with the systems analyst to show him that by making a small change to the requirements (i.e., by compromising the user's original requirements a little bit) an existing library function could be used *in situ.*

A.3.11   Project Team Blackboards

Some of the leading researchers in the country (e.g., at research labs like MCC in Austin, Texas) feel that the real productivity improvements in the 1990s will come from the synergistic effects of a project *team* rather than the individual; this is because today's large systems are not built by individuals, but rather by groups of groups of people (often in different companies). Most of the concepts described thus far concern the improved productivity of an individual worker, but the intelligence of the project-level minicomputer could be used to provide a convenient project-level view of an entire system as it gradually takes shape and grows.

This concept of a project blackboard is being implemented at MCC as part of the Leonardo project; it should provide fascinating results by the end of the decade. The research group is experimenting with the notion of a communal blackboard in the form of a *wall-sized* CRT. They are also investigating the idea of using the sense of smell and sound, as well as color, to add new dimensions to the graphical models described in this book. If it is successful, the Leonardo project will be the third- or fourth-generation automated workbench for software developers in the mid-1990s!

A.4   CONCLUSION

My bias and excitement for this aspect of software development is obvious; I cannot hide it. I do not apologize for it. I truly feel that it represents the only mechanism that can help us catch up and keep up with the hordes of programmers in countries around the world who would take away the magical industry we have created in the United States over the past 25 years.

Some will say that this technology is too expensive, that no programmer is worth an investment of $25,000. Perhaps not; but since hardware is getting cheaper all the time, today's $25,000 is tomorrow's $10,000 and next year's $5000. It strikes me as highly ironic that a country that invests $50,000 to $75,000 in capital equipment for its farm workers and factory workers should begrudge a few thousand dollars for its information workers. This reluctance, this grudging acceptance that investments may be necessary, is the last gasp of the Industrial Revolution, the last gasp of what Alvin Toffler calls the "Second Wave."

I will admit that a software profession dominated by automated workstations does raise some serious questions: Does it make programmers obsolete? Will it destroy our creativity? Can we afford the cost? And does it *guarantee* that we will make dramatic improvements in our ability to produce high-quality software more productively?

There is nothing magical about automated software tools; anyone with common sense can answer these questions. Automated tools will certainly not make programmers obsolete in the short term and will not make maintenance programmers obsolete for another 20 years or more. In the meantime, it should help de-emphasize the business of programming, which will continue a trend that has been in motion since the first high-level language was invented in the late 1950s. It does not threaten the job of any programmer; keep in mind that we have a backlog of seven years of systems development work in most organizations!

Will an automated workstation destroy the creativity of software developers? Bah! Humbug! Do CAD/CAM (computer-aided design) systems destroy the ability of a designer to design an esthetically beautiful automobile or airplane? *No!* A hundred times: No, no, no! Quite the contrary. The availability of automated support tools helps the programmer and systems analyst concentrate on the *truly* creative part of the job and spend less time worrying about the mundane parts of the job. Since an analyst workbench allows the systems analyst to spend *more* time inventing *more* models of the user's requirements, it makes him or her more creative.

Can we afford the cost of these workstations? The simple answer is this: we cannot afford the cost of *not* using these workstations! With these workstations, we have some chance of saving the American software industry; without them, there may be no hope. For those who want something more practical, keep in mind that the cost of a sophisticated workstation, assuming that we include the project-level minicomputer support, is about $25,000.[9] That is about equal to the annual salary, in 1987, of a typical computer programmer with one to two years of experience. If one includes the overhead cost (insurance, pension benefits of 100%), it represents about six months of the cost of a programmer. Since we can easily justify amortizing the cost of the hardware and associated software over 3 years, the cost is roughly equal to 15% of a programmer's annual cost. In other words, if it increases the programmer's productivity by 15% each year, it pays for itself.

But does an automated software development workbench *guarantee* to improve productivity by a factor of 10? Anyone who can seriously ask such a question must still believe in the Tooth Fairy and the Easter Bunny. Does going to church every Sunday guarantee that you will go to heaven? Stupidity, arrogance, laziness, and other human frailties will always make it possible to fail despite the best of tools and support; there is no way that we can preclude this possibility. But if we believe in the power of information systems and automated support for society and for business, we should believe in it for the profession that builds systems for the rest of the human race. It should not always be true that the cobbler's children are the last to wear shoes.

REFERENCES

1. Jack Crawford, speech at Wang Computer Company, May 6, 1985.

2. James Martin, *An Information Systems Manifesto*. Englewood Cliffs, N.J.: Prentice-Hall, 1984.

3. Paul Ward and Steve Mellor, *Structured Systems Development for Real-Time Systems*, Volumes 1-3. New York: YOURDON Press, 1985.

4. Meilir Page-Jones, *The Practical Guide to Structured Systems Design*, 2nd ed. New York: YOURDON Press, 1988.

5. Steve McMenamin and John Palmer, *Essential Systems Analysis*. New York: YOURDON Press, 1984.

6. Paul Ward, *Systems Development Without Pain*. New York: YOURDON Press, 1984.

7. Brian Dickinson, *Developing Structured Systems*. New York: YOURDON Press, 1980.

8. Edward Yourdon, *Managing the System Life Cycle*, 2nd ed. New York: YOURDON Press, 1988.

---

9 Simple drawing programs are available for under $100, and even the sophisticated drawing programs cost only a few hundred dollars. The cheapest analyst workstation, with the features described in Section A.2, costs about $895 in 1987; those prices will probably drop gradually over the next couple of years. Even an expensive workstation product is only about $8000 in 1987.

9. Edward Yourdon and Larry Constantine, *Structured Design*. Englewood Cliffs, N.J.: Prentice-Hall, 1979.

10. David King, *Current Practices in Software Engineering*. New York: YOURDON Press, 1983.

11. Tom DeMarco, *Structured Analysis and System Specification*. Englewood Cliffs, N.J.: Prentice-Hall, 1979.

12. Tom DeMarco, *Concise Notes on Software Engineering*. New York: YOURDON Press, 1979.

13. Chris Gane and Trish Sarson, *Structured Systems Analysis and Design*. New York: Improved Systems Technologies, 1977.

14. Ken Orr, *Structured Systems Development*. New York: YOURDON Press, 1977.

APPENDIX

B ESTIMATING GUIDELINES

B.1   INTRODUCTION

As a systems analyst, you will probably be called on to produce a number of *estimates* for your project. Indeed, you may be solely responsible for producing these estimates in some cases; in other cases, your project manager may ask you to develop estimates for his or her use.

What kind of things need to be estimated in a systems development project? This will vary from project to project, but typically the major things that need to be estimated are:

- *People resources.* How many programmers, systems analysts, database designers, telecommunications experts, user representatives, and other categories of people will be required for the project?

- *Schedule.* How long will the project take? How much time can be expected for each of the typical phases of the project (e.g., systems analysis, design, programming, testing, etc.)?

- *Staff scheduling.* In addition to knowing how many people the project will require, we need to know *when* they will be required. If the project requires ten programmers, will all ten be needed at the same time?

- *Budget.* How much money will it cost to develop the system? The major cost is likely to be the salaries paid to the development staff, and this can usually be computed directly once the staffing and staff scheduling is known. But, of course, there are other costs associated with a project; these are detailed in Appendix C.

Keep in mind that you will generally have to make these estimates more than once. A set of estimates will generally be made in the early stages of a project (e.g., during the feasibility study), but they may need to be made many times, as users and management explore the ramifications of different trade-offs. One obvious example of this is the trade-off between time and functionality (e.g., the project manager might say to the user, "I'm pretty sure we can deliver the system to you by January 1st if you leave out functions X, Y, and Z."); another example is the trade-off between time and people (e.g., the user might say to the project manager, "If you had three more programmers, would you be able to get the system done in time?").   It may take several iterations before the project team, management, and the user community have reached an acceptable compromise.[1]

B.2   ESTIMATING DANGERS

We have a great deal of common experience in the area of estimating; just think of all the situations typified by the question, "How long do you think it will take to drive to your grandmother's house?" And we are all intuitively familiar with the concept of an optimistic estimate and a pessimistic estimate.   But estimating a systems development project is somewhat different, because (1) the scope of work is much larger and more complex, and (2) the consequences of an estimating error are usually much more severe than that of being half an hour late to your grandmother's house.[2] There are a number of common problems that you should be aware of before you begin calculating estimated budgets, schedules, and resource requirements:

- The difference between estimating and negotiating

- The wide variation in technician skills

- The danger of estimating your own work

- The lack of an estimating database

- Management's insistence on premature, detailed estimates

- An industry-wide difficulty of measuring the unit of work

- Estimates based on assumptions of unpaid overtime

Depending on your seniority in your project, and your clout with management and users, you may be able to prevent some of these problems from becoming serious. But even if you are a junior systems analyst on the project, you should be aware of the estimating problems, for they can ultimately determine the success or failure of your project. We will discuss each of the problems in more detail next.

---

1 Keep in mind also that the estimates will almost certainly have to be revised during the project as circumstances change. External factors (business conditions, new competitors, mergers, etc.) may cause the user to change his or her mind about required functionality, budget expenditures, or required delivery date. And internal factors (staff turnover, unexpected difficulty of implementation, etc.) may also cause budgets and schedules to change, usually dramatically.

2 Some grandmothers may violently disagree with this assumption!

B.2.1   The Difference Between Estimating and Negotiating

There is often a great deal of negotiation at the beginning of a project (and often throughout the development phase of the project!). This is normal, because the user community often has little understanding of the amount of work involved in a complex information system and will thus "ask for the moon," that is, an enormous amount of functionality in an absurdly small amount of time, and for little or no money. Meanwhile, the project manager is faced with limited staff and a limited budget; hence, she or he needs to work with the users to help them see what trade-offs are possible.

But this negotiating process, so necessary and so common in systems development projects, must not be confused with *estimating.* What you must avoid is the conversation between user and systems analyst (or whoever does the estimating) that goes like this:

User: "So, how long is it going to take you to build the XYZ system?"

Analyst: "Well, it looks like we'll have it finished by April 1st."

User: "That's not good enough. We need it by January 1st."

without a willingness to discuss other trade-offs in functionality or resources.[3] This is sometimes followed by an appeal by the user to the project team's sense of devotion, duty, and patriotism, which we will discuss as a separate problem in Section B.1.8.

In some cases, this situation simply reflects a lack of understanding on the part of the user; it can usually be corrected by a careful explanation of the activities involved in developing a system. In other cases, though, it reflects the user's overall approach, his business "paradigm," for dealing with people and organizations that provide him with products and services. To the typical user, you see, the internal data processing organization is not that much different from an external vendor; negotiating, in an attempt to squeeze the price down or cut the schedule back a few months, is a very natural thing to do. And it is a reasonable thing to do (from his point of view) if the person or organization providing that service has a profit margin that can be cut down through skillful negotiation.

Even in the case of an internal data processing organization, negotiating (without accepting any trade-offs in functionality, resources, budget or schedule) *may* be reasonable if your estimates include a margin for error (otherwise known as a cushion or a contingency factor) that the user thinks is unreasonably large. But if you have provided careful, realistic estimates, and the user negotiates you down to a smaller staff, smaller budget, and tighter schedule, then your project has entered the realm of heavy-duty politics for which the techniques and tools discussed in this book probably won't help much. The time may have come to update your resume.

---

3 There is another trade-off, but hardly anyone ever talks about it explicitly: *quality.* Many project managers try to accomplish miracles by delivering all the required functionality within the user-imposed schedule and with the less-than-optimal resources provided; but the inevitable result is a system that has more bugs and is less maintainable than would otherwise have been the case.

B.2.2   The Wide Variation in Technician Skills

It is common to make estimates of the work to be done based on average talent (i.e., the typical programmer or systems analyst, who can write 15 lines of code, or draw four DFD bubbles, in an average day). It's important to keep in mind that numerous studies over the past 20 years have documented an order of magnitude difference between talented professionals and mediocre professionals in the field.[4] If your project has a group of so-called super programmers, you may drastically overestimate the amount of time and money that will be required to finish the project. Of more concern is the fact that a project team of dullards may cause your project to miss its schedule and exceed its budget by a substantial amount.

One major problem in this area is that the actual performance of experienced practitioners does not correlate strongly with most standard programming aptitude tests. Hence, you must base your estimates on each person's reputation or previous work experience, or you must simply assume that everyone on the project is average. Since most organizations don't keep careful, detailed records on the productivity of each person in a systems development environment, it will be very difficult for you to obtain documented evidence that you can trust. All you can do is make your best judgment and then modify the estimates, as appropriate, during the course of the project.

B.2.3   The Danger of Estimating Your Own Work

One of the worst mistakes that you can make is to estimate your own work; it is almost as bad to use the estimate of any one single person, since that person's judgment may be affected by a number of factors.

If you estimate your own work, you are very likely to fall prey to one or more of the following myths:

- *"I'm better than most of the other people around here, and I'm sure I can finish the project much sooner."* It's very common to overestimate one's ability. When estimating someone else's ability, you tend to be conservative; when estimating your own, you tend to be optimistic.

- *"I know that the boss needs this project done real fast, and I really want to help him out."* In most cases, this is an altruistic feeling; it's quite natural to want to help your boss succeed. But it can cloud your judgment about the actual amount of time required to get the project finished. In the worst case, optimistic estimates are made in an effort to impress your boss (keep in mind that he's doing the same thing to *his* boss, and his boss is doing

---

4 One of the first indications of this was a paper entitled "Exploratory Experimental Studies Concerning Online and Offline Programming Performance," by H. Sackman, W.J. Erickson, and E. E. Grant in the January 1968 issue of *Communications of the ACM.* Their study showed a 26:1 variation between the best programmers and the worst programmers, all of whom were given the same programming task. This variation between good programmers and bad programmers has been verified several times during the past 20 years.

the same thing to his boss, etc.) so that you can get that next raise or promotion. If you know what you're doing and are able to accept the risk, fine;[5] but keep in mind that you're playing with fire.

- *"I'm willing to work hard to get this project done on time."* The willingness to work overtime is commendable, but it is dangerous, as suggested earlier. Also, keep in mind that the commitment to put in long hours is often made in a moment of excitement at the beginning of the project; six months later, it may not seem like such a good idea.

- *"I've worked on systems like this before; this will be a piece of cake."* Well, maybe, if indeed you have worked on a project *exactly* like this one or very close indeed. However, there is a tendency at the beginning of a project to see superficial similarities with previous projects and to optimistically assume that you'll be able to do the new project even more quickly. You're likely to find that the new project is actually rather different, once you get into the details; and you're likely to forget all those problems you encountered in the last project.

For these reasons, it's very important that estimates be carried out by someone other than the person responsible for the work. It's also highly desirable if one does not have an estimating database (discussed in Section B.1.4) or a computerized estimating package (discussed in Section B.4) to obtain estimates from more than one person. At the very least, get estimates from three people; this will give you a best case and worst case estimate, along with an in-between estimate.

B.2.4   The Lack of an Estimating Database

When faced with a new project, one would like to use statistics from a hundred similar projects in order to produce accurate estimates. Some consulting firms and software houses are able to do this: when asked to estimate the time and cost for, say, an order entry system, they can say, "Well, this is almost exactly the same as the last 137 order entry systems we've built, so it should take X person-months, Y dollars, and Z people."

Even within your own organization, it's possible that there have been 137 order entry systems developed over the past decade or two. But this doesn't necessarily mean that it will be easy to estimate the budget or schedule for the 138th order entry system; if careful records have not been kept, all you can go on is hearsay and rumor. For a typical data processing organization, which acts as an internal service organization, without having to worry about profit/loss figures or cash flow considerations, there is no real incentive to keep such careful records.

---

5 God is looking over my shoulder as I write this, and He says, "No, it's *not* fine." Maybe you're willing to take the risk of not being able to deliver the project with the optimistic schedule and budget that you're promising, but a failure is likely to jeopardize much more than just your career. It's unethical, unprofessional, and intellectually dishonest to make unrealistically optimistic estimates when your boss, your users, and your entire organization might suffer a considerable loss by your inability to deliver what you promise.

Some large data processing organizations are beginning to change this attitude and have begun developing large, detailed databases that can be used to generate much more accurate estimates for future projects. And some consulting firms specializing in this area have developed databases of literally *thousands* of projects; these are usually used to provide parameters in the computerized estimating models discussed in Section B.4.

In the meantime, there is a significant likelihood that you will be faced with a one-of-a-kind estimate. You should certainly look for other, similar projects in your organization; but be aware that you may be in a situation analogous to the architect who was asked how long it would take build an underground house in a swamp.

B.2.5   Management's Insistence on Premature Detailed Estimates

As a general rule, it is almost impossible to produce detailed estimates of costs, time, and resource requirements for a project until a considerable amount of detailed systems analysis and design have been done. After all, how can you tell the user how much a system will cost if you don't know what the user wants? Nevertheless, there is often great pressure from both users and management to produce an estimate, which is presumed by both of those parties to be an accurate, detailed estimate, at a *very* early stage in the project. Why? Simply because they need to make a go/no-go decision to invest the time, money, and people required to build the system.

This demand for an early estimate is quite understandable; the only thing that is *not* realistic is the assumption that an early estimate can be detailed or accurate. It's more appropriate to give management a series of estimates throughout the project, with each one being progressively more detailed and more accurate. Thus, if the project team is developing a system for an application they are fairly familiar with, they might provide the following series of estimates:

- At the end of the survey or feasibility study: an estimate that may vary by plus or minus 50%. That is, the project team might tell management that the system will take one year and cost $200,000, plus or minus 50%. Management should thus realize the possibility of the project taking 18 months and costing as much as $300,000.

- At the end of the analysis phase: an estimate that may vary by ± 25%.

- At the end of the design phase: a revised estimate that may vary by ± 10%.

- At the end of the programming phase (when testing remains to be done): a final estimate that should not vary by more than ± 5%.

B.2.6   An Industry-Wide Difficulty of Measuring the Unit of Work

Many industries have standard ways of measuring the amount of work to be done in a project. Someone building a house, for example, might measure the work in terms of the number of bricks to be laid or the number of rooms to be built. But in the field of systems development, there is still no agreed-upon way of measuring the unit of work to be done.

The most common method is to measure the number of program statements to be written, otherwise known as lines of code. Thus, on some projects, you will see references to KLOC, which stands for kilo lines of code. But there are many problems with lines of code as a measure of the unit of work:

- Do comments in a computer program count as a line of code?

- Do we count only the code that is delivered to the user, or do we also count code that is written for testing, utility programs, and other support activities during the project? (And on a larger scale, do we count the code associated with canceled projects in an attempt to measure enterprise productivity?)

- What if the programmer has written more than one program statement on a single line of a program listing? And what about the complex statement that takes more than one line?

- Most important, how do we deal with the fact that some programmers will take more lines of code to accomplish the same function than other programmers? As we saw in Section B.1.2, this can represent an order of magnitude variation!

As Capers Jones points out in *Programming Productivity* ([Jones, 1985]) different ways of measuring the unit of work can distort the reported productivity results by two orders of magnitude; perhaps that's why some programmers can claim to be 10 times or even 100 times more productive than their colleagues! Because of these problems, some organizations are now beginning to use function points as the unit of work; this corresponds roughly to the bottom-level atomic bubbles in a DFD.[6]

B.2.7   Estimates Based on Assumptions of Unpaid Overtime

As mentioned earlier, users and project managers may react to scheduling conflicts by suggesting, implicitly or explicitly, that the project team put in extra hours, work on weekends, skip holidays, and postpone vacations. This is usually accompanied with appeals to the loyalty, professionalism, dedication, devotion, pride, honor, and patriotism of the project participants.

I'll leave it to you to decide whether a willingness to work extra hours is a necessary attribute of patriotism. In some organizations, this may be the case: *every*

---

6 The term function point was introduced by A.J. Albrecht to describe this; see "Measuring Application Development Productivity," *Proceedings of the Joint SHARE/GUIDE Application Development Symposium* (Chicago: GUIDE International Corp., 1979). Tom DeMarco uses the term function bang in much the same way; see his book, *Controlling Software Projects* (New York: YOURDON Press, 1982) for more details. Also, see Capers Jones' *Programming Productivity* (New York: McGraw-Hill, 1986) for a thorough discussion of the difficulties of measuring productivity, as well as the many factors that affect productivity.

project may be organized in such a way that it will only succeed if the project team regularly puts in an 80-hour week. And some projects (e.g., the NASA Apollo project that put the first men on the moon in the late 1960s) may be so exhilarating that everyone will be more than happy to sign up for the extra work required. And it's not uncommon to find that a project that *appeared* to be under control falls behind schedule during the last month, requiring a few weeks of late evenings and weekends.

But you have to remember that working is like running: you can sprint at top speed for a hundred yards, but you can't sprint at top speed for a 26-mile marathon. Similarly, you can work 14-hour days for a few weeks, but it's unrealistic, in most cases, to assume that you can work 14-hour days for a 3-year project. People with spouses (spice?), children, or other outside interests will simply refuse to continue working such hours after a few months; if necessary, they'll quit and find another job. Young, single people may be more willing to devote their entire waking lives (as well as their dreams) to the project, especially if they feel it will help advance their career or their knowledge of the profession.

Even if members of the staff are willing to work 14-hour days, there is no guarantee that they will be *effective* at their work. This is especially true if the overtime work continues for a period of several months: the long evening hours are often unproductive, and one usually finds that more errors are created as people do their work in an exhausted, frazzled state of mind.

B.3   ESTIMATING GUIDELINES

There are four important guidelines to keep in mind when you develop estimates for the amount of work to be done in a systems development project:

1.   Make the estimating units as small as possible.

2.   Make the units of work as independent as possible.

3.   Take into account the communication factor.

4.   Distinguish between new work and borrowed work.

These are discussed next.

B.3.1   Make the Estimating Units as Small as Possible

This should be an obvious suggestion, but it is not followed as often as you might think; it also has some pitfalls, as we shall see. But, in general, it's much better to estimate the budget and schedule for a one-week unit of work than it is to estimate a "man-millennium."[7] Large projects have large complexities; if you try to estimate the

---

7 A man-millennium is a thousand man-years of work. I use the term "man" deliberately, because I am convinced that women are far too intelligent to get enticed into estimating in such large, machismo units! The term "man-millennium" was originally suggested by one of my company's clients, a large public utility company in California.

amount of work involved, you are almost certain to make major errors. It makes much more sense to base your estimates on small amounts of work.

This implies, of course, that the overall project has been broken down into small units of work. This will normally happen quite naturally as a result of structured analysis, structured design, and structured programming; unfortunately, as discussed in Section B.1.5, you may be required to provide a detailed estimate of budget and resource requirements *before* this detailed work-breakdown has taken place. There is no magic solution to this problem; all you can do is try to impress upon your managers and the users that a detailed, accurate estimate requires some initial effort to identify the units of work to be done.

But how small should the units of work be? Some organizations measure work in units of one month; however, this seems too large—projects can get seriously out of control in the span of one month. It is perhaps more reasonable to measure work in units of one week; as one veteran project manager said to me, "Nothing useful ever gets done in less than a week." Perhaps the most common unit of work, though, is a day; this fits nicely with the way we organize our work life. A few organizations actually measure their work in units of an hour; while there are indeed many activities that take an hour or less (e.g., defining a single data element in the data dictionary), it seems too microscopic a unit to work with.

B.3.2   Make the Units of Work as Independent as Possible

A problem that has plagued many attempts at estimating is the interaction, or coupling, between one piece of work and another. If a system is divided into pieces with many, many interactions, then the total amount of work to develop the system will be far more than the linear sum of the work for each piece. If a change is made to piece 13, for example, the change may cause problems in piece 14, and a change to 14 could result in changes being made to 15, and so on. This ripple effect has wreaked havoc in many projects.

The solution is to divide the system into small, independent pieces that are only loosely coupled to other pieces. This requires careful work; we discussed it in Chapter 20 as the major rationale for grouping low-level bubbles in the preliminary behavioral model into higher-level aggregates. The notion of modular independence is also important during the design phase of the project; we discussed this in Chapter 22.

B.3.3   Take into Account the Communication Factor

Even in a project where all the modules are independent of one another, people have to talk to one another. If the project is carried out by one individual, then the only communications required are those that take place with the user (and perhaps some discussions with management). But a typical project has many systems analysts, designers, database specialists, and programmers; even worse, some of these people may work in different companies or even speak different languages.

Thus, your estimates will have to include some time for communication between all the project personnel. This communication will take the form of meetings, memos, telephone conversations, and so forth. Keep in mind also that the amount of communication increases sharply as the size of the project team increases: the number of communication paths between team members increases as the *factorial* of the number of individuals.

B.3.4   Distinguish Between New Work and Borrowed Work

If the project team is lucky, it will be able to make use of work that was done on previous projects; most often, this takes the form of modules in a common software library.[8] However, you should not assume that the reusable modules are free; it will take some amount of work to (1) find them, (2) investigate them to see if they perform the desired function, and (3) learn enough about them to understand how to use them. It's more appropriate to estimate that the borrowed modules will require some fraction (perhaps 25%, perhaps as low as 10%) of the work that would have been necessary to develop the modules from the beginning.

B.4   FORMULAS FOR ESTIMATING

During the past 20 years, the systems development industry has invested an enormous amount of time and effort developing *models,* or formulas, to help predict the time, resources, and cost of a system. Some of these models are now in widespread use; perhaps the best known model is the COCOMO model developed by Barry Boehm at TRW.[9] But as Tom DeMarco points out in *Controlling Software Projects,*

> *There are no transportable cost models.* If you wait for someone elsewhere to develop a set of formulas that you can use for cost forecasting in your own shop, you will probably wait forever. Much of our industry concluded, upon realizing this fact, that cost modeling was therefore irrelevant. I think that was the wrong conclusion. If locally developed cost models can be used to improve the precision of the cost-forecasting process, and if the improvement is worth the cost of developing the models, then the concept is viable.

However, it is interesting to see some of the formulas used in other organizations; if nothing else, they will give you a starting point for developing your own formulas. Some of the formulas involve as many as 40 factors or parameters; but, as we will see, some involve only one parameter.

B.4.1   Formulas for Estimating Work Time

Three common formulas for estimating the effort (described in person-months) are based on lines of code. Walston and Felix developed a model at IBM (see

---

8 But it may also be possible to reuse portions of a design portions of a model of user requirements, or even portions of a feasibility study. In the past, this was typically not done because the design model, analysis models, and feasibility studies were not well documented and were never maintained. Now, with the proliferation of analyst workstation products of the kind discussed in Appendix A, this is becoming more practical.

9 For a detailed discussion of this model see Barry Boehm's *Software Engineering Economics* (Englewood Cliffs, N.J.: Prentice-Hall, 1981).

[Walston and Felix, 1977]), based on observations of some sixty projects, which is expressed as

$$E = 5.2 * L^{0.91}$$

where E was measured in person-months, and L was measured in thousands of lines of code.

Similarly, Bailey and Basili developed a formula based on 19 projects; it is expressed as

$$E = 3.4 + 0.72 * DL^{1.17} \quad \text{plus or minus 25\%}$$

where effort was measured, once again, in person-months, and DL is thousands of lines of delivered code; see [Bailey and Basili, 1983].

Finally, Barry Boehm's COCOMO model has an effort formula for three different types of system: organic systems, semidetached systems, and embedded systems:

$$E = 2.4 * KDSI^{1.05} \quad \text{(organic systems)}$$

$$E = 3.0 * KDSI^{1.12} \quad \text{(semidetached systems)}$$

$$E = 3.6 * KDSI^{1.20} \quad \text{(embedded systems)}$$

where KDSI represents "kilo delivered source instructions;" see [Boehm, 1981] for details.

B.4.2   Formulas for Estimating Time

Once you have developed an estimate of the amount of work to be done, you might think that it's easy to estimate the length of time that the project will take. After all, if you have a project estimated at 10 person-months of work, and 5 people are available, then it should take 2 calendar months to finish the project. But what if only 2 people are available? Does the project then take 5 calendar months?

In general, what we are concerned with here is the trade-off between time and people. Many years of painful experience have taught us that the trade-off is not a simple one: doubling the number of people on a project does not necessarily cut the duration of the project in half. Indeed, Fred Brooks, the architect of the original OS/360 operating system, coined the phrase, "Adding more people to a late software project just makes it later." There are two reasons for this: (1) adding more people increases the required communication between team members, which reduces productivity, and (2) some work in the project is indivisible; it can only be done by one person and adding more people simply won't help.

While this is a useful concept, it does not tell us specifically how many people a project will need nor how long it will take. This area has also been the subject of research; Barry Boehm found, for example, that the calendar time for a project could be expressed by the following formula:

$$T = 2.5 * E^{0.33}$$

where E is the effort of the project measured in person-months; see [Boehm, 1981] for details..

Studies have also been made of the optimal "manpower loading" for a project; the three best known formulas are based on the work of Norden, Putnam, and Parr; see [Norden, 1963], [Putnam and Fitzsimmons, 1979] and [Parr, 1980]. Norden was the first to find that project staffing follows a curve similar to the one shown in Figure B.1.

The chart is often known as a Rayleigh distribution, based on the mathematical formula for the curve. Putnam provided a formula describing the number of people required on the project as a function of calendar time:

$$People(t) = 2K * a * t * exp(-at^2)$$

where K is the total effort of the project (expressed in people-months), and a is an acceleration factor that establishes the initial slope of the curve. (Note that K represents the total area under the curve.)

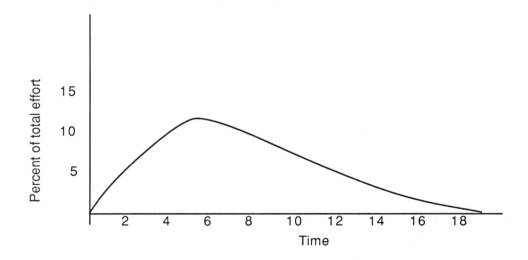

Figure B.1: **Typical project staffing**

An alternative model was developed by Parr [Parr, 1980]; while the overall shape looks similar to Figure B.1, it estimates a higher amount of staffing in the early phases of the project. The Parr model is described by the following formula:

$$People(t) = 1/4 \ sech^2((at + c)/2)$$

B.5   COMPUTERIZED ESTIMATING MODELS

The idea of using formulas with exponentials and hyperbolic secants is probably not very appealing; you can be sure that most veteran systems analysts have long since forgotten what a hyperbolic secant is and have no idea how to compute an exponential! But it's not necessary to remember any of the formulas, nor is it necessary to carry out any of the calculations by hand. There are now many computerized project estimating packages available; most run on PCs, and many of them utilize Boehm's COCOMO model, as well as the Putnam model described above. Some can also incorporate the PERT charts and GANTT charts discussed in Chapter 16.

If you are working on anything other than a trivial system, you should definitely investigate such packages. Not only will they carry out the calculations for you, but they will allow you to play "what-if" simulations to see the effect of adding people to the project or losing people because of sickness or other calamities.

REFERENCES

1. Tom DeMarco, *Controlling Software Projects.* New York: YOURDON Press, 1982.

2. Barry Boehm, *Software Engineering Economics.* Englewood Cliffs, N.J.: Prentice-Hall, 1981.

3. *Workshop on Quantitative Software Models for Reliability, Complexity, and Cost: An Assessment of the State of the Art.* IEEE Catalog No. TH0067-9. New York: Institute of Electrical and Electronics Engineers, 1979.

4. Victor Basili, *Tutorial on Model and Metrics for Software Management and Engineering.* New York: Institute of Electrical and Electronics Engineers, 1980.

5. C.E. Walston and C.P. Felix, "A Method of Programming Measurement and Estimation," *IBM Systems Journal,* Volume 16, Number 1 (January 1977), pp.54-73. Reprinted in *Writings of the Revolution,* Edward Yourdon (editor). New York: YOURDON Press, 1982, pp. 389-408.

6. J.W. Bailey and V.R. Basili, "A Meta-Model for Software Development and Resource Expenditures," *Proceedings of the 5th International Conference on Software Engineering.* New York: Institute of Electrical and Electronic Engineers, 1983.

7. P.V. Norden, "Useful Tools for Project Management," *Operations Research in Research and Development.* New York: Wiley, 1963.

8. Larry Putnam and A. Fitzsimmons, "Estimating Software Costs," *Datamation,* September 1979, pp. 89-98; October 1979, pp,171-178; November 1979, pp. 137-140.

9. F.N. Parr, "An Alternative to the Rayleigh Curve Model for Software Development Effort," *IEEE Transactions on Software Engineering,* Volume SE-6, Number 3 (May 1980), pp. 291-296.

10. T. Capers Jones, *Programming Productivity.* New York: McGraw-Hill, 1985.

APPENDIX

 COST-BENEFIT

CALCULATIONS

C.1   INTRODUCTION

This appendix is concerned with the techniques of cost-benefit calculations, an important part of any systems analysis effort. Its purpose, of course, is to demonstrate to the users of the new system, as well as other groups of managers throughout the organization, that the expected benefits of the new system exceed the expected costs.

As a junior systems analyst, you may not be involved in this effort at all, or you may be given the job of developing a cost-benefit model for a small part of the overall system. Even as a senior systems analyst in charge of the entire project, you may not be involved in the cost-benefit calculations; it may be done, for example, by a separate, independent financial group.

Or it may not be done at all! Many systems are developed in organizations simply to meet mandatory government requirements (e.g., reporting systems for the Equal Employment Opportunity Act or new systems to deal with the vagaries of tax legislation). Of course, even in these cases, when there is no benefit to be derived from the system (other than the luxury of avoiding penalties or being allowed to stay in business!), management generally wants to know what the cost of the system will be; but this may be carried out as part of the estimating activities discussed in Appendix B.

There is one other reason why the cost-benefit study may not be carried out: the user may not want one. Just as a consumer may not be able to cost-justify a Cadillac (i.e., he could have done just as well with a small Honda or even a bicycle), so many users are unable to cost-justify a new system they have asked for. Sometimes they ask for a new system for the same reason a consumer may buy an expensive car—keeping up with the Joneses.[1] In other cases, the user may feel that there is a le-

---

1 This is particularly true in some highly competitive industries where new computer systems are developed to provide additional kinds of services to the marketplace (e.g., new banking systems, credit card systems, and airline "frequent flyer" systems. Thus, *your* user may not be able to cost-justify such a new system on its own merits, but may feel that he or she has to develop it to keep up with the competition.

gitimate need for a new system, but may recognize that all the benefits are intangible or extremely difficult to quantify; the user may justify the request for the system by claiming an "entrepreneurial hunch" that it will pay off.

As a systems analyst, it is not your position to *insist* that a cost-benefit calculation be carried out; after all, it's the user's system, and if he wants to build it without any justification at all, that is his prerogative. However, it's a very good idea to find out whether a cost-benefit calculation for the project has been done and, if so whether it is a rational one.[2] If there is no cost-benefit study, or if the benefits are very fuzzy (or the costs glaringly underestimated), you should be aware that the project is vulnerable.

In the worst case, you'll find that the user is not terribly enthusiastic about the project, but has been talked into it by higher management, based on the optimistic calculations of the project manager who *really* wants to build the system (because it will enhance his career, because he thinks that all users should be fully computerized, or for a hundred other reasons). In the best case, you may find that the user has authorized the system and is very enthusiastic about it despite the lack of a rational cost-benefit calculation. But users are fickle: today's pet project becomes tomorrow's discarded project.

And users come and go: the user who authorized the project yesterday may be replaced by a new user tomorrow who takes a very different view of the desirability of the project. So, if there is no cost-benefit calculation (and it's evident that nobody wants to develop one), my advice is very simple; keep your resume up to date, for you may be looking for a new job before the project finishes.

In the sections below, we will examine several aspects of cost-benefit calculations:

- Cost analysis

- Benefit analysis

- How to express the savings

- Risk analysis

C.2   COST ANALYSIS

The purpose of this activity, of course, is to calculate all the anticipated costs associated with the system—not only the cost of *building* the system, but also the cost of *installing* the system and *operating* and *maintaining* the system, as well as ancillary costs. Each of these is discussed next.

---

2 As a senior systems analyst, you are in a position to know this right away, of course. But to a junior systems analyst, brought into the project after it has been underway for six months, it may not be so evident. At that point, the project has taken on a life of its own and will fight for its existence independently of the user and any other rational decision-making process.

C.2.1   The Cost of Building the System

In Appendix B, we discussed techniques for estimating the length of time required to build a system and the number of people required. Keep in mind that you need to calculate not only the cost of the programmers and systems analysts, but also all of the other people involved with the development of the system:

- Clerical people

- Managers

- Members of the user community

- Consultants and contract programmers

- Possibly members of the auditing, QA, or operations staff

In most cases, you can obtain from management (or from the accounting department) the average salary of the categories of people that are included in your project; this may be expressed in terms of hourly costs, monthly costs, or annual costs. Make sure that you take into account your company's overhead factor; that is, you will probably have to multiply each salary by a factor of, say, 150% to cover the cost of insurance, employee benefits, and various other corporate overhead factors. Again, you should be able to get this figure from your management or from the accounting department.

Keep in mind also that the people working on the project will not be available 100% of the time: some time will necessarily be lost because of illness, vacation, personal leave, and the like. Your company may have a standard factor to apply for this lost time; if not, a figure of 10% is the very least you should assume; 20% to 25% is not all that unrealistic. (It's possible that this has already been taken into account in the resource estimates carried out in Appendix B. Check to ensure that the lost time factor has not been left out and that it has not been applied twice.)

In many projects, you must also include the cost of training the development staff. Team members may need training in new development methodologies, new programming languages, or various hardware and software skills associated with the vendor equipment being used. Another cost that must be taken into account is that of computer time, terminals or workstations, and development tools (editors, testing packages, etc.) that are required for the development of the system. In some cases, the terminals and development tools may already exist and your project may not incur any additional charges; in virtually all cases, though, the project will have to include costs for the computer time involved. (Note that this may also include disk storage costs, telecommunication costs, as well as costs for paper, forms, and other ancillary supplies.)

Some new projects are developed with new people, that is, people who did not work for the organization prior to the project and for whom office space presumably did not exist. Thus, you may have to include recruiting costs (travel expenses for the job candidates, recruiting fees for employment agencies, etc.), as well as employee expenses associated with the initial orientation training that a new employee must go through. And you may need to include the cost of office space, desks, telephones, and other equipment for the new staff.

On some projects, there are also travel costs associated with visits that must be made to remote user sites in order to interview users. Obviously, this is not a factor on a project where all of the users are located in the same geographical area as the development team; but on projects where there are diverse groups of users in different locations (often in different countries), this can be a major expense. By the way, management will often assume that all the required information can be gathered in one trip; in real projects, subsequent trips are often necessary to resolve questions and misunderstandings.[3]

Thus, the costs for development of a system can be many and diverse. The following list summarizes the discussion above; it may not be a complete list, but it covers most of the major items:

- Salaries and overhead for all the personnel attached to the project

- Training costs

- Computer time and development tools for the staff

- Recruiting costs for new staff

- Office space and office equipment for new staff

- Travel expenses to visit remote users

C.2.2   The Cost of Installing the System

In a simple project, it may be sufficient to telephone the user and tell her or him that you have finished developing the system; you may be able to deliver it to him on a floppy disk, and let him install it on his own personal computer. But on a large, complex system, there is much more to the installation process, and there are many costs involved. Among them are the following:

- User training costs

- Database conversion costs

- Vendor installation costs

- Cost of regulatory approval

---

3 Sometimes this can be minimized if your organization has extensive electronic mail facilities or other forms of communication systems in addition to the telephone.

- Cost of parallel runs

- Cost of development team during installation

Typically, the entire user community will require some training to become familiar with the usage of the system. Additional training may be required for supervisory users; some training may also be required for the operations staff and various other ancillary personnel. Note that this means that we must also include the cost of developing the user training courses, the cost of training manuals or course documentation, as well as the cost of user training facilities (classrooms, etc.). Finally, don't forget the cost of the user's *time* during this training process; you may be asked to compute that in terms of the salaries of the users, or you may have to compute it in terms of the *replacement cost* of the people doing the users' jobs while the users are being trained.

Database conversion costs can be ignored if you are installing a new system for which there is no predecessor. But if the new system is replacing an existing system, then there will almost certainly be an existing database that needs to be brought over to the new system. If the existing database is noncomputerized (e.g., file folders full of scraps of paper), then there may be a substantial cost associated with data entry; that is, someone (or possibly a large group of people) will probably have to sit at a terminal and enter all the relevant data into a computer system. If the existing data are already computerized, there may be a somewhat smaller cost involved in mechanical translation of the old files into a new format.[4]

Vendor installation costs should not be ignored, especially if the system involves new hardware, new telecommunication equipment, and/or new software. The vendors will generally give you a good estimate of the installation costs, and you should be able to get them to quote a fixed cost.

For some systems, there may be a cost of licenses or other forms of regulatory approval, from various local, state, or federal governmental authorities. This could also include such things as environmental testing of radiation emissions from the CRT screens used by the user's data entry operators. If regulatory approval is a "cut and dried" procedure simply involving the filling out of forms, you should be able to estimate the cost fairly accurately; if instead it involves an open-ended testing process, your estimate may have to be much more approximate.

The cost of parallel runs, if any, must also be included in the estimate of installation costs. For many types of systems, the user will insist that the old system be carried on, in parallel with the new system, for some period of time. This may entail a

---

4 There is a hidden cost that you should be aware of: during the conversion of the old database to the new database, it is inevitable that errors will be found. This is particularly true, as you can imagine, if the existing database is manual and entries have been made by hand; you will find missing data, incomplete data, and data that are obviously incorrect. The more historical the data are, the more of these errors you're likely to find. In addition, the conversion process itself may be error prone, particularly if it is a manual process. Thus, there is likely to be a cost associated with *data correction*. It is probably a good idea to take a random sample of the existing database to get an estimate of the number of errors that will be found; then estimate the cost of correcting those errors (in most cases, the corrections will have to be made manually).

temporary doubling of user staff or other related expenses. You should be able to find out (hopefully in the specification for the system) how long the parallel run period will be; this should help you develop an appropriate estimate.

Make sure that you don't forget the cost of the development staff involved in the installation. Typically, the programmers and systems analysts who were involved in the development of the project will be heavily involved in its installation. Obviously, in addition to their salaries (and possible overtime) and overhead, you must also take into account any travel expenses required to install the system in a remote user location.

Finally, keep in mind that for large systems installation will not take place in one fell swoop; a new banking system, for example, may be installed in one branch office after another, over a period of several months. In general, this will mean that the installation cost of the initial branches (or user areas) will be more expensive than those of the subsequent ones, because the installation team will be more and more experienced and (hopefully) any initial problems with the system will have been shaken down after the first few installations. On the other hand, if the installation process goes on for several months (or even years), then you must take into account the possibility of staff turnover: people who have become experienced at installing the system and training user groups may get tired of the process and move on to a new job somewhere else.

C.2.3   The Cost of Money

The money required to develop and install a system does not grow on trees; it must either be borrowed by the organization, or it must be taken out of the organization's current funds. Thus, there is a cost associated with the use of the money. Depending on your organization, you may be asked to express this as the cost of borrowed money or in terms of the interest that the money *could* have been earning if it had been invested instead of being used for your project.

This is an area where you should turn to your accounting department for advice. They will almost certainly have a standard guideline for how such matters should be treated, and it's important that your project use the same approach.

C.2.4   Operational Costs

Once you have installed your system, it will cost money for the user to continue operating it. However, this should also represent an area where your new system will *save* money, since it will presumably be cheaper than the current system that the user has (unless you have added a great deal of functionality). Typical of the operational costs are:

- Hardware costs and related supplies and equipment

- Software costs

- People costs

- Maintenance costs

- Facilities costs

Hardware is a broad term here, including the cost of the computer equipment (assuming that it hasn't been purchased outright, but see also Section C.2.6), telecommunications equipment, terminals, workstations, and supplies (paper, forms, floppy disks, disk packs, printer ribbons, etc.). Keep in mind also that some hardware can be thought of as a consumable in the sense that it wears out and needs to be replaced. This includes terminals, some printers, and perhaps other types of hardware. Be sure that future periods reflect replacement costs as needed.

Software costs, in this discussion, mean the ongoing lease costs for operating systems, database management packages, and other system software that your system may have leased from a software vendor.

People costs include the operations staff, technical support personnel, maintenance programmers, and the cost of those users directly involved in the ongoing day-to-day operation of the system. As discussed above, you will probably have to express this as a loaded cost in order to take into account insurance, benefits, and corporate overhead.

Maintenance costs include the expected monthly (or annual) maintenance cost for the computer equipment; your estimate here should not only include the cost of preventive maintenance that the vendor provides, but also any extra costs associated with actual repairs if equipment breaks down. You should also include the maintenance costs of vendor-supplied software, if applicable; the maintenance contract offered by the software vendors usually includes a hot-line telephone number for technical support, as well as free (or reduced-cost) upgrades to new versions of their packages.

In addition, your maintenance costs should include an estimate of the maintenance cost for repairing and enhancing the application software. This can be a major cost factor, as evidenced by the fact that most organizations spend more than 50% of their data processing budget on maintenance. There are various ways that you can estimate the maintenance costs of the new system:

- If you system is replacing an old system, you might estimate that the new system will require the same amount of maintenance effort. This is a fairly conservative effort, for it implies that the old system was developed using fairly modern software engineering techniques and that the new system won't use techniques any more modern or efficient. This is unlikely if the old system is 10 to 15 years old, but it at least represents a sort of worst-case estimate.

- An optimistic estimate might be based on an expected *savings* over the maintenance of the current system. Many organizations have found, for example, that their maintenance costs have been reduced by a factor of five or more by careful use of structured analysis, structured design, and structured programming.[5] You should investigate other similar projects within your own organization to see whether savings of this kind have been achieved; if so, it may be reasonable to expect similar savings on your project. Be leery, however, of the temptation to show sizable personnel reductions based on the installation of your new system; it rarely happens, for reasons discussed in Section C.3.1.

- If there is no current system to use as a comparison (or if you want to avoid overly optimistic and overly pessimistic estimates), try to determine the *average* maintenance cost for similar systems in your organization. This will probably be based on some normalized unit (e.g., maintenance dollars per line of code per year or maintenance dollars per function point per year), but the estimates that you carried out in Appendix B should allow you to make the appropriate maintenance estimates for your project.

A final cost that must be estimated when calculating the operational cost of the new system is that of the physical plant (e.g., the computer room and the office facilities for operations staff, vendor maintenance people, and user staff). If the new system is going to operate on a centralized mainframe that is already in place, these facilities costs may already have been buried in the overall hardware cost discussed above. However, if you are developing a brand new system that will have its own operational facilities, this could well be a major cost.

C.2.5   The Cost of Failures

There is yet another cost that you must take into account: the cost of potential failures in the new system. It is convenient to bury this in the category of operational costs, but it tends to hide what will become an increasingly important aspect of information systems in the future: their reliability.

There are various forms of system failure, as you can imagine; in some cases, the system is entirely unavailable for operation until the error has been corrected, while in other cases, the system continues to operate, but one or more of its outputs are incorrect. In some cases, some functions in the system may be inoperable, and in other cases, some users may be unable to access the system. All these forms of failure have a cost associated with them: hardware costs, software costs, people costs associated with correcting the error, potential legal costs if the system has caused financial loss or some other grievous loss, and possibly loss of revenues or loss of customers.

How should one estimate this? It would be naive to ignore this area altogether, for we have not yet achieved the ability to build perfect systems; on the other hand, if you ask any of the programmers or systems analysts on the project how many failures they expect to have in their new system, they look at you as if you had just suffered a new form of senility.

---

5 For detailed calculations of this savings, see Capers Jones' *Programming Productivity*. (New York: McGraw-Hill, 1985).

Perhaps the most responsible thing you can do is to (1) look at the failure rate of the current system, if you are building a new system to replace an existing one, and (2) look at the failure rate of all other systems in your organization.[6]   You may then be able to make some reasonable assumptions about the failure rate that can be expected in your new system. Hopefully, your project can be built with substantially fewer errors than in the current system, or even the average system in your organization; indeed, you should be striving for a minimum of a factor of 10 improvement, if not more.

If there are no available statistics about software reliability of your organization's current system and no basis on which to make an estimate for your new system, then at the very least you must include this fact in your risk analysis document; see Section C.5 for more information. If you are building a large, complex system in which a failure would have potentially disastrous, far-reaching consequences, it is professionally unacceptable *not* to have a software reliability model, despite the fact that most organizations do not currently bother doing so. For more information on this area, see *Software Reliability* by Glen Myers (Reading, Mass.: Addison-Wesley, 1979).

C.2.6   Distinguish Between Capital Costs and Expensed Costs

Some of the costs associated with the new system will be expensed during the year in which they occur; that is, your organization will recognize those costs on their P&L statement (and in the tax returns they file with the IRS) during they year they occur. Other costs are capitalized; that is, the costs are spread over a period of several years. While this does not affect the aggregate cost of the system, the classification of a cost as expensed versus capitalized can have an enormous impact on the organization's tax position. Similarly, the decision to incur some costs on a *purchase* basis instead of a *lease* basis can have an enormous impact on the organization's cash flow, even if the total cost remains the same.

Typically, hardware purchases are considered a capital expense, and the cost is spread over a period of 5 to 7 years (depending on the prevailing tax regulations). The cost of developing the software may or may not be capitalized. And installation costs and operational costs are normally expensed in the period when they occur, though there may be minor variations in this area.

Obviously, this is not an area where you can invent your own accounting policy. It is important to find out what financial standards are used in your organization and follow them in a consistent fashion.

C.3   BENEFIT ANALYSIS

It is much more difficult to calculate expected benefits of a new information system than it is to calculate its costs. In some cases, as mentioned at the beginning of

---

6 This assumes, of course, that someone in your organization is keeping track of such things. A landmark survey of nearly 500 U.S. data processing installations conducted by Lientz and Swanson in 1980 suggests that approximately 50 percent of the organizations did *not* keep track of operational failures in their systems; see Lientz and Swanson, *Software Maintenance Management*, Reading, Mass.: Addison-Wesley, 1980.

this appendix, it may be impossible—because the system is mandatory or because the user has decided that he wants the system regardless of whether tangible benefits can be identified.

It is the attempt to calculate *tangible* benefits that causes so many problems. Users are likely to wax enthusiastically about "better control" or "more timely information" or "better decision-making scenarios," but if you ask them how much money they're going to save or how much profit it will add to the bottom line, they're likely to waffle and say, "Oh, lots and lots ... I just know that it's going to be terrific!" Indeed, the new system probably will be terrific—but words like terrific don't fit very well in a spreadsheet showing numerical comparisons of costs and benefits.

Thus, your biggest job in carrying out a cost-benefit calculation will be that of pinning the users down and getting them to commit to tangible benefits that can be measured and calculated in a quantitative way. If you are unable to do this (which is the case for many projects and many systems analysts), try to get the users to compare your new system with some other system with known benefits. Thus, you might say to your user, "Suppose you had to make a choice between the new system we're talking about and System X. Which one would you consider is most important? If we could only implement one of them, which one would you pick?" Assuming that System X has some tangible benefits associated with it, this should give you at least a crude way of determining the approximate value of the new system.

In the following sections, we will distinguish between tactical benefits and strategic benefits offered by the new system. In this context, a tactical benefit is one that allows the organization to continue carrying out the same business activity, but at a lower cost (or a higher profit); a strategic benefit is one that allows the organization to begin conducting an entirely new kind of business or to conduct business in a new area or with new clients.

C.3.1   Tactical Benefits

The tactical benefits are often associated with reductions in clerical or administrative personnel; while this is not music to the ears of the clerical users, it is nevertheless a fact of life. A new information system may allow the same function to be carried out with half the number of users or even less. This is generally because the users are currently carrying out calculations or data-recording activities by hand, when it could be computerized; or they are forced to carry out the same activities (or record the same data) multiple times, when it could be done *once* on a computer; or it takes them a considerable of time to retrieve data, when it could be done quickly by a computer.

Though this is an obvious benefit of the new system, be careful that you don't overestimate its effect. In some cases, there will be fewer savings than you might have estimated; union regulations and the good-hearted nature of middle ranks of management in the user organization may prevent some of those clerical-level users from being laid off. And, equally important, you should realize that more senior levels of management are less and less impressed by the savings of one or two clerks; they are looking for bigger and better benefits from the introduction of a new system.

A slightly more interesting form of tactical benefit is the savings that comes from being able to process business transactions more quickly. Faster turnaround (or being able to handle more transactions per second) not only affords the opportunity to reduce clerical costs, it can lead to better cash flow for the organization (i.e., getting the customer's order turned into cash more quickly, speeding up delivery time of customer orders, etc.). The trick, again, is quantifying this and expressing it as a dollar figure. But, as an example, consider the following dialogue between the systems analyst and the user:

Analyst: So, how many orders a day do you process?

User: Well, we process 10,000 orders a day. But there's always a backlog—so it takes a week, on average, before a customer's order is processed and shipped.

Analyst: And the invoice is sent to the customer along with his order, right? So the customer isn't expected to pay his invoice until he receives shipment of his order?

User: That's right.

Analyst: So, if we could reduce the order processing delay from five days to one day, we would get the customer's cash, on average, four days earlier. And if the average customer order is $1000 and we process 10,000 orders a day, that means we're talking about $10 million dollars a day. Getting our hands on $10 million four days earlier than before, for each day's orders, would be worth....

A new system may also bring about savings in computer equipment; the old system may be running on an expensive mainframe computer, while the new system runs on a small PC sitting on the user's desk. Such a change not only saves computer hardware costs, but it also saves money in the area of facilities costs, operator costs, and the like. And if the new system reduces the amount of paper and printed forms, that should also be reflected as a savings. Make sure your calculations are complete here; keep in mind that fewer file cabinets may be needed, less office space, fewer typewriters, possibly fewer telephone calls between your organization and the customers, and so on.

The maintenance costs of the new system should also provide a benefit, as discussed in the previous section. Hardware maintenance costs should be reduced (unless you are running your new system on the same computer equipment that is installed in the organization), and software maintenance costs will presumably be lower than that of a current system.

C.3.2   Strategic Benefits of the New System

In more and more cases, the truly interesting and important benefits of a new system are the *strategic* benefits—not only the opportunity to save a few clerical people or a few pieces of paper, but rather the ability to let the organization do things that would not be possible with the current system. There are several examples of potential strategic benefits:

- Identifying or attracting new customers that the organization would otherwise be unable to identify.

- Entering new markets or providing new products that were previously not available.

- Capturing, reproducing, or distributing knowledge and expertise that was previously known only to one or two people in the organization.

In an economy as competitive as today's economy seems to be, an information system that can attract new customers or prevent current customers from being lost to the competition is valuable indeed. In some cases, this may be possible because your new system offers functionality that was not available before; in other cases, it may result from your system's ability to identify potential new customers that the organization was previously unaware of. Whatever the situation, you should try to quantify this benefit in terms of increased customers or increased market share and, from that, ultimately in terms of revenues and profits.

A more difficult form of strategic benefit is the ability of the new system to provide information that was not previously available. The typical example of this is the ability of the system to identify trends and patterns (e.g. sales trends by territory or season or customer preferences for different products). This is possible in almost any automated system that replaces a manual system; and there is usually an opportunity for any type of on-line or real-time system to present such trends in a more timely fashion than would have been possible with a batch system. Similarly, a system with graphics capabilities can provide information in a more effective fashion than a current system that produces information in the form of tables and numerical printouts. And a system built with a fourth generation programming language and a modern database management system can permit ad hoc browsing through the database.

A relatively new form of benefit made possible by commercial expert systems is the encapsulation of knowledge that has previously been known only to one or two people. This knowledge is typically judgmental, diagnostic, or evaluative in nature, and the human expert who possesses these skills is usually considered a very valuable asset to the organization; hence the ability of the new system to replicate this expertise should be a benefit whose value can be calculated.

As artificial intelligence techniques continue to grow, we will find ourselves identifying, as a benefit, the ability of a system to *extend* the knowledge originally only known to one or two human experts in the organization. Thus, a human expert in the organization may have a number of rules of judgment that he or she uses to diagnose the likely cause of failures in some mechanical system (an oil drilling platform, for example). It would obviously be strategically beneficial to capture that human expert's knowledge and replicate it for others to use; but it may be an order of magnitude more valuable to be able to *extend* that expertise and increase the diagnostic ability to deal with system failures.

C.4   HOW TO EXPRESS THE COSTS AND BENEFITS OF THE SYSTEM

If all the system costs were incurred instantaneously and all the benefits realized instantaneously, it would be relatively simple to represent the value of the system as the difference of benefits and costs. But, as mentioned earlier, costs usually occur over a period of years; and even if a cost is actually incurred at one point of time (e.g., a hardware purchase), the organization's accounting policies may dictate that it be spread over a period of several years.

Thus, you will probably have to demonstrate the costs and benefits of your proposed new system over a period of time. There are four common methods for doing this:

- Cash flow

- Return on investment (ROI)

- Internal rate of return (IRR)

- Net present value (NPV)

Each of these is discussed next.

C.4.1   Cash Flow

Whether or not your system eventually shows a profit (benefits that exceed the costs), management may want to know how much cash will have to be invested before a positive cash flow can be expected; obviously, they will be more concerned about this for large projects than for small ones. Note that the project's cash flow may be quite different than the information officially reported as profits and losses for the organization. For example, the project team may spend $100,000 in salaries during a one-year systems development effort; but the tax laws may allow that cost to be depreciated (or amortized) over, say, a period of 5 years. Thus, the organization may report only $20,000 of costs on its tax returns for the year, but the $100,000 in cash is definitely gone. Similarly, the benefits of the new system may look quite different from a cash-flow point of view than from the point of view of the organization's profits and losses as reported to the Internal Revenue Service.

In most cases, it is appropriate to show both an annual and an aggregate cash flow. Your cost-benefit study might produce a table like this for management:

Project X Cash Flow Projections

	Year 1	Year 2	Year 3	Year 4	TOTAL
Cash Savings	0	10,000	50,000	100,000	160,000
Cash Expenses	50,000	30,000	20,000	10,000	110,000
Net Cash	-50,000	-20,000	30,000	90,000	50,000
Aggregate Cash	-50,000	-70,000	-40,000	50,000	50,000

C.4.2   Return on Investment

Another way of evaluating the costs and benefits of the system is to calculate the *return on investment.* Suppose, for example, that you invested $110,000 in some stock or real estate and that you were then able to sell it for $160,000. (Note that these are the same figures used in the cash flow example above.) This would mean that you made a $50,000 profit on a $110,000 investment; expressed in percentage terms, this means that your return on investment was 45%.

This sounds better than investing money in a savings bank! But wait; in the example above, that profit did not occur at the end of the first year; indeed, it took 4 years. So this makes the return on investment appear to be approximately 11% per year. Even this is somewhat misleading, though, because it does not take into account the present value of future money. This is discussed next.

C.4.4   Net Present Value

If someone gave you $100 today, you would know what the value of the money was: you would have a good idea of how much you could buy with that much money. But how much is $100 worth if you know that you're not going to get it for a year? This is known as the present value or the discounted value. The present value of money that you will receive in the future is defined as the amount that you would have to invest *today,* at current interest rates, in order to end up with the amount specified. Thus, the present value of next year's $100 is approximately $95.24, at interest rates of 5%.

In general, if we want to calculate the present value of some amount of money (which we will call F), n years into the future, we can use the following formula:

$$P = F/(1+i)^n$$

where i is the interest rate. Thus, in the example above, the present value of the benefits could be calculated as follows (assuming an interest rate of 5%):

Project X Present Value Calculations

	Year 1	Year 2	Year 3	Year 4	TOTAL
Cash Savings	0	10,000	50,000	100,000	160,000
Present Value	0	9,070	43,192	82,270	134,532

As you can see, this makes financial return on the project much less impressive, but it is much more realistic. To be even more realistic, though, we must realize that future *costs* need to be discounted in the same way as future benefits. Just as a benefit of $10,000 at the end of the second year is only worth $9070 today, so a cost of $10,000 that will be incurred at the end of the second year represents a *present* cost of only $9070.

This leads to the definition of *net present value* for a project: the difference between the present value of the the benefits and the present value of the costs. For our sample project, this would lead to the following calculations:

Project X Net Present Value Calculations

	Year 1	Year 2	Year 3	Year 4	TOTAL
Cash Savings	0	10,000	50,000	100,000	160,000
Present Value of Benefits	0	9,070	43,192	82,270	134,532
Cash Expenses	50,000	30,000	20,000	10,000	110,000
Present Value of Costs	47,619	27,211	17,277	8,227	100,334
Cumulative Net Present Value	-47,619	-65,760	-39,845	34,198	34,198

Thus, the net present value of the system—*today's* value of the profit we expect to get from the system at the end of 4 years—is $34,198.

C.4.4   Internal Rate of Return

The *internal rate of return* is analogous to the percentage rate that banks, money market funds, and other financial institutions advertise for their savings accounts and other investment opportunities. The internal rate of return (IRR) is defined as the interest rate that would be required in order to generate the cash savings each year (i.e., the benefits of the system, which we have already identified) given an investment equal to the cash expenses that we have identified. In the example above, imagine that we had invested a total of $110,000 in a make-believe savings account over a period of 4 years. The question is: what interest rate would we have to earn in order to be able to withdraw a total of $160,000 by the end of the fourth year, *with no money left in the "bank" at the end?* By comparing this against the prime rate and various other investment rates, management can see whether the new system is indeed a good investment.

Suppose that we describe the future benefits to be achieved at the end of year 1, year 2, ..., year N as B_1, B_2, ..., B_N; suppose also that the future costs are described as C_1, C_2, ..., C_N. Then, the following polynomial formula must be solved for the interest rate, i:

$$C_1/(1+i) + C_2/(1+i)^2 + ... + C_N/(1+i)^N = B_1/(1+i) + B_2/(1+i)^2 + ... + B_N/(1+i)^N$$

This is not the kind of formula that one can easily solve on the back of a napkin or even with a simple four-function calculator. However, specialized calculators can be obtained with IRR functions built in; also, a variety of special-purpose PC-based and mainframe-based programs exist for this kind of financial analysis. If you don't have such tools readily available, ask your financial or accounting department for assistance.

C.5   RISK ANALYSIS

As part of your cost-benefit calculations, you should be prepared to carry out a risk analysis for the new system; if management does not ask for one, you should do one anyway. The reason for this is that we cannot assume, with total certainty, that we will achieve the estimated benefits or incur the estimated costs. Things might turn out better than we estimate; of more concern is the fact that things might turn out far worse.

Management will generally want to know what the consequences are if things go wrong during the project; and they will want to know *what* things can go wrong. Specifically, they will want to know the conditions under which the estimated costs might be significantly higher and the conditions under which the benefits might be significantly lower than estimated.

How could the costs be higher than what you have estimated? Here are a few possibilities; it is up to you to identify specific risks for your own project:

- The computer hardware vendor might go bankrupt.

- The project team might suffer extreme turnover, illness, or other disruptions.

- The technology used for the project might not work as advertised, especially if it is new technology that has never been used before.

- The window of opportunity might be missed; for example, the system might not be ready for installation until January 2, and government regulations might prevent the system from actually being installed until the *following* January 1.

- Political or contractual problems might arise with unions, outside contractors, and others.

- The project team might not have the required knowledge of the application or might have other deficiencies (inadequate training and experience) that lead to lower-than-expected productivity.

- Turbulent business or economic circumstances might force the project to be canceled.

- A variety of hidden costs might appear, for example, additional overhead or paperwork that had not been necessary in the previous system.

Similarly, the estimated benefits might fail to materialize. Here are a few possible reasons:

- The operational users might find it more difficult than expected to use the new system, leading to delays and disruptions. (This is particularly important if the system benefits were predicated on higher user productivity.)

- Expected improvements in market share might not occur. The system might not produce more customers, more orders, more business, or more revenues.

- The system might not behave as expected; for example, it might not process as many transactions per second as had been expected.

- The value of the new information made available by the system might turn out not to have any tangible benefits.

To deal with these risks, it is often a good idea to put together a worst-case scenario, a best case, and an expected case. The more precise and realistic you can make this, the better: there is no point fooling yourself and your management with unnecessarily optimistic assumptions about costs and benefits. Similarly, though nobody expects the worst-case situation to occur, it is important for management to understand just how bad things *could* get.

A final note about risk analysis: management will often know of far more risks than you do (e.g., a potential merger between your company and another company that will render the system useless). They can evaluate these risks, and will often not even tell you about them; they need you to evaluate the technical project risks.

APPENDIX

WALKTHROUGHS AND INSPECTIONS

D.1 INTRODUCTION

This appendix provides a brief overview of a technique known as a *walk-through*. You may find it useful to conduct walkthroughs of the specifications developed during a systems analysis project. In order to use the concept, though, you need to know what a walkthrough is, why walkthroughs are held, who participates in a walkthrough, and what the procedures are.

After you have finished reading this appendix, you may need additional information. Two possible references are *Structured Walkthroughs*, 3rd edition, by Edward Yourdon (New York: YOURDON Press, 1985) and *Technical Inspections and Reviews*, by Daniel Freedman and Gerald Weinberg (Boston: Little, Brown, 1977).

D.2 WHAT IS A WALKTHROUGH?

As the term is used in the systems development industry, a walkthrough is a *peer group review of any technical product.* This means that the review involves other systems analysts who are working with you, as well as users, programmers, systems designers, operations people, and others who may be involved in various aspects of the project you are working on. But a walkthrough, under normal conditions, does *not* include your boss, or the head of the department, or the vice-president from the user organization.

Obviously, these eminent persons will want some opportunity to review various aspects of the project, including the specifications you are working on. But they are generally less involved in the technical details than your peers, and may not be able to offer any detailed suggestions. And politics is usually a factor in such high-powered reviews. This does not mean that such reviews are bad or that they are irrelevant, merely that they are *different* from the walkthroughs discussed in this appendix. The danger of allowing management in a peer-group review is that politics will generally intrude, and/or the walkthrough will turn into a performance evaluation of a *person,* rather than a technical review of a *product.*

Note that there can be many different types of walkthroughs in a typical project:

- Analysis walkthroughs

- Design walkthroughs

- Code walkthroughs

- Test walkthroughs

Since the subject of this book is systems analysis, we will concentrate here on analysis walkthroughs. In practical terms, this means that a group of systems analysts, together with other interested parties, gather together to review dataflow diagrams, entity-relationship diagrams, state-transition diagrams, data dictionary entries, and process specifications, i.e., all the technical products developed by the systems analyst.

D.3   WHY DO WE HAVE WALKTHROUGHS?

The primary reason for conducting a walkthrough is to spot errors as quickly and economically as possible. As mentioned earlier in this book, it is generally *much* cheaper to find and remove errors as early as possible, rather than waiting until a product has been finished and sent on to the next stage of development.

There are other ways of finding errors besides a walkthrough: the person who produced the product (e.g., a DFD) can review it himself and try to find his own errors. But common sense and many years of experience in the data processing field tell us that this is often a very uneconomical way to do things. People are often unable to find their own errors, no matter how much they study their work. This is true whether one is reading a text document for typographical errors, or reading a computer program to look for bugs, or reading a DFD to look for errors. A group of knowledgeable, interested peers can often find errors *much* more quickly.

Another way of finding errors is to use an analyst workstation of the sort discussed in Appendix A; this is roughly analogous to using a compiler to find syntax errors in a program, rather than desk-checking the program listing. If you have an analyst workstation, by all means use it to identify all of the syntax errors that it is capable of finding. But just as a compiler does not find *all* the errors in a computer program (e.g., it does not find run-time errors and logic errors, because it performs a static analysis rather than a dynamic analysis of the program), so an analyst workstation does not pretend to find *all* the errors in a set of specification models. A walkthrough is still a useful complement to any mechanical tools that are available.

Indeed, one of the things that the analyst workstation is highly unlikely to do is comment on the *style* of the products; this is something that people are eminently well qualified to do. Thus, when examining a DFD, the human reviewers may ask such questions as:

- Are there too many bubbles in the diagram?

- Have the process names been chosen in a meaningful way?

- Has the diagram been drawn so that it is esthetically pleasing? Is it likely that the user will actually read the diagram, or is he likely to be confused by it?

- Have dataflows been packaged in a meaningful way from one level to another?

- Have elementary activities been packaged together in an intelligent way to form higher-level bubbles?

In addition, there are other benefits that organizations generally find with a walkthrough approach: training, and insurance. A peer group review process is an excellent vehicle for teaching new, junior members of the project team (as well as older, burned-out members of the team!) details about the application, about systems analysis, or about the details of dataflow diagram notation. And because all the members of the review group become somewhat familiar with the product (and often intimately familiar with it), the walkthrough becomes an insurance policy against the unexpected, untimely departure of the producer from the project team; someone else should be able to pick up the work done by the producer and carry it forward.

The big danger with all this is that the producer may not agree with the benefits and may consider the entire walkthrough process to be an invasion of his privacy. If the producer considers the DFDs to be *his* property (as opposed to a corporate asset), then he may resent having to show them to someone else. If his notion of style differs widely from that of his peers, there may be violent arguments in the walkthrough. And if the producer is opposed to the notion of training and insurance, he may well reject the concept of a walkthrough.

In general, walkthroughs succeed in an environment where the notion of a team is already accepted and in place; in a typical project, it means that each individual must understand that a serious failure or error in *his or her* work could endanger the success of the entire project, which means that the potential of errors in his work is a legitimate concern of the other team members. For more on the notion of teams, especially so-called "egoless teams," you should read Gerald Weinberg's classic *The Psychology of Computer Programming* (New York: Van Nostrand Reinhold, 1971).

D.4   WHEN TO HAVE A WALKTHROUGH

A walkthrough can take place at virtually any point in the development of a technical product—from the moment that it first represents a gleam in the eye of the producer, to the point where the producer is absolutely convinced the product is finished and ready to be turned over to the customer (or to the next stage of the development process). In general, it is preferable to have a walkthrough as early as possible, but not so early that the product is incomplete or riddled with many trivial errors that the author could have removed.

Let's take the example of a dataflow diagram to illustrate this point. The producer will typically go through several iterations of (1) discussing the relevant area of the system with the user; (2) mentally visualizing a DFD; (3) sketching various incomplete versions of the DFD on paper napkins and the back of envelopes; (4) sketching a relatively clean version of the DFD on a clean sheet of paper; (5) entering the details about the DFD into an automated analyst workstation of the sort discussed in Appendix A; (6) conducting whatever error-checking operations are available in the workstation product to remove syntax errors; (7) printing out a final version of the DFD on a plotter or laser printer; and (8) delivering the final DFD to the boss with a triumphant announcement that the task was finished ahead of schedule.

In this case, it's too early to have a meaningful walkthrough at stage (1), (2) or (3); the walkthrough can be conducted effectively at stage (4), (5) or (6); and stages (7) and (8) are too late. Precisely when one has the walkthrough will depend on how much automated support is available, how quickly it can be made available (i.e., does the analyst have to wait for four days to get access to the analyst workstation, which is being shared with 27 other analysts?), and how much it costs to use the automated support.

The primary reason for avoiding a walkthrough at a late stage is that the producer will have invested so much of his ego in the product that he will generally be reluctant to make any changes, other than corrections of gross errors (and sometimes not even that!). Then, too, the producer may have needlessly wasted a lot of time removing errors from his product, when the review team could have done it more quickly and economically if they had seen the product at an earlier point.

And, finally, one must remember the psychology of the reviewers themselves: they are spending their own time to participate in finding someone else's errors, and they will feel this way to some extent, no matter how much of an egoless team they claim to be. Given this perception, the reviewers should not be shown a sloppy, incomplete product; but they should also not be shown a finished, frozen, perfect product.

If you are going to spend an hour of your time reviewing your colleague's DFD, it's nice to know that you've done something useful by finding an error that the producer had not seen on his or her own. If, on the other hand, you spend an hour staring at a product without finding anything to comment on, there is a natural human tendency to view the effort as somewhat of a waste of time and to be less available the next time you are asked to participate in a walkthrough.

D.5   ROLES IN A WALKTHROUGH

Many organizations conduct walkthroughs with no more training or formalism than what has been described above. But many have found that it helps to introduce some formalism or structure to the review; hence the common term structured walkthrough. One common characteristic of a structured walkthrough is a set of formal *roles* that are played by the reviewers. Different reviewers can play different roles from one walkthrough to the next; and in some cases a reviewer might play more than one role.

Here are the common roles found in a walkthrough:

- *Presenter*, the person who explains to the reviewing group what the product does, what assumptions were made when it was created, and so on. In many cases, the presenter is the producer, but not always. Some organizations feel that if the producer presents his or her own product, then (1) the product may be so cryptic that it would never stand on its own if the producer were not immediately available to explain it, and (2) the producer may subtly (and presumably innocently) brainwash the reviewing audience into making the same errors, oversights, and errors of omission and commission that *he* or *she* did.

- *Chairperson*, the person who organizes the meeting and runs it. His or her purpose is to keep the discussion moving along in an orderly, constructive way, to prevent tangential discussions, as well as critiques of the presenter. For obvious reasons, there is a temptation to let the project manager serve as the chairperson; but for reasons described earlier in this appendix, a manager's presence in the peer group review often changes the tenor of the review in a very negative way.

- *Scribe*, the person who makes a written record of the significant events of the review. Aside from such trivial things as recording when the walkthrough took place, whose product was being reviewed, and who attended the walkthrough, the scribe writes notes about significant technical questions that were raised, bugs that were found, and suggestions for improvement or modification made by the reviewers.

- *Maintenance oracle,* a reviewer whose main orientation is the long-term maintenance of the product. He will generally be concerned that the product is not too idiosyncratic or not sufficiently well-documented. He is likely to play a larger role in design walkthroughs and code walkthroughs than systems analysis walkthroughs.

- *Standards bearer*, the role of this person is obvious: to ensure that the product is consistent with the overall standards that have been adopted by the project and/or organization. Sometimes the primary role of this person is to advise the producer (and other members of the team) as to whether the product will ultimately be judged acceptable (in terms of adherence to standards) by a formal quality assurance group.

There are two last points to make about these roles: first, keep in mind that the roles can change from one walkthrough to the next. And, second, remember to include the user as one of these roles if the user is an active participant in the project.

D.6 WALKTHROUGH PROCEDURES

As indicated in the previous section, successful walkthroughs are generally characterized by a set of formal roles and procedures. The procedures vary from organization to organization, but the following list is typical:

1. Schedule the walkthrough a day or two in advance and distribute appropriate materials to the reviewers. If the walkthrough is scheduled without sufficient advance warning, the reviewers will not have the chance to study the product before they arrive at the walkthrough.

2. Ensure that the reviewers have indeed spent some time reviewing the product. One easy way of doing this is to ask each reviewer to bring to the walkthrough at least one positive comment and one negative comment about the product. The danger here is that some of the reviewers may be so busy or so uninterested in the product that they will do no advance work and just sit silently in the walkthrough without making any contribution.

3. Ask the presenter to make a brief presentation of the product. This is often done using flipcharts, overhead transparency projectors, and the like. This is where the group literally walks through the product.

4. Solicit comments from the reviewers. This is normally orchestrated by the chairperson, who may decide to go around the room, asking each reviewer in turn to point out a bug or make a comment about the product.

5. Ensure that issues are *presented,* but not *resolved,* in the walkthrough. This is especially important if a nontrivial bug has been pointed out; let the producer figure out how to solve it on his own time, rather than allowing an unstructured brainstorming session to ensue. This is also an important procedure when issues of style are raised: the producer may disagree with the comments, and it's better for him to consider them after the meeting (or talk separately with the person who made the style suggestion).

6. Keep the walkthrough relatively brief—no more than an hour. People cannot be expected to maintain a high level of concentration for more than about an hour; their attention will wander, and there is a serious danger that the walkthrough will degenerate into a bull session.

7. Take a vote on the results of the walkthrough meeting. The typical recommendations that are made by the walkthrough reviewers are (1) "We think the product is OK as it stands," or (2) "We think some errors should be fixed and some minor style issues should be addressed, but we trust the producer to make the appropriate changes without any further reviews," and (3) "We have found a sufficient number of bugs and/or style issues that we would like to have another walkthrough when the producer has made all the appropriate changes." Depending on the nature of the team and the way in which people are assumed to take responsibility for their work in the organization, this vote may be binding, or it may simply represent an optional suggestion made by the reviewers.

D.7 SUMMARY

Though the walkthrough approach is a simple and straightforward reviewing process, it is not used as widely as you might think. One reason for this is the apparent increase in time required to conduct the walkthroughs: it can take up as much as 5% to 10% of the total project time. On the other hand, most organizations that have used walkthroughs have reported dramatic reductions in the number of errors that go undetected.

Perhaps the most important reason for not using walkthroughs is that some programmers and systems analysts continue to regard their programs and their dataflow diagrams as their *personal* property, rather than a corporate asset. Thus, they prefer not to show their work to others and strongly resist any criticisms or suggestions for improvement. This is a dangerous point of view; more and more organizations are beginning to realize that they must introduce some form of peer group review if they are to succeed at improving the quality of the systems they produce.

APPENDIX

 INTERVIEWING AND

DATA-GATHERING

TECHNIQUES

E.1 INTRODUCTION

This appendix discusses a number of guidelines for the *interviews* that you will carry out during the systems analysis phase of a systems development project. You are likely to interviews users, managers, auditors, programmers who maintain existing computer systems, and a variety of others.

Why do we conduct interviews during systems analysis? The reasons are these:

- We need to gather information about the behavior of a current system or the requirements of a new system from people who have this information stored somewhere in their heads.

- We need to verify our own understanding, as systems analysts, of the behavior of a current system or the requirements of a new system. This understanding was probably acquired through previous interviews, together with independently gathered information.

- We need to gather information about the current system and/or systems in order to carry out cost-benefit studies (see Appendix C for more information in this area).

This appendix covers the following topics about the interviewing process:

- Types of interviews

- Fundamental interviewing problems to worry about

- General guidelines for conducting interviews

E.2 TYPES OF INTERVIEWS

The most common form of an interview is a live, face to face meeting between you (perhaps accompanied by one or more fellow analysts on the same projects) and one or more subjects (interviewees). Typically, notes will be taken with pencil and paper by one of the interviewers; less commonly, the interview will be recorded on a tape recorder or a secretary will take formal notes at the interview. Throughout this appendix, I will assume that your interview is of this general nature, but I will not make any assumptions about tape recorders or stenographers.

You should realize that the kind of information captured in an interview might also be obtained by other means, for example, by asking the subject(s) to respond to a formal, written questionnaire, or by asking the subject(s) to write a position paper describing the requirements of their new system. It's also possible that the interviews could be augmented by the presence of various specialists (who might even conduct the interview while the systems analyst plays a passive role), such as industry experts, behavioral psychologists, and union negotiators. And, finally, you should keep in mind that another data-capturing media (e.g., videotape) might be used to record the content of an interview.

During the 1980s, one specialized form of interviewing has become popular in some MIS organizations; it is known as JAD (for Joint Application Development) or accelerated design, or team analysis, and by various other terms. It consists of an accelerated interviewing and data-gathering process in which all the key users and systems analysis personnel are gathered together for a single, intensive meeting (which may last from one day to a week) to document user requirements. The meeting is usually supervised by a trained specialist who acts as a facilitator to encourage better communication between the systems analysts and the users.

While all these variations have indeed been used, they are relatively rare and will not be discussed further in this appendix. The most common interview is still the one-on-one meeting between a systems analyst and an end user.

E.3 FUNDAMENTAL PROBLEMS TO WORRY ABOUT

At first glance, it might seem that the process of interviewing a user is a simple, straightforward affair. After all, you're an intelligent, articulate person; and the user is an intelligent, articulate person. You're both rational people and you both want to accomplish the same thing: transfer information about a proposed new system from the user's mind to your mind. What's the problem?

In fact, there are *lots* of problems that can occur. In many high-tech projects, it has been observed that the most difficult problems do not involve hardware or even software, but rather "peopleware." The peopleware issues in systems analysis are often seen best in the interview situation: it is the interview where "the tire meets the road" between user and systems analyst. The most common problems that you must watch out for are these:

- *Interviewing the wrong people at the wrong time.* It's very easy, because of organizational problems and politics, to find yourself talking to the person who is the official expert on user policy, who turns out not to know anything at all about the true requirements of the system; it is also possible to miss the opportunity of talking to the unknown user who really *does* know what the requirements are. Even if you find the right person, you find yourself attempting to conduct an interview during a period when the user is unavailable or thoroughly swamped with other pressures and emergencies.

- *Asking the wrong questions and getting the wrong answers.* Systems analysis is, as Tom DeMarco likes to point out, a form of communication between aliens. Users and systems analysts have a different vocabulary, a different experience base, and often a different set of assumptions, perceptions, values, and priorities. Thus, it's easy for you to ask the user a reasonable question about the requirements of his or her system and for the user to completely misunderstand your question, without either of you being aware of the fact. And it's easy for the user to give you some information about his or her requirements and for you to misunderstand that information, again without either of you being aware of the fact. The modeling tools presented earlier in this book are an attempt to provide a common, unambiguous language in order to minimize these misunderstandings. But interviews take place largely in a common spoken language (English, Spanish, French, etc.), so the problem is a real one. This is why it is so important to schedule follow-up interviews to verify that both parties have understood both the questions and the answers.

- *Creating bad feelings between both parties.* As we will see in Section E.6, there are a number of reasons why a user might feel uncomfortable or even antagonistic about an interview with a systems analyst (e.g., because he feels that the whole purpose of the new system that the analyst is specifying is to take away his job). And the analyst may feel resentful about the way that the user is answering her questions (e.g., she may feel that the user is insulting her by suggesting that she is too young and inexperienced to offer any suggestions about the requirements for the new system). In either case, bad feelings can arise between the two parties, making communication that much more difficult.

There is no magic way of guaranteeing that these problems will not occur; they are the result of person-to-person interactions, and each such interaction is unique. However, the suggestions given next can help reduce the chances of these problems; other than that, you must depend on practice to get better and better with each succeeding interview.

E.4   GUIDELINES FOR CONDUCTING INTERVIEWS

The following guidelines can be helpful in conducting a successful interview with your user.

E.4.1   Develop an Overall Interview *Plan*

Before you get started, it's extremely important that you find out *who* you need to interview. Otherwise, you'll waste everyone's time, and create an enormous political backlash, by talking to the wrong people about the wrong things.

This will require that you obtain an organization chart showing the various people in the user organization, as well as their reporting hierarchy. If a formal organization chart has not been published, find someone who knows how the organization works and ask for help. If an organization chart *does* exist, make sure that it is accurate and up to date; organizations often change far more frequently than the annual publishing cycle in which the charts are produced!

Even knowing the organization chart doesn't necessarily tell you who you need to talk to; sometimes the most knowledgeable person about some aspect of a system will be an administrative or clerical person not even shown on the organization chart. As discussed in Chapter 3, there are often three levels of users in a large, complex organization—the real user, the operational supervisory user, and the executive supervisory user—and it's often important to talk with all three levels.

It's also important in many cases to talk to users in the proper sequence and in the right combination. That is, you may find yourself interviewing Martha, who says, "Well, of course, I get all of my input data from George; he can tell you what it looks like. And then I do the following...." In such a case, it is often helpful to talk with George first, then Martha. Or you may find yourself interviewing Frank, who says, "Well, actually, Susan and I work on this function together; she does part of it and I do the rest...." In this case, it would obviously be more productive to interview Susan and Frank together. Sometimes you can tell which users need to be interviewed in what sequence just from your general knowledge of the organization; sometimes the users themselves will tell you once they know you're going to be interviewing them.

E.4.2   Make Sure You Have Approval to Talk with the Users

In some informal organizations, there will be no restriction on your choice of which users to talk with or when the interviews should be scheduled. But in a large organization, this is unusual; it's politically dangerous to wander around the user organization conducting interviews without some advance approval.

In most cases, this approval will come either from the manager of a user area (a department or division or group) or it will come from a designated user representative who is attached to the systems development project. In any case, the users have legitimate reasons for wanting to approve, in advance, who you interview:

- They may feel that some users are not able to understand or articulate system requirements well.

- They may be worried that some of their operational-level users are "renegades" who will articulate false requirements (or, in any case, requirements that management doesn't approve of).

- They may be very worried that the interviews will interfere with normal work assignments that the users need to carry out. Thus, they will want to schedule the interviews at an appropriate time.

- They may be worried that the interviews will be perceived as the beginning of an effort to replace the human users with a computerized system, causing layoffs, and the like.

- They may feel that they themselves (the managers) know far more about the requirements of the system than anyone else. Thus, they may not want you to talk with *any* users at the operational level.

- There may be an ongoing political battle, at a much higher management level, between the user organization and your systems development organization. Thus, the user manager may not have any real objections to your interviews, but by preventing such interviews from taking place, he may be able to send a political message to your boss's boss's boss.

For all these reasons, it's a good idea to get approval in advance. In most cases, verbal approval is sufficient; if the organization is terribly bureaucratic or paranoid, you may even need to get it in writing. This also means, by the way, that you should be aware of and sensitive to the organizational politics if you feel strongly that you need to talk with a user (typically an operational-level user) that you have been told *not* to talk to. You may want to schedule some clandestine meetings off site, but it's usually safer to pass the request up through the chain of command in your department so that it can be passed down the chain of command in the user organization.[1]

E.4.3   Plan the Interview to Make Effective Use of Time

The main point of this suggestion is that you should realize that you're taking up the user's time and that he (or his boss) may even feel that you're *wasting* his time. Thus, it's important that you do as much advanced planning and preparation as possible so that you can make effective use of the interview.

The first thing to do is make sure that the user knows the subject of the interview. In some cases, this can be done by phone; in other cases, it might be appropriate to write a list of questions that you're going to ask, or topics that you're going to cover, or DFDs that you want to review, and send it to the user a day or two in advance. If you're not able to do this, it's an indication that you really aren't prepared for the interview. And if the user hasn't read the material you've sent, it means either that he's (1) too busy, (2) uninterested, (3) feeling hostile about the whole concept of the interview, or (4) unable to understand the questions that you've raised.

---

1 All this involves organizational politics that are beyond the scope of this book. For more information, read any of the standard textbooks on management and organizational theory; or consult Robert Block's delightful *The Politics of Projects* (New York: YOURDON Press, 1981).

A related point: gather as much pertinent data in advance of the interview as possible. If there are forms or reports that are pertinent to the discussion, you can generally obtain them in advance. If there are other written user documents describing the new system or the old system, make sure that you have gotten them and studied them before the interview.

If you have prepared your questions in advance, you should be able to keep the interview to an hour or less. This is important; not only is the user generally unable to spare more than an hour or so at a time, but also (as I pointed out in Appendix D, too) people generally can't focus and concentrate intently (especially if they are looking at somewhat unfamiliar diagrams) for more than about an hour. This means, of course, that you must arrange the interview to cover a relatively limited scope, concentrating typically on a small part of the system. It may also mean that you have to schedule several interviews with the same user to completely cover the area that she or he is involved in.

Finally, schedule a follow-up meeting to review the material that you have gathered. Generally, you will want to retreat to your desk with all the information that you have gathered from the interview, put on your "analyst's hat," and do a lot of work with the raw data. There may be DFDs to be drawn or data dictionary entries to be created; cost-benefit calculations may need to be done; the information from your interview may need to be correlated with data from other interviews, and so on. In any case, the data from that interview will be massaged, documented, analyzed, and *transformed into a form other than what the user may have ever seen before.* Thus, you need to schedule a follow-up interview to verify (1) that you did not make any mistakes in your understanding of what the user told you, (2) that the user hasn't changed his or her mind in the interim,[2] and (3) that the user understands the notation or graphical representation of that information.

E.4.4   Use Automated Tools as Appropriate, But Don't Overdo It

During the interview, you may find it convenient to use prototyping tools, especially if the purpose of the interview is to discuss the user's view of the person-machine interface. Similarly, if you are reviewing a dataflow diagram and discussing possible changes, you may find it convenient to use one of the CASE tools discussed in Appendix A.

Remember, though, that the purpose of such tools is to *facilitate* discussions, not to hinder them; it should allow you and the user to explore alternative and changes quickly and easily; it may help you record your understanding of a user requirement on the spot and immediately correct any errors that you have made.

If, however, the technology gets in the way, then it should be kept out of the interview. If the user is required to venture far away from his or her normal work environment (e.g., to another building, into the computer room), the user may view the tool

---

2 Why would the user change his mind from one interview to the next? Usually because the interview causes him to focus his attention on something that he has only thought about in a "fuzzy" way up to this point. Your questions during the interview may cause him to view his requirements in a different light.

as a nuisance. If the user is unfamiliar with computer technology and is asked to use the tool, he or she may reject it. And if you are unfamiliar with the tool, (or if the tool is slow, error prone, or limited in its use) then it will interfere greatly with the interview. In any of these cases, it's probably best to use the tool off-line *after* the interview has taken place; you can then show the user the output from the tool without causing any unnecessary problems.

E.4.5   Try to Judge What Information the User is Most Interested In

If you have to develop a complete system model for some portion of a system, you will eventually need to determine inputs, outputs, functions, time-dependent characteristics, and stored memory of the system. But the order in which you obtain this information usually doesn't matter all that much, or, at least, it probably won't matter that much to you.

But it may matter a lot to the user, and you should let him start wherever he wants in the interview. Some users will want to start with the outputs, that is, reports or data values that they want the system to produce (indeed, they may not even know what inputs will be required in order to produce those desired outputs). Other users may be more interested in inputs or in the details of a functional transformation. Still others will want to talk about the details of data in a data store. Whatever it is, do your best to see the system requirements from their perspective, and keep that perspective in mind when you ask them the questions required of your interview.

E.4.6   Use an Appropriate Interviewing Style

As William Davis [Davis, 1983] points out,

> Your attitude toward the interview is important in determining its success or failure. An interview is not a contest. Avoid attacks; avoid excessive use of technical jargon; conduct an interview, not a "snowjob." Talk *to* people, not up to them, down to them, or at them. An interview is not a trial. Do ask probing questions, but don't cross-examine. Remember that the interviewee is the expert, and that you are the one looking for answers. Finally, whatever you do, avoid attacking the other person's credibility. Don't say, "So and so told me something different," or "You don't know what you're talking about."

Asking probing questions is not always easy; depending on the personality of the interviewee and the subject matter of the interview, you may need a variety of styles for drawing out the necessary information. Here are some styles that can prove helpful:

- *Relationships:* Ask the user to explain the relationship between the item being discussed and other parts of the system. If the user is discussing an object (e.g., a customer), ask him to explain its relationship with other objects; if he is describing a function (i.e., a bubble in the DFD), ask him to explain its relationship with other functions. This will not only help you discover more about the item being discussed, but will also help you discover interfaces (e.g., dataflows from one bubble to another in the DFD) and formal relationships.

- *Alternative viewpoints:* Ask the user to describe the viewpoint of *other* users about the item being discussed. For example, ask the user what her boss thinks about a bubble in the DFD, or an object type in the ERD; or ask what her subordinates think.

- *Probing:* Ask the user for an informal, narrative description of the item you're interested in. "Tell me about the way you calculate shipping charges." Or, if you're talking to the user about an object type in the ERD, you might say, "Tell me about a customer. What things do you know (or need to know) about a customer?"

- *Dependencies:* Ask the user if the item being discussed depends for its existence on anything else. This is particularly useful when discussing potential object types and relationships in the ERD. In an order entry system, for example, you might ask the user whether it is possible to have an order (if that's the item you're currently discussing) without having a customer.

- *Playing it back:* Tell the user what you think you heard him say; use your own words instead of his and ask for confirmation. Thus, you might say, "Let me see if I understand what you just said: whenever a widget comes into the system, you always have to frogulate it and send a status message to the auditing department."

E.5   POSSIBLE FORMS OF RESISTANCE IN THE INTERVIEW

As mentioned earlier, you should be prepared for the fact that some users will be opposed to the very idea of an interview; this is one of the reasons for ensuring that their manager or someone in authority in their department is aware of and has sanctioned the interview. Some of the more common objections (and some possible answers to those objections) are listed next.

- *You're taking up too much of my time.* The answer to this is to tell the user that you're sympathetic, and apologize for the time you need to take, but that you've done as much advance preparation as possible and will keep the interview as short as possible. This requires, of course, that you arrive punctually for the beginning of the interview, keep the discussion on target, and finish the interview when you said you would.

- *You're threatening my job.* This is often a very emotional reaction, and it may or may not be well-founded. While you may be able to think of a number of replies to this comment, you must remember that you are *not* the manager of this person and that you are in no position to reassure him that his job is not in danger, or warn him that it is. You can try to disclaim responsibility by saying, "I have nothing to do with this; I'm merely documenting system requirements at the direction of management," but the user in your interview won't buy that. He will view you as the "efficiency expert" whose job is to advise management on how his job can be eliminated by computerization. The solution to this problem, if you run into it, is to let higher levels of user management know about it and get *their* official comment, either in person or in writing if at all possible.

- *You don't know our business, so how can you tell us what the new system should look like?* The answer to this question is, "You're right! That's why I'm interviewing you to find out what *you* feel the requirements should be!" On the other hand, if you're a clever analyst, you'll probably suggest various ways of "improving" things (particularly if part or all of the work done by the user *now* is a manifestation of an old, inefficient implementation of a system); so this kind of comment may be unavoidable. However, the real trick is to continue to be as deferential as possible and to constantly acknowledge the user's expertise in his own area, while continuing to ask him if he would be so kind as to explain to you (and thereby help educate you) why your idea won't work.

- *You're trying to change the way we do things around here.* A variation of the above comment. The trick here is to show the user that while you may be proposing some (radical) changes in the *implementation* of their current system, you're not trying to change the *essential* features of that system, except in the areas where they themselves have asked for a change. Keep in mind, though, that some of the implementation features of the current system may have to be preserved, because the current system interfaces with other external systems that require inputs or outputs to take prescribed forms.

- *We don't want this system.* This is a variation of the "you're putting me out of a job" complaint. The real answer is that you're there, conducting the interview, because user management wants the new system. It's not your place to convince the operational user that they should want the system (no matter how wonderful you may think it is); to do that is to put the burden of responsibility on your shoulders, where it does not belong.

- *Why are you wasting our time with this interview?* "We know what we want, and if you were competent, you would understand immediately what we want. Why don't you get on with it, and just *build* the system?" This is a difficult complaint to deal with, because it has to do with the basic fact that users and systems analysts are speaking different, alien languages; if the user doesn't recognize this fact, he's in for a lot of trouble. One possible solution is to draw an analogy: ask the user if he would let an architect begin building a house for the user without detailed discussions and blueprints, followed by close communication all during the construction. Ask the user if he would be willing to say to the architect, "Build me a nice three-bedroom house. You know what I mean, right?" However, keep in mind that with the widespread availability of fourth generation languages and personal computers, the user may feel that he can build the system himself; easy successes with simple projects (e.g., spreadsheets) may have given him the impression that *all* systems are easy to implement. This may explain his impatience with you.

E.6 OTHER PROBLEMS TO WATCH OUT FOR

The guidelines above have warned you of the many political problems you may face in an interview and the many reasons why a user may be resistant to an interview. But there are a few more problems that you should anticipate:

- *A discussion that focuses more on implementation issues than require-ment issues.* This will often happen when the user says, "This is how I would like you to build the system...." It happens quite often when the user is thinking in terms of the implementation of his current system; and it can happen if the user is somewhat familiar with computer technology (e.g., if he has his own PC or is an ex-programmer himself). Remember that it is not your job in an analysis interview to describe implementation features of the system unless they are so important that they truly belong in the user implementation model that we discussed in Chapter 21.

- *Confusion between symptoms and problems.* This is a problem in many fields, not just the computer field. Imagine a patient who is talking to a doctor and who says, "Doctor, my problem is that my face really feels hot. Can you solve that problem for me?" Presumably, this is a symptom, a fever of some sort, that is indicative of some kind of medical problem. The trick is to realize that it is a symptom and not the real problem, and then to find the real problem. The same happens over and over again in systems analysis interviews. However, much of it depends on where the *boundary* is drawn in the context diagram: whether the user's complaint is a symptom or a problem depends on whether it is associated with something *inside* the system boundary or outside. Thus, you must pay special attention to the development of the environmental model; this is discussed in detail in Chapter 18.

- *The user may be unable to say what she wants the system to do or she may change her mind.* This is a common problem, and the systems analyst must be prepared for it. The more extreme this problem is, the more important prototyping becomes. For more about prototyping, see Chapter 5.

- *Disagreement between user peers, subordinates, and managers.* Unfortunately, this puts the systems analyst into the role of negotiator between various disagreeing parties. As an analyst, you can't abdicate this role; you can't say, "When you guys figure out what you want and agree with each other, come back and tell me." Instead, you must act like a labor negotiator and bring all the concerned parties into a room and work with them to arrive at a consensus. Unfortunately, this involves skills and procedures beyond the scope of this book.

E.7 ALTERNATIVE FORMS OF DATA GATHERING

Interviews are not the only way to gather information about the requirements for a system. Indeed, the more information you can gather from other sources, the more productive your live interviews are likely to be. Among the alternatives to interviews are these:

- *Questionnaires:* You can send written questionnaires to users inside your organization, to the people (or organizations) who interact with the system, to managers who sanctioned the project, and others.

- *Vendor presentations:* Computer hardware vendors and software vendors may have already developed turnkey systems for the application you are interested in. Asking them to make a presentation of the features of their system may not only help you determine whether theirs is a good solution, but also point out functions and stored data requirements that you would otherwise have missed.

- *Visits to other installations:* Look for organizations that are in the same line of business or who have systems similar to the one you are working on. Arrange to visit the installation to get first-hand information on the features and capabilities of the system.

- *Data collection:* Look for forms, reports, manuals, written procedures, records, CRT displays, and program listings that already exist in the user organization. However, keep in mind that these are typically associated with the *current implementation* of the system; as discussed in Chapter 18, this will usually include redundant and/or contradictory and/or obsolete information. Nevertheless, it's often a good starting point in order to familiarize yourself with the terrain before conducting face to face interviews with the user.

- *External research:* If you are building a system for a new application, one for which the user does not have any hands-on experience for describing her or his requirements, then you may have to look for information from professional societies (e.g., the ACM, IEEE, or DPMA), or from technical journals, textbooks, and research reports.

E.8   SUMMARY

The communication skills, diplomacy, and other human issues involved in interviewing are not easily communicated in a book. It's something you have to learn by doing or by observing: as a junior systems analyst, it's a good idea to tag along with a veteran to watch a few interviews being conducted. Also, get feedback: ask your boss to find out how the users think you're doing with your interviews. And provide feedback to the users: tell them what will happen with the results of your interview, so they don't think the whole thing was a waste of time.

REFERENCES

1.   Abraham Maslow, *Motivation and Personality.* New York: Harper & Row, 1954.

2. Charles J. Stewart and Cash Stewart, *Interviewing Principles and Practices,* 2nd ed. Dubuque, Iowa: William C. Brown, 1978.

3. William S. Davis, *Systems Analysis and Design: A Structured Approach.* Reading, Mass.: Addison-Wesley, 1983.

APPENDIX

 THE YOURDON PRESS

CASE STUDY

F.1   INTRODUCTION

No discussion of systems analysis would be complete without at least one example to illustrate the various modeling tools and techniques discussed in this book. Unfortunately, almost any case study is likely to be either entirely fictitious or a grossly oversimplified and "sanitized" version of a real-world situation. Also, it is difficult to find an example that illustrates both a business- and scientific-oriented application.

This case study describes the requirements for computerization of the information processing activities for YOURDON Press. On the one hand, it is very indicative of a real-world publishing activity that operated for approximately 10 years. Indeed, one of the things I want to show in this case study is that things are not always done for rational reasons (including the formation of companies and the initiation of many systems development projects!), and that most systems have to deal with a lot of annoying unpleasant "glitches" in the real world.

On the other hand, YOURDON Press has now joined the ranks of fictitious examples, for it was acquired by Prentice-Hall in 1986, and its information processing activities have been subsumed into Prentice-Hall's.[1] Thus, this case study describes what YOURDON Press' information processing requirements *would* have been had it continued on as an independent publisher.

The following sections provide a brief background of the YOURDON Press operation, the environmental model of the system, the behavioral model, and the user implementation model.

---

1 Prentice-Hall's information processing activities, meanwhile, are being subsumed into its new parent company, Simon & Schuster. And Simon & Schuster is part of an even larger company, Gulf + Western, which all goes to show that systems are almost always part of larger systems.

F.2   BACKGROUND

To understand the workings of YOURDON Press, it is necessary to spend some time explaining the larger context of the corporation within which it existed: YOURDON inc. Without YOURDON inc., there would have been no YOURDON Press; though without YOURDON Press, it is fairly clear that YOURDON inc. would not have achieved the success that it has.

YOURDON inc. was formed as an outgrowth of independent consulting and lecturing activities that I had been carrying out for a number of years in the late 1960s and early 1970s. The company was formed in April 1973 because my accountant told me that a corporation offered some tax advantages that would not be available to me as a self-employed consultant. Notwithstanding this practical tax advice, the new corporation did not really begin conducting any business until April Fool's Day, 1974.

As is true in most companies (and most data processing projects!), one of the first activities was to think of a proper company name. My wife and I, who served as the company's sole stockholders, directors, officers, and employees, were rather fond of the name "Artichokes And Other Fur-Bearing Animals, Inc.," but decided that it would not fit onto our stationery. We finally settled on the name "Superprogrammers, Limited," and filed the appropriate papers with the State of New York to establish the name. About two weeks later, just as we were about to place some advertisements for our first series of seminars on structured programming, the state informed us that our company name had not been approved: it was too close to the name of an already extant company. When we investigated, we found that the other company was named "Supermarket Products, Inc."[2] Out of desperation, we quickly chose a name that we were reasonably certain would not be duplicated by any other company: my own name. Thus was YOURDON inc. born.

The company's initial activities were professional seminars on advanced programming techniques and on-line systems design aimed at veteran programmers and systems analysts in large organizations and government agencies. The seminars involved about 20 hours of classroom lectures and were accompanied by a few hundred pages of class notes; the class notes for the seminar on advanced programming techniques eventually became a textbook: *Techniques of Program Structure and Design,* published by Prentice-Hall in 1975.

Because of the large number of seminar attendees, it proved economical to print the class notes in moderate volume and to bind the pages together; thus, they bore some resemblance to a book, though some of the pages were printed upside down and other pages fell out of the book at the slightest provocation. Nevertheless, some of the seminar attendees asked to purchase additional copies of the class notes, and thus, as a sideline, YOURDON inc. found itself in the business of selling "books."

---

2 When we investigated, we found that Supermarket Products was located somewhere on the periphery of New York City and was chiefly involved in importing bananas from Guatemala. We didn't see what this had to do with computers or why the state felt that our name would impinge on poor old Supermarket Products, but we decided not to fight the bureaucracy.

However, YOURDON inc. concentrated primarily on training activities: the number of distinct training courses grew to approximately 50 by the mid-1980s, and the company has now trained some 250,000 data processing professionals throughout the United States and in over 30 other countries. Professional consulting activities also began to grow, and many of the company's technical staff now serve as consultants, project leaders, and systems analysts on major systems development projects in client companies throughout North America and Europe. And in the mid-1980s, the company entered the CASE market, with an analyst toolkit product of the nature described in Appendix A. In 1987, YOURDON inc. had offices in 8 cities, with a staff of approximately 150 people.

YOURDON Press began as a division of YOURDON inc. in 1976 with the softcover publication of three books: *Structured Design*, by Yourdon and Constantine; *Learning to Program in Structured COBOL,* by Yourdon, Gane, and Sarson; and *How To Manage Structured Programming,* by Yourdon. As with so many other real-world business operations, this happened without a great deal of planning or organized thinking: the books seemed like a good way of popularizing the structured techniques concepts being developed and marketed in YOURDON inc.'s training seminars.

The first three books were produced on a simple IBM Selectric typewriter and were bound in 8.5- by 11-inch sheets; all of this predated the days of convenient typesetting and desktop publishing. Advertising was rather modest, consisting of a few *Computerworld* ads and mailings to YOURDON's seminar customer list. Sales were equally modest; indeed, for the first several years of its existence, YOURDON Press represented only a tiny fraction of the company's overall revenues.

Consequently, the information system surrounding the early YOURDON Press activities was modest and entirely manual in nature. Orders were taken over the phone or by mail, but credit card orders were not accepted. Invoices were typed by hand on four-part invoice forms, and orders were individually packed by hand. The inventory was stored in one of the world's most elegant warehouse spaces: windowed offices of the 38th floor of YOURDON inc.'s offices at 1133 Avenue of the Americas, looking out over all of Manhattan.

Automation arrived at YOURDON inc. in the spring of 1976, in the form of a second-hand PDP-11/45 minicomputer and a mysterious operating system called UNIX.[3] A few months later, a phototypesetter, two dozen terminals, and the TROFF typesetting package were added. This immediately facilitated typeset production of YOURDON Press textbooks and eventually led to the automation of several aspects of YOURDON inc.'s training business and general accounting activities. But the YOURDON Press operational activities, the activities that could be considered as an "information system," continued to operate in a manual fashion for several more years.

---

3 UNIX is not so mysterious now, of course, but in the mid-1970s hardly anyone outside Bell Laboratories and a few universities had heard of it. Neither I nor most of my colleagues at YORUDON were all that prescient; we owed our decision, which we later came to appreciate very much, to the urgings of Dr. P.J. Plauger, who had joined the company from Bell Labs in 1975. Plauger is widely known for books co-authored with Brian Kernighan, including *The Elements of Programming Style* (Reading, Mass.: Addison-Wesley, 1973) and *Software Tools* (New York: McGraw-Hill, 1976).

In 1980, a limited number of computerized applications were developed for YOURDON Press, using the convenient pipeline features of the UNIX operating system. Between 1980 and 1985, the C programming language and a number of UNIX shell scripts were used to gradually add a number of simple programs for order processing, sales reports, shipping labels, and various accounting reports. Though these programs were easy to develop and reasonably reliable to operate, they were developed on a piecemeal basis, similar to what one often sees today in an EDP organization where the end users have access to spreadsheets, report generators, and fourth generation programming languages. They were also rather limited; for example, if the details of an order needed to be modified subsequent to its entry, the system was unable to accomplish it. Instead, the standard UNIX text editor was used to modify the order, which was stored in the computer as a simple ASCII text string, terminated by an end-of-line character.

One of the most difficult activities in the day-to-day operation of YOURDON Press was the task of producing an up to date statement showing all a customer's orders, payments, book returns, and credits for a given time period. Equally difficult was the process of reconciling these activities (which took place as interactions between the customers and YOURDON Press administrative personnel) with the financial records maintained by YOURDON inc.'s accounting department. For various reasons, YOURDON Press and the Accounting Department always seemed to be "out of synch" with one another. This was further complicated by the fact that YOURDON inc.'s London office had their own inventory of books and did their own shipping and invoicing independently of the New York office; prices were quoted in pounds sterling rather than dollars and were generally somewhat higher than the prices quoted from the New York office.[4] Once every quarter, when financial statements had to be prepared, long, frustrating, mind-numbing meetings took place in which computer printouts produced by the Accounting Department were manually compared with computer printouts produced by YOURDON Press in order to reconcile differences. Tempers flared; people shouted insults, obscenities, and various epithets at one another; blunt objects were sometimes thrown back and forth across the room. It was not a pleasant activity to look forward to each quarter.

Thus, by 1986, it was evident that a full-scale *system* would have to be developed if YOURDON Press was going to continue to grow; initial planning began for the new system. However, it was also evident that a substantial amount of capital would be required to continue growing the business, not only for additional computer equipment, but also to modernize the typesetting equipment (which was now obsolete) and enlarge the editorial and marketing activities of the division. It was finally decided

---

4 The issue of separate inventories, and sales from separate offices was looming on the horizon as a larger and larger problem. Each of the various YOURDON offices insisted that they needed to have a small, local inventory to service the walk-in customers who wanted to be able to get a book right away, rather than waiting several days (or weeks) for a shipment from Galactic Headquarters. And the Canadian office argued that it needed its own pricing structure (i.e., prices quoted in Canadian dollars rather than U.S. dollars) and its own marketing/advertising campaign to appeal to the Canadian market in a different way than the U.S. market. In some cases, the remote offices would simply give the book to the customer and ask the central New York office to generate the invoice. In other cases, the customer would pay for the book on the spot, and ask for a receipt. Sales from the London office accounted for roughly 10% of the overall YOURDON Press revenues, while sales from the other offices accounted for less than 1% of the overall YOURDON Press revenues.

that it would make more sense to have the publishing operation acquired by a larger organization, and this led to the merger with Prentice-Hall. Thus, the system models described below represent what the requirements would have been if YOURDON Press had continued to operate as an independent business.

The planning for a new information system also coincided with a series of organizational changes within YOURDON Press and the rest of YOURDON inc. From its inception in 1974 until approximately 1983, the company had the organizational structure shown in Figure F.1.

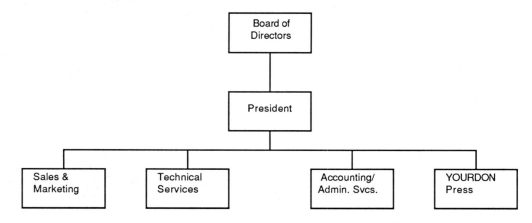

Figure F.1: **Organizational structure of YOURDON inc., 1974-1983**

Between 1984 and 1986, the company shifted to more of a regional organization, and added a new division for its software product, as shown in Figure F.2.

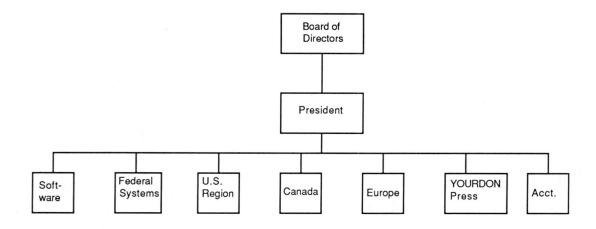

Figure F.2: **Organizational structure of YOURDON inc., 1984-1986**

And during this period, YOURDON Press gradually developed the organizational structure shown in Figure F.3.

As part of this reorganization, the YOURDON Press shipping operations were moved out of the elegant office space occupied by the rest of the staff, and into a warehouse in beautiful downtown Yonkers, New York. Thus, there was a physical separation of some 20 miles between the people entering orders and the people packing books into boxes and sending the orders to the customers.

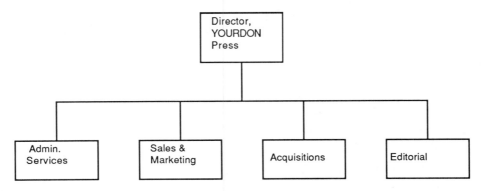

Figure F.3: **Organizational structure of YOURDON Press**

The four major groups within YOURDON Press had the following responsibilities:

- *Administrative services* was responsible for most of the day to day interactions between YOURDON Press and the customers. Thus, this group accepted orders; produced invoices; received payments, discussed book returns and credits with customers; interacted with the warehouse to arrange for shipments of books; and interacted with the Accounting Department, as discussed above.

- *Sales and marketing* was responsible for producing catalogs of the various YOURDON Press books; running ads in computer magazines and trade journals; sending promotional brochures to various mailing lists; and soliciting sales via telephone calls to large corporate purchasers of technical computer books.

- *Acquisitions* was responsible for finding new authors and new books. This part of YOURDON Press carried on all discussions with authors up to the point where a final manuscript was delivered by the author.

- *Editorial* was responsible for taking a final manuscript and turning it into a published book. This involved not only the copyediting of the book, but also interactions with printers to obtain proposals for the initial printing of the book. Editorial was also responsible for the artwork and production of the book cover, as well as the inside contents.

It should be kept in mind that YOURDON Press was a fairly small operation compared to such well-known publishing operations as McGraw-Hill, Harcourt Brace, Prentice-Hall, and Random House. An idea of the scale of the operation can be gleaned from the following statistics:

- YOURDON Press had approximately 50 books in its list; typically 4 to 6 news titles were added to the list each year.

- The books were written by approximately two dozen authors, and the acquisition group interacted with approximately 200 potential authors, that is, individuals who expressed interest in writing a book, but who had not yet actually finished writing anything.

- YOURDON Press processed approximately 50 orders a day.

- The average order was approximately $100, which typically represented three to four books. Some orders, of course, were for an individual book; some orders were larger. Wild celebrations and cheers broke out whenever an order larger than $5000 was received.

- Approximately 50,000 books per year were shipped.

Aside from its small scale, though, YOURDON Press operated in much the same way that other, larger publishers do. Sales were made via written orders, telephone orders, or walk-in orders (i.e., a customer coming into the YOURDON inc./YOURDON Press offices to purchase a book). Payment could be made in cash (which was rare), by check, or by credit card. As a matter of policy, orders under $100 had to be prepaid; larger orders, especially those from book stores and companies, generally required an invoice.

To understand the publishing business, one must also be familiar with the concept of *returns.* If an individual customer or corporation felt that a book was not suitable for their needs or if it was received in damaged condition, they could generally return the book and ask for a refund. This would normally happen within a matter of days after the shipment was received by the customer. Book stores, on the other hand, had the privilege of returning up to half of the books in an order within a year of the date that the order was placed; this is common within the publishing industry, because book stores often don't know in advance how much demand there will be for a book and want to avoid getting stuck with inventory that they can't sell.

F.3   THE ENVIRONMENTAL MODEL

F.3.1   The Statement of Purpose

The purpose of the YOURDON Press Information System (YPIS) is to maintain information needed to sell books to customers. This includes order entry, invoicing, generation of shipping documents, inventory control, and production of royalty reports and accounting reports.

F.3.2   The Context Diagram

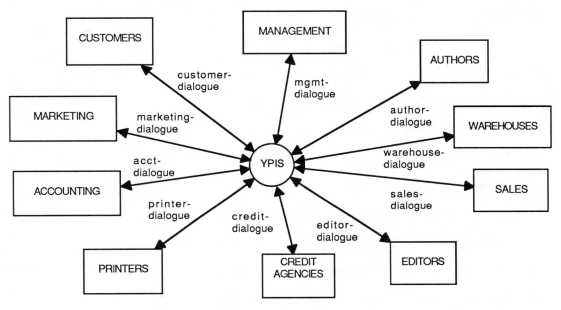

Figure F.4: **Context diagram for the YPIS system**

F.3.3   The Event List

The event list for YPIS consists of 40 events. Most of the events are flow-driven, though most of the events involving the Accounting Department are temporal. The events are listed next; temporal events are marked with a T notation following the description of the event.

1. Customer orders book (this includes special rush orders, too).

2. Customer sends payment.

3. Customer asks for book information (price, etc.).

4. Customer asks permission to return a book.

5. Customer asks about status of a book order.

6. Customer asks about status of an invoice.

7. Customer needs (monthly) statement. (T)

8. Customer asks for credit memo.

9. Customer wants refund check.

10. Accounting needs (daily) cash receipts. (T)

11. Accounting needs (daily) revenue reports. (T)

12. Accounting needs (monthly) net revenue report. (T)

13. Accounting needs (quarterly) author royalty report. (T)

14. Accounting needs (monthly) inventory data. (T)

15. Accounting needs (monthly) sales commission report. (T)

16. Management sets new credit limit for a customer.

17. Accounting needs (monthly) aged accounts receivable report. (T)

18. Printer offers quotation for print (or reprint) order.

19. Management authorizes a print order.

20. Printer advises exact print quantity and delivery date.

21. Printer sends invoice for print job.

22. Management asks for quotation on print order.

23. Marketing asks for mailing labels from customer database.

24. Marketing needs statistics on book sales.

25. Marketing needs in-stock date for new titles.

26. Editors announce new book title (date ready for printer).

27. Authors need quarterly royalty report. (T)

28. Warehouse needs shipping data and mailing labels. (T)

29. Warehouse receives books from printer.

30. Warehouse receives book returns from customer.

31. Warehouse conducts (monthly) physical inventory.

32. Warehouse makes shipment of book order to customer.

33. Warehouse announces that a book is out of stock.

34. Acquisition department announces new book project.

35. Salesperson places order on behalf of customer.

36. Marketing declares that a book is out of print.

37. Customer announces a change of address.

38. Author announces a change of address.

39. Customer elects to join agency plan.

40. Invoices need to be sent to customer. (T)

F.4　　THE BEHAVIORAL MODEL

F.4.1　　The Preliminary Behavioral Model: Dataflow Diagrams

Each of the 40 events listed in Section F.3.3 has an associated dataflow diagram. Of course, the logistics of printing a book make it unwieldy, to say the least, to connect all 40 diagrams together into a single, composite diagram representing the entire system. As we pointed out in Chapter 19, this is the sort of exercise that requires a very large sheet of paper—or several small sheets of paper taped together. I leave that as an exercise for the reader.

The diagrams were drawn with Version 2.0 the **Design** software package, available from Meta Systems Inc., in Cambridge, Mass. While it does not represent a full-fledged CASE toolkit, it is more sophisticated than most simple graphics packages; and it has the advantage of running on a Macintosh computer, which was used for the preparation of this book. To accommodate the **Design** program, I have shown stores in the DFDs with the notation given in Figure F.5.

STORE NAME

Figure F.5: **Notation for stores in the YOURDON Press case study**

As I drew the preliminary DFDs, I kept notes on errors that I found and changes that I suddenly found that I had to make in other parts of the model; these notes are itemized below each DFD. The reason for doing this is to emphasize that in a real-world project the systems analyst rarely draws a perfect DFD the first time; after thinking about the system and after follow-up interviews with the user, it is inevitable that errors will be found either in the DFD being examined or in some other part of the system model.

No attempt was made to create an organized data dictionary as the preliminary behavior model was developed. After the initial DFD model was created, process specifications were sketched out to see if there were any obvious errors; many such errors are shown as comments on the following pages. A leveled set of DFDs was then created and the data dictionary was then developed.

Event 1: Customer orders book.

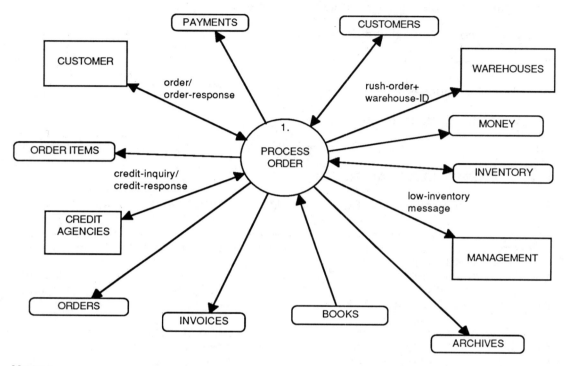

Notes

1. After the first version of this diagram was drawn, I remembered that credit card orders normally require an authorization if the amount is above some preset limit. YOURDON Press accepted orders paid with Mastercard, Visa, and American Express; hence the interface to the terminator labeled "CREDIT AGENCIES."

2. Some further thinking about the credit situation made it obvious that the definition of **customer** in the **CUSTOMERS** store would have to include **credit-limit** as a field. It also became evident that there was a required event to change the customer's credit limit (event 16), which had not been obvious before.

3. Note that orders are *not* shipped on a one-at-a-time basis, with the exception of rush orders. Details of a rush order are sent immediately to the warehouse; all other orders are simply stored in the **ORDERS** store. As a separate event (event 28), the warehouse receives mailing labels and shipping instructions for a group of orders (typically one day's worth of orders). I had forgotten the rush orders in the initial version of the diagram.

4.　When drawing this DFD, I also realized the need for an **ARCHIVES** store, which is a copy of the customer's original written order (or, in the case of a telephone order, the salesperson's order form), plus a copy of the invoice that was generated for the order. The invoice copy is not necessary in an essential model (since it could be regenerated), but the other documents are necessary in case of a subsequent dispute with the customer, and in case of audits or investigations from the tax authorities, and so on.

5.　Note that the order can be received by mail, by phone, or in person. We don't show this in the DFD above, since these are all transporter functions.

6.　Note that the system does not reorder books from the printer automatically. Instead, management is informed at various times that inventory has fallen below a preset threshold. This can occur as a result of event 1, as well as several other events.

7.　Orders may be received from new customers (especially new book stores or companies that will be doing ongoing business with YOURDON Press). Hence a new record will have to be created in **CUSTOMERS** with the standard discount rate, and so on. This is the reason for the double-headed arrow between bubble 1 and the **CUSTOMERS** store.

Event 2: Customer sends payment.

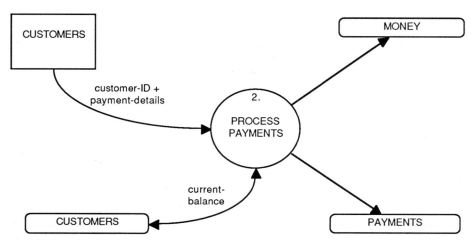

Notes

1. Payment may cover several different invoices, but it's not always clear which invoice(s) is/are involved. Sometimes the customers don't identify the invoice they are paying; sometimes they identify invoices that have already been paid; sometimes they reference nonexistent invoice numbers.

2. Sometimes it's not even clear where the payment is coming from. This is particularly true in the case of book store chains: XYZ book store in city A may be owned by a conglomerate, PQR, in city B. If a random check arrives from PQR Corp., addressed to YOURDON Press, we may not be able to determine which invoice or even which company is involved. Payments of this kind are put in an accounting category called unapplied cash. The assumption is that if we continue sending overdue invoices to XYZ book store they will call us and tell us that the invoice was paid by PQR.

3. There is no guarantee that the payment will be for the exact amount of the invoice. Some payments are high or low by a small, random amount. Some customers try to avoid paying the sales tax or the shipping and handling fees; this usually results in payments that are one or two dollars too low.

Event 3: Customer asks for book information.

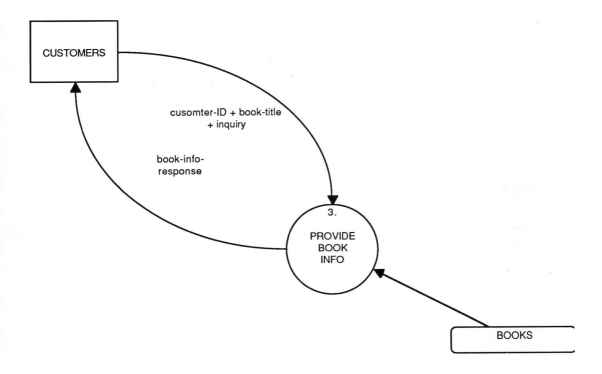

Notes

1. The customer is generally asking for such things as the price of the book, or when a new book is expected to be in stock, or the schedule for volume discounts.

Event 4: Customer asks permission to return a book.

Notes

1. Customers are supposed to get approval from YOURDON Press before returning the books. They don't always do it.

2. Actual returns arrive later on (event 30) and may or may not match the requested return that has been authorized here.

3. Note that a requested return has to be matched up with an original order.

Event 5: Customer asks about status of a book order.

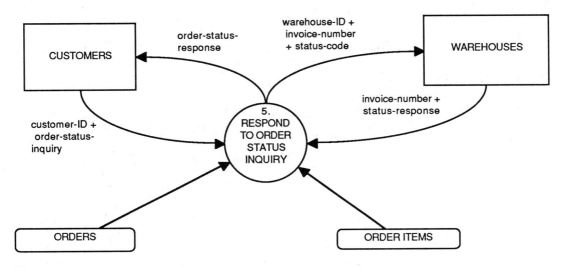

Notes

1. Shipment of a customer's order may have been delayed because of a backlog in the warehouse or because the book is out of stock. It is this potential delay that typically leads to a customer inquiry.

2. If the customer decides to cancel the order at this point, it is treated as a separate event (event 8).

3. Another possibility is that the order has not been received by YOURDON Press (either because it was lost by the Post Office or somewhere within the mailroom at the customer's office or at YOURDON's office).

4. The order may have been received by YOURDON Press and processed; indeed, it is possible that the warehouse even shipped the order, but it may have been lost by the Post Office (or other shipping agency) en route to the customer. This is treated in the same way (e.g., the customer may decide to cancel the order at this point or may ask for a credit and place the order again).

5. While developing this DFD, I realized that invoices have not been sent to the customer (shipping of the books by the warehouse and mailing of the invoice by the main YOURDON Press office are two separate events). Thus, we need a separate store for invoices, and a temporal event to cause the invoices to be sent.

Event 6: Customer asks about status of an invoice.

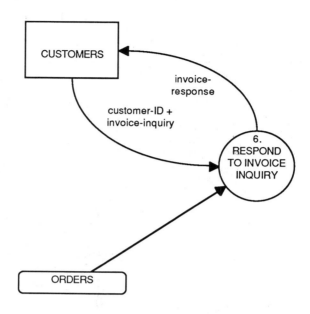

Notes

1. The customer's question may have to do with the discount rate that was quoted on the invoice, or with shipping charges, sales tax, or other aspects of the invoice.

2. If the customer is asking a more general question about all of his orders, payments, and the like, event 7 is the part of the system that handles it.

3. For this event, an **invoice-number** is necessary in order to retrieve information about the individual order. (**invoice-number** is a component of **invoice-inquiry**, as will be seen in the data dictionary.)

Event 7: Customer needs (monthly) statement.

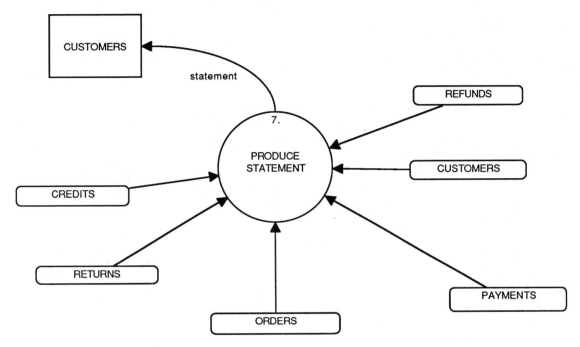

Notes

1. While working on this DFD, I discovered the need for an event to let the customer ask for a credit (event 8).

2. Note that this event is temporal (i.e., statements are generated on a regular basis, once a month).

Event 8: Customer asks for credit memo.

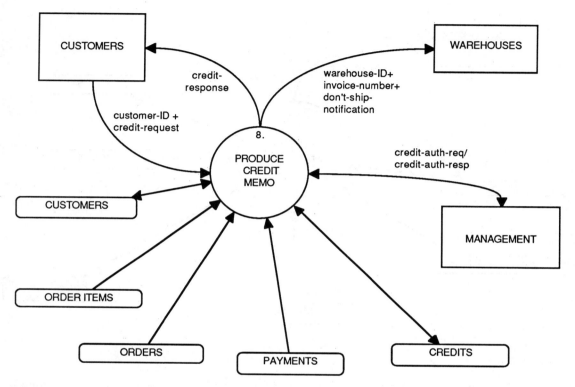

Notes

1. A credit may be given to the customer for a number of different reasons:

    *   An error in the original order (perhaps the customer was given the wrong discount, or charged the wrong price, etc.)

    *   The customer received damaged goods (e.g., the books were mangled by the Post Office).

    *   The customer received an undershipment because of an error in the warehouse. At this point, he wants a credit for the books that he did *not* receive, rather than having the rest of the order filled.

    *   The customer overpaid one or more previous invoices and has just discovered that fact (normally the overpayment would become obvious when he received his next statement).

    *   There has been an excessive delay in shipment, so the customer has decided to cancel the order.

2. The main thing that has to be done by this bubble is to update the customer's credit balance.

3. However, note that management must authorize the credit. This event has been drawn to show an immediate response from management, so that a response can be made to the customer. This avoids a "pending" store of credit authorization requests, which would otherwise be necessary.

4. Note that this activity has nothing to do with book returns; those are handled separately.

Event 9: Customer wants refund check.

Notes

1. This is OK if the customer does indeed have a credit balance. In most cases, the customer will apply an outstanding credit balance against future purchases. However, sometimes they want a check, either because they don't plan any future purchases or for some other reason.

Event 10: Accounting needs (daily) cash receipts.

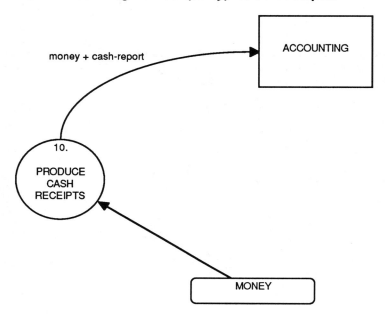

money + cash-report

ACCOUNTING

10.
PRODUCE
CASH
RECEIPTS

MONEY

Event 11: Accounting needs (daily) revenue reports.

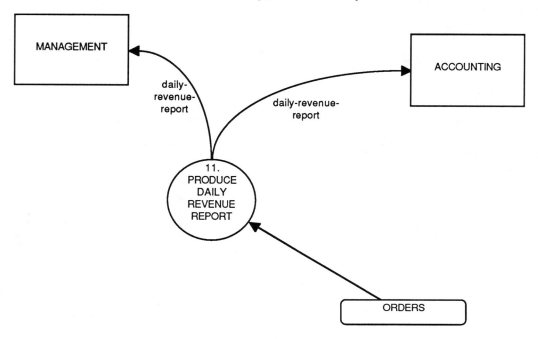

MANAGEMENT

daily-
revenue-
report

daily-revenue-
report

ACCOUNTING

11.
PRODUCE
DAILY
REVENUE
REPORT

ORDERS

Event 12: Accounting needs (monthly) "net" revenue report.

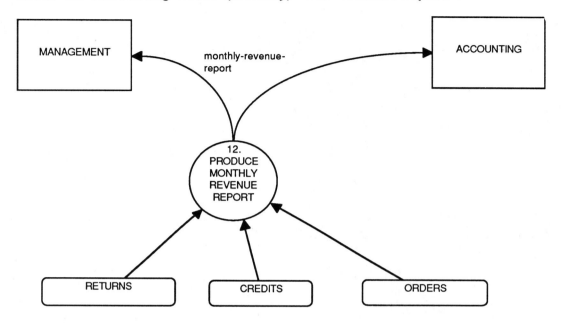

Event 13: Accounting needs (quarterly) author royalty report.

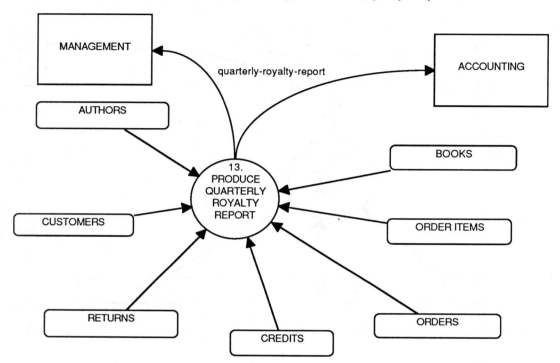

Notes

1. We need access to the **BOOKS** store to get the author's royalty rate for the book (the same author may have different royalty rates for different books).

2. We need access to the **AUTHORS** store to get the author's Social Security number, address, and so on.

3. We also need access to the **BOOKS** store to see if there is an outstanding advance (which may have been granted as a result of event 34) and to update it to reflect the current cumulative royalty owed.

4. Note that royalties for any given period could be negative if book returns for that period exceed the number of new books ordered.

5. We need the **ORDERS** store because accounting wants details on *who* bought the books. We don't need this in event 27.

Event 14: Accounting needs (monthly) inventory data.

Notes

1.   Inventory is updated asynchronously as a result of orders, returns, receipt of new shipments from the printer, and physical inventory.

2.   Note that this report shows books that have been ordered, but that may not have been shipped by the warehouses. It would not necessarily correspond with a physical inventory taken at the same instant because of the pipeline of orders that have been processed but not yet shipped.

Event 15: Accounting needs (monthly) sales commission report.

Notes

1. This assumes that salespeople are paid a commission even if the customer hasn't paid for the order. It ignores the real-world issue of reversing a commission if the customer never does pay for the order, and the associated invoice has to be written off.

2. Note many sales are not associated with any individual salesperson; they are received, unsolicited, as a result of direct mail campaigns, reviews in the computer literature, and the like.

3. This model also assumes that all salespeople are paid at the same commission rate, and that the commission is the same for all books. However, the commission rate can be changed by management each time this event occurs.

4. The model also assumes that we have to show the *details* of the order to the salespeople, because (being typical paranoid salespeople) they don't believe the computer.

Event 16: Management sets new credit limit for a customer.

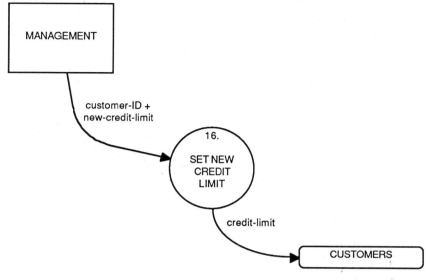

Notes

1. Management may decide to change the credit limit of a customer for a variety of reasons, the most common of which is slow payment of previous invoices. However, it could also be done if the customer has gone bankrupt or if management feels that general business conditions have changed.

Event 17: Accounting needs (monthly) aged accounts receivable report.

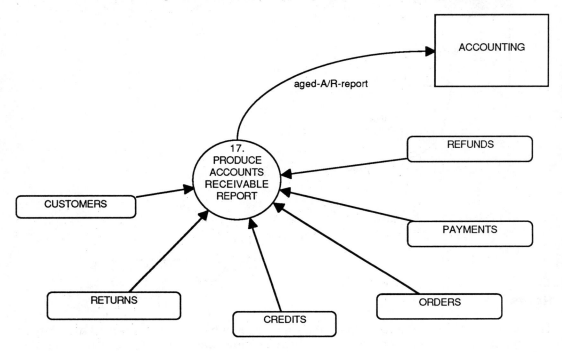

Event 18: Printer offers quotation for print (or reprint) order.

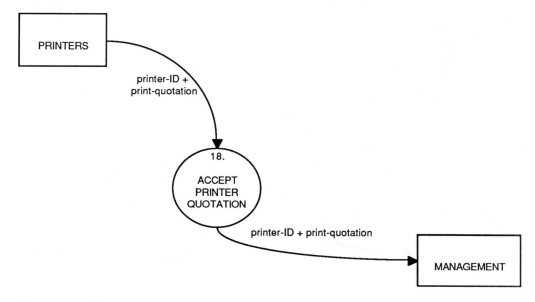

Notes

1. Note that the system does no processing of the printer's quotation; it is simply passed on to management.

2. Since the system does no processing, it is not clear why this event needs to occur at all. (On the other hand, one could argue that the system does have the responsibility to serve as the conduit, or interface, between external printers and management within YOURDON Press.) In any case, it provides for the future capability of the system to do automated ordering, based on preset criteria.

Event 19: Management authorizes a print order.

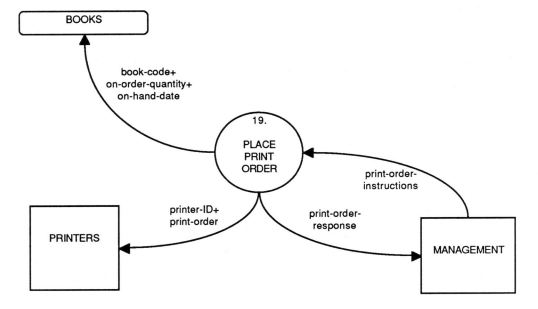

Event 20: Printer advises exact print quantity and delivery date.

Notes

1. Accounting needs the revised book order information so that they can keep track of unit costs. This, together with event 14, allows accounting to keep track of the value of the inventory on a first-in-first-out (FIFO) basis.

2. Note that this assumes that the printer won't make major changes to his initial quotation. In practice, the printer typically underprints or overprints the quantity originally quoted by 1% to 2% (e.g., a print order for 2000 copies of a book might actually result in a print run of 2037 books). Typically, the printer also waits until this point to quote shipping and other charges.

Event 21: Printer sends invoice for print job.

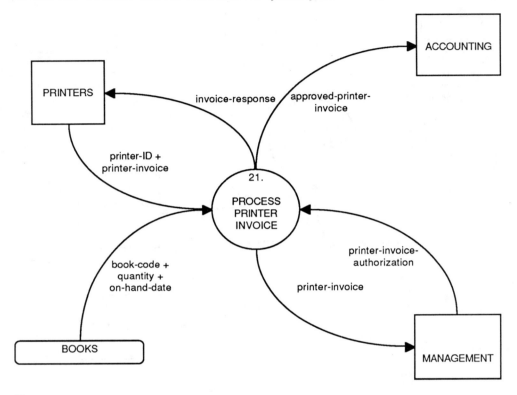

Notes

1. This assumes that management will respond to the printer's invoice immediately. Note that YPIS does not produce a check, but merely informs accounting that a check should be cut.

2. This model assumes that there will be a separate invoice for each print order. It also assumes that there is only one print order outstanding at any given time.

3. Note that invoicing is asynchronous from the shipment of books by the printer. As a separate event, the warehouse informs the system that books have been received from the printer.

4. This also assumes that the invoice amount is the same as that shown on the revised estimate (event 20).

5. Note that some printers insist on partial prepayment of invoices; this model does not take that into account.

Event 22: Management asks for quotation on print order

Notes

1. Note that multiple printers are generally queried in order to get a range of price quotations. These quotations are received as an asynchronous event, and each quotation is sent to management (event 18).

2. Note that the printers do not respond with a quotation right away; however, we assume that they eventually will respond.

Event 23: Marketing asks for mailing labels from customer database.

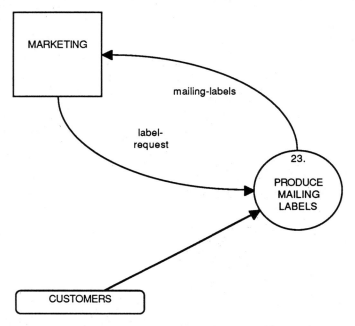

Event 24: Marketing needs statistics on book sales

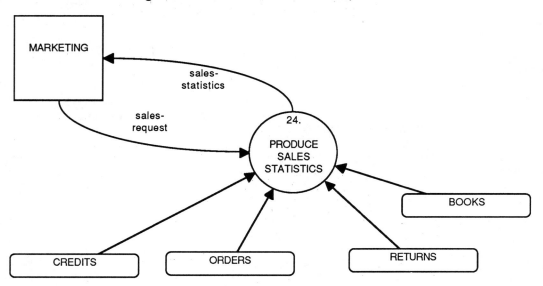

Event 25: Marketing needs in-stock date for new titles.

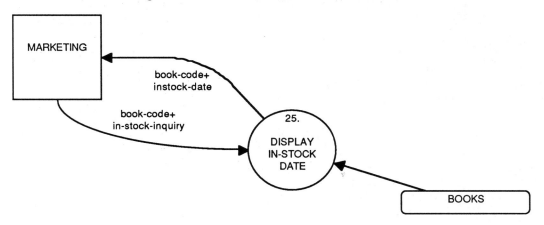

Event 26: Editors announce new book title (date ready for printer)

Notes

1. While developing this model, I saw the need to eventually delete books from the system. This happens rarely, but marketing eventually decides when to "kill" a book by declaring it out of print (event 36).

2. While this event actually creates a new **book** record (the book is not considered real and part of the system until the editors have substantially finished editing the book and are about ready to send it to a printer), we must also create an **author** record. This is done by event 34.

Event 27: Authors need quarterly royalty report.

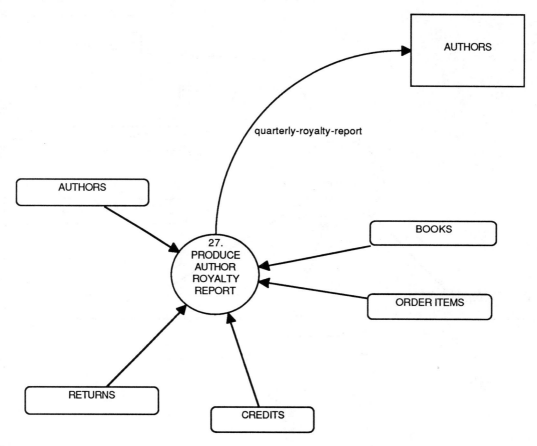

Notes

1. This is similar to event 13, except that the report goes to the authors rather than to accounting.

2. Note that accounting wants to see detailed information, including an identification of the customers to whom a book was sold. Authors are not given this information.

Event 28: Warehouse needs shipping data and mailing labels.

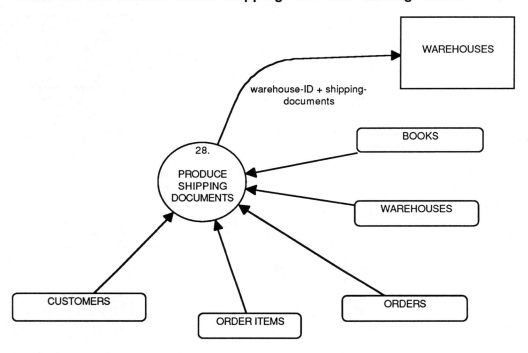

Event 29: Warehouse receives books from printer.

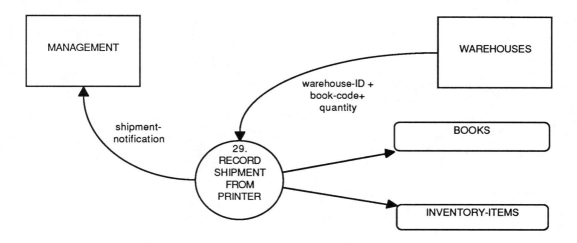

Notes

1. This does not take into account the possibility of a partial shipment from the printer. This does occasionally happen: if there is a tremendous demand for a new book (or for a reprint of an existing book), the printer might rush-ship the first few hundred copies (perhaps by air freight) and then forward the rest of the print order later.

2. This assumes also that the amount received by the warehouse is the same as the amount specified in event 20.

Event 30: Warehouse receives books from customer.

Notes

1. The system may instruct the warehouse to refuse the book returns if they have not been authorized. This means that the warehouse will notify the Post Office (or whatever shipping agency brought the books) that the package(s) should be returned to the sender.

2. Note that it is sometimes impossible to tell who sent the books back; that is, the information that the warehouse finds in the package of books may not correspond to any known customer.

Event 31: Warehouse conducts (monthly) physical inventory.

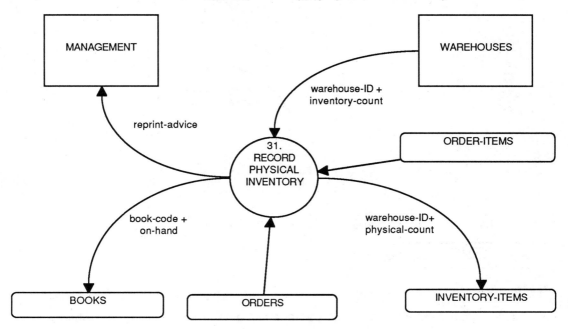

Event 32: Warehouse makes shipment of book order to customer.

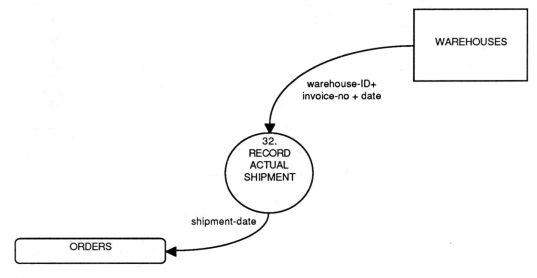

Note

1.   This assumes that there are no partial shipments of an order to a customer.

Event 33: Warehouse announces that book is out of stock.

Notes

1. Note that the out-of-stock situation could occur either because a previously ordered reprint has not yet arrived; or because of an unexpectedly large order; or because of pilferage within the warehouse, and so on.

2. As a result of the out-of-stock situation, subsequent processed orders may not be filled for the time being, but that's the warehouse's problem to manage.

Event 34: Acquisition department announces new book project.

Notes

1. This shows that event 13 must read the **BOOKS** store to see if there is an outstanding advance.

2. This event also creates a new **author** record if it is a new author.

Event 35: Salesperson places order on behalf of customer.

Notes

1.   Note that this is the same as event 1, except that the order is placed by a salesperson instead of the customer.

Event 36: Marketing declares that a book is out of print

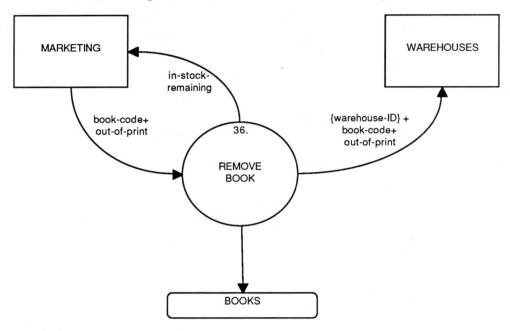

Notes

1.   This can be accomplished externally by simply stopping all advertising for a specified book. Eventually the orders will trickle away to zero.

2.   When it is accomplished as shown here, it precludes further orders. The assumption is that the warehouses will dispose of the remaining stock in order to free up inventory space.

3.   In real-world situations, provisions are often made to "remainder" the existing stock of the book at this point. Either the author or a discount book store may be allowed to buy the remaining stock for, say, $0.10 per copy.

4.   Note that the **book** record cannot be deleted from **BOOKS** until at least after the monthly accounting reports and the quarterly royalty statement has been produced. In addition, there may still be a pipeline of outstanding orders that have not yet been shipped by the warehouse.

5.   Note that *all* the warehouses need to be informed when this event occurs.

6.   We are assuming at this point that there are no outstanding orders due from the printer: if sales have been slow enough to consider putting the book out of print, it is virtually impossible to imagine that a reprint order would have been issued.

Event 37: Customer announces a change of address.

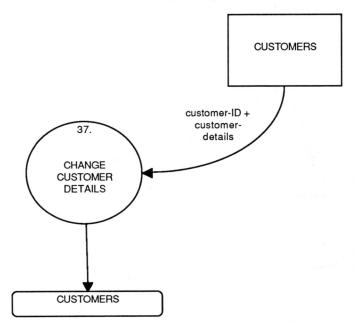

Event 38: Author announces a change of address.

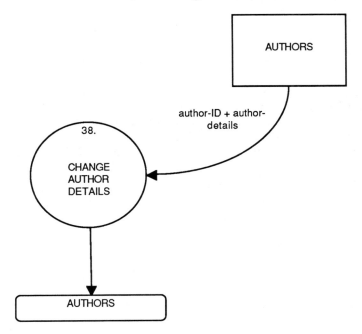

Event 39: Customer elects to join agency plan.

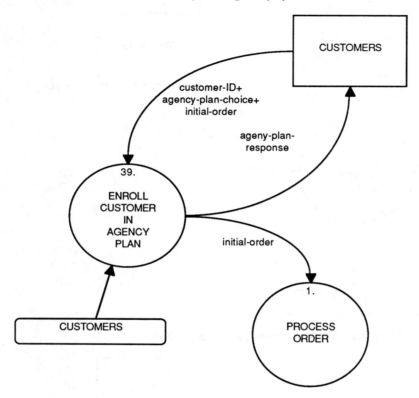

Notes

1. The agency plan is known by a number of other names in the publishing industry (e.g., "standard shipment plan," "guaranteed shipment plan," "standing order plan," etc.). It is used almost exclusively by book stores. The book store places an initial order for a certain number of books and agrees that it will accept a certain number of copies of each new book that YOURDON Press publishes.

Event 40: Invoices need to be sent to customer.

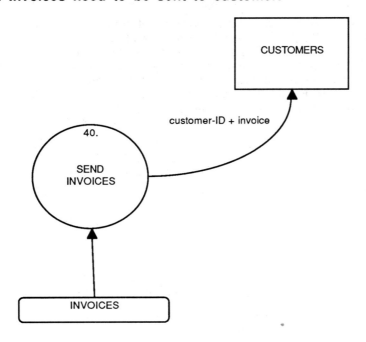

F.4.2   The Final Behavioral Model: Dataflow Diagrams

The initial behavioral model shown on the last several pages was transformed into a leveled set of DFDs. Upward leveling produced the Figure 1 diagram shown on the next page; it is sufficiently complex that I didn't show the details of all the inputs and outputs to each bubble. Subsequent figures then show which events were grouped together. In one case, a single event (event 26) was not leveled upward, and appears as process 5 in Figure 1. And in one case (event 1) additional downward leveling was required because of the complexity of the processing.

Figure 0:   The top-level DFD

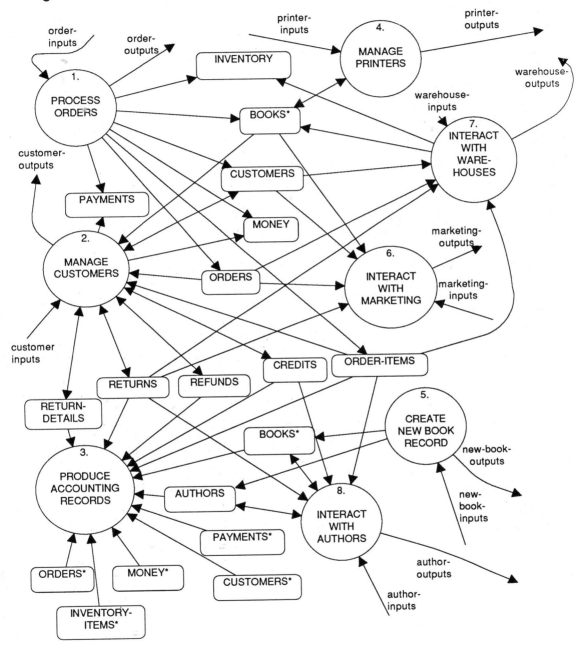

Figure 1: Process orders

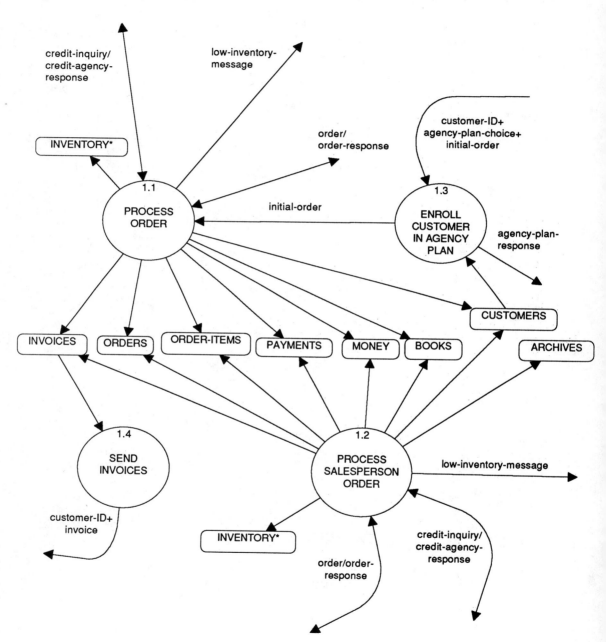

Figure 1.1: Process orders

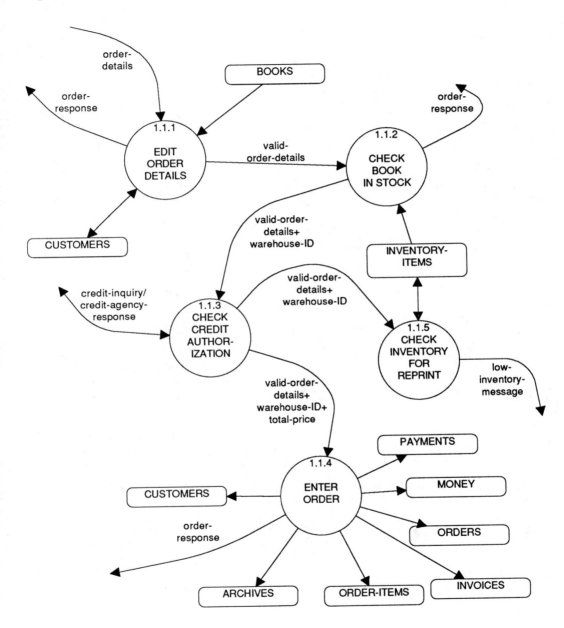

Figure 2: Manage customers

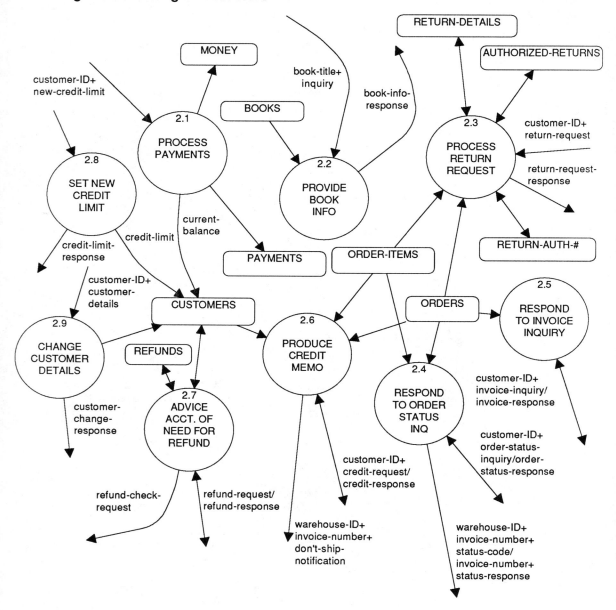

Figure 3: Produce accounting reports

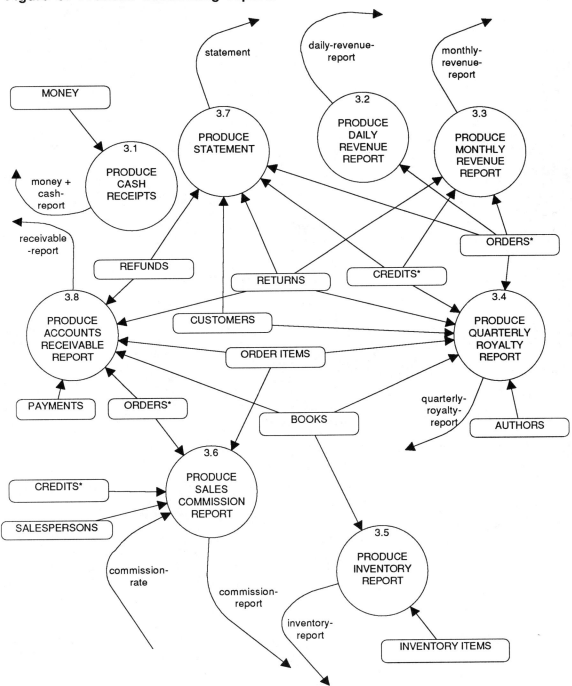

Figure 4: Manage printers

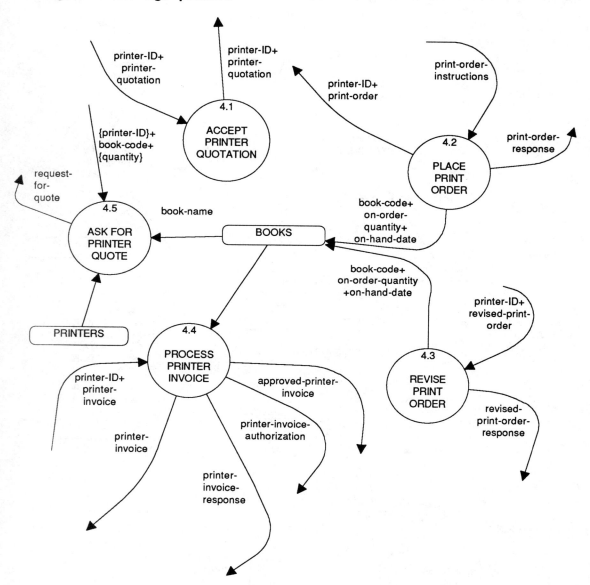

Figure 6: Interact with marketing

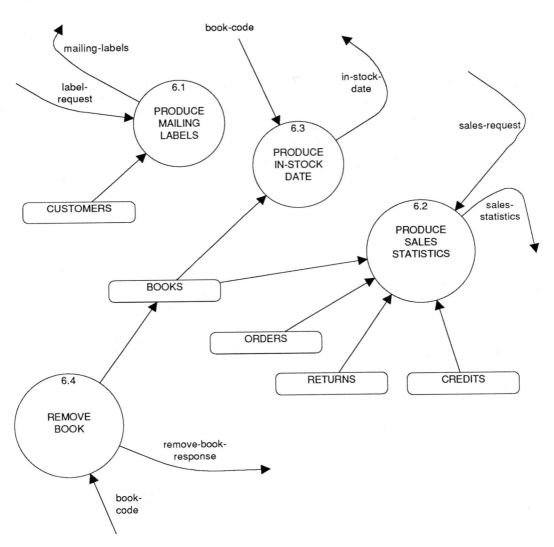

Figure 7: Interact with warehouses

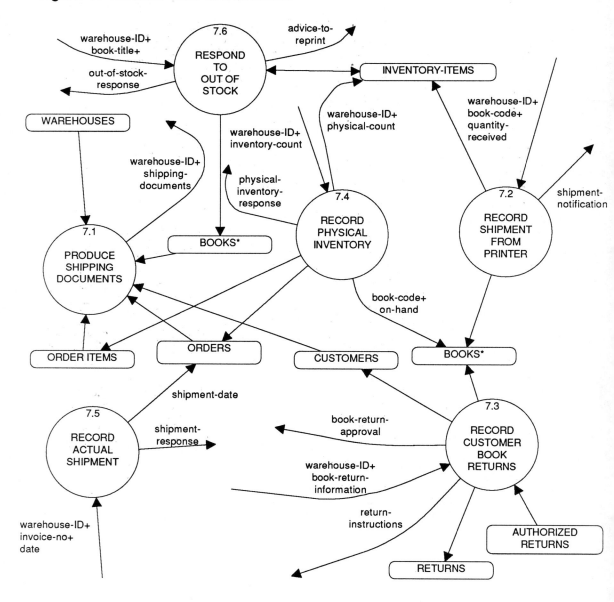

Figure 8: Interact with authors

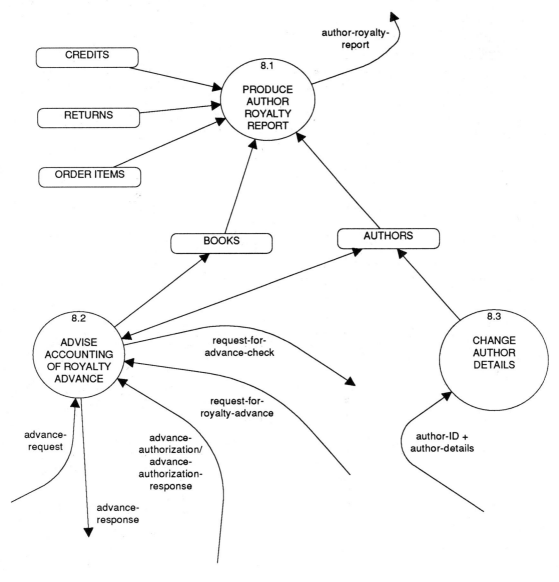

F.4.3   The Data Dictionary

The data dictionary is organized in the fashion described in Chapter 10. Self-defining terms (data elements whose meanings are sufficiently well known that no explicit definition is required) are entered with a definition of **. See, for example, the definition of "country" and "state."

advance-amount   = *amount of money requested for a royalty advance*
                              units: dollars

advance-authorization-response
                            = *response from management to a request for a
                              royalty advance for an author*
                              ["Yes" | "No"]

advance-response   = *response to acquisitions editor when he makes a
                              request for an royalty advance for an author*
                              ["No such author" | "No such book" |
                              "Advance approved" | "Advance denied"]

agency-plan-choice   = *customer's choice of which level of agency plan to
                              join*
                              range: 0-4

agency-plan-level   = *code to indicate what level of "standing orders" the
                              customer has chosen for forthcoming YOURDON Press
                              books*
                              range: 0-4

alphabetic-character   = *a letter in the English alphabet*
                              **

alphanumeric-character   = *either a number or a letter or a punctuation mark*
                              [alphabetic-character | numeric-digit |
                              punctuation-mark]

approved printer-invoice   = *a printer invoice which has been approved by mgmt*
                              book-code + invoice-amount

as-of-date   = *the date that a physical inventory was taken*
                              **

AUTHORS   = {author}

author   = *information maintained about each author*
                              @author-ID + author-details + royalty-balance

author-details   = courtesy-title + first-name + last-name + street-address+
                              city + postal-code + (country) + phone-number

author-ID = * identification of each YOURDON Press author
Social Security numbers are not used because not
all authors are American citizens*
last-name + first-name

author-royalty-report = *report for authors showing royalties
earned or lost on sales, credits, and returns of each
book during a three-month period*
{book-copies-total +book-revenue-total +
book-royalty-total}

AUTHORIZED-RETURNS = {authorized-return}

authorized-return = *information about a group of books that YOURDON
Press has authorized a customer to return for credit*
@return-auth-# + return-details

back-order-OK = *an indication of whether a customer will place an
order even if there are not enough books currently
in stock*
["Yes" | "No"]

BOOKS = {book}

book = *information maintained about a YOURDON Press
book*
@book-code + book-title + author-ID + total-in-stock +
on-order-quantity + on-hand-date + royalty-rate +
out-of-print-indicator + reorder-threshold

book-code = *a numeric code the identifies each book*
1{numeric-digit}

book-code-request = *message to management asking for a book-code to
be assigned to a new book*
"Please assign new book code for following book:"

book-copies-total = *total number of copies of a single book sold, taking
into account returns and credits, during a
three-month period*
**

book-info-response = *information about the title, price, etc. of a book*
book

book-return-approval = *response to customer when warehouse notifies the
system that book returns have been received*
["This return is not authorized" | "This return is OK"]

book-return-information = *information about a group of books that have been returned to the warehouse by a customer* (customer-ID) + (customer-name) + {book-code + quantity-returned} + return-auth-#

book-revenue-total = *total revenues earned for sales of a single book during a three-month period, taking into account credits and returns* *units: dollars*

book-royalty-total = *total royalties earned (or lost) from sales or returns or credits on a single book during a three-month period* *units: dollars*

book-title = *the full title of a YOURDON Press book* 1{alphanumeric-character}

commission-quantity = *the amount of commission paid to a salesperson for an individual book order; calculated in process 3.6* **

commission-rate = *the commission rate paid to salespeople for book sales. This is expressed as a fraction* *range: 0 - 0.25*

commission-report = *sales commission report* {{salesperson-ID+invoice-number + commission-quantity} + total-commission}

company-name = *the name of a company or organization* **

country = *the name of a country, e.g., "Canada"* **

courtesy-title = *the prefix in front of a person's first name* ["Mr." | "Mrs." | "Ms." | "Miss" | "Dr." | "Prof."]

CREDITS = {credit}

credit = *an individual credit given to a customer because of a problem with an order* @invoice-number + customer-ID + credit-date + book-code + credit-book-quantity + credit-amount

credit-agency-response = *response from a credit card agency to a request for charge authorization* ["Yes" | "No"]

credit-amount	=	*the amount of money given in a credit* *units: dollars*

credit-amount-requested = *the amount of money requested for a credit*
units: dollars

credit-book-quantity = *the number of copies of a book for which a credit is being sought*
**

credit-card-number = *a credit card number supplied by a customer if he wants to charge an order of books to his credit card*
**

credit-date = *the date that a credit was given*
**

credit-inquiry = *a request for authorization to a credit card agency for the purchase of an order of books*
"Request for authorization" + credit-card-number+ order-total

credit-limit = *amount of credit that will be extended to a customer for orders that are not prepaid*
units: dollars; range: 1-10,000

credit-limit-response = *response to management instructions to change the credit limits for a customer*
["No such customer" | "illegal credit limit" | "New credit limit is OK"]

credit-reason = *customer's reason for requesting a credit*
["Overpayment" | "Excessive delay" | "Undershipment" | "Damaged books"]

credit-request = *request made by a customer for a credit on an order*
customer-ID + invoice-number + book-code + credit-book-quantity +credit-reason + credit-amount-requested

credit-response = *response to customer who wants a credit memo*
["No such order for this customer" | "Credit has already been given" | "No payment was made for that invoice number" | "Credit will be shown on next statement" | "Invoice was not overpaid" | "Full amount of order credited" | "Credit for undershipment: " + credit-amount | "Credit for damaged books: " + credit-amount]

current-balance	=	*amount of money currently owed by a customer,* *AS OF THE THE CURRENT-BALANCE DATE* *units: dollars; range: 1-10,000*
current-balance-date	=	*the date on which the customer's current balance was last computed (usually while producing a statement for the customer* **
CUSTOMERS	=	{customer}
customer	=	*a YOURDON Press customer* @customer-ID + (company-name) + customer-name + customer-address + current-balance + credit-limit + agency-plan-level
customer-address	=	*"bill-to" address: where we send the cust. invoices* street-address + city + state + postal-code + (country)
customer-change-response	=	*response to customer when he notifies system of a change of address, etc.* ["No such customer"	"Change accepted"]
customer-details	=	*information provided by a customer to change info already on his record, e.g., new cust. address* (customer-name) + (company-name) + (customer-address)
customer-ID	=	*identification of a YOURDON Press customer unknown or unidentified customers are known as "unapplied cash," especially regarding payments* [{numeric-digit}	"unapplied cash"]
customer-name	=	courtesy-title + first-name + last-name
daily-revenue-report	=	*report sent to Accounting Department each day* {invoice-number + customer-name + company-name + order-total} + daily-revenue-total
daily-revenue-total	=	*the total amount of new sales recorded each day* *units: dollars*
discount	=	*the discount percentage offered on a volume order, expressed as a fraction of the price to be paid, i.e., a 10% discount would be expressed as 0.90* *range: 0 - 1.00*

first-name   =   *a person's first name*
                                  **

in-stock-response   =   *response to marketing when they ask for the in-stock
                                  date for a shipment of books from the printer*
                                  ["No such book" | "No shipment due" | on-hand-date]

inventory-book-total   =   *the total number of books, of a given title, in all of
                                  the YOURDON Press warehouses*
                                  **

inventory-count   =   *information about a physical inventory count that
                                  has been taken by a warehouse*
                                  {inventory-detail} + as-of-date

inventory-detail   =   *physical inventory count for a single book title*
                                  book-code + physical-count

INVENTORY-ITEMS   =   {inventory-item}

inventory-item   =   *a group of books, with the same title, located in a
                                  single warehouse*
                                  @book-code + @warehouse-ID + inventory-quantity

inventory-quantity   =   *a count of the number of books, with the same title,
                                  located in a single warehouse*
                                  **

inventory-report   =   *a report produced for Accounting Department*
                                  {{warehouse-ID + book-code + inventory-quantity} +
                                  inventory-book-total}

INVOICES   =   {invoice}

invoice   =   *information contained in a YOURDON Press invoice*
                                  @invoice-number + customer-name +
                                  customer-address + order

invoice-amount   =   *the amount of money charged by a printer on an
                                  invoice that he submits for a printing order*
                                  units: dollars

invoice-number   =   *a unique number assigned to each invoice;
                                  a typical invoice number is B88-5067*
                                  "B" + year-code + {numeric-digit}

invoice-response   =   *response to a customer's inquiry about an invoice*
                                  ["no order exists with that invoice number" | order-date
                                  + {order-items} + shipping-charges + sales-tax]

item-revenue = *gross revenue from the sale of one or more copies of the same book in a single order*
units: dollars

item-royalty = *royalties earned from the sale of one or more copies of the same book in a single order*
units: dollars

label-request = *request from Marketing to produce mailing labels*
"Please produce mailing labels"

last-name = *a person's last name*
**

low-inventory-message = *a message sent to management when the system discovers that the total inventory of a book has dropped below a prescribed threshold*
book-code + total-in-stock + "time to reprint"

mailing-labels = *mailing labels produced for marketing department*
{customer}

MONEY = {money}

money = *information about checks, cash or other monies*
@money-date + @customer-ID + {invoice-number} + money-amount

money-amount = *amount of money collected in a single payment*
units: dollars

monthly-revenue-report = *report of total revenues, returns and credits for a single month, sent to Accounting Department*
total-revenue + total-returns + total-credits

numeric-digit = *a plain old numeric digit!*
**

on-hand-date = *the date that a book printing order is expected to arrive at the warehouse*
**

on-order-quantity = *the number of copies of a book that are currently on order from a printer as part of a printing order*
**

ORDERS = {order}

order = *an order for a YOURDON Press book*
@invoice-number + customer-ID + order-date +

		{order-item} + shipping-charges + sales-tax + shipment-date + (salesperson-ID) + order-total + warehouse-ID
order-details	=	*the raw data from which a valid order will be constructed and put into the ORDERS store* tentative-customer-ID + {order-item} + sales-tax-rate + shipping-charges + payment-type + (order-payment) + (credit-card-number) + back-order-OK + order-type
ORDER-ITEMS	=	{order-item}
order-item	=	@invoice-number + @book-code + quantity-ordered + unit-price + discount
order-payment	=	*payment supplied by the customer WITH the order* *units: dollars*
order-response	=	*response to the customer when he places an order* ["Purchase price exceeds amount paid" | "Credit request denied" | "Order exceeds your credit limit" | "Not enough books to fill your order"| "No such customer" | "No such book" | "Illegal sales tax rate" | "Illegal shipping charges" | "Order accepted"]
order-status-response	=	*response to a customer who has inquired about the status of an order he has placed* ["No order exists for that invoice number" | order-date + {order-items} + shipment-date]
order-total	=	*total amount of money invoiced for an order* *units: dollars*
order-type	=	*an indication of whether the order was placed over the phone, by mail, or a "walk in"* ["Phone" | "Mail" | "Walk-in"]
out-of-print-indicator	=	*a binary indication of whether a book is out of stock so that subsequent orders (if any) are rejected* [YES|NO]
out-of-stock-response	=	*message to warehouse in response to their indication that a book title is out of stock at that warehouse* ["No such book"| "Error: inventory item cannot be found" | "Out of stock message accepted"]
PAYMENTS	=	{payment}

payment = *payment made for a book order or to pay an invoice*
(customer-ID) + payment-date + payment-details

payment-date = *the date that a payment is made*
**

payment-details = *detailed information about an item or invoice being
paid for*
{invoice-number} + total-amount

payment-type = *the way the customer intends to pay for his purchase
of books in an order*
["Cash" | "Check" | "Credit card" | "Bill me"]

phone-number = *a phone number*
**

physical-count = *a count of the number of copies of a single book title
found during a physical inventory taken by a
warehouse*
**

physical-inv-response = *message to a warehouse by the system in response to
a physical inventory that has been taken*
["No such warehouse" | "Illegal book code" + book-code]

pick-list = *an indication of the number of copies of each book
that a warehouse needs to pick in order to fulfil a
day's orders*
{book-title + pick-quantity}

pick-quantity = *the number of copies of an individual book that need
to be picked to fulfil a day's orders at the warehouse*
**

postal-code = *American, Canadian, or British postal code*
**

PRINTERS = {printer}

printer = *information maintained about each of the printers
with whom YOURDON Press does business*
@printer-ID + printer-name + printer-address

printer-address = *the address where the printer can be contacted*
street-address + city + state + postal-code

printer-ID = *a unique code that identifies a printer*
{numeric-digit}

printer-invoice   = *an invoice received from a printer for a print order*
                                book-code + invoice-amount

printer-invoice-authorization = *response from management after they review a
                                printer invoice*
                                ["YES" | "NO"]

printer-invoice-response   = *response to the printer from the system when the
                                system receives a printer invoice*
                                ["No orders outstanding for this book"|

printer-name   = *the name of the printing company*
                                **

printer-quotation   = *a quotation from a printer, an offer to print a
                                certain quantity of books at a certain price
                                book-code + printer-price

printer-price   = *the price associated with a printer quotation*
                                **

print-order   = *a printing order given to a printer*
                                book-code + print-quantity

print-order-instructions   = *instructions from management to reprint a book*
                                printer-ID + book-code + print-quantity + on-hand-date

print-order-response   = *response from system to reprint order from mgmt*
                                ["No such book" | "Illegal printing quantity" |
                                "Print order accepted"]

print-quantity   = *the number of copies of a book to be printed*
                                **

punctuation-mark   = *a comma, period, exclamation point, etc.*
                                **

quantity-ordered   = *the number of copies of a book that has been ordered*
                                **

quantity-received   = *the number of copies of a book that have actually
                                been received from the printer as a result of a print
                                order*
                                **

quantity-returned   = *the number of copied of a book that have been
                                to the warehouse by a customer*
                                **

quantity-to-return   =   *the number of copies of a single title that a customer
                                wants to return for credit*
                                **

quarterly-royalty-report   =   *report for Accounting Department showing royalties
                                earned or lost on sales, credits, and returns of each
                                book during a three-month period*
                                {{customer-ID + customer-name + invoice-number +
                                item-revenue + item-royalty} + book-copies-total +
                                book-revenue-total + book-royalty-total}

receivable-report   =   *report for Accounting showing current balance for
                                each customer
                                {customer-ID + current-balance}

REFUNDS   =   {refund}

refund   =   *information about a refund*
                                @refund-date + @customer-ID + refund-amount

refund-amount   =   *amount of money to be refunded to a customer*
                                units: dollars

refund-check-request   =   *message to Accounting Department asking for a
                                refund check to be written for a customer*
                                "Please pay" + customer-ID + refund-amount

refund-date   =   *the date the refund was approved*
                                **

refund-request   =   *request from a customer for a check in the amount of
                                his current credit balance*
                                customer-ID + "refund request"

refund-response   =   *response to the customer who has asked for a refund*
                                ["no such customer" | "No refund is due" + "Current
                                balance is " + current-balance | "refund approved"]

remove-book-response   =   *response to marketing when they indicate that a
                                book should be considered out of print*
                                ["No such book" | "Book has been marked as out of
                                print"]

request for advance-authorization =
                                *message to management, asking for approval for a
                                royalty advance for a book project*
                                author-ID + book-code + advance-amount

| request-for-advance-check | = | *message to Accounting Department, requesting that an authorized royalty advance be paid* author-ID + book-code + advance-amount |

request-for-advance-
check
= *message to Accounting Department, requesting that
an authorized royalty advance be paid*
author-ID + book-code + advance-amount

request-for-royalty-
advance
= *a request from the acquisitions editor for a royalty
advance for an author—associated with a book*
author-ID + book-code + advance-amount

RETURNS
= {return}

return
= *information about a group of books that have been
returned and accepted by YOURDON Press*
return-date + book-code + quantity-returned +
return-value

RETURN-AUTH-#
= *a store that is used to keep track of the next available
authorized return number*
return-auth-#

return-auth-#
= *a sequential number used identify a specific set of
returned books that have been authorized*
{numeric-digit}

return-date
= *the date that a group of books was returned*
**

return-details
= **
{return-item}

return-instructions
= *instructions to the warehouse about how to deal with
a set of books that the customer has returned*
["Cannot identify customer; accept books anyway" |
"This return is not authorized; please send back" |
"No such book" | "Return is authorized"]

return-item
= *information about one or more copies of a single
title that the customer wants to return*
book-code + quantity-to-return

return-request
= *information about one or more books that a customer
wants to return for credit*
invoice-number + return-details

return-request-response
= *response to customer who wants to return a book*
["Cannot find this order" | "Books were shipped more
than a year ago" | "Can't return that many books" |
"Return is OK" + "Please identify actual return with" +
return-auth-#]

return-value	=	*value of a group of books that have been returned* *units: dollars*
revised-date	=	*a new date quoted by the printer for the delivery of a batch of books which he is currently printing* **
revised-print-order	=	*revision to a print order, made by a printer. Usually involves minor changes to quantity to be printed* book-code + revised-quantity + revised-date
revised-print-order-response	=	*response made by the system when a revised order is received from a printer* ["No such book" | "Revised print order OK"]
revised-quantity	=	*a revision to the number of books to be printed by the printer as part of a print order* **
royalty-rate	=	*royalty rate paid to an author for a book expressed as a percentage, e.g., 10 means 10%* *range: 5-25*
royalty-rate-request	=	*message to acquisitions department asking for royalty rate of a new book* "Please indicate royalty rate for following book:"
SALESPERSONS	=	{salesperson}
salesperson	=	@salesperson-ID + salesperson-name
salesperson-ID	=	*identification of a YOURDON inc. salesperson* **
salesperson-name	=	*name of a YOURDON inc. salesperson* **
sales-credits	=	*credits associated with an individual book during a specified time period* *units: dollars*
sales-date	=	*the date after which all orders, credits and returns should be included in the sales statistics report* **
sales-request	=	*a request from the Marketing department to produce a sales report for all orders, credits, returns that occurred after the specified date* sales-date

sales-returns | = | *returns associated with an individual book during a specified time period*
units: dollars

sales-revenues | = | *gross revenues from sales of an individual book during a specified time period*
units: dollars

sales-statistics | = | *report for Marketing on net sales of books for a given time period*
{book-code + sales-revenues + sales-returns + sales-credits}

sales-tax | = | *local and state sales tax associated with an order*
units: dollars

sales-tax-rate | = | *the sales tax percentage, expressed as a decimal fraction, e.g., a 7% sales tax would be 0.07*
range: 0.00 - 1.00

shipment-date | = | *the date the warehouse ships an order*
**

shipment-notification | = | *message from warehouse when a print order is received from the printer*
["No such book" | "Received from printer" + book-code + quantity-received]

shipment-response | = | *error message to warehouse in response to their notification that they have shipped a customer's order*
"No such order can be found"

shipping-charges | = | *the amount charged for shipping a book to the cust. it may be a standard amount, e.g., $1.50, or it may be *based on actual charges imposed by a shipper*
units: dollars; range: 0 - 100

shipping-documents | = | *picking list and mailing labels sent to the warehouses so they can pick enough copies of each book and ship the day's orders, plus a copy of each order so the warehouse know what books to pack for each customer*
{warehouse-ID + pick-list + {shipping-label} + {order}}

shipping-label | = | *mailing labels for a day's orders for the warehouse*
customer-name + customer-address + invoice-number

state   =   *a state or province in an address*
                                   **

tentative-customer-ID   =   *information about a customer when an order is
                                   first placed*
                                   [customer-ID + (customer-name)| "new" +
                                   customer-name + (company-name) + customer-address]

total-commission   =   *the total commission paid to a salesperson during a
                                   one-month period based on all of the books he sold.
                                   Calculated in process 3.6*
                                   **

total-credits   =   *the total amount of credits given to all customers
                                   during a single month*
                                   units: dollars

total-in-stock   =   *the number of copies of a YOURDON Press book title
                                   that we have in stock in all the warehouses*
                                   range: 1-10,000

total-returns   =   *total amount of money associated with books that
                                   have been returned by all customers during a
                                   single month*
                                   units: dollars

total-revenue   =   *total amount of gross revenues from all book orders
                                   in a single month*
                                   units: dollars

unit-price   =   *the price charged for a single copy of a YOURDON
                                   Press book on an individual order; note that it may
                                   not be the same as the "standard" or "retail" unit
                                   price advertised for the book*
                                   units: dollars

unit-price-request   =   *message to marketing to get unit price for new book*
                                   "Please indicate unit price for following book:"

valid-order-details   =   *the raw data from which a valid order will be
                                   constructed and put into the ORDERS store*
                                   customer-ID + {order-item} + sales-tax-rate +
                                   shipping-charges + payment-type + (order-payment)
                                   + (credit-card-number) + back-order-OK + order-type

warehouse-ID   =   *identification of the various warehouses where
                                   YOURDON Press books are stored*
                                   ["NYC" | "LON" | "DC" | "SFO" | "YONKERS" | "OTTAWA"]

year-code   = *the last two digits of the current year, e.g., "88"
                      if the current year is 1988*
                      2{numeric digit}2

F.4.4   The Entity-Relationship Diagram

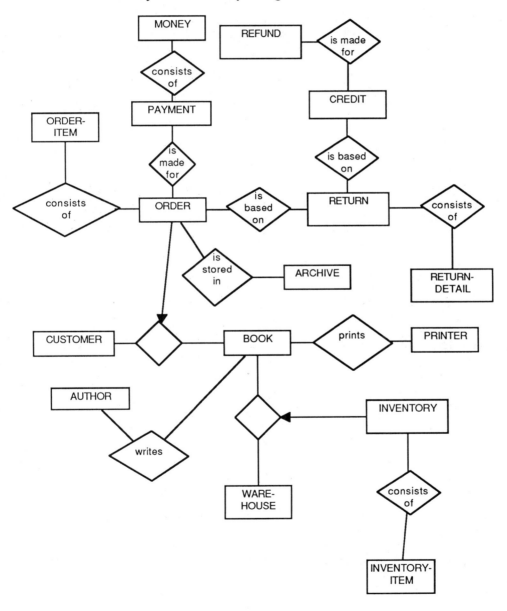

F.4.5   The Process Specifications

PROCESS 1.1.1:   **EDIT ORDER DETAILS**
BEGIN
IF **tentative-customer-ID** = "new"
        customer-ID = next available customer-ID
        credit-limit = standard credit limit
        current-balance = 0
        agency-plan-level = 0
        customer = customer-ID + customer-name + (company-name) +
                customer-address + current-balance + credit-limit +
                agency-plan-level
        APPEND new **customer** record to **CUSTOMERS**
ELSE
        FIND **customer** in **CUSTOMERS** with **customer-ID = customer-ID**
                in **order-details**
        IF record cannot be found
                order-response = "No such customer"
                DISPLAY **order-response**
                EXIT
                note: this means the order will not be processed any further
        ENDIF
DO WHILE there are more **order-item**s in **order-details**
        FIND **book** in **BOOKS** with **book-code = book-code** in **order-item**
        IF record cannot be found
                order-response = "No such book"
                DISPLAY **order-response**
                EXIT
                note: this means the order will not be processed any further
        ENDIF
END DO
IF **sales-tax-rate** is out of range
        order-response = "Illegal sales tax rate"
        DISPLAY **order-response**
        EXIT
        note: this means the order will not be processed any further
ENDIF
IF **shipping-charges** are out of range
        order-response = "Illegal shipping charges"
        DISPLAY **order-response**
        EXIT
        note: this means that order will not be processed any further
ENDIF
valid-order-details = customer-ID + {order-item} + sales-tax-rate +
        shipping-charges + payment-type + (order-payment) +
        (credit-card-number) + back-order-OK + order-type
DISPLAY (to process 1.1.2) **valid-order-details**
END

PROCESS 1.1.2:   CHECK BOOK IN STOCK
BEGIN
IF **back-order-OK** = "Yes"
        DISPLAY (to bubble 1.1.3) **valid-order-details** + "YONKERS"
ELSE
        IF order-type = "Walk-in"
                DO WHILE there are more **order-item**s in **valid-order-details**
                        FIND **inventory-item** in **INVENTORY-ITEMS** with **book-code**
                                = **book-code** in **valid-order-details** and
                                warehouse-ID = the location where this walk-in
                                order was received
                        READ **inventory-item** record
                        IF **inventory-quantity** < **quantity-ordered**
                                order-response = "Not enough books to fill your order"
                                EXIT
                                *note: this means no further processing of this order
                        ENDIF
                END DO
                DISPLAY (to bubble 1.1.4) **valid-order-details** + **warehouse-ID**
                        (of the warehouse at the location where this walk-in order
                        was received)
        ELSE
                enough-books = "Yes"
                REPEAT UNTIL there are no more **warehouse**s in **WAREHOUSES** or
                                enough-books = "Yes"
                        note that this means we will examine at least one warehouse
                        enough-books = "Yes"
                        DO WHILE there are more **order-item**s in **valid-order-details**
                        FIND **inventory-item** in **INVENTORY-ITEMS** with **book-code**
                                = **book-code** in **valid-order-details** and
                                warehouse-ID = **warehouse-ID** of current
                                warehouse record
                        READ **inventory-item** record
                        IF **inventory-quantity** < **quantity-ordered**
                                enough-books = "No"
                        ENDIF
                        END DO
                END REPEAT
                IF enough-books = "No"
                        order-response = "Not enough books to fill your order"
                        DISPLAY **order-response**
                ELSE
                        DISPLAY (to bubble 1.1.4) **valid-order-details** +
                                warehouse-ID of current **warehouse** record
                ENDIF
        ENDIF
ENDIF
END

PROCESS 1.1.3:   **CHECK CREDIT AUTHORIZATION**
BEGIN
total-price = 0
REPEAT UNTIL there are no more **order-item**s in **valid-order-details**
ADD (**quantity-ordered * unit-price * discount**) to total-price
END REPEAT
MULTIPLY total-price by (1 + **sales-tax-rate**)
ADD **shipping-charges** to total-price
credit-OK = "Yes"
CASE **payment-type** of
    CASE **payment-type** = "Cash" or payment-type = "Check"
        IF total-price > **order-payment**
            order-response = "Purchase price exceeds amount paid"
            DISPLAY **order-response**
            note: this means no further processing of the order will
            take place at this point
            credit-OK = "No"
        ENDIF
    CASE **payment-type** = "Credit card"
        credit-inquiry = "Request for authorization" + total-price
        DISPLAY (to credit card agency) **credit-inquiry**
        ACCEPT (from credit agency) **credit-agency-response**
        IF **credit-agency-response** = "No"
            order-response = "Credit request denied"
            DISPLAY **order-response**
            credit-OK = "No"
            note: this means no further processing of the order will
            take place at this point
        ENDIF
    CASE **payment-type** = "Bill me"
        FIND **customer** in **CUSTOMERS** with **customer-ID = customer-ID**
            in **valid-order-details**
        READ **customer** record
        IF **current-balance** + total-price > **credit-limit**
            order-response = "Order exceeds your credit limit"
            DISPLAY **order-response**
            credit-OK = "No"
            note: this means no further processing of the order will
            take place at this point
        ENDIF
END CASE
IF credit-OK = "yes"
    DISPLAY (to bubble 1.1.4) valid-order-details + total-price + warehouse-ID
    DISPLAY (to bubble 1.1.5) valid-order-details + warehouse-ID
ENDIF
END

PROCESS 1.1.4:   ENTER ORDER
BEGIN
DO WHILE there are more **order-item**s in **valid -order-details**
      CREATE **order-item** record from next **order-item** in **valid-order details**
      APPEND **order-item** record to **ORDER-ITEMS**
END DO
CREATE **order** record from **valid-order-details** and **warehouse-ID**
APPEND **order** record to **ORDERS**
CREATE **invoice** record from **valid-order-details**
APPEND **invoice** record to **INVOICES**
IF **payment-type** = "Cash" or "Check" or "Credit card"
      CREATE **money** record from **valid-order-details**
      APPEND **money** record to **MONEY**
      CREATE **payment** record from **valid-order-details**
      APPEND **payment** record to **PAYMENTS**
ENDIF
APPEND **valid-order-details** to **ARCHIVES**
order-response = "Order accepted"
DISPLAY **order-response**
END

PROCESS 1.1.5:   CHECK INVENTORY FOR REPRINTING
BEGIN
DO WHILE there are more **order-item**s in **valid-order-details**
      FIND **inventory-item** in INVENTORY-ITEMS with **book-code** = book-code in
            order-item and **warehouse-ID** matching **warehouse-ID** provided as
            input to this process
      READ **inventory-item** record
      SUBTRACT **quantity-ordered** from **inventory-quantity**
      Note: this could result in a negative inventory; it simply means that the
      warehouse won't be able to fill the order until a reprint arrives
      WRITE **inventory-item** record
      FIND **book** in BOOKS with **book-code** = **book-code** in **order-item**
      READ **book** record
      SUBTRACT **quantity-ordered** from **total-in-stock**
      WRITE **book** record
      IF **total-in-stock** < **reorder-threshold**
            low-inventory-message = **book-code** + **total-in-stock** +
                "time to reprint"
            DISPLAY **low-inventory-message**
      ENDIF
END DO
END

PROCESS 1.2: PROCESS SALESPERSON ORDER

      At the present time, the policy for processing a salesperson order is the same as
that for processing a normal customer order. See Figure 1.1 for details.

PROCESS 1.3: ENROLL CUSTOMER IN AGENCY PLAN
Precondition-1.
There is a **customer** in **CUSTOMERS** which matches **customer-ID** with
　　agency-plan-level = 0 and with **agency-plan-choice** > 0
　　and **agency-plan-choice** less than or equal maximum agency level.

Postcondition-1.
agency-plan-level in **customer** is set to **agency-plan-choice**.

PROCESS 1.4: SEND INVOICES
BEGIN
DO WHILE there are more **invoice**s in **INVOICES**
　　READ next **invoice**
　　DISPLAY **invoice**
END DO
END

PROCESS 2.1:   PROCESS PAYMENTS
BEGIN
IF **customer-ID** is present
　　FIND record in **CUSTOMERS** with matching **customer-ID**
　　IF record cannot be found
　　　　WRITE **payment-details** to **PAYMENTS** with **customer-ID** =
　　　　　　"unapplied cash"
　　ELSE
　　　　SUBTRACT **total-amount** from **current-balance**
　　　　WRITE record to **CUSTOMERS**
　　　　WRITE **payment-details** to **PAYMENTS**
ELSE
　　WRITE **payment-details** to **PAYMENTS** with **customer-ID** =
　　　　"unapplied cash"
　　WRITE today's date + **customer-ID** + **payment-details** to **MONEY**
ENDIF
END

PROCESS 2.2: PROVIDE BOOK INFO
BEGIN
FIND **book** record in **BOOKS** with matching **book-title**
book-info-response = contents of entire **book** record
DISPLAY **book-info-response**
END

PROCESS 2.3: PROCESS RETURN REQUEST
BEGIN
FIND **order** in **ORDERS** that matches **invoice-number** in **return-request**
IF record is not found
　　return-request-response = "Cannot find this order"
　　DISPLAY **return-request-response**
ELSE

```
         READ  order record
         IF shipment-date is more than one year ago
                 return-request-response = "Books were shipped more than a
                         year ago"
                 DISPLAY return-request-response
         ELSE
                 everything-OK = "yes"
                 REPEAT UNTIL  no more return-items in return-details
                         FIND order-item in ORDER-ITEMS that matches
                                 invoice-number in return-request and
                                 book-code in return-item
                         IF no record is found
                                 DISPLAY "This book was not part of the order"
                                 everything-OK = "no"
                         ELSE
                                 READ order-item record
                                 IF quantity-to-return in return-item is more than
                                         half of quantity-ordered in order-item
                                         return-request-response = "Can't
                                           return that many books"
                                         DISPLAY return-request-response
                                         everything-OK = "no"
                                 ENDIF
                         ENDIF
                 END-REPEAT
                 IF everything-OK = "yes"
                         READ return-auth-# from RETURN-AUTH-#
                         return-request-response = "Return is OK," + "Please
                                 identify actual return with" + return-auth-#
                         DISPLAY return-response-request
                         WRITE return-details, return-auth-# to
                                 AUTHORIZED-RETURNS
                         ADD 1 to return-auth-#
                         WRITE return-auth-# to RETURN-AUTH-#
                 ENDIF
         ENDIF
 ENDIF
 END
```

PROCESS 2.4: RESPONSE TO ORDER STATUS INQUIRY

```
BEGIN
FIND order in ORDERS with matching invoice-number
IF record cannot be found
         order-status-response = "No order exists for that invoice number"
         DISPLAY order-status-response
ELSE
         READ order record in ORDERS with matching invoice-number
         order-status-response = order-date + {order-items} + shipment-date
         DISPLAY order-status-response
```

ENDIF
END

PROCESS 2.5: RESPOND TO INVOICE INQUIRY
BEGIN
FIND **order** in **ORDERS** with matching **invoice-number**
IF record cannot be found
    invoice-response = "no order exists with that invoice number"
    DISPLAY **invoice-response**
ELSE
    READ **order** record
    invoice-response = **order-date** + {**order-item**} + **shipping-charges** +
        sales-tax
    DISPLAY **invoice-response**
ENDIF
END

PROCESS 2.6: PRODUCT CREDIT MEMO
BEGIN
FIND **order** in **ORDERS** with matching **customer-ID** and
        invoice-number matching **invoice-number** in **credit-request**
    IF record cannot be found
        credit-response = "No such order for this customer"
        DISPLAY **credit-response**
    ELSE
        FIND **credit** in **CREDITS** with **invoice-number** matching
        invoice-number in **credit-request**
    IF record is found
        credit-response = "Credit has already been given"
        DISPLAY **credit-response**
    ELSE
        CASE **credit-reason** OF
        CASE **credit-reason** = "Overpayment"
            FIND **payment** in **PAYMENTS** with **invoice-number**
            matching **invoice-number** in **credit-request**
        IF record cannot be found
            credit-response = "No payment was made for
                that invoice number"
            DISPLAY **credit-response**
        ELSE
            read **payment**
            FIND **order** in **ORDERS** with **invoice-number** =
            invoice-number in **credit-request**
            IF **total-amount** > **order-total**
                credit-response = "Credit will be shown on
                    next statement"
            ELSE
                credit-response = "Invoice was not
                    overpaid"

```
                              ENDIF
                              DISPLAY credit-response
                      ENDIF
              CASE credit-reason = "Excessive delay"
                      credit = invoice-number + customer-ID +
                              today's-date + order-total
                      APPEND credit to CREDITS
                      credit-response = "Full amount of order credited"
                      DISPLAY credit-response
              CASE credit-reason = "Undershipment"
                      IF order-total > credit-amount-requested
                              credit = invoice-number + customer-ID +
                                      today's-date + credit-amount-requested
                              credit-response = "Credit for undershipment: "+
                                      credit-amount-requested
                              DISPLAY credit-response
                      ELSE
                              credit = invoice-number + customer-ID +
                                      today's date + order-total
                              credit-response = "Credit for undershipment: " +
                                      order-total
                              DISPLAY credit-response
                      ENDIF
                      APPEND credit to CREDITS
              CASE credit-reason = "Damaged books"
                      IF order-total > credit-amount-requested
                              credit = invoice-number + customer-ID +
                                      today's-date + credit-amount-requested
                              credit-response = "Credit for damaged books: "+
                                      credit-amount-requested
                              DISPLAY credit-response
                      ELSE
                              credit = invoice-number + customer-ID +
                                      today's-date + order-total
                              credit-response = "Credit for damaged books: " +
                                      order-total
                              DISPLAY credit-response
                      ENDIF
                      APPEND credit to CREDITS
              ENDCASE
          ENDIF
      ENDIF
END
```

PROCESS 2.7: ADVICE ACCOUNTING OF NEED FOR REFUND

```
BEGIN
FIND customer in CUSTOMERS with customer-ID matching customer-ID in
    refund-request
```

```
IF record cannot be found
        refund-response = "no such customer"
        DISPLAY refund-response
ELSE
        READ customer record
        IF current-balance is greater than or equal to zero
                refund-response = "No refund is due" + "Current balance is " +
                current-balance
                DISPLAY refund-response
        ELSE
                refund-response = "refund approved"
                refund-check-request = "Please pay" + customer-ID
                        + current-balance
                DISPLAY refund-response
                DISPLAY refund-check-request
                WRITE zero to current-balance in customer record
                WRITE today's date + customer-ID + current-balance to REFUNDS
        ENDIF
ENDIF
END
```

PROCESS 2.8: SET NEW CREDIT LIMIT

```
BEGIN
FIND customer in CUSTOMERS with matching customer-ID
IF record is not found
        credit-limit-response = "No such customer"
ELSE
        read customer record
        IF new-credit-limit < 0
                credit-limit-response = "illegal credit limit"
                DISPLAY credit-limit-response
        ELSE
                credit-limit-response = "New credit limit is OK"
                DISPLAY credit-limit-response
                REPLACE credit-limit with new-credit-limit
                WRITE customer record
        ENDIF
ENDIF
END
```

PROCESS 2.9: CHANGE CUSTOMER DETAILS

```
BEGIN
FIND customer in CUSTOMERS with matching customer-ID
IF record cannot be found
        customer-change-response = "No such customer"
        DISPLAY customer-change-response
ELSE
        read customer record
        REPLACE customer-name, company-name, customer-address with
```

        customer-name, company-name, customer-address in
        customer-details
    customer-change-response = "Change accepted"
    DISPLAY **customer-change-response**
ENDIF
END

PROCESS 3.1: PRODUCE CASH RECEIPT<u>S</u>
BEGIN
cash-collected = 0
DO WHILE there are more records in **MONEY**
    READ next **money** record
    DISPLAY **money**
    cash-collected = cash-collected + **money-amount**
END DO
cash-report = cash-collected
DISPLAY **cash-report**
END

Process 3.2:   PRODUCE DAILY REVENUE REPORT
BEGIN
daily-total = 0
DO WHILE there are more **orders** in **ORDERS** with **order-date** = today's date
    READ next **order** with **order-date** = today's date
    ADD **invoice-number,customer-name, company-name,**
        order-total as a new line in **daily-revenue-report**
    ADD **order-total** to daily-total
END DO
ADD daily-total as a new line to **daily-revenue-report**
DISPLAY **daily-revenue-report**

PROCESS 3.3: PRODUCE MONTHLY REVENUE REPORT
total-revenue = 0
total-returns = 0
total-credits = 0
DO WHILE there are more **orders** in **ORDERS** with **order-date** in this month
    ADD **order-total** to **total-revenue**
END DO
DO WHILE there are more **returns** in **RETURNS** with **return-date** in this month
    ADD **return-value** to **total-returns**
END DO
DO WHILE there are more **credits** in **CREDITS** with **credit-date** in this month
    ADD **credit-amount** to **total-credits**
END DO
monthly-revenue-report = total-revenue, total-returns, total-credits
DISPLAY **monthly-revenue-report**
END

PROCESS 3.4: PRODUCE QUARTERLY ROYALTY REPORT

```
BEGIN
DO WHILE there are more books in BOOKS
        total-books = 0
        total-revenue = 0
        total-royalty = 0
        READ next book record
        DO WHILE there are more orders in ORDERS with order-date in this quarter
                READ next such order record
                DO WHILE there are more order-items in ORDER-ITEMS with
                        invoice-number matching invoice-number in
                        current order record and book-code matching
                        book-code in current book record
                    READ next such order-item
                    ADD quantity-ordered to total-books
                    this-revenue = quantity-ordered * unit-price * discount
                    ADD this-revenue to total-revenue
                    ADD (this-revenue * royalty-rate) to total-royalty
                    APPEND customer-ID, customer-name, invoice-number,
                        this-revenue, (this-revenue * royalty-rate) to next line
                        of quarterly-royalty-report
                END DO
        END DO
        DO WHILE there are more credits in CREDITS with book-code matching
                book-code in current book record and credit-date in this quarter
                READ next such credit
                SUBTRACT credit-book-quantity from total-books
                    SUBTRACT credit-amount from total-revenue
                    SUBTRACT (credit-amount * royalty-rate) from total-royalty
                    APPEND customer-ID, customer-name, invoice-number,
                        credit-amount, (credit-amount * royalty-rate) to
                        next line of quarterly-royalty-report
        END DO
        DO WHILE there are more returns in RETURNS with book-code matching
                book-code in current book record and return-date in this quarter
                READ next such return
                SUBTRACT quantity-returned from total-books
                SUBTRACT return-value from total-revenue
                SUBTRACT(return-value * royalty-rate) from total-royalty
                APPEND customer-ID, customer-name, invoice-number,
                        return-value, (return-value * royalty-rate) to next
                        line of quarterly-royalty-report
        END DO
        APPEND total-books, total-revenue, total-royalty to next line of
                quarterly-royalty-report
END DO
DISPLAY quarterly-royalty-report
END
```

PROCESS 3.5: PRODUCE INVENTORY REPORT
BEGIN
REPEAT UNTIL there are no more **book**s in **BOOKS**
      READ next **book** in **BOOKS**
      inventory-total = 0
      REPEAT until there are no more **inventory-item**s in INVENTORY-
            ITEMS with **book-code** that matches **book-code** in **book**
           ADD **inventory-quantity** to inventory-total
           ADD **warehouse-ID**, **book-code**, **inventory-quantity**
                to next line of **inventory-report**
      END REPEAT
           ADD inventory-total to next line of **inventory-report**
END REPEAT
END

PROCESS 3.6: PRODUCE SALES COMMISSION REPORT
BEGIN
DO WHILE there are more **salesperson**s in **SALESPERSONS**
      READ next **salesperson** record
      salesperson-commission = 0
      DO WHILE there are more **orders** in **ORDERS**
             with **salesperson-ID** matching **salesperson-ID** in
             salesperson and with **order-date** within this month
           READ next such **order** record
           commission = **commission-rate** * **order-total**
           ADD commission to salesperson-commission
           APPEND **salesperson-ID**, **invoice-number**, commission
                to next line of **commission-report**
      END DO
      APPEND salesperson-commission to next line of **commission-report**
END DO
END

PROCESS 3.7: PRODUCE STATEMENTS
BEGIN
REPEAT UNTIL there are no more **customer**s in **CUSTOMERS**
      READ next **customer** record
      new-balance = **current-balance**
      DO WHILE there are more **orders** in **ORDERS** with **customer-ID** =
           customer-ID in current **customer** record and
           order-date later than current-**balance-date**
         READ next such **order** record
         ADD **order-total** to new-balance
         APPEND **order** to next line of **statement**
      END DO
      DO WHILE there are more **payment**s in **PAYMENTS** with **customer-ID** =
           customer-ID in current **customer** record and
           payment-date later than **current-balance-date**
         READ next such **payment** record

```
            SUBTRACT total-amount from new-balance
            APPEND payment to next line of statement
        END DO
        DO WHILE there are more refunds in REFUNDS with customer-ID =
                customer-ID in current customer record and
                refund-date later than current-balance-date
            READ next such refund record
            ADD refund-amount to new-balance
            APPEND refund to next line of statement
        END DO
        DO WHILE there are more credits in CREDITS with customer-ID =
                customer-ID in current customer record and
                credit-date later than current-balance-date
            READ next such credit record
            SUBTRACT credit-amount from new-balance
            APPEND credit to next line of statement
        END DO
        DO WHILE there are more returns in RETURNS with customer-ID =
                customer-ID in current customer record and
                return-date later than current-balance-date
            READ next such return record
            SUBTRACT return-value from new-balance
            APPEND payment to next line of statement
        END DO
APPEND new-balance to next line of statement
DISPLAY statement
SET current-balance-date in current order record to today's date
SET current-balance in current order record to new-balance
END REPEAT
END
```

PROCESS 3.8: PRODUCE ACCOUNTS RECEIVABLE REPORT

```
BEGIN
REPEAT UNTIL there are no more customers in CUSTOMERS
    READ next customer record
    new-balance = current-balance
    DO WHILE there are more orders in ORDERS with customer-ID =
            customer-ID in current customer record and
            order-date later than current-balance-date
        READ next such order record
        ADD order-total to new-balance
    END DO
    DO WHILE there are more payments in PAYMENTS with customer-ID =
            customer-ID in current customer record and
            payment-date later than current-balance-date
        READ next such payment record
        SUBTRACT total-amount from new-balance
    END DO
    DO WHILE there are more refunds in REFUNDS with customer-ID =
```

                customer-ID in current **customer** record and
                refund-date later than **current-balance-date**
      READ next such **refund** record
      ADD **refund-amount** to new-balance
  END DO
  DO WHILE there are more **credits** in **CREDITS** with **customer-ID** =
                customer-ID in current **customer** record and
                credit-date later than **current-balance-date**
      READ next such **credit** record
      SUBTRACT **credit-amount** from new-balance
      APPEND **credit** to next line of **statement**
  END DO
  DO WHILE there are more **returns** in **RETURNS** with **customer-ID** =
                customer-ID in current **customer** record and
                return-date later than **current-balance-date**
      READ next such **return** record
      SUBTRACT **return-value** from new-balance
  END DO
END REPEAT
APPEND **customer-ID**, new-balance to next line of **receivable-report**
DISPLAY **receivable-report**
END

PROCESS 4.1: ACCEPT PRINTER QUOTATION
BEGIN
ACCEPT (from printer) **printer-ID**, **printer-quotation**
DISPLAY (to management) **printer-ID**, **printer-quotation**
END

PROCESS 4.2: PLACE PRINT ORDER
BEGIN
FIND **book** in **BOOKS** with **book-code** that matches **book-code** in
    print-order-instructions
IF record cannot be found
    print-order-response = "No such book"
    DISPLAY **print-order-response**
ELSE
    IF **print-quantity** < 0
        print-order-response = "Illegal printing quantity"
        DISPLAY **print-order-response**
    ELSE
        print-order-response = "Print order accepted"
        DISPLAY **print-order-response**
        SET **on-order-quantity** in **book** to **print-quantity**
        SET **on-hand-date** in **book** to **on-hand-date**
            in **print-order-instructions**
        WRITE **book** record
        print-order = book-code + **print-quantity**
        DISPLAY **print-order**, **printer-ID**

```
        ENDIF
ENDIF
END
```

PROCESS 4.3: REVISE BOOK ORDER

```
BEGIN
FIND book in BOOKS with book-code that matches
        book-code in revised-print-order
IF record cannot be found
        revised-print-order-response = "No such book"
        DISPLAY revised-print-order-response
ELSE
        Read book record
        Set on-order-quantity to revised-quantity
        Set on-hand-date to revised-date
        Write book record to BOOKS
        revised-print-order-response = "Revised print order OK"
        DISPLAY revised-print-order-response
ENDIF
END
```

PROCESS 4.4: PROCESS PRINTER INVOICE

```
BEGIN
FIND book in BOOKS with book-code matching book-code in printer-invoice
IF record cannot be found
        printer-invoice-response = "No orders outstanding for this book"
        DISPLAY printer-invoice-response
ELSE
        DISPLAY printer-invoice (to management for approval)
        ACCEPT printer-invoice-authorization
        IF printer-invoice-authorization = "YES"
                printer-invoice-response = "Invoice rejected; please contact
                        management to discuss"
                DISPLAY printer-invoice-response
        ELSE
                printer-invoice-response = "Invoice accepted"
                DISPLAY printer-invoice-response
                approved-printer-invoice = printer-invoice
                DISPLAY approved-printer-invoice
        ENDIF
ENDIF
END
```

PROCESS 4.5: ASK FOR PRINTER QUOTATION

```
BEGIN
DO WHILE there are more printers in PRINTERS
        READ next printer record
        IF printer matches any of the printer-IDs in the input to this process
```

           request-for-quote = **book-code** + {**quantity**}
           DISPLAY **request-for-quote**
       ENDIF
ENDDO
END

PROCESS 5:   **CREATE NEW BOOK RECORD**
BEGIN
DISPLAY (to management) **book-title** + **book-code-request**
ACCEPT (from management) **book-code**
DISPLAY (to acquisitions) **book-title** + **royalty-rate-request**
ACCEPT (from acquisitions) **royalty-rate**
DISPLAY (to marketing) **book-title** + **unit-price-request**
ACCEPT (from marketing) **unit-price**
book = **book-code** + **book-title** + **author-ID** + **royalty-rate**
SET **total-in-stock** to zero
SET **on-hand-date** to **in-stock-date**
APPEND **book** to **BOOKS**
END

PROCESS 6.1: PRODUCE MAILING LABELS
BEGIN
SORT **CUSTOMERS** by **postal-code** into **mailing-labels**
DISPLAY **mailing-labels**
END

PROCESS 6.2: PRODUCE SALES STATISTICS
BEGIN
REPEAT until there are no more **books** in **BOOKS**
       sales-revenue = 0
       sales-returns = 0
       sales-credits = 0
       DO WHILE there are more **orders** in **ORDERS** with **order-date**
                 after **sales-date**
             read next such **order** record
             DO WHILE there are more **order-items** in current **order** record with
                     book-code = **book-code** in current **book** record
                 READ next such **order-item** record
                 ADD (**quantity-ordered** * **unit-price** * **discount**) to
                     sales-revenue
           END DO
       END DO
       DO WHILE there are more **returns** in **RETURNS** with **return-date**
             after **sales-date** and **book-code** = **book-code** in current **book** record
             ADD **return-value** to **sales-returns**
       END DO
       DO WHILE there are more **credits** in **CREDITS** with **credit-date** after
             sales-date and **book-code** = **book-code** in current **book** record
             ADD **credit-amount** to **sales-credits**

```
        END DO
        APPEND book-code, sales-revenue, sales-returns, sales-credits
                to next line of sales-statistics
END REPEAT
DISPLAY sales-statistics
END
```

PROCESS 6.3: PRODUCE IN-STOCK DATE

```
BEGIN
FIND book in BOOKS with matching book-code
IF record cannot be found
        in-stock-response = "No such book"
        DISPLAY in-stock-response
ELSE
        read book record
        IF on-hand-date = "null"
                in-stock-response = "No shipment due"
        ELSE
                in-stock-response = on-hand-date
                DISPLAY in-stock-response
        ENDIF
ENDIF
END
```

PROCESS 6.4: REMOVE BOOK

```
BEGIN
FIND book in BOOKS with matching book-code
IF record cannot be found
        remove-book-response = "No such book"
        DISPLAY remove-book-response
ELSE
        READ book record
        SET out-of-print-indicator to YES
        WRITE book record
        remove-book-response = "Book has been marked as out of print"
        DISPLAY remove-book-response
ENDIF
END
```

PROCESS 7.1: PRODUCE SHIPPING DOCUMENTS

```
BEGIN
REPEAT UNTIL there are no more warehouses in WAREHOUSES
        READ next warehouse record
        *note: this part produces the pick list for the warehouse*
        REPEAT UNTIL there are no more books in BOOKS
                books-to-pick = 0
                DO WHILE there are more orders in ORDERS with order-date =
                        today's date and warehouse-ID matching warehouse-ID
                        in current warehouse record
```

          READ next such **order** record
          DO WHILE there are more **order-item**s with **invoice-number** =
               invoice-number in **order** record
             READ next such **order-item** record
             ADD **quantity-ordered** to books-to-pick
          END DO
       END DO
       APPEND **book-title** , books-to-pick to next line of
           shipping-documents
    END REPEAT
    note: this part produces the shipping-labels
    DO WHILE there are more **orders** in **ORDERS** with **order-date** = today's
            date and **warehouse-ID** = **warehouse-ID** in
            current **warehouse** record
       READ next such **order** record
       APPEND **customer-name, customer-address, invoice-number**
           to next line of **shipping-documents**
    END DO
    note: this part produces a copy of the original order for the warehouse
    DO WHILE there are more **orders** in **ORDERS** with **order-date** = today's date
         and **warehouse-ID** = **warehouse-ID** in current **warehouse** record
       READ next such **order** record
       APPEND **customer-ID, order-date, shipping-charges, sales-tax**
           to next line of **shipping-documents**
       REPEAT UNTIL there are no more **order-item**s in **ORDER-ITEMS** with
              invoice-number matching **invoice-number**
              in current **order** record
           APPEND **order-item** to next line of **shipping-documents**
       END REPEAT
    END DO
END REPEAT
END

PROCESS 7.2: RECORD SHIPMENT FROM PRINTER
BEGIN
FIND **book** in **BOOKS** with matching **book-title**
IF record cannot be found
    shipment-notification = "No such book"
    DISPLAY **shipment-notification**
ELSE
    shipment-notification = "Received from printer" + **book-code** +
        quantity-received
    DISPLAY **shipment-notification**
    READ **book** record
    ADD **quantity-received** to **total-in-stock**
    SET **on-order-quantity** to zero
    WRITE **book** record to **BOOKS**
    READ **inventory-item** in **INVENTORY-ITEMS** with
        warehouse-ID = "YONKERS" and matching **book-code**

```
        ADD quantity-received to inventory-quantity
        WRITE inventory-item record
ENDIF
END
```

PROCESS 7.3:   RECORD CUSTOMER BOOK RETURNS
```
BEGIN
FIND customer in CUSTOMERS with customer-ID matching customer-ID
        in book-return-information or with customer-name matching
        customer-name in book-return-information
IF record cannot be found
        return-instructions = "Cannot identify customer; accept books anyway"
        DISPLAY return-instructions
ELSE
        FIND authorized-return in AUTHORIZED-RETURNS with return-auth-#
                matching return-auth-# in book-return-information
        IF record cannot be found
                return-instructions =
                        "This return is not authorized; please send back"
                DISPLAY return-instructions
                book-return-approval = "This return is not authorized"
                DISPLAY (to customer) book-return-approval
                EXIT
        ELSE
                return-instructions = "Return is authorized"
                DISPLAY return-instructions
                book-return-approval = "This return is OK"
                DISPLAY (to customer) book-return-approval
        ENDIF
ENDIF
REPEAT UNTIL there are no more book-codes in book-return-information
        FIND inventory-item in INVENTORY-ITEMS with matching
                warehouse-ID  and with book-code matching book-code
                in book-return-information
        IF record cannot be found
                return-instructions = "No such book"
                DISPLAY return-instructions
        ELSE
                READ inventory-item record
                ADD quantity-returned to inventory-quantity
                WRITE inventory-item record
                FIND book in BOOKS with matching book-ID
                READ book record
                ADD quantity-returned to total-in-stock
                WRITE book record
        ENDIF
END REPEAT
APPEND book-return-information to RETURNS
END
```

PROCESS 7.4: RECORD PHYSICAL INVENTORY
BEGIN
FIND **warehouse** in **WAREHOUSES** with matching **warehouse-ID**
IF record cannot be found
      physical-inv-response = "No such warehouse"
      DISPLAY **physical-inv-response**
ELSE
      REPEAT UNTIL there are no more **inventory-detail**s in **inventory-count**
          FIND **inventory-item** in **INVENTORY-ITEMS** with
          matching **warehouse-ID** and **book-code**
        IF record cannot be found
          physical-inv-response = "Illegal book code" +
          DISPLAY **physical-inv-response**
        ELSE
          variance = **inventory-quantity** - **physical-count**
          SET **inventory-quantity** to **physical-count**
          FIND **book** in **BOOKS** with matching **book-code**
          READ **book** record
          SUBTRACT variance from **total-in-stock**
          DO WHILE there are more **orders** in **ORDERS** with **order-date**
             later than **as-of-date** and matching **warehouse-ID**
             READ **order** record
             DO WHILE there are more **order-items** in **ORDER-**
                 ITEMS with **book-code** = **book-code** in
                 inventory-detail and **invoice-number** =
                 invoice-number in **order**
               READ **order-item**
               SUBTRACT **quantity-ordered** from
                 inventory-quantity
               SUBTRACT **quantity-ordered** from
                 total-in-stock
             END DO
           END DO
          WRITE **inventory-item** record
          WRITE **book** record
         ENDIF
      END REPEAT
ENDIF
END

PROCESS 7.5: RECORD ACTUAL SHIPMENT
BEGIN
FIND **order** in **ORDERS** with matching **invoice-number**
IF record cannot be found
      shipment-response = "No such order can be found"
      DISPLAY **shipment-response**
ELSE
      READ **order** record
      SET **shipment-date** to today's date

        WRITE **order** record
ENDIF
END

PROCESS 7.6: RESPOND TO OUT OF STOCK
BEGIN
FIND **book** in **BOOKS** with matching **book-title**
IF record cannot be found
        out-of-stock-response = "No such book"
        DISPLAY **out-of-stock-response**
ELSE
        READ **book** record to get **book-code**
        FIND **inventory-item** in **INVENTORY-ITEMS** with matching
                warehouse-ID and matching **book-code**
        IF record cannot be found
                out-of-stock-response = "Error: inventory item cannot be found"
        ELSE
                READ **inventory-item**
                SET **inventory-quantity** to zero
                WRITE **inventory-item**
                out-of-stock-response = "Out of stock message accepted"
        ENDIF
ENDIF
END

PROCESS 8.1: PRODUCE AUTHOR ROYALTY REPORT
BEGIN
DO WHILE there are more **book**s in **BOOKS**
        total-books = 0
        total-revenue = 0
        total-royalty = 0
        READ next **book** record
        DO WHILE there are more **order**s in **ORDERS** with **order-date** in this quarter
                READ next such **order** record
                DO WHILE there are more **order-item**s in **ORDER-ITEMS** with
                                invoice-number matching **invoice-number** in
                                current **order** record and **book-code** matching
                                book-code in current **book** record
                        READ next such **order-item**
                        ADD **quantity-ordered** to total-books
                        this-revenue = **quantity-ordered** * **unit-price** * **discount**
                        ADD this-revenue to total-revenue
                        ADD (this-revenue * **royalty-rate**) to total-royalty
                END DO
        END DO
        DO WHILE there are more **credit**s in **CREDITS** with **book-code** matching
                book-code in current **book** record and **credit-date** in this quarter
                READ next such **credit**
                SUBTRACT **credit-book-quantity** from total-books

```
                    SUBTRACT credit-amount from total-revenue
                    SUBTRACT (credit-amount * royalty-rate) from total-royalty
          END DO
          DO WHILE there are more returns in RETURNS with book-code matching
                    book-code in current book record and return-date in this quarter
                    READ next such return
                    SUBTRACT quantity-returned from total-books
                    SUBTRACT  return-value from total-revenue
                    SUBTRACT(return-value * royalty-rate) from total-royalty
          END DO
          APPEND total-books, total-revenue, total-royalty to next line of author-
                    royalty-report
END DO
DISPLAY author-royalty-report
END
```

PROCESS 8.2: ADVISE ACCOUNTING OF ROYALTY ADVANCE

```
BEGIN
FIND author in AUTHORS with author-ID matching author-ID in
          request-for-royalty-advance
IF record cannot be found
          advance-response = "No such author"
          DISPLAY advance-response
ELSE
          FIND book in BOOKS with book-code matching book-code in
                    request-for-royalty-advance
          IF record cannot be found
                    advance-response = "No such book"
                    DISPLAY advance-response
          ELSE
                    request-for-advance-authorization =
                              request-for-royalty-advance
                    DISPLAY (to management) request-for-advance-authorization
                    ACCEPT (from management) advance-authorization-response
                    IF advance-authorization-response = "Yes"
                              advance-response = "Advance approved"
                              DISPLAY advance-response
                              request-for-advance-check=request-for-royalty-advance
                              DISPLAY (to Accounting) request-for-advance-check
                              read author record
                              ADD advance-amount to royalty-balance
                              WRITE author record
                    ELSE
                              advance-response = "Advance denied"
                              DISPLAY advance-response
                    ENDIF
          ENDIF
ENDIF
END
```

PROCESS 8.3: CHANGE AUTHOR DETAILS
BEGIN
FIND **author** in AUTHORS with matching **author-ID**
IF record can be found
        WRITE **author-details** to **author**
ENDIF
END

APPENDIX

G

CASE STUDY: THE ELEVATOR PROBLEM

G.1   INTRODUCTION

This appendix shows the essential model for an elevator scheduler and controller. Its primary purpose is to illustrate the use of structured analysis models for real-time systems; you will see examples of control flows, control processes, and state-transition diagrams that would typically *not* be used in a business-oriented system.

In the next section, a narrative description of the problem is given. Following that are the various diagrams that make up the essential model, as well as the data dictionary and process specifications. Note that most of the process specifications use the precondition/postcondition approach discussed in Chapter 11.

The elevator problem was used in a workshop sponsored by the Washington, D.C., chapter of the ACM in 1986. The models provided here were originally developed by Dennis Stipe, formerly of YOURDON inc. The dataflow diagrams and data dictionary were produced on a Macintosh II computer with MacBubbles from StarSys, Inc.; the state-transition diagrams were produced with MacDraw.

It is important that you see how different the diagrams in this chapter are from the diagrams in Appendix F, which were produced by Design from Meta Software. MacBubbles is a CASE product that is specifically tailored for drawing dataflow diagrams (with balancing between parent and child diagrams, etc.). Design is a more general-purpose object-oriented drawing program, which can be used to draw flowcharts, data flow diagrams, or virtually any other software diagram. From an aesthetic viewpoint, the diagrams produced by the two programs are very different; I think that the editors who produced this book would have preferred a reliable human artist to both packages. As mentioned in Chapter 9, the style and format of dataflow diagrams can be a sensitive issue with many users; when you compare Appendices F and G, you will see why.

G.2   A NARRATIVE DESCRIPTION

The general requirement is to design and implement a program to schedule and control four elevators in a building with 40 floors. The elevators will be used to carry people from one floor to another in the conventional way.

Efficiency: The program should schedule the elevators efficiently and reasonably. For example, if someone summons an elevator by pushing the down button on the fourth floor, the next elevator that reaches the fourth floor traveling down should stop at the fourth floor to accept the passenger(s). On the other hand, if an elevator has no passengers (no outstanding destination requests), it should park at the last floor it visited until it is needed again. An elevator should not reverse its direction of travel until its passengers who want to travel in its current direction have reached their destinations. (As we will see below, the program cannot really have information about an elevator's actual *passengers;* it only knows about destination button presses for a given elevator. For example, if some mischievous or sociopathic passenger boards the elevator at the first floor and then presses the destination buttons for the fourth, fifth, and twentieth floor, the program will cause the elevator to travel to and stop at the fourth, fifth, and twentieth floors. The computer and its program have no information about actual passenger boardings and exits.) An elevator that is filled to capacity should not respond to a new summon request. (There is an overweight sensor for each elevator. The computer and its program can interrogate these sensors.)

Destination button: The interior of each elevator is furnished with a panel containing an array of 40 buttons, one button for each floor, marked with the floor numbers (1 to 40). These destination buttons can be illuminated by signals sent from the computer to the panel. When a passenger presses a destination button *not already lit,* the circuitry behind the panel sends an interrupt to the computer (there is a separate interrupt for each elevator). When the computer receives one of these (vectored) interrupts, its program can read the appropriate memory mapped eight-bit input registers (there is one for each interrupt, hence one for each elevator) that contains the floor number corresponding to the destination button that caused the interrupt. Of course, the circuitry behind the panel writes the floor number into the appropriate memory-mapped input register when it causes the vectored interrupt. (Since there are 40 floors in this application, only the first six bits of each input register will be used by the implementation; but the hardware would support a building with up to 256 floors.)

Destination button lights: As mentioned earlier, the destination buttons can be illuminated (by bulbs behind the panels). When the interrupt service routine in the program receives a destination button interrupt, it should send a signal to the appropriate panel to illuminate the appropriate button. This signal is sent by the program's loading the number of the button into the appropriate memory-mapped output register (there is one such register for each elevator). The illumination of a button notifies the passenger(s) that the system has taken note of his or her request and also prevents further interrupts caused by additional (impatient?) pressing of the button. When the controller stops an elevator at a floor, it should send a signal to its destination button panel to turn off the destination button for that floor.

Floor sensors: There is a floor sensor switch for each floor for each elevator shaft. When an elevator is within eight inches of a floor, a wheel on the elevator closes the switch for that floor and sends an interrupt to the computer (there is a separate interrupt for the set of switches in each elevator shaft). When the computer receives one of these (vectored) interrupts, its program can read the appropriate memory mapped eight-bit input register (there is one for each interrupt, hence one for each elevator) that contains the floor number corresponding to the floor sensor switch that caused the interrupt.

Arrival lights: The interior of each elevator is furnished with a panel containing one illuminable indicator for each floor number. This panel is located just above the doors. The purpose of this panel is to tell the passengers in the elevator the number of the floor at which the elevator is arriving (and at which it may be stopping). The program should illuminate the indicator for a floor when it arrives at the floor and extinguish the indicator for a floor when it leaves a floor or arrives at a different floor. This signal is sent by the program's loading the number of the floor indicator into the appropriate memory-mapped output register (there is one register for each elevator).

Summons buttons: Each floor of the building is furnished with a panel containing summon button(s). Each floor except the ground floor (floor 1) and the top floor (floor 40) is furnished with a panel containing two summon buttons, one marked UP and one marked DOWN. The ground floor summon panel has only an UP button. The top floor summon panel has only a DOWN button. Thus, there are 78 summon buttons altogether, 39 UP buttons and 39 DOWN buttons. Would-be passengers press these buttons in order to summon an elevator. (Of course, the would-be passenger cannot summon a *particular* elevator. The scheduler decides which elevator should respond to a summon request.) These summon buttons can be illuminated by signals sent from the computer to the panel. When a passenger presses a summon button *not already lit,* the circuitry behind the panel sends a vectored interrupt to the computer (there is one interrupt for UP buttons and another for DOWN buttons). When the computer receives one of these two (vectored) interrupts, its program can read the appropriate memory mapped eight-bit input register that contains the floor number corresponding to the summon button that caused the interrupt. Of course, the circuitry behind the panel writes the floor number into the appropriate memory-mapped input register when it causes the vectored interrupt.

Summon button lights: The summon buttons can be illuminated (by bulbs behind the panels). When the summon button interrupt service routine in the program receives an UP or DOWN button vectored interrupt, it should send a signal to the appropriate panel to illuminate the appropriate button. This signal is sent by the program's loading the number of the button in the appropriate memory-mapped output register, one for the UP buttons and one for the DOWN buttons. The illumination of a button notifies the passenger(s) that the system has taken note of his or her request and also prevents further interrupts caused by additional pressing of the button. When the controller stops an elevator at a floor, it should send a signal to the floor's summon button panel to turn off the appropriate (UP or DOWN) button for that floor.

Elevator motor controls (Up, Down, Stop): There is a memory-mapped control word for each elevator motor. Bit 0 of this word commands the elevator to go up, bit 1 commands the elevator to do down, and bit 2 commands the elevator to stop at the floor whose sensor switch is closed. The elevator mechanism will not obey any inappropriate or unsafe command. If no floor sensor switch is closed when the computer issues a stop signal, the elevator mechanism ignores the stop signal until a floor sensor switch is closed. The computer program does not have to worry about controlling an elevator's doors or stopping an elevator exactly at a level (home) position at a floor. The elevator manufacturer uses conventional switches, relays, circuits, and safety interlocks for these purposes so that the manufacturer can certify the safety of the elevators without regard for the computer controller. For example, if the computer issues a stop command for an elevator when it is within eight inches of a floor (so that its floor sensor switch is closed), the conventional, approved mechanism stops and levels the elevator at that floor, opens and holds its doors open appropriately, and then closes its door. If the computer issues an up or down command during this period (while the door is open, for example), the manufacturer's mechanism ignores the command until its conditions for movement are met. (Therefore, it is safe for the computer to issue and up or down command while an elevator's door is still open.) One condition for an elevator's movement is that its *stop button* not be depressed. Each elevator's destination button panel contains a stop button. This button does not go to the computer. Its sole purpose is to hold an elevator at a floor with its door open when the elevator is currently stopped at a floor. A red emergency *stop switch* stops and holds the elevator at the very next floor it reaches irrespective of computer scheduling. The red switch may also turn on an audible alarm. The red switch is not connected to the computer.

Target machine: The elevator scheduler and controller may be implemented for any contemporary microcomputer capable of handling this application.

G.3   THE ESSENTIAL MODEL

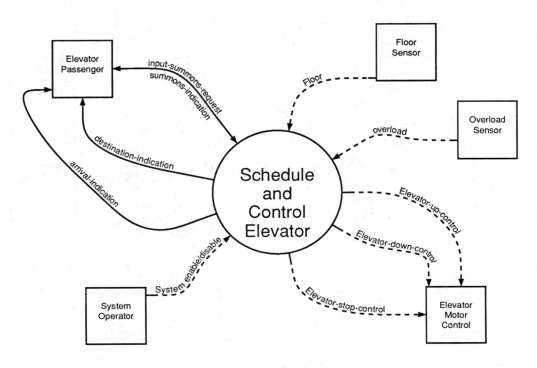

Context Diagram
Elevator Essential Model

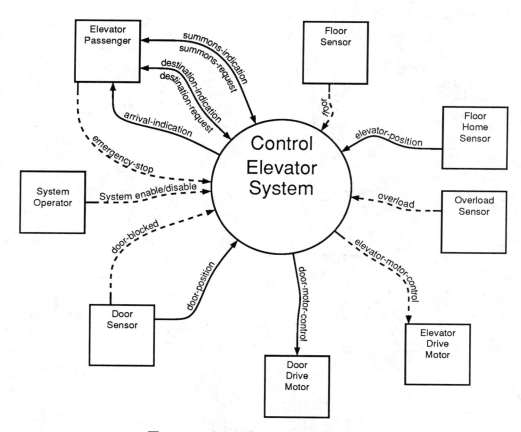

Expanded Context Diagram

The Event List

1. Passenger issues up summons request.

2. Passenger issues down summons request.

3. Elevator reaches summoned floor.

4. Elevator not available for summons request.

5. Elevator becomes available for summons request.

6. Passenger issues destination request.

7. Elevator reaches requested destination.

8. Elevator arrives at floor.

9. Elevator departs floor.

10. Elevator fails to move (goes out of service).

11. Elevator returns to normal service.

12. Elevator becomes overloaded.

13. Elevator load becomes normal.

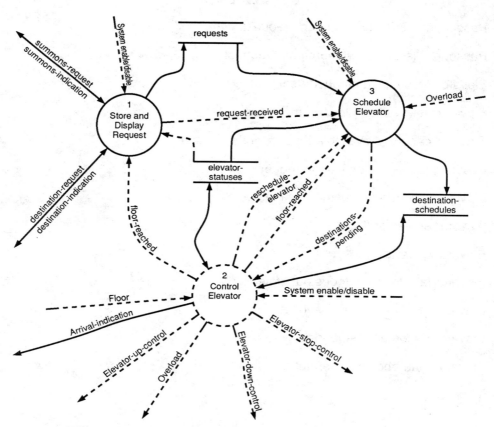

Figure 0: Schedule and Control Elevator: Elevator Essential Model

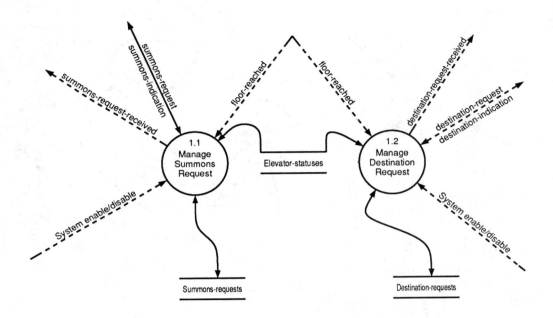

Figure 1: Store and Display Request

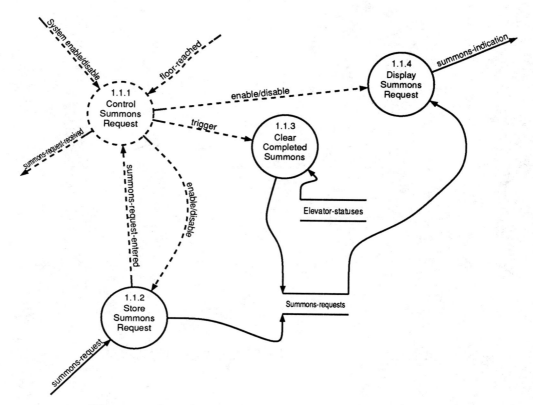

Figure 1.1: Manage Summons Request

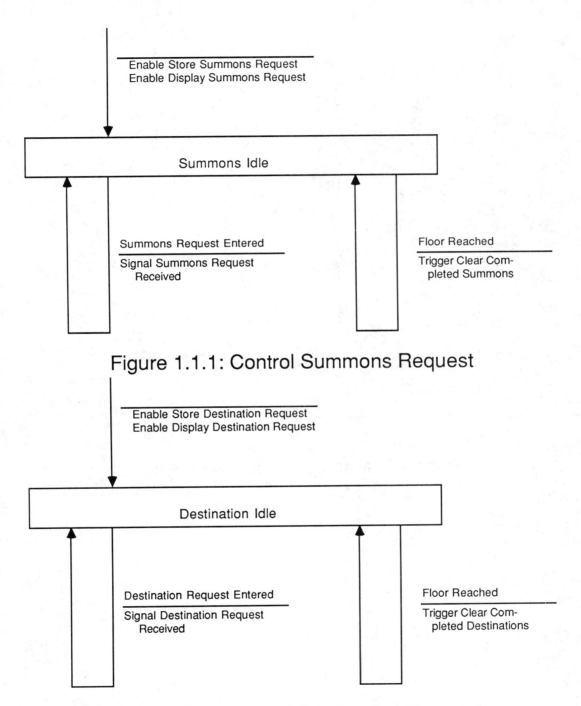

Figure 1.1.1: Control Summons Request

Figure 1.2.1: Control Destination Request

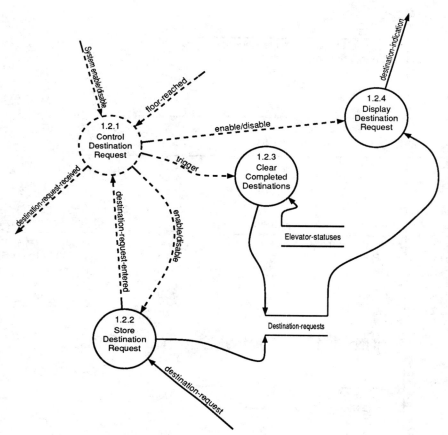

Figure 1.2: Manage Destination Request

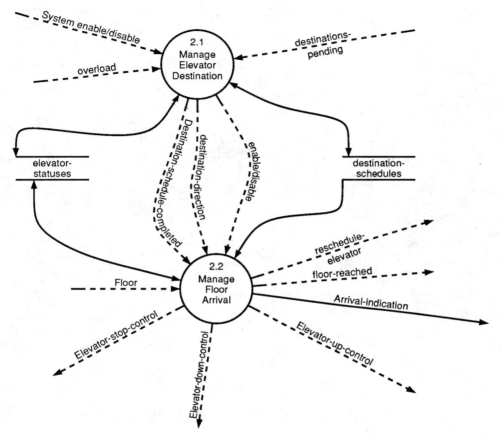

Figure 2: Control Elevator

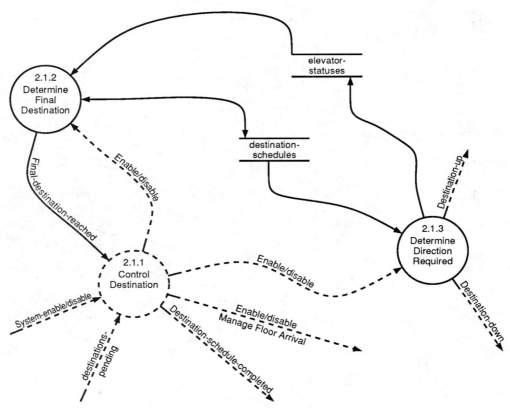

Figure 2.1: Manage Elevator Destination

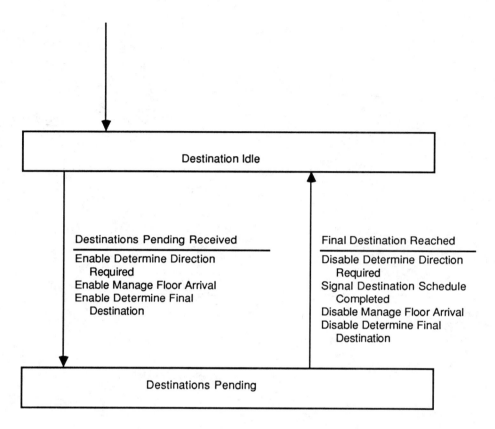

Figure 2.1.1: Control Destination

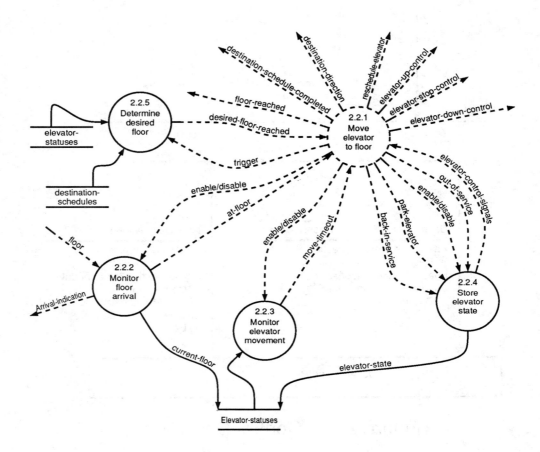

Figure 2.2: Manage Floor Arrival

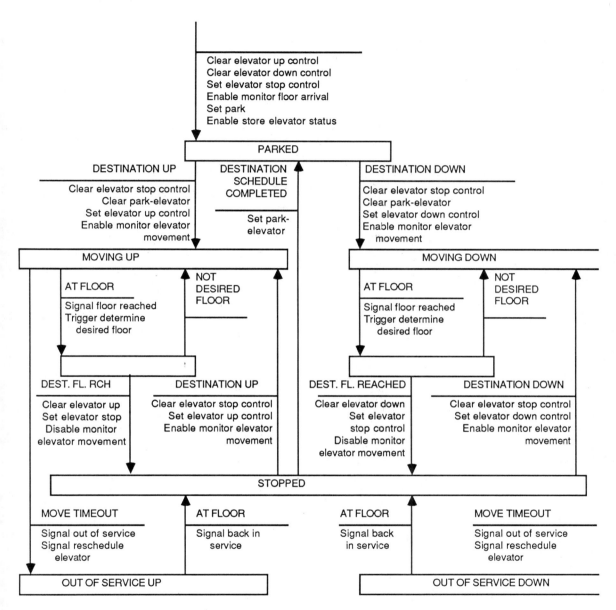

Figure 2.2.1: Move Elevator to Floor

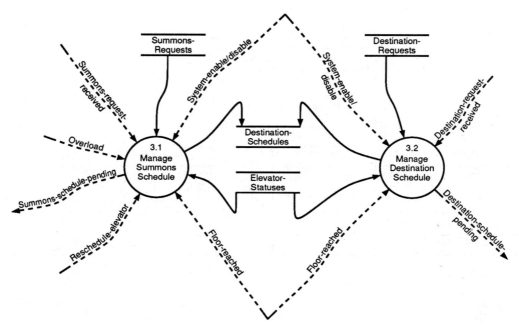

Figure 3: Schedule Elevator

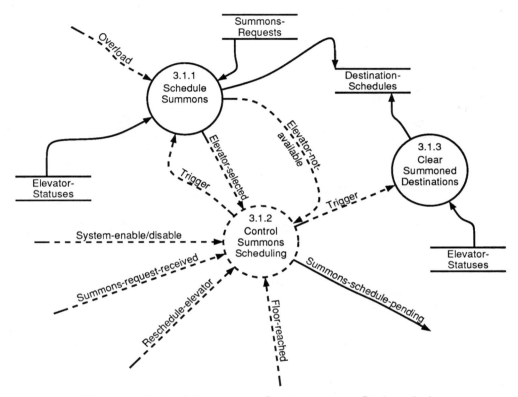

Figure 3.1: Manage Summons Schedule

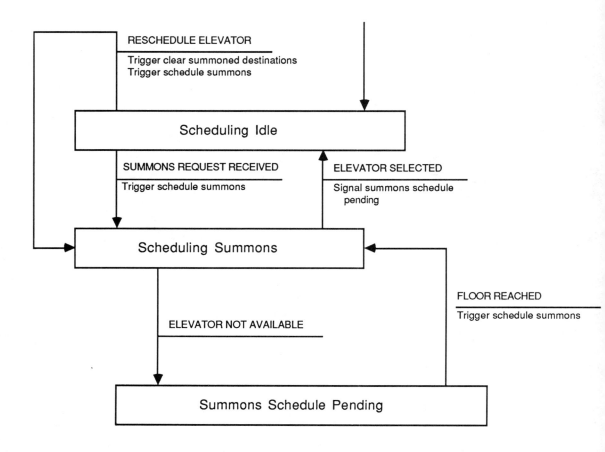

Figure 3.1.2: Control Summons Scheduling

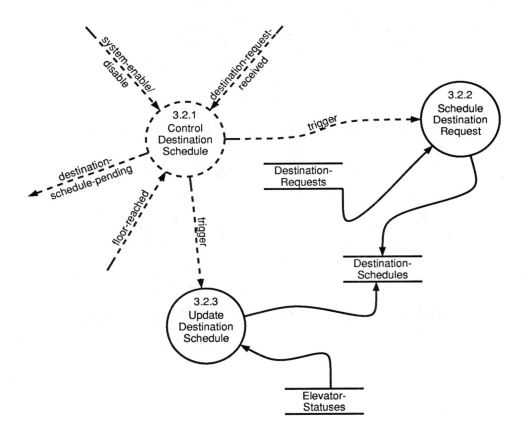

Figure 3.2: Manage Destination Schedule

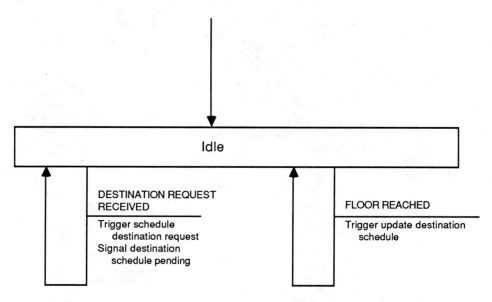

Figure 3.2.1: Control Destination Schedule

DATA DICTIONARY LISTING   Page: 1
for
Elevator Control System

arrival-indication = values: 1-40
              NOTES: indication of floor at which elevator has arrived

at-floor
              NOTES: signal that elevator reached a floor

current-floor = values: 1-40
              NOTES: floor number where an elevator floor is currently located

desired-floor-reached
              NOTES: signal

destination-direction = [destination-up|destination-down]

destination-down
              NOTES: signal that required direction is down

destination-floor = values: 1-40
              NOTES: floor numbers where an elevator is scheduled to stop

destination-indication = values: 1-40
              NOTES: indication of floor numbers where an elevator is scheduled to stop

destination-pending = values: [on | off]
              NOTES: indication that elevator has destinations subsequent to current
                      floor

destination-request = @elevator-number+{floor-number}

destination-request-entered
              NOTES: signal that passenger has entered request

destination-request-received
              NOTES: signal that request is ready for scheduling

destination-requests = {destination-request}

destination-schedule = @elevator-number+{destination-floor}+request-source+destination-pending

destination-schedules = {destination-schedule}

destination-up
              NOTES: *** Generated Entry ***

destinations-pending = [summons-pending | destination-pending | summons-pending + destination-
              pending]
              NOTES: signal that a destination schedule exists

DATA DICTIONARY LISTING
for
Elevator Control System

down-direction
> NOTES: *** Generated Entry ***

elevator-control-signal = elevator-up-control+elevator-down-control+elevator-stop-control

elevator-down-control
> NOTES: signal to hardware

elevator-floor = values: 1-40

elevator-not-available
> NOTES: signal that an elevator is not available to honor a summons request

elevator-number = values: 1-4

elevator-selected
> NOTES: signal that an elevator has been scheduled for a summons
> request

elevator-state = [parked|moving-up|moving-down|stopped|out-of-service]

elevator-status = @elevator-number+elevator-state+current-floor

elevator-statuses = {elevator-status}

elevator-stop-control
> NOTES: signal to hardware

elevator-up-control
> NOTES: signal to hardware

floor-number = values: 1-40
> NOTES: *** Generated Entry ***

moving-down
> NOTES: *** Generated Entry ***

moving-up
> NOTES: *** Generated Entry ***

off
> NOTES: *** Generated Entry ***

on
> NOTES: *** Generated Entry ***

out-of-service
> NOTES: signal that elevator has failed to respond to movement command

DATA DICTIONARY LISTING
for
Elevator Control System

overload
> NOTES: signal from hardware

parked
> NOTES: signal

request-received = summons-request-received + destination-request-received

request-source = [summons | destination-floor | summons + destination-floor]

requests = summons-requests + destination-requests

reschedule-elevator
> NOTES: signal to initiate rescheduling summons assigned to failed
> elevator

stopped
> NOTES: *** Generated Entry ***

summons
> NOTES: *** Generated Entry ***

summons-indication = values: 1-40
> NOTES: indication of floor numbers where an elevator is scheduled to stop

summons-pending = values: [on | off]

summons-request = @elevator-floor + [up-direction | down-direction | up-direction + down-direction] +
elevator-number

summons-request = @elevator-floor + [up-direction | down-direction | up-direction + down-direction] +
elevator-number

summons-request-issued
> NOTES: signal

summons-request-received
> NOTES: signal

summons-requests = {summons-request}

up-direction
> NOTES: *** Generated Entry ***

values
> NOTES: *** Generated Entry ***

Process Specifications

1.1.2 STORE SUMMONS REQUEST
Precondition
input-summons-request occurs
Postcondition
input-summons-request is stored
summons-request-entered is produced

1.1.3 CLEAR COMPLETED SUMMONS
Precondition
There is an **elevator-number** in **elevator-statuses** that matches
elevator-number-assigned in **summons-request**
and
There is a corresponding **current-floor** in **elevator-statuses** that
matches **floor-number** in **summons-requests**
Postcondition
Corresponding entry in **summons-request** is null

1.1.4 DISPLAY SUMMONS REQUEST
Precondition
None
Postcondition
summons-requests are displayed

1.2.3 CLEAR COMPLETED DESTINATIONS
Preconditon
There is an **elevator-number** in **elevator-statuses** that matches
elevator-number in **destination-requests**
and
There is a corresponding **current-floor** in **elevator-statuses** that
matches **floor-number** in **destination-requests**
Postcondition
Corresponding entry in **destination-requests** is null

1.2.4 DISPLAY DESTINATION REQUEST
Precondition
None
Postcondition
destination-requests are displayed

2.1.2 DETERMINE FINAL DESTINATION
Precondition
There is an **elevator-number** in **elevator-statuses** that matches
elevator-number in **destination-schedules**
and
There is a corresponding **current-floor** in **elevator-statuses** that
maches **destination-floor** in **destination-schedules**
and

corresponding **destination-pending** = **off** in **destination-schedules**
Postcondition
  final-destination-reached is produced

2.1.3 DETERMINE DIRECTION REQUIRED
Local term **match** is a matching **elevator-number** in **destination-schedules** and **elevator-number** in **elevator-status**
Precondition 1
  match exists
  and
  There exists in **destination-schedules** a **destination-floor** >
  current-floor in **elevator-status**
Postcondition 1
  destination-up is produced
Precondition 2
  match exists
  and
  There exists in **destination-schedules** a **destination-floor** <
  current-floor in **elevator-status**
Postcondition 2
  destination-down is produced

2.2.2 MONITOR FLOOR ARRIVAL
Precondition 1
  floor occurs
Postcondition 1
  arrival-indication is cleared for previous **floor**
  and
  arrival-indication is produced for corresponding **floor**
  and
  at-floor is produced
  and
  current-floor is updated in **elevator-statuses**

2.2.3 MONITOR ELEVATOR MOVEMENT
  current-floor is read from **elevator-statuses**
Precondition
  10 seconds elapse and **current-floor** is unchanged
Postcondition
  move-timeout occurs

2.2.4 STORE ELEVATOR STATUS
Precondition
  input signal is received
Postcondition
  elevator-state is updated in **elevator-status**

2.2.5 DETERMINE DESIRED FLOOR
Precondition

There is an **elevator-number** in **elevator-statuses** that matches
elevator-number in **destination-statuses**
and
There is a corresponding **current-floor** in **elevator-statuses** that
matches **destination-floor** in **destination-schedules**
Postcondition
desired-floor-reached is produced

3.1.1 SCHEDULE SUMMONS
BEGIN
with **summons-request, elevator-status,** and **overload**
DO WHILE **elevator-selected** has not been signaled
    Find closest **elevator**
    IF **elevator** is moving in correction **direction** or **elevator** is **parked**
        IF **elevator** is not **overloaded**
            enter **summons-request** by **elevator-number** in
                destination-schedule
            set **request-source** to **summons** or **summons +**
                destination
        ENDIF
        IF **destination-pending = off**
            set **destination-pending = on**
        ENDIF
        signal **elevator-selected**
    ELSE
        Find next closest **elevator**
END DO
IF no **elevator** found
    Signal **elevator** not available
ENDIF
END

3.1.3 CLEAR SUMMONED DESTINATIONS
Precondition
There is an **elevator-number** in **elevator-statuses** that matches
elevator-number in **destination-schedules**
and
corresponding **elevator-state = out-of-service** in **elevator-statuses**
and
corresponding **request-source = summons** in **destination-schedules**
Postcondition
Corresponding entries of **destination-floor** are null

3.2.2 SCHEDULE-DESTINATION-REQUEST
Precondition
    None
Postcondition

destination-schedules is updated by **destination-requests**
matching **elevator-number**
Set **request-source** = destination or **summons** + **destination**
IF **destination-pending** = off
  Set **destination-pending** = off
ENDIF

3.2.3 UPDATE DESTINATION SCHEDULE
Precondition 1
  There is an **elevator-number** in **elevator-statuses** that matches
  elevator-number in **destination-schedules**
  and
  There is a corresponding **current-floor** in **elevator-statuses** that
  matches **destination-floor** in **destination-schedule**
Postcondition 1
  Corresponding **destination-floor** entry is null
Precondition 2
  same condition as Precondition 1
  and
  no other corresponding **destination-floor** entries are present
Postcondition 2
  corresponding **destination-floor** entry is null
  and
  corresponding **destination-pending** is set to **off**

INDEX

Structured analysis (continued):
   human interface, 387–401
   impact on organizational structure, 428–29
   interviews, 522–32
   maintenance of specifications, 446–63
   modeling, 24, 65–76, 126
   modeling tools, 65–66, 132–38
   move toward, 123–25
   past changes in, 453–55
   process specifications, 68–69, 198,
     203–32, 326
   programming, 426–35
   project life cycle, 77–104
   prototyping, use of, 128–29
   prototyping life cycle, 78, 97–100
   state-transition diagrams (STDs), 24, 71,
     72, 126, 173, 198, 259–74, 326
   structured project life cycle, 88–94
   systems design, 410–25
   systems development, 40–63, 105–20
   testing, 82–83, 428–29, 435–39
   user implementation model, 25, 60, 295,
     321, 380–409
   users, 41–50
   walkthroughs, 439, 515–21
   Yourdon Press Case Study, 534–630
   See also specific topics
Structured English, 206–14, 220
   definition of, 206–7
   objects, 208–9
   sentences, 209–10
     compound sentences, 212–13
   verbs, 208
Structured programming, 434
Structured project life cycle, 88–94
   acceptance test generation, 92
   database conversion, 93
   design, 91
   implementation, 92
   installation, 93
   quality assurance, 92
   summary of, 93–94
   survey, 88–90
   systems analysis, 90–91
Sun Computer, 467
Supervisory users, 44–46
Survey, structured project life cycle, 88–90
Synchronous hierarchy of modules, 299
System flowcharts, 294–96
Systems
   automated systems, 16–33
   building costs, 500–501
   definition of, 9–12
   getting input into system, 401–2

   getting output out of system, 402
   installation costs, 501–3
   manmade systems, 15–16
   natural systems, 12–15
   operational costs, 505–6
   similarities among, 10
   types of, 12–16
Systems analysts
   programming/testing and, 427–29
   roles of, 56–57
   workstation vendors, 468–69
Systems design, 410–25
   guidelines for, 420–23
     cohesion, 421–22
     coupling, 422
     module size, 422
     scope of effect/scope of control, 422–23
     span of control, 422
   programming/testing, 426–45
   stages of, 411–20
     goals/objectives, 420–23
     processor model, 411–16
     program implementation model, 417–20
     task model, 416–17
Systems designers, 57
Systems development
   major issues in, 105–20
     efficiency, 116
     maintainability, 114–16
     portability, 116
     productivity, 106–12
     reliability, 112–14
     security, 116
   players in, 40–63
     auditors, 53–56
     management, 50–53
     operations personnel, 59–60
     programmers, 57–59
     quality assurance staff, 53–56
     standards department, 53–56
     systems analyst, 56–57
     systems designers, 57
     users, 41–50
   relationship between management and, 52
System states, 260–62
   changes of state, 262–64

Task model, 416–17
Telephone, 389
Terminals, 390
   definition of, 23
   and personal computers (PCs), 388–89
   time-sharing terminals, 464–65

TEAR OUT THIS PAGE TO ORDER THESE OTHER HIGH-QUALITY YOURDON PRESS COMPUTING SERIES TITLES

Quantity	Title/Author	ISBN	Price	Total $
_____	Building Controls Into Structured Systems; Brill	013-086059-X	$35.00	_____
_____	C Notes: Guide to C Programming; Zahn	013-109778-4	$21.95	_____
_____	Classics in Software Engineering; Yourdon	013-135179-6	$39.00	_____
_____	Concise Notes on Software Engineering; DeMarco	013-167073-3	$21.00	_____
_____	Controlling Software Projects; DeMarco	013-171711-1	$39.00	_____
_____	Creating Effective Software; King	013-189242-8	$33.00	_____
_____	Crunch Mode; Boddie	013-194960-8	$29.00	_____
_____	Current Practices in Software Development; King	013-195678-7	$34.00	_____
_____	Data Factory; Roeske	013-196759-2	$23.00	_____
_____	Developing Structured Systems; Dickinson	013-205147-8	$34.00	_____
_____	Design of On-Line Computer Systems; Yourdon	013-201301-0	$48.00	_____
_____	Essential Systems Analysis; McMenamin/Palmer	013-287905-0	$35.00	_____
_____	Expert System Technology; Keller	013-295577-6	$28.95	_____
_____	Concepts of Information Modeling; Flavin	013-335589-6	$27.00	_____
_____	Game Plan for System Development; Frantzen/McEvoy	013-346156-4	$30.00	_____
_____	Intuition to Implementation; MacDonald	013-502196-0	$24.00	_____
_____	Managing Structured Techniques; Yourdon	013-551037-6	$33.00	_____
_____	Managing the System Life Cycle 2/e; Yourdon	013-551045-7	$35.00	_____
_____	People & Project Management; Thomsett	013-655747-3	$23.00	_____
_____	Politics of Projects; Block	013-685553-9	$24.00	_____
_____	Practice of Structured Analysis; Keller	013-693987-2	$28.00	_____
_____	Program It Right; Benton/Weekes	013-729005-5	$23.00	_____
_____	Software Design: Methods & Techniques; Peters	013-821828-5	$33.00	_____
_____	Structured Analysis; Weinberg	013-854414-X	$44.00	_____
_____	Structured Analysis & System Specifications; DeMarco	013-854380-1	$44.00	_____
_____	Structured Approach to Building Programs: BASIC; Wells	013-854076-4	$23.00	_____
_____	Structured Approach to Building Programs: COBOL; Wells	013-854084-5	$23.00	_____
_____	Structured Approach to Building Programs: Pascal; Wells	013-851536-0	$23.00	_____
_____	Structured Design; Yourdon/Constantine	013-854471-9	$49.00	_____
_____	Structured Development Real-Time Systems, Combined; Ward/Mellor	013-854654-1	$75.00	_____
_____	Structured Development Real-Time Systems, Vol. 1; Ward/Mellor	013-854787-4	$33.00	_____
_____	Structured Development Real-Time Systems, Vol. II; Ward/Mellor	013-854795-5	$33.00	_____
_____	Structured Development Real-Time Systems, Vol. III; Ward/Mellor	013-854803-X	$33.00	_____
_____	Structured Systems Development; Orr	013-855149-9	$33.00	_____
_____	Structured Walkthroughs 3/e; Yourdon	013-855248-7	$24.00	_____
_____	System Development Without Pain; Ward	013-881392-2	$33.00	_____
_____	Teams in Information System Development; Semprivivo	013-896721-0	$29.00	_____
_____	Techniques of EDP Project Management; Brill	013-900358-4	$33.00	_____
_____	Techniques of Program Structure & Design; Yourdon	013-901702-X	$44.00	_____
_____	Up and Running; Hanson	013-937558-9	$32.00	_____
_____	Using the Structured Techniques; Weaver	013-940263-2	$27.00	_____
_____	Writing of the Revolution; Yourdon	013-970708-5	$38.00	_____
_____	Practical Guide to Structured Systems 2/e; Page-Jones	013-690769-5	$35.00	_____

Total $ _____

Discount (if appropriate) _____

New Total $ _____

AND TAKE ADVANTAGE OF THESE SPECIAL OFFERS!

a.) When ordering 3 or 4 copies (of the same or different titles), take 10% off the total list price (excluding sales tax, where applicable).

b.) When ordering 5 to 20 copies (of the same or different titles), take 15% off the total list price (excluding sales tax, where applicable).

c.) To receive a greater discount when ordering 20 or more copies, call or write:

Special Sales Department
College Marketing
Prentice Hall
Englewood Cliffs, NJ 07632
201-592-2498

SAVE!

If payment accompanies order, plus your state's sales tax where applicable, Prentice Hall pays postage and handling charges. Same return privilege refund guaranteed. Please do not mail in cash.

☐ **PAYMENT ENCLOSED**—shipping and handling to be paid by publisher (please include your state's tax where applicable).

☐ **SEND BOOKS ON 15-DAY TRIAL BASIS** & bill me (with small charge for shipping and handling).

Name _____

Address _____

City _____ State _____ Zip _____

I prefer to charge my ☐ Visa   ☐ MasterCard
Card Number _____ Expiration Date_____

Signature _____

All prices listed are subject to change without notice.

Mail your order to: Prentice Hall, Book Distribution Center, Route 59 at
Brook Hill Drive, West Nyack, NY 10995

Dept. 1   D-OFYP-FW(1)